# Management in Canada:

## The Competitive Challenges

**Bruce Partridge**
Camosun College

**John M. Ivancevich**
University of Houston

**Peter Lorenzi**
Loyola College in Maryland

**Steven J. Skinner**
University of Kentucky

**with Philip B. Crosby**

**McGraw-Hill
Ryerson**

Toronto Montréal New York Burr Ridge Bangkok Bogotá Caracas Lisbon London Madrid
Mexico City Milan New Delhi Seoul Singapore Sydney Taipei

*McGraw-Hill*
*Ryerson Limited*
A Subsidiary of The **McGraw·Hill** Companies

## Management in Canada: The Competitive Challenges

ISBN: 0-07-560766-2

1 2 3 4 5 6 7 8 9 0   VH   0 9 8 7 6 5 4 3 2 1 0

Editorial Director and Publisher: Evelyn Veitch
Marketing Manager: Bill Todd
Sponsoring Editors: Evelyn Veitch/Susan Calvert
Developmental Editor: Karina TenVeldhuis
Manager, Editorial Services: Kelly Dickson
Senior Supervising Editor: Margaret Henderson
Production Co-ordinator: Nicla Dattolico
Production Editor: Susan Broadhurst
Art Director: Dianna Little
Cover Design: Barry Mortin
Cover Image: Boden/Ledingham/Masterfile
Inside Design: Liz Harasymczuk
Typesetter: Bookman Typesetting Company
Printer: Von Hoffman Press

**Canadian Cataloguing in Publication Data**

Main entry under title:

Management in Canada: the competitive challenges

1st Canadian ed.
Includes bibliographical references and index.
ISBN 0-07-560766-2

1. Management.   I. Partridge, Bruce, 1946–   .

HD31.M2936   1999         658         C99-931782-2

# Contents

| CHAPTER 2 | The Environments of Business, Culture, Social Responsibility, and Ethics | 40 |
|-----------|--------------------------------------------------------------------------|----|

**CHAPTER 4**     **Planning**     **126**

**CHAPTER 6** | **Leading** | **204**

## CHAPTER 7    Controlling    244

## CHAPTER 8    Human Resource Management    278

# Preface

## Focus on Canada

In writing this book I found that my efforts, like the work of most managers, underwent considerable change in direction from the original concept. The original intention of "Canadianizing" a leading management text from the United States grew to a complete rewriting of the text to address issues that are uniquely Canadian. The result is *Management in Canada: The Competitive Challenges* and its supplementary material. This is a truly Canadian text that is based on Canadian experience, uses Canadian examples, and, most of all, reflects Canadian thinking.

## The Concept

The philosophy that is reflected in this text can be summarized in three sentences:

- Management is both an intellectual discipline and a practice that can be learned.
- Students who are conversant with a wide spectrum of management principles are best prepared to function in any size or type of organization.
- Accepted principles of management are constantly changing, but certain concepts shine through all of the fads and innovations that periodically refresh and expand management thinking.

The subtitle of this text, "The Competitive Challenges," was carefully chosen. It reflects the realization that the fundamental question facing any organization in today's world is whether it can become and remain competitive. Competitiveness is not a single challenge, but is better referred to in the plural. Every organization, regardless of size or type, faces competitive challenges in terms of suitability of management styles, product or service obsolescence, the availability of human resources, changes in the economy, and countless other factors. Although each factor includes some elements that are beyond the organization's control, harmful effects can be limited by imaginative and effective actions by its managers. This text was written to help students be better prepared to meet these challenges. It was also written for those preparing themselves to become managers and for those who are already managers, so they can gain new perspectives and understandings of the challenges they face.

One of the challenges faced in writing this text was to strike a balance between describing management theory and "practical" methods. It is my hope that, after numerous revisions and reviews, I have provided sufficient theory to ground the subsequent descriptions of real world applications, providing students with the balanced understanding they'll need to meet the challenges of management.

Few students will leap into managerial positions immediately after graduation. It is a truism that the most effective employees are usually those who understand how managers think and act, and those employees are the ones most likely to be selected for positions of greater responsibility. With this in mind, the principles of management set out in this text should help students in their first professional jobs to be prepared for promotion, serving them well even before they become managers.

An increasing number of today's students will spend much of their careers working for governments or not-for-profit organizations. Another large number will start as entrepreneurs whose enterprises soon grow and demand managerial talent. *Management in Canada* stresses that the same principles of management apply equally to small as well as to huge organizations; to not-for-profit and government organizations as well as to business enterprises; and to those who deliver services as well as to those who manufacture and market products.

## Learning Elements

Jargon is avoided, and language style and vocabulary level respect the abilities of my intended audience. My goal is to explain complex concepts clearly and simply without becoming simplistic. New terms that might not be familiar to students are defined in the margin and repeated in the end-of-chapter glossaries with accompanying page references. Endnotes are used to direct students and faculty to original sources.

Each chapter begins with an overview of key concepts. These concepts reappear at the end of the chapter, with suitable summaries that students can use to check their comprehension.

A full-colour presentation and rich and relevant photo program help convey the excitement and fascination offered by challenging aspects of business management.

"Management in the Real World" boxed segments illustrate concepts as they appear in the world outside the classroom. "What Managers Are Reading" boxes provide brief reviews of current books on management, directing students who wish to become more familiar with current thinking and influences in the field.

"Real World Reflection" boxes illustrate real world concepts, in brief scenarios. These boxes, as well as some of the end-of-chapter material, were contributed by Sherry Campbell, Sydney Scott, and Marnie Wright, all from the Faculty of Management of the British Columbia Institute of Technology.

Each chapter concludes with:

- "The Workplace of Tomorrow"—brief discussions that examine how management and managers will likely be changing in the years immediately ahead, when most students will be applying their learning.
- Review and Discussion Questions to test students' understanding of chapter content.
- Internet Application questions that can be used to challenge students to research concepts presented in the chapter on the World Wide Web.
- Case studies to provide for more in-depth application of chapter context.
- Application Exercises that can be used for class discussion or independent study.

## Instructor's Support Materials

### Instructor's Manual

The Instructor's Manual contains chapter summaries, complete lecture outlines, additional materials to reinforce concepts presented in the textbook, and answers to end-of-chapter questions.

## Computerized Test Bank

Brownstone's Diploma Testing is the most flexible, powerful, and easy-to-use computerized testing system available in higher education. The Diploma system allows the test maker to create a test as a Print version, as an Online version (to be delivered in a computer lab), and as an Internet version. Diploma includes a built-in Gradebook for instructors.

The text bank contains over 2000 questions, including multiple-choice questions, true/false questions, and essay questions.

## PowerPoint® Presentations

The PowerPoint® presentation package includes a series of slides for each chapter of the textbook. These are keyed directly to the lecture outlines.

## Videos

A series of video segments are provided that tie concepts from the text directly to a real company profile.

## Online Support

### Online Learning Centre

*www.mcgrawhill.ca/college/partridge* Contains instructor and student resource material linked to Partridge's *Management in Canada: The Competitive Challenges.*

### The McGraw-Hill Ryerson Management Web Community

*www.communities.mcgrawhill.ca* Free to adopters, this moderated Web site is a place for management instructors across Canada to share course ideas, papers, and teaching strategies as they relate to the discipline.

## Student Support

### Study Guide

Contains chapter overviews, key terms, chapter synopses, practice matching questions, multiple-choice questions, true/false questions, and answer keys—all designed to enhance the independent learning process.

The supplements listed here may accompany *Management in Canada: The Competitive Challenges.* Please contact your local McGraw-Hill Ryerson representative for details concerning policies, prices, and availability as some restrictions may apply.

## Academic/Professional Content

If the teaching term is scheduled for 15 weeks, one of the 15 chapters of the text may be assigned each week. If the teaching term is longer, there are ample Application Exercises and Cases to extend assignments over the longer period. If it is shorter, some Application Exercises may be omitted, and some of the simpler chapters may be combined in a given week. Each chapter is written so that it can stand alone, making it easy for the instructor to alter the order of topics. It is suggested, however, that students will have a better grasp of fundamentals if the first seven chapters are taught in the order presented.

The first three chapters of *Management in Canada* lay the groundwork for understanding the principles within which management theory and practice have their bases.

*The Management Challenge: Chapter 1* discusses how management fits into today's world. It starts with a discussion of the relationship between management and competitiveness, and why competitiveness is crucial. It differentiates the roles played by and the skills required of successful managers. Then, having set the stage, the development of management theory is briefly traced from Frederick W. Taylor, through such discoverers as Elton Mayo, Joan Woodward, and Chester Barnard, to contemporary writers such as Michael Porter, Tom Peters, and Peter Drucker. The chapter closes with a description of how management theories are applied in the real world.

*The Environments of Business, Culture, Social Responsibility, and Ethics:* With the background understanding provided by the first chapter, the student is prepared for *Chapter 2*. It addresses the external and internal environments within which an organization functions. Differences in culture are described, and their effects on management are explored. These ideas lead to a pointed discussion of various levels of social responsibility. Ethical concepts and practices are set forth in the context of workable social responsibility.

*Decision Making—The Essence of Management:* Then comes an exposition of the fundamental tool of managers: decision making. In *Chapter 3* it is pointed out that every effect that a manager has on an organization or environment is the outcome of a decision, whether conscious or unconscious. The decision-making process is exemplified in both individual and group decisions. Innovative methods of unleashing innovative potential are described. The discussion points out the need for decisions to be grounded in reliable information, and describes the development and use of Management Information Systems.

These three chapters, having embraced the broad concepts of the manager's thought processes and actions, provide the grounding for the next four chapters. They are devoted, respectively, to each of the four elements of management: planning, organizing, leading, and controlling.

*Planning: Chapter 4* discusses the qualities of effective planning that distinguish it from less effective planning. This discussion leads to descriptions and examples of mission statements, and explicit statements of goals and objectives, and how to develop them. Benefits and hazards of both centralized and decentralized planning are presented.

*Organizational Structure and Design:* The material in *Chapter 5* is presented as one logical application of the planning process. Structure is connected with delegation of authority, and with various forms of departmentalization. A comprehensive description and evaluation is given of the relatively new, but increasingly popular, matrix organizational structure.

*Leading: Chapter 6* makes a clear distinction between *managing* and *leading* and discusses the points at which the two may be effectively merged. Comparisons are made of the theories of trait, behavioural, and contingency or situational leadership. Transformational leadership introduces the concepts of self-leadership and self-management.

*Controlling:* The imaginative Red Bead Experiment introduces *Chapter 7*. The management element of controlling is presented as the effort to ensure that all of an organization's activities are focused on its mission, goals, and objectives. The discussion of quality control closes with a description of ISO 9000.

The remaining eight chapters reflect a change in emphasis, from what might be termed the foundation coverage of the first seven chapters to theory and applications in specific areas.

*Human Resources Management: Chapter 8* points out the fallacies in the common misconception that this is a topic only for large corporations that have HR departments. It is stressed that regardless of size or type of organization, HR management is a crucial aspect of every manager's responsibilities, and cannot be left just to HR professionals. Job analysis, job specification, and job enrichment and enlargement are presented in some detail. Methods are suggested for the successful recruitment and selection of employees. Future managers are warned of the hazards of condoning sexual and other forms of harassment, and suggestions are made as to how these sensitive issues can be handled. Compensation plans are described, as are personnel benefits plans, including flextime and telecommuting.

*Managing Organizational Change: Chapter 9* is timely in the order of the chapters, because it follows eight chapters whose applications would, in the case of most organizations, result in changes and the need to manage those changes. Some manifestations of resistance are presented as natural concomitants of any change in people's lives. Change forces are discussed, as well as means of intervening and reducing resistance to change without being manipulative.

*Interpersonal and Organizational Communication: Chapter 10* stresses the importance of communication, and how to overcome some of the barriers to its effectiveness. Verbal and nonverbal clues are identified, and specific suggestions are offered to convert language to non-offensive gender-inclusive terms. The grapevine is recognized as a potent force, and methods to decrease its potentially negative effects are discussed.

*Managing Production and Operations:* The roles of production and operations managers are described in *Chapter 11*. Explicit methods are presented to facilitate site selection and operations layouts. Emphasis is placed on safety—both for employees and for those outside the organization. Production control devices such as PERT charts and statistical displays are explained and illustrated.

*The Management of Services:* A large proportion of today's Canadian students will be employed (or will be employers) in service industries. *Chapter 12* covers this area of management that is all too often ignored, or mistakenly assumed to be identical to that for an organization that manufactures and markets a tangible product. This chapter makes the distinction on the grounds of intangibility, inseparability of production and consumption, perishability, and homogeneity. The discussion of means to improve service quality and productivity have particular relevance to the service industries, but are equally applicable to the service components of manufacturing corporations.

*Entrepreneurship and Growth: Chapter 13* recognizes that nearly one in five gainfully employed Canadians are self-employed. It addresses the aspects of management that are uniquely adapted to entrepreneurship. The point is made that intrapreneurship, or the exercise of similar qualities within an organization, has been found to benefit both the organization and the individual. A brief exposition of the need for a business plan is followed by illustration of an adaptable *pro forma* plan. The growing popularity of franchises is noted, and some cautions are presented to the potential franchisee.

*Canadian Business in the Global Economy:* No management text in Canada today would be complete without a brief exposition of Canada's involvement in management on an international scale, and the particular challenges that arise from that practice. *Chapter 14* provides an overview of these challenges, the environments for international operations, and international organizations and trading blocs such as NAFTA. Without taking a judgemental or political position on these controversial issues, the chapter highlights for the student the salient features and the undoubted impact on all Canadian organizations, from the largest to the smallest.

*Technology and Innovation: Chapter 15* focuses on the management challenges that arise from the development of new technologies, as well as on managing innovators and innovations. A look is provided at various means that have been used to try to identify potentially creative individuals, and to stimulate their creativity. The chapter, and the text, closes with a brief discussion of some of the new dilemmas that technology poses for managers—from the accelerating pace of change of all kinds, to the apparent failure of most investments in technology to reduce costs, to the ubiquitous deluge of e-mail. It brings the thinking back to the initial concept—that effective management is the means by which an organization of any type becomes and remains competitive.

# Acknowledgements

THE ORIGINAL CONCEPT FOR THIS TEXT CAME FROM EVELYN VEITCH, then Sponsoring Editor for Times Irwin. Fortunately, she continued in that role after the merger with McGraw-Hill Ryerson. Those who know her will understand when I say that it was the contagion of her enthusiasm, as well as her professionalism, that undergirded the project from start to finish. After Evelyn's well-deserved appointment to Editorial Director and Publisher of the College Division, Karina Ten Veldhuis, in her role as Development Editor, ably fulfilled the combined tasks of nurturing and keeping me on track. She also gave time and energy beyond the call of duty, searching out suitable photos, acquiring the necessary permissions, and bringing everything together. Susan Broadhurst's skill and care show in her detailed editing, chasing punctuation and generally cleaning up manuscript glitches. Margaret Henderson was a gem in keeping it all together, a not inconsiderable task. Susan Calvert and Carole Marche relieved me of some of the tasks that were testing my time and my sanity in the last frantic months. I cannot express my appreciation sufficiently to these remarkable people.

A large and devoted group of individual faculty members reviewed successive drafts of the manuscript, offering explicit and helpful comments and suggestions, many of which have been incorporated into the final version. They constitute a roster that reflects many years of teaching, and in many cases direct experience as managers. My appreciation goes to: Kathryn Arnold, Grant MacEwan College; Kirk Bailey, Ryerson Polytechnic University; Lewis Callahan, Lethbridge Community College; Nina Cole, Brock University; Brian Harrocks, Algonquin College; Martha Reavley, University of Windsor; Sydney Scott, British Columbia Institute of Technology; Bernie Villeneuve, Douglas College; and Leslie Wilder, Red River College.

It would be uncharitable of me as well as inaccurate, however, if I did not point out that while they offered corrections where they saw that I had gone astray, any errors remaining are not theirs, but are solely my responsibility.

Finally, I could not close this recognition of my indebtedness if I did not acknowledge the patience with which my wife, May, put up with my long hours closeted with my computer. Although buried in her own teaching and writing, without interfering she continued to provide silent but crucial moral support throughout the long months. Every aspiring author should hope for such support!

Bruce Partridge
Camosun College
Victoria, British Columbia

# Management in Canada: 🍁
## The Competitive Challenges

# The Management Challenge

After studying this chapter, you should be able to:

▶ Define the terms *management, competitiveness,* and *quality*;

▶ Explain why a competitive focus has become imperative in a globalizing world;

▶ Identify the traditional functions and purposes of management;

▶ Explain the types of skills that managers need to achieve their goals;

▶ Discuss the major theories of management, and their relevance to management today;

▶ Contrast management in a small business with that in a large corporation; and

▶ Discuss why it is important for management students—tomorrow's managers—to develop their own personal theories of management.

## Managing the Future

WHAT DOES IT MEAN TO "MANAGE THE FUTURE"? IT means paying attention to the past, to the present, and to patterns of change in the world around us. In managing the future, understanding and initiating action are top priorities. For any organization, constant innovation and improvement are essential. Relying solely on the past is neither possible nor is it good management. Using a past orientation results in missed opportunities and a failure to keep up with changes in today's emphasis on the customer. The past-oriented manager wants to attract and retain customers, but focuses primarily on other parts of the organization, such as the accounting system, environmental and tax laws, and the sources and flow of funding. All of these are important, but they are only means to the end, rather than ends in themselves. ▶

McDonald's Corporation is one future-oriented company that respects and has learned from the past, but knows that the past can't be repeated. In the notoriously competitive fast-food business, McDonald's has managed to grow from its founding in 1955 to a massive worldwide organization that has more than 15,000 franchises and wholly owned outlets, spread among many different countries, and employing more than 183,000 staff members.[1] Behind the well-known Golden Arches is an innovative management, continually watching consumer trends and searching for ways to remain competitive. When McDonald's was planning its first outlet in Moscow, managers discovered that the potatoes grown in Russia did not meet their specifications for fibre and water content. A management decision was made to enlist a number of Russian potato growers, to provide them with new varieties of potatoes, and to guarantee them a market for their new product. McDonald's innovations in Canada include the Big Mac (1968), the Egg McMuffin (1973), Chicken McNuggets (1983), salads (1987), and the McChicken Sandwich (1989). The McDLT was first offered in 1985, but was not widely accepted; in the early 1990s it was replaced with the McLean, a low-fat burger, which McDonald's launched with a $50 million advertising campaign. This product did not catch on either, and was dropped in early 1996.

In May 1996, after extensive test marketing and what is reported to have been a $200 million advertising campaign, McDonald's launched the Arch Deluxe, a premium hamburger designed to attract more adults to supplement McDonald's already successful hold on the children's market. This innovation was only moderately successful,[2] and was followed by the introduction of pizza to attract teenagers and young adults. Then, in 1998, to stay abreast of food fashions, McDonald's introduced the McWrap. This brief synopsis illustrates the McDonald's approach—to try innovations, continue with them if they succeed, and drop them if they do not. It recognizes that innovation is likely to result in some mistakes, but that the biggest mistake is not to innovate at all.

While McDonald's founder Ray Kroc got his ideas for fast and efficient service from the original McDonald brothers, he quickly expanded on the theme, and began to offer franchises, in what for 1955 was almost a completely new concept of food sales. In effect, he used the past (the McDonald brothers' emphasis on fast and pleasant service) as well as the present and a look to the future to manage his and McDonald's future. We can't all be Ray Krocs, but we can prepare ourselves to be successful managers by learning from the successes and failures of those who have gone before us.  ■

## Management and Managers in Canada

Before embarking on the study of management, it is reasonable to ask what management is, and why it exists. Practitioners and scholars have suggested any number of definitions, the flavour of which has changed over the years. In a simple form, we can look backwards nearly a century to Henry Ford, the founder of the Ford Motor Company, and the "inventor" of mass production. He has been quoted as having said that management consists of causing average men to do the work of superior men. While there is an element of truth in this statement, the basic concepts underlying it are as inappropriate today as the gender-specific language in which he expressed himself. No longer is the manager's sole purpose to extract more production from workers. True, no organization can function effectively for long if it permits inefficiencies to continue, but the scope of management today is much broader than it was in Ford's time.

### Managers and Management

**planning**
The function of management that determines the objectives of the business, and how best to achieve those objectives.

In general, a manager is someone who directs and oversees the work and performance of other individuals. Even in a one-person company, however, success depends on other management skills that in many ways are analogous to those required in the largest of global corporations. In the simplest terms, today it is generally recognized that management responsibilities can be categorized into four fundamental functions: **planning,**

**organizing**
The function of management that arranges appropriate staffing and assigns responsibilities and tasks to individuals and groups, in order to best achieve the objectives established by planning.

**leading**
The function of management concerned with demonstrating by example and by teaching, directing, and motivating employees to perform effectively to achieve the objectives of the organization.

**controlling**
The function of management that involves monitoring performance, comparing results with planned objectives, and providing feedback and, if necessary, correction.

**organizing, leading,** and **controlling**. This book will treat each of these functions separately, and in some detail.

Planning determines *what* results the company wishes to achieve and *how* those results may be achieved. Organizing establishes and operates the structures, policies, and procedures through which the results will be achieved. Leading consists of motivating and providing examples to encourage people to work harmoniously and effectively towards the desired ends. Controlling includes establishing the frameworks within which tasks will be done, monitoring the performance of those tasks, and providing feedback and corrective action to maximize efficiency and effectiveness. These functions in combination constitute the acts of management, and the people who perform them are managers.

In a large organization, these four functions may be distributed among a number of divisions or departments. In the smallest business, a one-person entrepreneurship, the owner/manager must perform all of the functions. Yet the scope of the functions and how they can be performed are fundamentally the same, regardless of the size of the organization, or whether it is a business organized for profit, a not-for-profit organization, or a governmental department, division, or agency.

## The Management Challenge in Canada

Although some management principles are almost universal, each economy and society has its own distinct features that require adaptations in the actual practice of management. As will be discussed in Chapter 14, cultural differences from country to country have a profound impact on which management approaches and techniques will be effective in a particular location. It is important, then, to consider the unique features of Canada that have an influence on Canadian management.

First, as is well known but often disregarded, individual and family incomes in Canada far exceed those in most of the rest of the world. As a result, Canada maintains a high level of literacy and specialized education, an enviable standard of health care with its resulting long life expectancy, and relative freedom from political unrest and upheavals. In some respects, these factors assist Canadian managers, but at the same time they offer challenges because, unlike the situation in some societies, employees expect and demand a higher degree of participation in management decisions than would have been thought possible even a few years ago.

Geography also plays a significant role in Canadian management. Canada's population is one of the smallest among "industrialized" nations; at some 30 million people, it is roughly equal to the population of California. Moreover, most of Canada's relatively small population is spread in a band only 100 kilometres wide and some 6000 kilometres long. Because of Canada's wide distribution of population and industrial activity, Canadian managers must plan well ahead, because they cannot always count on quick delivery of needed products, as would be the case for many managers in the United States and in Europe, whose sources of supply are often within an overnight truck haul.

*In Canada, family income exceeds that of most other countries in the world and affords Canadian families an enviable standard of living.*

Canadian managers also must tailor their thinking to the fact that most Canadians live and work within only two or three hours' drive from the United States. This means that Canadian consumers have relatively easy access to the products produced and marketed in the much larger economy of the United States. This proximity creates significant competitive pressures. It also means that because of the size of the economy in the United States, Canadian managers have to be alert to changes in that country as well as in our own.

From its earliest days, Canada has been heavily dependent on resource-based industries—from the early dependence on fish and furs, through the provision of masts and spars to the British navy and the subsequent forest products industries, to the growth of the industries based on mineral, agricultural, and fisheries products. As recently as 1970, 42.8 percent of Canada's exports were classified as food and agricultural products and ores and metals. Even though that proportion dropped by almost half, to 23.5 percent, in the following quarter-century, the total output is even greater than it was at the earlier date.[3] As a result of this emphasis on these industries, Canadian managers have had to cope with the resource industries' typical boom-and-bust cycles, and have often had to operate in remote and relatively inaccessible locations.

Still another complicating factor is Canada's heavy dependence on foreign trade. As will be discussed in Chapter 14, this dependence has profound implications for Canadian managers even if their markets are solely within Canada and they do not directly import or export products.

These and other factors contribute to the challenges facing Canadian managers. All must be recognized and accounted for if Canadian organizations are to be competitive in the world market, as well as in the domestic market.

## Competitiveness

**competitiveness**
The capacity of an organization, in a free and fair market, to produce goods and services that meet the needs and wishes of customers, without causing environmental degradation, while simultaneously maintaining or expanding the real incomes of its employees and owners. It is the ultimate measure of potential for effective operations.

An enterprise, whether a business or a not-for-profit organization, whether large or small, must be competitive to stay alive. To be competitive, an organization must offer its products or services in ways that are better, less expensive, or more readily available, than those of its competitors. Those organizations that do not remain competitive soon lose the sales or other forms of support on which they depend in order to meet their payrolls and pay their other expenses. When they fail, their employees lose their jobs. In addition, shareholders or other owners lose the money they have invested. As a consequence, they do not want to, or they are unable to, invest more money in other business enterprises that could otherwise be the sources of Canadian job opportunities.

One aspect of competitiveness is how much an organization decides to invest in enhancement of quality, thus driving up the selling price of products and services and inhibiting potential purchasers or users of the service. Managers must decide on the optimum balance between higher quality and quicker service on the one hand, and lower selling price on the other. These decisions are almost daily challenges for managers as customer expectations increase due to improved products and services that become available from competitors. For example, the computing power of a small notebook computer is many times that of the room-size computers that were the state of the art only 20 or 30 years ago. No computer manufacturer could remain in business today if its products were only as good as those that were state-of-the-art a few years, or perhaps even a few months, ago. Similar improvements in other industries, while perhaps not quite as dramatic, still pose challenges to managers not to be left behind in quality enhancements.

*Managers must adapt to an unprecedented rate of change. One example of rapid change is that the laptop computer is many more times powerful than the room-sized computer that was state of the art a few years ago.*

**efficiency**
The ability to achieve business objectives with the minimum of effort, expense, or waste.

**effectiveness**
Doing the right thing, at the right time, to achieve the right results.

## Management for Efficiency

One of the most easily recognized responsibilities of the manager is to promote **efficiency**. This term means to obtain desired results with the least expenditure of money, effort, and time. A single-minded concentration on cost cutting can often increase efficiency substantially. There remains, however, a challenge to management to know which cost cutting method is desirable, and which would lead to savings in the short term but ultimately would lead to inefficiency, erosion of quality, and other unanticipated problems. Another challenge to management is that any move towards efficiency entails change. If change is not managed skilfully, it may be delayed or even prevented by subtle and not-so-subtle opposition on the part of those affected by it. The management of change will be considered further in Chapter 9. For now it is sufficient to point out that improvements in efficiency are often more difficult to achieve than might seem likely on first thought, and in some circumstances may even prove to be counterproductive.

## Management for Effectiveness

Efficiency addresses whether a task or a program is being conducted in the optimum and least costly manner. A more difficult question is whether it is being conducted in such a way as to ensure **effectiveness.** Whereas efficiency addresses the question of *how* something is being done, effectiveness asks *why* it is being done. Even if something is being done in absolutely the most efficient manner, it still may be contributing little or nothing to the purposes of the organization. With the advent of computers, and the ease with which numbers can be crunched and reports can be generated, many managers are deluged with statistical reports—all impressive, all correct, and many absolutely useless. Massive, figure-laden reports, while useful tools, are never a substitute for management skill and management thinking. A good test is whether a given report actually leads to a decision being made; if not, managers should question whether the report should be produced at all.

Other examples of ineffectiveness are the ritual meetings that fill many managers' calendars. Often someone will attend a meeting solely to be able to communicate the results to those who do not attend, or worse, to provide nominal "representation" from a constituent body. Again, the test is whether everyone attending a particular meeting can either contribute necessary information or be helpful in arriving at the collective decision that is the purpose of the meeting. It is the effective manager's challenge to use meetings when they are appropriate, but to avoid them when they do not serve a demonstrable purpose, and to limit attendance to those who have a real reason for being there.

## Special Features of Management in Small Business

Some multinational corporations have larger annual revenues than the Gross Domestic Product of a number of small countries (see Exhibit 1-1). It is tempting to think of management in terms of these huge companies. Nevertheless, as has been said, the fundamental principles do not depend on size, so even a small business must address the same aspects of management. In the small business, one or a few individuals must provide or find ways of providing expertise in all of the different areas that specialists provide in a

**Exhibit 1-1**

*Twenty Companies with Largest Revenues and Twenty Representative Countries with Lower Gross Domestic Product (US$ billion)*

| Company | Nationality | Revenues | Country | GDP |
|---|---|---|---|---|
| Mitsubishi | Japan | 175.8 | Bangladesh | 24.8 |
| Mitsui | Japan | 171.5 | Bolivia | 6.3 |
| Itochi | Japan | 167.8 | Bulgaria | 9.6 |
| Sumitomo | Japan | 162.5 | Chile | 41.2 |
| General Motors | U.S. | 155.0 | Columbia | 43.4 |
| Marubeni | Japan | 150.2 | Cuba | 16.6 |
| Ford Motor | U.S. | 128.4 | Egypt | 40.9 |
| Exxon | U.S. | 101.5 | Ethiopia | 2.7 |
| Nissho Iwai | Japan | 100.9 | Guatemala | 10.4 |
| Royal Dutch Shell | Netherlands | 94.9 | Hungary | 35.5 |
| Toyota Motor | Japan | 88.2 | Ireland | 50.5 |
| Wal-Mart Stores | U.S. | 83.4 | Israel | 69.4 |
| Hitachi | Japan | 76.4 | Malaysia | 58.0 |
| Nippon Life Insurance | Japan | 75.4 | Nicaragua | 1.5 |
| AT&T | U.S. | 75.1 | Nigeria | 29.6 |
| Nippon Tel & Tel | Japan | 70.8 | Pakistan | 56.4 |
| Matsushita Elec. | Japan | 70.0 | Peru | 44.7 |
| Tomen | Japan | 70.0 | Philippines | 52.6 |
| General Electric | U.S. | 64.7 | Singapore | 46.0 |
| Daimler-Benz | Germany | 64.2 | Uruguay | 11.0 |

Source: United Nations Statistical Division, *Statistical Yearbook 1995*, 40th edition (New York: UN Secretariat, 1995).

large corporation. Although there are compensating factors, this difference poses a major challenge for the managers of small business. Further discussion of this management challenge appears in Chapter 13.

## Characteristics of Successful Managers

A study by Harbridge House, a consulting firm, identified ten behavioural characteristics of a successful manager, regardless of age, sex, industry, organization size, or corporate culture.[4] Those characteristic behaviours are:

1. *Provides clear direction.* An effective manager needs to involve people in establishing explicit goals and standards for groups as well as for individuals, and must be clear and thorough in delegating responsibility.
2. *Encourages open communication.* Managers must be candid, honest, and direct in dealing with people, establishing a climate of openness and trust.
3. *Coaches and supports people.* Managers must work constructively to correct performance problems, and go to bat with superiors for subordinates. (The latter "was consistently rated as one of the most important aspects of effective leadership," says Robert Stringer, senior vice president of Harbridge House.)
4. *Provides objective recognition.* Managers must recognize employees for good performance more often than they criticize them for problems, with rewards being related to the quality of job performance, rather than to seniority or personal relationships.

## Management in the Real World　1-1

### The Management Challenge: Quality and Competitiveness: Reflections by Philip Crosby

Getting an organization to do things right the first time is obviously a good idea. Naturally it's cheapest to do something only once. Along those lines, it seems apparent that happy customers are a company's primary objective. Yet the conventional way of managing isn't automatically tilted towards these objectives. Management is full of "old wives tales"—ideas that are accepted as true without investigation. Management has its own agenda, which is usually very short-term oriented.

Executives used to tell me that I would bankrupt the company if I insisted on getting everything perfect. They had a vision of work slowing to a crawl while each step was inspected and tested several times. They talked about the perils of babying the customer. They wanted to grant permission to deliver materials and services that weren't absolutely correct—merely fit to be used.

People who talk about the good old days, when everything was done better, have selective memories. Nothing was made right the first time years ago—it was reworked until it was acceptable, which was part of the plan. Management knew in its heart that the problem was the workers, so they kept making systems to reduce labour's effect. This discouraged people and led to a self-fulfilling prophecy of even more separation of the workforce from product and service quality. I found myself trying to explain the people to the management and vice versa.

One day, when I was a quality engineer, I was asked to attend the monthly management review and say a few words about quality. I put on my good suit and appeared at the proper time, sitting in the back of the room. The meeting began with the comptroller breaking down revenue by product line and services. There was an animated discussion about each item, particularly those not meeting the objectives. Charts and discussion on profitability, inventory, employee compensation, purchasing, accounts receivable, and debt followed for three hours. Then the personnel director presented a new hospitalization plan. Next the industrial relations director talked about labour negotiations and the possibility of a strike. Then there was a pause.

The general manager checked his watch and noted that they had "invited Phil Crosby to come and talk about quality."

"We've used up most of the time, Phil," he said. "Could you limit your remarks to five minutes or so?"

I noticed that the attendees were busily putting their papers away and checking things out with each other. This wasn't going to be an attentive group, I thought, but I nodded and stood up.

When they quieted down I smiled and said, "Quality can be measured by money also. If we added up the expenses of doing things wrong and over—like rework, customer service, inspection, excess inventory, unplanned overtime, accounts receivable overdue, engineering change notices, purchasing change notices, and such—it comes to over 20 percent of revenue. These are my figures put together without benefit of the accounting department, but I think if they're calculated properly the number will be much higher. Roughly the price of nonconformance, as I call it, is five times the pretax profit I saw reported earlier. Thank you."

When I sat down the group just stared at me. The general manager turned to the comptroller, "Five times pretax profits?" he asked.

"Anyway," said the comptroller, "I've mentioned it before."

The meeting continued for another hour and ended with the price of nonconformance (PONC) becoming a regular part of the accounting and reporting process. From that moment on, management's interest in quality was focused; the old beliefs disappeared and were replaced by management attention on a management subject. They reduced the PONC expense by half in a year just by changing their attitude and attacking problems that measurement showed to be important. They even started talking to their employees.

Measure quality by money, not by statistics. Be real.

"Most managers don't realize how much criticism they give," the study says. "They do it to be helpful, but positive recognition is what really motivates people."

5. *Establishes ongoing controls.* This means following up on important issues and actions and giving subordinates feedback on their individual and collective performance.
6. *Selects the right people to staff the organization.* Managers must attract and select the best people in terms of skills and competencies to accomplish the organization's mission and goals.
7. *Understands the financial implications of decisions.* This quality is considered important even for managers of support departments, such as personnel/human resources and research and development, whose connection to the organization's profit margin is only indirect, albeit just as important as that of the primary operating departments.
8. *Encourages innovation and new ideas.* Employees rate this quality important in even the most traditional and conservative organizations.
9. *Gives subordinates clear-cut decisions when they're needed.* "Employees want a say in things," the report says, "but they don't want endless debate. There's a time to get on with things, and the best managers know when that time comes."
10. *Consistently demonstrates a high level of integrity.* The study shows that most employees want to work for a manager they can respect.

Many of these attributes reflect the application of basic communication and human relations principles. Others reflect analytical and conceptual thinking. Still others require the courage to make decisions when decisions must be made. All depend on the practice of time-management techniques, for time is the one resource that cannot be stretched, so its effective use is paramount. These skills and techniques are not innate—that is, no one is born with them—but they can be learned.

## Levels of Management

**managers**
Top-level managers are responsible for developing long-range plans for the business; middle managers are responsible to top-level managers for directing and managing one or more business units or functions; first-line managers are responsible to middle managers for direct supervision of the performance of non-management employees.

All **managers** perform the four basic functions of management—planning, organizing, leading, and controlling. Each manager's job, however, reflects different proportions of these basic areas of responsibility, depending on such factors as the manager's level in the organization; the kind of business, industry, or organization; the culture of the organization; and even the personal skills and interests of the manager. For convenience, those who study management, and those who actually practise it, usually divide the levels of management on the basis of their vertical rank in the organization. These categories are top management, middle management, and first-line management.

**Top management.** As might be expected from the term, top management refers to the most senior officers of the organization. In a large corporation this may include several *vice presidents*, the *president*, and a *chairman and chief executive officer (CEO)*. Bombardier, Inc., one of Canada's largest companies, provides an example, with a slight variation. In 1995 Bombardier had a chairman and CEO, a president and Chief Operating Officer (COO), an executive vice president, and seven vice presidents. The task of this company's top management structure is to guide and direct a Canadian corporation whose 40,000 employees are engaged in worldwide operations that generate more than $7 billion in revenues. By contrast, in a relatively small business, which might have 15 or 20 employees and only $1 of revenues for every $10,000 of Bombardier's, the top management typically might consist of the owner or owners, and perhaps one or two heads of divisions such as sales and production. The behaviour and attitudes of top management set the tone for the whole enterprise, regardless of its size. In the small business,

---

**Real World Reflection    1-1**

## Encouraging Self-responsibility

Self-responsibility means that employees take 100 percent of the responsibility for their work. Gerald Ksushel, author of *Reaching the Peak Performance Zone*, says:

> (Self responsibility) means simply that *you* decide how good you want to be, how hard you want to work, how thoroughly you want to do something, how far you want to go. Not your boss, not the shop steward, not your colleagues, not the president of the company. And when things don't work out as planned, you take responsibility for your mistakes and setbacks.

Employees may enjoy having a bigger "piece of the action" because they are trusted with a higher level of decision making. Their problem-solving ideas are solicited and implemented more regularly. An end result hopefully will lead to employees believing that their work is valuable and important. An intangible benefit is the individual taking pride in performing at a new level of excellence.

### MANAGEMENT STRATEGY
All of the individuals working for you are unique. Each person is going to respond differently to the question "What's in it for me?"

---

Contributed by Marnie Wright, British Columbia Institute of Technology.

---

the top manager's leadership has a direct impact on nearly every employee. In the large corporation, on the other hand, the direct impact of top management's leadership is often largely restricted to contacts with other top managers and with people in the upper levels of middle management. They, in turn, convey the patterns of behaviours and attitudes to those with whom they have most contact, and so on down the hierarchical structure of the organization.

**Middle management.** People at the *middle management* level typically have one of two main roles. One is to manage a particular operation of the business, such as a mine, factory, retail outlet, or region of operations. The other is to manage a specific support function, such as accounting, purchasing, or human resource management. Typical position titles are *department manager, area sales manager, plant manager, director of procurement,* or *human resource manager.* In a small organization, one individual may fulfil several of these roles. Middle managers are accountable to top managers or to other middle managers, and often must coordinate their work with that of other middle managers.

Competitive pressures have caused many organizations to "downsize" their management cadres, especially at the middle management level. In the past ten years many middle management positions have been eliminated in companies such as Cominco, Nortel, and Canadian Pacific. Competitive pressures indicate that the shrinking of management in large companies likely will continue throughout the foreseeable future. As these middle management positions disappear, top managers either have to take on the functions formerly performed by middle managers or have to permit some tasks to be left undone.

**First-line management.**  Managers classified as *first line* coordinate the work of others who aren't themselves managers. They work much closer than top or middle managers to the people who actually produce the products or provide the services for which the organization exists. First-line managers may have titles such as *supervisor, office manager,* or *foreman* (a title that seems to persist even when the "foreman" is a woman). In small organizations the first-line manager may be accountable directly to the top manager or managers. In a larger organization accountability probably will be to a middle manager. In either situation, the first-line manager probably will oversee the work of skilled or unskilled workers, salespeople, accounting clerks, or scientists, depending on the subunit's particular tasks (in these examples, production, marketing, accounting, or research). First-line managers are responsible for the organization's basic work and are in daily or near-daily contact with the staff members accountable to them. They must work with their own staff and with other first-line supervisors whose tasks are related to their own.

**The mix of responsibilities.**  The extent to which a manager is involved in each of the four basic areas of management is dictated in part by the manager's position in the hierarchy of an organization. In one study, reported more than a decade ago but doubtless still representative of the situation today, managers were asked what activities were most important in their jobs. From the responses, it is clear that as an individual is promoted up the organizational ladder, planning takes on more and more importance in that person's workload, while less time and energy are devoted to organizing and controlling. The extent of involvement in direct leadership varies considerably from individual to individual.[5] Exhibit 1-2 illustrates a typical mix of activities at each of the three levels.

## Managerial Skills

**skill**
Ability or proficiency in performing a particular task or kind of task.

**conceptual skill**
The ability to think in abstract terms, to analyze and diagnose problems, and to make use of lateral thinking when appropriate.

**analytical skill**
The ability to solve problems by applying basic principles in a logical manner.

Regardless of the level at which managers perform, they must learn and develop many skills.[6]

**Conceptual skill.**  This skill consists of the ability to see the big picture as well as the complexities of the overall organization. To keep an organization focused, managers must conceptualize how each part of the organization fits and how those parts interact with each other to accomplish goals and operate in an ever-changing environment.

**Analytical skill.**  This skill involves solving management problems by applying logic to relevant information, and reaching a conclusion. It requires the ability to identify key factors, to understand how they interrelate, and to apply them in a given situation.

Long-range planning requires a combination of both conceptual and analytical skills, to look forward and project how prospective actions may affect an organization five, ten, or even twenty years in the future. Although events will not turn out exactly as planned, the long-range vision helps the company to plot its present courses of action in such a way as to provide the flexibility required to meet changing conditions and remain competitive.

**Exhibit 1-2** *Typical Mix of Skills Required at Three Organizational Levels*

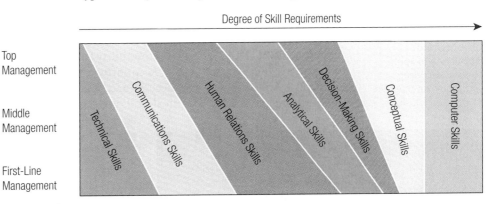

**Decision-making skill.** All managers must make decisions by choosing from alternatives. The quality of these decisions determines the manager's effectiveness. In addition to skill in decision making, managers have to develop the courage actually to *make* decisions. This may be more difficult that it seems, because the manager knows that any change might lead to unforeseen outcomes, and it often seems safer to postpone making a definitive decision, or to avoid making it altogether. Effective managers realize, however, that *not* making a decision is actually *making* a decision—a decision to continue with the status quo, whatever it may be.

**People skill.** Since all managers must accomplish much of their work through other people, it is vital that they work effectively with those other people, both inside and outside of the organization. One aspect of **people skill** is effective communication—the written and oral transmission of information, instructions, criticism, or praise, and a genuine indication of interest in the other person as an individual.

**Communication skill.** The ability to communicate accurately and concisely is critical to success in every field, but it is perhaps even more important for managers than for non-managers. This skill involves the ability to convey ideas and messages in ways that other people understand and to seek and use feedback from employees to ensure that the messages have been understood. This subject is discussed further in Chapter 10.

Lewis Lehr, chairman and CEO of 3M, demonstrates one form of effective people and communication skills. He spends six months of every year away from 3M's headquarters, visiting the company's numerous plants in several countries. There, he participates in question-and-answer sessions with employees, building the employee trust and cooperation that are essential to 3M's success. Lehr also requires the other 3M executives to visit frequently with representatives of the media, government, and education to talk about 3M.[7]

**Computer skill.** In a study of 100 personnel directors from some of North America's largest corporations, 7 of every 10 directors reported that they classified computer skills as *important*, *very important*, or *essential* for advancement in management.[8] This does not mean that managers must be able to write computer programs, or even have a high degree of competence in operating a computer, although the latter is becoming increasingly useful. Instead, middle managers are required to have enough knowledge of

**decision-making skill**
The ability to choose solutions from alternatives, and to have the courage to take definitive action when required.

**people skill**
The ability to work effectively with and motivate others.

**communication skill**
The ability to listen actively and to transmit to others ideas, concepts, and directions.

**computer skill**
Having sufficient understanding of how computers can facilitate decision making, in order to be able to make effective selection and use of hardware and software.

computers and what they can do, to oversee the selection and application of computer hardware and software, and to ensure that computer-generated reports are as effective as possible in facilitating management decision making.

**technical skill**
The ability to apply specific knowledge, technique, or expertise to perform a task.

**Technical skill.** This skill reflects the ability to use *specific* knowledge, techniques, and resources in performing work. Accounting supervisors, engineering directors, and nursing supervisors, for instance, all need highly specific technical skills to perform their management jobs. Technical skills are especially important at the first-line management level, since daily work-related problems must be solved. Middle managers need to marshal sufficient technical skills to be able to monitor the work of supervisors and of those they supervise, and to offer guidance when serious problems arise, but they do not need complete technical mastery of all of the skills that are required in the areas for which they are responsible. Top managers, similarly, need enough technical skill to understand operations and to distinguish between technical competence and incompetence in their subordinates. Top managers, however, need not be (nor could they be) technically competent in all of the areas of knowledge required throughout a large organization.

It is not a coincidence that technical skill is the last to be identified in this list of managerial skills. It is widely recognized that when a manager fails, it is seldom caused by a lack of technical skills, but rather by a lack of other managerial skills.

**Skills required by managers at various levels.** While the preceding skills are all important, just as with the functions of management, the importance of each kind of skill varies with the level of the manager in the organization. Exhibit 1-2 illustrates the skills required at each level. For example, technical and human relations skills are usually highly important at lower levels of management. These managers have greater contact with the actual production of products or delivery of services, and with the people doing these tasks. Communication and computer skills are equally important at all levels of management. Analytical skills are slightly more important at higher levels of management where the environments are less stable and problems are less predictable. Finally, decision-making and conceptual skills are extremely critical to top managers' performance. Top management's primary responsibility is to make decisions that are implemented at lower levels, and to foster a climate throughout the organization that enhances its ability to meet its goals.

*Managing a construction project requires the application of all kinds of skills: conceptual, analytical, decision-making, people, communication, and technical. Detailed plans help to focus how these skills are applied, but are not substitutes for them.*

## What Managers Are Reading　1-1

### The Witch Doctors: Making Sense of the Management Gurus

So many management fads and theories have surfaced within the past century that one could say that Frederick W. Taylor opened a floodgate. John Micklethwait and Adrian Wooldridge have observed this deluge from their vantage points as business editor and managing editor, respectively, of the *Economist*. From this book it would seem that their observation has ranged from amused toleration to outright disdain.

In this well-written volume, they attempt to sort through some of the most important of the current and recently discarded management fads, and to make sense out of them as a whole, without espousing any one as the final answer. They skilfully avoid succumbing to what must have been a strong temptation to skewer some of the more assertive and now-discredited of the management gurus. Instead, they calmly express rather pointed opinions as to which theories have made significant contributions to management understanding, and which have proven to be at best damp squibs, and at worst the cause of management disasters. For instance, they rush in where proverbial angels fear to tread by taking a few shots at best-selling Tom Peters, whom they dub "the middle manager's pinup." They award plaudits to true innovators such as Canada's Henry Mintzberg (some of whose works are briefly reviewed elsewhere in this text). They mercifully do not assign any ranking order to those whose works they believe might better have been left unpublished.

In one of the more cogent passages, the authors attribute the plethora of management books and their amazing popularity to two human emotions—fear and greed. In their view, many managers fear that they will be left behind if they do not know about, and indeed often appear to put into practice, the latest in management fads. They also say that many managers expect miraculous bottom-line results if they can only latch on to the latest in management theories, or at least the latest versions of management theories that may have been known for many years.

The authors do not promise that those who buy their book will have a transformation in their thinking or their actions. Instead, a major theme is to warn that *no* book will accomplish this sought-after answer to all management problems. And that warning, in itself, may be the greatest value in the book, which has received favourable reviews all over North America and topped several best-seller lists for many weeks.

Source: John Micklethwait and Adrian Wooldridge, *The Witch Doctors: Making Sense of the Management Gurus* (London: Random House, 1998).

## Roles Played by Managers

**role**
A behaviour pattern expected of, or exhibited by, an individual in a given situation.

**managerial role**
The behaviour pattern of a manager, incorporating interpersonal, informational, and decisional roles.

A **role** is the behaviour pattern exhibited by an individual or that is *expected* of an individual within a unit or position. One of the most frequently cited studies of **managerial roles** was conducted by Henry Mintzberg, a Canadian who published what has become recognized worldwide as a classic management source. He interviewed and observed five chief executives from different industries, each for a two-week period. He determined that managers serve in ten different but closely related activities.[9] Exhibit 1-3 on page 17 summarizes some of his findings. Mintzberg categorizes these ten activities into three broadly described groups of roles: *interpersonal* roles, *informational* roles, and *decisional* roles.[10]

### Interpersonal Roles

The three interpersonal roles of *figurehead*, *leader*, and *liaison* grow out of the manager's formal authority and focus on interpersonal relationships. By assuming these roles, the

## Real World Reflection    1-2

### Management Skills

Most people can easily name a manager they have worked for who does not personify the picture of the effective manager. While most managers have a sense of their "end result" responsibilities, not all demonstrate the behaviours that will achieve these goals efficiently. There are many skills that, if mastered, create stepping stones from objectives to results. These skills include:

- Listening
- Questioning
- Giving and receiving feedback
- Planning
- Team building
- Coaching
- Delegating

These behaviour-based skills are often referred to as "soft skills." As you develop as a manager, you will find your own natural style of delivery. If you are an aspiring manager, you can begin your training now, by mastering these skills in your personal life.

Contributed by Marnie Wright, British Columbia Institute of Technology.

---

manager also can perform informational roles that, in turn, lead directly to performing decisional roles. All managerial jobs require some duties that are symbolic or ceremonial in nature. Examples of the *figurehead role* include that of the college dean who reads the names of students at graduation, the manager who "makes an appearance" at the wedding of a subordinate's daughter, and the CEO whose name appears on the letterhead of a charitable organization in an honorary capacity.

The manager's *leadership role* involves directing and coordinating the activities of subordinates. One part of this role is to lead by personal example. Another part probably involves staffing (hiring, training, promoting, disciplining, and dismissing) and motivating employees. The leadership role also involves controlling, or making sure that things are going according to plan. Chapter 6 explores a number of aspects of the leadership role.

The *liaison role* involves managers in interpersonal relationships outside their area of command, both inside and outside of the organization. Within the organization, managers must interact with numerous other managers and other individuals. Many managers must maintain relationships with customers or officers of customer corporations, with officials of governmental agencies, and in some cases with representatives of the media.

### Informational Roles

As a result of the three interpersonal roles just discussed, managers develop informal networks of interpersonal contacts. As a result of these contacts the managers gather and receive information and transmit it both upwards and downwards in the hierarchy. In

**Exhibit 1-3**   *Mintzberg's Ten Managerial Roles*

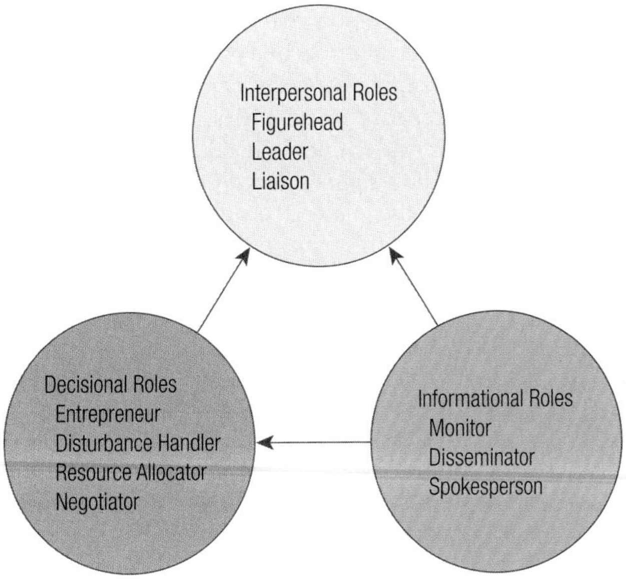

this activity the manager is acting in an *informational role*. One of the perplexities of management is that the higher one goes within a hierarchy, the less contact one has with the majority of the staff of the organization, and the greater is the tendency of others to shield the manager from "bad news." As a consequence of these two factors, an important goal of any manager wishing to perform effectively is to transcend these restrictions and to enhance the free flow of information.

The *monitor role* involves observing the internal and external environments to discover information, changes, opportunities, and problems that may affect the unit. The information gathered may concern competitive moves that could influence the entire organization, such as observing young people wearing a new fashion that suggests a change in a product line, or noting changes in the rejection rate of items being produced.

The *disseminator role* involves providing important information to subordinates and to peers. It may be done formally in writing or in a meeting, but more often information is disseminated informally.

In the *spokesperson role*, the manager represents the unit to other people. This representation may be internal, such as when a manager makes a case for salary increases to top management. Equally important, the manager represents and speaks for top management in explaining company policy to the people in the manager's unit. The spokesperson role also may be external, such as when an executive speaks to a local civic organization or to representatives of a governmental agency or the news media.

## Decisional Roles

Developing interpersonal relationships and gathering information are important, but they aren't ends in themselves. They serve as the basic inputs to the process of decision making. Some people believe that *decisional roles*—as entrepreneur, disturbance handler, resource allocator, and negotiator—are a manager's most important roles.

The *entrepreneur role's* purpose is to improve performance and effectiveness by innovative means. Entrepreneurial behaviour is discussed in Chapter 13.

In the *disturbance handler role*, managers make decisions or take corrective action in response to pressures and conflicts that arise either internally or externally. When an emergency room supervisor responds quickly to a local disaster, a plant manager reacts to a strike, or a first-line manager responds to a breakdown in a key piece of equipment or to a conflict between members of the staff, they are dealing with disturbances in their environments. Because these situations require prompt responses, often the disturbance handler role temporarily takes priority over all of the other roles.

In the *resource allocator role*, a manager decides who will get what resources (money, people, time, materials, and equipment). Invariably, there aren't enough resources to go around, so the manager must allocate scarce goods among competing requests. Top managers must decide which departments and activities will receive more or less resources, thus determining which will expand or contract. These allocations set the course for the whole organization. A first-line supervisor must decide whether to set up overtime schedules or to hire part-time workers. Any manager responsible for several tasks or projects must decide daily how much time to spend on each, thus allocating the precious resource of time.

In the *negotiator role*, managers must bargain with other units concerning the allocation of staff and other resources, or anything else influencing the unit. A sales manager may negotiate to convince the production manager to amend a production schedule to complete a special order for a valuable customer. A first-line supervisor may negotiate for new work schedules for employees, while a top-level manager may negotiate with labour union representatives or government officials.

Mintzberg suggests that recognition of these ten roles helps to explain the job of managing and illustrates that all of the roles are interrelated. This interrelationship is illustrated in Exhibit 1-4, and applies as well in a small business as in the largest of organizations, and not only in businesses organized for profit, but also in not-for-profit and government agencies and bodies.

## The Classical Approaches to Management

**classical theories of management**
The general category describing early studies of management.

The history of management as a *practice* goes back into the mists of antiquity, whenever and wherever people attempted to work together to accomplish a common purpose. Complex planning and coordination must have been required to design, shape, transport, and erect the stones at Stonehenge, or to construct the pyramids of the ancient Egyptians and of the Maya in Central America. Even in the simplest of prehistoric communities, some form of management has always been required. Otherwise, people could not have coordinated their efforts to avoid chaos and to overcome the hazards posed by the life-threatening environments in which they existed. Yet, even though management was being practised, it was not recognized either as a distinct function or as an academic discipline until early in the twentieth century.

### Frederick Taylor (1856-1915) and Scientific Management

**scientific management**
The theory that there is one best way to do any particular job, that it can be ascertained and taught to employees, and that workers are motivated primarily by money.

One of the earliest to recognize management as a discipline was Frederick Taylor. He has been called "the father of **scientific management**," because of the influence of his book *Principles of Scientific Management*, published in 1911.[11] Based on his experience as the chief engineer in a steel plant, he believed that management's primary objective should be to secure the maximum prosperity for both the employer and each employee. To achieve these two objectives, Taylor applied what he called "management science," or an approach based on systematic observation and measurement of worker activities. Tay-

**Exhibit 1-4**    *The Interrelationship of Skills, Roles, and the Functions of Management*

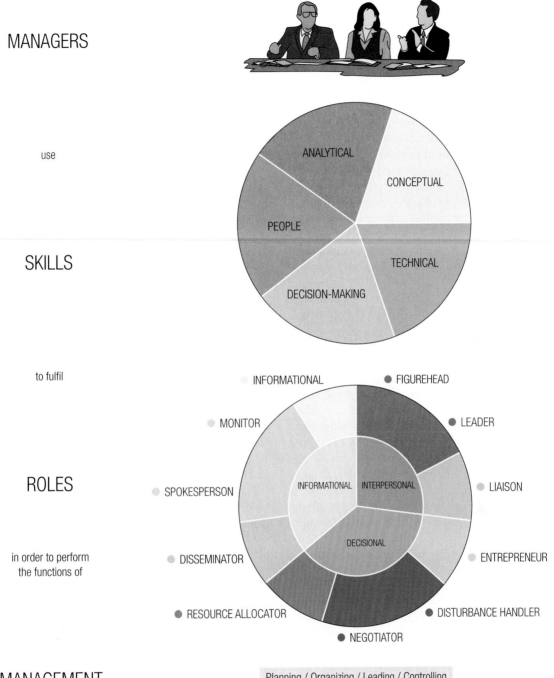

MANAGERS

use

SKILLS

to fulfil

ROLES

in order to perform
the functions of

MANAGEMENT

Planning / Organizing / Leading / Controlling

**time and motion studies**
Timing each aspect of a
job to determine the
actual physical move-
ments that will allow it to
be done most efficiently.

lor concluded that there must be "one best way" to do every task, and that production
would be increased if every worker were taught that best way and required to follow it.
Taylor used a stopwatch and later a movie camera to do what are called **time and motion
studies.** In order to encourage worker cooperation, Taylor advocated an incentive pay

## Management in the Real World    1-2

# The Evolution of Management: Reflections by Philip Crosby

Soon after I gained employment as a quality technician back in 1952, the company sent me to quality control school. There I learned that each process had its own lifestyle and results based on the laws of probability. I also learned that we should assign acceptable quality levels (AQL) to know how many good things would emerge from the process. But the people conducting the process weren't to be trusted, so all output had to be examined carefully and protected from use if it was found to be wanting. Little work was done properly the first time but this was attributed to humans' built-in error factor. All in all, error was inevitable and it was up to the science of quality control to protect the world.

My education and military experience were in medicine where the main effort was to keep people from getting sick. For this reason, vaccines had been developed to spare people smallpox, diphtheria, polio, and other disagreeable diseases. So all of this scientific determination that things could never be done right the first time on a regular basis didn't make sense to me. But my teachers and co-workers believed it all and so were upset with my deductions. They would point to the statistics and results.

Sure enough, the manufacturing operations were struggling to raise their quality to the AQLs assigned —indicating that more charts and more control were necessary. However, I thought things should be the other way around. The human element was completely missing: these beliefs assumed that "people were no damn good" and that was the end of it.

I felt that the concepts of quality control and of quality assurance (which checks on quality control) were fatally flawed. I felt that the defect rates were self-fulfilling, caused by the concept rather than the process.

Since I was on the absolute bottom of the organization chart, my concerns had little effect except to generate some fatherly lectures from my superiors. But these only encouraged me since they were offering advice, not hemlock.

I felt that the main problem was that "quality" was considered to be "goodness" and was therefore negotiable. I proposed that we define the word as meaning "conformance to requirements." That way we could spend our time teaching and helping people to do their jobs right the first time, rather than just treating the wounded. As we learned, we could then improve the requirements. Requirements, I thought, originated when we determined what the customers needed and described the actions necessary to produce that. We weren't talking just about the shop workers here—most of the expensive problems were caused by errors originating in the white-collar and other service areas.

A paper I wrote on these ideas met with a complete lack of support. The conventional wisdom of quality control couldn't accept it. A few years later when I brought the idea of zero defects as a performance standard, it was completely rejected—even though it worked.

But ideas that deserve to live, live. And now we see that the concept of preventing has become a normal part of management's lifestyle. Relationships with employees, suppliers, and customers are beginning to be a priority of management. The old "do a good job and you get to keep it" style is gone. But there are those who still think doing things right the first time costs more.

We need to continually test the concepts put forth by business practitioners and philosophers. People who would become effective and prosper can't just accept whatever has been believed before. Personal success comes from applying an open mind to current attitudes. A large chest of unsound concepts is waiting to be challenged.

After all, not too long ago tomatoes were considered poisonous.

*The "Father of Scientific Management," Frederick W. Taylor, inaugurated a revolution in thinking about management.*

**classical organizational theory**
The management theory that is primarily focused on the organization, its functions, and how it should be organized for greatest efficiency.

system in which any worker who produced more than the predetermined quantity would be paid more than workers who merely fulfilled their quotas.[12]

For the sake of "efficiency", Taylor advocated that jobs be broken down into simple, repetitive tasks. Then each worker would be required to learn and practise what managers had decided was the "best way" to do each task, taking no longer than the prescribed time allotted for it. Not surprisingly, workers resisted his methods. First, they feared, with some justification, that if they produced too much they would "work themselves out of a job." Second, the rigid specialization meant that they quickly became bored with their jobs. Another weakness in Taylor's thesis was his assumption that money was the only way to motivate workers—a fallacy that will be discussed further in Chapter 8. In addition, Taylor has been accused of having misinterpreted or even of having falsified some of his research data, and of having plagiarized material written by a colleague.[13] Despite these criticisms and the fact that in his day Taylor's proposals met with little enthusiasm from practising managers, the study of management owes a significant debt to him for having proclaimed the need to consider management as something that could and should be studied.[14]

## Henri Fayol (1841–1925) and Classical Organization Theory

Another approach focused on the management of *organizations*, as contrasted with Taylor's focus on the management of *tasks*. This **classical organization theory** was directed primarily to large organizations, but most of the principles enunciated are equally applicable to small business enterprises. Among several authors taking this approach,[15] Henri Fayol was one of the more influential.[16] Fayol divided an organization's activities into six categories, which he said were essential and present in all organizations. They are:

1. Technical (production, manufacturing);
2. Commercial (buying, selling);
3. Financial;
4. Security (protecting property and persons);
5. Accounting; and
6. Managerial (planning, organizing, commanding, coordinating, and controlling).

Fayol proposed the 14 *principles* shown in Exhibit 1-5 on page 22. He suggested that a manager's "experience and sense of proportion" should guide the degree of application of any principle in each particular situation.

## Max Weber (1864–1920) and Bureaucracy

Born in Germany, Max Weber (pronounced VAY-ber) was interested in the authority structures in organizations. He made a distinction between power (the ability to force people to obey) and authority (where orders are voluntarily obeyed by those receiving them). According to Weber, the first mode of exercising authority is based on the qualities of the leader. The second mode of exercising authority is through precedent and usage; that is, by virtue of the status the manager has acquired.

**Exhibit 1-5**

*Fayol's 14 Principles of Management*

1. *Division of work.* Specialization of labour is necessary for organizational success.
2. *Authority.* The right to give orders must accompany responsibility.
3. *Discipline.* Obedience and respect help an organization run smoothly.
4. *Unity of command.* Each employee should receive orders from only one superior.
5. *Unity of direction.* The efforts of everyone in the organization should be coordinated and focused in the same direction.
6. *Subordination of individual interests to the general interest.* Resolving the tug of war between personal and organizational interests in favour of the organization is one of the management's greatest difficulties.
7. *Remuneration.* Employees should be paid fairly in accordance with their contribution.
8. *Centralization.* The relationship between centralization and decentralization is a matter of proportion; the optimum balance must be found for each organization.
9. *Scalar chain.* Subordinates should observe the formal chain of command unless expressly authorized by their respective superiors to communicate with each other.
10. *Order.* Both material things and people should be in their proper places.
11. *Equity.* Fairness that results from a combination of kindliness and justice will lead to devoted and loyal service.
12. *Stability and tenure of personnel.* People need time to learn their jobs.
13. *Initiative.* One of the greatest satisfactions is formulating and carrying out a plan.
14. *Esprit de corps.* Harmonious effort among individuals is the key to organizational success.

**bureaucracy**
Management of an organization by specialization of labour, a hierarchy of authority, specific selection and promotion criteria, and adherence to a rigid set of rules; also the people who manage an organization that follows this pattern.

Weber believed that the "bureaucratic" organization is the dominant institution in society because it is the most efficient. As he used the term, **bureaucracy** refers to a management approach based on formal organizational structure with set rules and regulations that relies on specialization of labour, an authority hierarchy, and rigid promotion and selection criteria. He considered bureaucracy inevitable, but cautioned that it was the "iron cage within which humanity will be stifled and die." While he was speaking of the Germany of his day, his recognition both that some bureaucracy is necessary and that it embodies hazards is still relevant today. Another of his contributions, which was almost revolutionary when he proposed it, was the concept of management as a career, instead of something into which someone might just happen to stumble.[17]

## Contributions and Limitations of the Classical Approaches

The greatest contribution of the classical approaches was that they identified management as a subject that—like law, medicine, and other occupations—should be practised according to principles that managers can learn. In addition, many of the management techniques used today (such as time and motion analysis, work simplification, incentive wage systems, production scheduling, personnel testing, and budgeting) are derived from the classical approaches. One major criticism of the classical approaches is that the majority of their insights are too simplistic for today's complex organizations in a constantly changing world. The approaches were simplistic by today's standards, but they provided an invaluable start.

## The Behavioural Approaches to Management

The behavioural approaches to management developed partly because managers found that employees didn't always behave as they were "supposed to." These approaches fall into two separate branches. The first branch, the *human relations approach*, became popular in the 1940s and 1950s, although it was first proposed several decades earlier. The second branch, the *behavioural science approach*, received little attention until the 1950s.

## Elton Mayo (1880-1949) and the Human Relations Approach

**human relations approach**
The management approach that focuses on the interaction of individuals within groups, and pays heed to the individual's needs, goals, and expectations.

In the **human relations approach**, managers and other employees are studied in terms of what occurs within the group. It is argued that to develop good human relations, managers must know which psychological and sociological factors influence the behaviours of employees and how employees are influenced by the group within which they operate. Thus, while scientific management concentrates on the job's *physical* environment, human relations concentrates on the *social* and *psychological* environments. Elton Mayo placed his focus on the *informal group* as an outlet and a source of motivation for workers. His work also led to an emphasis on the importance of an adequate upward-flowing communication system. His Hawthorne studies are among the most famous in management literature.[18] The studies are named for the Hawthorne Works of Western Electric Company, where they took place from 1927 through 1932. The original aim was to determine whether production workers would assemble more electric instruments if the level of illumination was raised from the existing dark and gloomy levels. The first studies showed that with each increase in light levels, production went up. As the researchers proceeded, they found, to their amazement, that when they progressively *lowered* the light levels, with each change, production went *up* still further. After initial confusion, the researchers concluded that the employees were reacting in the ways they thought the experimenters wanted them to react, because they were so grateful that someone was paying attention to them. These influences are called the **Hawthorne effect**, which will be discussed in greater detail in Chapter 6. For now, the important fact is that the research established new principles of human resource management, stressing the impact of group dynamics and motivation, and that employees may be motivated by more than economic factors.[19]

*It was at the Hawthorne Works of Western Electric Company that Elton Mayo and his colleagues formulated concepts that subjects of experiments often react in ways "they think the researchers want them to."*

## Mary Parker Follett (1868-1933) and Group Dynamics

**Hawthorne effect**
The tendency of workers to increase their productivity when management pays attention to them, and also to respond as they believe researchers intend them to.

Follett laid the foundation for studies in group dynamics, conflict management, and political processes in organizations. She and other early human relations writers served as a counterbalance to the impersonal approaches of the scientific management theorists.

## Joan Woodward and the Behavioural Science Approach

Behavioural science scholars argue that employees are much more complex than the "economic man" described in the classical approaches or the "social man" described in the human relations approach. Behavioural science concentrates more on the nature of work itself and the degree to which it can fulfil the human need to use skills and abilities.

**behavioural science approach**
The approach to management that attempts to incorporate findings of social scientists, recognizing the complexity of individuals and what interests and motivates them.

From 1953 to 1957, Joan Woodward led a research team studying 100 English manufacturing companies. She found significant differences from company to company in characteristics such as span of control (number of workers reporting to a manager), number of levels of authority, the extent of written communications, and the clarity of job definitions. She concluded that the more an organization employs technological methods in its operations, the more it tends to shed middle managerial positions, thus altering its organizational structure and managerial culture. In contrast with the teachings of Frederick W. Taylor, she concluded that there is no one best way to manage or structure an organization, but that a pragmatic approach should be applied, to combine features that best fit the particular organization.

## Contributions and Limitations of the Behavioural Approaches

The behavioural approaches stress that since managers must get work done through others, they must understand interpersonal relations, and must both motivate and lead. But management is more than applied behavioural science, as it must reflect the gathering and application of reliable and specific information, and also the interactions within the organization.

# The Systems Approaches to Management

**systems approaches**
Approaches to management based on the assumption that an organization is a collection of parts, and that is primarily concerned with the interactions of those parts.

**system**
A collection of individual parts that are coordinated to accomplish a common purpose.

The **systems approaches** to management consider organizations and management problems by focusing on the interaction of the individual components to form a functioning whole. A useful metaphor is a car. It has wheels, an engine, some form of transmitting power from the engine to the wheels, and a steering wheel to direct the movement. These are all components, and the car as a whole is the system. A **system** is greater than the sum of its parts, although each part contributes to achieving the goals of the organization.[20] For example, Finning Tractor has production, sales, and marketing departments, accounting and human resource functions, sales agencies, and offices in Edmonton, Kamloops, Grande Prairie, Fort McMurray, Victoria, and several other cities in western Canada, as well as in Chile, Scotland, England, and Poland.[21] Finning Tractor, however, is more than the sum of these individual components—it is a whole that encompasses all of these and brings meaning to them because of their interrelationships.

From the systems perspective, management involves managing and solving problems in each part of the organization, but doing so with the understanding that actions taken in one part will affect other parts of the organization. For example, if the production manager decides to shut down an important production machine for repair, this decision likely will have an effect on marketing, finance, personnel, and other segments of the organization. When a sales representative promises quick delivery to a customer, meeting this commitment may disrupt production schedules, increase costs, and create employee resentment that will have to be dealt with by the human resources department. As this example illustrates, managers must view the organization as a dynamic whole and try to anticipate the unintended as well as the intended consequences of their decisions.

## Chester Barnard (1886-1961) and the Systems Approaches

In his classic management book, *The Functions of the Executive*, Chester Barnard, the president of New Jersey Bell Telephone, emphasized the importance and variability of individuals in the work setting. He believed that an essential element for an organization to be successful is its people's willingness to contribute their individual efforts for the benefit of the whole system.[22]

**inputs**
The influences on an organization from various aspects of its environment, including reactions of suppliers, customers, the general public, shareholders, and employees; effects of competition; governmental actions; and economic factors.

**transformation**
The process of change that occurs as an organization processes inputs and changes a product or service from the form in which it was received to the form in which it is delivered to a customer, or to the next stage of production.

**outputs**
The products or services produced by an organization.

**feedback**
The response of those who receive a message or become aware of a situation, communicated back to the originator of the message or the creator of the situation.

The systems approaches stress that organizational effectiveness, even survival, depends on the organization's interaction with its environment, as well as its own internal operations. The organization receives **inputs** from the external environment, causes a **transformation** in materials or by preparing to offer a service, and then issues **outputs** in the form of products or services.

Important in these interactions is the concept of **feedback.** Feedback can be received directly, from information such as cost analyses and records of defects and scrap, or it can be received from observing whether customers continue to buy its products or services. In the case of not-for-profit organizations, the ultimate feedback may be whether the intended "publics" use the services, accept the information disseminated, or continue to provide support through donations. Because of the tainted blood episode, the Canadian Red Cross received feedback in several ways—unfavourable publicity in the media, public criticism, demands from government to reorganize, and reduced donations of both blood and operating funds. Finally, it had to relinquish its blood collection and distribution activities entirely. Exhibit 1-6 on page 26 provides an illustration of the interactions described in the systems approaches.

According to systems theories, it is the task of management not only to ensure effective planning, organizing, leading, and controlling, but also to seek, and to be alert to, feedback from a multiplicity of sources, and then to make appropriate accommodations to changes in the organization's environments.

## Contributions and Limitations of the Systems Approaches

The systems approaches make an important contribution by emphasizing that the decisions made in one part of the organization will affect other parts of the organization, as well as the environment beyond the organization. Recognizing these interrelationships, managers understand that they must think broadly about a problem, rather than concentrate only on immediate results. The systems approaches provide a framework within which competing pressures within the organization can be resolved—for example, the production objective of low manufacturing costs and the marketing objective of offering a broad product line (which requires high production costs). Seldom can both objectives be fully achieved at the same time. The challenge for managers is to balance the low-cost objectives of the production department against the customer-appeal objectives of the marketing department, in order to remain competitive in the external environment within which the company operates.[23]

Critics have argued that the systems approaches are abstract and not very practical. Talking about inputs, transformations, and outputs isn't how everyday managers discuss problems, make decisions, and face reality. Managers must think, respond, and observe. For them, the systems approaches are good for classroom analysis, but being in the middle of daily decision making precludes deep systems-like analysis and thinking. True as this is (and the criticism applies equally well to all management theories), there is also some merit in

*Feedback comes in many forms. In the case of the Canadian Red Cross it has been in the form of a decrease in public support as a result of allegations that its officials made decisions that placed the public at risk. This has led to other agencies taking over the blood supply from the Red Cross.*

**Exhibit 1-6**    *The Four Parts of Organizational Activity*

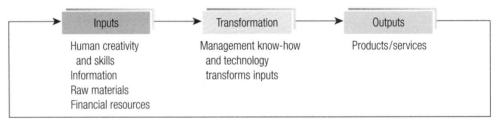

Environmental feedback serves as a response to products/services

managers being reminded of the interconnectedness of all elements of the organization, and of the organization with its external environment.

## The Contingency Management Approach

### Fremont Kast, James Rosenzweig, and Contingency Management

**contingency management approach**
The theory of management that recognizes that the appropriate managerial response to a particular situation is contingent on the specific characteristics of the situation.

In a seminal article in a 1972 issue of the *Academy of Management Journal*, Kast and Rosenzweig described the **contingency management approach** as follows:

> [T]he organization is a system composed of subsystems.... The contingency view seeks to understand the interrelationships within and among subsystems, as well as between the organization and its environment.... Contingency views are ultimately directed toward suggesting organizational designs and managerial systems most appropriate for specific situations.[24]

**universalist management approach**
The theory of management that presupposes that for every problem there is a "best" answer, and that the manager's task is to find that answer and apply it universally.

While Frederick W. Taylor argued that there exists a single best way to perform each different management function (the **universalist management approach**), contingency management theorists believe that although there are some generally applicable principles, management response must reflect the unique aspects of each particular situation, and the differences among the individuals involved.

It would be futile to try to manage Memorial University with all of the same management techniques that would be appropriate for Pizza Pizza Ltd., or to apply the same disciplinary action to a senior computer researcher who is perennially late for "normal" work hours but who works well into the night and to a ferry worker who frequently misses the sailing to which he or she is assigned. Contingent factors such as the kind and size of the organization, the necessity for promptness, and the seriousness of an error must be taken into account in deciding which management principles should be applied, and to what extent.

Time is also a factor. If a particular solution resolved a problem last month, and what appears to be the same problem arises today, that same solution may no longer be the optimum solution, and may not even work at all. In the month that has elapsed since the problem last arose, economic pressures may have worsened or lessened, production schedules may have become looser or tighter, competition may have changed, and there may be different people involved.

According to this approach, it is the manager's task to identify the changes that have occurred, to evaluate the effects of these changes, and to choose what action to take in the new situation. Contingency theorists do not assert that *all* managerial situations are unique. Rather, they argue that situations are often similar to the extent that some of the same principles of management can be effectively applied.[25]

## Theory Z

In 1981 William Ouchi, a professor of management, introduced what he termed Theory Z management.[26] Theory Z is an attempt to amalgamate what Ouchi sees as the best aspects of both Japanese and Western-style management. An example of the differences between the two is illustrated by the practices relating to an individual's career path. In large Western companies, each individual tends to have a relatively defined career path, progressing from one level in a specialty (such as accounting or production) to a higher level in the same specialty. In contrast, the usual Japanese practice ensures that each individual who is destined for promotion is first exposed to several different specialties, all at roughly the same level, before progressing to the next level in the hierarchy. The Japanese practice provides broader exposure, but results in much slower promotion than might occur in the West. Ouchi's ideal is a middle ground—where an individual's career path is not as unidirectional as in the Western-style management, but not as diverse and slow as in the Japanese style.

Although Ouchi's writings generated considerable discussion among business academics, few Western companies have attempted to adopt Theory Z principles. As was mused in 1984 by Harold Geneen,[27] then-CEO of ITT, at that time few Western middle managers would have wanted to exchange their personal freedom to better themselves by changing employers for the longer-term commitments required in the Theory Z approach. Even so, Ouchi has contributed useful concepts to add to the arsenal of management tools, and in one sense he reinforces the validity of the contingency theories—that solutions must fit current circumstances.

## Practical Application of Management Theories

The preceding discussion touches on only a few of the highlights in the development of management theory. Practical limitations on space preclude reference to many other scholars and managers, each of whom contributed something to the understanding of management as an essential activity in any organization. The modern manager has the opportunity to choose relevant features of classical management theory, overlay them with some of the behavioural approaches, apply pragmatic systems usages and some ideas from Theory Z, adapt them in a contingency form to the culture of the organization and the personality of the individual manager, and mix in a generous measure of what we might call common sense, all the while watching the professional literature for new refinements that might be tried cautiously in the hope that some will prove useful.

## Contemporary Management Writers Who Influence Today's Managers

### Michael Porter and Comparative Advantage

Michael Porter, a professor of industrial organization and a consultant at the Harvard Business School, was one of the first contemporary scholars to apply traditional economic thinking to management problems. Porter explains corporate strategy in terms of a competitive marketplace. He identifies four generic strategies: (1) cost leadership, (2) differentiation, (3) cost focus, and (4) focused differentiation. In Porter's lexicon, cost leadership means achieving lower costs per unit of production or service than can be achieved by competitors, while still making a profit.

*Porter's concept of differentiation is illustrated by the Coca-Cola Company, which offers what is considered by many to be unique taste throughout most of the world.*

Differentiation is the practice of providing superior quality to customers or users. Cost focus refers to controlling costs in a restricted market area. Focused differentiation is the application of differentiation in a limited area or in a unique product or service. These strategies are illustrated in Exhibit 1-7. Porter's attention to competitive advantage has had a significant impact on practising managers as well as on academics, as it helps to focus thinking on key elements of planning. Porter's hypotheses will be discussed at greater length in Chapter 4.

## Tom Peters and "Excellence"

In 1982, Tom Peters and Robert Waterman wrote *In Search of Excellence*.[28] It rapidly became a best-seller, and developed a huge cult-like following. In that and later books, and in workshops that he conducted, Peters attempted to identify the qualities and characteristics of companies that were unusually successful. He states that although there is much diversity among the management practices of companies, there are nine aspects that are almost universally found in companies that are well-managed. They are:

1. *Managing ambiguity and paradox.* The business climate is always uncertain and always ambiguous. The rational, numerical approach doesn't always work because we live in irrational times.
2. *A bias for action.* Do it, try it, fix it. The point is to try something, without being dissuaded by the fear of failure. Sootier Honda, founder of Honda, said that only 1 out of 100 of his ideas worked. Fortunately for him, he kept trying after his ninety-ninth failure.
3. *Close to the customer.* Excellent companies listen closely to their customers, and have an almost uncanny feel for what they want.
4. *Autonomy and entrepreneurship.* "Ownership" of a department, task, or problem is essential in motivating employees. Desire for autonomy is the most frequently cited reason for entering into self-employment. Excellent companies allow and encourage autonomy and within-company entrepreneurship.

**Exhibit 1-7**    *Porter's Competitive Strategy Matrix*

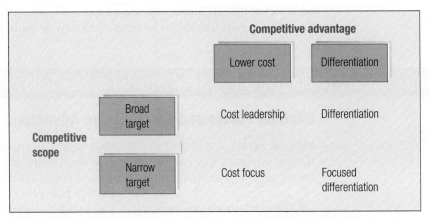

Source: Reprinted with permission of *The Free Press*, a Division of Macmillan, Inc., from *The Competitive Advantage of Nations* by Michael E. Porter. Copyright © 1990 by Michael E. Porter.

5. *Productivity through people.* Not surprisingly, people act in accordance with the way they are treated. Treat them as untrustworthy, and they will be; treat them as business partners, and they will be. Excellent companies have taken the leap of faith required to trust their employees to do the right thing right.
6. *Hands-on, value-driven.* Constantly ask the value added of every process and procedure.
7. *Stick to the knitting.* Stay close to your organization's basic industry. The skills or culture involved in a different industry may be a shock that is fatal to the organization.
8. *Simple form, lean staff.* Excellent companies are characterized by organizations with few layers of management unencumbered by a bloated headquarters.
9. *Loose-tight properties.* Tight control is maintained while at the same time allowing staff far more flexibility than is the norm.

A later book by Peters, *Liberation Management,*[29] takes his thinking further, and states that trying to be close to the customer isn't enough. He adds that management must remove structural impediments such as rigid rules, hierarchies, stilted policies, and stifling demands. He proposes a symbiosis (that is, mutual helpfulness and interdependence) with both domestic and foreign customers.

Critics have pointed out that some of the companies identified by Peters and Waterman as "excellent" actually may not have been applying the principles described by the authors![30] In addition, whether they were actually applying those principles, some of the companies identified as excellent have subsequently failed financially. Nevertheless, the lines of thought brought together by Peters and Waterman have stimulated managers, researchers, and theorists to think more seriously about organizations, the tasks of managers and other employees, and how to improve management practices. In a sense, they have popularized the study of management, and have made management theories background knowledge for most managers in North America today.

## Peter Drucker and Management for Long-term Success

Although Peter Drucker's many works are known to most thoughtful managers, they have not achieved the public acclaim (nor perhaps the lucrative sales volumes) of such writers as Tom Peters. Drucker describes the role of managers as follows:

> Managers practice management. They do not practice economics. They do not practice quantification. They do not practice behavior science. These are the tools for the manager.… As a specific discipline, management has its own problems.… Specific approaches … distinct concerns … a man who only knows the skills and techniques, without understanding the fundamentals of management, is not a manager. He is, at best, only a technician.[31]

Throughout his writing, Drucker has stressed that the search for profit is not the major objective of business. In one of his works, he writes:

> There is only one valid definition of business purpose: to create a customer.… What the business thinks it produces is not of first importance—especially not to the future of the business and its success. What the customer thinks he is buying, what he considers "value" is decisive—it determines what a business is, what it produces, and whether it will prosper."[32]

Drucker considers the present to be an era of transformation, and believes that businesses inevitably will fail if they do not change with the times. He states that to stay current, management must engage in three key practices. First, it continually must implement improvement in everything the organization does. Second, it must learn to apply and make use of its knowledge. Third, it must innovate constantly.[33] Drucker argues that an organization can accomplish these practices only by acquiring the most essential resource: knowledgeable people.[34]

## W. Edwards Deming, Total Quality Management, and Leadership

The late W. Edwards Deming is known for developing the concept of total quality management, which emphasizes employee involvement, leadership, and continuous improvement. He writes: "People are born with intrinsic motivation.... People are born with a need for relationships with other people and with a need to be loved and esteemed by others.... One is born with a natural inclination to learn and to be innovative. One inherits the right to enjoy his work."[35]

Deming states that the role of a company is not only to make money, but to stay in business and provide jobs through innovation, constant improvement, and maintenance.[36] His approach to leadership is to help people do a better job, to employ objective methods to find out who needs help, and to provide that help by giving adequate instructions and offering appropriate training.

## Philip B. Crosby and "Zero Defects"

Philip B. Crosby, who has contributed insights found throughout this book, brought new emphasis to the question of quality, through his innovative application of the term "zero defects." The genius of this approach is to teach managers that they do not have to accept defects as normal. Crosby proposes that top management must make the commitment that the whole organization will function with zero defects. He says that when this commitment is made, the other managers will create quality improvement teams and quality councils, establish quality measures for every activity, train employees in quality management, and generally celebrate quality.[37] He makes the seemingly obvious, but usually disregarded, point that if the job is done correctly the first time (that is, if it meets the zero defects standard), the cost of achieving quality will be reduced to its lowest possible level.

## The Workplace of Tomorrow

Management theory often may seem to be far removed from the day-to-day activities of managers. Yet many of the principles that we take for granted today were startling and innovative when they were first proposed. Typically, management theorists study a problem, formulate hypotheses, test the hypotheses against what actually happens in companies and other organizations, and then publish findings and proposals. Managers who take their responsibilities seriously read a wide range of these publications, and decide whether the principles enunciated seem to make sense for them. Eventually, those principles and theories that stand the test of time become the accepted norm, and those managers who do not practise them are increasingly seen as behind the times and unacceptably old-fashioned. Finally, the principles that started as new and innovative ideas become part of "what everyone knows," and we wonder how anyone could think otherwise. In this manner, management is constantly in a state of change—often slow and not everywhere simultaneously, but change nonetheless.

No one can safely predict which of the latest management theories will stand the test of time and which will be relegated to the dustbin of fads. As Henry Mintzberg says

## Management in the Real World   1-3

### We've Always Done It This Way

A story has been told in management circles that might be apocryphal but might well be true. It illustrates the hazards of adhering too long to a management practice that was once useful but that has outgrown its usefulness. It is said that in 1860, when Prince Otto von Bismarck (later the "Iron Chancellor" of the newly unified Germany) was ambassador to the court of Czar Alexander of Russia, he asked why there was always an armed guard standing sentry at a particular spot in the lawn of the Kremlin. When the Czar inquired, he found that no one seemed to know the reason for the sentry. The commanding general is reported to have said, "… it is in accord with ancient custom." The Czar demanded that a search be made of the records. After three days of digging through volumes of standing

military orders, the answer was discovered. In 1780, 80 years before Bismarck's question and near the end of a harsh Russian winter, Catherine the Great had seen some lovely crocuses poking up through the patches of melting snow. To keep the blossoms from being trampled, she had ordered that a guard be mounted there. Unfortunately, no one provided for the order to be rescinded when its need passed, so for the ensuing 80 years, there had been a 24-hour guard for the crocuses that had been there for only a few days. This story, apocryphal or not, stands as a reminder to all managers that what was once a fine solution to a problem may no longer be valid. How many management practices are continued because "We've always done it this way"?

in *The Rise and Fall of Strategic Planning,*[38] management theories have their place, but managers cannot rely on them as substitutes for judgement and adaptability. In one of his more trenchant observations, he says, "Strategies grow initially like weeds. They are not cultivated like tomatoes."

One of the certainties is that management 25 years from now will be different from what it is today. What is equally certain is that even if a particular theory does not survive intact, it will have made some impact on thinking and on management practices. As a consequence, those managers who keep up with serious reading on management issues will be among those who are best equipped to adapt and to innovate, while those managers who ignore these opportunities will gradually slip behind their competition. As almost any student of management would agree, knowledge is an indispensable cornerstone of good management.

## Summary of Learning Objectives

▶ **Define the terms** *management, competitiveness,* **and** *quality.*
This chapter introduces a number of key terms that are fundamental to the study of management. *Management* is the process by which one or more persons coordinate their own activities and the activities of other persons to achieve business objectives. *Competitiveness* is the capacity, in a free and fair market, to produce goods and services that meet the needs and wishes of customers, without causing environmental degradation, while simultaneously maintaining or expanding the real incomes of its employees and its owners. It is the ultimate measure of potential for effective operations. *Quality* is the inherent nature of goods and services that compares with a norm or standard of fitness for the intended use.

▷ **Explain why a competitive focus has become imperative in a globalizing world.**

The organization that does not provide goods or services that are better, more available, more attractive, or less expensive, than similar offerings of competitors, either domestic or foreign, will inevitably lose customers or other forms of support, and eventually will fail.

▷ **Identify the traditional functions and purposes of management.**

*Planning* is the determination of objectives, and discerning and organizing the activities that will achieve them. *Organizing* is creating the policies and procedures, and assembling and training the staff to achieve the objectives. *Controlling* involves monitoring activities and providing feedback and motivation for all people involved to ensure effective application of resources towards the achievement of objectives. *Leading* consists of showing by example and helping people to know how to contribute most effectively to achieving the objectives of the organization.

▷ **Explain the types of skills that managers need to achieve their goals.**

Depending on their level in the organizational structure, and on their specific responsibilities, managers need to be able to apply to various extents all or most of the following skills: conceptual, analytical, interpersonal (including communication) and technical (including computer) skills.

▷ **Discuss the major theories of management, and their relevance to management today.**

The *classical approach* to management focuses on the tasks being performed; the *behavioural approach* emphasizes the responses and actions of people. Frederick W. Taylor introduced "scientific" (that is, quantified) methods to the study of management; Joan Woodward, among others, showed that empirical research can be helpful in this study. The *systems approach*, as exemplified by Chester Barnard, views organizations as a collection of its parts and their interrelationships. The *human relations approach*, of which Elton Mayo and Mary Parker Follett were early proponents, focuses on the behaviour of individuals in groups. The *contingency management approach* recognizes that there are some universal principles, but that it is not a case of "one size fits all"; instead, solutions to specific management problems must be tailored to the surrounding circumstances. Michael Porter, in advancing a theory of competitive advantage, urges the need to adapt to circumstances in order to be competitive. W. Edwards Deming stresses the importance of quality and Philip B. Crosby is best known for his advocacy of a zero defects approach. Peter Drucker offers broad-ranging concepts of management, many of which are based on the need for innovation, and choosing the right person for the job.

▷ **Contrast management in a small business with that in a large corporation.**

Management of any enterprise, regardless of size, consists of varying parts of planning, organizing, leading, and controlling. The major difference that stems from size is that in a small organization, one or more individuals must cover all four of these fundamental functions, while in a large organization, many of the tasks associated with each function are carried out by separate departments and different individuals. As a consequence, large organizations have potential for specialization, while small organizations require more generalists. Small organizations, however, have an advantage in that they are less likely to have problems in coordinating the thinking and efforts of the smaller number of people involved in the various functions. From a theoretical standpoint, management is essentially the same regardless of size; differences occur in the application and implementation of the theories.

▶ **Discuss why it is important for management students—tomorrow's managers—to develop their own theories of management.**

Each of the management theorists described in this chapter has brought some worthwhile concepts to the thinking both of management students and of actual managers. For today's student—tomorrow's manager—these concepts will remain purely academic unless the student formulates a personal approach to management, and thinks clearly about how this composite approach can and will be applied, as opportunity arises in the student's personal and business life.

## *KEY TERMS*

analytical skill, p. 12
behavioural science approach, p. 24
bureaucracy, p. 22
classical organizational theory, p. 21
classical theories of
    management, p. 18
communication skill, p. 13
competitiveness, p. 6
computer skill, p. 13
conceptual skill, p. 12
contingency management
    approach, p. 26
controlling, p. 5

decision-making skill, p. 13
effectiveness, p. 7
efficiency, p. 7
feedback, p. 25
Hawthorne effect, p. 23
human relations approach, p. 23
inputs, p. 25
leading, p. 5
managerial role, p. 15
managers, p. 10
organizing, p. 5
outputs, p. 25

people skill, p. 13
planning, p. 4
role, p. 15
scientific management, p. 18
skill, p. 12
system, p. 24
systems approaches, p. 24
technical skill, p. 14
time and motion studies, p. 19
transformation, p. 25
universalist management
    approach, p. 26

## *REVIEW AND DISCUSSION QUESTIONS*

### Recall

1. What are the four basic functions of management, and how do they relate to each other?
2. Why is it that efforts to improve efficiency may not improve effectiveness?
3. What skills does every modern manager have to exercise, to a greater or lesser degree, depending on the manager's level in the organizational structure, specific responsibilities, and other environmental factors?
4. What did each of Frederick Taylor, Joan Woodward, Elton Mayo, Chester Barnard, Fremont Kast, Michael Porter, and Henry Mintzberg contribute to the development of modern theories of management?
5. What refinement and extension did Philip B. Crosby contribute to the principles enunciated by W. Edwards Deming?

### Understanding

6. What is the Hawthorne effect, and how does it impinge on other management theories?
7. If you have solved a problem once, and it arises again, can you safely apply the identical solution that was successful before? Explain, and suggest hypothetical examples of your point.
8. What would be the effects on a business if it attempted to function as a closed system?

9. Tom Peters has been criticized as offering only anecdotes, rather than giving specific advice to managers. Of what value are such anecdotes, if any, to practising managers?

10. How can you best prepare yourself for a future managerial role?

## Application

11. In one page or less, write a summary of your personal theories of management, drawing as much as you wish on any one or more of the theorists quoted in this chapter. Give appropriate credit to your sources.

12. Select from the library one article or book by Peter Drucker, W. Edwards Deming, or Philip B. Crosby, and choose a single sentence from it that conveys an important idea. Copy the sentence, restate it in your own words, and in a single page or less, either discuss in what way it enhances your understanding of management or, alternately, in what way you believe it to be an oversimplification or even an incorrect analysis.

13. Arrange to meet with a manager of a business, not-for-profit organization, or governmental agency. Ask to what extent that manager plans, organizes, leads, and controls, and how these functions are accomplished. Take notes at the interview, and add an evaluation of the responses you receive.

# CASE 1-1

## Russian Workers and North American Managers

Managing is a difficult job, wherever it is practised. Managers have trouble satisfying everyone—their peers, subordinates, superiors, and the public. If Canadian managers have a difficult job, Russian managers may face the impossible. In Russian enterprise, managers are confronted with poor machinery, a lack of raw materials, and a workforce whose work ethic has been suppressed since the 1917 revolution. But opportunities to locate plants, offices, and buildings in Russia are thought to be so attractive to foreign investors that learning about Russian management thinking and practice has become important.

Polaroid Corporation has a circuit board plant about 100 kilometres south of Moscow in Obninsk. The plant produces about 70,000 circuit boards a month for the company's instant cameras. In the plant, Polaroid has introduced new equipment and standards of cleanliness that far exceed the norm in Russian plants. After all, old equipment and messy work areas have been the rule for over 75 years in the Russian republic. North American managers staff a number of key positions in the Obninsk plant, which has a reputation of being efficient and able to produce high-quality circuit boards. In other plants that are still state-controlled and managed by Russians, the circuit board defect rate is 10 percent. A zero defect level is considered a foolishly unattainable goal. In the Obninsk plant, the defect rate is one-half percent. Not yet at zero defects, but very close, and the plant is still trying.

Is it the technology, the management, the workforce's morale, or a combination of these factors that have made the Obninsk plant a success story? The circuit boards produced at the plant have resulted in discussions about customer satisfaction, fun in the workplace, and reasonably priced products. A decade or more ago, plant managers in what was then the Soviet Union were not interested in such issues. The Russian economy must produce many more examples like Obninsk to turn itself around.

The joint American-Russian venture has resulted in the sale in Russia of 24,000 cameras—less than half a month's production, the rest being exported. However, it is estimated that 100 times as many, or 2.4 million cameras, could be sold if quality is maintained and the cameras are priced reasonably. Lines form early every morning at Polaroid's shop. Sales personnel have been trained by Polaroid to be courteous and responsive. These sales characteristics, like the sparkling plant, are new experiences in Russia. Of course, many other new thoughts and events are occurring in Russia.

For years, Soviet workers were depicted by the Western press as loafers and thieves. Polaroid executives heard these stereotypes before setting up the Obninsk plant. However, after meeting some Russian workers, they decided that clean workplaces, equitable pay, and teamwork would be as effective in Russia as elsewhere. Polaroid pays workers almost twice the average of Moscow factory workers. Furthermore, they are paid on time! These "innovations" have led potential employees to want to work for Polaroid, and when they do so, they respond positively to incentive pay plans.

Years of central command control in the Soviet Union appear to have devastated the economy, but haven't entirely eliminated Russian workers' enthusiasm for work, quality products, and learning. Managing the Russians has been an illuminating experience for North American expatriates in Obninsk. Still, sceptics question whether Russian managers can take over key positions and operate the plant without any Western managerial guidance. There is also the question of whether the new ways of thinking will last in the social and economic turmoil now being experienced in Russia. Only time will tell.

### Questions

1. What roles must a North American manager practise in the Russian Obninsk plant?
2. Should Polaroid use Russian managers in all managerial positions? Why or why not?
3. How will competition influence the managerial practices of Western managers in the Obninsk plant?

---

Source: Adapted from "Privatization in Russia: Bargain Debasement," *The Economist* (May 8, 1993): 79; John M. Ivancevich, Richard S. DeFrank, and Paul R. Gregory, "The Soviet Enterprise Director: An Important Resource Before and After the Coup," *Academy of Management Executive* (February 1992): 42-55; and Steven Greenhouse, "Polaroid's Russian Success Story," *The New York Times, Business Edition* (November 24, 1991): 5-6, 17.

## CASE 1-2

### A Competitive Advantage: Treating Women Fairly

The evolution of management has been presented in this chapter. As management knowledge and practice have evolved, so has the composition of the Canadian workforce. Significant shifts have occurred in demographics—the baby boomers, Generation X, the empty nesters, the changing gender mix, the changing racial and language mixes, the changing educational levels. Managers today must relate to an entirely different workforce than their predecessors did a generation ago. It can no longer be assumed that the workforce is a homogeneous, predictable group. Each of the diverse segments consists of people who want to be, and deserve to be, valued for themselves.

To acquire and keep a competitive advantage, managers must understand, address, and respect diversity. Women have increasingly entered the workforce, and some have reached levels in the hierarchy that would have been almost unheard of even as little as 20 years ago. But for every Margaret Witte (CEO of Royal Oak Mines) and every Madame Justice Beverly McLachlan (Puisne Justice, Supreme Court of Canada) there are a thousand women who are being recognized and marked for promotion in less visible positions. Even so, in many organizations there is still the "glass ceiling," the invisible but real barrier that keeps women from rising in the hierarchy. Managers must consider to what extent this glass ceiling and other forms of subtle discrimination exist in their workplaces. Gender bias or preconceptions that result in unequal treatment of women are documented in recruitment, selection, promotion, salary allocation, performance appraisal, and management development. To be competitive, it is not enough for an organization to eliminate these kinds of discrimination. This change in attitudes and practices also must be seen as having occurred. If an organization is viewed as a fair place for women to work, qualified women will be attracted to it; conversely, if it is viewed as a place that clings to old, discriminatory attitudes and practices, it will be denied the benefit of being able to recruit from half of the population. It is a challenge for managers to work effectively in this direction, while countering the resistance that faces this or any other change. An organization that effectively shuts off the creativity and energy of half of the potential workforce will suffer against the competition, and ultimately will pay a large price for having failed to break free from gender stereotypes and old habits.

### Questions

1. What have been the effects on management of the increase in workforce diversity since the days of Frederick Taylor?
2. Do you believe that women can be as good managers as men? Why? Is your answer limited by circumstances in which women find themselves?
3. What is the role of managers in addressing workforce diversity—not only gender diversity but all of the other facets of diversity in today's workforce?

## APPLICATION EXERCISE 1-1

### Managerial Behaviour Self-assessment

Managers are likely to apply any of the following 20 statements, depending on the situation. Consider how you believe you would act in each of the situations presented, and assign a number from 1 to 9, where 1 represents "not very often," 4 "sometimes but not often," 7 "occasionally," and 9 "very often." There are no right or wrong answers, but to the extent that you are able to analyze your reactions accurately, this exercise may help you to find something about your "natural" style of management.

#### When (if) I work as a manager, I (will):

1. Carefully set clear goals for the group.
2. Represent the group with enthusiasm to outsiders.
3. Carefully review the group's performance.
4. Intervene to handle internal conflicts.
5. Attempt to receive the best work schedules for the group.
6. Motivate the group to perform at optimum level.
7. Examine the group's past and present performance.
8. Transmit relevant information to the group.
9. Positively influence how top managers view the group.

10. Find opportunities for the group to excel.

11. Take on difficult projects with risks so that the group can make an impact.

12. Make sure that the group is represented at important social events.

13. Pass along relevant group information to top managers.

14. Discipline individuals who purposefully disrupt the group.

15. Reward good performers equitably.

16. Bring recognition to outstanding group members.

17. Provide needed time, materials, or resources on the request of members.

18. Provide needed data to help members complete a project.

19. Represent the group when requests for information are made.

20. Help group members with other groups' and outsiders' requests.

After having assigned a number to each statement, place those numbers in the following table, total the two numbers for each characteristic, and divide by two to arrive at the averages.

## Interpersonal

| FIGUREHEAD | LEADER | LIAISON |
|---|---|---|
| #12 _____ | #1 _____ | #2 _____ |
| #19 _____ | #6 _____ | #20 _____ |
| Total ÷ 2 = _____ | Total ÷ 2 = _____ | Total ÷ 2 = _____ |

## Informational

| MONITOR | DISSEMINATOR | SPOKESPERSON |
|---|---|---|
| #3 _____ | #8 _____ | #9 _____ |
| #7 _____ | #18 _____ | #13 _____ |
| Total ÷ 2 = _____ | Total ÷ 2 = _____ | Total ÷ 2 = _____ |

## Decisional

| ENTREPRENEUR | DISTURBANCE HANDLER | RESOURCE ALLOCATOR |
|---|---|---|
| #10 _____ | #4 _____ | #15 _____ |
| #11 _____ | #14 _____ | #17 _____ |
| Total ÷ 2 = _____ | Total ÷ 2 = _____ | Total ÷ 2 = _____ |

**NEGOTIATOR**
# 5 _____
#16 _____
Total ÷ 2 = _____

Plot the ten averages on Exhibit 1-8, which is the Mintzberg role profile diagram. With a coloured pen, connect the points that represent the averages. Would the people who work with you (fellow students, subordinates, friends) rate you the same way?

**Exhibit 1-8**   *Mintzberg Role Profile Diagram*

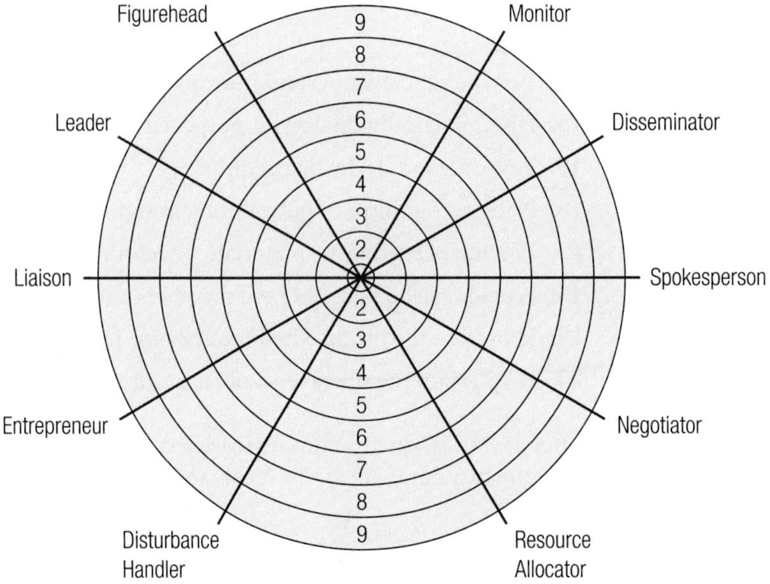

Source: This exercise is based on the Mintzberg management role study and description.

## APPLICATION EXERCISE  1-2

### Working with People Is Never Efficient

With all of the time-management tools available on the market today, filling each time slot with constructive and important work seems easier than ever. But there is one reason why even the most effective manager can never plan a perfectly productive day: Working with people is never efficient.

While corporate problems can be neatly outlined and resolved strategically, *people* require unlimited time. Listening to and working towards resolving "human" issues is possibly the most difficult job a manager faces. Such problems are never resolved with reactions, snap decisions, or delegation.

The manager must find a way to "move" or motivate the employee from the ineffective place towards increased productivity, without a guidebook or manual with all the answers. It is a day-to-day aspect of management where planning strategies often fall short.

#### Questions
1. What types of "skills" would be helpful when dealing with the "people side" of management?
2. Think of your favourite boss or teacher. What did that person do to motivate you?
3. What do you do in your personal life that builds relationships?

Contributed by Marnie Wright, British Columbia Institute of Technology.

## *INTERNET APPLICATION*   **1-1**

Enter Bombardier's Web site (www.bombardier.ca). Check out the information in this site, especially its Corporate Profile and Annual Report sections.

1. What are the building blocks of Bombardier's competitive advantage? Continue to explore the Web site and identify other aspects of the company's approach to doing business.

Search for the Web site of an organization in which managers discuss their approach to planning, organizing, leading, or controlling. What is that organization's approach to management? What effects has this approach had on the organization's performance?

# The Environments of Business, Culture, Social Responsibility, and Ethics

After studying this chapter, you should be able to:

▶ Distinguish between the terms *internal environment* and *external environment*;

▶ Explain why managers must consider their environments in all of their activities;

▶ Explain why workforce culture is such an important issue for managers to understand;

▶ Discuss how a person's values are formed, and how they influence behaviour;

▶ Explain social responsibility as social obligation, social reaction, and social responsiveness;

▶ Discuss why companies are becoming more interested in producing environmentally friendly products;

▶ Describe how an organization can best develop an effective code of ethics; and

▶ Explain why ethical behaviour is important in shaping work life.

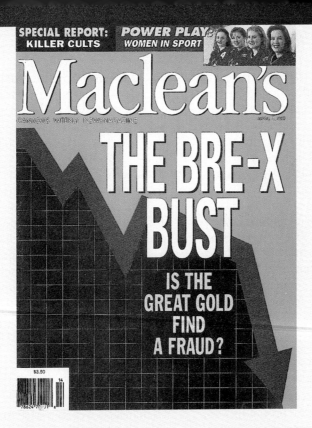

## Environments and Ethical Issues

NO ORGANIZATION EXISTS IN A VACUUM; RATHER, IT is shaped and constrained by external forces. At the same time, some of those external forces may offer opportunities. The external environments include economic and social conditions; government regulations and initiatives; pressures from competitors, suppliers, and customers; and countless other influences. At the same time, every organization is constantly shaping and reshaping its internal environment, which includes its product or services, its workforce, its level of technology, and its access to financing. While the organization is shaping its internal environment, the internal environment is also shaping the organization. It is important for managers to identify the parameters of the various environments within which the organization functions. Then the managers must find ways to adapt behaviour, change the environments, or as a last resort, move to a more compatible situation. ▶

How an organization responds to its external and internal environments will depend on its leadership and its culture. The responses are reflected in both its short-term and its long-term plans and actions. One important manifestation of an organization's responses to its environments may be seen in the ethical standards it reflects. Some individuals, whether managers or non-managers, and some organizations, whether large or small, business or not-for-profit, exhibit the highest standards of behaviour; others do not operate within well-defined ethical standards, or may even consistently behave outside accepted norms. Those individuals and organizations that fail to appreciate the damage done to themselves by unethical practices usually survive for a while apparently unscathed, but eventually succumb to the bad reputations they earn even if they escape actual legal sanctions.

Prudent managers will select employers whose ethical standards are congruent with their own. To do otherwise is to subject oneself to continual conflict between one's own standards and the prevailing culture of the employing organization. Such a mismatch creates painful tension within the manager and confusion within the organization.

The broadcast and print media often publish examples of unethical behaviour. Concerns about ethics in business are reflected in reports of situations such as those in which B.C. Hydro executives were said to have taken advantage of insider information. In recent years, four cement companies were convicted of price fixing and fined $5.8 million in Quebec Superior Court.[1]

Recently there have been widely publicized examples of some of the world's oldest scams. Who would have believed that in today's world, in which scientific testing is highly accurate and communication is quick, that such scams could have fooled investors? Based on little more than well-orchestrated hype, investors rushed to buy Bre-X shares. They apparently believed reports that a massive gold deposit had been discovered, when the only "verification" came from tainted reports by those who stood to make a fortune if the public could be persuaded to invest. Then, too late, eager investors learned that the test drill cores had been "salted" with gold granules and that there was no gold at Bre-X.[2][3] People who lost money in Bre-X could have taken warning from the widely publicized scam, only a few months earlier, involving Calgary-based Timbuktu Gold Corp[4] that also was based on "salting" of gold samples. Instead,

investors learned the truth of the old adage: "If something looks too good to be true, it probably is."

On a less dramatic note, frequently a news story will report a situation in which a business manager or employee has been caught doing something illegal or unethical. But how many unethical acts aren't reported? No one knows for sure. There is a widespread perception that although the public, the courts, and corporate officers treat employees who are caught falsifying credentials on résumés or padding expense accounts harshly, they are lenient with those who manipulate financial reports and mislead shareholders and the public or who use insider information for personal profit.[5] Whether this perception is accurate or not, it is clear that reputations of individuals and of organizations can be ruined by revelations of unethical or even questionable behaviour.

Some business practices come close to the line of unethical behaviour, and their evaluation depends on the standards of the beholder. For example, Toys "R" Us managers were reported to have sent employees to rival Child World stores around the country to buy large quantities of items that Child World was selling at greatly reduced prices. These toys, purchased at loss leader prices, were then resold at a markup in Toys "R" Us stores. Was this behaviour unethical?

Sun Life, Crown Life, and other life insurance companies have been faced with massive class action lawsuits for allegedly unethical sales presentations in the 1980s and early 1990s. Policyholders claimed to have understood sales representatives to promise that in a few years dividends on the policies would pay all remaining premiums. When interest rates dropped throughout Canada, these expectations did not materialize. After several years of litigation, settlements were reached. This example raises the question of whether unrealistic sales presentations are unethical or just a case of *caveat emptor* ("let the buyer beware").

In recent years, many Canadian companies have entered foreign markets for the first time. They have found that in many countries little can be accomplished unless they pay bribes to people closely connected with host governments. Some Canadians belatedly may have recognized the extent of corruption that exists in some of those countries as they followed the ludicrous claims made by relatives of Indonesia's president for ownership of what was then thought to be the massive gold discovery by Bre-X.[6]

Some people, and some country's laws, distinguish between out-and-out bribery on the one hand and what is variously described as "grease," "kumshaw," or "facilitating payments." Bribes are disapproved of or even prosecuted, but "facilitating payments" are permitted. In this context, bribery means giving something of value to decision makers to cause them to change their decisions. "Facilitating payments," by contrast, encourage an official to make the same decision as would have been made without the payment, but to do it more promptly. A typical example of a facilitating payment would arise when a ship is anchored in the harbour of Lagos, Nigeria, awaiting a routine customs clearance before it can unload its cargo. The customs official eventually will clear the ship and cargo, but may take several weeks to do so. Meanwhile the company with cargo onboard is paying hundreds or thousands of dollars a day in demurrage while the ship is sitting idle. It is tempting to slip the customs agent a $100 bill so that the necessary papers will be pulled from the bottom of the pile and given the required stamps of approval immediately instead of after a costly delay. Managers responsible for foreign operations must consider whether to accede to local custom or to abide by standards that are taken for granted in Canada. And what happens when the manager returns to Canada? Is the manager so habituated to an atmosphere of corruption that something seems "normal" when in fact it violates Canadian standards? The reputation of the Canadian Olympic Committee has suffered immeasurably as a result of allegations that its members received benefits to choose a particular host city over another.[7]

There is no perfect solution to what some commentators have dubbed the "ethical crisis." Managers must set the tone, serve as a role model, and lead in a positive way. Managers can reward and call attention to examples of ethical behaviour. No code of ethics and no amount of cajoling by managers will have much influence if organizational rewards go to people who cut corners. Managers must communicate in unmistakable terms what is expected of employees. When all employees understand and internalize the organization's ground rules, the corporate culture will shape ethical behaviour. Like many organizations, Canadian Pacific Hotels & Resorts gives each employee a Code of Business Conduct stating that its provisions are mandatory and that "full compliance is expected in all circumstances."[8]

Like many other aspects of the modern organization, significant changes are occurring in concepts of business ethics. The successful manager and the forward-looking organization will serve as bellwethers, leading the charge towards improved ethical standards and, with that, towards improved public acceptance and a better society. ■

---

Source: Adapted from "How to Be Ethical, and Still Come Out on Top," *The Economist* (June 5, 1993): 71; Brian Dumaine, "Times Are Good? Create a Crisis," *Fortune* (June 28, 1993): 123-24, 126, 130; Kenneth Labich, "The New Crisis in Business Ethics," *Fortune* (April 20, 1992): 167-76; Andrew Willis and Douglas Goold, "Bre-X: The One-Man Scam," *Globe and Mail* (July 22, 1997): A1, A10; Paul Waldie and Allan Robinson, "Timbuktu Tampering Preceded Test," *Globe and Mail* (June 12, 1996): B1; James Christie, "Samaranch Linked to Olympics Scandal," *Globe and Mail* (January 6, 1999): S1.

## The Environments of Business

**environment**
The factors that affect an organization, and the situations within which the organization functions.

**external environment**
All factors, such as laws, competition, technology, social-cultural norms and trends, and ecology, that are outside the organization and that may affect it.

For convenience, business writers usually refer to the organizations, institutions, and forces that affect an organization as its **environment.** Those influences outside the organization are referred to as the organization's **external environment.**

Managers cannot control some of the external environmental forces that shape how an organization and its resources are managed. Sometimes unexpected events require businesses to make radical changes in the ways they operate. For example, in 1993, in a widely publicized case, a two-year-old child died after eating hamburgers tainted with deadly *E. coli* bacteria. Before the source of the bacteria had been identified, some 300 other people had been made seriously ill. Although this tragic event arose in a single fast-food outlet (Jack-in-the-Box), its effects were far-reaching throughout the whole fast-food industry. Not only did Jack-in-the-Box franchises suffer a massive drop in customers but also the entire meat inspection system was called into question.[9] As a

*Inspectors grade and inspect for possible contamination all meat sold through normal market channels, protecting the consumer.*

**internal environment**
The factors within an enterprise, such as employees, structure, policies and practices, and system of rewards, that influence how work is done and how goals are accomplished.

**culture**
An organization's way of life, including the meanings and practices shared by members of the organization, as shown in common ways of thinking, traditions, customs, manners, and ways of dealing with each other and with "outsiders," all of which are transmitted to new members of the organization by example, and sometimes by directives.

result of consumer concern in both Canada and the United States (where the problem arose), federal meat inspection procedures were tightened, and the restaurant industry took further steps to ensure the safety of the meat it serves. Since fast-food chains spend about $3 billion per year on ground beef, their demands for more stringent safety measures got the attention of meat packers. Some restaurant chains have developed in-house techniques for detecting and killing *E. coli*, and for ensuring that ground beef is fully cooked before being served. The publicity arising from this one tragic incident has influenced the ways in which managers function.

Besides the external environment, an **internal environment** also exists in every organization. Managers must recognize and adapt their behaviour to aspects of the organization's internal environment, such as the mood and morale of its employees, its financial strengths and weaknesses, and its organizational structure and style of management.

This chapter first examines the internal environment and then reviews the external environment. It then discusses social responsibility and ethics. To function effectively in today's world, managers must consider and understand their environments, the issues of social responsibility, and the ways in which to respond to ethical dilemmas.

## The Internal Environment

An organization's internal environment directly influences how work is done and how goals are accomplished. Factors that make up the internal environment include employees' attitudes and perceptions, work flow, office and plant layout, managers' style, and the reward system. The internal environment factors together constitute the organization's **culture**.

An organization's culture embraces the behaviour, rituals, and shared meaning held by employees that distinguishes that organization from all others.[10] Managers develop employees by training them, setting goals, and rewarding good performance. All members of the organization, from the chief executive officer (CEO) to the newest office clerk, from the warehouse staff to the outside sales representatives, share responsibility for the organization's products and services. Consequently, all share in creating and sustaining the organization's culture.

Culture is perpetuated because, through their own behaviours and sometimes through oral admonitions, current employees pass the "accepted" traits and behaviours along to new employees. Culture serves as a guideline for what is appropriate and acceptable behaviour because it provides an identity for employees. Culture is reflected in the formal and informal "rules" that employees must follow in order to "belong."

As stated in a thoughtful discussion in the *Journal of Applied Behavior Science*, "Culture by definition is elusive, intangible, implicit, and taken for granted. But every organization develops a core set of assumptions, understandings, and implicit rules that govern day-to-day behavior in the workplace.… Until newcomers learn the rules, they are not accepted as full-fledged members of the organization."[11]

When a strong positive culture emerges, organizational commitment, loyalty, and cooperation can help make the organization strong and effective. However, culture can be a liability when behaviours and work patterns are not congruent with values and actions that enhance performance. Changes in the external environment may require rapid responses and adaptation. However, an ingrained culture may inhibit or block necessary changes. IBM developed a strong culture that apparently could not adapt when new competitors created the need for rapid changes. The resistance of the IBM culture slowed the firm's ability to respond to strong competitors like Apple and Compaq, which were able to capture market share. IBM is still attempting to gain back some of the market share that it lost to these quicker-responding competitors.

## Multiple Cultures

**dominant culture**
An organization's core values that are shared by a majority of its members.

Research suggests that most organizations have a dominant culture and a set of subcultures.[12] The **dominant culture** designates the core values shared by the majority of employees. It represents the distinct mark of a company such as McDonald's, which emphasizes quick and efficient service, and of credit unions, which are known for their personal approach to banking services. *Subcultures* develop because of common situations or problems faced by a group of employees. Subcultures are likely to occur in separate units, groups, or departments. The finance department, sales department, or production department, for example, can have a subculture shared by members of the unit but different in significant respects from the subcultures that prevail in the rest of the organization.

### Real World Reflection    2-1

#### How Do You Define Culture?

The culture of a work group may act as an invisible force that influences behaviour. Culture goes beyond policy to demonstrate what actually happens in an organization, and the only way to really understand it is often to experience it. Therefore, culture becomes a representation of understandings, norms, values, and beliefs that are shared by organizational members. You can, however, get a measure of the organization's culture by considering the following aspects:

- *Symbols:* What are the shared "things" in an organization—anything from open offices to casual clothing;
- *Language:* What shared language is used in the organization—abbreviations, common words, technical language;
- *Activities:* Are there shared rituals or actions—masses of meetings, personal relationships and communications, close ties to the union, long-service recognition teas;
- *Stories:* What stories are told and shared in this organization—gossip, "horror" stories, celebrations of success.

Now, to take one step closer to the culture of the organization, what do each of these areas tell you about how the organization really operates? What is the view of top management? How do employees feel about the organization? What are the organizational priorities? What is valued and rewarded? How is status distributed? What are operations like on a day-to-day basis?

Contributed by Sherry Campbell, British Columbia Institute of Technology.

There are strong and weak dominant cultures.[13] In an organization with a strong culture, core values are intensely held and widely shared. In such an organization, employees' or members' behaviours can be dramatically affected by the values of other employees and role models. In Apple Computer's early days, it was a common practice to work long after the shift was over to complete the job, especially when a group was attempting to solve a problem. In other organizations, it is part of the culture to leave at the official quitting time regardless of the work load, and any employees who frequently work later are considered suspect by their fellow employees.

Cultures vary from organization to organization. For example, Bausch & Lomb has a very strong dominant culture, reflecting the personality of its tenacious CEO,

## Management in the Real World    2-1

### Total Ethics at Traidcraft

Simply having a code of ethics doesn't make a business ethical. Neither does an ethical response in reaction to consumers' demands or to political pressure. Instead, argues Richard Evans (external affairs director of Traidcraft Plc.), the ethics movement in business should be motivated by a vision of "total ethics" on the order of the total quality and zero defects movements. Evans says that to develop total ethics, managers must be trained and encouraged to get out of the habit of viewing ethical strategy in terms of responses to internal and external threats to the business. Managers must be encouraged to take an active role in creating an ethical society.

Evans has developed a new total ethics program for Traidcraft, a limited company selling craft products from Bangladesh. Begun in 1979, it seeks to redress the imbalance in wealth and opportunity between people in developing countries and people in the rich industrialized countries. In its first 12 years, the company sold more than $20 million worth of products from the Third World.

Evans points out that the Traidcraft view is that "businesses are not distinct social entities, but merely activities of society as a whole." In addition, the company believes that "business plays a major social role in human development: through the way people at work are taught to, and then enabled to, fulfill their economic role in society or in its effects on those it excludes from an economic role."

To take into account this broad social responsibility, Traidcraft operates with the interests of multiple stakeholders in mind. Evans said, "If business is regarded as an activity of society, we can define a much larger number and range of stakeholders than the shareholders with the financial interest." Stakeholders that Traidcraft takes into account include lenders, creditors, employees, managers, government, consumers, suppliers, and others.

The company's total ethics culture was created within its overall mission:

> Traidcraft promotes practical service and partnership for change, which will characterize the organization that puts people before profits.

Evans states that total ethics is manifest in Traidcraft's business practices as it aims to be one of the agencies that will change society through the nature and manner of its business activity. Its founders and directors do not claim to know what is best for society and have, therefore, encouraged the participation of all stakeholders in developing the company objectives and have made its policies and practices open for public scrutiny.

Public demand for ethical business practices has deep roots in Western ethical traditions. With the complex and competitive new global marketplace, a new view of total ethics founded on continuous improvement and taking the views of various stakeholders into account seems to be a workable alternative.

Source: Adapted from Richard Evans, "Business Ethics and Changes in Society," *Journal of Business Ethics*, 10 (1991): 871-76; and David Vogel, "Business Ethics: New Perspectives on Old Problems," *California Management Review*, 33(4) (1991): 101-17.

*The success of some businesses depends largely on whether customers feel that they are being served in a friendly manner. Forward-looking organizations devote considerable effort, and invest in expensive training, for front-line employees to instill positive attitudes.*

Dan Gill. He began his career as an auditor and even after having been promoted through several positions, still closely examines each division's financial report every month.[14] Partly as a consequence of Gill's attention to financial details, Bausch & Lomb managers at all levels know that they must be completely familiar with the financial aspects of their parts of the company. In contrast, the culture at Microsoft apparently is more laid back and entrepreneurial, reflecting the personality of its CEO, Bill Gates. Even though Microsoft seems to have a more casual culture, in fact it is just as competitive as Bausch & Lomb, and Gates does not brook carelessness on the part of his managers. Gates' relationship to his company has been described as "more like a headmaster or supervisor than a tycoon. To be questioned by him is like a final university examination. But behind that discipline is still the ultimate motivation of profit."[15]

## External Perceptions of Culture

Some aspects of an organization's culture are readily apparent to outsiders. When a patron encounters a surly waiter in a restaurant, the patron knows immediately that unless that particular waiter is new to the job (and will not last long), the surliness is indicative of the culture of that restaurant. The same attitude is likely to be found in almost all of that restaurant's staff. These readily identified reflections of culture, however, are like the proverbial tip of the iceberg—perhaps one-ninth of the culture is visible, while the great bulk lies invisible beneath the surface. Exhibit 2-1 on page 48 illustrates the relationship between the visible and unseen portions of organizational culture.

## Building Culture

Management success at building a positive culture requires selecting, motivating, rewarding, and retaining high-performing employees. In some companies, there is a healthy competition among employees to outdo each other in providing service. For instance, one Air B.C. employee chased down a mislaid briefcase for a worried lawyer, and got it to her in time for an important appearance she was scheduled to make. At Best Western Hotels, there is an oft-recounted story about a desk clerk who took the computer disc of a guest home to print out its files on his personal computer because the software in the hotel's business office was not compatible. In doing so, the hotel employee saved the guest from the terrible embarrassment that would have resulted from not having the necessary printed material for a vital sales presentation. In both companies, this kind of service is celebrated, and each incident begets others like it.

By observing companies with positive cultures, managers will find three distinct characteristics that result in culture building: *commitment*, *competence*, and *consistency*. In building a positive culture, managers continually must strive to instill commitment to a common philosophy and service, develop and reward competence, and consistently find and retain the right people. *Organizational socialization* is the process through which a newcomer is transformed into an accepted member of the team. Most of this socialization occurs inadvertently, and results from the new employee observing how other employees act in given situations. When an organization grows very rapidly, the new members of the group may outnumber those who have worked longer within the

**Exhibit 2-1**    *The Iceberg Metaphor for Corporate Culture*

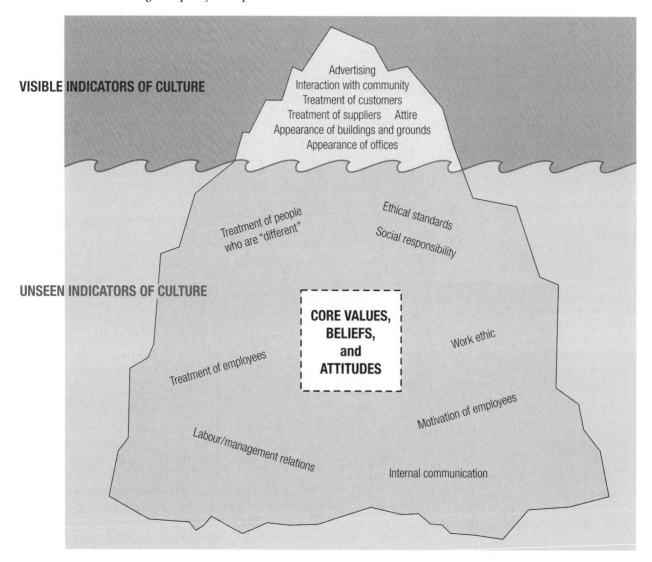

prevailing culture. The result may be a change in the corporate culture to reflect the attitudes and practices of the newcomers, or in more extreme cases, the "old" and the "new" cultures may exist side by side, creating disharmony and tension.

## Values as a Source of Organizational Culture

**values**
Convictions about what is good or desirable; beliefs that a specific mode of conduct is personally or socially preferable to other modes of conduct.

The values held by the individuals within an organization are fundamental to its culture. **Values** constitute personal convictions that a specific mode of conduct is personally or socially preferable to another mode of conduct. Individuals hold values quite deeply, even when they do not recognize that they are doing so. For some individuals, certain values are extremely important, while for others the same values are less important. The intensity with which a particular value is held often will be a source of conflict between individuals.

**beliefs**
Conscious or subconscious convictions or expectations that something is true.

Whatever values are held, however, they are fundamental to a person's personality, lifestyle, and reactions to particular situations. Values underlie and give credence to **beliefs**—sometimes recognized as such, and at other times taking the form of unrecognized assumptions. An individual may believe that people who are newcomers to the organization, or who are just "different" (whether of a different race, gender, sexual orientation, or educational and economic background), are inferior. A person also may assume that members of a particular group automatically share certain undesirable characteristics, such as laziness, selfishness, greed, dishonesty, and immorality, or conversely (and rarely) that they are endowed with superior knowledge and wisdom, social sense, and high standards.

**attitudes**
A manner of thinking, feeling, or holding an opinion.

The natural result of beliefs is that the individual holding them exhibits corresponding **attitudes**. If the beliefs about an identifiable group are negative, members of the identified groups become the targets of harassment, and friction inevitably results. In some organizations, beliefs may be positive, such as believing that top managers know all that is happening in the organization. Although such a belief may be gratifying to top managers, it may have negative effects. When middle managers and other employees have this belief, they are likely to feel it is not necessary to communicate problems to top managers. Then, if those problems are not actually recognized by senior managers, those who believe that top managers know all believe that the top managers know about the problems and simply are failing to correct them. More often, of course, non-managerial employees begin with the assumption that management is oppressive and unreasonable. Therefore, when managers suggest changes, those changes are viewed with suspicion and are assumed to be for ulterior motives.

Thus, the behaviours of people in an organization depend on their attitudes, which are based on their beliefs, which in turn arise from the values they hold. From this it can be seen that, to an extent not often recognized, the internal environment of an organization will depend on the values held by the individuals who make up the organization.

Exhibit 2-2 illustrates the progression from values through beliefs and attitudes to behaviours. These interrelationships emphasize the need for managers to recognize and be sensitive to values, so they can better interpret and predict employees' attitudes, motivations, and possible reactions. Failure to recognize value differences may lead to an organizational culture in which friction and harassment are everyday occurrences, and managers and non-managerial employees think the worst of each other.

## Emphases in Values

The values that employees bring to the workplace were largely established in their early years by observing the values held and demonstrated by parents, teachers, relatives,

**Exhibit 2-2**

*The Importance of Values*

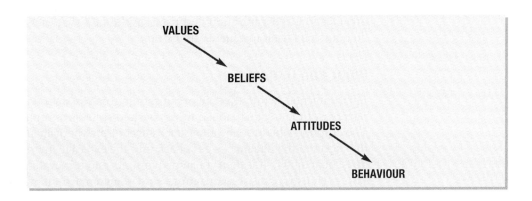

VALUES → BELIEFS → ATTITUDES → BEHAVIOUR

*Managers are recognizing that having the time and resources to enjoy a vacation is an important benefit to many employees.*

friends, and other peers. The discussions a young person hears at home, in the street, or at school provide a basis for the values that may be carried throughout life. A workforce that includes a range of people from a variety of national, cultural, economic, and religious backgrounds will possess a variety of values spanning many issues that arise in everyday life.

As a consequence, today's manager deals with a workforce whose reactions to events may differ considerably from person to person. Some employees will place most value on economic recognition in the form of direct wages and various personnel benefits; some will value time off to be with their families; others will seek to work overtime to increase their earnings. Most employees value opportunities to interact socially in connection with their jobs, but these interactions often will focus on a relatively homogeneous grouping of other employees who have similar ethnic, educational, or age characteristics, and who have similar levels of responsibility within the organization. Often, people will accord a higher value to matters that have been lacking (such as opportunity for promotion, respect, autonomy, and power) than to matters that have been resolved to their satisfaction (and consequently may be taken for granted). Values often change with age (few 60-year-olds enjoy ear-splitting audio!), with significant life experiences (losing a job changes one's attitude towards job security), with increased education, and with personal success. Since values differ, managers must use care in assuming what employees' values are on an issue. In particular, managers must resist the temptation to think that people at other levels in the organization will automatically share their own values.

## The External Environment

Managers also must be aware of, and adapt to, the external environments that affect the organization. Exhibit 2-3 on page 52 presents some of the components of external environments that face managers. For convenience, they can be divided into two interrelated categories: *general factors* (forces that have an impact on a number of companies) and *specific factors* (forces that can directly affect a particular enterprise or task in ways that are different from the impacts on other enterprises or tasks). In this chapter, the five general factors will be discussed in some detail, but the specific factors vary so much from organization to organization and from task to task that each is effectively unique and does not lend itself to general discussion.

### Input and Output

Environmental factors affect an organization from two directions: input and output. The purpose of the organization is to receive and transform inputs to produce an output. The output—whether it be a toaster, a sheet of plywood, an automobile part, or an airline ticket to the Bahamas—goes back into the external environment if it is sold, given away, or accepted. It is then consumed or used, and it is evaluated, either consciously or unconsciously. Thus, organizations and their environments are inseparable—each

## Management in the Real World    2-2

### Mary Kay Leads by the Golden Rule

Mary Kay Ash founded her company on the Golden Rule—do unto others as you would have others do unto you. She believes that to apply the golden rule, to make it powerful in your life, you must develop a sense of empathy for other people. Empathy is an essential ingredient of ethics as well as an important attribute of leadership. Ethical leaders can create an ethical corporate culture that brings out the best in people. Ethical behaviour takes on a life of its own and grows, if given a chance.

Mary Kay Ash believes that ethics is good business. However, an ethical company doesn't exist in a vacuum. To make ethical decisions, businesses must consider the impact on the larger society of which they are a part.

In the case of Mary Kay Cosmetics, the larger society includes independent entrepreneurs—the company's beauty consultants, its employees, the communities in which the company is located, and business partners such as suppliers, scientists, medical professionals, the cosmetics industry, and pharmaceutical industry, and the direct-selling industry.

All of these factored into a decision Mary Kay made in May 1989. The company announced a moratorium on animal testing while it developed and evaluated new testing technology. Mary Kay Cosmetics was one of the first companies to take such a step. The corporate goal was to take the high ground. The decision meant putting a hold on new products for a while, which meant lost sales. It also meant additional investment in evaluating alternatives.

Ethical corporate conduct is not easy and can be costly, but Mary Kay believes that ethics is good business. And the company believes that ethical conduct can be measured. Although accountants have given the company many ways to measure goodwill for the balance sheet, loyalty and trust of employees, shareholders, and business partners are important measures too. Mary Kay believes that loyalty and trust are probably the greatest assets a company can have, especially a company where independent entrepreneurs are not tied to the corporation through a paycheque. Loyalty and trust are built on a base of everyday ethical conduct. The ethics of people management has to be based on the fact that the truth is the only way people can trust each other.

Mary Kay Cosmetics prides itself on being a "caring" organization. People still laugh, even as they admire her success, when Mary Kay tells them that her ideas on people management are based on the Golden Rule—management by caring and sharing. Mary Kay's "core values" are a foundation for that approach:

- We believe in integrity and fairness in every aspect of our lives as expressed by the Golden Rule.
- We believe that service and quality are essential to our success.
- We believe that enthusiasm produces a positive, can-do attitude, which is a real source of inspiration in working toward our goals.
- We believe that leadership among our sales force and employees is the key to personal and corporate growth.
- We believe the priorities of faith, family, and career lead to a balanced life.

People want to work, they want to create, they want to produce, they want families, and they want their families to live well. They want to live in peace, in a clean, safe world. They want someone to care for; they want someone to care about them, to recognize them and reward them for their contributions. Caring competence allows Mary Kay Cosmetics to quickly take the high ground, to use its ethical framework to influence constituents, and to help make its communities better.

Sources: Adapted from Richard C. Bartlett, "Mary Kay's Foundation," *Journal of Business Strategy* (July/August 1995): 16-19; Alan Farnham, "Mary Kay's Lessons in Leadership," *Fortune* (September 20, 1993): 68-77.

**Exhibit 2-3**    *External Environmental Factors Facing Managers*

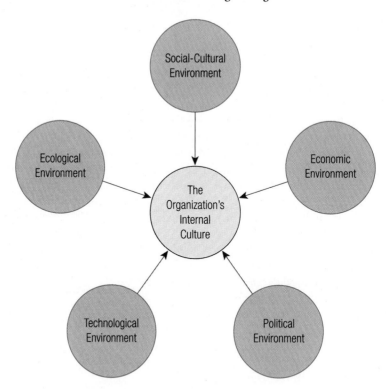

affects the other. It also will become apparent that managerial skills in observing, analyzing, and forecasting the environment may mean the difference between success and failure, or even between survival and disappearance.

**environmental analysis**
Applying rationality to understand the sources and possible effects of environmental factors and to determine the organization's opportunities and threats.

## Environmental Analysis and Diagnosis

**Environmental analysis** is the act of monitoring external environmental forces and applying a rational approach to assessing their effects. It is designed to determine the organization's opportunities and threats and to decide on managerial and strategic decisions that take into account these analyses.

## The Social-Cultural Environment

The social-cultural environment involves institutions, people, and their values, and the norms of behaviour that are learned and shared. Since social structures and culture are constantly changing, managers must examine trends, forecasts, and other forms of information. Social-cultural dimensions that are important for managing and remaining competitive include workforce diversity, employees' perceptions of their family responsibilities, the nature of work, and employees' health, among countless other factors.

## Workforce Diversity

As mentioned in Chapter 1, the Canadian workforce is changing both in terms of structure and of composition. At the beginning of the twentieth century, most women worked only in the family home; only one in six women worked for wages outside the home. Of those who did work outside the home, 42 percent were hired as domestic workers, presumably in the homes of the more well-to-do, and only 5 percent were in clerical occupations, presumably in business enterprises. Seventy-five years later, the proportion of women in the workforce had doubled, and the clerical component had grown sixfold, while the domestic component had shrunk by one-half.[16] By the early 1980s, two-thirds of Canadian women under the age of 55 were employed for wages outside the home.[17] By 1992, this percentage had increased even further, to approximately three-quarters.[18] Managers who fail to take account of this trend and its implications will find themselves at a competitive disadvantage in attracting qualified employees at all levels.

Another significant factor is that the workforce is aging, and the number of younger, entry-level workers available is shrinking. The aging of the baby boom generation is raising the median age of the Canadian population. By the second decade of the twenty-first century, more than one-quarter of the Canadian population will be at least 55, and 1 in 6 or 7 Canadians will be 65 or older. As older Canadians become a larger proportion of the population, economic and political power will shift. Consumer buying habits, preferences, and attitudes towards spending will profoundly affect the economy. The Canada Pension Plan will be making payments to an increasing number of claimants, and there will be an accompanying decrease in the size of the employed, tax-paying workforce. These changes will have profound effects on the perceptions of the public, and hence of politicians and governments. More and more employees will opt for some form of job sharing, and it is conceivable that legislation will mandate some accommodation to these requests. Managers will have to take account of changes in laws affecting mandatory retirement, provisions for health care, and perhaps provisions for both child and elder day care, as well as provisions for time off for family responsibilities.

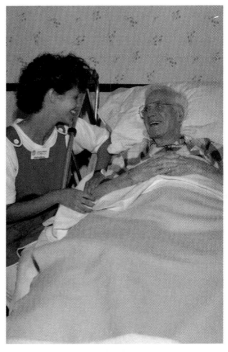

*More and more organizations are making provisions to allow employees to cope with personal issues such as elder care and child care.*

Educational levels are increasing and many factors contribute to the growing sophistication of employees. An increasing number of employees at all levels come from different cultures, many of whom claim neither English nor French as their mother tongue.

All of these changes place a responsibility on managers to recognize diversity in the workforce, to adapt to it, and to find ways to reduce the resistance that inevitably accompanies any fundamental change. Managing change will be discussed in detail in Chapter 9.

## Family Responsibilities of Employees

In the last decade, many businesses have created policies and programs to help employees balance their home and work roles. Several provinces have enacted broad provisions for maternity and paternity leaves, and for leaves for other family responsibilities. Although the growth of day care has been slow, many companies are finding that providing on-site facilities, or subsidizing the cost of day care elsewhere, can result in increased employee loyalty and enhanced morale, with a resulting decrease in absenteeism. Little thought has been given to the increasing responsibilities of active employees to care for elderly parents, but provisions for such responsibilities will increase the need

*With improved transportation and communication facilities, many Canadians have become almost nomads, moving because of changes in job assignments, in order to find better job opportunities, or to retire and either be with family members or enjoy a different part of the country.*

for job sharing and flexible work schedules, each of which brings its own management challenges. The availability of computers and access to networks makes it possible for some employees to work at home part-time, but most companies have not solved the problems of communication and monitoring work and productivity. (The relatively new phenomenon of telecommuting will be discussed in Chapters 11 and 15.)

Until the mid-1980s, the average Canadian moved every 6 years—11 times in a lifetime. Then, as jobs became more difficult to get and real estate prices rose, employee mobility reduced markedly. Even now, however, Canadians are still much more mobile than members of older, more traditional societies. New management approaches are needed because of the growing number of dual-career couples, for whom it is necessary to make some accommodation if one spouse is transferred to a distant location or offered a job that entails moving.

## The Nature of Work

A number of surveys have identified the basic skills that employers want their workers to possess. The results of some of these studies are reported in Chapter 8. As might be expected, the kind of business determines some of the factors, but regardless of the type of business, employers reported almost uniformly that they want workers with a solid basic education plus skills in human relationships and self-management. Employment opportunities are quickly disappearing for the unskilled and for those with only minimal formal education. Thus, managers are finding that the employees they supervise are increasingly better educated, better able to accept responsibility for their own work, and less willing to accept thoughtless, impersonal, autocratic styles of management. Effective managers recognize these changes in the expectations of the workforce, and adapt in socially responsible ways.

## Employees' Health

Canada has become an increasingly sedentary society. It is not just the inordinate amount of time that many Canadians spend in front of television, but also the fact that most of our daily activities—eating, sleeping, dressing, talking, reading, and commuting—are almost entirely non-athletic. Aside from the small minority who exercise conscientiously, most Canadians are inviting the illnesses that stem from poor physical fitness. An increasing number of forward-looking companies are encouraging their employees to give up smoking, to take part in some form of exercise, to have regular physical examinations, and to follow sensible, healthy diets. Some large companies, such as British Columbia Telephone Company, provide fully equipped fitness facilities and encourage employees to make full use of them. The managers of these companies recognize the payoff in reduction of lost time and in increased morale and motivation.

Attention to employee safety is another managerial approach that shows a positive cost-benefit return. Improved accident prevention results in better employee attendance, reduced retraining costs, and improved employee morale, not to mention reduced premiums for workers' compensation. The challenge for managers is to design accident prevention programs and to motivate employees to follow them, dispelling the natural assumption that "it can't happen to me."

## Government Intervention

At the time of Confederation, Canadian governments had very little involvement in the affairs of business. Environmental regulations, labour standards, truth-in-advertising regulations, control of monopolies, health and safety standards, zoning and building codes—all of these were almost completely nonexistent. In the period since 1867, governments have responded to public demands for protection in these and other areas. Providing these services and protections costs money, so taxes have become ever more of a factor in business planning and operations. Government has become at least a partner in business (even if not, as some people complain, the *managing* partner). There is a widespread belief that government intervention should control everyone else, but that we (whoever "we" are) should be freed from restrictions. It is tempting for managers to let this kind of irrational thinking colour their relations with governments and governmental agencies. Another challenge facing managers is to ensure that resentment does not reduce an organization's willingness to be socially responsible and to comply with laws and regulations, and does not create a psychological barrier between the organization and government officials.

These examples of social-cultural factors point out that the external environment presents largely uncontrollable factors, but that some steps can be taken to ameliorate their most damaging effects. Managers need to be aware of trends, values, and forecasts to be prepared for changes in the mix of employees, consumer preferences, governmental involvement, and the availability of skilled employees.

## The Economic Environment

The economic environment has a marked impact on management decisions and plans. An expanding economy directly affects demand for an organization's products or services. If demand increases, the workforce probably will need to expand or new shifts may have to be added. During a recession, decisions may have to be made about layoffs, downsizing, cutting back on the size of the organization, or even closing plants and offices.

Changes in the levels of employment, in economic growth, in inflation, and in consumer optimism are difficult to predict. Still, effective managers constantly keep themselves informed of trends and the predictions of a variety of "experts"—assessing the information available and trying to foresee how changes will affect the organization in order to make informed decisions.

## Productivity

Most economists agree that decreasing productivity worsens inflation. A sluggish, or flat, productivity rate can slow the growth of the entire economy. During most of the 1960s the Canadian economy grew rapidly, with low unemployment and low inflation. But in the 1970s and 1980s the economy grew much less rapidly, with significantly higher unemployment and inflation.

Productivity is an estimate of output per hour of labour worked, or per unit of cost applied. It is a crude measure, and may be misleading in the short term. But over the longer term, productivity measures can reveal informative trends. For years, overall Canadian productivity increased at an annual rate of between 2 and 3 percent. However, the rate of productivity growth slid below 2 percent from 1970 to 1978. The rate then picked up again, aside from setbacks during the recessions of the early 1980s, late 1980s, and early 1990s. Now, once again, the productivity rates are falling behind those that would best stimulate the economy and provide employment. When employees produce more, total output grows and employers can increase wages without raising prices. The rise in revenue from increased output offsets the higher wage costs. But if productivity is flat, almost every dollar of wage gains has to be reflected in price increases. Goods and services that cost more won't be purchased as readily by consumers, because they find alternatives or decide that they can't afford to purchase them. Thus, a self-sustaining downward spiral begins and continues.

Across different industries, it is interesting to examine white-collar and blue-collar productivity rates. When additional capital investment is made in automation and control systems, production per blue-collar employee will increase. In contrast, while the advent of computers has made many things feasible, by the usual measures of productivity—that is, units of production per hour of work—it is difficult to cause a measurable increase in the "productivity" of white-collar, managerial, and professional employees. Largely as a result of increased capital investment, blue-collar productivity has increased by 28 percent in the past decade, while white-collar productivity, to the extent that it is measurable, has decreased by 3 percent. In roughly the same period, white-collar employment has increased by more than 30 percent, while blue-collar employment has grown by only 2 percent, and even that growth has come largely in the service industries, where automation has little effect. It may be seen, then, that contrary to widely held perceptions, major economic problems have not stemmed from falling blue-collar productivity, and managers must look elsewhere for solutions.

*Many Canadians invest in the stock market. Even those who do not invest are affected indirectly by share prices because their retirement income usually depends on pension funds that are invested, and because any major change in share prices will influence business decisions made by their employers.*

## The Global Economy

In generations past, economic activity took place within the well-defined and circumscribed boundaries of nation-states. Now, by contrast, as will be discussed in Chapter 14, even if a business enterprise does not engage in importing or exporting, it is still profoundly influenced by what goes on in other countries. We all operate in a truly global economy.

There are now three main economic regions in the world: North America, the European Union (EU), and Southeast and East Asia including Japan. Rationalization and coordination in all three regions, and indeed in other areas that are less significant economically, are moving ever closer to some forms of integration. Rationalization within the EU has proceeded further than in the other two regions. Within the EU, it is possible to move merchandise and people across borders with little hindrance. A company based in one EU country can establish branches in other EU countries and function almost as if national borders did not exist. On January 1, 1999, a single currency, the "euro," came into being for accounting and pricing purposes, as the first step towards the elimination of national currencies such as the German mark and the French franc. International rationalization and integration offer formidable complications to the problems of management. These issues will be discussed at length in Chapter 14; it is sufficient for our present purposes simply to point out the broad implications for managers in Canada as part of the emerging global economies.

## Small Companies

**technology**
The aggregate competence to produce goods and services.

As discussed in Chapter 1, management theories initially were directed primarily to management in large corporations and other large enterprises. The same basic principles underlie the management of small companies, with the main differences being that in the small company, people necessarily are closer to each other and specialization is less pronounced. In a small business one person does many different kinds of tasks that in the large corporation would be divided up, with each part delegated to a different person or group. The importance of small business to the Canadian economy and the special problems of small business managers will be discussed in Chapter 13.

## The Technological Environment

*Technological innovations, such as those used to allow astronauts to work in space, take years of research and development.*

Technological changes are the most visible of all the environmental changes, but public pride in controlled progress in the early 1900s appears to have changed to apprehension, or even fear, by the 1980s and 1990s. After two world wars, a depression, and many unresolved economic problems, only an unthinking person could believe that all change is positive and that increasing technical knowledge will produce still better technology that inevitably will improve the human condition.

Technology has touched almost every aspect of life in industrialized nations. In the process, it has made affluence possible for many. Because the benefits of technology have not been evenly distributed among the people of the world, it can be seen that technology also has created some new ethical dilemmas. In addition, the very existence of technological innovations has created new dimensions of communication, dissemination of information and misinformation, and difficult questions for managers, as is illustrated in Management in the Real World 2-3 on page 58.

**Technology** is the totality of the means employed by people to accomplish desired tasks and to provide comfort and human sustenance. The term is broad enough to include everything from the methods of shaping flint learned thousands of years ago to the latest discoveries in cloning and redesigning biological cells. Therefore, it is hardly valid to think of technology itself as a problem or as the cause of problems. Civilization and individual people can be helped or hurt by technology.

## Management in the Real World     2-3

### Ethics in the Digital Age

Microsoft Corporation's dominance in the software industry has inspired more than its share of critics. On the Internet, those potshots are beginning to attain a new level of polish and professionalism, due in part to technology offered by the World Wide Web. The kinds of messages—positive or negative—made possible by new Internet technologies raise concerns about decency, responsibility, and competitive ethics.

A prime example of the technical sophistication and scope of company bashing on the Internet is a World Wide Web site called the "Microsoft Hate Page," which invites people worldwide to submit comments, essays, jokes, graphics, and criticism related to the Redmond-based software company. The Web site was designed with a professional look and feel that provides colour graphics, "hot" links to other pages, games, and e-mail capabilities to communicate with the site's creator. The site's content harshly criticizes Microsoft, in some instances with censurable language and graphics.

A Microsoft spokeswoman said that the company's position about complaints against it is that people have the right to voice their opinions. If they have problems with specific products, they should contact the company's customer support group, she said. Regarding the company's online detractors, the spokeswoman said Microsoft has not pursued any legal action against them; nor does it have any official policy on the matter.

The high level of commitment and resources needed to create a Web site easily may fuel suspicions about the motives behind certain Web sites and the messages they are sending. Hence, even though Web sites such as Microsoft Hate Page may be created by individuals exercising their freedom of speech, the World Wide Web has given those messages a weight and reach similar to those of large corporations. Thus, the Internet has created a channel for market parity that may be used by companies and individuals to undermine their competition.

As one Internet engineer pointed out, the Internet is considered by many to be "the largest functioning anarchy in the world"—an anarchy that already has attracted debates about regulation, ethics, responsibility, and accountability.

Rushworth M. Kidder, president of the Institute of Global Ethics, believes we are moving into an age of greater self-regulation of digital technology. He suggests that the answer may lie in both moral strictures as well as legal injunctions. "As we move from tangible assets to intangible ideas, truth will become more crucial," Kidder declares. "How can we use the information highway when we can't tell what's true on it?"

Sources: Adapted from Ken Yamada, "World Wide Web Raises Issues of Decency, Ethics," *Computer Reseller News* (September 4, 1995): 43-44; Eileen McMorrow, "Will Digital Technology Impact Ethics?" *Facilities Design & Management* (May 1995): 9.

## Technological Innovation

**technological innovation**
The translation of technical knowledge into physical reality that can be used to achieve a purpose.

**Technological innovation** involves all of those activities that translate technical knowledge into a physical reality that can be used. In a real sense, the discovery of how to make fire and the invention of the wheel are both examples of technological innovation. In today's more sophisticated world, however, the process of technological innovation usually progresses from basic research through testing and production to marketing.[19] The automobile was a technological innovation that had a long-term irreversible effect on the mobility of society and the purchasing patterns of consumers. The telephone, airplane, radio, television, computers, antibiotics, and X-ray and CAT scans also have influenced society significantly. Peter Drucker notes that three great industries and their technologies—agriculture, steel, and automobiles—have powered the growth of the Western world, and that these effects are likely to continue in the foreseeable future. All three of these industries have experienced such profound changes as to make them almost unrecognizable to a Canadian whose mind was frozen in the mid-twentieth century.

It takes time and money to carry out technological innovation and marketing. Years may pass before an innovation in biomedicine, energy, or any other sector reaches the marketing stage. As a significant environmental force, technology causes change in industries and relationships between companies and customers, and it creates new competitors. To meet competition and continue in business, managers must use technology effectively. Astute managers employ technology to improve their services to customers, find new customers, lower costs, and speed the introduction of new products. When effectively used, technology is a major force in competitiveness.

## The Political-Legal Environment

The political-legal environment consists of the government rules and regulations that apply to organizations. The very words *rules and regulations* often make managers uneasy and resentful. No one likes being regulated. For years, the typical Canadian manager has been a staunch *theoretical* advocate of a "hands-off" government policy (a policy of not interfering with business activity). Yet most managers know that the business system can't work without some government rules and regulations to organize and monitor the external environment, and to protect consumers and companies from possible predatory action by others.

There is a huge number of and much variety in government programs affecting business. Programs are directed towards goals as disparate as economic growth, job security, and environmental pollution control. These regulations and government programs can be divided into those that are designed specifically to *support* business and those designed to *control* various business activities.

Business support programs are designed around one or more of several different forms. They may consist of direct subsidies, indirect subsidies through tax relief, publicity and promotion, granting of contracts, or support of research and development. The meaning of *subsidy* was once restricted to the provision of public funds to preferred users—for example, to support agriculture, to stimulate exports, and to encourage research. Today the term *subsidy* may be used to describe the allowance of any benefit to politically determined business activities. The government provides subsidies directly in the form of guaranteed and insured loans, and through tax breaks for specific kinds of business or in selected geographic areas, as in the federal Regional Development Programs. It even can be argued that government expenditures for highway construction are a form of subsidy, because while highways provide benefits to almost all members of society, the benefits are greater for some than for others.

The meaning of *subsidy* has been expanded to include what are seen as decisions by governments not to collect "enough" from various fees. An example is the long-running dispute with forestry companies in the United States, who claim that Canadian governments' fees for "stumpage" (that is, fees based on the amount of timber cut) are too low, and result in unfair competition for companies in the U.S. when Canadian products are exported. While this argument has some obvious logical flaws, it illustrates the difficulty of defining precisely what is meant by the term *subsidy*—a question with which negotiators for Canada and the U.S. have been wrestling for nearly two decades.

The government is actively involved in *promoting* business through such devices as tariffs and quotas designed to protect home industries from foreign competition. From time to time both the federal and provincial governments have operated programs not only of direct grants but also of increased benefits, such as in the Employment Insurance program, for areas that are economically depressed and that have higher-than-average unemployment rates. For many years, native-owned businesses have been eligible for startup grants, preferential or zero tax rates, and other financial benefits not available to others. Substantial grants and tax concessions are often made by governments to encourage resource development or research and development.

A third type of support takes the form of government *contracts* for the construction of buildings and highways, the purchase of goods, and consulting services of various kinds. These contracts are designed to stimulate business, and because of their volume are a significant economic force. Not surprisingly, businesses that wish to be awarded contracts for government work often have to submit to conditions that would not be required for contracts with private contractors. An example is the Fair Wage Act, in which the British Columbia government requires all contractors working on provincial highways to pay all wages at union rates, whether the companies are unionized or not.

Contracts and grants for *research and development* are designed to encourage the development of new products and services, and sometimes to provide financial support for educational institutions and companies interested in high-tech fields. In other instances, grants that are identified as being for research and development are thinly disguised methods to supply financial support for companies that might otherwise fail, causing unemployment and creating hardships in communities that depend on them.

## Government Control

There are three primary areas of government control: investigation and publicity, legislation, and regulatory enactments and rulings. By means of Royal Commissions and other types of hearings and their reports, governments attempt to influence managers' behaviours and attitudes. For example, the 1997 report by Mr. Justice Krever on supplying tainted blood has had a profound effect on procedures for handling blood, and on the reputations of the organizations and individuals who were involved.[20] It also has given considerable impetus to research that seeks ways to reduce the need for transfusion of blood products. Other government initiatives, for example, *investigating* and *publicizing* findings about the health effects of aerosol sprays and smoking and the devastating atmospheric effects of the diminishing ozone layer, have influenced public opinion about certain products and about the industries and companies producing and selling those products. Of course, when significant numbers of the public form a negative opinion, managers must abandon or adapt the product or see their sales decrease, even though, as in the case of smoking, other factors may mask the effects for many years.

Legislation mandates certain behaviours and prohibits others. For nearly a century, under the Competition Act (and Combines Acts, the name by which similar legislation has been known at various times), various anti-competitive practices such as bid-rigging, exercise of monopoly power, and misleading advertising have been prohibited, with possible penalties ranging upwards to $10 million and two-year prison terms.

The third type of control—regulatory enactments and rulings—is less obvious to the public, but actually is more extensive than the statutes under which the regulations and rulings are issued. For example, the Transportation of Dangerous Goods Act gives rise to hundreds of pages of regulations, which define items that are classified as dangerous and set out the exact precautions and labelling required when transporting each one. Similarly, the various provincial motor vehicle and highways acts are extended by regulations that specify the exact locations of controlled speed zones, authorize the placing of stop signs at rural intersections, and other details that would be too voluminous to include in the legislation itself. This type of regulation is issued by the federal or provincial Cabinet, and becomes effective when published in the *Gazette* for that jurisdiction.

Municipal regulation is also pervasive. Zoning rules and decisions of zoning boards, orders of boards dealing with business licences, building heights and standards, and noise control all have immediate and crucial impacts on business within the areas covered.

From these few examples, it can be seen that government is involved in the daily operation and managerial decisions of every business, often to the frustration of the managers whose decisions are being limited. Yet, as is so often the case, the same managers who complain about regulation and control often will turn to government agencies to seek regulation and control of competitors. Perhaps, in the words of the old saying, "It depends upon whose ox is being gored."

## The Ecological Environment

The ecological environment consists of our natural surroundings. Ecology is the branch of natural science devoted to the relationship between living things and their environments. The production of most goods and services create problems in waste disposal; air, water, and ground contamination; and other sources of degradation of the natural environment. As far back as 1962, Rachel Carson's best-selling book *Silent Spring* alerted the general public to the dangers of widely used chemical pesticides, particularly the organochlorine types such as DDT and its related compounds, DDE and dieldrin. These compounds interfere with life processes. Carson pointed out that their uncontrolled use, without concern for harmful effects, promised future soil, water, and human health problems.

The tragic impact of chemicals on the ecological environment and on human life was brought into focus when a cloud of poisonous methyl isocyanate gas was accidentally released in December 1994 from the plant of a subsidiary of the Union Carbide Company in Bhopal, India. More than 2000 people were killed and 200,000 others apparently were injured to some extent.[21] Methyl isocyanate was used to manufacture Sevin, a plant pesticide distributed throughout India to protect corn, rice, soybean, cotton, and alfalfa crops. Manufacturing the product, which reduced insect infestations that were destroying much-needed food, certainly had a positive social benefit. But no one would have intentionally created the situation that caused the spill and such widespread misery.

*Outdated design, poor maintenance, inadequate safety procedures, and the exercise of bad judgement in the early stages of the emergency all seem to have contributed to a nuclear disaster at Chernobyl that almost caused worldwide radioactive pollution.*

Another celebrated case was the Chernobyl nuclear disaster, which affected radiation levels and food supplies in countries all over the Northern Hemisphere, and which, unfortunately, seems to be representative of conditions throughout the former Soviet Union.

The current ecological problems of energy shortages, pollution, and poor planning didn't arise overnight. They result from years of almost uncontrolled economic growth, affluent lifestyles, urbanization, and technological development with little concern for ecological consequences. No nation is free from responsibility or from criticism. Canadians often tend to feel rather smug and to point to environmental problems in other countries. To realize that the problems are not all elsewhere, we only have to look at the "mountains of the moon" landscapes surrounding some of Ontario's big smelters, and at the ecological disaster that is Lake Erie. The teeming landfills in developed countries, the slash-and-burn agriculture in some less developed countries, and the unchecked population growth in many less developed and developing countries all endanger critical natural resources.

The world now faces problems in deforestation, species loss, soil erosion, and water and air pollution. In June 1992, 140 world leaders and 30,000 other participants met in Rio de Janeiro for the Earth Summit to discuss and find solutions for ecological problems. The world had changed dramatically since the first Earth Summit 20 years earlier in Stockholm. Since then, 115 nations, including Canada, have created environmental agencies and ministries. Laws have been promulgated in many countries to punish irresponsibility in these areas, although enforcement is often less than vigorous. Much more must be done to solve environmental problems. Managers will play a prominent role in resolving these problems.

## Ecological Dilemmas

Ecological decisions are seldom easy to make. Protective equipment and measures are expensive, time and money spent in treating waste products may have an adverse effect on the company's bottom line, and some particularly harmful products (such as dioxins and freon) may have to be abandoned altogether. Even the protective actions may have unintended adverse effects. The history of DDT is a case in point. For a number of years after it was synthesized, DDT was widely used, especially in tropical countries that were plagued with hordes of malaria-carrying mosquitoes. DDT seemed the perfect solution. When sprayed over large areas, the mosquito populations declined precipitously, with accompanying decreases in the incidence of malaria. For a time, it was thought that malaria would follow polio and smallpox into oblivion. Then DDT began to appear in the food chain in the fatty tissues of animals, birds, and fish, and it was having potentially deleterious effects on humans who consumed them. DDT was banned in most countries. Almost immediately the mosquito populations burgeoned, and so did the number of people infected with malaria. Once again, according to the World Health Organization, 300 to 500 million new cases of malaria are occurring worldwide every year, and malaria is the third leading cause of death in developing countries.[22] The public health question "To DDT or not to DDT?" is one that defies a simplistic answer. As this example illustrates, managers have to weigh the consequences of their decisions, and the outcomes may not always be foreseeable.

It is this sort of dilemma that faced government officials and managers of Komineft, the company that operates the pipeline that connects Moscow with the Vozey oil field in the northern Komi Republic. In late 1994, the poorly constructed pipeline had become so rusty that it began hemorrhaging. To shut it down would have meant a massive loss of revenues, as well as a serious disruption of the oil supply to millions of Russians who depended on it for heating throughout the bitterly cold Russian winters. Furthermore, a prolonged shutdown would have allowed the hot oil in the pipeline to cool and harden in the frigid Siberian winter, perhaps ruining the pipeline irreparably. Managers were reluctant to shut down the pipeline, so pollution of the fragile Arctic environment continued for weeks before managers finally succumbed to the pressure of the worldwide horror at the ecological disaster.[23]

Not every environmentally sound decision causes a negative financial result. In the 1920s and 1930s, residents of Washington state who lived downwind from the lead-zinc smelter of the Consolidated Mining & Smelter Company (now Cominco) in Trail, British Columbia, complained bitterly to a binational commission about the pollution to which they were being subjected. (People in Trail did not seem to complain, perhaps because most of them or members of their families were employed by the company and were willing to tolerate conditions that the employees of a polluting company would not accept today.) After much international discussion and negotiation, the company agreed to install baghouses and other scrubbers to remove most of the particulate matter and sulphur from the stack gases. The company then investigated potential agricultural uses of sulphur, and eventually developed a market for some of the products that previously had been discharged into the atmosphere. After many years, and imaginative research and marketing, the recaptured sulphur has become an important source of revenue for the company. Unfortunately, such a happy outcome is not always available, so in many cases managers are faced with the need to balance environmental protection against cost—a question that will be developed further in subsequent pages.

It is not hard to see that there are no easy solutions to some ecological issues concerning business and the environment. The best that managers can do is learn about the aspects that affect their own businesses, be alert to the potential for problems, identify problems quickly when they arise, and make the best decisions they can in light of the information available.

## Social Responsibility

**social responsibility**
The practices of a company for which it is accountable, in relation to other parties such as customers, competitors, governments, employees, suppliers, creditors, and the general public.

Laws set the *minimum* standards for responsible and ethical business practices and employer and employee behaviour. Within an organization, there is a philosophy that reflects the company's approach to social responsibility. The company's **social responsibility** is demonstrated by its practices in dealing with other parties such as customers, competitors, the government, employees, suppliers, and creditors. Actions interpreted as being socially responsible differ across industries and from company to company. Some managers view social responsibility to be an obligation reluctantly accepted, others view it as something required in reaction to pressures, and still others consider proactive behaviour to be the proper position.

### Social Responsibility as Social Obligation

When social responsibility is viewed as a social obligation, it is assumed that a corporation engages in socially responsible behaviour when it pursues profit, while doing as much as but not more than the law requires. The theory is that because society supports business by allowing it to exist, business is obligated to repay society by making profits to encourage further investment and job creation. Thus, according to this view, legal behaviour in pursuit of profit is socially responsible behaviour, and any behaviour that is illegal or isn't in pursuit of profit is socially irresponsible.

This view is espoused by economist Milton Friedman and others who believe that society creates companies to pursue two primary purposes: to produce goods and services efficiently and to maximize profits.[24] As Friedman has stated, "There is one and only one social responsibility of business—to use its resources and engage in activities designed to increase its profits so long as it stays within the rules of the game, which is to say, engages in open and free competition without deception or fraud."[25]

Proponents of social responsibility as social obligation offer four primary arguments in support of their views. First, they assert that businesses are accountable to their shareholders, the owners of the corporation, and that their sole responsibility is to serve the shareholders' interests by producing profits. If a corporation does not make profits, it will not attract investors, and the business ultimately may starve financially. If this occurs, employees lose their jobs and society suffers.

Second, they argue that as representatives of the people, the government (through legislation and allocation of tax revenues) is best equipped to determine the nature of social improvements and to realize those improvements in society. Businesses contribute in this regard by paying taxes to the government, which rightfully determines how they should be spent.

Third, if management allocates profits to social improvement activities, these economists say that it is abusing its authority. As Friedman notes, management is taking the shareholders' profits and spending them on activities that have no immediate profitable return to the company. And management is doing so without input from shareholders. Managers also are taking actions that affect society without being accountable, because managers aren't elected public officials. Further, according to Friedman, this type of not-for-profit-seeking activity may be both unwise and unworkable because managers are not trained to make non-economic decisions.

Fourth, according to this view, these actions by management may hurt society. The financial costs of social activities over time will cause the price of the company's goods and services to increase, and customers must pay the bill. Thus, managers have acted in a manner contrary to the interests of the public—that is, customers and, ultimately, the shareholders.

It is sometimes argued that this view of corporate responsibility is mandated by the federal and provincial statutes under which corporations are formed. The Canada Business Corporations Act, and each of the provincial enabling acts, includes words to the effect that corporate directors and officers must act "… in the best interests of the corporation." The question, however, is whether this phrase would preclude acting on a broader definition of social responsibility. It can be argued that it *is* in the best interests of the corporation to act in socially responsible ways. In May 1996, a group of academics from across North America met at the University of Toronto to initiate a three-year project to examine aspects of this and related questions. One of the leading participants, Professor Michael Deck, executive director of the Centre for Corporate Social Performance & Ethics at the University of Toronto, said, "The notion that the modern corporation is constituted of shareholders and managers and nobody else is bankrupt."[26]

## Social Responsibility as Social Reaction

A second view of social responsibility is that it is in reaction to "currently prevailing social norms, values, and performance expectations."[27] This assumes that society is entitled to more from a business than the mere provision of goods and services. As a minimum, business must be accountable for the ecological, environmental, and social costs incurred by its actions. At a higher level, business must react and contribute to solving society's problems (even those that can't be directly attributed to business). Thus, this

*A growing number of socially responsible corporations encourage their employees to assist with the leadership of youth groups that provide socially acceptable outlets for the energy and interests of young people.*

viewpoint holds that corporate contributions to charitable organizations are socially responsible, even though the money donated "belongs" to the shareholders.

A somewhat restrictive interpretation seeks to separate corporate actions that are required by economic or legal imperatives from those that are initiated by voluntary, altruistic motives. This narrower view implies that a corporation that is only doing what it is *obligated* to do is not socially responsible because its behaviour is required, not voluntary.

A broader interpretation of this view identifies actions as socially responsible whether they are required or voluntary. In this interpretation, it is socially responsible to react to specific groups—for example, unions, shareholders, social activists, and consumer advocates—even though they expect more than the legal minimum. A company can decide not to react, but favourable reaction, in this view, is considered to be the ideal reflection of social responsibility.

## Social Responsibility as Social Responsiveness

According to this view, socially responsible behaviours are anticipatory and preventive, rather than just reactive and restorative.[28] The term *social responsiveness* has become widely used in recent years to refer to actions that exceed social obligation and social reaction.[29] Socially responsive behaviour includes taking stands on public issues, accounting for actions to any who inquire, anticipating society's future needs and moving towards satisfying them, and communicating with governments about existing and potential legislation that is socially desirable.

A socially responsive corporation actively seeks solutions to social problems. According to this view, progressive managers apply corporate skills and resources to every problem—from conditions on native reserves to youth employment and from local schools and hospitals to environmental cleanup. Such behaviour reflects the "true" meaning of social responsibility for social-responsiveness advocates. Corporate executives who commit their organizations to such endeavours are likely to receive substantial public approval,[30] although they may risk criticism from those who disagree with the positions they have taken.

In the words of The New Academy of Business, a registered charity that conducts workshops in Wales on social responsibility in business, "Sound environmental management is a key component of socially responsible business practice…. [I]t is no longer just visionary leaders who appreciate the necessity for action. It is becoming a business fact … and pressure from lawmakers and consumers will ensure that change comes sooner rather than later."[31]

Social responsiveness is the broadest meaning of social responsibility. It removes managers and their organizations from the traditional position of solely being concerned with economic means and ends. This view rests on two premises: (1) organizations should be involved in preventing, as well as solving, social problems, and (2) business organizations "… are perhaps the most effective problem-solving organizations in a capitalist society."[32]

## What Managers Are Reading    2-1

### The Ethical Imperative: Why Moral Leadership Is Good Business

Starting from his convictions as a conservative business-oriented consultant and former corporate executive, John Dalla Costa states baldly that private conscience and business practice cannot be divorced. He argues that business practices in the ethical realm mirror the standards of society as a whole, as well as our personal beliefs, but he takes little comfort from these connections. In the first third of the book Dalla Costa explores the current situation and the relationship between business and ethics.

Drawing on concepts from Dr. Hans Kung, a Swiss theologian, and Dietrich Bonhoeffer, a philosopher martyred by the Nazis, Dalla Costa attempts to offer a world model for leadership in the redefinition of business ethics. He acknowledges that changing an organization is always difficult, and that courageous and effective leadership is required to accomplish any transformation of substance.

Dalla Costa expresses gratification that public opinion is now coalescing around eco-friendly views that a few years ago were voiced only by a tiny group of people outside of the mainstream. He cites as an encouraging indication that even though it took many years, the managers of Nike finally succumbed to the effects of widespread and damaging publicity and began to change their practices in impoverished countries. Another positive sign is the decision by the World Bank and the International Monetary Fund in 1997 to mount a vigorous campaign against graft throughout the world. (One can see the effects of this decision, as these organizations recently have refused loans to desperately needy countries until they take initial steps to curb corruption. The effect may be less immediate on countries that do not need IMF or World Bank loans, such as Germany and Denmark, which still allow bribes to be used as tax-deductible expenses.)

In terms that should catch the attention of business leaders, Dalla Costa states that only two-thirds of the *Fortune 500* companies from the 1970s still existed 13 years later—proving, he says, that in today's society, "short-termism" is profitable. And civilization is at long-term risk from just such "short-termism."

Dalla Costa offers Hewlett-Packard's efforts on "ethical alignment." From that source he quotes two truisms that too often are disregarded. The first is: "The judgment of the company is only as good as the judgment of the individual." The second is: "Profitability is imperative, but equally so is character." Business leaders could do worse than to adopt just these two principles, and to build on them solid ethical standards that constitute, according to Dalla Costa, *good business.*

Source: John Dalla Costa, *The Ethical Imperative: Why Moral Leadership Is Good Business* (Toronto: HarperCollins, 1998).

Choosing among these three types of social responsibility will still leave managers with only an abstract set of guidelines. Those who define social responsibility determine what is considered responsible. The importance of social responsibility has increased the attention paid to ethics and ethical dilemmas. Social responsibility deals primarily with the external environment, while ethics deals with both the internal and external environments of the organization.

## Ethics

What is meant by the term **ethics**? Opinions differ, but a working definition might be that ethics is a rule or standard of desirable conduct. Immanuel Kant, Thomas Hobbes, John Locke, and others argued that there is a *system of moral imperatives* (directives, rules, or principles) that are self-evident and universal. Religious leaders often expound

**ethics**
Standards of conduct that are reflected in behaviour that is fair and just, including but also extending over and above what is required by laws and regulations.

this view, but there is considerable disagreement as to the details of these moral imperatives. Jeremy Bentham and John Stuart Mill reduced the moral imperative to the need to act in such a way as to create the *greatest good for the greatest number*. This formulation might seem attractive until one realizes that if carried to its utmost, it would mean disposing of all weak and infirm people, those who lack skill or motivation, and perhaps even all children who are unable to support themselves. Presumably these people are a minority of the population, and by disposing of them, the "greatest number" of the population would seem to benefit from not having to support them. Seen in this light, most thinking people would reject this simplistic definition of ethics.

## Management in the Real World          2-4

### The Intelligence-Gathering Choice

Competition has created combative adversaries in many industries. No-holds-barred competition for human resources, ideas, innovations, data, and market information has led to numerous instances of illegal behaviour and many unethical procedures. Beating "them" (e.g., a competitor, the Japanese, the government, Revenue Canada) is an obsession in some organizations.

It came as a shock to a large U.S. manufacturer of medical supplies when a Japanese competitor, Kokoku Rubber Industry, was boosting output at a new plant in Kentucky. The U.S. firm had to cut prices drastically as it struggled to survive. Kokoku has gathered information (intelligence) for years from legal sources (newspapers) about its U.S. competitor. Kokoku used information gathering to gain an edge and beat the competitor.

Intelligence involves gathering information about competitors and customers. It ranges from Kokoku's methods (reading, filing, and analyzing published reports and data) to illegal spying. The heat of competition unfortunately has spawned more and more illegal and unethical intelligence gathering.

Companies have been known to sift through competitors' garbage to find information. Others have instructed executives (using disguised names or positions) to take competitors' plant tours just to acquire information. Kellogg has stopped granting plant tours because competitors were observing and collecting information on manufacturing technology.

Is intelligence gathering necessary? Most firms would state that gathering intelligence in a legal manner is part of management's fiduciary responsibility to its employees, shareholders, and customers.

Ethical methods of intelligence gathering include review of public documents, financial report analysis, legitimate employment interviews with people who worked for a competitor, attending trade fairs, market surveys, and analyzing competitors' products and services.

Unethical intelligence gathering has taken many routes: bribery, planting spies in a competitor's business, wire tapping, theft, blackmail, and extortion. Cordis Corporation, a Miami-based heart pacemaker manufacturer, introduced a superior product. Sales, however, worsened. Cordis management was baffled by the lack of positive response to its superior product, but found that competitors were offering physicians cars, boats, and trips to use their pacemakers. Cordis responded by increasing educational support for doctors and by adding salespeople so that more time could be spent explaining the product to physicians. This dramatically increased sales. Cordis took the high road and responded to unethical behaviour with a set of steps that by most standards were ethical.

Intelligence gathering is now part of competition. But will the methods be ethical or unethical? Each person making a decision on how to conduct intelligence gathering must answer this question.

Source: Adapted from Richard S. Teitebaum, "The New Race for Intelligence," *Forbes* (November 2, 1992): 104-07; and Patrick E. Murphy and Gene R. Lacznack, "Emerging Ethical Issues Facing Marketing Researchers," *Marketing Research* (June 1992): 6-11.

For our purposes, perhaps we should avoid the intricacies of philosophical debate and recognize that an ethical standard would have to reflect what have been identified as modern versions of classical principles: justice and fairness, non-discrimination, utmost honesty and integrity, an ability to keep confidences, respect and caring for others, and the courage to pursue the right path.

Most of us behave reasonably well in dealing with big and obvious ethical decisions. We tend to judge ourselves and would like others to judge us by these intentional decisions, in which we have consciously weighed the ethical issues. Where we may fall down, and in fact where we are more likely to be judged by others, is in the day-by-day conduct of our business and personal lives—the little things that, taken together, describe our characters. Even the appearance of impropriety can sully our reputations, and in the long run can damage the organizations with which we are associated. Truly ethical people do not measure their conduct by minimal standards, but instead they do more than they *have* to do, and less than they have a strict *right* to do. Although there may be several ethical responses to a particular situation, they are not all equal—some are more ethical than others. An ethical person often must sacrifice short-term benefits to achieve long-term advantages. By behaving ethically, a business, acting through the people associated with it, can establish and maintain a reputation for fair dealing and integrity—the value of which cannot be measured and the loss of which can have far-reaching negative effects.

What constitutes ethical behaviour seems, like beauty, to rest in the eye of the beholder. And while most people consider themselves highly principled, they view their co-workers more suspiciously. A survey conducted by the Ethics Resource Center, a not-for-profit educational organization, found that more than half of the 4035 respondents said that their own standards of ethics were higher than those of their co-workers. More than half of the respondents thought that their own companies were more ethical than the average North American company, but they felt that ethical conduct is not rewarded in business today. Nearly six out of seven respondents said that North American managers choose profits over doing the right thing! In an analysis of a study of Canada's largest companies, Janet McFarland concluded that: "A study by EthicScan Canada of 114 Canadian companies often found low standards and little concern."[33] She quotes David Nitkin, the president of EthicScan Canada, who found that for many of the companies surveyed, ethical issues were not a top priority.

The picture is not all black, however. Some corporations are beginning to give serious consideration to ethical issues, in part because of recently publicized examples of unethical behaviour, but also because it is beginning to be recognized that behaving ethically is good business.[34] General Motors, for instance, issued a new ethics policy that strictly forbids employees from accepting "entertainment" from suppliers. One might even hope that the increasing attention to ethical standards may result in part from the recognition by some managers that ethical behaviour is essential if a better society is to be created, and that achieving a better society will improve the quality of life for everyone.

A first step has been taken by a number of corporations, which have developed codes of conduct for all of their employees. A study conducted in 1991 of 1900 corporations in Canada, the United States, Mexico, and Europe found that more than three-quarters of the North American companies surveyed had adopted codes of ethics, and that nearly half of these companies had done so in the preceding four years.[35] A similar survey of United Kingdom companies conducted in the same year by the London-based Institute of Business Ethics found that 71 percent of its respondents had adopted codes of conduct, up from 55 percent four years earlier. In light of increasing media attention to unethical behaviour, it can probably be assumed that the trend has continued, and that today only a few companies do not at least have nominal codes of ethics.

Unfortunately, adopting a code of conduct and acting on it may be two different things. KPMG recently surveyed 1000 of Canada's largest companies, and received 251 responses. Of those responding, two-thirds had codes of conduct, but only about one-fifth had training programs in ethical behaviour and only one-fifth had a confidential hotline for employees to report unethical behaviour.[36]

Ideally a code of ethics should (1) give employees specific direction in dealing with ethical dilemmas, (2) clarify the organization's position regarding areas of ethical uncertainty, and (3) help achieve and maintain ongoing conduct that the organization views as ethical and proper.[37] It should cover such broad issues as compliance with law and regulations and honesty in communications, as well as everyday issues such as workplace equity and how to handle "gifts" and "entertainment" offered by suppliers. Of course, adoption and publication of a code of ethics does not ensure that everyone will act ethically, but it is a start, and it does let employees know that the official policy of the company is that behaviour will be ethical.

Codes are often ineffective because once they are established in written form, management doesn't follow through and proactively implement them in the organization. The written code lies dormant and ultimately serves little more than a public relations function.[38] However, organizations can achieve effective, "living" codes of ethics by following a multistep implementation strategy. First, managers involve people at several levels of the organization in discussing and formulating the values and ethical standards that they believe are desirable and appropriate. Then they translate values and beliefs into specific ethical standards of behaviour, both in general terms and in very specific terms, for the issues that executives and employees are most likely to face in their work. Then they offer all members of the organization the opportunity to comment on the draft policy, before it becomes the company's official code of ethics. When the code has been agreed upon and approved by top management *and* the company's board, it is distributed throughout the company, and seminars are held to discuss how the principles embodied in the code are to be applied in day-by-day activities. Positive provisions are made for periodic review, and possible amendment, as new situations arise and as standards and emphases change in the society in which the organization functions. The final test, however, is whether everyone in the company, from the top down, accepts and lives by the code.

## Reporting Unethical Behaviour

Studies have confirmed that one-quarter of respondents say that their companies look the other way and ignore unethical conduct in order to meet business objectives. Slightly more than one-quarter of respondents say that they sometimes feel pressure to act in ways that violate their own organizations' codes of behaviour! Nearly one-third of respondents report having seen misconduct at work in the preceding year. The three top misdeeds were lying to supervisors, lying in reports or falsifying records, and theft. Of those who observed misconduct, fewer than half reported it. More than half of those who reported misconduct were not satisfied with the resolution (or lack of resolution). Those who observed misconduct but failed to report it gave these three top reasons: "I didn't believe corrective action would be taken," "I feared retribution or retaliation from my supervisor or management," or "I didn't trust the organization to keep my report confidential."[39]

This reluctance to report unethical behaviour is even more prevalent in cases of sexual harassment. Not only do those who observe this type of unethical behaviour hesitate to report it, but the person who is the recipient of the unwanted behaviour often tolerates it, because of fear that reporting it will not result in any corrective action and

## Paradigms and Parables: The Ten Commandments for Ethics in Business

What principles should guide decision making? Look on the shelves of any airport bookstore and you're sure to find dozens of choices. Countless self-help books tell the history of a particular company or how some historical figure "got it right." Yet few writers take the trouble to explore the general principles of ethical behaviour against which managers might measure their actions.

In *Paradigms and Parables* the authors aren't merely talking about being truthful with customers or following the law. They're touting a global approach to capitalism with a conscience: "Act so that the largest number of people receive the maximum benefit from every decision and action ... Remember: Peace and prosperity in the world are created by ethical business practice."

The idea is that organizations can put social justice first if they integrate ethics and finance through the acceptance of "commandments" that shape the belief that "we are all part of one world,

and we can help one another to make it a better place."

Although it's as hard to disagree with this philosophy as it is to denigrate Mom and apple pie, you may find reading this book uncomfortable. Some reviewers have complained that the book preaches. The parables use case study situations of a Wall Street trading firm—written in Biblical language—to illustrate the authors' commandments. The authors may make you feel guilty, or they may inspire you. Yet even if you buy into the commandments, you may discover they are as elusive as a sermon you agree with on Sunday, but find hard to live by on Monday.

Sources: Brother Louis Dethomasis, FSC, and William Ammentorp, *Paradigms and Parables: The Ten Commandments for Ethics in Business* (Amherst, MA: Human Resource Development Press, 1995). Adapted from Lin Standke, "Paradigms and Parables: The Ten Commandments for Ethics in Business," *Training* (October 1995): 121-22.

may bring about subtle or not-so-subtle retribution. Some managers recognize that it is generally to the advantage of the organization to have instances of misbehaviour reported to those who want to act on it and who have the authority to correct it. These forward-looking, ethical managers are beginning to take steps to protect whistle-blowers, not only from misguided organizational sanctions, but also from the criticism and shunning that fellow employees often direct at anyone who violates the presumed code in which unethical behaviour is condoned and even subtly applauded. In a large organization, a whistle-blower can be transferred laterally to another division to build relationships with a new set of co-workers. In a small organization this option is seldom possible, so managers have to make it clear that any negative behaviour towards the whistle-blower will be subject to discipline. This critical issue will be discussed in greater detail in Chapter 8.

## Application of Ethical Standards

Questions of ethics are major considerations for organizations today. Ethics is an area fraught with uncertainty, ambiguity, and occasionally anxiety. Managers must face ethical questions squarely, set the pattern for the corporate culture of their organizations, and demonstrate by their own actions that they mean what they say. If top managers accept lavish hospitality from officers of other companies with which they deal, soon the most junior buyers in the purchasing department will be seeking "freebies" from suppliers. If top managers charge personal holidays as business trips, it will not be long

## Management in the Real World 2-5

### The Role of Leadership in Corporate Ethical Behaviour

For many years, a common assumption among researchers in organizational behaviour was that leaders influence organizational performance. This assumption was based primarily on intuitive feelings, and little empirical research had been done on the subject. Now that more empirical research has been done, it seems puzzling to discover mixed results. Some studies have discovered the expected relationships; in other studies, the relationships seem either weak or non-existent.

One possible explanation for the seemingly contradictory results is that when the impact of leadership is measured across different organizations, the outcomes may be obscured by variations in the sizes of the organizations studied. It is reasonable to assume that in a small organization, with perhaps 20 employees, everyone is almost completely aware of the actions of everyone else. If the owner/manager uses the company minivan as a personal vehicle, employees will begin to disregard the difference between personal property and company property. The outcome, of course, may be use of company machines and supplies for personal purposes, and eventually outright theft of supplies, tools, and products. By contrast, if the manager is meticulous about arriving on time in the morning, attends consistently to duties, avoids long personal calls, and makes conservative use of the organization's supplies and facilities, these behaviours, too, will be observed and copied by the other employees. The corporate culture will have been established, and most members of the group will conform to it without giving it much thought.

The situation is quite different in a larger enterprise that has 1000 or more employees. In such an enterprise, the average production worker or clerk does not know whether the CEO and vice presidents are allowed to drive company cars as part of their compensation packages. Thus, the actions of the "leaders" may not have a direct impact on those employees at the lower end of the hierarchy. If the researchers identify the CEO and vice presidents as the "leaders," it is not surprising that they may not be able to confirm widespread direct impact on the ethical behaviour of production workers.

More sophisticated and longer-term research, however, might come to different conclusions. If the relationships studied were restricted to those in which informed observation is possible—for instance, the vice presidents' observations of the CEO's behaviour—the results likely would show that what the CEO does has a direct impact on the ethical standards of the vice presidents. The actions of the vice presidents then would be observed to affect the general managers, whose actions would then affect the managers, whose actions would then affect the supervisors, whose actions would then affect the production workers, who would have no way of knowing that the pattern of behaviours was established by top managers. Ultimately, the CEO's behaviour becomes pervasive throughout the organization. But given the relatively short tenure of CEOs in today's business world, the wave of effects may not reach the bottom of the organization before the CEO has departed and been replaced by another person, whose standards of behaviour may be different. If this hypothesis is correct, it may account for the failure of some studies to find that the standards of behaviour of "top managers" will be reflected throughout the organization.

Although it would be difficult to formulate, the research design would be more effective if it could focus on interpersonal relationships in which a person who is superior in the hierarchy is observed on a day-to-day basis by those individuals who are peers or subordinates. In such a research design, the contagion of high or low ethical standards might be traceable. In the meantime, useful findings may be limited to studies of behaviour in relatively small organizations. Those findings can be extrapolated to larger organizations, with the cautionary realization that extrapolation is always dangerous and may prove to be misleading in the long term.

before middle managers take personal friends to lunch on the organization's expense accounts and non-managers use company supplies for personal purposes. Examples of such creeping misbehaviour can be found in many organizations, and pose difficult problems for managers, especially if they are personally dissatisfied with the corporate cultures in which they find themselves.

The top managers who publish codes of conduct and exhort employees to act ethically are wasting their time if they, themselves, do not keep higher standards than those they set for their employees. It serves a manager well to remember Ralph Waldo Emerson's statement: "What you *are* thunders so loudly in my ears that I cannot hear what you *say*."

In the end, managers must be comfortable with the fact that they will constantly face questions about the ethics of their actions. To function under these potential constraints, managers must examine their own motivations, attempt to predict the consequences that may flow from their decisions and who may be injured by them, and apply the "newspaper test." That is, they should ask themselves, "If my actions were described by an unsympathetic reporter on the front page of tomorrow's *Globe and Mail*, would I be comfortable having breakfast with my friends, my parents, or my spouse?" There are no perfect answers to ethical questions, but being aware of the questions and having a plan for dealing with them will help managers make decisions that are most likely to meet ethical standards and least likely to injure society, the organization, the manager, and other individuals.

## The Workplace of Tomorrow

In the years immediately ahead, an organization's external environment will become a greater consideration in the thinking that drives managerial decisions. Media inquiry, government regulation, and public expectations are becoming ever more important in organizational planning. Even if managers in bygone days could act as if they were unaffected by public interest (a doubtful proposition), by now they should have abandoned that misapprehension.

There is little doubt that organizations increasingly will be faced with ethical dilemmas. Those that seek to expand operations into countries such as Indonesia and China, where bribery is common, will have to decide whether to risk losing the business opportunities or to succumb to the temptation to "buy" support by whatever means may be available. Subtler, and consequently more difficult, questions concerning business "entertainment" arise in Canada. Organizations frequently will have to decide how much information to make public, either voluntarily or in response to questions. Whatever these decisions may be, it is certain that organizational behaviour will be under closer scrutiny than it has been in the past, and that reputations may be built or destroyed by seemingly minor decisions.

## Summary of Learning Objectives

▶ **Distinguish between the terms** *internal environment* **and** *external environment.*
*Internal environment* refers to the factors within the organization, such as rules (both formal and informal), people, structure, and reward systems that influence how employees work to accomplish goals. *External environment* refers to all factors outside the organization, such as social-cultural trends, laws, technology, and environmental issues that have direct or indirect impact on the organization.

▷ **Explain why managers must consider their environments in all of their activities.**

Every organization is shaped by external factors, and by the elements of the internal environment. Some environmental factors require certain decisions and preclude others; other environmental factors make a specific course of action much more effective than the alternatives.

▷ **Explain why workforce culture is such an important issue for managers to understand.**

Employees' backgrounds, values, experience, age, gender, and racial makeup are changing. All members of an organization act in ways that reflect their own attitudes and perceptions. These attitudes and perceptions are based on their individual values, which in turn stem from their backgrounds and their particular situations in life. To manage a diverse workforce, managers must be aware of these differences and develop management styles and methods that accommodate them and that are tailored to the mix of employees in the particular organization.

▷ **Discuss how a person's values are formed, and how they influence behaviour.**

Values are typically formed in a person's early years. Teachers, relatives, parents, friends, and other peer group members—by example, discussions, and responses—illustrate various values that are observed, modified, and adopted. Once values are formed, it is unusual for them to be changed appreciably, unless there is a major upheaval that profoundly affects the individual's life. These values lead to beliefs, which shape attitudes and ultimately determine behaviour.

▷ **Explain social responsibility as social obligation, social reaction, and social responsiveness.**

Some argue that an organization should act in society within the law, but only to the extent required by law. Others say that an organization should react to its environments, and act accordingly in socially acceptable ways. Still others advocate that an organization should act as a concerned member of society and seek out and help to ameliorate unacceptable conditions. These three views are described, respectively, as those of social obligation, social reaction, and social responsiveness.

▷ **Discuss why companies are becoming more interested in producing environmentally friendly products.**

Some managers recognize that the capacity of the environment is becoming overloaded, and that it cannot absorb even the present levels of toxic and other destructive impacts. To preserve the quality of life for all members of society, managers realize that their organizations must adopt better ways of controlling these impacts. Other managers see expanding markets for environmentally friendly products and services, and are motivated by opportunities for profit. Still other managers are beginning to realize that their organizations will be called to account by government regulatory agencies and consumers to improve their ways.

▷ **Describe how an organization can best develop an effective code of ethics.**

Developing a code of ethics requires broad involvement, from every level of the organization. To be effective, the code must be accepted by executives and other employees, and must become part of their working tools. A code of ethics will be no better than the degree to which top and middle managers adhere to it and demonstrate that it is important to them.

▶  **Explain why ethical behaviour is important in shaping work life.**

At the very least, ethical behaviour is essential in building a good reputation and earning trust—both of which are attributes of the effective manager. Managers illustrate by their own actions the ethical standards they expect of their subordinates, their colleagues, and their superiors. Most people find that living and working in an unethical atmosphere is unpleasant, if not intolerable, and that the best way to avoid this kind of an atmosphere is to have one's own standard of behaviour.

## KEY TERMS

attitudes, p. 49
beliefs, p. 49
culture, p. 44
dominant culture, p. 45
environment, p. 43

environmental analysis, p. 52
ethics, p. 67
external environment, p. 43
internal environment, p. 44

social responsibility, p. 63
technological innovation, p. 58
technology, p. 57
values, p. 48

## REVIEW AND DISCUSSION QUESTIONS

### Recall

1. What is an organizational culture and how does it influence employees' performance? What effect does it have on the organization's competitiveness?
2. In ecological terms, how can a product be environmentally friendly?
3. What are the implications of a sluggish productivity rate for a manager facing employees' demands for wage and salary increases?

### Understanding

4. Values are important to every individual. Why would the values of an increasingly diverse workforce be difficult to determine?
5. What does the concept of "learning to learn" have to do with the need for a workforce that must use a range of skills to perform their jobs?
6. Why are some codes of ethics not effective?
7. Many organizations are considered to be socially reactive. What does this mean in practical terms?

### Application

8. List the specific ways in which your educational institution or workplace exhibits diversity. Consider what effect this diversity has had on the organization, and what effects it may have in the future.
9. Ask a friend, a respected peer, and a person engaged in business to describe what each thinks constitutes the culture of an organization. What did you find in the terms and phrases they use? Is there confusion about what is meant by the term *culture*?
10. Draft a one-page code of conduct for a hypothetical small business—for example, a carpet-cleaning company that is owned by two people and employs ten people, who go to various houses each day to sell the service, clean carpets in place, issue invoices, and collect payments. Then, with two or three other students, compare and discuss your drafts, and decide what items you wish to add to your draft, and which, if any, you might modify. Did you omit some subjects that others identified as important? Would your wording convey your intentions to employees, suppliers, and customers? How would your code of conduct affect the day-to-day operations of your company?

# CASE 2-1

## Booth Pharmaceutical Corporation

You are a member of the board of directors of Booth Pharmaceutical Corporation. You have been called to a special board meeting to discuss what should be done with the product Vanatin. Vanatin is a "fixed-ratio" antibiotic sold by prescription. That is, it contains a combination of drugs. On the market for more than 13 years, it has been highly successful. It now accounts for about $18 million per year (12 percent of Booth's gross income in Canada and a greater percentage of net profits). Vanatin is marketed in the United States, and the identical product is marketed in other countries under a different name. Profit margins in the U.S. and other foreign markets are comparable to those in Canada.

Over the past 20 years, a large number of medical scientists have objected to the sale of most fixed-ratio drugs. The arguments have been that (1) there is no evidence that fixed-ratio drugs are more beneficial than single drugs, and (2) the possibility of detrimental side effects, including death, is at least double that of drugs prescribed singly. For example, scientists have estimated that Vanatin and its foreign counterparts are causing about 30 to 40 unnecessary deaths per year (deaths that could have been prevented if the patients had been prescribed a substitute made by one of Booth's competitors). Despite recommendations to remove fixed-ratio drugs from the market, doctors have continued to use them. They offer a shotgun approach for doctors who are unsure of their diagnoses.

A government-funded panel of impartial scientists carried out extensive research studies in the U.S. and recommended unanimously that the sale of Vanatin be banned. One respected panel member was quoted by the press as saying, "There are few instances in medicine when so many experts have agreed unanimously and without reservation [about banning Vanatin]." Other panel members made similar comments. In fact, these remarks were typical of comments that had been made about fixed-ratio drugs over the past 20 years. These impartial experts believe that while all drugs have some possibility of side effects, the risks associated with Vanatin far exceed the possible benefits.

The special board meeting has arisen out of an emergency situation. The U.S. Food and Drug Administration has notified the president of Booth that it plans to ban Vanatin in the United States, which is Booth's major foreign market. The agency will delay its final decision to allow Booth a final appeal. Should the ban become effective, Booth would have to stop all sales of Vanatin in the United States, attempt to remove inventories from the market, and provide refunds for those recalled inventories. Booth has no substitute for Vanatin, so consumers will switch to substitutes currently marketed by rival drug companies, some of which apparently have no serious side effects. Booth's management believes that it would be extremely unlikely that bad publicity from this case would have a significant effect on the sale of Booth's other products or the company's long-term profits.

The board is meeting to review and decide on three issues:

1. What should be done with Vanatin in the U.S. market (the immediate problem)?
2. Assuming that Vanatin is banned from the U.S. market, what should Booth do in Canada, where there is as yet no great pressure to have it banned?
3. What should be done in foreign markets, where scrutiny of drugs is quite lax and no concerns have been expressed?

Decisions on each of these issues must be reached at today's meeting. The chairman of the board has sent out background information. He suggests that the following options are available separately for each of the U.S., Canadian, and foreign markets:

A. Recall Vanatin immediately and destroy it.

B. Stop production of Vanatin immediately, but allow sale of what has been produced to continue in Canada and countries where it has not been banned.

C. Stop all advertising and promotion of Vanatin, but provide it to doctors who request it.

D. Continue efforts to market Vanatin until its sale is actually banned, country by country.

E. Continue efforts to market Vanatin and take legal, political, and other necessary actions to prevent the authorities in the U.S. from banning Vanatin.

### Questions

1. Which of the options, A through E, would you choose (and try to convince the other board members to choose) for Booth for each of the U.S., Canadian, and foreign markets?

2. What effect would your choice have on Booth's financial results? Would it be neutral, slightly negative, extremely negative, slightly positive, or positive, in both the short term and the long term?

3. If there is a difference in your decision for the three markets? Why did you choose those different options? Is it ethical or unethical to choose such differences? Why or why not? If there are no differences, how does your choice in this regard reflect ethical principles?

4. What arguments would you use to persuade the other board members to accept your preferred choice?

5. Assuming that Booth directors, and Booth as a corporation, have exhibited ethical standards that are about the norm for Canadian companies, what do you think the final decision of the board would be?

6. If the board decision is different from the one you chose, what action, if any, would you take?

Source: This case is based on an exercise adapted by Roy J. Lewicki, Duke University, from an exercise developed by J. Scott Armstrong, University of Pennsylvania. It is adapted from Douglas T. Hall, Donald D. Bowen, Roy J. Lewicki, and Francine S. Hall, *Experiences in Management and Organizational Behavior*, 2nd ed. (New York: John Wiley & Sons, 1982).

## CASE 2-2

## Pacific Arts & Crafts Faces Some Ethical Dilemmas

Peter Campbell has just been appointed chair and CEO of Pacific Arts & Crafts Limited, after a successful career in theatre management and organizing entertainment events throughout Canada. PACAL, as the company is known, is a publicly traded company with nearly 2000 shareholders. It is a leading factor in the import and distribution of all kinds of textiles, pottery and ceramics, carvings, and other artworks, largely from Asia. The company owns and maintains six high-quality retail stores that are spread across Canada from St. John's to Victoria. It also sells a much lower quality of goods to independent stores that are typically located in resort and entertainment areas that cater to tourists and fun-seekers. PACAL has grown in its 40 years of existence from a one-person entrepreneurship to a solid but unspectacular corporation with annual revenues of more than $140 million.

When the previous CEO had announced his impending retirement, Alex Winter, a relatively new member of the 12-person board of directors, had suggested that PACAL retain the services of an executive recruiting firm, known jocularly as a headhunter, to comb the market for the "right" CEO. Josh Finnerty, a long-term director, countered with: "Alex,

PACAL has done pretty well without calling in outsiders in red suspenders who charge a fat fee for telling us what we already know. Some of us on the board have contacts all over the country. We can find the right person ourselves." Josh then said, "I move that we constitute a three-man search committee of directors to find the best CEO and bring him into the company." Sheila Carpenter, the sole woman on the board, mildly muttered, "Did you say three-*man*?" Josh laughed and said, "Sheila, you shouldn't be so sensitive. You know what I mean. If you had a lot of contacts, I wouldn't object to you being on the committee." The matter was dropped, and on a perfunctory vote the motion was passed. As could have been predicted, Josh Finnerty was made chair of the search committee, and two other long-term members were named to work with him.

Finnerty and his fellow committee members phoned several of their many friends in corporations all over Canada, and developed a short list of five men whom they thought might be qualified. When they phoned the first candidate they learned that a year or so ago he had suffered a severe heart attack and had retired to his summer home in the Gatineau Hills. The second candidate expressed interest, as did the next two. The final person on the short list told the committee that he had no interest in leaving his present post.

The committee interviewed the three remaining candidates, but almost immediately it was clear that they would recommend to the board that Peter Campbell be appointed as chair and CEO of PACAL. They were fully aware that Peter had had no experience in importing or marketing of products. This negative factor was balanced because they were tremendously impressed with his energy at the age of 37, with his obviously successful career in the highly demanding entertainment area, and with his description of how he saw himself as a manager—"Someone who gets the best out of people by leading not by pushing, and most of all by constantly setting a good example." They believed that his approach would bring new ideas and stimulation to PACAL, making it a more aggressive seeker of opportunities and growth. It also helped in their decision that Peter's father-in-law was the company's major shareholder—owning 32 percent of its outstanding shares.

Peter had decided to leave his former career because he had become increasingly disenchanted with what he saw as unethical behaviour, and an obsession with greed, on the part of many people in the entertainment world. He was not quite sure what ethical standards would be viable in a business environment, but he was committed to making that determination and then ensuring that it was followed without exception in any business in which he was involved.

One of the first major decisions Peter made after assuming office was to issue a three-month contract to Ethics Unlimited, a consulting firm that specialized in corporate ethical audits and in offering advice as to how a corporation could improve its ethical standards. Two EU partners and two of their salaried associates spent the next three months going to all of PACAL's retail stores, and to several of the independent outlets that were customers of PACAL. They interviewed nearly everyone in PACAL's home office in Vancouver, and in its sales office in Toronto.

When they presented their report to Peter at the end of the review period, he found it difficult to separate truly important matters from those that seemed to be trivial. Among a large number of examples with which the report was peppered, he was struck by several that involved individuals with whom he had come into contact in his half-year at PACAL. He highlighted them, to serve as reminders to himself that they were ones that he might or might not want to pursue. The items he highlighted were:

14. Staff in the sales office seem always to have lunch with customers or with people they identify as potential customers. They go to the most prestigious and expensive restaurants in Toronto, and in some cases even have their "special" table always set aside for them. This practice seems to be confined to guests who are from Toronto or environs.

15. Sales staff make monthly visits to their assigned territories, and entertain customers and potential customers at lavish local restaurants.

21. When out-of-towners come to Toronto, sales staff provide them with free hotel accommodation and with tickets to plays, etc.

33. At Christmas, sales staff receive from suppliers (from whom PACAL purchases goods) great numbers of "baskets" containing liquor, specialty cheeses, and other specialty foods. To avoid being personally influenced, the buyers insist that the donors do not identify the gifts they bring. They also issue a blanket invitation to all of their suppliers to attend the annual party for staff and their spouses and partners that is held in the office.

39. When head office personnel travel on business, they are always booked in first class, but often trade in their tickets for business or economy class and pocket the difference. It is generally understood that this practice is acceptable, because the company doesn't pay any more than if the personnel are actually in the first class cabin of the aircraft.

43. The head office maintains box seats at B.C. Place for basketball and hockey games. Occasionally customers or suppliers are invited, but most of the time the boxes are occupied by PACAL staff and managers and directors.

49. Last year PACAL gave more than $86,000 to local junior hockey teams, the Calgary Symphony, and art galleries in Winnipeg and Moncton. In several of these cases, we found that relatives of the directors or officers of PACAL were connected with the organizations that received the grants.

63. The bookkeeper in the store in Saskatoon described how she urges suppliers to bill in advance in December so she can record the expenditures in the tax year, even though the products or services are not delivered until January. She explains that this reduces the year's income and therefore the income tax payable. In her view this is legitimate, because the tax is paid in the following year, so the only difference is that tax is deferred, not avoided.

74. Pottery from Asia is sometimes cracked or broken in shipping. PACAL maintains a very efficient repair shop that glues together those that can be salvaged. These pieces are then sold as sale items, at reduced prices but without notice that they have been damaged. The repairs are so skilfully done that no one can tell they have been damaged unless they know to tap them and hear that they do not "ring" as a perfect piece would do.

82. Company policy regarding packaging material and other waste is that it is to be recycled if it can be sold for the cost of handling, or discarded in landfills if recycling is too expensive in the local manager's estimate.

88. Buyers who circulate around Southeast Asia frequently are confronted with requests for bribes. Company policy, which is strictly adhered to, is to refuse to give bribes. It is common practice, however, to hire on retainer "company facilitators" who know local customs and local officials. They are paid substantial fees for these services. Annually they are asked to sign a statement that they have not issued any bribes on PACAL's behalf.

92. PACAL buys large quantities of pottery from Indonesia. Each shipment has to be cleared by an official "export officer." If the export officer is given a gift worth perhaps $20 in Canadian funds, the papers for thousands of dollars' worth of goods will be cleared in a day or so. If there is no gift, the papers and the shipments will often be held up for several weeks. PACAL's local buyers are asking for instructions on this matter.

96. PACAL officers from vice president up are allowed to take a member of the family on a business trip to a foreign destination at company expense, once each year.

## Questions

1. How would you describe the internal climate of PACAL, and particularly of its senior management?

2. Which, if any, of these examples describe unethical behaviour? Which, if any, are totally ethical? Which are borderline?
3. How would you rate PACAL's ethical standards—excellent, acceptable in a highly competitive environment, or unacceptable? Are these standards better, the same as, or worse than those in most of Canada's large corporations?
4. If Peter wishes to raise PACAL's ethical standards, how can he go about it? What obstacles will he face?
5. Three years ago PACAL published a code of conduct that clearly stated that the company is determined to pursue the highest of ethical standards, and that no exceptions will be tolerated. What might have kept this code from having the effect that its authors might have desired?
6. Based on the information described above, why do you think that the PACAL management and board might have issued the code of conduct?
7. What level of social responsibility does PACAL seem to be exhibiting?
8. What advice would you give to the buyers described in item 92?

## APPLICATION EXERCISE 2-1

### Rokeach Value Survey

Milton Rokeach is a researcher who has done much work in explaining and measuring values. He separates values into two categories: *instrumental* and *terminal*. An instrumental value is the belief that a way of behaving fits every situation. For example, it would be an instrumental value to want "to be logical" no matter what the situation. A terminal value is a belief that a certain end state (terminal) is worth attaining. One person may strive for "happiness," while another strives to be "socially recognized." Each individual has a set of instrumental and terminal values.

The Rokeach Value Study is presented here.

Study the two lists of values presented below. Then rank the instrumental values in order of importance to you (1 = most important, 18 = least important). Do the same with the list of terminal values.

#### Instrumental values

**RANK**

_____ Ambitious (hard-working, aspiring)
_____ Broad-minded (open-minded)
_____ Capable (competent, effective)
_____ Cheerful (lighthearted, joyful)
_____ Clean (neat, tidy)
_____ Courageous (standing up for your beliefs)
_____ Forgiving (willing to pardon others)
_____ Helpful (working for the welfare of others)
_____ Honest (sincere, truthful)
_____ Imaginative (daring, creative)
_____ Independent (self-sufficient)
_____ Intellectual (intelligent, reflective)
_____ Logical (consistent, rational)
_____ Loving (affectionate, tender)

_____ Obedient (dutiful, respectful)
_____ Polite (courteous, well-mannered)
_____ Responsible (dependable, reliable)
_____ Self-controlled (restrained, self-disciplined)

**Terminal values**

**RANK**

_____ A comfortable life (a prosperous life)
_____ An exciting life (a stimulating, active life)
_____ A sense of accomplishment (making a lasting contribution)
_____ A world at peace (free of war and conflict)
_____ A world of beauty (beauty of nature and the arts)
_____ Equality (brotherhood, equal opportunity for all)
_____ Family security (taking care of loved ones)
_____ Freedom (independence, free choice)
_____ Happiness (contentedness)
_____ Inner harmony (freedom from inner conflict)
_____ Mature love (sexual and spiritual intimacy)
_____ National security (protection from attack)
_____ Pleasure (an enjoyable, leisurely life)
_____ Salvation (being saved, having eternal life)
_____ Self-respect (self-esteem)
_____ Social recognition (respect, admiration)
_____ True friendship (close companionship)
_____ Wisdom (a mature understanding of life)

Try the Rokeach Value Survey again in about three months and compare your rankings. Are they the same? Are you surprised by your rankings? Do you think that reading about ethics and social responsibility in this chapter and class discussion of these issues had any influence on your rankings?

## *APPLICATION EXERCISE* **2-2**

### A Personal Code of Ethics

Write a code of ethics by which you wish to govern your own behaviour as an entrepreneur, employee, or manager. Your code should express the broad principles you wish to follow, and then illustrate these principles with specific examples of ethical dilemmas you think you might face and descriptions of how you will handle them. Put your code aside for a week, then review it. Amend it if you feel it is too general, too specific, or incomplete. Put it away again until a week or so before the end of this course. Review it again, and decide whether it is something you wish to keep to remind you of how you now feel about ethical issues.

## *APPLICATION EXERCISE* **2-3**

### Ethical Dilemmas Facing Managers

The following are some representative examples of the kinds of ethical dilemmas frequently faced by middle managers in both small and large organizations. The issue, of course, is what to do, considering the many implications both of acting and of not acting. Read each example, then write in a sentence or two how you would act and when and to whom you would speak, if anyone. Then compare what you decided with two other class members, and discuss the implications of each course of action.

1. A supplier phones to say that he has two tickets to an important game of your favourite professional sports team and that he has the flu and can't use them. He wonders if you would like them so that they won't go to waste.

2. You have written a detailed memo to your boss describing your concerns that a product sold by your company may not do what it is claimed to do. Your boss instructs you to destroy all copies of your memo and drop the matter.

3. The son-in-law of your organization's CEO has been working in your section and makes a serious error, but he blames it on another member of the group.

4. You have been interviewing consultants to assist your group with the design of important software, and have narrowed the choice to two candidates, whom you believe to be equally qualified. Before anyone knows of your choices, you receive a call from a member of your organization's board of directors, expressing the strong hope that you will choose a specific candidate, whom the director names, because that candidate is a friend of the director. It happens that the named candidate is one of the two whom you had selected.

5. The situation described in item 4 above occurs, except that the friend of the director is one of the candidates who was eliminated before the list was narrowed to two. You believe that the director's friend is slightly less well qualified than the two candidates you have selected, but probably could do the work reasonably well.

6. The CEO has asked you to be present while some senior officers are interviewed by a financial columnist. During the interview the CEO states that no one has been fired from the research division. You know that yesterday the vice president of research, who is not present at the interview, gave a research scientist an ultimatum: "Resign or you will be fired."

7. You own a small company. One of your employees has been interviewed for a job with a larger competitor, and tells you "in confidence" that during the interview one of the competitor's senior managers described plans to take away one of your major customers by offering a below-market price for a large contract.

8. As head of the art department of a small company that screen prints T-shirts, you are not responsible for inventory. However, you have seen the inventory manager taking several garments out the back door, presumably for personal use or even for resale.

9. As a sales representative for a food wholesaler, you get your first contract with a large supermarket that you have been trying to attract as a regular customer. The order is for $20,000, which is very attractive to your company. As you leave the supermarket, the meat manager hands you a slip of paper, on which is written a home address, and asks that a large ham be delivered there.

10. While browsing the Internet you run across a copy of a three-page report that someone apparently has released accidentally. From the title you see that it describes a plan of your major competitor to make a bid to buy out another of your competitors, but unless you read the whole report you will not know who the target is or any other details.

11. As a middle manager, your company rules entitle you to fly in business class for all overseas business trips. Your travel agent suggests issuing you an invoice for the business class fare (to submit to your employer for reimbursement), but issuing you two tickets in economy class for yourself and your spouse. The two economy class tickets will cost the same as the one business class ticket.

## APPLICATION EXERCISE  2-4

### Researching "Ethical" Companies

Many companies offer products that are sensitive to the environment or promote or support ethical causes with part of their revenue. Ethics can be the basis for a profitable marketing strategy. Companies such as the Body Shop and Lush and products such as green mutual funds and organic groceries, to mention a few, are positioning themselves as "do good" companies and products.

#### Questions

1. Identify a company that has appeared to take an ethical stand and develop a marketing strategy from it.
2. Try to determine which came first: the ethical stance or the marketing strategy?
3. Identify a company that has been criticized in the press for unethical behaviour.
4. Have they been unfairly targeted by the press for these practices?
5. Has the unethical behaviour appeared to have done harm to their bottom line?

Contributed by Sydney Scott, British Columbia Institute of Technology.

## INTERNET APPLICATION  2-1

Explore the Body Shop's Web site (www.bodyshop.com) and, in particular, its Values Report.

1. How does the company approach social responsibility? Why does the company have this stance, and how appropriate do you think it is?

Search for an organization Web site that has an explicit statement of its approach to ethics and social responsibility. What is its approach and why does the organization have this approach?

# Decision Making— The Essence of Management

After studying this chapter, you should be able to:

▶ Compare programmed and non-programmed decisions;

▶ Contrast intuitive and systematic decision making;

▶ Identify and explain the nine steps in the decision-making process;

▶ Explain the differences between individual and group decision making, and how each may be applied in business;

▶ Explain the terms *cognitive dissonance* and *escalation of commitment*;

▶ Describe process improvement teams, brainstorming, the Delphi technique, and the nominal group technique; and

▶ Describe how an MIS can facilitate informed decision making, and what difficulties may be encountered with it.

## Manufacturers Use Simulations to Aid in Decision Making

ONE OF TODAY'S RAPIDLY EXPANDING TECHNOLOGIES is manufacturing simulation. Using this technique managers, engineers, and shop floor employees can "design" a part, a component, or a complete item of equipment or other product by entering detailed specifications on a computer program. They can then experiment with any number of "what if" possibilities by varying one or more dimensions or shapes. With each change the computer program redesigns the whole component, showing how that change affects other parameters, dimensions, and shapes. The technique saves immense amounts of time, and permits designers to test ideas without having to build working prototypes. It also reduces the chance for the kind of error that might occur if one parameter were changed without reflecting that change in other parameters. Using computer simulation, designers can easily and quickly evaluate several possible solutions to a problem and make informed decisions as to which combinations are optimal. ▶

Using this technique, automobile manufacturers have been able to design new models, create the necessary machine tools, jigs, and dies to construct them, and bring them to market in less time and with less cost than was formerly possible. In a roundabout manner, computer simulation in design illustrates the fundamental principle of decision making—that best decisions usually can be made when the decision makers have been able to choose among several solutions. ■

## The Basic Management Activity—Making Decisions

As the opening vignette indicates, decision making in organizations is an essential part of the management process. Every action is preceded by a decision, whether carefully studied, intuitive, or arrived at casually with little thought. Decision making, therefore, is a critical management tool, and the quality of an action inevitably is determined in part by the quality of the decisions that led to it. Consequently, it is incumbent upon managers to improve the quality of their decision making.

Informed decision making requires the weighing of relevant information. Increasingly managers are turning to technology to help them sift through the vast amount of information available to them. Decision making involves a complex mixture of knowledge, experience, creativity, and calculated risks. In some organizations today, many decisions are made by groups or teams. In organizations that have not embraced the concept of shared management, decisions are made by top and middle managers and their implementation depends on subsequent decisions made by managers and non-managers at lower levels of the organization. If the CEO decides that production rates must increase, only subsequent decisions by managers and non-managers will change practices in such a way as to cause the desired improvement. In one sense, the study of management is in essence the study of decision making and its effectiveness. The contents of this chapter, therefore, underlie almost all that follows. Although the emphasis is on decision making by managers, the same principles, perhaps at a simpler level, apply to decision making by non-managers, and indeed to all of us in our daily lives.

**decision**
A choice, whether conscious or not, among available alternatives.

Managers in every type of organization—business, hospitals, government, educational institutions—make decisions every day that require choices between competing goals and objectives and that involve risk and uncertainty. A **decision** is the act of making a conscious choice among alternatives. To be effective, the decision must be followed by action to implement it. Thus, managerial decision making entails both a process and subsequent action. Although we often think of a decision as requiring some degree of analysis of the available alternatives, failing to make a conscious decision may have the same results as making a conscious decision. A **decision-making process** is a series or chain of related steps or interconnected stages that lead to an action or to an outcome and assessment.

**decision-making process**
A series of related steps that lead to a decision, its implementation, and follow-up.

In today's complex, information-rich organizations, managerial decision making is often a fragmented, rapid process. In the modern work environment it is becoming less likely that a single individual can process enough information to make the best decisions for the organization. Besides the vast amount of data available for most decisions, managers respond to interruptions and unexpected events and find that most decision making, rather than being a single event, is a series of efforts to come closer to organizational goals. Managers must learn how to work in a decision-making environment that emphasizes oral communication, brief meetings, incomplete information, and close approximations, with decisions often having to be based on impressions, estimates, and personal experience. Decision making often reflects the manager's effort to make sense of the complicated environment, to attain some control over the uncontrollable, and to achieve some sense of order.

Managers in any organization must identify, solve, and prevent problems. An organized approach to decision making—including a clear understanding of the current state of affairs, the historical basis for improving decisions, and the possible errors that can be made—enables managers to make better decisions and to reach personal and organizational goals.

Management theorists have investigated decision making from many different perspectives and have developed a set of useful concepts to understand the phenomenon. In this chapter, several of the more important concepts will be explored to illustrate the complexity of this highly social process that involves reason and emotion, risk and uncertainty, creativity and knowledge. Exhibit 3-1 presents these and other factors that influence the decisions that managers and other employees make.

Decision making can be understood as a series of steps that progress from the initial identification of a problem to selecting solutions, implementing them, and evaluating actions and reflecting feedback. Using such a systematic approach to decision making ensures that relevant information has been gathered, alternatives have been considered, and possible consequences have been foreseen. This chapter describes a nine-step decision-making process for improving organizational effectiveness.

Individual decision making differs from group decision making, and each has its own strengths and weaknesses. Separate sections of this chapter are dedicated to these different types of decision making. The chapter concludes with an overview of the infor-

**Exhibit 3-1**    *The Decision-Making Influencer Environment*

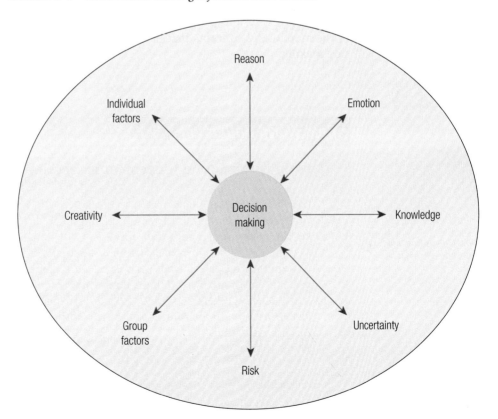

mation technology available to assist managers with decision making. Managers today are confronted with an overwhelming amount of information and a bewildering variety of tools to help them manage it. It is a challenge to use information technology effectively to ensure that the right information is made available to the right people at the right time.

## Types of Managerial Decisions

Given that decision making is an entirely human process, it is fraught with complexities and ambiguities that are reflective of human beings themselves. By gaining some understanding of the different concepts that researchers have used to understand decision making, the practising manager often can avoid difficulties. For example, a manager who is used to making decisions based on intuition may notice that those decisions are less effective than they used to be. This may be in part because the intuitions on which the decisions are based reflect personal experiences that no longer may be relevant in a changed environment. It also may be in part because business and life in general has become more complex. First World War flying aces flew their tiny wood-and-canvas aircraft "by the seat of their pants" (that is, knowing that they were climbing when they felt heavier in their seats, and were losing altitude when they felt lighter). It would be absurd for anyone today to try to fly a 747 by physical feeling, rather than by the vast array of instruments and controls available to highly trained pilots. So it is with business. The manager of a little store in the middle of the prairies in 1880 could rely largely on common sense. Today, the manager of a modern Loblaws or Bay store, with hundreds of employees and tens of thousands of items in stock, must call upon more sophisticated management aids and techniques. Switching to a more systematic approach may make more effective decisions possible (but does not guarantee them). Following are just some of the more useful concepts that have been studied and applied to management decision making.

### Real World Reflection    3-1

#### Tips on Using Sound Judgement in Decision Making

1. Use your best time of day for decision making.
2. Give yourself the right to feel emotions, but do not act on them.
3. Look at issues from many perspectives.
4. Determine whether immediate action is required.
5. To keep moving, ask yourself what is the worst thing that could happen if you make the decision now with limited information.
6. Put yourself in others' shoes and try to foresee their reactions.
7. Put the decision in the context of the big picture.
8. Discuss with others.
9. Think in practical, workable terms.

Contributed by Sydney Scott, British Columbia Institute of Technology.

## Programmed versus Non-programmed Decisions

In an organization, some decisions are made in routine operations; others are required in unexpected situations. Management thinker Herbert Simon has distinguished between two different types of decision making in these different conditions.

**programmed decision**
A decision for repetitive or routine problems, for which the responses have been decided already and made known to the persons who will make the decisions.

**Programmed decisions.** If a particular situation occurs often, a routine procedure can be worked out for solving it. This procedure can be communicated to all employees involved, and their actions can be "preprogrammed" accordingly. After this has been done, when the situation arises again, no one has to delay action while waiting for a decision to be made. Furthermore, those who otherwise would have to take time to consider the facts and make decisions in a multiplicity of situations are freed to do other, more useful tasks. Decisions are programmed to the extent that they address problems that are repetitive and routine, and a definite procedure has been developed to handle them.

---

**What Managers Are Reading    3-1**

### Innovation: Breakthrough Thinking at 3M, DuPont, GE, Pfizer, and Rubbermaid

Popular business writer and Harvard Business School academic Rosabeth Moss Kanter teams up with John Kao, the academic director of Stanford University's Managing Innovation program. Together they provide what appears to be a piercing internal look at the five massive corporations named in the subtitle of this book. Since both Kanter and Kao have become well known by espousing the benefits of innovation, it is not surprising that this is the focus of their book.

According to the authors, innovation is the essence of success—that is, becoming and remaining competitive. In their view the long-term viability of each of these five companies has depended on freeing their innovative people to do what they do best—that is, to find creative ways to develop new products. Innovation, however, goes far beyond product development and involves the whole culture of the corporations.

In particular, Kao stresses that for innovation to flourish, the creative projects that spring up in a corporation must be insulated and protected from the natural bent of most corporate denizens to criticize whatever is not in accord with known parameters, and consequently to stifle whatever is truly creative! Inside these five corporations, it appears that innovation occurs not in the central corridors of power but in fringe areas that are almost out of sight and ignored. In this way, the innovators can be somewhat removed from the deadening effects of the bureaucracy without which the corporation could not function and the in-house politics that inevitably accompanies any aggregation of people.

Corollary to this observation, however, is the understanding that these fringe areas would not be allowed to exist for long unless those in power had a marked tolerance for the truly creative people who make innovation happen, but who are unlikely to be conformists. After reading this engaging book, one would have to conclude that innovation does not stem so much from flashes of inspiration as from concerted effort and intention that requires both financial and emotional support from senior management. And this support can only be provided if conscious decisions are made to do so.

Although the book deals directly only with massive corporations, the same principles would appear apt in the decision making that shapes a small business or a not-for-profit organization. The lessons are: "Innovate or become irrelevant" and "Provide facilities, time, and encouragement so that innovation can occur."

Source: Rosabeth Moss Kanter and John Kao, with Fred Wiersma, *Innovation: Breakthrough Thinking at 3M, DuPont, GE, Pfizer, and Rubbermaid* (New York: HarperBusiness, 1998).

**Non-programmed decisions.** Decisions are non-programmed when they are unstructured. In these situations, there is no established procedure for handling the problem, because it is either complex or extremely important or because the circumstances arise only occasionally. Such decisions require special treatment.

Managers in most organizations face many programmed decisions in their daily operations. Such decisions should be made without expending unnecessary time or other organizational resources. Best of all, it is often possible to delegate most programmed decisions to subordinates, freeing the manager to tackle the non-programmed decisions.

In contrast, each non-programmed decision must be properly identified as such, since this type of decision can involve significant risk and uncertainty. Exhibit 3-2 provides examples of each type of decision in different kinds of organizations and illustrates that programmed and non-programmed decisions require different procedures and apply to distinctly different types of problems.

Some managers, reminiscent of Frederick W. Taylor, hope to place all organizational processes under rigorous and invariant control regimens. In today's workplace this is seldom successful, because variation, complexity, and ambiguity are the rule rather than the exception. Much day-to-day variation can be accommodated with routine responses, yet a creative response or non-programmed decision of some sort is often needed. Non-programmed decisions involve searching for information and alternatives that lie outside of the routine decision-making process. These decisions are often time-consuming and, unlike routine decisions, demand that managers and other employees be prepared to create alternative solutions, analyze them critically, and choose a course of action.

Most large organizations, and even many of the smallest, use computers and software to assist with complex, non-programmed decisions. As illustrated in the opening vignette, simulation techniques assist managers in understanding the possible consequences of various courses of action and choosing those that appear to provide optimum outcomes.

**Exhibit 3-2**

*Types of Decisions*

|  | Programmed Decisions | Non-programmed Decisions |
|---|---|---|
| Type of Problem | Frequent, repetitive, routine, much certainty regarding cause-and-effect relationships | Novel, unstructured, much uncertainty regarding cause-and-effect relationships |
| Procedure | Dependence on policies, rules, and definite procedures | Necessity for creativity, intuition, tolerance for ambiguity, creative problem solving |
| Examples | *Business:* Periodic reorders of inventory | *Business:* Diversification into new products and markets |
|  | *University:* Necessary grade point average for good academic standing | *University:* Construction of new classroom facilities |
|  | *Hospital:* Procedure for admitting patients | *Hospital:* Purchase of experimental equipment |
|  | *Government:* Merit system for promotion of state employees | *Government:* Reorganization of government agencies |

Source: John M. Ivancevich and Michael J. Matteson, *Organizational Behavior and Management*, 3rd ed. (Burr Ridge, IL: Richard D. Irwin, 1993): 584.

Programmed decisions that do not allow for flexibility can inhibit creativity to such an extent that outdated, inapplicable responses are applied to what may have seemed to have been uncomplicated problems, but that have grown in importance and perception. For example, product design engineers still may be directed by management to create product assembly processes so simple that they require no input from assemblers on the factory floor. While such a design may be valuable to an untrained customer assembling a product at home (for instance, a modular bookcase), the same attitude reflected in the instructions for a trained assembly worker fails to take advantage of the ability of most employees to act independently and make effective non-programmed decisions.

One company that has succeeded in employing an innovative form of Frederick Taylor's time-and-motion regimentation on the factory floor is New United Motor Manufacturing, Inc. (NUMMI), a joint venture of Toyota and General Motors. NUMMI has used the principles of scientific management to create a highly programmed process flow and to increase quality, productivity, and employee motivation. NUMMI has accomplished this by allowing the production-line workers themselves to design the formal work standards and to establish the programmed decisions. As Professor Paul Adler stated following a two-year study of the company, "Procedures that are designed by the workers themselves in a continuous, successful effort to improve productivity, quality, skills, and understanding can humanize even the most disciplined form of bureaucracy."[1]

Programmed and non-programmed decisions affect organizations daily. Sometimes managers need to react promptly to events and make decisions. At other times they can anticipate changes and make decisions before the events arise. This distinction is captured in two more decision types: proactive and reactive.

## Proactive versus Reactive Decisions

**proactive decision**
A decision made in anticipation of an existing situation or an expected change in conditions.

A decision made *before* the occurrence of an external or internal change is called a **proactive decision**. Managers who use a systematic, proactive approach often can prevent problems from developing, or at the very least can ameliorate their effects if they do arise.

**reactive decision**
A decision made in response to a change or situation.

A **reactive decision** is one made in response to changes that have occurred or are occurring. Using a reactive approach, a city street department may wait for citizens to complain about poor street conditions before a crew is sent to repair potholes. A manager may initiate action to correct product defects only after customer complaints have surfaced. Rather than apply preventive maintenance (proactive), a machine shop manager may spend money only to repair machines after they break down (reactive).

Managerial vision provides the context for proactive decision making. If the vision is clear enough and communicated effectively, many employees will intuitively make decisions that support that vision.

## Intuitive versus Systematic Decisions

**intuitive decision**
A decision based primarily on an almost unconscious reliance on the decision maker's experience, without a conscious rational analysis having been made.

**Intuitive decisions** are based on experience and often are made in situations where there is little time for analysis. Intuitive decision making involves the use of estimates and "best guesses" to choose from alternative courses of action. Most managers realize that many of their decisions are influenced to a great extent by their intuitions. Intuition should not be ignored because it can reflect the manager's knowledge and the wealth of experience the manager has had. Nonetheless, decisions based entirely on intuition often will be uninformed, ineffective, and even counterproductive. For example, one common flaw in the application of merit pay systems is that managers may falsely assume that they can sense meaningful individual differences among employees' performances. If these

systematic decision making
An organized, exacting, information-driven process, applying logic in choosing among alternatives.

differences are determined more by personal opinion and human biases rather than by systematic data collection and analysis, the concept of merit may be lost. Such biased pay raise decisions can be destructive rather than productive in encouraging employees to perform at high levels.

In contrast to intuitive decision making, **systematic decision making** is an organized, exacting, data-driven process, as illustrated by the comparisons in Exhibit 3-3. Systematic decision making requires developing a clear set of objectives, assembling a relevant information base, and instituting an effective implementation and evaluation process.

**Exhibit 3-3**

*Intuitive versus Systematic Decision Making*

| Intuitive | Systematic |
| --- | --- |
| My hunch is that we should improve customer support after we sell our product. | Our customer surveys show that we should improve post-sale support. |
| This process is out of control; it needs some adjustment. | Control charts show that this process has been out of control for the past seven shifts; it needs to be corrected. |
| My feeling is that our company could benefit by greater attention to quality. | Having observed our major competitor, it seems clear that we are falling behind in quality, and that we must improve. |

It is often facilitated by using a team-based, consensus-seeking sharing of ideas and creativity. In the consensus-seeking approach, the manager discusses the perceived problem with those who are affected by it, asking for ideas and suggestions. Only after the group members involved reach a reasonable level of agreement on a proper course of action is a decision actually made. It requires considerable self-discipline for the manager to withhold reaching a decision until consensus is reached, but the outcome is often that other managers and non-managers will be more likely to accept the decision and be more willing to implement it without reservations. Consensus seeking is most successful in relatively small organizations, where the people involved have relatively broad responsibilities, but it also can be effective in large organizations if those involved are a clearly defined work group or a group of individuals who are at roughly the same level in the administrative hierarchy.

W. Edwards Deming calls the systematic approach to decision making "management by fact." Another term in common use is "data-based decision making." Manufacturing, commerce, agriculture, retailing, not-for-profit organizations, and indeed almost all enterprises of all sizes can use sophisticated econometric analyses to improve productivity, quality, customer satisfaction, and, in fact, all forms of competitiveness.[2] Not all decisions will be improved by these analyses, but all organizations can benefit by focusing on management by fact. Some of the variables to be considered when using this approach are listed in Exhibit 3-4.

Some decisions may be best made intuitively, others systematically, and most by some combination of the two. In any event, judgement is always required to decide to what extent a decision should be intuitive or systematic. At times managers must react quickly and intuitively. Sound intuition, however, is developed from experience and training as well as from practice in systematic decision making. For example, a service repair manager may have to react immediately to an angry customer who is dissatisfied with a product. If the manager doesn't react appropriately, the customer may be lost per-

**Exhibit 3-4**

*Management by Fact*

- Identify the source of the material and as much as possible about the time and manner in which the information was collected.
- Don't be seduced by dramatic graphics or charts, or the appearance of sophistication in statistics or other data presentations.
- Don't succumb to the persuasiveness of the presenter's communication skills without retaining an appropriate level of scepticism about the content of the message.
- Always be wary of situations where the presenter has a vested interest in convincing you of the conclusions.
- Particularly in the case of survey research, consider how the data were compiled.
- Look for some level of statistical checks on the reliability, accuracy, and meaningfulness of findings whenever possible. In some cases, this may require an exploration of what is not reported.
- Learn to discern whether the data are being overinterpreted and overextended.
- Always consider the relevance and applicability of the results to your situation.
- Remember that the results of a single study, no matter how well done, should be used with extreme caution.
- Be cautious in making changes in response to simple data. There is often greater underlying complexity than meets the eye.

Source: Adapted from Stephen A. Rubenfeld, John W. Newstrom, and Thomas B. Duff, "Caveat Emptor: Avoiding Pitfalls in Data-Based Decision Making," *Review of Business* (Winter 1994): 20-23.

manently. Even in such stressful situations, the manager's reactive, intuitive decision will be better if it is based on training and experience with similar situations than if it reflects the manager's sense of having been unfairly criticized.

Continuous improvement in organizational performance requires creativity in making programmed and non-programmed decisions. But decision-making creativity must be tempered with a well-developed decision-making process. One author has called such an approach "disciplined creativity."[3] The next section will address a decision-making process that managers and other employees can follow to make creative, yet sound, organizational decisions.

## The Decision-making Process

Decision making is a sequential *process* rather than a single, fixed event,[4] even when a decision appears to have been made instantaneously. In making a decision, managers go through a series of steps or stages that help them identify the problem, develop alternative strategies, analyze these strategies, choose among the alternatives, implement the choice, and evaluate the results and provide appropriate feedback. A good decision requires the application of each of the stages, even though attention to some stages may only be momentary. The quality of the decision will suffer if any stage is omitted. The stage most often omitted, with damaging consequences, is the last—feedback. Identifying steps in the decision-making process is valuable since it helps the decision maker to structure the attempt to solve the problem situation in a meaningful, systematic way.

Exhibit 3-5 on page 94 shows the segments of one common progression of events leading to a decision. The basic steps in this model are (1) establishing specific goals and objectives, (2) identifying and defining the problem, (3) establishing priorities, (4)

**Exhibit 3-5**   *The Decision-Making Model: A Sequence of Steps*

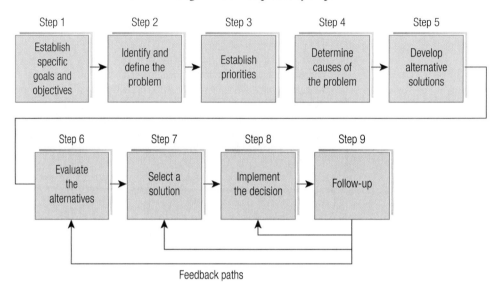

Feedback paths

determining the causes of the problem, (5) developing alternative solutions, (6) evaluating the alternatives, (7) selecting a solution, (8) implementing the decision, and (9) follow-up. The first seven steps are the **decision formulation** stages; the last two steps are the **decision implementation** stages.

## Step 1: Establishing Specific Goals and Objectives

Effective decision making always should be done in the context of goals and objectives. Chapter 4 will discuss setting goals and objectives. Here, it is important to point out that all behaviour is basically goal-oriented.[5] We only do something because we want to accomplish some purpose. If goals and objectives are adequately established and communicated, they will dictate the results that must be achieved and the measures that indicate whether they have been achieved. The mutual acceptance of goals and objectives tends to bind people in the organization together—a crucial factor in organizational success.

## Step 2: Identifying and Defining the Problem

When clear goals and objectives are established, problems become apparent when goals are not being met. For example, a problem in quality would be readily identified if the established quality standard is a defect rate of only three parts per million units produced and, in fact, there are ten defective units per million. But if no standard has been established, managers and other employees may not realize that the ten-parts-per-million rate reflects a problem that requires attention.

Difficulties may arise in identifying a problem from any of the following factors:

1. *Perceptual inaccuracies.* Individual attitudes, feelings, or mental models may prevent people from seeing problems. For example, prior to 1968 the Swiss dominated the world of watch making. They continuously had improved their products and were constant innovators. Yet by 1980 their market share had collapsed from 65 percent to 10 percent because they did not recognize that world demand was changing from

**decision formulation**
The process of (1) establishing specific goals and objectives; (2) identifying the need for a decision; (3) establishing priorities; (4) determining the causes of the problem; (5) collecting information and developing possible alternative courses of action; (6) evaluating the alternatives; and (7) selecting one of the alternatives.

**decision implementation**
The process of putting the decision made into action, and of following up the results and possibly communicating feedback and deciding on modifications in the ways in which the decision is being applied.

mechanical to electronic inner works. The Swiss themselves had invented electronic quartz movements; yet when Swiss researchers presented the revolutionary development in 1967, Swiss manufacturers rejected it. The new quartz movement did not fit their mental model of watches, so they were unable to see its potential for the future.[6]

2. *Defining problems in terms of assumed solutions.* This is a form of jumping to conclusions. For example, prior to any research a quality engineer may state, "The excessive rework we're experiencing is due to bad quality of material from the suppliers." Here the quality engineer is suggesting a solution before the problem has been adequately identified. The supplies may be of low quality, but there may be other explanations for the need for excessive rework. Some of these explanations might be that there has been inadequate employee training, that the technology is out of date, or that the work flow is cumbersome. Research is needed to identify the problem before any solutions are suggested.

3. *Identifying symptoms as causes.* Some companies with ongoing quality problems blame their employees. Their managers will argue that the employees lack appropriate motivation, or that absenteeism is high, or that the employees are not good workers and don't care about the quality of the product or service. More successful organizations realize that low employee morale is a symptom rather than a cause, and recognize the need to treat this symptom by correcting its underlying causes.

Problems usually are of three types: crisis problems, routine problems, and problems of failing to take advantage of opportunities. By their very nature, most crises demand immediate attention. Opportunities, on the other hand, often go unnoticed and eventually are lost by an inattentive manager. Unless this difference in visibility is recognized, a manager may spend more time handling problems than pursuing important new opportunities. This is a common failing of organizations, and can be summed up by the aphorism "The *urgent* takes precedence over the *important*." Well-managed organizations try to find ways to deal efficiently with the urgent crises and routine problems in order to save managers' time, energy, and attention for important longer-range issues.

*Organizations must take into account the possible consequences of deviations from desirable practices. A seemingly slight lapse in food-handling techniques may cause unintended disasters.*

## Step 3: Establishing Priorities

Not all problems are of the same importance. Deciding whether to launch a new product in response to a competitor's move is probably more significant than deciding whether the employee lounge should be repainted. On the other hand, if employee morale has suffered because the lounge is dingy, it may be advisable to correct this problem before seeking employee support for a new product. The process of decision making and solution implementation requires resources—time, money, skill, and personal energy and attention. Consequently, an organization must deliberately assign priorities to its problems. This means being able to determine each problem's significance, which involves considering three issues: urgency, impact, and growth tendency.

*Urgency* is the degree of pressure on time for a prompt decision. Some companies have learned that urgent problems are best dealt with at their source. For example, Avcorp Industries, an aircraft parts manufacturer, has instituted a program that ensures that urgent decisions are made on the factory floor. When there is a production snag or a technology-related problem that could upset a delivery schedule, the production employee who notices the problem literally raises a red flag. Then, an alarm sounds every 30 seconds until a supervisor arrives to offer assistance and either resolves the problem or starts the process to find a solution. Using this system, Avcorp's delinquency on orders from Bell Helicopter Textron, Avcorp's major customer, fell in two years from 18 percent to less than 1 percent.[7]

*Impact* refers to the seriousness of a problem's effects. Effects might be on people, sales, equipment, profitability, public image, or any number of other organizational resources. A suspicion that a food product has been contaminated is more urgent than the knowledge that production is slowing down, and may have a much greater impact on the organization. Other key questions are whether problem effects are short- or long-term and whether the problem is likely to create other problems.

*Growth tendency* refers to future consequences of a problem. A problem currently may be of low urgency and have little impact, but if it is allowed to go unattended, its consequences may become more severe over time. For example, a decision to cut back on routine preventive maintenance of plant equipment as a cost-cutting measure may not create a significant problem immediately, but may cause major difficulties over time.

The more significant the problem, as determined by its urgency, impact, and growth tendency, the more important it is that it be addressed promptly.

## *Real World Reflection*    3-2

### When to Use Creative Decision-making Skills

Use creative decision-making skills when:

- Problems are recurring
- You want to do things differently
- The standard way is no longer working
- Problems are ambiguous
- The cause of a problem is unknown
- Feelings abound; facts are scarce
- Situation allows for uncertainty and risk taking

How to use creativity in problem solving:
- Look at problems as opportunities
- Define aspects about problems you will be working on. Adapt this mind set to problems you see as more mundane or disruptive.
- Define the problem in different ways rather than solving the problem as first defined.

Contributed by Sydney Scott, British Columbia Institute of Technology.

## Step 4: Determining Causes of the Problem

It is usually difficult and unwise to determine a solution to a problem until its causes are known. The employees who deal with the situation in which the problem arises are often best qualified to discover its causes. For instance, the employees who have frequent contact with customers often have a better understanding of customer needs and problems than others who are more remote from customers. Recognizing this fact, some companies are empowering front-line employees to decide what solutions to offer when customers complain. This allows decisions to be made quickly, and helps to satisfy those who make complaints, often retaining a customer who might be lost if there were delays in responding. It also avoids the "ping-pong" effect in which a dissatisfied customer is shunted from person to person, aggravating an already tense situation.[8] In addition, open communication between managers and contact employees can improve service quality and customer satisfaction.[9]

---

### *What Managers Are Reading*  3-2

### Zapp! and Heroz

William C. Byham enlisted the help of a professional writer to pen the book *Zapp! The Lightning of Empowerment*. The book went on to become an underground bestseller. *Zapp!* was initially published by Byham, who started with 200,000 copies. He gave away 7000 to clients. Many more were sold by direct mail before the book was commercially published in 1991.

Byham claims that 1.5 million copies of *Zapp!* have now gone into print. Written in Dick and Jane prose, it's a fictionalized story of how employees can play a more meaningful role in companies if they're empowered to make more decisions. The following companies have purchased Byham's book: IBM (40,000 copies), General Electric (30,000 copies), DuPont (25,000 copies), Pepsico (23,000 copies), Wal-Mart (10,500 copies), and KFC (8500 copies).

Capitalizing on the success of *Zapp!* Byham has come out with the sequel, titled *Heroz, Empower Yourself, Your Coworkers, Your Company*. (The z after *Hero* is supposed to stir memories of *Zapp!*) Byham's latest fable is set in the imaginary medieval castle of Lamron. The story features heroic knights who defend the kingdom's citizens from fire-breathing dragons by using magic arrows. However, the arrow producers become dispirited, and the citizens begin to flee to other kingdoms that offer better protection and cheaper arrows. Employees in the new kingdom control their jobs and relentlessly improve the way they work so that, in the end, everybody wins. Throughout the story these employees empower themselves and show what must be done to spread empowerment to their co-workers and their bosses.

Sound corny? Not to the managers and corporations that are snapping up *Heroz* almost as fast as *Zapp!* Byham hopes *Heroz* "will inspire people at all levels of a business organization to envision themselves as heroic knights charged with the glorious duty of slaying the dragons that block the way to a prosperous future."

---

Sources: William C. Byham, *Zapp! The Lightning of Empowerment* (New York: Harmony Books, 1988); and William C. Byham, *Heroz, Empower Yourself, Your Coworkers, Your Company* (New York: Harmony Books, 1994). Adapted from John A. Byrne, "See Bill. See Zapp! See the Sequel," *Business Week* (May 16, 1994): 42; Theodore B. Kinni, "Zapp! You're Empowered," *Industry Week* (September 19, 1994): 40-41; "Books," *Training & Development* (June 1994): 61-62.

## Step 5: Developing Alternative Solutions

Before a decision is reached, alternative solutions must be explored. This step involves examining the organization's internal and external environments for information and ideas that may lead to creative solutions to a problem. One source of alternative solutions that is coming into wider use is **benchmarking**.[10] This method consists of visiting operations of other organizations and observing how they do things, with the hope of gaining new ideas that can be adapted for use. This technique will be expanded on in Chapter 11, in the discussion of managing operations.

**benchmarking**
Observing and analyzing activities in another organization to try to discover different methods or ideas that could assist the company doing the benchmarking.

## Step 6: Evaluating the Alternatives

Once alternatives have been developed, they must be evaluated and compared. Whenever a decision is required, the objective is to select the alternatives that will produce the most favourable outcomes and the least unfavourable outcomes, all at the least cost in time, energy, and money. In selecting among the alternatives, the decision maker should be guided by the organization's previously established goals and objectives.

In any situation, it is unlikely that the decision maker can be absolutely certain of all of the outcomes that possibly may result from any of the available alternatives, to say nothing of the uncertainty surrounding a whole series of alternatives. Therefore, most management decisions are based on a combination of systematic and intuitive modes. Often the decision maker will suspect that if given more time, further information could be gathered that would strengthen the systematic aspects of the decision-making process. Yet, at some point there is no more time, and the decision has to be made using only the information available at that moment. People new to management soon discover, often to their horror, that most major decisions have to be made with incomplete information. Unfortunately, decisions have to be made when they have to be made, and managers must do the best they can within the time constraints. Managers cannot avoid applying the concept of *satisficing*—that is, accepting a solution that is adequate, even though it may not be ideal.

In evaluating alternative solutions, two cautions should be kept in mind. First, this phase of the decision-making process must be kept separate and distinct from the previous step—especially in a group decision-making context. When alternatives are evaluated as they are proposed, this may stifle the process and limit the number of alternative solutions suggested. If evaluation of one alternative is reasonably positive, there is a tendency to end the process prematurely without continuing to explore other alternatives that might turn out to be even better. On the other hand, negative evaluations make it less likely for someone to risk venturing what may be an excellent solution for fear of being criticized or looking foolish.

Second, be wary of solutions that are evaluated as being "perfect." If a solution appears to have no drawbacks, it is highly likely that some potentially unfavourable outcomes have been overlooked. Similarly, in a group setting, if there is unanimous agreement on a course of action, it may be useful to assign someone to be a devil's advocate—a thorough critic of the proposed solution. Research supports the benefits of using a devil's advocate.[11]

## Step 7: Selecting a Solution

It must be kept in mind that a decision is not an end in itself but only a means to an end. Although the decision maker chooses the alternative that is expected to result in achieving the objective, the selection of that alternative should not be thought of as an isolated act. If it is, the factors that led to the decision likely will be excluded. Specifically, the steps following the decision should include implementation and follow-up.

Unfortunately, the choice of an alternative that achieves a desired objective will often have a negative impact on another objective. In a business, for example, if production efficiency is optimized, customer service may deteriorate, and employee morale may suffer. In a hospital, the superintendent may optimize a short-run objective such as reducing maintenance costs at the expense of the long-run objective of excellent patient care. Thus, the interrelatedness of organizational objectives complicates the decision maker's job.

In managerial decision making, the decision maker cannot possibly know all of the available alternatives, the consequences of each alternative, and the probability that these consequences will occur. Thus, rather than being an optimizer, the decision maker is usually a satisficer, selecting the alternative that meets a satisfactory standard. As already noted, a *satisficer* is a person who accepts a reasonable alternative that in many cases is not the optimal alternative. This is not a criticism of managerial decision making. Rather, it is an acknowledgment that the urgency of the decision may not allow enough time to search for the absolutely optimal solution. And besides, the cost of the effort to find the best solution may not be justified by the incremental difference between the best solution and a satisficing solution. Managers must be prepared to act by making decisions that may, in fact, have some unforeseen negative outcomes, in addition to the positive outcomes that are intended.

## Step 8: Implementing the Decision

Any decision is little more than an abstraction if it is not implemented, and that implementation must be effective if it is to achieve the desired objective. It is entirely possible for a good decision to be negated by poor implementation. In a sense, the actual alternative can be no more beneficial than its implementation.

The test of a decision's soundness is the behaviour of the people who put it into action or who are affected by it. While a decision may be technically sound, its benefits can be undermined easily by dissatisfied employees or by those who do not understand it. A manager's job is not only to choose good solutions but also to transform them into effective behaviour in the organization. This is aided considerably by empowering employees to make decisions that affect work processes.

## Step 9: Follow-up

Effective management involves periodic measurement and evaluation of results. Actual results are compared with planned results (the objective). If deviations exist, changes must be made in the solution chosen, in its implementation, or perhaps in the original objective if it is found to be unattainable. If the original objective must be revised, the entire decision-making process is reactivated. The important point is that once a decision is implemented, a manager cannot assume that the outcome will meet the original objective. Some system of control and evaluation is necessary to make sure that the actual results are consistent with the organization's objectives.

Sometimes a decision's outcome is unexpected or is perceived differently by different people. Dealing with this possibility is an important part of the follow-up phase in the decision process. The potential for differences in perception may be reduced by setting readily measurable objectives, and by ensuring that not only the objectives but the means of measurement have been fully understood and accepted by those who will be affected by them.

## Summary of the Decision-making Process

The nine-step decision-making process is an outline of how managers in the modern workplace spend much of their time. In an increasingly technological world, work has become less a matter of physical effort and more a matter of processing information, even in traditional "sweat" industries such as agriculture, forestry, and mineral development. Yet making effective decisions requires more than just the ability to process information and then to choose among and manage alternatives. It requires effective post-decision implementation, usually involving employees from various levels and functions within the organization.

## Bounded Rationality

This discussion could lead to the commonly held misconceptions that the ideal decision is the one that is best from all standpoints and arrived at on a completely rational basis, and that managers can make purely rational decisions if the proper principles and techniques are applied. Nothing could be further from the truth. Instead, since organizations cannot exist in a vacuum, there are external and internal constraints, as discussed in Chapter 2. Given the existence of these constraints, it is logical to assume that they must be taken into consideration in making any decision. For instance, the owner of a small bakery might decide on a rational basis that by hiring a second baker, production capacity would increase and the additional sales would soon more than make up for the additional cost and, therefore, would add to profit. Yet, if there is no qualified baker in the community who will accept the job, the owner's rational analysis leads to what is called **bounded rationality.** A decision must be implemented within the bounds permitted by the external environment. Similarly, if the bakery is experiencing cash flow problems, even though sales eventually would pay for the second baker, bounded rationality would dictate that hiring an additional baker be postponed until finances permit. It's also possible that the baker already on the job would resign in a huff if another baker were hired. That would be another bound, and the owner would have to decide whether to accede to the new bound or break through it and risk having to replace the first baker as well. This example illustrates that a manager will be able to make a major decision on the basis of pure rationality only occasionally, if ever.

*In making crucial decisions, a farmer has to consider many factors: possible weather, comparative costs, personal and employee time to accomplish tasks in a short time, competition, and potential market conditions for the planned crops.*

**bounded rationality**
The concept that a manager's freedom to make totally rational decisions is restricted by internal and external environmental factors and by the manager's own characteristics and decision-making abilities.

One of the greatest dangers of recognizing this fact, however, is that timid managers often will assume that they cannot implement a decision because of perceived bounds, when with a bit more courage they could transcend the bounds, accept whatever consequences might arise, and proceed with the decisions that they believe are best in the long term.

No matter what steps are involved, decision making always involves people. Some decisions are made by individuals acting alone. Today, much decision making occurs in groups. The next two sections explore how decision making by individuals and group decision making differ.

# Individual Decision Making

In today's workplace, managers make many decisions in groups, but other decisions must be made by an individual acting essentially alone. By their very nature, decisions often involve change. Change, in turn, usually creates some degree of discomfort for those who are affected. To be an effective manager requires the ability and the courage to make individual decisions, despite knowing that those decisions are likely to result in some criticism, either expressed or implied. Understanding the decision-making process may give managers the confidence to overcome their natural reluctance to make decisions.

Several behavioural factors influence the decision-making process. Some influence only certain aspects of the process, while others influence the entire process. Each behavioural factor must be understood if managers are to gain a full appreciation of decision making as a process involving individuals in organizations. These factors include values, personality, and potential for dissonance.

## Values

In the context of decision making, values are the guidelines a person uses when confronted with a situation in which a choice must be made. Most of an individual's enduring values are formed early in life and are a basic part of the person's personality. Other values can be acquired in adulthood and usually are associated with membership in a group.

Organizational values and objectives are presumed to be overriding, but individual interpretations invariably will influence day-to-day decision making. Personal values determine how the decision maker decides what is right, what is questionable, and what is downright wrong. But few solutions can be so easily categorized. A manager is often faced with a choice between "driving a hard bargain" and "preserving a business relationship" with the other party. The manager's personal values often will dictate the choice selected, without the manager having even been aware that a choice has been made—after all, "it was just the natural thing to do in the circumstances."

Values may have a subtle effect on assumptions about a person as a result of that person's appearance or race, on attitudes about the "proper" role of a manager, and on ethical questions such as whether to shade the truth to achieve an objective. No one can be completely free of personal values that create unconscious bias, so the manager's challenge is to identify personal values and to assess how they may affect performance.

## Personality

Many psychological forces influence decision makers. One of the most important is the decision maker's own personality, which is reflected in the choices made. Several studies have examined the effect of selected personality variables on the decision-making process.[12] These studies generally have focused on three sets of variables:

1. *Personality variables.* These include the individual's attitudes, beliefs, and needs;
2. *Situational variables.* These pertain to the external (physical and social) situations in which individuals find themselves; and
3. *Interactional variables.* These pertain to the individual's momentary state as a result of the interaction of a specific situation with characteristics of the individual's personality.

The most important conclusions concerning the influence of these personality variables on the decision-making process are:

- It is unlikely that one person can be equally proficient in all aspects of the decision-making process. The results suggest that some people will do better in one part of the process, while others will do better in another part. Some managers are excellent leaders (discussed in Chapter 6) but tend to dislike detailed financial analyses, while others excel in financial projections but do not handle complaints well. And so it goes, reflecting individual personality differences.
- Such characteristics as risk tolerance are associated with different steps in the decision-making process. In some situations, a mistake would have little adverse effect, so it would be reasonable to save time by making a decision without exhaustive study, even though this might entail a risk that the decision will be wrong. In other situations, in which errors could lead to serious consequences, it is reasonable to decrease the risk factor by careful advance study, and even by implementing the decision only incrementally in order to try it out gradually, thus minimizing potential negative impact.
- The relation of personality to the decision-making process will vary from individual to individual. Some managers tolerate risk to the verge of being foolhardy; others are so cautious as to defer or avoid decisions whenever possible. As might be expected, the successful manager tends to fall between these two extremes. Other factors that influence the extent to which a manager may be comfortable with risk include the manager's race, cultural or ethnic background, age, level of education, gender, and social status, as well as these same characteristics in the persons with whom the manager is dealing at the particular time.

## Potential for Dissonance

Much attention has been focused on the decision itself and on the forces and influences affecting the decision maker before the decision is made. But it is also important to consider what happens *after* a decision has been made. Behavioural scientists have called attention to post-decision anxiety.

**cognitive dissonance**
The mental state caused by the realization that the current situation is different from what has been desired.

Post-decision anxiety is related to what Leon Festinger and others call **cognitive dissonance**.[13] As in music, the term *dissonance* refers to a situation that is the opposite of harmony. Thus, the term refers to a lack of consistency or harmony among an individual's various cognitions (attitudes, beliefs, etc.) after a decision has been made. In cases of cognitive dissonance, there is a conflict between what the decision maker believed or hoped would happen and the actual consequences. For instance, a manager may decide to accept an opportunity to head a task force to prepare a special report, thinking that it will offer a career opportunity by providing visibility with senior management. After accepting, the manager may have doubts as to whether the task force's report will have to be so negative that it could antagonize senior managers, hurting the manager's career. These "second thoughts" cause a conflict within the manager's thinking—the current negative assessment of the situation is in conflict with the earlier positive assessment. This cognitive dissonance will create doubts and anxiety about the choice that has been made.

Another example occurs in all types of organizations, but may be felt more acutely in a small organization, where personal relations tend to be closer. This situation occurs when a manager decides that for the good of the organization, it is necessary to dismiss an employee. The decision often will create a serious cognitive dissonance, because the manager may know the employee's family, and at least feels compassion for the difficulties the dismissed employee faces. In such instances, the cognitive dissonance reflects the conflict between the manager's concept of duty to the organization and loyalty to the individual.

The intensity of the anxiety in any instance of cognitive dissonance is likely to be greater when any of the following conditions exist:

1. The decision is important psychologically or financially;
2. There are a number of foregone alternatives; or
3. The foregone alternatives have many favourable features, which will be lost.

A manager who has a high tolerance for risk is less likely to experience post-decision cognitive dissonance than another manager who is more bothered by risk. Conversely, a manager who habitually takes few chances is more likely to experience post-decision cognitive dissonance than one who frequently takes calculated risks.

Often managers want to reduce cognitive dissonance to feel comfortable that they are behaving consistently. This desire for personal consistency can have a negative effect because it can lead to inflexibility. The modern decision-making environment requires flexibility and adaptability. The desire to reduce cognitive dissonance becomes dysfunctional when it leads to what has been called **escalation of commitment**—an increased commitment to a previous decision despite having received information that raises questions about the correctness of that decision. Research has shown that individuals often will escalate their commitment to a failing course of action when they view themselves as having been responsible for the action. According to dissonance theory, this behaviour results from the individual trying to demonstrate that the original decision was correct.[14] It also may reflect fear that the decision maker will suffer consequences from a "bad" decision. Understanding that a common response to cognitive dissonance is escalation of commitment to a bad decision should help a manager to feel greater freedom to change the bad decision and maintain essential flexibility.[15] Otherwise, a bad decision may be allowed to stand, perhaps doing damage that could have been avoided if it had been reversed at an early stage.

Different people engage in different thought processes to reduce the cognitive dissonance they are experiencing. Some of the most common dysfunctional thought process methods are shown in Exhibit 3-6. A few of them may be relatively benign, but many of the methods can be quite destructive to organizational effectiveness. They may lead to confusion or resentment on the part of those who are close to the decision and its implementation. In their worst form, some of the methods may cause decisions to be implemented only half-heartedly, or even sabotaged entirely. Effective managers will seek

**escalation of commitment**
An increased desire to support a decision that has been made, despite having received evidence that it may not be the optimum decision.

**Exhibit 3-6**

*Thought Processes Often Employed to Reduce Cognitive Dissonance*

- Seek information to show that the decision was right.
- Reinterpret or distort information to show that the information was right.
- Suppress information that shows defects in the decision.
- Denigrate the alternatives that were foregone.
- Exaggerate the benefits to be obtained from the decision.
- Try to discredit anyone who questions the decision.
- Create distractions, so the decision becomes less noticeable.
- Become so involved in different activities that the decision fades in significance.
- Excuse the decision by emphasizing that there was insufficient information.
- Explain the decision's failings by attributing them to faulty implementation.
- Blame someone else for the decision.

to minimize the extent to which they and others resort to the more negative methods of reducing cognitive dissonance, and will guard against being unduly influenced when it does occur. To achieve relative freedom from cognitive dissonance, a manager has to accept the unwelcome fact that some decisions will be found to have less-than-optimum or even markedly negative consequences.

The individual forces discussed in this section are likely to be intensified in a group decision-making environment. The next section discusses some of the forces that affect groups as they wrestle with decision making.

## Group Decision Making

In most organizations today, many major decisions are made through teams, task forces, and committees. This tendency towards group decision making is due in part to organizations' increased complexity and to the large amount of information needed to make sound decisions. This is especially true for the non-programmed decisions, which typically have the greatest uncertainty of outcome. By its very nature, a non-programmed decision may require innovation and creativity, because it may require solutions that have not been tried before. The complexity of many of these problems may require specialized knowledge in several fields, knowledge that is usually not possessed by any one person. This requirement—coupled with the fact that decisions eventually must be accepted and implemented by many units throughout the organization—has increased the use of the team approach to decision making.

### Individual versus Group Decision Making

Considerable debate has centred on the relative effectiveness of individual decision making as opposed to group decision making. Certain decisions appear to be better made by groups, while others appear better suited to individual decision making. Bringing together individual specialists and experts has its benefits, since the mutually reinforcing impact of their interaction often results in better decisions. In fact, some research seems to have shown that on problems that have major impact, consensus decisions with five or more participants often produce more satisfactory results than any of individual decision making, majority vote, or leadership decisions.[16]

The following are some of the benefits claimed by proponents of group decision making:

1. In establishing goals and objectives, groups may be superior to individuals because of their wider knowledge;
2. In developing alternatives, groups are often able to provide input from several functional areas of the organization;
3. In evaluating alternatives, the collective judgement of the group, with its wider range of viewpoints, may be superior to that of the individual decision maker;
4. In selecting a solution, some research has shown that group interaction and the achievement of consensus may result in the acceptance of more risk than an individual decision maker would accept; and
5. The group decision may be more likely to be accepted widely as a result of the participation of more of those affected by its consequences.

Despite these claimed benefits of group decision making, there are some potential disadvantages. Groups usually take more time to reach a decision than do individuals, and sometimes timing is crucial. The dynamics of some groups may lead them to select

*As organizations and operations become more complex, more and more decisions have to be made by informed groups, rather than by an individual.*

a solution solely because, unlike the other possible solutions considered, it does not offend anyone in the group—the *lowest common denominator syndrome*. Research has also found that group decision making is often negatively influenced by the following behavioural factors:

- Pressure to conform to the group norms, sometimes called "group think";
- The presence in the group of someone who has a domineering personality;
- The tendency of group members with relatively low status in the hierarchy to defer to the opinions of those who have higher status, called "status incongruity";
- Uncritical acceptance by the group of the opinions of members who are thought to have special expertise or knowledge; and
- The development of a competitive atmosphere in which some group members try to "win" rather than accepting other points of view.

Another potential problem is that it is difficult to hold a group accountable for its decisions. Who *really* made the decision, and who "went along" only reluctantly? Who provided inadequate or inaccurate information? Who had a vested interest in a particular outcome, and consequently leaned heavily towards it rather than towards alternatives? And, conversely, who sparked the discussion and initiated the solution? Without knowing the answers to these questions, all of which are homogenized within the group, it would not be fair to assign blame or give credit to specific individuals. This weakened accountability may be somewhat alleviated if implementation is expressly assigned to an individual or to an identifiable unit within the organization. Even so, it is hardly fair to fix blame on those implementing a group decision if the decision was faulty in the first place.

Techniques have been developed to capture the inherent benefits of group decision making, while compensating for its inherent weaknesses. These include process improvement teams, brainstorming, the Delphi technique, and the nominal group technique, each of which will be discussed in the sections that follow.

## Process Improvement Teams

**process improvement team**
A group brought together from different functions and levels of an organization, to consider ways in which the organization's activities could be improved.

One form of group decision making that has been used effectively in a number of companies is the **process improvement team.** These teams consist of employees from throughout the organization and are often made up of people from interacting functional areas (such as sales and marketing). Everyone on the team is treated as having equal status; the leader is not automatically appointed solely because of position in the hierarchy of the organization.

The manager who originates the process improvement team gives it a well-defined problem to solve, and a time period in which it should be solved. In an effective organization, no team is chartered without ensuring that team members have received training in basic team processes, and in the tools and techniques of group facilitation. Successful process improvement teams are usually limited to six or eight people. The originator or the group selects a convener, a facilitator, and a recorder. The convener is responsible for seeing that the group sets the agenda and arranges meeting times and places. The facilitator is charged with seeing that the meetings stay focused on the problem and that everyone has an opportunity to be heard. In a small group one person may have both of these responsibilities, but if the size of the group permits, it is better to assign them to two different people. The recorder takes the minutes and reports after each meeting to the manager who chartered the team. Since it is almost impossible to facilitate a meeting and to concentrate on recording its decisions, the recorder and facilitator should always be two different people.

In situations where groups are better suited than individuals to non-programmed decisions, an atmosphere fostering group creativity must be developed. All group members must participate, and the evaluation of individual ideas must be suspended from the beginning to encourage participation and to discourage immediate rejection of novel ideas merely because they are novel. When properly used, three techniques—brainstorming, the Delphi technique, and the nominal group technique—may unleash a group's creative ability to generate ideas, understand problems, and reach better decisions.

**brainstorming**
A process in which a group of individuals generate and state ideas, but in which the rules prohibit questioning, evaluating, or rejecting any ideas, even if they seem ridiculous.

**Brainstorming.**  In many situations, groups are responsible for producing imaginative solutions to organizational problems. To meet this need, **brainstorming** was introduced in the 1950s and was in vogue through the 1960s.[17] After the original enthusiasm faded a bit, it was observed that brainstorming did not provide all of the benefits originally ascribed to it. Subsequently, the technique evolved into a more structured form that was designed to incorporate the creativity released, yet use it to reach prioritized, useful decisions. In its more structured form, brainstorming can be useful in some situations as a means of generating possible alternatives to the "obvious" solution. It can only be successful if the brainstorming group adheres to a firm set of rules designed to promote the generation of ideas and avoid the inhibitions that face-to-face groups can easily create. The basic rules are:

- Group members are encouraged to state any idea, no matter how extreme or outlandish. No idea is too ridiculous, and no one is to discount or criticize it at this stage.
- Each idea presented belongs to the group, not to the person stating it. In this way, group members can build on the ideas of others, and the originator of an idea does not feel the need to defend it.
- The session's purpose is to generate ideas, not to evaluate them, so evaluation only occurs after the brainstorming session ends.

Brainstorming seems most effective in advertising, the media, and similar creative fields. In other situations, it has been less successful because it has not been followed by the essential step of evaluating and ranking the ideas generated. When brainstorming seems to become an end in itself the group may never reach any viable conclusions. Nevertheless, when properly used the technique may bring to attention some novel ideas that otherwise might never have surfaced, but that can be properly evaluated after the brainstorming session.

**Delphi technique**
A process for arriving at an evaluation of decisions, in which selected individuals are asked to respond individually to key questions about a problem, then are provided with a summary of the responses all members have given and invited to respond again.

**The Delphi technique.** The **Delphi technique** involves soliciting and comparing judgements from a group of acknowledged experts, whose identities are not necessarily known to the evaluators. It takes its name from the ancient Greek temple complex at Delphi, where specially trained people provided answers to questions about the future. In this technique, the experts are asked to complete a set of questionnaires, which are summarized by staff members. The summaries are then fed back to the original respondents without identifying who has made which suggestions. The experts are then asked to complete a second questionnaire for reassessment. Based on this feedback, respondents independently evaluate the responses they and the other members of the group have submitted. Although it is possible to continue the procedure for several rounds, research has shown that, typically, no significant changes occur after the second round of feedback. The rationale for the technique is that the consensus estimate may result in a better decision after two rounds of anonymous group judgement, because the biasing effects of the group interactions are eliminated. Of course, another factor is introduced by the biases of the person or persons summarizing the questionnaire responses, but with great care this effect can be minimized.

**nominal group technique (NGT)**
A group decision-making process in which selected individuals each submit possible solutions to a problem, then discuss them and attempt to reach consensus.

**The nominal group technique (NGT).** NGT has gained increasing recognition in health, social service, education, industry, and government organizations. The term **nominal group technique** was coined by researchers to refer to processes that bring people together in what is only nominally a group, that is, a group in name only.

The "group" meeting proceeds as follows: Seven to ten individuals sit around a table, each writing ideas on pads of paper but not communicating with each other. After five or ten minutes, a structured sharing of ideas takes place. Each person, in turn, presents one idea. A person designated as recorder writes the ideas on a flip chart in full view of the entire group. This continues around the circle until all of the participants indicate that they have no further ideas to share. There is still no discussion.

The output of this phase is a rather lengthy list of ideas. The next phase involves structured discussion in which each idea receives attention before a vote is taken. Discussion includes asking for clarification and stating the degree of support for each idea on the flip chart. In the next stage, independent voting, each participant privately selects priorities by ranking or voting. The group decision is the pooled outcome of the individual votes.

There are two basic differences between the Delphi technique and NGT: (1) In the Delphi technique, all communication between participants is by way of written questionnaires and feedback from the monitoring staff. In NGT, after the initial listing of ideas, communication is direct among the participants. (2) NGT participants meet face to face around a table, while Delphi participants are physically distant, never meet face to face, and are typically anonymous to one another.

Practical considerations, of course, often influence which technique is used. These considerations can include the number of working hours available, costs, the extent of technical knowledge required, the importance of the issues being considered, and the participants' physical proximity.

## The Information Age

Canada has become an information society. According to Tom Healey, general manager of the Infoscam Division of Anderson Consulting Canada, a surprising 29 percent of Canadian adults have used the Internet,[18] and the number is increasing daily. Businesses today have access to more information than ever before. The abundance of newspapers, journals, magazines, TV and radio programs, seminars, and reports from business and government has led many commentators to label this the *Information Age*. The sheer volume of information available presents a real challenge to business managers, raising important questions about the impact of information technology on the management of organizations. Understanding this impact becomes even more critical as organizations struggle to improve quality and competitiveness in the face of relentless challenges from domestic and foreign companies.[19] Obviously no manager can use all of the information that is available from countless sources. The challenge is to collect, store, process, use, and report the most relevant information to make more effective decisions.

One of the challenges facing organizations is to communicate useful information to managers in a timely fashion. Organizations must be able to make decisions quickly to keep pace with competition. Yet if an organization isn't prepared to handle a large volume of information, or if the information doesn't reach key decision makers, the volume of information and its speed of dissemination are of no value whatsoever. Two important points for managers to remember is that not all information is useful and that useful information is usually better if it is widely shared.

### Attributes of Useful Information

Not all information is appropriate for decision making. For information to be truly useful, it must be accessible, timely, relevant, accurate, verifiable, complete, and clear.[20] Exhibit 3-7 summarizes the attributes of useful information. As the table shows, the requirements are fairly rigorous and may be difficult to meet. When information is needed quickly, accuracy may have to be sacrificed for speed. Information obtained quickly may contain errors. Statistics Canada has a well-deserved worldwide reputation for precision, breadth, and accuracy. Probably no other country in the world gathers and makes available to its citizens such a wealth of statistical information. This quality of output, however, comes at a cost—the rather lengthy periods required for the processing of statistics before they are published. As a consequence, Statistics Canada reports

**Exhibit 3-7**

*Attributes of Useful Information*

| Attribute | Description |
|---|---|
| Accessible | Information can be obtained easily and quickly. |
| Timely | Information is available when needed. |
| Relevant | Managers need the information to make a particular decision. |
| Accurate | Information is error-free. |
| Verifiable | Information can be confirmed independently. |
| Complete | All details needed are available. |
| Clear | Information is stated in such a way that no facts are misunderstood. |

*Managers of the W.A.C. Bennett Dam in British Columbia had to balance the cost and inconvenience of greatly reducing the amount of impounded water against the slight possibility that the dam might fail if the water were not released. They opted to "act now, study later" because of the potential for disaster.*

are comprehensive and reliable, but may not be published until other factors have superseded them.

Similarly, at times a manager has to make a decision between comprehensiveness and accuracy, on the one hand, and speed on the other. For instance, in July 1996, when B.C. Hydro was advised of a "sink hole" in the huge W.A.C. Bennett dam, a decision was made immediately to spill large amounts of the impounded water, to reduce hydrostatic pressure and avoid even the slight chance of dam failure. This decision was made on what was known to be inadequate information, since the managers did not yet know whether the defect was potentially hazardous—information that could only be known after lengthy study. Nevertheless, the possible consequences of delay made it imperative to "act now, study later." In fact, after immediate protective action was taken, detailed studies were initiated, and several months later the company discovered that the perceived risk had been minimal. But surely no one at B.C. Hydro would have condoned delaying the protective action, because of what was even a slight risk of catastrophe. Similar examples, although perhaps not quite as dramatic, face managers almost every day. The question often is: Do I make the decision now or await further information?

## Information Sharing

A major problem facing organizations is the manner in which information is shared. Because of the abundance of data, much valuable information never reaches the person who can benefit from it the most. In one survey, 66 percent of employees said that their main source of information was the grapevine.[21] In such cases, decisions affecting millions of dollars may be based on rumour. The grapevine, which exists in every organization, is discussed in greater detail in Chapter 10.

In today's economy, information—more than factories and products—is the key to growth and competitiveness. Some managers withhold information from employees because they are afraid employees will use the information to contradict or embarrass managers or even disclose it to competitors. Unfortunately employees cannot respond to the need for continued improvement without adequate information. Organizations that train people in the value of information and how to use it gain a competitive advantage over those failing to share information.

The key to sharing information is to put it in the hands of the people who can use it, in a form those people can understand. For example, client/server technology is enabling the gas industry to reorganize and revolutionize the workplace so teams of employees can work on the same task simultaneously. The result is unprecedented levels of efficiency and new highs in customer service. With client/server computing, personal computers perform functions that once could be handled only by mainframe computers.[22]

Another innovation allowing for the wide sharing of information is groupware, which helps organizations to build integrated work group and work flow systems. These systems include electronic mail (e-mail), scheduling, and group conferencing.[23] In the highly competitive groupware industry, powerful new additions to this type of software will continue for at least the next decade or so. Netscape, for example, has been applied inside organizations to create intranets, which allow employees with disparate computer platforms to share information.[24] These powerful new tools will create productivity enhancement opportunities for companies by expanding their ability to share information.

## Management Information Systems

**management information system (MIS)**
A composite system that entails collecting, recording, and storing information for later retrieval to assist in management decision making.

A **management information system (MIS)** uses the capabilities of computers through regular, organized procedures to provide managers with information needed to make decisions. An MIS is critical for decision making in all aspects of management: organization and job design, human resource decisions, strategic planning, customer service, cash management, and so on. Hogg Robinson Travel, one of Britain's largest travel agencies, developed an MIS that permits the detailed analysis and planning of corporate clients' travel needs. Hogg Robinson captures 99 percent of its management information electronically at the point of sale and transmits it for storage on a central computer. This information is analyzed and the trends identified allow travel policy to be recommended and agreed on for each large customer. Similarly, many large organizations have their own in-house travel departments that are connected to the major commercial reservation systems. With this online capability, company executives can check availability of airline seats, car rentals, and hotel reservations, and can make immediate confirmed bookings from their offices or homes.[25] It is even possible for a passenger on a delayed flight to use a laptop computer, modem, and the telephone provided on many planes to change reservations for connecting flights, thus minimizing the inconvenience arising from the delay. This is possible because the airlines have comprehensive MIS databases that can be tapped from external sources.

### MIS Functions

An MIS is used to collect data, store and process those data, and then present useful and timely information to managers. This section discusses these functions.

**Collection of data.** As noted above, a massive amount of information is available to organizations—personnel records, information about customers and competitors, sales and accounting data, current interest rates, and so on. The first step in designing an MIS is to determine what information is needed to make informed decisions. This informa-

*Airlines have comprehensive MIS databases that can be tapped into by travel agents and by customers themselves, providing a useful service and, at the same time, reducing salary costs for the airlines.*

tion must then be organized into a *database*, an integrated collection of data stored in one system for efficient access and information processing.[26]

Usually, sources from within the organization provide most of the data collected for an MIS. These sources include company records and reports and information compiled by managers themselves. External sources include trade publications, customers, consultants, updated industry and market studies, Statistics Canada, and periodical and newspaper articles.[27] Managers must thoughtfully specify the information they need to make decisions and then identify the sources of that information.

Information available in even the most sophisticated databases is no better that the accuracy of the information that is input into the system. In addition to applying quality control methods to inputs, managers must screen the kinds of information entered to avoid the database being so full that it is difficult to separate out useful information.

A survey of information managers at 50 large companies made by MIT researchers reported that half of the managers believed that the corporate information in the company's central database was less than 95 percent accurate. This may sound good until one realizes that it means that the remaining 5 percent, or 1 in 20 entries, is incorrect! This inaccuracy limits the usefulness of the central database. More discouraging, nearly all of the respondents said that databases kept by individual departments (rather than in a central system) were seldom reliable enough to use for important decisions.

It has been said, only partially in jest, that the advent of the computer database has made the escalation of little mistakes into big mistakes possible. For example, one of the major banks was creating fictional transactions to test its readiness for the year 2000 problem. Unfortunately, the transactions were actually entered in the system. As a result, 2000 overdraft notices were sent out to real, not fictional, customers.[28] Similarly, a major airline made thousands of phantom entries while testing its reservations system. When the test was completed, no one thought to clear the phantom entries, which looked just like real entries from real customers. Consequently, until the error was discovered several months later, the airline was turning down passengers wishing to buy tickets because the system told managers that the seats were fully booked, even though many spaces were available. The system was working perfectly. However, because the phantom information had been put into the system, incorrect information was being provided by the system. A large manufacturer developed a database to consolidate its sales records by customer number. But salespeople, not having been properly instructed, created a new customer number for each sale, including sales to existing customers. As a result, a single customer, McDonnell Douglas Corp., was listed in the database under more than 7000 customer numbers.[29] The software functioned well, but operators were not given adequate instructions on how to use it.

No matter how good the system is, the results can be no better than the quality of the information put into the system. MIS managers often ruefully refer to this principle as "garbage in, garbage out" (GIGO). Software is constantly being developed that uses statistical control to analyze big databases and help detect inaccuracies, but the human factor cannot ever be entirely eliminated.

## Management in the Real World    3-1

### Information for Decision Making: Reflections by Philip Crosby

There are many systems of accumulating and distributing information, and there is a lot of information. For the purpose of this reflection I counted how many newspapers and magazines I receive each month: 108 papers and 42 magazines. Add to that the mail I receive and the TV shows I watch and it's apparent that a lot of data come across the bow of my life.

In the business world there is a great deal of formal information development and transmission. Understanding all of this is a burden for managers and subordinates alike. However they can sometimes delude themselves into believing that this is all there is, and that it is the most important part of their job.

I recently visited a plant that made chlorine gas. As an example of a quality project they had me sit with a team investigating cases where gas had escaped and injured employees. There were 42 such happenings in the past year—6 of them quite serious. The team showed me their computer analysis of the movement of the tanks containing the gas and the various pressures involved. They lost me after about ten minutes, but since they all seemed to understand it, I hung in there. The study would be finished in a few more months, I was told, and then they would know why these exposures had happened.

After the meeting, I was taken on a tour by a shop worker and shown the area where the leaks had occurred.

"Those leaks happened while gas was being transferred from these big tanks to the little ones we send the customers," he said.

"Can you show me how the transfer is made?" I asked.

He nodded and grabbed a nozzle attached to a hose fitted into the large tank. He took a washer off the nozzle and replaced it with a new one from the open box sitting on a bench.

"Why did you replace the washer?" I asked.

"Have to do that every time," he replied. "The chlorine eats these washers right up. If you use one too many times it will leak."

"Is that how the gas escapes happen?" I queried.

He nodded briskly. "Gets them every time they don't want to bother to change the washer."

"Have you told the task team about this?" I asked.

He shook his head. "I gave it a try a couple of times, but they're so involved in their computer they aren't really interested in what goes on out here."

I thanked him and then relayed his story to the general manager who found it all to be true. The problem was solved, the worker was rewarded, and the information crunchers were embarrassed. Procedures and training were changed and that was the last of the gas escapes.

Collecting data is more important than processing it, particularly when the real stuff might not be written down.

**Storing and processing data.**  Once created, a database must be stored and processed in a form useful to managers. Data generally are stored on magnetic tape or hard disks when mainframe computers are used and on hard disks or "floppy" disks or CDs when minicomputers or microcomputers are used.

Data for an MIS must be current, which requires periodic updating of the database. In some systems, all updating is done manually by an operator; in other systems, information is entered automatically from sensors and monitors that are integral parts of the production control process. In an efficient MIS, when a particular item of information is entered in one segment of the system, that information is automatically carried forward to all other segments in which it is relevant. This single-entry feature eliminates the need for the same information to be manually entered again, thus preventing errors in copying for subsequent entries.

For example, even relatively small companies often have systems that follow an order from its initial receipt until all activities relating to it have been completed. When an order is received from a customer, it is entered in the MIS. It then automatically generates a production work order, allocates the appropriate amounts and kinds of inventory, and establishes a control schedule for all steps in the process. If properly configured it can also create shipping documents, prepare invoices and accounts receivable records, and set up follow-up notices in case the customer does not pay promptly. It can even alert the person responsible for ordering inventory that it is time to replenish stock. All of this work, formerly done manually and thus prone to omissions and errors, is done from only the first manual entry. Once the first entry is made, there can be no chance that the order will be mislaid between steps in the process, and it is easy to trace the progress and status of any order if necessary.

**Presenting information to managers.**     Processed data must be put in a form useful to managers. Verbal (as distinguished from "oral") information can be presented in text format in reports, outlines, lists, articles, and books. Numerical information can be presented in table or graph format. Computer programs offer numerous graphic options and sound and visual displays of all kinds. Data can be illustrated in bar charts, pie charts, or line graphs (see Exhibit 3-8 on page 114). A bar chart uses vertical or horizontal bars to represent values at a particular time, with longer bars representing greater values. A pie chart is a circle divided into segments, or "slices," each representing a different proportion of the whole. Bar charts and pie charts help the reader to visualize the relative size or importance of various items. A line graph is used to illustrate how results change over time, or how a stated condition changes. A number of software programs make it possible for the operator to enter data in numeric values, then command the computer to represent those data in one or more of the chart forms.

Charts create a visual impact that is more easily grasped by the reader than tables of numbers, so they are often used to supplement text and numeric tables. Care must be taken in selecting scales for charts so that they portray an accurate representation of the facts, rather than subtle but real distortions. The *"fantastic charts"* shown in Exhibit 3-9 on page 115 illustrates how a chart with an improperly chosen scale can be misleading, however inadvertently. Exhibit 3-9(b) is a fantastic chart; Exhibit 3-9(a) shows exactly the same data, but with a left-hand scale properly based on zero. Of course, 3-9(b) shows the minor variations that are not readily evident in 3-9(a), but it also gives the impression of fantastic fluctuations. In contrast, a manager who reviews 3-9(a) may say "Ho hum, things are going along quite smoothly," because in fact the variations all fall within a very narrow range. Exhibits 3-9(c) and 3-9(d) illustrate another common form of fantastic chart. Both show exactly the same values— 1, 2, 4, and 2. The simple bars in Exhibit 3-9(c) convey visually the exact relationships among these values. In Exhibit 3-9(d) the figures of men have the same comparative heights, but they convey quite different relationships. Our minds are trained to think of the figures as if they were in three dimensions—in a sense, we are comparing volumes rather than heights when we look at Exhibit 3-9(d). The man representing 4 does not appear to be twice the size of the one representing 2, but rather something like six or eight times it. Charts using pictures of three-dimensional objects, such as bags of money to represent costs, expenses, or taxes, often are used intentionally to distort the perceptions of those who see them. The wise and ethical manager will seek both to avoid publishing misleading charts of the "fantastic" nature and to guard against being misled by others' use of "fantastic" charts.

**Exhibit 3-8**   *Commonly Used Forms of Graphical Presentation*

a) Bar chart

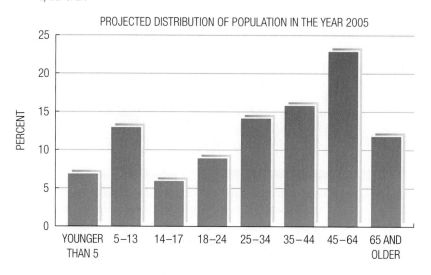

b) Pie chart

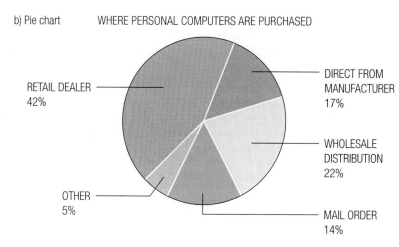

c) Graph

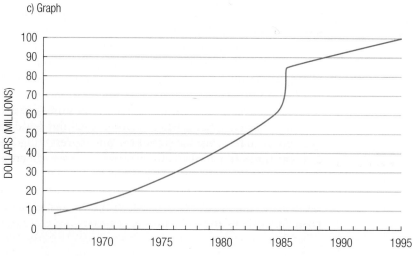

**Exhibit 3-9**   *Charts That Distort the Perceptions*

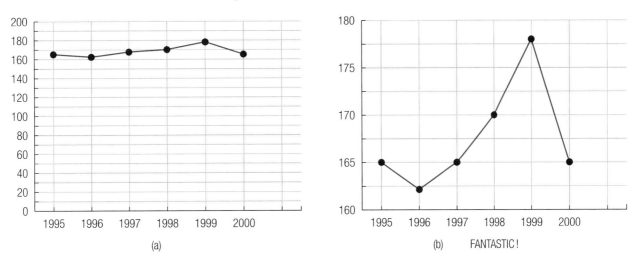

Both charts reflect the same figures. The "fantastic" chart suppress the origin point (the zero), so it exaggerates the amount of variation.

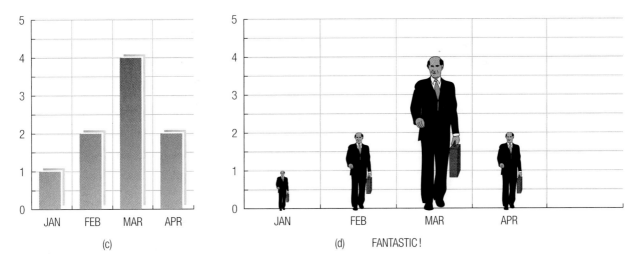

The images in the "fantastic" chart are the same height as those in the plain bar chart, but the reader's mind perceives the figures in three dimensions, so it exaggerates the differences between 1, 2, and 4.

## Upgrading Hardware and Software

Hardware and software are being designed and marketed so rapidly in the present highly competitive environment that whatever is chosen by the manager seems to have become obsolete almost before it is installed. It is incumbent on the manager to keep abreast of new developments in the computer industry, and to judge whether those new developments would assist in managing the organization to such a degree that their purchase would be warranted. Massive advertising programs and the uncritical enthusiasm of in-house computer experts often lead the unwary manager to feel that it is essential to equip the organization with the latest software and the fastest, most sophisticated hardware. The prudent manager will resist this temptation. Every decision relating to hardware or software purchase should be subjected to the same tests as any other capital purchase: Will it permit us to function *better*—that is, more *accurately*, more *quickly*, or more *easily*—and is the added accuracy, speed, or convenience sufficient to *justify the additional cost?*

## Computer Networks

A computer network is a collection of computers connected in a manner that allows them to function individually, yet communicate with each other. Computer networks usually include a mainframe or server as the foundation of the system. Other mainframes, servers, or microcomputers can communicate with the central mainframe or network server, or with each other. Networks link computers within an office, across the country, or even worldwide—in which case the computers are linked by telephone lines, microwaves, or satellites.

**local area network (LAN)**
A system in which separate computers are linked for communication.

A **local area network (LAN)** is a system of telecommunications links that connect all computers in one company directly without using external telephone lines.[30] Because computers in the network can communicate with one another, members of an organization can send information back and forth instantly. In 1993, securities brokerage Machaira Group, Inc. installed its first LAN. This installation allows Machaira's account representatives to execute buy and sell orders electronically through their individual PCs, reducing time on each transaction and locking in the prices quoted on fast-moving stocks, while the customer waits on the telephone. Now, only a few years later, any securities broker that did not have a similar network would be considered completely out of date, and would soon succumb to the competition.

## Trends in Information Systems

The amount of information available to managers will continue to increase dramatically, making information systems even more crucial to organizations. Virtually no organization, regardless of size, will be able to function efficiently or effectively without a computer-based information processing system. Some early enthusiasts predicted a "paperless" society in which computers would replace hard copy for nearly all letters, memos, reports, and other business correspondence. Of course, computers are being used for an increasing proportion of internal and external correspondence, but this probably has not reduced the amount of paper generated. After all, for important communications, both the sender and receiver need a hard copy, so even though the message was conveyed electronically, the same amount of paper is still required.

The amount of computer power a dollar can buy has grown a thousand times every two decades, and this shows no sign of slowing.[31] The trend towards smaller, faster, and less costly computers also will continue, fuelled by advances in three areas: smaller computer chips, new operating systems, and better, faster communications technology. It was only a few years ago that it was considered quite innovative when the B.C. Ferry Corporation installed work carrels with power sources for computers in its ferries. Satellite phone technology has made it possible for most major airlines to provide in-seat telephones for the use of passengers. Also, most major hotel chains in the Western world routinely provide facilities for guests to plug in their laptop or notebook computers so they can communicate with their offices and other associates while travelling on business. These facilities also permit the travelling business person to access home office databases, so that informed decisions can be made no matter where the managers happen to be.

## The Internet

Perhaps the most profound information-related development for decision making in the last few years has been the explosive growth of the Internet. Since 1994 the World Wide Web (WWW) has been available to the most unsophisticated users of the Internet. There are tens of thousands of Web sites, and the number is reported to be growing exponentially.[32] For business the implications are almost incalculable, as this new communications medium reaches most of the world's largest organizations and most people in the world with middle or upper incomes. According to BIS Strategic Decisions, $20 to $30 billion of business-to-business merchandise was sold through electronic catalogues as early as 1993,[33] and the amount has grown prodigiously since. In June 1994, GM's Saturn division began advertising on Prodigy,[34] and other major manufacturers soon followed. Sony New Technologies coordinates different divisions and makes their products available to computer users on the WWW. Sony offers an Internet access service called Sony Online, which constitutes a direct marketing channel and bypasses conventional retail distribution channels.[35]

*Even small companies routinely use computers for efficient information processing.*

Business creates a presence on the WWW by establishing a "home page." These home pages can be linked to other databases and computers called "servers." People who "visit" a home page on the Internet are offered a variety of subtopics from which to choose. The hypertext markup language (HTML) used to create home pages makes point-and-click navigation of the WWW possible.

The Internet affects decision making because it offers the potential for worldwide information gathering and discussion groups. At the same time, the fact that in a majority of cases access to the Internet is unregulated permits irresponsible users to publish unsupported, inaccurate, and even intentionally false "information." As a consequence, the prudent manager will view with healthy scepticism any material culled from the Internet and will scrutinize it and seek to find its real source, and thus possibly acquire enough information to evaluate its reliability.

## Data Security

A major concern is the vast amount of personal and other confidential information that is stored on computers, which is available to unauthorized users who manage to break into computer systems. Computers linked together in networks are especially vulnerable, because a breach of security anywhere in the system may lay the whole system open to unauthorized access. The true story of such a breach and its frightening implications appears in Cliff Stoll's 1990 best-seller, *The Cuckoo's Egg*.[36]

By assigning a secret password to each individual who is authorized to have access to particular classes of information, organizations can institute a measure of control. For example, the password assigned to the manager of human resources might permit access to payroll and personnel records, but not to a secret biochemical formula or to details of a production process. On the other hand, the production manager's password might permit access to the secret formula, but not to personnel records.

Of course, the degree of confidentiality afforded by the use of passwords is directly related to the extent to which passwords are difficult to guess and the extent to which authorized users actually keep their assigned passwords secret. Passwords should not contain personal dates, licence numbers, addresses, or telephone numbers, all of which can be guessed by someone attempting to break into the system. Powerful computers can search for passwords by trying all of the known words in an unabridged dictionary, so security experts recommend assigning meaningless jumbles of letters and numbers that will be difficult for all but the most sophisticated and persistent computer users to discover.

The best choice of password can be foiled by vagaries of human nature. Even senior scientists and executives who are otherwise security conscious may write their passwords on slips of paper that can be found by someone diligently seeking to break into the system. Even more surprising, many of those entrusted with a password "lend" it to friends and colleagues, effectively eliminating the purpose of the password and completely compromising security. Thus, the safeguards built into any computer system can be so easily and thoughtlessly compromised that the question of computer security (for which one can substitute "data security") is one that managers everywhere find perplexing, and almost impossible to solve with any degree of confidence.

## Viruses

Another serious threat to computer security is the so-called virus, which is a destructive program that can be unintentionally inserted into a system and then replicate itself to other programs, destroying or distorting data or even causing the system to crash. Viruses often are introduced into a system when an employee, without authorization, downloads a pirated program (that is, an illegal copy of software that violates the original copyright). While use of pirated copies largely can be controlled by rigorous company security, it is more difficult to prevent viruses being introduced from the Internet or through the exchange of data and communications by multiorganizational connections. Fortunately, there are a number of programs available that detect all *known* viruses. Of course, these virus detectors have to be upgraded frequently if they are to identify new viruses.[37] And despite all of these safeguards, one virus spread quickly across the Internet and paralyzed 6000 computers in businesses, universities and colleges, and government offices. Obviously, the problems have not been completely solved, and caution must be exercised in downloading *any* information from an outside source.

## The Workplace of Tomorrow

As management information systems become more common, and more information becomes available from such sources as the Internet, managers increasingly will face the problem of having too much information, rather than too little. A key management skill will be to sift through the available information and disregard what is least relevant, using the rest to make necessary decisions. Along with the plethora of information may come an increasing reluctance by some managers to make decisions, knowing that if they only spend more time, they may be able to acquire even more information, and possibly make a better decision.

With all of the new sources and techniques, there still will be a pressing need for managers who have the courage to make decisions, and who know how to synthesize information and make good decisions. Managers also will have to learn how to discriminate between decisions that are best made individually, and those that are best made by group process. This discrimination, too, will require the exercise of decision-making skills.

No matter how sophisticated the information-gathering process becomes, and regardless of refinements in theories of decision making, nothing will replace the need for what might be called the garden variety of personal decision making. As managers hone this skill, they will become ever more capable as managers, and ever more effective in all that they do.

## Summary of Learning Objectives

▶ **Compare programmed and non-programmed decisions.**

Decisions are programmed to the extent that they are repetitive and routine and a definite procedure has been developed for handling them. Decisions are non-programmed when the problems they address are novel and unstructured and no solutions have been prearranged.

▶ **Contrast intuitive and systematic decision making.**

Intuitive decision making involves the use of estimates or hunches to decide among alternative courses of action. Many managerial decisions are influenced to a great extent by the manager's intuitions. Systematic decision making is an organized, exacting, data-driven process. Systematic decision making requires the development of a clear set of objectives, a relevant information base, a consensus-seeking sharing of ideas and creativity, and exacting implementation, assessment, and feedback.

▶ **Identify and explain the nine steps of the decision-making process.**

(1) Establish goals and objectives. Decision making is always conducted in the context of goals and objectives. (2) Identify and define the problem. A problem is defined as the realization that the current situation does not reflect the desired state. (3) Establish priorities. Because resources are never unlimited, an organization must assign priorities to its problems. (4) Determine causes of the problem. It is ill-advised to try to find a solution to a problem when the cause of the problem is not yet known. (5) Develop alternative solutions. Before a decision is reached, alternative solutions need to be created and developed, and their potential consequences must be explored. (6) Evaluate alternative solutions. Once alternatives have been developed, they must be evaluated and compared. (7) Select a solution. The purpose of selecting a particular solution is to solve a problem in order to achieve a predetermined end. (8) Implement the decision. Any decision is little more than an abstraction if it isn't implemented. (9) Follow up. Effective management involves periodic measurements of results and feedback to initiate any required modifications.

▶ **Explain the differences between individual and group decision making, and how each may be applied in business.**

Individual decision making is subject to behavioural factors involving a person's values, personality, and toleration of uncertainty and dissonance. These forces are heightened but tend to be "averaged out" in a group decision-making environment. Groups usually take more time than an individual to reach a decision. There is a tendency for a group to select a solution that does not offend any members of the group, rather than one that might be a better solution but that is objected to by a group member. However, bringing together specialists in a group situation may offer benefits because of the mutually reinforcing effects of their interaction. Research has shown that for complex and crucial matters, consensus decisions made by five or more participants may be superior to those formed through individual decision making, majority vote, or leader decisions. Individual decision making can be much quicker than group decision making, and therefore will be the mode of choice when speed is necessary. An organization is more likely to use group decision making for problems that affect many different groups of people, that may be sensitive, or that require a broad spectrum of knowledge.

▶ **Explain the terms** *cognitive dissonance* **and** *escalation of commitment.*

Cognitive dissonance refers to a lack of consistency among a person's perceptions after a decision has been made. Escalation of commitment occurs when a decision maker develops an increased commitment to the decision that was made despite having received information that may bring into question the wisdom of that decision.

▶ **Describe process improvement teams, brainstorming, the Delphi technique, and the nominal group technique.**

A process improvement team consists of people selected from all levels within an organization who may have knowledge about the problem in question. It sets out to make decisions to solve organizational problems within the context of the organization's objectives. In brainstorming, a group of individuals get together to generate ideas, but do not evaluate them, no matter how ridiculous they initially may seem. Evaluation occurs after the brainstorming session, sometimes by the same people that participated in the session, sometimes by other people. The Delphi technique consists of soliciting from experts and comparing anonymous opinions through a sequence of questionnaires, circulation of a summary of responses, and iterative feedback. In the nominal group technique, individuals are brought together and their opinions are solicited without interaction among themselves. Later in the process they are invited to participate in structured discussion.

▶ **Describe how an MIS can facilitate informed decision making, and what difficulties may be encountered with it.**

Information is essential for informed decision making. A well-designed and functioning MIS can provide the essential information by gathering it from a multiplicity of sources, sorting and analyzing it and reporting it in a useful form. Because an MIS can store and process such a large volume of information, sometimes the essential information for a decision is buried in a welter of irrelevant or peripheral data, making it difficult to extract what is required. An MIS is only as helpful as the effectiveness of its design, and as the focus of that design on the information that is actually needed and on the form in which it is most useful.

# KEY TERMS

# REVIEW AND DISCUSSION QUESTIONS

## Recall

1. Why is decision making sometimes called the essence of management?
2. Identify and connect the nine steps in making a decision.
3. Name the different types of decisions.
4. What are the three components of decision making?

## Understanding

5. Decision making occurs at both the individual and the group levels in most organizations, and managers need to know the strengths and weaknesses of each approach. Explain and provide examples of situations where managers should use individual or group decision making.
6. Why does decision making in a well-managed organization focus on continual improvement? Why can't a manager simply make one right decision for a particular problem, and have that problem be solved completely and permanently?
7. To be effective, decision making must continue with implementation and follow-up. Why are these so important to the process? Describe a hypothetical situation in which the lack of effective implementation or follow-up would cause greater problems than the original problem that the decision was intended to solve.

## Application

8. Imagine that you manage 50 people in a department of a major retail discounter. You have recently learned that the customer service centre has been receiving complaints about the quality of goods in your department. What steps would you take to decide what to do, if anything, with this information?
9. Much of what we believe about decision making has a basis in history, and does not come just from research. From the business section of a recent issue of a major newspaper, identify an important decision facing a local politician or nationally known business figure. Develop a list of goals that you might establish if you were faced with that decision. How might the goals of the public figure or the business executive differ from yours? How can a decision maker in that situation combine many different people's goals and make a decision that will satisfy most of them? Make a list of the information you would want to make an effective decision in that situation. Are any of those items unattainable? Why? What information is the public figure likely to have that you do not have, and that as a private citizen you might be unable to acquire?
10. Describe an experience in which you have decided to stop doing business with a company. What led to your decision? Did you make the decision consciously or did you just stop patronizing that company? Did you let the manager of the business know of your decision and the reason for it?
11. How can a manager use an MIS system to improve decision making?

# CASE 3-1

## Mastic Corporation Satisfies Its Customers

Satisfying customers requires quick response to their needs. One way for a business to stay close to its customers is through a management information system. Mastic Corporation, a leading supplier of vinyl siding, has 16 percent of industry sales. Competition is keen in this

$500 million industry. To stay on top, Mastic developed a computer-based MIS to react more quickly to changing customer needs. Market research and planning manager Andrew P. Panelli says, "As the industry becomes competitive, you have to direct sales campaigns to where they're going to generate the most business and create the most impact. That becomes harder to do if you don't have a feel for what your customers want and need."

Mastic's managers developed an MIS to monitor market share and sales performance by territory and to determine the market potential for various territories. The MIS compiles information from several sources. It collects sales data from the county level up to the national level and then converts the information to the territorial level. It gathers information on market trends, such as housing starts, ages and values of homes, changes in home style, and acceptability of vinyl siding—all of which helps in estimating potential demand.

The company surveys dealers to determine how much vinyl siding they sell, how much of it is made by Mastic, how much is used for new construction, and how much is used for remodelling. This information enables Mastic to rank competitor strength by territory and to keep track of where its siding is sold: at lumber yards, factory warehouses, or other outlets.

The MIS helps Mastic improve its sales coverage and set up new, more efficient sales territories. It provides sales managers with monthly and annual performance reports comparing current sales to the previous period's sales. Information in the MIS also led Mastic to become more aware of ethnic populations, and to print promotional materials in other languages. Mastic officials, pleased with their MIS, are expanding the system to other divisions producing vinyl materials for windows, new construction, and mobile homes.

### Questions

1. Reflecting Mastic's experience, how can an MIS bring a business closer to its customers?
2. Why did Mastic Corporation managers develop an MIS?
3. How has Mastic benefited from the MIS, and how might the benefits compare with the costs?
4. What problems is Mastic likely to have encountered in instituting the MIS?

Source: Adapted from Tom Eisenhart, "Faced with Limited Resources, the Computer Is Becoming a Key Tool in Staying Close to the Customer," *Business Marketing* (May 1998): 49-52.

## CASE 3-2

## Expert System Design at Cadila Laboratories

Cadila Laboratories is a major pharmaceutical company in India. Top managers felt the company could gain a competitive advantage over competitors by designing an expert system to help scientists preformulate drugs. Preformulation involves investigating a drug's physical, chemical, and biological properties in combination with other chemicals called excipients. Drugs can be formulated as tablets, capsules, injectables, liquid orals, or drops. Most drugs end up in tablet form. In addition to the main active ingredient, tablets contain many excipients, such as a binding material to hold the tablet together and a disintegrator to break the tablet up after it is swallowed. A preformulation study identifies compatible, potentially useful excipients and determines their relative proportions in the final formulation.

The release of the active drug from a drug product is greatly influenced by the method of formulation. Cadila Laboratories believed that a computer-based expert system for preformulating drugs would reduce total costs by reducing research and development (R&D) time.

R&D time (and thus cost) is cut by using the expert system to incorporate knowledge about preformulations. Developing an expert system for drug preformulation included three stages: acquiring information about the main drug, the excipients, and their interactions; organizing the knowledge base; and designing a mechanism for drawing inferences and conclusions.

Information about the main drug includes its physical, chemical, and biological properties as well as its solubility, melting point, dissolution rate, absorption rate, and so on. The therapeutic and production-process properties of excipients are included. For instance, disintegrants like cornstarch ensure that a tablet crumbles after it is swallowed. Binders and adhesives such as gelatin are used to compress particles together to form a tablet.

The knowledge base contains the information that experts need to draw inferences and conclusions. Cadila's expert system contains the information needed to select compatible excipients for a main drug. Thus, the expert system's knowledge base consists of data on the interaction between main drugs and their excipients. The knowledge base about the excipients carries excipients' names, properties, and proportions relative to the main drug.

The MIS was designed to draw inferences in two steps. First, it infers the desirable properties of the excipients for compatibility with the main drug. This is accomplished by matching the main drug's properties with those of the excipients using the knowledge base on interactions. Second, the expert system selects the appropriate excipients and the recommended proportions by consulting the knowledge base on excipients.

The expert system is interactive and driven by various menus. For instance, the Consult menu lets the software consult the knowledge base on the interaction between the main drug and the excipients and identifies the properties of desirable excipients. The system then consults the knowledge base and identifies compatible excipients from the list of excipients possessing the required characteristics. The system then suggests a preformulation consistent with the knowledge already built in. Alternative preformulations can be provided if needed.

The lab has reported a 35 percent reduction in total R&D time needed for preformulations since using the system. The knowledge base is still being developed. When completed, the system will be able to identify fully compatible excipients, and save even more time.

### Questions

1. Why did Cadila Laboratories need such a system?
2. Why did Cadila Laboratories approach the MIS in stages, and what might have happened if one stage had been omitted, or if the stages had occurred in a different order?
3. How could the system be even more beneficial for Cadila in the future?

---

Source: Adapted from K.V. Ramani, M.R. Patel, and S.K. Patel, "An Expert System for Drug Preformulation in a Pharmaceutical Company," *Interfaces* (March-April 1992): 101-108.

## *APPLICATION EXERCISE* **3-1**

## Meeting Managers' Information Requirements

Catherine Roberts, director of information systems for a large chain of discount stores, has received several complaints from store managers that the monthly reports don't provide useful information. In addition, store managers say that receiving reports on a monthly basis is not timely. They would like access to useful information on demand. Store managers want to be able to track sales of all products, follow the competitors' activities, and stay in touch with environmental factors such as economic and social trends. Many managers also have specific information needs. Roberts wants to be responsive to managers' needs, so she is considering several options, including a complete overhaul of her company's management information system.

### Questions

1. How can Roberts determine exactly what type of information would satisfy managers' needs?
2. If she decides to redesign the MIS, what steps should she take to develop the system?
3. What other options might be considered to meet store managers' information needs?
4. What implications do Roberts' actions have for the overall effectiveness of the discount chain? What morale problems and losses from disruption of operations might be expected?

## APPLICATION EXERCISE  3-2

### Creative Decision Making

Connect all of the dots, using only four straight lines. Lines must touch connecting one end to the other. When drawing the lines, do not lift your pencil from the paper and do not retrace the same line.

Having applied the solution, what does this exercise say about problem solving?

_____

Contributed by Sydney Scott, British Columbia Institute of Technology.

## INTERNET APPLICATION  3-1

Visit the Web site for New United Motor Manufacturing Inc. (www.nummi.com).

1. What type of decision making does this company use? What are the pros and cons of this form of decision making?

Search for a Web site that describes an organization whose managers have just made a major decision. What was the decision and why did they make it? Do you think it will be successful? Why or why not?

# Planning

After studying this chapter, you should be able to:

▶ Define *planning* and discuss the characteristics of effective planning that distinguish it from less effective planning;

▶ Describe at least four factors that underscore the need for planning in any organization, regardless of type or size;

▶ Discuss the benefits organizations may gain from effective planning;

▶ Describe the steps in the planning process and explain why each is important;

▶ Explain the following approaches to planning: (1) plan, do, check, act (PDCA); (2) time-based planning; and (3) planning for continuous improvement;

▶ Discuss quantitative measures for different types of business objectives;

▶ Discuss the possible advantages and disadvantages of centralized and decentralized planning;

▶ Describe each of and explain the interrelationships among the *mission statement*, *goals*, and *objectives*;

▶ Explain the differences between *variable* and *rolling* budgets; and

▶ Explain the differences among *strategic*, *operational*, and *tactical* planning.

## Canadian Airlines International Successfully Launches Service Quality Program

IN MANY ORGANIZATIONS, QUALITY INITIATIVES HAVE as their principal focus an improvement in service and operations. However, Canadian Airlines International's "Service Quality" program also was the basis for carrying out one of the largest employee training projects in North American business annals. Planning played a major part in the successful delivery of the training program. It helped organize tasks, kept people focused, and delivered the needed training to the right people at the right time.

In 1994, after a year and a half of preparation and training, CAI switched over its entire reservations, airport, cargo, and financial information systems to a new supplier. For those involved in planning, developing, and delivering the training to prepare CAI's employees, contractors, and suppliers, this was a major feat of logistics and coordination. The project scope included the following: ▶

- The total transition project comprised 13,000 milestone events, with 50,000 tasks.
- 12,000 people attended training in a 96-day "window" for a total of 50,000 days of training.
- 26 classrooms were in use in Canada, London, Beijing, Tokyo, and Hong Kong.

The real beginning of this story was in 1990, when CAI was coming to terms with the impact of five recent mergers, which reformed the company. Routes, aircraft configurations, facilities, and collective agreements had to be standardized while management and many employees were resolving cultural differences and coping with staffing redundancies. To turn the situation around, a new strategy, called *service quality*, was adopted. The new focus on quality was aimed at enhancing service standards and reducing costs by regaining customer focus and improving core business processes.

The Employee Training and Development group played a key role in supporting the new strategy. Employees were provided with quality skills training and were brought together in teams to change the systems and processes they worked with. For the training group, this meant launching a whole new spectrum of services to deliver quality skills and assist improvement teams throughout the company. The overall result was a tremendous leap in customer approval ratings, as well as increased employee involvement in improvement initiatives and in the developing of a unified culture to provide quality service.

Because CAI had to keep running while the training progressed, a limited number of people could be released for training at any one time. Even with training running in two shifts, some employees would be trained up to three months ahead of time. They would go back to using the existing system and then, on cut-over weekends, switch back and apply their new skills and knowledge while ensuring seamless customer service.

The training group's earlier involvement with quality improvement efforts meant that standardization of the basic processes was in place. In particular, a core "training for impact" strategy focused all development around analyzing and solving business problems. Until this time, training productivity had been measured by activity. That is, how many seats had been filled, how many courses given, and how many annual days of training delivered per employee. By moving away from routine activity-based training, CAI was able to install a regimen where each training activity was tested against the value added to customer service.

This shift in the measure of success affected the overall outcome of the transition training project. For example, with the training courses for the new airport reservations systems averaging three weeks each, it was daunting to consider the logistics of training over 4000 agents. With the adoption of the training-for-impact strategy, the task became to identify those competencies that were needed to allow basic operation of the systems, leave out the "nice to know," and ensure employees weren't retrained in skills they already possessed. Each day of unnecessary training saved was equal to savings of 16 person-years of production plus 66 weeks of instructor time—or approximately $850,000.

Planning and executing the change effort at CAI was aided by the overall focus on customers. The focus on internal customers ensured the early and continuous involvement of future trainees. External customer focus provided a guiding hand when the volume and complexity of issues to be resolved became daunting.

Project planning also played a big part. In an organization whose operation is schedule driven, the urge to leap into action—and not be late—is constant. The significant amount of time spent on planning and reviewing the plan for completeness and connectivity to 25 other plans created some frustrations. However, this approach did ensure that the training plan coincided with the overall corporate plan and ongoing operations. The discipline to stick to the plan and a significant change process put a damper on endless requests for individual variations.

CAI has suffered serious financial problems, attributed by some analysts to having maintained unprofitable routes, by others to the aggressive competition of Air Canada, and by still others to the on-again-off-again agreements for cooperation with other airlines. In view of all of these difficulties, it is reasonable to suggest that it is only because of customer loyalty that flowed from CAI's "Service Quality" program that the company was not forced into bankruptcy as early as 1995. ■

Source: Adapted from Rob Muller, "Training for Change," *Canadian Business Review* (Spring 1995): 16, 19; Cecil Footer, "Tough Guys Don't Cuss," *Canadian Business Review* (February 1995): 22-28.

## Planning as a Crucial Management Function

Planning is the part of the management process that attempts to define the organization's future,[1] and influence that future in ways that the managers wish. A good manager has a vision, but that vision is unlikely to be achieved unless it is reflected in sound planning. All organizations operate in uncertain environments, although some are less predictable than others. For an organization to succeed, its managers must find ways to cope with and adapt to change and uncertainty.[2] If managers fail to plan, they will be forced to respond to current pressures rather than be able to achieve the organization's long-range goals. The opening vignette shows how Canadian Airlines International used planning to organize and implement a major training initiative that has had profound impact on the company and its survival.

The approach to planning, the comprehensiveness of plans, and the manner of arriving at them can differ greatly from manager to manager and from organization to organization. This chapter examines planning and its uses for modern organizations, regardless of their type and size. It discusses strategic, operational, and tactical plans, and describes a six-step planning process. The chapter concludes with an overview of several planning methods, some tools used in planning, and applications of planning.

## What Is Planning?

Change is a constant, but as technology expands, the pace of change increases dramatically. Planning can help an organization to be more competitive in this volatile environment. Planning enables a company to respond quickly to changing business demands, market conditions, and customer expectations. To be effective, planning must be flexible and responsive, and should include input from persons at all levels of the organization. Planning is unlikely to be successful if it is totally controlled by a few people at the top of the hierarchy. Nevertheless, planning is unlikely to gain much attention in an organization unless it is initiated by top managers, and then is actively supported at all levels of management.

As noted in Chapter 1, *planning* is the process by which managers examine their internal and external environments, ask fundamental questions about their organization's purpose, formulate a mission statement, and establish goals and objectives. Planning includes all of the activities that lead to the definition of objectives and to the determination of appropriate courses of action to achieve those objectives.

Armand Feigenbaum defined planning as "thinking out in advance the sequence of actions to accomplish a proposed course of action . . . to accomplish certain objectives."[3] Ultimately, the true test of managerial competence is whether the manager is able to achieve results that are aligned with the values and mission of the organization. Planning helps organizations achieve results. Effective planning guides decisions made today so that they can produce useful results at a later date. The planning process must be systematic and dynamic, and must incorporate many variables from the organization's internal and external environments, as well as from its central or core values.

**centralized planning**
A system in which responsibility for planning lies with the organization's highest level, or top management.

### Centralized versus Decentralized Planning

In **centralized planning**, responsibility for planning lies with the highest level of the organization. In the former Soviet Union, the People's Republic of China, and other

## Management in the Real World     4-1

### Information Infrastructure: A New Source of Global Competitive Advantage

For the past decade or so, many political, business, economic, and sociological thinkers have asserted that knowledge and information are becoming the primary resources in the global economy. Across a range of industries from banking and retail to automotive and aerospace, information technology is increasingly instrumental in product development, manufacturing, marketing, sales, and service. The flow of information has become the foundation for improving productivity and increasing innovation in almost every enterprise.

As we enter the twenty-first century, North America has the lead over foreign competitors in computing and communications technologies. But to remain on top, experts argue, it must continue to develop its "information infrastructure." This infrastructure refers to an international system of fibre-optic "information superhighways" that will allow everyone to take advantage of communication and computing technologies. The information infrastructure, used in conjunction with a collection of "information appliances"—tools that will combine computing, communications, and video technologies, for example—will give people ready access to libraries, museums, job information, medical care, and other things. By making information resources readily available and easy to use, the information of the future will revolutionize the ability to access information needed to collaborate and cooperate with others.

How does a nation plan for an information infrastructure? Should Canada adopt a centralized approach (i.e., let government direct it)? Or should the country leave construction of this important new national resource to private interests?

Despite its current lead in computing and communications, many experts believe that North America is lagging behind its trading partners in building an information infrastructure—a failing that could reduce Canada's competitiveness. Corning, the number one maker of optical fibre, estimates that if telephone companies upgrade existing installations at their historical pace, rewiring will take until the year 2037.

Japan, in contrast, has made a national commitment to completing a national fibre network by 2015. Further, government leaders believe the resulting productivity gains will boost Japan's GNP by 30 percent or more. Its information infrastructure is being planned at the federal level.

Germany, France, and Singapore are not far behind in their plans for national information superhighways. These countries are all using centralized planning to direct the construction of their information infrastructure. As Michael Morrison (manager of advanced operations testing at GTE) observed, "These nations see how attracting and keeping companies with telecommunications helps them be competitive."

Foreign competition is forcing Canadian companies to choose between centralized or decentralized planning for their information infrastructure. Choices in the coming years will affect the project's pace and progress for generations. Which way will they choose to go? Will they opt for a mix of government and private industry? Major foreign competitors—Japan, Germany, France, Singapore—have already opted for a centralized approach. Without question, the project's complexity requires long-term planning. The question is, who should do the planning?

Source: Adapted from *Perspectives on the National Information Infrastructure* (New York: January 12, 1993), Computer Systems Policy Project; and Andrew Kupfer, "The Race to Rewire America," *Fortune* (April 19, 1993): 42-61.

countries that have what is known as command economies, this has meant the central government. In an organization, whether large or small, centralized planning would limit involvement in planning to a few top managers. In an organization that is loosely structured, as are many not-for-profit institutions, this means leaving planning by default to a small clique of "insiders." These insiders may operate behind the scenes, and consequently be less accountable than in an organization where the responsibility for planning is clearly lodged in those who are personally identified with planning. It has been suggested that many of the problems discovered in Ontario Hydro's nuclear energy plants stemmed largely from lack of adequate planning and, as a consequence, lack of accountability.

**decentralized planning**
A system in which responsibility for planning lies with employees at several levels of the organization and participation in the planning process is widespread.

By way of contrast, in **decentralized planning,** responsibility for planning is distributed and includes people at all levels of the organization, although overall coordination still rests with top managers.

Many organizations have found that moving from a centralized to a decentralized structure can improve quality, productivity, and competitiveness. A number of speakers at the 1994 convention of the American Production and Inventory Control Society addressed the future of large organizations. Alvin Toffler, author of books such as *Future Shock* and *The Third Wave*, said that large organizations of all types must "de-massify" because they cannot effectively process all of the information available today. To avoid being stifled by rigid bureaucracies (as predicted long ago by Max Weber in his warning about the "iron cage" of bureaucracy), forward-looking corporations are working hard to become more flexible and agile and are responding to changing environments.[4] There have even been whole books written on the theme that the path to success is for the organization to become "nimble," or flexible.[5]

The federal and provincial governments have announced various plans to downsize, which may, to the extent actually implemented, result either in a slowing of the civil service growth or in some cases even in actual reductions in overall numbers. In the process called *devolution*, the federal government passes certain responsibilities to the provincial governments. In turn provincial governments pass certain responsibilities to municipalities. This results in decentralization, because authority for policy decisions will be more widely distributed and there can be less centralized control over those decisions.

Although politically it may be good public relations to decentralize, both in government and in corporations, decentralization has its hazards, and for various reasons is not universally accepted. Of course, resistance may come from some of the individuals who will lose personal power when decision making is decentralized. Individuals with less at stake personally, however, also express more objective reservations. Decentralized planning requires a well-developed communications network so that independent units don't spin out of control.

Equitable Life Insurance Company embarked on a program to decentralize decision making out of head office to operatives in the field. As a result, various field officers took actions that top managers considered to be ill advised and contrary to the company's overall objectives. Reflecting this concern, since taking over as Equitable's chief agency officer, Joe Sequet has made changes that put the home office in more firm control of what happens in the field. Reversing the previous company trend, the changes brought in by Sequet create a more uniform way of recruiting, training, and supervising agents,

*For many decades, banks have been decentralized, such as at this branch, to make it possible for customers to do their banking business close to home. Now, as other industries begin to decentralize for other reasons, banks are considering whether it would be feasible to consolidate some tiny, unprofitable branches and rely ever more on cash machines and electronic banking.*

and provide structure for greater interaction between field management and executives in head office.[6]

Whatever the direction taken by a company, reorganization, and particularly downsizing, creates additional work for managers who must restructure their operations to accommodate the reduced numbers of employees or to reassign tasks and responsibilities as the locus of authority changes. For many managers, however, the greatest stresses that arise from downsizing are the emotional and ethical tensions between their desire to make the organization more efficient and effective (which may be essential to permit it to survive) and their empathy for the personal difficulties created for the individuals who lose their jobs.

Joseph Juran, a writer and speaker who was important in the quality movement of the 1980s and early 1990s, suggests ten objectives of planning. They apply equally to all types and sizes of organization. These ten objectives appear in Exhibit 4-1.

**Exhibit 4-1**

*Juran's Planning Objectives*

1. Build awareness for opportunities to improve quality.
2. Set specific goals for quality improvement.
3. Organize resources to meet the goals.
4. Provide worker training.
5. Conduct projects to solve quality problems.
6. Report on progress towards goals.
7. Give employees recognition.
8. Communicate results.
9. Keep score.
10. Maintain momentum by institutionalizing improvement as part of the regular systems and procedures for the company.

## Why Planning Is Necessary

Planning is central to competitiveness for organizations of all sizes and types. Through planning, an organization links its decision-making process to its fundamental values and mission and establishes its goals and objectives. Planning puts purpose into action. Without planning, organizations can only react after changes have occurred in the environment, in technology, and in customer demands. With careful planning, an organization can both anticipate and influence many upcoming events. In other words, planning may permit an organization to become proactive instead of merely reactive.

Four characteristics of the modern organization underscore the need for planning: (1) pressure to reduce cycle times; (2) increased organizational complexity; (3) increased global competition; and (4) the impact of planning on other management functions.[7] Planning is an effective way that managers can address each of these characteristics.

### Pressure to Reduce Cycle Times

**cycle time reduction (CTR)**
Actions to reduce the time required to complete a process and to be ready to begin the cycle anew.

**Cycle time reduction (CTR)** has become a key goal of organizations. Cycle time refers to the length of time required to complete a process and to be ready to begin another process or a second round of the same process. In a software company, one example of cycle time might be the time required to develop, test, and market a new program. In a fish processing company it might be the time required to unload the catch from fishing vessels and to clean, freeze, and ship the fish. In a not-for-profit hospital, it might be the time required to prepare a patient for discharge, clean and disinfect the room and change the bedding, and assign the space to a new patient. Even in a one-person entrepreneurship, cycle time is important. For example, in a tiny shoe repair shop the proprietor has to assemble materials, repair the customer's shoes, and return them to the customer before receiving pay for the work. If this cycle time is reduced, money is received more quickly, reducing the amount of working capital needed from a bank loan, or in the proprietor's own investment in the business. Not surprisingly, in each of these cases reduced cycle time may enhance customer satisfaction, leading to repeat business or to other forms of tangible support.

*Although Wal-Mart's success is often attributed to economies of scale, its founder, Sam Walton, gives more credit to economies of time.*

**economy of time**
Saving time through reducing lost time, as in having faster inventory turns or quicker turnover of customer seats in a restaurant.

High-performing, competitive organizations have realized that although in the past economy of scale was a key to success, today **economy of time** is the key. Sam Walton, the founder and guiding light of Wal-Mart, said that everyone thought the success of his chain was the result of placing large stores in small towns and superstores in large cities. True, these actions provided some economies of *scale*, but as Walton pointed out, the real key was achieving faster inventory turns, that is, achieving economy of *time*. Like Wal-Mart, organizations of all types are putting significant planning effort into providing faster service to the people who interact with them.[8] These themes will be developed further in Chapter 11.

## Increased Organizational Complexity

As organizations and economies become larger and more complex, so does the manager's job. Few decisions made in one division of an organization—research and development, production, finance, or marketing, for instance—can be made independently of decisions made in other divisions. More products and more services add to the complexity of managing the business. The more markets a company competes in, or the more products it offers, or the more competitors there are in the market, the greater the complexity of both the internal and the external environments. In his book *The Fifth Discipline*, Peter Senge makes the point that to remain competitive in the global economy, organizations must learn to be comfortable with uncertainty and complexity. Managers must develop a capacity for thinking clearly and continuously about the unknown future.[9] Planning helps an organization deal with complexity and uncertainty by providing a road map for change. With this road map an organization can adapt to the forces of competition without making wrong turns and straying off course.

New customers, new markets, and new parts of the world pose both opportunities and competitive threats to a firm. Planning is vital to survival in this expanded marketplace. In the last several years, satellite countries of the former Soviet Union have entered the global economy in a more meaningful way as restrictions have been lifted on trade and transportation. Smaller, dynamic Asian countries such as Hong Kong, South Korea, Singapore, and Taiwan (the so-called *little tigers*, or as they are also called, *little dragons*) have learned to compete vigorously and successfully in worldwide markets. Despite their manifold problems, China, India, Indonesia, Malaysia, possibly Vietnam, and some of the countries of Latin America and Africa may offer similar market opportunities to Canadian organizations and pose major competitive threats in the future.

The more diverse consumer population in Canada also has created new market opportunities. Canadian companies have been able to expand their opportunities by addressing domestic ethnic markets—immigrants from China, India, Pakistan, the Philippines, and the Caribbean islands—and demographic market segments such as single parents, empty-nesters, retirees, and single professionals. This diversity of population also has created a challenge to traditional hiring and managing practices. Companies have had to reexamine and adjust their hiring, managing, and benefits plans.

Global competition is forcing companies to change at an unprecedented rate, becoming more flexible and client-oriented while simultaneously lowering costs.[10] Being able to manage change effectively has become the key to success. Every change represents an opportunity to increase the quality and competitiveness of the company.[11] Planning is the key to ensuring an adequate business response to global competition. This issue will be explored more fully in Chapter 9, which discusses managing change, and in Chapter 14, which explores some of the implications of management in a global economy.

## Impact on Other Management Functions

A large organization consists of many different divisions, departments, and other units. A small organization that does not have these subdivisions still has many of the same internal functions as a larger organization. In either type of organization, all of the functions may be working cooperatively towards common organizational goals and objectives. Regrettably, in some organizations the opposite is true. In those organizations, each unit may single-mindedly pursue its own goals because they seem appropriate for that unit, despite the possibility that they may impede other segments of the same organization. Of course, this internal conflict produces results that are contrary to the goals of the organization as a whole. The result, of course, is that the organization cannot be as effective and competitive as it might have been if all functions and units had subordinated their individual goals to the overall goals. Only when there is comprehensive planning and the results of that planning are communicated to everyone in the organization can individuals know where they fit in the overall scheme of things and how they can best contribute to success.

Thus, it may be seen that both internal and external forces have made planning necessary for the modern organization to become and remain competitive. The next section highlights some specific benefits that may accrue from planning.

## Benefits of Planning

Some specific benefits of planning include (1) coordination of effort, (2) preparation for change, (3) development of performance standards, and (4) development of managers.

### Coordination of Effort

Management exists in organizations because it is necessary to coordinate the work of individuals and groups. Planning is one important technique for coordinating effort. An

## What Managers Are Reading    4-1

### Boom, Bust & Echo 2000: Profiting from the Demographic Shift in the New Millennium

Foot and Stoffman argue that to understand the past and to predict the future it is essential to consider the effects of changes in demography—the study of human populations. The authors then illustrate their point by discussing in specific terms the changes that have occurred already and that they predict will occur because of the changing demographics of the Canadian population. As one of many examples, they cite the fact that according to Statistics Canada participation in tennis by people 18 to 24 is nearly five times that by people 45 to 64. Therefore, it seems a foregone conclusion that as the bulge in population moves up from the younger to the older age ranges, the popularity of tennis will decline, and commercial tennis clubs will have to change their focus to attract a different clientele. The authors also predict that industries that offer less strenuous activities such as cross-country skiing, walking, and gardening have an opportunity to expand in the years up to 2012, when the baby boomers will reach 65.

Looking at another effect of demographic change, the authors discuss the difficulties facing middle managers in corporations, who can no longer expect steady progress up the corporate ladder. They conclude that not only must individuals reshape their thinking, but that organizations must do so as well. As they point out, "Corporations don't grow and develop in isolation from the rest of society." As a result, say Foot and Stoffman, organizations must develop flatter organizational structures and make horizontal mobility more readily available to employees. They stress the value of providing educational and job training opportunities to help prevent employees from feeling stuck in a rut. They also seemingly favour incentive compensation plans, and close coupling of employee growth and reward systems.

Foot and Stoffman examine the changing birth and fertility rates in Canada. Canadian couples are no longer, on average, replacing themselves. This has far-reaching implications for the need for elementary schools, and later for secondary and post-secondary educational institutions. They trace the changing emphases on government funding of the various levels of education and warn that similar mistakes are likely to continue to be made if demographics are disregarded. And they remind readers that every decade has seen an increase in the educational requirements for job entry.

Dispelling a commonly held assumption, the authors point to Statistics Canada figures to support their contention that young people who are now entering the job market are in a more favourable competitive position than their predecessors who are 10 to 15 years older. While this contention may be questioned on the basis of economic conditions, from the standpoint of demographics alone, their view is unassailable.

All organizations, from commercial and industrial behemoths to hospitals, educational institutions, government agencies, and the smallest of entrepreneurial enterprises, should consider demographic predictions when planning or they will be caught by surprise and suffer in the competitive race.

Source: David K. Foot, with Daniel Stoffman, *Boom, Bust & Echo 2000: Profiting from the Demographic Shift in the New Millennium* (Toronto: Macfarlane Walter & Ross, 1998).

effective plan specifies goals and objectives both for the total organization and for each of its parts. By working towards planned objectives, each part contributes to and is compatible with the entire organization's goals.

## Preparation for Change

An effective plan of action allows room for change. The longer the time between completion of a plan and when the objective is expected to be met, the greater the necessity to include contingency plans that permit flexibility to adapt to unforeseen changes in the environment. If the plan helps managers to foresee the potential effects of the change, they can be better prepared to deal with it. History provides vivid examples of what can result from failure to prepare for change. The collapse of many property development companies, junior mining companies, and regional airlines in the past few years was due in large part to lack of preparedness, that is, faulty planning on the part of the managers, and to an inability to become and remain competitive.

## Development of Performance Standards

Plans define expected behaviours. In management terms, expected behaviours are **performance standards**. As plans are implemented throughout an organization, the objectives and courses of action assigned to each individual and group are the bases for standards and provide benchmarks for evaluating actual performance.

A slightly different approach to planning is to define the *competencies* required for each job, instead of establishing performance standards. The competencies are the things that the worker must be able to do, or must be able to learn to do. These job-specific competencies then form the basis for screening, hiring, training, and establishing compensation for employees. This approach requires that managers:

1. Define the mission for each job;
2. Describe the major outcomes required to achieve the mission;
3. Define performance standards for each major outcome;
4. Identify known barriers to achieving the performance standards;
5. Determine which barriers will be best overcome by training the worker; and
6. Design and deliver appropriate training.[12]

Through planning, management derives a basis for developing performance standards or competencies based on organizational goals and objectives. Without planning, performance standards are difficult to define, and the standards that are developed may be in conflict with the organization's values and mission.

## Development of Managers

Planning is intellectually demanding. Those who plan must be able to deal with abstract ideas and information that is usually incomplete and often unreliable. These ideas must be juggled in a variety of ways to produce a range of *what if* questions. Addressing these questions helps managers to be prepared if any of the scenarios come to pass.

Planning also involves managers in concrete action. Through planning, the organization's future can be enhanced if its managers take an active role in moving the organization towards that future. Thus, planning implies that effective managers will be proactive and *make* things happen, rather than reactive and *let* things happen.

Through planning, not only do managers develop their ability to think about what may occur in the future, but also, to the extent that their plans lead to effective actions, their motivation to plan is reinforced. Thus, both the results and the act of planning benefit not only the organization but also its managers personally in meeting their career goals.

Finally, every organization that intends to remain competitive for more than a brief period constantly must develop its managers. In Chapter 8, which discusses human resource management, it is emphasized that it is desirable to establish career paths for promising managers, to provide for orderly succession as older managers leave or retire, and to keep managers motivated and enthusiastic. Organizational planning is a key ingredient for career planning and development of managers. If the organization is not clear about where it is going, there is little point in trying to plan where its managers' paths might lead.

## Types of Planning

**scope**
In planning, the range of activities covered by a plan.

**time frame**
The period of time covered.

**level of detail**
The degree of specificity.

Planning activities differ in scope, time frame, and level of detail. **Scope** refers to the range of activities covered by the plan. **Time frame** is the period covered by the plan, ranging from the immediate short term to the future longer term. **Level of detail** concerns the degree to which the plan is specific. All plans must be specific enough to direct actual decisions, but multiple contingencies and uncertainties in the future require that some plans be more flexible than others. For example, plans for a mineral exploration company, which must adapt actions frequently to reflect ever-evolving discoveries and disappointments, will need to be more flexible than those for a building contractor's production schedule for the coming month, where construction plans are explicit and subject to fewer surprises.

### Strategic Planning

**strategic planning**
Comprehensive, long-range planning, focusing on broad, enduring issues to increase the organization's effectiveness.

The broadest form of planning is at the strategic level. It is comprehensive, long-term, and relatively general. Strategic plans focus on the broad, enduring issues for ensuring the organization's effectiveness and survival over many years. A strategic plan typically states the organization's mission and describes a set of goals to guide the organization as it moves into the future. For example, a company's strategic plan might state that its mission is to be pre-eminent in marketing a particular class of products throughout the Atlantic provinces. It would set goals to establish outlets, city by city, based on targeted consumer research and development. Equally valid, Foster Parents Plan of Canada might articulate its mission as alleviating poverty in less-developed countries by assisting with the education of children and by teaching women the essentials of family hygiene and how to market their craft products. For a small business, such as a local Ukrainian restaurant, the strategic plan might describe the mission of developing and promoting a wider variety of food and set a goal to test customer acceptance of three different kinds of kielbasa.

**price penetration strategy**
The strategy of setting low prices to create a mass market rapidly.

**Price penetration strategy.** Whether the organization furnishes a product or a service, an important aspect of strategic planning is to choose the approach it will take to its pricing and marketing functions. At least three possible approaches may be taken. The one that comes quickest to mind is generally known as *cost leadership* or **price penetration strategy**. This strategy reflects a plan to market a product or service at a lower price than the competition. For the company to cover its costs, the lower prices usually will require a large volume of sales to make up for the low profit margin per unit. Unfortunately, in order to keep costs down, the quality of the product or service may have to be sacrificed. If large sales volumes can be maintained, the price differential may be sufficient for customers to overlook the lower quality. Discount consumer chains such as Zellers, Costco, and Wal-Mart have shown that in the absence of direct competition within their respective niches, they can generate the necessary high volumes by appealing to a mass market of cost-conscious customers. However, when new entrepreneurs choose this strategy, as they often do, they frequently find that they cannot build the large volumes necessary in time to survive the low profit margins.

*Owning a well-recognized status symbol such as Callaway golf clubs justifies the application of prestige pricing.*

**prestige strategy**
The strategy of setting high prices relative to the competition on the basis of high quality or an unusually attractive image in the market.

**skimming strategy**
The strategy of setting a high price when a product is new and before competitors enter the market, with the realization that the high price will attract competitors, and that when they enter the market the price will have to be lowered.

**niche strategy**
The strategy of finding a unique characteristic such as design, form and speed of service, or attractiveness to a particular segment of the market.

### Prestige strategy.

The second pricing and marketing approach is variously known as the differentiation or the **prestige strategy**. It is the exact opposite of the cost leadership or price penetration strategy. Using the prestige strategy, a company deliberately sets prices higher than those of its competitors. Obviously, in order to attract customers at the higher prices, the company must provide some compensating features. One feature may be superior quality, recognizable by customers as exceeding that offered by lower-priced competitors. Another feature may be prestige, such that customers are willing to pay a premium to be seen driving, wearing, or using the well-known and respected name brand. For example, the Rolls Royce is priced so far above a mass-produced consumer automobile that it must offer something special to justify the price differential. It is generally acknowledged to be of superior quality, but that is not all. The Bentley, which is made in the same factories as the Rolls to the same exhaustive standards, costs tens of thousands of dollars less and looks almost identical to the Rolls, except for its hood ornament and hubcaps. But the Rolls sells at the higher price because most customers would rather pay more to be able to drive the Rolls, with its *reputation* for luxury, than the Bentley, which is less well known and has less prestige.

When one thinks of prestige, one does not immediately think of T-shirts and sweatshirts, but Club Monaco has successfully used the prestige strategy in pricing their garments. The clothing is of reasonable quality, but probably no better than some less expensive brands. The difference, however, is that the Club Monaco name is widely known and has an appeal that causes some customers to be willing to pay the premium price in order to be seen wearing the name.

### Skimming strategy.

The third major approach to pricing strategy is called **skimming strategy**. This strategy is particularly applicable to a new product that may catch on as a fad, but it can be used with any new product or service. Applying this strategy, an organization plans to deluge the market with the product or service before competitors enter the market. Usually a massive advertising campaign is required to inform potential buyers that the product or service is available and to attract their interest. The organization sets prices that are considerably higher than cost, so the promoters who are first on the scene can benefit from a generous markup and profit margin. It is understood that unless there are patents or other forms of protection, the initial high prices will quickly attract competitors, so that the high prices cannot be maintained after the first rush of sales. The basic strategy is to make large profits quickly and then either settle for much lower margins or abandon the market entirely.

### Niche strategy.

Whichever form of pricing strategy an organization chooses for a particular product or service, it must be done with a view to the **niche** that it intends to fill. In initiating a new product or service, the first question the manager must ask is "Why will customers buy from us rather than from other suppliers from which they are already buying? If they are not now buying the product, what will cause them to start doing so?" To be successful, the company must offer a unique product or service—one that is not readily available or one that is better, more attractive, easier to use, less expensive, or in some other way convinces the customer that it is an improvement over what is already available. Decades ago, when PaperMate first offered the ballpoint pen, it was a marked improvement over the fountain pen, with its potential for leaking ink. PaperMate created a highly successful niche. It could charge a premium price for this unique product (that is, employing the skimming strategy). Then Bic started offering an inexpensive throwaway pen that constituted a different niche and greatly diminished the attractiveness of PaperMate's niche. Now, with countless competitors offering all kinds, shapes, and designs of ballpoint pens, both PaperMate and Bic have lost their exclusive niches and are facing broader competition. At this stage of the history of ballpoint pens, neither company has an exclusive niche, and neither could succeed with a skimming strategy.

The niche strategy is applicable not only to products but to organizations that provide services. Organizations that usually are not seen as businesses also must consider niches and pricing strategy. A community centre must decide how much to charge users for its services. If it has a special niche—because it offers facilities not available elsewhere or it does so in a different location—it still must decide how high prices can go without deterring people from using the services. At the other end of the equation, if the centre does not take in enough revenue, it will have to restrict services or perhaps eventually close its doors. Thus, it may be seen that almost any type of organization, whether organized for profit or not, must be sensitive to pricing issues and must establish its own niche.

Whichever of these strategies or whatever combination of them an organization chooses, strategic planning helps to identify the components and to focus efforts on making the plan successful.

## Operational Planning

Planning at the operational level is relatively short-term and specific. Operational planning shapes the day-to-day operations of the organization, reflecting overall strategies and goals. It translates the broad concepts of the strategic plan into clear numbers, specific steps, and measurable objectives for the short term. **Operational planning** includes the efficient, cost-effective application of resources to solving problems and meeting objectives.

## Tactical Planning

**Tactical planning** falls on the continuum between strategic planning and operational planning. It is narrower, shorter-term, and more specific than strategic planning and broader, longer-term, and more general than operational planning. Tactics usually deal more with issues of efficiency than with long-term effectiveness.

The type of planning process followed is determined by the goals and objectives to be achieved by the plan. Broad, long-term goals require strategic planning, while short-term, narrower objectives demand tactical and operational planning.

## Single-use and Standing Plans

A **single-use plan** has a relatively narrow scope and goals and a clear time frame. An example would be a plan to develop a new product or accomplish a specific project such as furnishing a new college building or hotel. This single-use plan will no longer be needed once the product has been developed or the project has been completed. In contrast, a **standing plan** has ongoing meaning and application. It constitutes the framework within which goals and objectives are formulated, and in a sense it defines the organization. In the history of the development of a product, a single-use plan is designed to take the product from the idea stage to actual production. Then that plan is no longer relevant and must be replaced by a standing plan. The standing plan covers the promotion,

**operational planning** Short-term, focused, specific planning that provides direction for implementing the organization's broad concepts in the strategic plan into clear objectives for operations.

**tactical planning** Planning that is more specific and for a shorter period than strategic planning but less specific and for a longer period than operational planning.

**single-use plan** A plan for a defined project or purpose that will exist for a short period and become redundant when the project is completed or the purpose is fulfilled.

**standing plan** A plan intended to have ongoing meaning and to be applied in an organization for a significant period.

## Success with a Niche Strategy

As the Great Depression was drawing to a close in the late 1930s, Edward B. Ratcliffe, Jr., with the help of scholarships and his own summer earnings, managed to scrape together enough money to enrol in the chemical engineering department of the University of Toronto. After graduating in 1941 he worked for others for five years, first at Welland Chemical, and then at DuPont Canada. At DuPont he observed and became interested in the effect of enlightened personnel policies on an organization, which was later a positive factor as he built his own business. Then his father died of a heart attack and left a small home-building company leaderless. Ratcliffe saw it as an opportunity to own, manage, and work in a small company. A significant event in his career was the decision to add stone to the building materials the company was using. However, he was not satisfied with the quality and appearance of the stone or artificial stone that could be bought in Ontario.

In 1949, stretching his available capital to the limit, Ratcliffe built a small plant in Hamilton and began developing the building material that become known as Angelstone throughout central and eastern Canada. In 1952 Ratcliffe put three sales representatives on the road, and sales burgeoned so that the plant had to operate on three shifts. In 1957, aided by loans from banks and the government, he established a sophisticated and expensive manufacturing plant in Cambridge, Ontario, which is still the company's central facility, now called Arriscraft International. In 1990 Arriscraft constructed a second manufacturing facility in Trois Rivières, Quebec. After having made several unsuccessful attempts to find and operate quarries, the company finally purchased and now successfully operates a marble quarry near Hope Bay, Ontario. Several years of experimentation and innovation have led to the development of a product that is no longer "artificial stone" but superior in durability, strength, workability, and appearance to both natural stone and the "artificial stone" that some competitors were offering to the construction industry. The ultimate product, made of fine silica sand, limestone, and several proprietary ingredients, is formulated under a proprietary process that requires extremely high pressure (1000 tonnes of force) and carefully controlled temperatures. Colour is blended directly into the formulation, and there is no need for any waterproofing treatment.

Success did not come easily or quickly. By working long hours, dedicating all efforts to the company's purposes, and concentrating on both quality and customer service, Edward Ratcliffe's Arriscraft International has achieved worldwide recognition and financial stability. Generous profit-sharing plans and humane treatment of employees have created a loyal workforce. Now celebrating its fiftieth anniversary, to date Arriscraft has manufactured and shipped more than eight million tonnes of their products. They have provided the material for the exteriors of such prestigious structures as the Canadian Embassy in Washington, D.C., the Convention Centre in London, Ontario, the Santirario del Valle in Santiago, Chile, the new Unitarian Church in Montreal, and the new Republic of Korea Embassy in Ottawa. Award-winning architects, such as Arthur Erickson, Douglas Cardinal, Smit & Diamond, and many others, choose Arriscraft's products over those offered by many eager competitors. Reflecting the financial success of the enterprise, Edward Ratcliffe, his wife, Elinor, and a foundation they established for Arriscraft generously support a large number of charities worldwide.

Randy White, a 20-year veteran with the company and now its president, attributes Arriscraft's growth and success to the fact that the founder "… knew his markets, understood and respected his customers, and knew the real costs and margins." In recalling his half-century of experience with Arriscraft, Ratcliffe muses that "we did not fall for the latest fads in business management." Instead, in the words of Randy White, "they operated around sound economic and business principles, knowing that if a decision made sense, even though it might be costly today, it would pay off in the long run." As in all successful planning, the company principals

*Continued*

based their thinking on what they knew about the past and present, and accurately forecast the future.

Arriscraft and its principals are classic examples of entrepreneurs/managers who identify a niche in the market and then work hard to find ways to fill that niche. Applying sound business principles and the highest of ethics, functioning in socially responsible ways, and staying within their chosen niche, they have achieved what many managers only dream of—creating a successful, respected, and forward-looking organization. Because of the quality of their planning, there is every indication that Arriscaft International can look forward one day to celebrating its one-hundredth anniversary.

---

Adapted from conversations with Edward and Elinor Ratcliffe and Randy White, December 1998 to May 1999.

marketing, and continuing production of the product—all of which are activities that will continue throughout the life of the product, although they often will be modified as time goes on.

## Steps in the Planning Process

The planning process, regardless of which type it is, resembles the decision-making process described in Chapter 3. This is not surprising, since planning is basically a specialized application of the decision-making process. Planning usually consists of six steps: (1) assessing the organization's environments; (2) deciding on a mission statement and establishing goals and objectives; (3) creating an action plan; (4) allocating resources; (5) implementing the plan; and (6) monitoring, controlling, and providing feedback (see Exhibit 4-2). Each step will be discussed in turn. At every step, those involved in planning must keep in mind that their purposes can be summarized in two questions:

1. What do we want the future to be?
2. What must we do now to increase the chance that this desired future will be achieved?

### Step 1: Assessing the Organization's Environments

This preliminary step covers all of the organization's environments—internal as well as external. A systemic situation analysis requires attention to four environmental

**Exhibit 4-2** *Steps in the Planning Process*

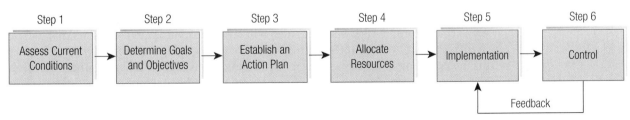

elements: internal *strengths* and *weaknesses*, and external *opportunities* and *threats*. The process of assessing these four elements is often referred to as a *SWOT analysis*, from the initial letters of these four elements.[13] Internal strengths and weaknesses may be found in financial, human, physical, and other resources. These resources might include strengths such as having a positive organizational culture, a loyal customer base, strong financing, or a desirable location. Specific weaknesses might be limitations from inadequate physical or equipment facilities, severe labour problems, or a shortage of finances. Financial strengths and weaknesses are relatively easy to assess; human resource assessment involves many intangibles and issues of judgement.

External *opportunities* include any factors that have the potential to increase the organization's strengths. These might include the potential for new products or for new markets because of a reduction in trade barriers, the departure of a competitor, or the discovery of a market that is not well served. A *threat* is anything that has the potential to hurt or destroy the company. One threat might be a damaging change in tax laws. Another could be an unanticipated increase in costs of supplies or production. Still another could be the entry into the market of a strong competitor, as Zellers experienced when Wal-Mart opened stores within what had been Zellers' niches.

Change is almost the only constant in modern societies. Strategic planners must be able to identify and predict changing social and cultural conditions that will have an impact on the organization. The transition of the *baby boomers* to the *empty nesters* has profound implications for any Canadian business, as does the rapidly increasing population of seniors. John Naisbitt and Patricia Aburdene's popular book *Megatrends 2000*[14] identifies ten megatrends that will be influential as Canada enters the twenty-first century. Four of these megatrends are sociocultural: global lifestyles, cultural nationalism, religious revival, and the rise of women in leadership positions. One can argue that the pace of any of these four changes is too fast or too slow, but one cannot escape the fact that they are having and will continue to have profound influences on the environments in which organizations function.

*Technological innovation* is creating whole new industries. Who would have dreamed of the growth of the computer industry when Chairman Thomas Watson of IBM first thought of converting mechanical bookkeeping machines into record-keeping machines for the New York Public Library? In 1949 *Popular Mechanics* forecast the relentless march of science, predicting that computers would continue to become more efficient so that "… in the future computers may weigh no more than 1.5 tons." It is safe to say that the author of that prediction did not foresee the development of the desktop computer, not to mention the notebook or palmtop computer! In the 1920s David Sarnoff tried to convince his associates to make an investment in the development of radio broadcasting. Their response was, "The wireless music box has no commercial value. Who would pay for a message sent to nobody in particular?"[15] Since these and other equally wrong forecasts were made, electronic banking has reduced costs for financial institutions and offered convenience to customers, and broadcasting has become one of North America's largest and most lucrative industries. Clearly, science, technology, and innovation will continue to be compelling factors for change, and managers must heed these changes and include them in their planning.

In the next few years the economy will be increasingly global and business will be increasingly competitive. These changes will create economic environments that will be more complex and more difficult to predict. Technological innovations have their impact on the economy as money managers communicate with each other around the world, and money is transferred instantaneously to take advantage of slight differences in interest rates and demands for money in the different financial markets. The coming

*Changes in the economy have encouraged organizations to flatten their structures, causing many people to seek employment elsewhere.*

shortages of food in China will affect wheat prices in Canada.[16] The frequent flare-ups in the Middle East will influence availability and cost of petroleum products. Any recession in Canada will affect competition, wages, and consumer buying decisions.

The *political climate* is still influenced by "little" wars that have been endemic for generations, even though the countries of the industrialized world have avoided "major" wars for more than half a century. On the other hand, with increased globalization these sporadic local conflicts will affect sources of supply, transportation, and world tensions. Any disruptive change in the government of a country, such as occurred twice in Chile more than two decades ago, will have material effects on Canadian companies interested in developing natural resources in that country.

These and many other manifestations of change have to be taken into account by managers seeking to initiate effective planning.

## Step 2: Deciding on a Mission Statement and Establishing Goals and Objectives

Every organization should have a vision—a positive view of the future. This vision must then be reflected in a mission statement to initiate the planning process. An organization's mission is its reason for existing, and reflects the vision of those who are guiding it. While a strategy addresses ongoing goals, objectives, and practices, the organization's **mission statement** describes its fundamental rationale for existence. Without a sense of mission, the organization's efforts become diffuse and unfocused. As a cynical pundit has observed, "If you don't know where you're going, any route is as good as any other." No organization can afford to be wandering on routes that lead nowhere. A mission statement helps to avoid this aimlessness. It also helps managers, other employees, suppliers, customers, the general public, and government officials to know what the organization is about and what it intends to accomplish.

**mission statement**
A statement of the organization's purpose and intentions, its long-term vision, that distinguishes it from other organizations.

There are rather indeterminate dividing lines between a mission statement and a set of goals, and between goals and objectives. In general, however, in the progression from mission to goals to objectives, the time lines get shorter, the elements become more easily measurable, and the details become more specific.

It is essential for a mission statement to be customer focused. The business that does not keep its customers constantly in mind is doomed to ultimate, and perhaps even prompt, demise. Successful businesses formulate mission statements and strategies on the premise that customer satisfaction and, better yet, customer delight and loyalty are necessary for enduring success. It is far less expensive, and more certain, to *keep* a customer than to *attract* a new one to replace a dissatisfied customer. As Deming notes, "[N]o one can guess the future loss of business from a dissatisfied customer."[17]

For a business organization, the customer is, of course, the person who buys the product or service being offered. For a non-profit organization, identifying the customer is more difficult. For example, for an educational institution the customer that comes immediately to mind is the student. But the institution has other customers as well. One is the arm of government that provides most of the institution's funding. Another is the future employer of the institution's graduates. Still another might be the donor of a building or operating funds that help to keep tuition from rising at quite such a rapid pace. Sometimes, actions taken to satisfy one customer may alienate another. Similar dilemmas face the managers of almost any non-profit organization. It is a challenge for the managers of an institution to identify clearly the individuals and groups that constitute its customers. It is even more challenging to balance the needs and expectations of different classes of customers and arrive at reasonable compromises.

The mission statement must state aspirations that are achievable. It hardly would be useful for an auto body shop based in St. John's, Toronto, or Winnipeg to define its mission as acquiring the contract for maintenance of Pacific Coast Lines buses in British Columbia. A less obvious weakness that is revealed in some mission statements is that of the diversified organization that decides to acquire a large number of businesses to expand into several different industry fields at once. As a paper by a respected business research centre reported, "The greater the number of industries in which the parent firm operated, the lower the productivity, and thus the profitability of plants."[18]

**Exhibit 4-3**

*Examples of Mission Statements from Three Canadian Corporations*

**Abitibi Consolidated**

Our vision is to be the world's preferred marketer and manufacturer of papers for communication.

**Canadian Western Bank**

Mission: To provide competitive full service consumer and commercial banking to Western Canadians. In doing so we aim to provide our shareholders with a sound and profitable return on their investment.

**Canada Trust**

Mission: To be the best Personal Financial Services Company.

A mission statement should serve as a source of motivation at all levels. If it is to be successful, a mission statement should have meaning to every manager and non-managerial employee. It should allow each worker to translate the mission statement's words into their own motivation, and to serve as a guide for decisions and actions. Philip Crosby describes what he calls the "three phases involved in getting an organization or a person to be productive in the very best meaning of the word: *conviction, commitment* and *conversion.*"[19] Conviction means that the employee is dedicated to the idea. Commitment is the behavioural expression of the psychological conviction. Conversion means that the employee has rejected outdated, noncompetitive notions of success.

Finally, the mission statement should describe strategies that are *specific*. It must be clear enough to allow employees and customers to know in what business the company operates, as well as in what businesses it does not. Generalized "motherhood" statements (for instance, "to provide the highest quality for the lowest price") do not make a useful mission statement. By attempting to be all things to all people, a company's energy is scattered, making it less able to develop distinctive competence and making it nearly impossible to please anyone.

The three corporate mission statements shown in Exhibit 4-3 illustrate how three different corporations have elected to state their missions. Abitibi Consolidated packs a lot of information into one sentence. It refers to its manufacturing and marketing, to worldwide markets, and to a specific category of paper products. Canadian Western Bank uses two sentences to state its aim for full service banking, consumer and commercial customers, and sound profits for shareholders. Canada Trust, by way of contrast, uses a phrase that has little firm direction, but in its financial report, from which the statement is taken, the concepts are amplified.

**goal**
Specific achievements that the organization intends to accomplish, based on its mission statement.

A mission statement must be particularized into meaningful **goals** that specify in concrete detail the organization's long-term aspirations. These are the specific results that exemplify the organization's mission. Goals define what the organization seeks to accomplish. Effective goals are capable of being converted into precise actions and shorter-term objectives. Goals facilitate management control and serve as standards against which performance will be measured. They provide precise and measurable targets and time spans in which each target is to be achieved. The most useful goals include intermediate goals that permit early identification if overall goals are not likely to be met. Equally important, but easily overlooked, intermediate goals also provide warnings if overall goals are likely to be exceeded, and thus require allocation of additional resources.

**Exhibit 4-4**

*Examples of Statements of Goals for Two Canadian Corporations*

---

**Scotiabank**

Scotiabank's goal is to be Canada's best and most successful financial services company. We will achieve this by focusing on our core strengths: diversification, risk management, productivity, customer satisfaction and our Scotiabank team.

**Scott Restaurant**

1998 Objectives: We will maintain operating earnings at 1997 levels. We will maintain cash flow at 1997 levels. We will improve Customer Service Index ratings by 2%. We will increase same-store sales at KFC restaurants by 2%. We will increase overall Travel Centre sales by 9%.

The statements of goals shown in Exhibit 4-4 illustrate two approaches. Scotiabank's statement appears to be designed primarily for external consumption, explaining to current and potential shareholders what the company is about, much in the nature of a mission statement. Scott Restaurant's statement, by way of contrast, is specific both as to numeric values and as to the time within which those figures are expected to be achieved. It can be seen that there may be considerable variation from organization to organization. Each statement reflects the culture of the organization, its approach, perhaps the industry in which it operates, and most of all, the audience to which the statement is directed.

The terms *goal* and *objective* are often used almost interchangeably, so it is not always clear which is being named. In this text, however, the two will be distinguished. **Objectives** relate to a term that is shorter than that of mission statements or goals. Objectives are measurable targets that are to be achieved to accomplish organizational goals. The interaction between goals and objectives is illustrated by a company that now operates in Montreal and sets a goal to operate nationwide within ten years. An objective might be to open sales offices the following year in Halifax and Toronto. The next objective towards this goal might be to expand operations in these two centres by stated percentages, and to open yet another office in Calgary. Thus, just as goals are derived from the organization's mission, objectives quantify the goals. Objectives must be relevant, focused, timed, and somewhat challenging to managers and other employees. The ideal objective is one that requires effort, but that those working towards it can see is fair and reasonable. An objective that can be achieved easily will stifle motivation but one that is almost impossible to achieve will also stifle motivation, so a middle ground must be found, and built into the statement of objectives.

**Priority of objectives.**  An organization is likely to have multiple goals and objectives that contribute to its mission and that recognize some of the interests of different stakeholders, including suppliers, customers, employees, investors, and the public.[20] For instance, a business must balance the objective of increasing wage levels on the one hand, and increasing service to customers, decreasing prices, or increasing dividends to shareholders on the other hand. These objectives may not be in conflict if higher wages make it possible to recruit more productive employees, but that is a judgement call that will require careful consideration.

Managers of non-business organizations likewise are faced with ranking seemingly interdependent but competing objectives.[21] For example, managers of a teaching hospital have to decide whether to allocate more of their scarce resources to trauma wards, acute care, long-term care, or palliative measures. The decisions made will determine, perhaps for a long time, not only the shape of the institution but also the extent to which it will garner and keep public support.

**Conflicts among objectives and setting priorities.**  The process of establishing objectives and setting priorities must not overlook any of the organization's stakeholders, and plans must accommodate their interests to the extent feasible. If customers are not happy with the company's products or services, they will stop buying them. If the company has decided to conserve cash by deferring payments to suppliers, those suppliers may cut off credit or refuse to ship supplies. If employees are dissatisfied, labour strife may erupt and, at the very least, morale and productivity will plummet. Government officials often have considerable latitude in their enforcement practices; if they gain the impression that a company is evading regulations, they may redouble their enforcement efforts and decline to give the company the benefit of doubt, which they might otherwise have done.

**objective**
Detailed steps that the organization intends to take in achieving its goals, stated in specific terms and accompanied by the dates on which each step is to be commenced and completed.

Often a company's future depends on satisfying some or all of these stakeholders, while remaining competitive.[22]

Studies of organizations' objectives confirm the difficulty of balancing the concerns of interest groups. These studies also suggest that the more successful companies consistently emphasize profit-seeking activities that maximize shareholder return, while providing reasonable satisfaction to its other constituents. This is not to say that successful companies seek *only* profit-oriented objectives, but rather that such objectives are dominant.[23] Chapter 2 discusses ethics and issues of social responsibility relating to actions that reflect organizational objectives.

The weight to be given to the views of any particular interest group is a matter of managerial judgement. Managers often have to decide between pairs of alternatives such as those in the following list.

1. Short-term profits versus long-term growth;
2. Profit margin versus competitive position;
3. Direct immediate sales effort versus development effort;
4. Greater penetration of present markets versus development of new markets;
5. Achieving long-term growth through related businesses versus achieving it through unrelated businesses;
6. Profit objectives versus non-profit objectives (that is, social responsibilities);
7. Growth versus stability; and
8. Low-risk environment versus high-risk environment.

**Measuring objectives.** Objectives must be clear, achievable, and measurable to be effective. A number of measurements are available to quantify objectives in some of the general areas of business.

**Profitability objectives.** This type of objective is designed to evaluate return on invested capital in order to attract funds required for innovation and possible future expansion. To illustrate, few prudent investors would invest funds in a company whose return on investment is expected to be less than interest on a savings account or on Canada Savings Bonds. It would be absurd for the investor to assume the risks of failure that are inherent in any business, unless there was a potential reward that exceeds what might be gained from an equal investment guaranteed by a bank or a government.

Stock markets tend to react to even slight changes in profit from one quarter to the next. As a consequence, managers are under strong pressure to emphasize short-term profit figures to the exclusion of other indicators that may be more meaningful as management tools. For management purposes, three standardized ratios are more indicative of financial health or weakness in the organization. The ratio of profit to sales reflects the effectiveness of the price strategies being applied. By comparing this ratio with that of other organizations in the same field, it may help to measure efficiency. The ratios of net profit to total assets or of net profit to fixed assets are indicators of how effectively the facilities and equipment are being used. The ratio of net profit to net worth or capital indicates the rate of return being experienced by the investors and other owners. These measures are not mutually exclusive. All three ratios may be specified as profitability objectives because each measures, and therefore evaluates, different yet important aspects of profitability.

**Marketing objectives.** Marketing objectives measure performance relative to products, markets, distribution, and customer service. They focus on prospects for long-term profitability. Thus, well-managed organizations measure performance in areas such as market share, sales volume, number of outlets carrying the product, number of new products developed, and number and desirability of customers.

Although the terminology may sound as if these concepts were related solely to businesses that are organized for profit, the same objectives are relevant in non-profit organizations and government agencies. No charitable enterprise or government would survive for long if it continually disregarded the interests of its customers as reflected in participation or support levels.

## Planning: Reflections by Philip Crosby

Those who plan for something to happen inside an organization sometimes become so involved in the process and mechanics of creating a plan that they forget the obvious, and the results they obtain are not what they had hoped for. The obvious is that no plan works unless those who have to execute it understand their personal roles, and have had an opportunity to contribute some information to the creation of the plan. Simply, if plan requirements are not understood in detail, they can never be accomplished properly.

Elaborate computer-driven planning and control systems, such as PERT, have been created over the years in an attempt to make plans more comprehensive. Many companies now have planning departments that plaster the walls with diagrams and issue hourly status reports. But these approaches are often much like taking a physical several times a day rather than learning how to prevent illness. Prevention consists of taking actions that head off difficulty, rather than learning how to identify and treat it.

Recently I was involved in a video project in which we were planning to create a dozen sessions, each complementary to the others. We planned to market them through national advertising and allow people to call an "800" number and order the product with a credit card. We resolved that we were going to use the project as an example of how to plan something so that each and every action was completed according to requirements the first time. There would be no wasted effort or money.

Rather than lay everything out on some process plan with a lot of arrows and diagrams we decided to bring the people involved together before any funds were expended. First we wrote a two-page description of the project, complete with the dates we would like to have it on the market. Then we invited the video producer, the advertising agency, the fulfilment house, the public relations person, the accounting firm, the members of Career IV staff who would be involved, and the studio people.

In an hour-long meeting, with plenty of time allotted, we laid out the project as we saw it and obtained agreement on the various completion dates. Each attendee was asked to think through their operation over the interval before the next meeting and return with suggestions and questions. We went around the room making certain we worked out the implementation details and wrote them carefully into a plan.

A great many preventive and money-saving actions came out of that meeting. For instance, the studio people said that they could take my computer disk containing the scripts and transmit them directly to the teleprompters. We also would be able to make changes easily at their terminal. The advertising people learned that the box they had designed was not the best size for processing and packaging. The fulfilment people suggested that we hire a company of handicapped workers to do the packaging.

The result was a plan everyone understood, with clear and measurable requirements that everyone agreed to meet, and a completely hassle-free execution. The participants subsequently knew each other well enough to deal directly with one another when they had questions. Nothing had to be done over, except for a few takes during the video shoot.

Quality, after all, means conformance to the agreed requirements.

**Productivity objectives.** Productivity objectives are based on the ratio of output to input. This ratio effectively tells how much value is added to the product or item as the company or department of a company works on it.[24] Other factors being equal, the higher the ratio, the more efficient is the use of inputs. If the amount of value added in a step in the process is greater than the total cost attributable to that step, the step is contributing to the profit of the company. A decline in this ratio for a particular step in the process, or worse, for the whole company, is a cause for managerial concern. Thus, by setting objectives that reflect productivity ratios, managers are able to monitor activities and take corrective action before the decline becomes too pronounced to be reversed.

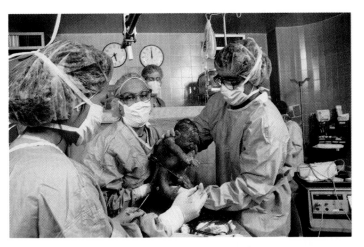

*Unlike their counterparts in business, managers of not-for-profit organizations do not have a financial bottom line to measure success, so they must seek other less tangible evaluative measures.*

Managers of non-profit organizations have a difficult time setting productivity objectives. A hospital might be measuring the wrong things, and encouraging disregard of more important matters, if it evaluated its productivity in terms of how quickly a surgical team could do a triple heart bypass, for example. It can, however, pay attention to how long it takes to make an operating room available for the next scheduled operation, or to the time required to launder bed linens and get them back in use. An educational institution would be misleading itself if it measured productivity in terms of how many students receive an A. Instead, it can monitor student retention and the number of graduates who are employed in their chosen fields or who go on to further education. Like most productivity measures, these factors are not enough to measure management effectiveness, but any change in them should alert managers to seek reasons for the change and assess its implications.

**Financial objectives.** Objectives also can be set for financial measures such as current ratio, working capital turnover, debt/equity ratio, inventory turnover, and aging of accounts receivable. Like other objectives, these help to evaluate performance and to predict and plan financial requirements. Financial objectives and profitability objectives will be expanded on in Chapter 11 in the discussion of managing operations.

**Quality objectives.** As Philip Crosby has pointed out elsewhere in this book, quality of performance is becoming increasingly important to establish and maintain competitiveness. Many objectives based on quality of product are readily measurable. They include statistics such as the proportion of spoiled or rejected items, the value of other forms of wastage, and failures to meet technical specifications. Objectives based on quality of service are often difficult to state in measurable terms, because there are no precise measures of customer satisfaction. Statistics such as the number of customer complaints may reveal long-term trends, but even this measure is imprecise, given that studies have shown that only 1 in perhaps 20 dissatisfied customers will communicate dissatisfaction to the organization. Instead, customers just take their business elsewhere, and the company never becomes aware of having failed to meet the customers' expectations.

Service quality measures must be stated in rather generalized terms, but nonetheless they are just as important for a service company as the more precise measures of

**Exhibit 4-5**

*Measures of Service Quality Objectives*

| Concept | How It Is Measured and Demonstrated |
|---------|-------------------------------------|
| 1.  Access | Availability to customers |
| 2.  Communication | Providing clear descriptions to customers, answering their questions |
| 3.  Competence | Proven expertise at a task |
| 4.  Courtesy | Friendliness, respect for customer |
| 5.  Credibility | Believability, meeting promises |
| 6.  Reliability | Error reduction |
| 7.  Responsiveness | Speed at meeting customer requests |
| 8.  Security | Maintaining customer safety and privacy |
| 9.  Tangibles | Physical appearance of workplace |
| 10.  Knowing the customer | Demonstrated capacity to listen to, respond to, and satisfy the customer |

product quality. Parasuraman, Zeithaml, and Berry offer ten dimensions that help to define customer satisfaction (see Exhibit 4-5).[25] It is a challenge for managers of service companies and not-for-profit organizations to find ways to monitor these indicators and to interpret them to help keep track of the quality of the organization's performance.

**Other objectives.**  Objectives for profitability, market standing, productivity, and physical and financial resources are amenable to measurement. But objectives for innovation, employee attitudes, managerial behaviour, and social responsibility are less easily measured or even identified. This is important, because without measurement it is not possible to monitor and evaluate performance to see if objectives are being met—the very essence of planning.

## Step 3: Creating an Action Plan

Once the organization's goals and objectives have been established, the next step is to develop an action plan. The most carefully written mission statement, goals, and objectives do little good if the organization does not act on them. Specific actions must be decided on and prescribed as means to achieve objectives. It is the actions taken that determine success or failure in meeting objectives. In some instances, managers must make choices among alternative actions, selecting some and rejecting or deferring others. For example, productivity increases might be achieved through a variety of means, including improving technology, offering employee and management training, instituting reward systems, improving working conditions, and purchasing more sophisticated or more efficient equipment. Managers must select the most effective alternatives from those available. Often several possible courses of action exist for top managers who are planning for the total organization. As the plan becomes more localized to a simple unit in the organization, the number of alternatives tends to become fewer yet more familiar, and the results become more readily predictable.

**forecast**
A prediction of future events, based on experience, past and current, and expectations for the future.

**Forecasting.**  Usually managers test the possible effects of a course of action by making a **forecast**, which is the process of predicting future events and situations based on past and current information. Unlike planning, in which the emphasis is on what the organization wishes to accomplish and how this may be done, forecasting is an attempt to predict what will happen as a result of implementing plans, within predicted environmental situations. Its purpose is to attempt to determine the likely outcome of alternative courses of action. For example, a sales forecast would include past and current information about the company's product or service, price levels, advertising methods and results, and costs. External conditions to be considered include the prices of competing products, the levels of consumer income, consumer credit interest rates, and other measures of local economic activity within the organization's sphere of activities.

The manager of a regional library would take into account demographic trends in their customers, trends in government funding, and expected population growth in the area. From these and other factors, the manager could forecast staffing, space, and acquisition needs, and prepare submissions to funding agencies for budget support.

Based on carefully constructed forecasts, and in communication with people at all relevant levels of the organization, managers can establish action plans that prescribe specific actions, their timing, and who or what unit in the organization will do them. This latter element is often overlooked, causing the plan to fail. It is essential for those charged with implementing an action plan to identify clearly who is responsible for taking each required action, and when. If this clarity is lacking, either an action will not be done because "no one is responsible" or, conversely, two or more people or units will attempt to accomplish the same task and come into conflict because their assumed responsibilities overlap.

The final requirement in establishing the action plan is to communicate it clearly and precisely to those who are expected to take actions, and to others who may be affected by those actions.

## Step 4: Allocating Resources

**resources**
Financial, physical, human, time, and other assets of an organization that can be used to fulfil its mission, goals, and objectives.

**budget**
A document that both predicts future resources and allocates resources for various purposes within the organization.

The fourth step in the planning process is budgeting resources for each important aspect of the plan. The term **resources** includes all of the financial, physical, human, time, and other assets of an organization. Expenditure of resources is usually controlled by use of a budget. A **budget** is a document that allocates resources to each activity. For example, as part of the plan to bring a new product to market, a budget likely will include facilities, salaries and associated costs of personnel, and expenses for materials and facilities, travel, promotional activities, and all other resources required to bring the plan to fruition.

A budget is a tool both for planning and for monitoring and control. Periodically, actual results are compared with budgeted (planned) results, which may lead to corrective action. This is one aspect of controlling, as will be discussed in Chapter 7.

In a company that sells a product or service, sales forecasts play a key role, because they are the starting point for almost all other plans and budgets. Similarly, in a non-profit organization, user numbers and trends are one factor used to determine the level of financial, physical, and human resources required to accomplish goals.

Forecasts are assumptions about the future, based on informed analysis. If these assumptions prove wrong, budgets may have to be amended. So the usefulness of financial budgets depend on how flexible they are to changes in conditions.

**variable budget**
A budget that reflects the fact that actual results are likely to deviate from those predicted and that allows for adjustment accordingly.

Effective budgets are either variable or rolling. A **variable budget** provides for the likelihood that actual output may not be exactly as planned. It also distinguishes between *variable costs* (such as those for purchases of materials, packaging, and shipping), which are directly related to level of output, and *fixed costs* (such as rent, interest on loans, and administrative costs), which likely will not change with moderate increases or decreases in sales. Because fixed costs continue even when there are changes in sales levels, if actual sales are higher or lower than planned, the variation in profit is likely to be greater than the percentage increase or decrease in sales. For example, between two consecutive years, Magna International's sales doubled, causing a 15-fold increase in profits. Major adjustments were required in the company's planning and budgets to accommodate this huge change in volume.[26]

**rolling budget**
A budget that is set for a period such as a year, and then is adjusted after each period of operations, such as a month, to reflect actual results and to function for the succeeding 12 months, until amended the following month.

A **rolling budget** is one in which a budget is prepared for a fixed period (say, one year) with periodic updating at fixed intervals (such as every month). For example, a budget is prepared in December for the next 12 months (January through December). At the end of January, the budget is revised and projected for the succeeding 12 months (February through January of the following year). This process of revision continues every month throughout the year so that the budget always reflects the latest experience and covers the succeeding 12 months. Premises and assumptions are revised constantly as management learns from experience.

Another form of rolling budget is one that covers the current year and the next two years. Each year the current year's budget governs financial activity, while the budgets for the next two years help the organization to recognize trends and take long-range factors into account when making financial decisions.

Rolling budgets have the advantage of requiring systematic reexamination; they have the disadvantage of being costly to maintain and revise. Although budgets are important instruments for implementing a firm's objectives, they must be viewed in perspective as one item in a long list of demands for a manager's time. Consequently, procedures must be devised to make it relatively easy to revise rolling budgets.

Some writers have created a stir by questioning the value of budgets.[27] Their major criticism is that by strictly adhering to a planning process based solely on numbers and dollars, organizations tend to overlook critical variables such as quality, customer service, and technological change. For example, organizations have to be able to adapt to technological innovation or their competitors will surpass them. To keep abreast of changes, managers must find ways to improve technological forecasting and translate these forecasts into plans that enable the organization to maximize its opportunities to gain from these technologies.[28] The payoff from dedicating resources to technological innovation may not appear immediately, so paying too much attention to short-term budgets may stifle desirable change. This hazard does not minimize the need for careful budgeting, but only suggests a caution as to how the budgets are to be viewed and applied.

## Step 5: Implementing the Plan

Developing an action plan is only part of the planning process. Effective managers also must have a strategy for implementing the action plan.

**implementation**
Putting a plan into action by assigning people and other resources to it, and by acting to achieve its design.

**Implementation** consists of the delegation of tasks, taking objective-driven action, and working to achieve desired results. Without effective implementation, the four preceding steps of the planning process are pointless. Implementation means using resources to put a plan into action. In some instances, such as with small businesses and entrepreneurial ventures, the manager carries out each step of the planning process, including implementation. Even in a small business, however, it is helpful for the manager to have a written implementation plan, rather than rely on memory and instinct. In most large organizations, the manager must implement plans through others, motivating them to carry out the plan, rewarding them for successful performance, and redirecting them when their actions lead to outcomes that differ from the objectives. Managers have at least three ways to implement plans through others: authority, persuasion, and policies.

**authority**
Decision-making power that stems from a formal position in the hierarchy of an organization, as contrasted with persuasive power that stems from the personal attributes of the person holding the position.

**Authority** is a form of power that attaches to a position in the organization, and does not solely reflect the person who occupies the position. The nature of authority in organizations involves the right to make decisions and to expect subordinates to comply with those decisions as long as they do not require illegal or unethical behaviour. Some decry the existence of authority as being impersonal, and assume that the power it carries will be used for improper ends. This view is rather shortsighted because, whether acknowledged or not, authority exists; the real question is how a person uses it. Authority alone may be sufficient to implement simple plans, but a complex plan seldom can be implemented through authority alone.

**Persuasion** is the process of convincing others to accept a plan on its merits rather than on the authority of the manager. There is a danger in depending solely on persuasion. If persuasion fails initially and is crucial for implementation, management must implement the plan by use of authority, perhaps in the face of resistance that might have been intensified during the attempt to persuade. If persuasion alone has failed to achieve its purpose, it is usually good advice that managers should not rely exclusively on it in the future,[29] until conditions are more favourable.

A **policy** is a statement that reflects a plan's basic values and provides guidelines for selecting actions to achieve objectives. Policies are "a guide to managerial action."[30] Some policies direct certain action; other policies prohibit certain action. When plans are expected to be rather permanent, policies are developed to implement them. Standard operating procedures (often referred to as SOPs) are formal guidelines designed to direct the decisions that should be made and the actions that should be taken by managers and other employees faced with situations that arise repeatedly. Related policies are often gathered in policy manuals, which are made available to all employees responsible for administering a particular group of activities. Some examples of policy statements include:

- "All customer returns will be accepted without question."
- "We will maintain a lifetime of service support for any product we produce."
- "If a reservation is cancelled 48 hours before flight time, the passenger will be entitled to a full refund."
- "Immediately upon arrival in the emergency ward, each patient shall be screened and a priority will be assigned for treatment by the appropriate attending physician."

These policies are stated in unequivocal terms; that is, they seem to allow for no managerial discretion. Yet, to function effectively, the administration of any policy must allow for the unexpected and for emergencies. Effective policies should have several common characteristics:

- *Flexibility.* An effective policy achieves a balance between rigidity and flexibility. In the most successful organizations, policies leave some room for managers and other employees at all levels to exercise discretion within understood guidelines.
- *Comprehensiveness.* A policy must cover multiple contingencies. No policy can cover all possible situations, but policies must be broad enough to cover a large proportion of the situations that are likely to be encountered. The degree of comprehensiveness depends on the scope of action controlled by the policy. Narrow issues require narrow policies and broad issues require broad policies.
- *Coordination.* A policy must be easily coordinated among divisions, teams, and departments. Activities must be able to conform to the policy without creating conflict among different organizational units.
- *Clarity.* A policy must be stated clearly and logically. It must specify the aim of the action, define appropriate methods, and set limits of discretion on those applying the policy.
- *Ethical standards.* A policy must reflect ethical standards and be responsive to cultural differences. This may be most difficult to follow when an organization is operating in a foreign country because local standards may be inconsistent with the organization's standards in the home country. In such circumstances, a policy may

**persuasion**
The process of convincing others to accept one's ideas, beliefs, or plans for the future.

**policy**
A governing principle, either written or simply understood by the individuals in an organization, that is intended to guide individual or group action in specific circumstances.

have to be adapted to local conditions. For example, in Canada an organization may have an invariable policy that every job vacancy must be "posted." This policy requires that whenever a position becomes open, a description must be published internally, inviting current employees to apply for it. While this policy may be ideal in Canada, it would be ineffective, and might be offensive, in Zambia, where most employees are illiterate and would resent being expected to understand a written notice.

As mentioned in Chapter 2, it is well known that in countries such as Indonesia and China, and those that were formerly part of the Soviet Union, it is almost impossible to obtain major contracts without bribing government officials. Many Canadian companies have policies that prohibit offering or receiving bribes. Do those policies apply while negotiating for a mining concession, for example, when some competitors are not constrained either by national laws or by company policies?[31] This question is too important to be left to an individual manager's discretion. It must be resolved by senior management and communicated to everyone who deals with other countries. Some senior managers intentionally hedge the issue by publishing vague guidelines, such as "Managers must use their own discretion …" This kind of "policy" provides little guidance and exposes associates to severe criticism after they have acted on their own discretion. When Foreign Affairs Minister Lloyd Axworthy announced the newly drafted code of ethics for federal Crown corporations, he pointed to the provision that says that they should "… refrain from paying bribes or engaging in unethical business practices." Then he effectively vitiated the policy by announcing that adoption of the code of ethics would be optional![32]

*The uniform ethical guidelines that are being adopted by Canada and several other industrialized countries inexplicably do not apply to Canadian Crown corporations.*

For several years, under pressure from the United States, the Organization for Economic Cooperation and Development (OECD) has been attempting to develop an international code of ethics so that nationals of all countries will operate under the same rules when operating in foreign countries. Unfortunately, some members of the U.S. Congress have tried to tie a provision relating to anti-trust rules to the enabling bill. This has become a roadblock, setting back, probably for several years, any international agreement on this delicate subject.[33]

As may be seen from these examples, if managers wish their policies to be understood and followed, they must communicate them clearly and unequivocally, and allow for appropriate feedback.[34]

**regulation**
A ruling, often relating to administrative procedures, that specifies how individuals within an organization shall act when certain foreseen circumstances arise.

While a policy is a general guide to decision making, a **regulation** (or standard procedure) either provides details amplifying the policy or provides instructions for implementing the policy. For example, a policy covering customer returns would have associated with it various regulations, directing the company's employees as to what to do with returned merchandise, how to make a record of the transaction, and how to issue refunds.

**Exhibit 4-6**

*Key Managerial
Planning Issues*

| Planning Element | Key Managerial Decisions |
|---|---|
| Objectives | 1. Which objectives will be sought? |
| | 2. What is the relative importance of each objective? |
| | 3. What are the relationships among the objectives? |
| | 4. When should each objective be achieved? |
| | 5. How can each objective be measured? |
| | 6. Which person or organizational unit should be accountable for achieving the objective? |
| Actions | 1. Which important actions bear on the successful achievement of objectives? |
| | 2. What information exists regarding each action? |
| | 3. What is the appropriate technique for forecasting the future state of each important action? |
| | 4. Which person or organizational unit should be accountable for the action? |
| Resources | 1. Which resources should be included in the plan? |
| | 2. What are the interrelationships among the various resources? |
| | 3. Which budgeting technique should be used? |
| | 4. Which person or organizational unit should be accountable for preparing the budget? |
| Implementation | 1. Can the plan be implemented through authority or persuasion? |
| | 2. What policy statements are necessary to implement the overall plan? |
| | 3. To what extent are the policy statements comprehensive, flexible, coordinative, ethical, and clearly written? |
| | 4. Who or what organizational units would be affected by the policy statements? |

Source: James H. Donnelly, Jr., James L. Gibson, and John M. Ivancevich, *Fundamentals of Management,* 8th ed. (Homewood, IL: Richard D. Irwin, 1992): 151.

Exhibit 4-6 summarizes some of the most important decisions that must be made in effective planning. First, objectives must be identified and made specific. Next, it must be decided what action will be required to accomplish the objectives. The next step is to decide what resources will be needed, and if sufficient resources are not available, to modify the objectives. Finally, the implementation plan must be designed. If planners have failed to answer any of these questions, the plan is likely to be unsuccessful.

## Step 6: Controlling Implementation

After completing the first five steps in the planning process, management must control implementation. The organization must manage ongoing work activities to ensure that the intended objectives are met or adjusted if necessary. Controlling includes all managerial activities dedicated to ensuring that actual results conform within reasonable limits to the planned results. Controlling and implementing occur almost simultaneously. As actions are taken to implement the plan, actual results are compared with those predicted. Prompt **feedback** is given, to take any corrective action that is thought to be desirable. In this way, the plan is adjusted to reflect actual experience before it has done serious damage, and before habits are so ingrained that later adjustment is difficult.

More will be said about issues of control in Chapter 7, but it is important to note here that the line between planning and controlling is largely a theoretical distinction

**feedback**
Information concerning results of activity that is conveyed to the policymakers or authority figures, enabling them to confirm, amend, or abandon the policy in question.

and that the two must complement each other and be integrated to the extent that they almost merge.

## Total Quality Approach to Planning

Companies that use the total quality management approach employ a number of specific planning methods. This section examines three of those methods: the plan, do, check, act cycle; time-based planning; and planning for continuous improvement. These approaches form the basis for quality planning.[35] W. Edwards Deming described quality planning as the activity of (1) determining customer needs and (2) developing the products and processes required to meet those needs. Quality planning is required for every product and service within an organization, not only for goods and services sold or provided to external customers. Many internal processes (such as writing purchase orders, sending reports, recruiting new employees, preparing sales forecasts and budgets, and monitoring the credit of customers) are overlooked in the planning process because they are not seen to be directly affecting external customers. A number of forward-looking companies have revised their operations to link internal work processes and business planning strategy to customers.[36] Each of the quality approaches to planning discussed in this section emphasizes the value of exceeding customer expectations, making continuous improvement, and organizing for team-based problem solving. Additionally, although each of these planning approaches is based on a similar concept of quality, each was developed by a different thinker and has some unique aspects.

### The Plan, Do, Check, Act Cycle

The *plan, do, check, act (PDCA)* planning process introduced the concept of planning as a cycle that forms the basis for continuous improvement.[37] In the PDCA cycle (also called the *Shewart cycle*, after its originator, Walter Shewart), the first step is to plan the quality improvement. Second, employees perform or produce a small version or batch of the procedure or product. Third, workers check the results of this pilot project. (The word *study* is sometimes used in place of *check* to reduce some of the negative ideas associated with checking work.) Fourth, workers implement the tested process. The PDCA cycle (set out in Exhibit 4-7) is then repeated.[38]

Employees at Procter & Gamble (P&G) use the PDCA cycle to manage environmental quality efforts. First, they develop a *plan* to remove pollutants from each stage of production as well as from packaging and the final product. Next (the *do* stage) they

**Exhibit 4-7**    *The PDCA Cycle*

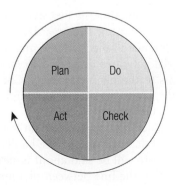

*Before a new product is marketed by a wholesale food manufacturer, it is tested in test kitchens. Planning must take into account the time required for a new recipe to be tested and checked, for operators to be trained in its production, and perhaps for new equipment or unaccustomed supplies to be purchased.*

reduce discharges to the environment and correct other potentially harmful environmental defects. Then they *check* the results, using sophisticated measuring devices and charting the results. Once the results are assessed, employees *act* by installing permanent systems to maintain the quality improvement and to apply it to other aspects of the business. Using this technique, a P&G pulp mill cut landfill dumping by 75 percent and a coffee-processing plant added a machine to compact chaff from coffee beans, cutting solids in sewage by 75 percent. New packaging cut 1.5 million kilograms of waste in deodorant product cartons. In another application of the PDCA process, P&G's redesigned Crisco bottle uses 28 percent less plastic than the earlier bottle, yet performs the same function.[39]

## Time-based Planning

Speed often can determine the success or failure of a plan's implementation. In a manufacturing company, the important period in product development occurs between the time the product is first seriously considered and the time it is ready to be sold to the customer. Throughout this period, the company has expended development money, but until sales are made the company has received no cash in return. Speed in planning and delivering a product or service also can help a company to meet or pre-empt competition. All other things being equal, market share often goes to the fastest organization. Further, paying attention to time usually forces managers to look at other issues affecting the quality of products and services. For example, it is not uncommon for a product to lay idle during 90 percent of the time allocated for its assembly, thus delaying receipt of sales revenues and tying up the company's funds in nonproductive investment. Paying attention to production speed can help to reduce these idle periods and develop greater customer loyalty.[40]

By examining its product design cycle, a boot manufacturer found that seven weeks usually elapsed between receipt of an order and delivery of the product to the customer. Yet only two days were required for actual production. Over 95 percent of the time was accounted for by paperwork and especially by delays that occurred between consecutive steps in the process. A telecommunications company found a similar costly delay in simply converting a customer's order into a work order for the factory. Here, too, 95 percent of the time was lost in delays between consecutive processes or departments.[41] By eliminating the time when a product or process lays idle, unproductive costs are reduced and customer satisfaction is enhanced.

## Planning for Continuous Improvement

Effective planning and plans can lead to quality outcomes and to continuous improvements in performance. Quality pioneer Joseph M. Juran notes three main negative outcomes resulting from a lack of attention to quality in the planning process:

- *Loss of sales due to competition in quality.* In North America this has affected almost every product, from televisions to lawn mowers to cars to fresh fruits and vegetables.
- *Costs of poor quality.* These include customer complaints, possible product liability lawsuits, the need to redo defective work, and waste through scrapping defective products. Juran estimates that typically 20 to 40 percent of all costs of doing business are from redoing work that was not done right initially.
- *Threats to society.* These include minor annoyances such as home appliance breakdowns, as well as matters of worldwide concern. Examples of the latter are the destruction of the ozone layer because of use of certain refrigerants, global disasters such as the poison gas release in Bhopal, India, and the nuclear reactor explosion in the Ukraine and the subsequent worldwide contamination.[42]

Managers can minimize the possibility of negative outcomes by using quality-based planning methods and by establishing quality goals. The primary outcome expected as a result of quality planning is customer satisfaction and, it is hoped, repeat business. To Juran, quality planning includes the following fundamental actions:

- Identify customers, both external and internal;
- Determine the customer's needs;
- Develop product features that satisfy customer needs;
- Establish quality goals that meet customers' and suppliers' needs at a minimum combined cost;
- Develop a process to produce the needed features; and
- Prove that the process can meet the quality goals under operating conditions, that is, prove process capability.[43]

To achieve customer satisfaction, work processes must be improved on a continuous basis. According to Juran, planning for continuous improvement in the production process requires the following steps:

- Prove the need for improvement;
- Identify specific projects for improvement;
- Organize to guide the projects;
- Organize for diagnosis (the discovery of causes);
- Analyze to find the causes;
- Provide remedies;
- Determine if the remedies are effective under operating conditions; and
- Provide for control to maintain the gains.[44]

Planning for continuous improvement recognizes that customer expectations are a moving target. There is no single, ultimate solution that will permanently meet customer demands.

Some managers mistakenly assume that to be successful planning must identify major changes. They look for a one-time, massive change in the production process, in the product, or in the delivery of service that will reduce costs materially or result in some other significant improvement. Then no other changes or improvements are made until another planning cycle results in another massive change. In this approach, the benefits from the original improvements tend to dissipate between planning cycles. Furthermore, opportunities for small improvements probably have been missed, even though cumulatively they may have made a substantial difference. Instead of this sporadic approach to planning, in the most successful organizations the planning cycle is continuous. Most improvements are not dramatic. Instead, they occur only incrementally, but consistently. There is no backsliding, and no satisfaction with the status quo.

By following these approaches to planning and implementing plans, an organization can set the stage for becoming and remaining competitive.

## The Workplace of Tomorrow

In the 1970s and 1980s, strategic planning was touted by some experts as a panacea for all of the problems that beset organizations. Many large corporations created strategic planning departments, and some managers of small businesses devoted countless evenings and weekends to detailed strategic planning. Then managers found that the benefits of strategic planning had been oversold. Not surprisingly, a backlash occurred. For a brief period, planning had a bad name among managers in the field.

Then reason prevailed, as it often does after a period of excess, and managers came to realize that while planning does not invariably lead to perfection, some formalization of planning practices and techniques are almost essential in the fast-changing environments in which they were operating. Planning began to make a comeback. Even corporations that had scrapped their strategic planning departments reinstituted the functions that those departments had provided. The difference was that instead of planning being seen as an isolated function carried on by specialists, it was recognized as an essential part of the responsibilities of line and staff managers. Planning no longer was divorced from daily operations; it began to be closely linked to all activities within the organization.

This relatively "new" approach, while lacking some of its previous excitement, drama, and exotic mystery, began to meld planning theory with practical management. Results began to reflect the operational realities more clearly than did some of the relatively esoteric output of earlier planning departments. Non-profit organizations, which had missed some of the furor that attended the "planning revolution" of the 1970s, began to think seriously about and formulate mission statements and articulate goals and objectives.

So what is the future of planning in tomorrow's organization? Now that the undoubted benefits of sound planning have become better recognized, the pendulum may swing back a bit. Once again, planning will be seen not only as a short-range operational necessity, but also as a means of setting a pattern for organizational direction and development. Managers will be expected to plan for their own areas of responsibility, and periodically the organization will dedicate staff to comprehensive planning efforts, involving employees at all levels. And perhaps most importantly, what might be called *microplanning* (that is, tactical and operational planning) will be better integrated with what might be called *macroplanning* (that is, overall institutional goal and objective setting).

Planning, therefore, may not have the visibility that it had in many organizations in the 1970s, but as a continuous process it may have even more effect on how organizations conduct themselves. Organizations that achieve the micro/macro integration and balance will have a good chance of thriving; those that do not will be less successful than they might otherwise have been.

## Summary of Learning Objectives

▷ Define *planning* and discuss the characteristics of effective planning that distinguish it from less effective planning.

Planning is a key managerial activity that looks at past and current situations, attempts to predict future events, determines where the organization wishes to be in the future, and combines these into a coherent method of achieving the desired future. Planning means that decisions made today will be most likely to produce results at a later date. The planning process is dynamic, involving many variables that must be considered and linked in designing the plan. Effective planning requires consistency in pursuing the plan's objectives and flexibility in its implementation. Planning, like decision making, must be proactive and systematic. Effective planning requires clear priorities and flexibility.

▷ Describe at least four factors that underscore the need for planning in any organization, regardless of type or size.

Factors that underscore the need for planning include: (1) pressure to reduce cycle times on key organizational processes; (2) increased internal complexity of organizational processes; (3) increased external change in markets and other parts of the external environments; and (4) the impact of planning on other management functions. Considerable time often passes between decisions and results. Careful planning can help an organization to allocate and control the expenditure of resources during this time period.

▷ Discuss the benefits organizations may gain from effective planning.

The fact that most successful organizations actively plan and that many unsuccessful organizations plan only sporadically or not at all suggests the importance of planning in management. Four specific benefits of planning are: (1) coordination of effort; (2) preparation for change; (3) development of performance standards; and (4) development of managers.

▷ Describe the steps in the planning process and explain why each is important.

The planning process consists of six steps: (1) assessing the organization's environments; (2) deciding on a mission statement and establishing goals and objectives; (3) creating an action plan; (4) allocating resources; (5) implementing the plan; and (6) monitoring, controlling, and providing feedback.

▷ Explain the following approaches to planning: (1) plan, do, check, act (PDCA); (2) time-based planning; and (3) planning for continuous improvement.

In the PDCA cycle, the first step is to plan the changes and improvements desired. Second, employees perform or produce a small version or batch of the procedure or product. Third, managers and other employees check the results of this pilot project. Fourth, managers and other employees implement the tested process. The PDCA cycle is then repeated.

Speed in planning and delivering a product or service—time-based planning—can be a strategic, competitive advantage. Time is important in the planning cycle. Often a market opportunity is lost through delay.

Planning for continuous improvement revolves around the realization that customer expectations are a moving target. There is no single, ultimate solution that will meet customer demands permanently.

▷ **Discuss quantitative measures for different types of business objectives.**

For the objectives of profitability, possible quantitative measures include profit/sales ratio, profit/total assets ratio, and profit/capital ratio. For the objectives of marketing, possible quantitative measures include market share, sales volume, rate of new product development, number and retention rate of customers, and number of outlets. For the objectives of productivity, possible quantitative measures include ratios of output to labour costs, output to capital costs, and value added to profit. For physical and financial objectives, possible quantitative measures include current ratio, working capital turnover, debt/equity ratio, accounts receivable aging, and inventory turnover.

▷ **Discuss the possible advantages and disadvantages of centralized and decentralized planning.**

Centralized planning has the merit of keeping the organization focused on goals. This cohesion tends to disregard the ideas and enthusiasms of employees at all but the highest levels in the organization, and tends to be so unwieldy that minor details are overlooked to the detriment of the whole operation.

Decentralized planning allows employees to make decisions and to plan at all levels of an organization. This means that people who are most directly involved in specific activities have primary responsibility to control and improve them. However, decentralized planning can lead to loss of control of lines of communication and to diffuse efforts that are not focused on the organization's mission and goals.

▷ **Describe each of and explain the interrelationships among the** *mission statement, goals,* **and** *objectives.*

A mission statement sets out the organization's purposes and its long-term vision in terms that distinguish it from other organizations. Goals are the achievements that the organization intends to accomplish. Its objectives are the detailed steps that it will take to achieve the goals, with specific achievements and the times when they are to be achieved. Objectives are the shortest-term of the three, and describe the plan of action that is to be followed. Goals are longer-term and fit within the principles stated in the mission statement.

▷ **Explain the differences between** *variable* **and** *rolling* **budgets.**

Variable budgeting recognizes that variable costs are related to output, whereas fixed costs continue almost independently of the volume of output. It reflects the possibility that actual results may vary considerably from those predicted, and that budgets will have to be adjusted to reflect these differences. Rolling budgets are updated after each fiscal period, to reflect actual results.

▷ **Explain the differences among** *strategic, operational,* **and** *tactical* **planning.**

Strategic planning reflects a long-term perspective; operational planning takes a focused, specific, short-term perspective; and tactical planning takes an intermediate-term perspective.

## KEY TERMS

authority, p. 152
budget, p. 151
centralized planning, p. 129
cycle time reduction, p. 132
decentralized planning, p. 131
economy of time, p. 133
feedback, p. 155
forecast, p. 150
goal, p. 145
implementation, p. 152
level of detail, p. 137

mission statement, p. 143
niche strategy, p. 138
objective, p. 146
operational planning, p. 140
performance standards, p. 136
persuasion, p. 153
policy, p. 153
prestige strategy, p. 138
price penetration strategy, p. 137
regulation, p. 154

resources, p. 151
rolling budget, p. 152
scope, p. 137
single-use plan, p. 139
skimming strategy, p. 138
standing plan, p. 139
strategic planning, p. 137
tactical planning, p. 139
time frame, p. 137
variable budget, p. 151

## REVIEW AND DISCUSSION QUESTIONS

### Recall

1. Name the elements of a successful planning process.
2. What are the important outcomes of planning?
3. What does PDCA mean, and what is its purpose?

### Understanding

4. What is the difference between a plan and an objective? Which do you feel is more difficult to develop and apply on a consistent basis? Why?
5. Even with a carefully constructed plan, managers and other employees are often required—or they demand—to change the plan. What would cause the people who made the plan to want to change it? Are there good and bad reasons to change a plan? Who should decide to make the change—those who made the plan or those who are putting the plan into action?
6. What is a rolling budget? How would it be implemented in a large organization? In a business with only three or four owner/managers?
7. How does global competition affect the planning process?
8. Identify three businesses, of any size, that illustrate each of price penetration, prestige, and skimming strategies. What niche or niches does each business fill? Consider how the three businesses differ from their competitors.

### Application

9. Write a mission statement for your business school. What are the key elements in the statement? Who are the customers to whom it is addressed? Who are the other stakeholders who have an interest?
10. Prepare a five- to ten-step action plan for writing a term paper for this course. Be sure to identify each step in the plan so that you know when you have completed the step. After putting the steps in order, assign a date or deadline to each step, using the current school term as the overall time frame, with the paper being due one week before the last day of class.
11. In a scheduled personal interview, discuss with a manager how planning is used in that person's organization, and what benefits or disadvantages may arise from the planning process.

**CASE** 4-1

# Harley-Davidson

Harley-Davidson (H-D) is a widely known, revered name in manufacturing. The company produces what has been called the "Cadillac of motorcycles," a symbol of strength, style, and machismo. A classic success story, H-D began by building the simplest of motorized bicycles almost 100 years ago. After the Second World War, Harleys became a symbol of freedom and spirit, an image immortalized in movies and spread around the globe. By 1973 Harley had 75 percent of the super-heavyweight motorcycle market in North America. Inroads made by Japanese manufacturers in the 1960s and early 1970s were minor; their bikes were small and lacked the power, appearance, and exciting throaty roar of the Harleys.

With the first global oil crisis in 1973, H-D began to slip. Customers no longer pined for the big, powerful Harley look. Smaller bikes, even mopeds (many from Japanese manufacturers), began to earn the attention of energy-conscious consumers. Worse, Harley quality was abysmal. Half of the motorcycles had parts missing as they came off the assembly line. Dealers told of having to wipe oil drips off their showroom floor, thanks to leaks from brand-new bikes. Sales were sustained by a small, loyal group. Ironically, Robert Pirsig's cult classic, *Zen and the Art of Motorcycle Maintenance*, described the author's fascination both with quality and with the need to maintain his motorcycle with utmost care.

H-D responded late and defensively. Soon it was spending an additional $1000 on each $4000 bike just to put it in adequate shape to sell. The company survived on makeshift designs—culled from existing patterns, pieces, and parts. Customers began to look elsewhere.

Then H-D realized that its Japanese competitors were now well ahead, if not in style then surely in quality. After visiting Japanese manufacturers, H-D realized it had to overhaul its assembly line completely, adding just-in-time (JIT) inventory control, employee participation, and decision making by consensus. Everyone received training on statistical quality control. Managers learned to become team leaders, rather than supervisors of shoddy work. The transformation began. In a short time, rework declined by 70 percent and morale improved. Harley's "productivity triad" consisted of employee involvement, JIT, and statistical process control training. In 1982 a full 50 percent of finished motorcycles had defects; by 1986 only 1 percent of finished bikes contained defects.

Revitalized marketing and short-term quota protection against imports helped H-D through its worst years. Celebrities "found" motorcycling, Harley-style, once again. Malcolm Forbes, Liz Taylor, Jay Leno, and others displayed their Harleys proudly. And H-D executives formed the Harley Owners Group (HOG) to promote their image. Driving a big, powerful machine once more became a sought-after symbol; HOG had 100,000 members, and Harley executives mingled with yuppies at HOG events around the country, listening closely and responding quickly to customers. By 1991 H-D had to add a second production line—a unique, small, automated electrified monorail (AEM)—supporting dedicated assembly for the plant's two engine types. An employee-controlled start-stop system also helped increase product quality. Despite booming demand, H-D declined to stretch production, fearing a return to old days and old ways of high production and low quality.

Recovering from its near-death experience, by the late 1980s Harley came to represent the resurgence of pride in workmanship, of responding to the market, and of meeting the global challenge. When import restrictions were lifted, permitting more foreign bikes to be imported, Harley was able to meet the competition head on. Formerly sloppy assembly had been replaced by precision work performed by assembly workers organized in small work "cells" rather than on long, impersonal production lines. Retired production workers volunteered to provide interested visitors with tours of the new Harley production process.

Harleys once again ruled the road and the market. Foreign sales boomed, and Harleys even became a Japanese favourite.

By 1992 H-D had recaptured more than 60 percent of the market for motorcycles with engine displacements over 900 cc—the true big-ticket bike. Sales in 1992 increased over 1991, despite a sluggish economy and a ten-week strike at one of its two plants. Selling lifestyle, not transportation, H-D expected to hold onto a greying market of middle-aged men and women. "Harleys make the same kind of statement as wearing a Rolex watch or driving a classic wing-tailed Cadillac," says one enthusiast. With this customer attitude and remarkable new quality, H-D has big plans for the future.

### Questions

1. How has planning restored Harley-Davidson to its previous prominence among those wishing to buy a large motorcycle?
2. How has H-D employed quality planning principles to recapture flagging sales?
3. If you were in charge of long-term planning for H-D, what sorts of environmental factors would you consider for the next five years?

Source: Gary Slutsker, "Hog Wild," *Forbes* (May 24, 1993): 45-46; Kevin Kelly and Karen Lowry Miller, "The Rumble Heard Round the World: Harleys," *Business Week* (May 24, 1993): 58, 60; "Harley-Davidson: Going Whole Hog to Provide Stakeholder Satisfaction," *Management Review* (June 1993): 53-55; Joseph H. Boyett and Henry P. Conn, *Workplace 2000: The Revolution Reshaping American Business* (New York: Dutton, 1991): 329-32; Michael L. McCracken and Brian H. Kleiner, "Enhancing Quality Control: New Developments," *Industrial Management & Data Systems*, 91(6): 20-23; Karen A. Auguston, "Overhead Monorail Revs Up Plant Capacity at Harley Davidson," *Modern Materials Handling* (October 1991): 38-41; and Richard L. Stern, "The Graying Wild Ones," *Forbes* (January 6, 1992): 40.

## CASE 4-2

## Toyota

To North American auto makers, Toyota symbolizes the rapid rise of Japanese automotive clout. Its introduction of the Lexus in 1989 showed how an economy-minded corporation could build luxury cars. Yet much of Toyota's post–Second World War history, chronicled in books such as *The Reckoning* and *The Machine That Changed the World*, is marked by pressure, frustration, and the occasional failure. For instance, its first imports to the United States in 1957 failed their basic market test. Toyota's cars were unable to sustain necessary, extended freeway driving speeds common to Americans—speeds yet unheard of in tiny, traffic-choked Japan. Also, in the late 1970s Toyota found that distributing and selling a car cost twice as much as manufacturing it. Toyota's solution was to merge its manufacturing and sales companies. Within 18 months all of the directors of the sales company had been retired; their jobs were left unfilled or were staffed by personnel from the manufacturing company.

Toyota's greatest impetus was the simple fact that following the Second World War the company literally had to build from the ground up. Often working and assembling cars in factories with dirt floors, Toyota could not afford to build large, mass-production, Western-style assembly lines. Factories had to be focused and flexible. Machines had to be able to make several models and their changeover to another model had to be done quickly.

Toyota is known for its development of the "lean production process," which contradicts much of the mass-production mentality that prospered in the Western world following the war. North American assembly lines worked to produce volume, generating profits through massive economies of scale. Quantity triumphed over quality. In the early 1950s General Motors could build over a million units of a single Chevrolet model to feed an insatiable consumer appetite for cars in the post-war boom. Today a quarter of a million units mark a best-seller; even as few as 40,000 units of a particular model may mean a successful sales year.

By the early 1960s Toyota had mastered lean production. On the manufacturing side, lean production meant low overhead. Lower overall costs were achieved with just-in-time parts supply, few supervisors, limited inspection, and very limited finished products inventory. Employees had broad responsibility for building and managing the process. Quality circles grew in abundance. Lean production also put the power to stop the assembly process in the hands of the assembly workers. If a defect is noted, the line is halted, and the defect is tracked to its source and fixed. Almost every employee can be seen directly adding value to the car. A 1986 comparison of Toyota's Takaoka assembly plant with GM's Framingham, Massachusetts, plant found that, by dividing the total number of hours of work in the plant by the number of cars produced, Toyota consumed 18 hours per car, while GM took 41 hours. Defects were also lower at Toyota: 45 assembly defects per 100 assembled cars, versus 130 at the GM plant.

Toyota used teams operating independently, instead of rigid assembly lines and fixed job titles. Cross-training was the standard and, typical of most Japanese auto firms, employees received up to ten times the training of their Big Three auto maker counterparts. Little space was set aside for fixing mistakes; few occurred, so even more money was saved. Workers made scores of suggestions, many of which improved the process and further reduced costs. Measuring value added per employee, Toyota workers were four to five times more productive than General Motors workers.

The Toyota production process actually begins with its sales approach. Toyota starts with highly developed databases on households and buying patterns in Japan. Salespeople do not wait for customers; they go calling, targeting their efforts on carefully selected buyers and honing customer loyalty. Customers become part of the entire planning process and are tracked carefully by lifestyle and purchase patterns.

The introduction of the Lexus in 1990 and publication of the Massachusetts Institute of Technology's five-year $5 million study of global automaking, *The Machine That Changed the World*, finally silenced any remaining sceptics who believed that Toyota's success was limited to small, inexpensive cars. While Ford purchased Jaguar and General Motors purchased Lotus, Toyota jumped into the luxury car market and shot to the top of the respected J.D. Power customer satisfaction measures. Not until GM's success with Saturn did an American car company make such a stellar introduction.

### Questions

1. Do you think that Toyota would have planned to use the manufacturing techniques that made it famous if its industrial plants had not been devastated during the Second World War?
2. What are some important issues that North American auto makers need to consider in long-range planning?
3. How can planning help North American auto makers become more competitive in the future?

---

Source: James P. Womack, Daniel T. Jones, and Daniel Roos, *The Machine That Changed the World* (New York: HarperPerennial, 1990); David A. Garvin, *Managing Quality: The Strategic and Competitive Edge* (New York: Free Press, 1988); Joseph Blackburn (ed.), *Time-Based Competition: The Next Battleground in American Manufacturing* (Homewood, IL: Business One Irwin, 1991).

## APPLICATION EXERCISE  4-1

### Team Planning

As the project development manager (PDM) for a $14 billion, global, high-tech communications company, you are responsible for managing a team of engineers, marketing directors, manufacturing reps, legal staff, financial analysts, and other key personnel as they take an idea from the basic research and development stage to the marketing and sales stage. You have been assigned to lead a team that will soon pick up a project from research and development. As part of their efforts to train new PDMs, management has asked you to prioritize the list of activities your team will follow. The 16 steps outlined below are required to do the job. Read the following instructions and complete this exercise in team planning.

### Instructions

1. On your own, order the activities from first (1) to last (16) in the sequence you feel they need to be completed. Write your numbers in column 1.
2. As part of a small group, agree on a sequence of activities. Record it in column 2.
3. The instructor will provide an expert's recommended rank ordering. Write these numbers in column 3.
4. Compute your individual accuracy by calculating the absolute difference between the numbers in columns 1 and 3. Write these numbers in column 4. Then add the figures from column 4 to determine your personal score.
5. Compute your group's accuracy in the same way, using the numbers in columns 2 and 3. Write the differences in column 5 and add these numbers to determine your group's score. Write the personal scores of other team members below, along with your team score.

| Activity | Your personal score | Your group's score | Expert's score | Your personal differences | Your group's differences |
|---|---|---|---|---|---|
| Find qualified people to fill the team positions. | | | | | |
| Measure team progress towards project goals. | | | | | |
| Identify all of the tasks needed to complete the project. | | | | | |
| Develop your team strategy and major priorities. | | | | | |
| Recognize and reward team performance. | | | | | |
| Prepare team members for their responsibilities. | | | | | |
| Gather and assess the facts of the current situation. | | | | | |
| Establish the qualifications for each team position. | | | | | |
| Take corrective action on project, and recycle plans. | | | | | |
| Lead and coordinate ongoing team activities. | | | | | |
| Allocate the team's operating budget. | | | | | |
| Compare actual team results to original objectives. | | | | | |
| Set team performance goals. | | | | | |
| Define the scope and authority of each team position. | | | | | |
| Decide on a basic course of action for the team. | | | | | |
| Determine checkpoints for intermediate review. | | | | | |

## APPLICATION EXERCISE  4-2

### *Clicking* with Market Trends

A key to understanding any manager's client base is following general consumer trends or market trends. Faith Popcorn writes books that break these concepts down into easy-to-understand general statements. In her recent book, she describes *Clicking* as being in control, in focus, and in sync with life. Popcorn's marketing company uses the trends identified to help businesses "click" with their customers.

Consider two of the trends identified by Popcorn:

- Cocooning—one of Popcorn's most famous catchwords—explains consumers wanting products for the home, so that they can remain in the safe, comfortable oases of their private domains.
- Ego-nomics—Connecting with "Me"—A trend towards personalized and specialized products designed for each individual consumer. Movement towards conveniencing the consumer on all levels (24-hour customer service).

#### Exercises

1. Identify one general consumer trend you see occurring today.
2. Create a catchy name for the trend and explain how consumers are behaving and what is causing the trend.
3. Identify how this consumer trend is going to affect the way business happens in the future.
4. List and explain some ways that Canadian businesses can prepare for the trend you have identified.

Contributed by Marnie Wright, British Columbia Institute of Technology.

## APPLICATION EXERCISE  4-3

### Understanding Your Circle of Concern

A key issue for effective managers is to focus their energies on problem areas that they have the power to resolve. In his best-selling book, *Seven Habits of Highly Effective People*, Dr. Stephen Covey calls this strategy *working within your circle of concern*.

Managers must accept that there are issues and problems that will remain unchanged, despite tremendous and tireless efforts. These roadblocks are a fact of life for everyone. Learning how best to use your time by working on areas that will yield the most positive results and walking away from issues that cannot be changed is a crucial first step.

#### Exercises

1. Consider your own "circle of concern" on a more personal level. Identify three issues you are currently focusing on that fall outside your control.
2. Identify who is really in control of the problem (that is, who can solve the problem)?
3. Is there any aspect of the problem that you can affect?
4. How can you redirect your actions to become more effective by focusing only on the aspects that fall within your "circle of concern"?

Contributed by Marnie Wright, British Columbia Institute of Technology.

## APPLICATION EXERCISE  4-4

### Strategic Thinking—Skill Development

To evaluate your strategic thinking skills, answer yes or no to the following questions:

1. Do you focus on the future?
2. Do you ask "what if"?
3. Are you curious about who is doing what?
4. Do you plan ways to get your ideas accepted?
5. Are you a tracker of trends?
6. Are you flexible in your daily routine?
7. Are you curious or focused on customer needs?
8. Do you build on other ideas?
9. Can you brainstorm without bias towards your ideas?
10. Can you list your competition's strengths and weaknesses?

If you answered yes to most of these questions you have some of the skills needed to become a strong strategic thinker.

To be a good strategic thinker one needs:

- Curiosity
- Future focus
- Potential focus
- Broad base of knowledge and skills
- Ability to challenge the paradigms
- Ability to see the big picture

Contributed by Sydney Scott, British Columbia Institute of Technology.

## INTERNET APPLICATION  4-1

McDonald's Corporation is vertically integrating on a global level. Visit its Web site (www.mcdonalds.com). Look at the company's most recent annual report and its descriptions of the company's goals and objectives.

1. What are the main elements of McDonald's strategy at the corporate, business, and functional levels?
2. How successful has the company been lately? What are the reasons for its success or failure?

Search for a Web site that contains a good description of an organization's strategy. What is the organization's mission? How does the organization's strategy help it to achieve its mission?

# Organizational Structure and Design

After studying this chapter, you should be able to:

▶ Define the terms *organizing* and *organizational structure*;

▶ Determine when organizational structure is a problem;

▶ Explain how managers decide on organizational structure;

▶ Distinguish between the principles of scientific management and craftsmanship;

▶ Discuss the significance of work teams and quality circles;

▶ Discuss how authority can be delegated;

▶ Describe the most common bases for departmentalization and their respective strengths and weaknesses;

▶ Describe the matrix form of organization, and discuss its advantages and disadvantages;

▶ Discuss how organizational structure can help or hinder an organization's quest to fulfil its mission and meet its goals and objectives; and

▶ Explain why there is no perfect form of organization.

## The Organization of Tomorrow

THE ORGANIZATION OF TOMORROW WILL BE STRUCtured much differently than that of today. The organizations that are most successful will be those that are highly competitive and that can adapt quickly to their customers' demands and changes in the environment. Often their organizational structure will help to determine their degree of competitiveness. According to David Nadler, president of Delta Consulting Group, who represents such clients as AT&T, Xerox, and Corning, "CEOs feel that companies need to be structured in dramatically different ways." Although there is no agreement on exactly what this organization will look like, a picture of a flat, lean, high-performance workplace is emerging. A decade from now, the average company will be smaller and employ fewer people and the traditional hierarchical organization often will be modified by the development of other forms such as the network of specialists. The model of doing business will shift from making a product to providing customer service, and work itself will be redefined to include constant learning and more innovative thinking.  ▶

One trend is the use of an organizational structure that includes teams of employees. It has been estimated that about one in five North American employers has self-managed teams in some areas of their operations. This approach is used in a General Electric factory in Puerto Rico. There, 172 hourly workers, 15 salaried advisers, and 1 manager produce surge protectors that guard power stations and transmission lines against lightning strikes. There are three layers of employees, no supervisors, and no supporting staff functions. A similar plant in a traditional Canadian company typically would employ about twice as many salaried people at various managerial and supervisory levels. But at the GE plant each hourly worker is on a team with about ten people that meet weekly. Each team "owns" some portion of the work—assembly, shipping, receiving, and so on. Team members come from all areas of the plant so that each team has representatives from all facets of operations. An adviser attends the meetings but sits in the back of the room, speaking up only if the team needs help.

The Chrysler Corporation also uses teams at its component plant in New Castle, Indiana. In the mid-1980s the company was about to shut down the plant because it was experiencing continual problems. According to machine shop worker John Pennington, "If they wanted us to run five parts, we would run two. I missed work when I wanted to. We would drink coffee and just wait for the problem to get corrected." In 1986 Chrysler initiated self-management teams in a last-ditch effort to save the plant. Workers were renamed "technicians" and line supervisors became "team advisers." Time clocks were removed. Employees were organized into 77 teams that assign tasks, confront lazy workers, order repairs, and even alter working hours. Employees took responsibility for the plant and absenteeism dropped from 7 percent to less than 3 percent. Equally important, the number of defects fell from 300 parts per million to 20 parts per million, while production costs dropped. ■

Source: Adapted from Walter Kiechel III, "How We Will Work in the Year 2000," *Fortune* (May 17, 1993): 38-52; Thomas A. Stewart, "The Search for the Organization of Tomorrow," *Fortune* (May 18, 1992): 92-98; Joann S. Lublin, "Trying to Increase Worker Productivity, More Employees Alter Management Style," *The Wall Street Journal* (February 13, 1992): B1, B7; Michael F. Dealy and Frederico DeAlmeida, "Changing Organizational Structure," *Fortune* (July 13, 1992): Advertisement section.

Competitiveness is a key to success in today's complex global environment. Organizations that can react promptly and adapt to the constantly changing environment will survive. They must be designed so that all employees are committed to satisfying customers. Only with this commitment can the organization become and remain competitive.

This chapter presents the basic elements of organizing. It first discusses the concept of organizing and organizational structure, including some of its myths and problems. It then examines four options about which managers must make decisions in determining organizational structure: specialization of jobs, delegation of authority, departmentalization, and span of control. The question of centralization versus decentralization is examined, as are various types of organizational design.

## Organizing and Organizational Structure

In Chapter 1 it was noted that the organizing function provides a structure of task and authority relationships. *Organizing* is the process of structuring both human and physical resources to accomplish organizational objectives. Thus, organizing involves dividing tasks into jobs, delegating authority, determining the appropriate bases for departmentalizing jobs and coordinating tasks, and deciding the optimum number of jobs in each department.[1]

Developing a responsive organizational structure is one of the most critical challenges facing managers today. Yet there is often an obvious a gap between what managers say and what they do. This gap is particularly evident when linking quality performance with customer satisfaction.[2] One study found that:

- Eighteen percent of North American companies report that senior management evaluates quality performance less than annually or not at all, compared with only 2 percent of Japanese companies.
- Twenty-two percent of North American companies regularly translate customer expectations into the design of new products or services, compared with 58 percent of Japanese companies.
- Twenty-two percent of North American companies report that technology is of primary importance in meeting customer expectations, compared with 49 percent of Japanese companies.[3]

Some large corporations such as Home Depot and Microsoft have succeeded because, despite their size, their organizations are nimble and can respond quickly to changes in the market.[4] In many other companies, however, managers recognize that their organization is not responsive and flexible, that it doesn't move quickly when it must. Some of this rigidity stems from organizational inertia. But these same managers often attribute this problem to people—departments that cannot get along with each

---

### *Real World Reflection*    5-1

## Implementing Workplace-based Teams

Four stages of team development are identified in *The Team Handbook* by Peter R. Scholtes.

- Stage 1: Forming—Team members cautiously explore the boundaries and limitations of acceptable behaviour within the group. Individuals begin to get a sense of their status as part of the group, and the guidance of a leader often takes shape.
- Stage 2: Storming—This is a difficult stage for most teams as team members try to clarify the task and objectives of the team, how decisions will be reached, and how personal and professional experience will determine which actions the team should take. This is a time when progress towards the team goal may be sacrificed in order to begin to understand how the members will work together.
- Stage 3: Norming—During this stage, the needs of individuals become subverted to team roles and objectives. Ground rules and roles within the team may allow members to exercise their individuality while becoming more collaborative and less competitive within the team environment.
- Stage 4: Performing—The team finally begins to perform when the relationship and expectations of the team become solidified. Diagnosing and solving problems becomes the focus, as well as implementing changes. An acceptance of team members' strengths and weaknesses assists the team in further development. All members become a cohesive whole.

Contributed by Sherry Campbell, British Columbia Institute of Technology.

other, uncommitted or unmotivated employees, or a general inability to develop new products in a timely fashion. These deficiencies may well be indicators of problems with organizational structure.

**organizational structure**
The framework of inter-relationships among individuals and departments that describes relationships of reporting and accountability.

**Organizational structure** is the framework of jobs and departments that directs the behaviour of individuals and groups towards achieving the organization's objectives. An effective organization is one that leads to customer satisfaction. When customers are not satisfied, there is a chance that the fault is with the organizational structure. While the organizing *function* refers to the decisions made by managers, organizational *structure* reflects one outcome of those decisions.

Organizational structure must be consistent with an organization's strategy. Strategic planning specifies *what* will be accomplished and *when*; organizational structure specifies *who* will accomplish what and *how* it will be accomplished. Many organizations, unfortunately, try to implement a new strategy with an obsolete organizational structure. The result becomes the failed "initiative of the month." For instance, an organization may recognize a need to be more market driven or more quality conscious. The result is often the announcement of a new program designed to enhance customer satisfaction or quality improvement. But an organization doesn't simply *become* quality conscious. Rather it must develop an organizational structure that results in the behaviours that the strategy calls for. In developing an effective organizational structure, managers must be aware of several myths and avoid the problems associated with organizational structure.

## Overcoming Myths about Organizational Structure

An effective organizational structure does not result from chance, or by historical accident. It is the responsibility of management to make deliberate decisions to develop a structure that enhances the organization's overall strategy, taking into consideration factors such as competition and both external and internal environments. Managers, in attempting to implement a new program or directive, often encounter resistance to change. Over time, organizational structures become quite ingrained and resistant to change. This behaviour is not consistent with an environment that is constantly changing and it can place an organization in a weak position relative to competitors. To keep in step with the constantly changing environment, many organizations find themselves reorganizing on a regular basis.[5]

Managers also must recognize that there is no single best structure for an organization, even among similar types of organizations. What works at Placer Dome may be different from what works at Teck Corporation or Inco, even though all three are multinational mineral development companies. The challenge that managers face is to design the best structure for a specific organization, a structure that facilitates getting work done well. If structure impedes the completion of work and hence the achievement of the organization's objectives, this situation constitutes a management failure. If a bank teller cannot respond to a customer's request because of lack of authority, this probably represents a structural problem that management must address if the bank is to

*Structural changes in an organization may allow employees to achieve greater efficiency.*

be competitive. Likewise, if an assembly line worker does not have the knowledge or ability to correct minor problems that occur frequently, managers should consider how structural changes could correct this bottleneck in efficiency. Often employees cannot function to their greatest potential because the organization's structure gets in their way.

## Detecting Problems in Organizational Structure

When is organizational structure a problem? Ultimately, whenever work is not getting done well, there likely is a problem with organizational structure. Many factors or circumstances may account for such problems. Conflicts between departments or groups within an organization suggest a structural problem. It is tempting to attribute these conflicts to personality differences but often such differences would not have arisen if the organizational structure had been more appropriate to the circumstances and understood by everyone involved. Conflicts also may arise because of differences in the goals of different departments. For example, the marketing department is usually most concerned with sales, introducing new products, and keeping customers satisfied, while the production department is most concerned with quality control, maintaining production schedules, and keeping costs down. These differing priorities must be resolved. The organization's structure can either facilitate or exacerbate the differences. Difficulty in coordinating work among related departments, slowness in adapting to change, and ambiguous job assignments also indicate problems with organizational structure. If employees are unsure what goals are most important or what work they should concentrate on, organizational structure may be the underlying problem.

Structural problems can be disastrous for an organization. When structure has failed to keep up with changing conditions, the organization may become little more than a collection of departments or independent groups, each pursuing its own goals rather than the common goals of the overall organization. When this happens, an organization's structure determines what it does, rather than vice versa. It is an important principle of management that strategy should dictate structure. If, on the contrary, structure is allowed to dictate strategy, it can prevent innovation and change. Structure must be consciously designed so that it reflects the organization's goals and objectives and facilitates rather than impedes activities that best accomplish those goals and objectives.

General Motors illustrates how structural problems can damage an organization. In 1979 GM had a 46 percent share of the North American market for cars and light trucks. Twelve years later its share had fallen below 35 percent. Many factors contributed to GM's problems, including failure to anticipate the drop in demand for large cars, retention of obsolete factories, and marketing what was seen as a relatively poor-quality product. All were symptoms of a nonresponsive organizational structure that was failing. Efforts to change GM's structure have been hampered by a stubborn middle-management bureaucracy and by lack of cooperation from the United Auto Workers union. In addition to eliminating 74,000 jobs (including thousands of white-collar jobs) and 21 factories, many observers believe that GM needs to restructure its entire organization to survive. Restructuring may include doing away with six separate operating divisions—Buick, Pontiac, Chevrolet, Oldsmobile, Cadillac, and Saturn—even while retaining the brand names.[6] Although GM may face other problems, those problems resulting from structure can be addressed, albeit with care and subject to opposition from those employees who resist change. Chapter 9 discusses philosophies and techniques for managing change, but before they can be employed, decisions must be made about what organizational structure will be selected from the many choices available.

Organizational structure is one of the major influences on employees' perception of their work and on their behaviour. One important management job is to design an organizational structure that enables employees to do their best work and to achieve the organization's objectives. The next section examines the fundamental considerations or decisions that determine organizational structure.

## Determining Organizational Structure

Most people who have worked in some type of organization tend to think of structure in narrow terms. From this perspective, several questions arise, all of which have a personal focus. These questions include:

1. What is one's own job task?
2. To whom does one report?
3. How much responsibility does one have?
4. Is one's authority commensurate with one's responsibility?

Managers responsible for designing organizational structure must think in much broader terms that describe the entire structure, not just the jobs that comprise it. In determining which type of structure might enable people to do their best work, managers make many decisions. The four major decisions pertain to the degrees of specialization of jobs, delegation of authority, departmentalization, and span of control.

Exhibit 5-1 summarizes some of the choices that managers face while addressing these decisions. In general, the structure of an organization falls on roughly the same part of each continuum. In other words, an organization structured for employees to do highly specialized jobs also will tend to group jobs according to homogeneous or common functions and assign each manager to supervise a few employees, who collectively have only minimal authority. The following sections examine each of these decisions in greater detail.

## Specialization of Jobs

Managers must decide the degree of specialization to reflect in job descriptions and assignments. Most organizations operate with some degree of specialization, with different employees performing different tasks. For example, nurses in a hospital may be assigned to operating rooms, pediatric service, emergency wards, intensive care wards, or any number of other specialities. All have comparable basic nursing education, but have different specialized training in their assigned tasks. By dividing tasks into narrow

**Exhibit 5-1**

*Designing Organizational Structure*

Specialization of jobs:

High _____Low

Delegation of authority:

Centralized _____Decentralized

Departmentalization:

Homogeneous_____Heterogeneous

Span of control:

Narrow_____Wide

specialties, the organization may gain the benefits derived from division of labour. Among other possible benefits, specialization reduces the time and effort required for employee training because each nurse needs to learn fewer skills than if all of them were responsible for all tasks in the hospital. Frederick Taylor predicted that a high degree of specialization would result in greatest efficiency and cost effectiveness.[7] But with these expected benefits, there come some disadvantages.

## Scientific Management versus Craftsmanship

As described in Chapter 1, Taylor's system of scientific management required that tasks be divided into the smallest possible elements and that problem solving be left to managers. Taylor, through his time and motion studies, identified basic movements that were designed to minimize effort and maximize the output of lathe operators, iron workers, and bricklayers. Taylor's thinking has permeated our entire society. Specialization now applies to employees as diverse as retail clerks, nurses, and accountants. People learn a job routine and repeat the required tasks over and over. If they experience problems, they consult a supervisor or manager. Work or execution is clearly separate from thinking or planning.

It is not hard to understand why this system replaced the craftsmanship system, which for many years was considered the only alternative to scientific management. According to quality expert Joseph Juran, "Taylor's concept of separating planning from execution fitted our culture and, at the time, was very logical. You had a lot of immigrants … some of them were completely illiterate. And they were in no position, in [Taylor's] opinion, to make decisions on how work should be done."[8]

Taylor reflected the view commonly held in his day that anyone coming from another country inevitably must be uneducated, unskilled, and worthy of little respect. In today's workplace, many managers still cling to that misconception, even though Statistics Canada consistently has revealed that immigrants in recent decades have had higher average educational levels than second-, third-, and fourth-generation Canadians. Failure to recognize this fact has led many managers to retain increasingly outmoded structures and has caused many organizations to fall behind in the competitive race. This failure illustrates the wisdom of the reworded adage that "what you don't know *can* hurt you."

**Exhibit 5-2**

*Scientific Management versus Craftsmanship*

| | Scientific Management | Craftsmanship |
|---|---|---|
| *Strengths* | | |
| | High productivity | High skill |
| | Lower cost | High-quality output |
| | Higher wages | Pride in work |
| | Unskilled workers | High job interest |
| | Predictable scheduling | Control by worker |
| *Weaknesses* | | |
| | Low morale and boredom | Low productivity |
| | Poor quality | Higher cost |
| | Lack of pride | Lower wages |
| | Low job interest | Poor control |
| | Control by managers | Scheduling problems |

Craftsmanship is based on principles that are opposite to those prescribed by Taylor in his scientific management theories. The employee who is engaged in a craft tends to be responsible for a series of tasks, rather than the few tasks typical of specialization. In the craftsmanship mode, the quality of the product produced is the responsibility of the craftsman. Management coordinates and provides the means and facilities for the craftsman to perform the entire operation. Craftsmanship can produce high-quality products but is expensive and may result in low output. At one extreme, the scientific management approach, the highly specialized employee tightens one bolt or assembles one part. At the other extreme, the craft approach, the employee starts with raw material, then shapes, assembles, and applies finishes to it, only relinquishing the product when it is completed and ready to be delivered to the customer. Exhibit 5-2 on page 177 illustrates some of the strengths and weaknesses of each approach.

The development of the assembly line replaced craftsmanship in many industries, and gave way to scientific management and greater specialization. For many years, it was assumed that the strengths of scientific management would overcome the deficiencies of craftsmanship. It has since been recognized that each approach has its strengths and weaknesses, and that some combination of the two may produce optimum results.

As noted earlier, many think of organizational structure in terms of their own jobs. Specialization has in some instances inspired a damaging attitude of "that's not my job." This rigid compartmentalization has seriously hurt some organizations. Many organizations are now searching for an alternative approach.

## Teams

As they rebuilt after the devastation of the Second World War, many Japanese companies decided that there were problems with the mindless, repetitive assembly-line jobs that grew out of the Industrial Revolution and that were endorsed and advocated by Taylor. The strong Japanese unions found common cause with Japanese managers in iden-

*Most furniture is produced on assembly lines, but for those willing to pay premium prices, hand construction and finishing may produce unique products of particularly high quality.*

tifying Taylor's concepts of time and motion with their concomitant effects on employees: high rates of absenteeism, low morale, and poor-quality output. While some parts of the world were experiencing the benefits of specialization, Japan was experiencing its disadvantages and moving away from the concept of specialization. Managers in Western nations are now recognizing these same disadvantages and, like the Japanese, also will have to make changes if they are to remain competitive.

In his seminars, W. Edwards Deming argued for the right of all people to have "joy in their work."[9] He emphasized that to continue to survive and be able to provide employment, companies must make money. At the same time, according to Deming, unless people enjoy their work there will be little commitment to the organization and to quality of output—key factors among the many that contribute to greater profit. Deming drew an analogy between designing an organizational structure and designing a good orchestra. In both activities, the players exist to support each other and to contribute to a harmonious result. According to Deming, an organization is "a network of people, materials, methods, equipment, all working in support of each other for the common aim."[10] Thus, managers must determine the appropriate degree of specialization without creating a demotivating and demoralizing environment in which employees do not do their best work.

Many organizations are modifying and redesigning jobs so that they can be performed by teams.[11] The most popular type of team is the *problem-solving team,* which is comprised of knowledgeable employees who gather to solve a specific problem that has developed. A *work team,* as noted in the discussion of decision making in Chapter 3, is a group of employees who work closely together to pursue common objectives.[12] Some organizations use teams in many areas of their operations. Others use teams more selectively, perhaps just for special projects. Some teams are directed by a manager while others are self-managed. In self-managed work teams, to a large extent the workers effectively become their own managers. This change in responsibility may help to unlock

## Real World Reflection    5-2

### What Are the Different Kinds of Teams? What Are They Used For?

The following are various types of teams:

- task teams (formed for the purpose of achieving a specific task);
- project teams (with the purpose of planning, implementing, and/or evaluating projects);
- communication teams (designed for the exchange of information);
- design teams (with a focus on preparation and design of projects, operations, and systems);
- quality teams (with ongoing objectives for quality improvement);
- unit teams (team-based operational groups with ever-changing objectives).

Teams may be short-term, temporary, or formed for a specific purpose and duration, or they may be longer-term, ongoing, and a standardized means for reaching organizational, professional, and related workplace objectives.

Contributed by Sherry Campbell, British Columbia Institute of Technology.

their creative and intellectual capabilities. At W.L. Gore & Associates—a manufacturer of a wide range of electronic, medical, fabric, and industrial products—*associates* (the term *employee* is not used) work on self-directed teams without managers or bosses.[13]

Regardless of which type of team is used, teams must be able to operate flexibly and effectively to produce innovative products. If the team is properly structured and has been delegated appropriate authority, it sometimes can make decisions quicker than can be done in the more traditional hierarchical organization. If the team has a faulty structure or is not accorded authority, it may become little more than a repository for expired ideas and lost dreams. Ideally, team members learn each other's jobs and bring their ideas together, capitalizing on each other's creativity. When truly empowered, a work team can change bored and demoralized *workers* into innovative and productive *partners*. Johnsonville Foods was a pioneer in the use of self-managed teams to run a factory. Teammates were given the power to hire and fire members and to award bonuses to one another.[14]

If team members are drawn from several different departments or units, they may feel a conflict between their "traditional" reporting relationships and their responsibilities to the team and its sponsor. This causes confusion in the organizational structure and may lead to a loss of accountability. On the other hand, if a team's members are all from a single department or unit, simply renaming it as a team will not cause it to function any differently than when it was organized in the more traditional hierarchy. In moving from a traditional form of organization to teams, managers are effectively asked to transform themselves into team leaders. This is not a simple process. Individuals thrust into this new role of team leader require behavioural skills—coaching, motivating, and empowering—and a change in mind set. The skills needed most by team leaders are:

- the ability to admit comfortably that they don't know everything;
- the good sense to know when to intervene with the team and when not to do so;
- the personal confidence to share power;
- the self-discipline to focus on the power they take on, not on what they give up; and
- the habit of learning while on the job.[15]

Making the transformation to this type of role does not come easily to anyone, but these skills can be learned, and innovative organizations provide relevant training and mentoring for managers who are facing these changes.

## Quality Circles

It has come to be recognized that in many situations, the people who work with the process are often best able to identify, analyze, and correct any problems that arise. In 1962 some Japanese companies began to experiment with a structure that reflected this belief. They expanded what is known as the quality circle into a highly developed system. A **quality circle** is a small group of people, usually fewer than ten, who do similar work and meet about once a week to discuss their work, identify problems, and present possible solutions.[16] Participation in the quality circle is voluntary and the members select their own moderator or team leader to lead discussions. The group's findings and proposals are forwarded to management for consideration.

A few North American companies began using quality circles in the mid-1970s and the concept grew in popularity during the next 15 years. Unfortunately, some efforts to use quality circles failed because they were merely cosmetic adaptations of the scientific management system. In some cases the aim of the manager was only to increase the productivity of employees. Not surprisingly, the employees recognized this sham and

**quality circle**
A group of perhaps six to ten employees who do similar work within an organization and meet regularly to discuss the effectiveness of their work and possible solutions to problems that arise.

*Japanese cultural norms lend themselves to decision making by consensus, called* ringisei, *more readily than do the North American cultural norms that stress individuality.*

refused to cooperate. But these failures appear to have resulted from how the concept was applied, rather than from flaws in the concept itself. In particular, problems in implementation often have stemmed from managers being unwilling or unable to change their mind sets from the "traditional" hierarchical approach to one of greater equality with non-managerial employees. The quality control concept has been most successful when used as part of an organization-wide improvement effort. Quality circles cannot simply be "installed" in an organization. If managers still control the thinking that takes place within quality circles, they have instituted quality circles in name only. More will be said about quality circles in Chapter 11.

The extent to which jobs are to be specialized is a critical managerial decision. The important point here is that jobs may vary considerably in this respect. By changing the degree to which jobs are specialized, managers change the structure of the organization. Chapter 8 discusses job design in further detail.

## Delegation of Authority

When designing an organizational structure, managers also must consider the extent to which authority will be distributed throughout the organization. As discussed in Chapter 3, *authority* is the organizationally sanctioned right to make a decision. Managers delegate (assign) certain tasks to others, simply because no one person can get all the work done. When delegating authority, managers must weigh the pros and cons of decentralization and centralization and strike an appropriate balance for the organization.

**decentralization**
Distributing authority throughout the organization, reducing the degree of direct control exerted by senior executives and other central figures; also, developing semi-autonomous divisions in which decisions are made within only general guidelines.

**centralization**
Assigning most authority to senior executives and other central figures, so that they make most major decisions; also, consolidating decision-making authority in a central core of the organization.

### Decentralization and Centralization

Authority can be distributed throughout the organization or held in the hands of a few. **Decentralization** is the process of distributing authority throughout the organization. It delegates to an organization member (historically, a manager) the right to make a decision within parameters (which may be either explicit or implicit but are clearly understood) without obtaining approval from a higher-level manager. The authority to identify problems or issues and to recommend solutions is delegated as well. By way of contrast, **centralization** is the process of retaining authority in the hands of a few high-level managers, who make all important decisions.

Decentralization has several advantages. Managers develop their own decision-making skills and may be motivated to perform effectively because advancement is related to performance. Managers also can exercise more autonomy, which usually increases job satisfaction and motivation, contributing to the organization's profitability. Decentralization is one of the factors suggested by managers as having contributed to the profitability of companies such as Bombardier, Imasco, Motorola, and United Parcel Service, all of which created nearly autonomous divisions.[17]

Decentralization also has a number of disadvantages. The most obvious is that when the same problem faces different people, they may make different decisions. This can

## Management in the Real World　5-1

### Elements of Organizing: Reflections by Philip Crosby

One thing we all learn as we practise the art/science of management is that it is very hard to process information through a system. Once we get past the level where we see each employee several times a day, it becomes necessary to rely on other people or systems to get the word out.

When I started Philip Crosby Associates (PCA), I decided that we would have a way of working that guaranteed each associate all the information and direction they needed at all times. Traditionally the way to attempt this is to have layers of supervision and pass things along like a chain letter. However supervisors, at all levels, only look up. They worry about their boss(es) more than they worry about their employees. All of the bosses I worked for in the early stages of my career spent their time staying out of trouble and keeping us away from what was happening. Any information they were supposed to transmit was edited severely. Their main source of intimidation and control was that they knew more than their subordinates about what was going on. However, when we think that their bosses were doing the same thing, we realize that they also were rather uninformed.

I didn't want a system of supervision in PCA for the purpose of control. Rather we would set it up so people would have leaders who helped them. Management would take on the job of communicating with people. The quality improvement team would be responsible for recognition, and the supervisors would concentrate on supporting and helping associates. The key to it all would be openness; that is why we concentrated on the word *associate* rather than *employee*.

For the routine life of the company we set up a weekly newspaper (when there were only 30 associates) and monthly Family Council meetings. At that time everyone, including the switchboard operator, came to a session lasting about an hour where all was revealed. Anyone could ask anything or write it down so they didn't have to speak up. Management gave status reports; committees or teams revealed their status. A weekly informal newsletter took care of personal announcements.

We set up a Systems Integrity Board consisting of senior management. Every change that was going to be made was approved by this board, which then let everyone know about it. When you are operating 25 or so classrooms and teaching in several languages, changing the words on one chart can cause chaos if it isn't managed. Procedural changes were accomplished by the procedures committee, which represented all departments. We held all company meetings on one day each month; the rest of the month was meeting-free. As a result of these efforts and more, the associates did not have to rely on their supervisors for general information, there were virtually no rumours (any that came up could be addressed at the Family Council), and everyone knew what was going on. Senior management was scheduled by the Quality Improvement Team to get around and see everyone regularly. The president had a dinner at each location every year to present awards and such, and we had an annual company black tie get-together. All of this was to let people know that it was all right for them to participate in running the company. And they did.

create confusion or even conflict within the organization. Furthermore, those charged with making decisions may hesitate to do so, because they fear that they will make the "wrong" decisions and be subject to criticism or discipline. To overcome these defects, delegation requires costly management training. If delegation is instituted in name only, with the organization retaining real hierarchical control, top managers may require extensive (and sometimes stifling) planning and reporting procedures. If this occurs, the purposes of delegation are defeated.

Some companies have moved towards decentralization, but are now drawing back, having experienced some of its disadvantages. KFC envisioned tastier food and happier customers when it decentralized several years ago. But the company's regional divisions apparently failed to coordinate their efforts, resulting in so much redundancy that restructuring was a failure.[18] Aluminum Co. of America (Alcoa) found that customers' rejections increased and customer satisfaction decreased after the firm decentralized.[19] Other companies, including Levi Strauss, have experienced similar problems with decentralization—overlap in functions and a lack of coordination. Following an experiment with decentralization of its order-processing system, Levi Strauss reverted to centralized control after retailers complained that they had to work with multiple divisions, each of which had its own procedures.[20]

In 1982, Peters and Waterman's book, *In Search of Excellence,* took the North American business world by storm. It created a following of almost cult-like characteristics. Now, with the passage of time, the enthusiasm has faded somewhat. Even so, it is instructive to consider the concepts the authors described. They identified eight attributes that they said characterized North America's best-run companies.[21] One of these attributes is that each company they identified as excellent was at the same time both centralized and decentralized. Those companies were said to delegate authority all the way to the shop floor yet insist on centralizing certain decisions that they believed to be critical to the company's core values. For instance, 3M was, and still is, recognized for encouraging engineers to *bootleg,* by which they mean to explore new product ideas using time, energy, and funds borrowed from other assignments. Yet a select group of engineers at 3M retains relatively tight control over *funding* new product development projects after the initial bootleg phase. Some companies are decentralizing operations closest to the customer to remain responsive in the marketplace. Less visible internal functions (such as personnel or order processing, as in the case of Levi Strauss) are centralized. In essence, what Peters and Waterman were describing, and what seems to be most successful, is the coexistence of firm, centralized direction and adequate individual autonomy—a difficult balance for managers to strike.

## Empowerment

**empowerment**
Delegating decision-making authority to individuals, usually to people in what traditionally were relatively subordinate positions.

Some organizations have begun to empower employees to make decisions that typically have been made by superiors. **Empowerment** involves giving to employees responsible for hands-on production or service activities the authority to make decisions or take action without prior approval.[22] For instance, a machine operator can stop production if a problem is detected, or a ticket agent can give a customer a refund without calling a supervisor. When discussing decentralization, one usually refers to the delegation of authority from managers to other *managers.* Empowerment means that process control, quality assessment, and customer relations become part of *everyone's* responsibility and that all individuals are given the ability and authority to take positive actions that will lead to superior company performance. This is the case for workers at both UPS and Federal Express. For example, at Federal Express, "all workers are routinely expected to take whatever initiative is required to fix problems and/or extend first rate service to a customer."[23]

Empowerment is at the heart of any total quality management program. It helps to accomplish many points advocated by leading quality experts. One of Philip Crosby's 14 points is to define the type of training employees need to carry out their roles in the quality improvement process.[24] Deming's points include removing barriers that rob employees of their pride of workmanship and making everyone responsible for the quality transformation.[25] The goal of employee empowerment is to stop depending entirely on extrinsic incentives such as money to motivate employees, and instead to build a work environment that motivates them from within through intrinsic incentives such as pride

*At UPS, employees are empowered to make decisions that address immediate problems, and this ultimately leads to success for the company.*

in their work and a sense that they personally matter.[26] McGregor, with his Theory X and Y, argued a similar case more than 30 years ago.[27]

Employees' lack of literacy is a major drawback to quality programs and to the competitiveness of an organization. Studies show that 2 percent of Canadians are totally unable to read or write in either of Canada's official languages. However, the ability to read simple passages is not enough to make it possible for an employee to read, understand, and put into practice the kind of instructions that appear in manuals or in memos circulated within an organization. Many sociologists have found that to be functionally literate a person must have acquired the equivalent of a grade nine education, and that if less than a grade five ability has been acquired, the person is "functionally illiterate."

Applying these standards, one in every five Canadians is functionally illiterate. A study conducted two decades ago that tested actual ability found that 19.6 percent of males 15 years of age and older were functionally illiterate; for females, the rate was 20.5 percent.[28] A more recent study by the United Nations Development Program confirms these figures and indicates that the situation has not improved materially. That study shows that no matter how long individuals had gone to school, 16.6 percent of adult Canadians still lack "adequate literacy skills."[29] These are shocking figures, but the essential message for managers is that they cannot rely solely on written communication to deliver messages to employees. Not being aware of this fact has been the underlying cause of many failures in well-meaning attempts at empowerment. More will be said about communication in Chapter 10.

If companies want to be competitive and empower employees, they may need to educate them. With layers of supervisors being eliminated, assembly line workers are being asked to make decisions that they have never had to face before. This requires them to have at least basic education skills. At automotive plants, for instance, production line workers are being asked to assemble the product, inspect it for quality at every stage of production, and fix any problems. It is not possible for them to follow plans and written directions unless they can read and understand them. Neither is it possible for them to communicate problems they encounter or to make coherent suggestions. Recognizing this problem, a number of organizations have developed in-house education programs or have subsidized outside programs to teach employees to read, write, and apply basic mathematical skills.

*More and more companies encourage employees to upgrade their skills by offering courses in-house or by supplying tuition assistance.*

## Chain of Command

The delegation of authority creates a **chain of command**, the formal channel that defines the lines of authority from the top to the bottom of

**Exhibit 5-3**   *Chain of Command*

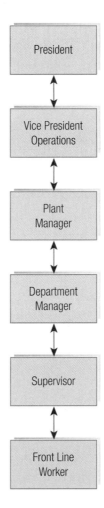

chain of command
The formal channel that
defines the lines of
authority and account-
ability in a hierarchical
organizational structure.

the organization. An example is illustrated in Exhibit 5-3. The chain of command reflects the formal communication links among all positions in the organization. It specifies to whom each employee is accountable and from whom each employee is to receive direction. Although the chain of command may be modified in certain matrix-type organizations, the basic rule is that no individual should report to more than one supervisor. Modern organizations are empowering employees to communicate with persons outside of the chain when circumstances warrant it. Communication both within and outside the chain of command is discussed in Chapter 10.

## Line and Staff Positions

line position
A position to which deci-
sion-making authority
has been delegated,
within the chain of com-
mand from senior man-
agers to front-line
production or service
employees.

The chain of command includes both line and staff positions. A **line position** is one that is in the direct chain of command from front-line employees to top management. In the simplified organization chart shown in Exhibit 5-4, the president, the vice presidents of operations and marketing, and the positions shown at the director and manager levels are classified as *line* positions. In practice, there would be several managers and other line positions, but the number has been reduced in this chart to avoid clutter and

**Exhibit 5-4**   *Differentiation Between Line and Staff Positions*

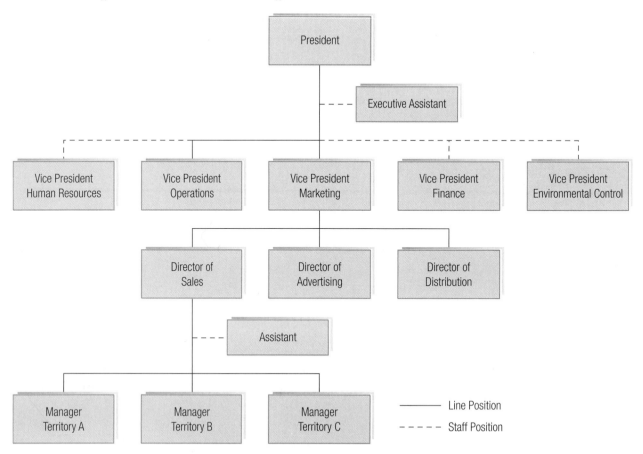

confusion. In line positions, directions could emanate from top management and progress down to the people at the front-line positions of machine operators and, along another line, to sales personnel who deal directly with customers. **Staff positions**, on the other hand, are occupied by those who facilitate the work of or provide advice to those in line positions but who do not control mainstream operations. This is not to say that they are less important, but only that they do not directly "produce" the product or service. In Exhibit 5-4, the executive assistant to the president, the vice presidents of human resources and environmental control, and the assistant to the director of sales are classified as *staff* positions, as would be the directors and managers who are accountable to these executives. People in staff positions provide support to others but do not directly produce the product or service for which the organization exists.

An organization's finance functions illustrate both the difficulty and the futility of making rigid distinctions between line and staff positions. In a manufacturing establishment, there could be no production unless someone procured the necessary raw materials and components. Procurement is usually a finance function, so by this reasoning, finance would be a line function. Another finance function, payroll, is just as essential, since employees would not stay long if they were not paid. Yet the payroll function is usually considered a staff function. Similarly, the accounting function of finance generally is thought of as staff, because in theory (although not in practice) production and sales could continue even if no accounting records were being kept. From these

**Real World Reflection**    **5-3**

## How Do You Know If Your Team Is Effective?

Most teams exist and persist because individuals working on their own could not accomplish the same work and because the involvement of individuals in teams encourages satisfaction for individuals in collecting resources and belonging to the team.

What are the factors that lead to team development and effectiveness?

- Shared goals and objectives: Do the team members understand and agree on goals and objectives?
- Use of resources: Are the resources of all team members fully recognized and used?
- Trust and conflict resolution: Is there a high degree of trust among team members, and is conflict dealt with openly and worked through?
- Leadership: Is there full participation in leadership, with leadership roles shared by team members?
- Control and procedures: Are there effective procedures to guide team functioning? Do team members support these procedures and regulate themselves?
- Interpersonal communications: Are communications between team members open and participative?
- Problem solving/decision making: Does the team have well-established and agreed-upon approaches to problem solving and decision making?
- Experimentation/creativity: Does the team experiment with different ways of doing things and is it creative in its approach?
- Evaluation: Does the team regularly evaluate its functioning and processes?

Contributed by Sherry Campbell, British Columbia Institute of Technology.

---

examples, it can be seen that essentiality is not a basis for distinguishing line positions from staff positions.

Another test is whether directions or orders progress through a function as they are being transmitted from the CEO downward through the hierarchy to the front-line workers. By this measure, finance would have to be classified as a staff function, since it would not be in this direct line. It is only within the finance function itself that line authority exists; for instance, from the CEO to the vice president of finance to the comptroller to the chief accountant to each accountant or accounting clerk.

Although making the distinction between line and staff positions may be useful for some purposes, many companies are now recognizing that it is not helpful to create, even by implication, two classes of managers and other employees. It is harmful to overall morale, and can lead to jealousy and conflict, if line and staff employees consider themselves to be of two different types. All too often sales people may think or say to others in the organization, "There wouldn't be any money to pay your salaries if we didn't sell the product." In response, production people may think or say, "If we didn't produce the product (or deliver the service) the company wouldn't even exist." When those attitudes persist, the natural reaction among staff personnel is to feel superior to line people, thinking that line people do not have the finely tuned understanding of the overall organization that staff personnel at head office have. And it is equally likely for line people to scorn staff people, "who are in an ivory tower and don't understand the real world!" Such divisions may be *fostered* by managers who are somewhat jealous and protective of their own turf. To avoid this destructive atmosphere, managers have to help all workers understand that if a position exists in the organization—whether it be an accountant, an order clerk, a telephone operator, or a machine operator—that position is considered essential to the organization's well-being. All employees, whether in line or staff positions, work towards common goals and are equally important to their achievement.

## Departmentalization

**departmentalization**
Grouping jobs according to some similarities, in order to simplify and clarify the chain of command and authority and to facilitate cooperation among those with similar responsibilities or tasks.

**Departmentalization** is the process of grouping jobs according to some logical arrangement of segments or units. As an organization grows in size and as job specialization increases, the organization's structure becomes more complex. In a very small organization, such as a mom-and-pop grocery store or an entrepreneurship with only a handful of employees, the owner/manager can supervise everyone. In a large grocery chain, managerial positions are created according to some plan, perhaps creating separate meat, deli, bakery, produce, and dairy departments, each headed by a manager who reports to the overall store manager. The most common bases for departmentalization are function, product, customer, and geographic area.

**functional departmentalization**
Departmentalization by function, such as finance, human relations, production, and marketing.

Grouping jobs together according to the functions of the organization is called **functional departmentalization**. A business may include functions such as production, finance, marketing, law, research and development, and human resources. Each function is headed by an individual who may carry the title of vice president (see Exhibit 5-5). Each is (theoretically) equal to the others, and all are accountable to the president or CEO. The president, in turn, may be accountable to the CEO, who is accountable to the board of directors. (In a technical sense, the board is accountable to the shareholders, but that accountability is different in kind as well as in degree from the accountabilities within the organization.)

**product departmentalization**
Departmentalization by type of product, such as men's suits, women's shoes, housewares, and hardware.

In companies that adopt the principle of **product departmentalization**, jobs associated with a particular product or product line are grouped in a department, while those associated with another product or product line fall within another department (see Exhibit 5-6). This form of organization enables all of the people working with a product or related products to cooperate in using their skills and expertise. For example, a manufacturer of home appliances might have a division for large appliances such as refrigerators and washing machines, another for small appliances such as toasters, and still another for power tools. Product departmentalization gives an organization the flex-

**Exhibit 5-5**  *Functional Departmentalization*

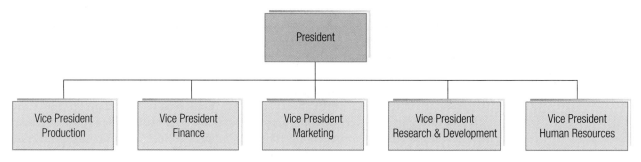

**Exhibit 5-6**   *Product Departmentalization*

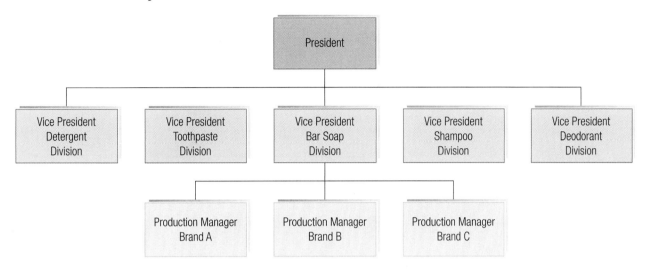

customer
departmentalization
Departmentalization by
type of customer, such as
industrial, retail outlets,
consumer, government,
hospitals, and, in some
cases, a single major customer.

ibility to develop specific strategies for different products, and is most appropriate in companies that have distinctly different product lines.

Organizations using **customer departmentalization** employ a structure that forms departments and divisions by classification of customer (see Exhibit 5-7). For example, a pharmaceutical company might have one division for consumer products, another for hospitals, another for other industrial products, and still another that specifically targets government agencies. Organizations that have a few extremely large customers or that serve diverse groups are most likely to use this approach. Banks might have separate departments for consumer accounts, commercial accounts, and relations with individuals who have large sums on deposit and who warrant (and expect) personalized treatment.

Organizations using **geographical departmentalization** employ a structure that forms departments and divisions by geographical area (see Exhibit 5-8). A company

**Exhibit 5-7**   *Customer Departmentalization*

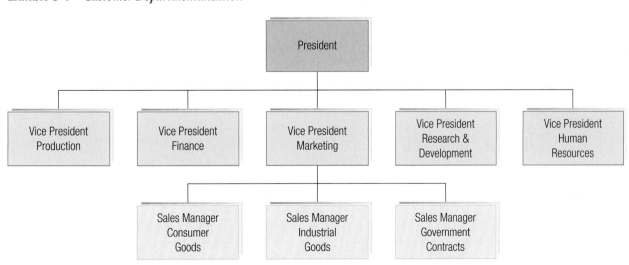

**Exhibit 5-8**    *Geographical Departmentalization*

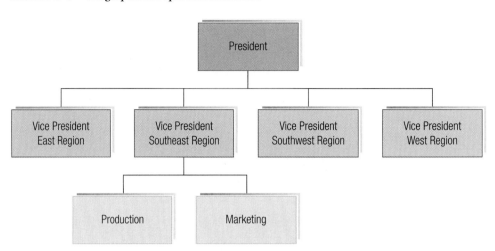

geographical
departmentalization
Departmentalization by
municipality, province,
region, country, or international region.

whose customers are all in Canada might establish separate departments for the Atlantic provinces, Quebec, Ontario, the two prairie provinces and Alberta, and British Columbia. A company that has foreign customers might add an international division or a separate division for each of the general areas in which it does business, such as Europe, Southeast Asia, and Australia/New Zealand.

Each type of departmentalization has one major strength and one major weakness. The strength of each is that it brings together specialists in the particular function, product, customer type, or geographic area. These specialists focus on the particular aspect of company activity that forms the basis for the organizational format. Communication and cooperation *within* the department is enhanced by this closeness. The weakness is that members of a particular department may focus so intently on the department's primary reason for being that communication with other departments is neglected. In such cases the interests of the department itself become paramount over the broader interests of the organization as a whole.

mixed
departmentalization
A hybrid form in which
more than one type of
departmentalization is
employed within the
same organization.

In most companies these types of departmentalization do not appear in their pure form, and a hybrid form of organization, called **mixed departmentalization**, has developed. In some cases it has resulted from accidents of history and interpersonal relationships. In others it has been the result of conscious decisions, and the recognition that all forms of departmentalization have strengths and weaknesses.

Because departmentalization reinforces specialization, some organizations are trying to involve everyone in the decision-making process by breaking down the barriers that often divide departments. Steelcase, Inc., the large office furniture company, actually did away with formal departments. People work in multidisciplinary teams that encourage interaction. Steelcase's physical facilities are not divided into departments. Instead, they contain areas for teams to work and space for working on special projects. Executives are located in the centre of the building, where everyone has equal access to them. This complex change from the traditional layout of offices took several years to implement but has been credited with cutting delivery cycles in half and dramatically reducing inventory.[30]

Another approach is that taken by Hallmark Cards, in which departmentalization is based on *process* or a specific outcome. At Hallmark, project teams are formed to develop greeting cards for each holiday—Mother's Day, Valentine's Day, Christmas, Hanukkah, and so on. Each team includes artists, writers, lithographers, marketers, and

*Project teams, such as this one, come together for a specific purpose and are disbanded once the project is completed.*

accountants. When a project has been completed, the employees return to a common pool for training or other work assignments.[31]

## Matrix Form of Organization

**matrix form of organization**
A cross-functional organizational structure in which individuals performing one function, such as accounting, are accountable to the senior executive in finance and also to the senior executive in a geographical, product, or customer department.

Still another form of organization that seems to be gaining in popularity is the **matrix form**. This form of organization is superimposed on and supplements an existing product, customer, or geographic departmentalization. In the matrix form, some employees of the staff or support functions are assigned or *seconded* (seh-KON-ded) on a relatively permanent basis to work closely with specific line departments, and are usually located physically in the offices of those line departments.

To illustrate, Exhibit 5-9 on page 192 shows the relationships in the corporate finance department of a hypothetical company that is fundamentally organized on a geographical basis and that employs the matrix form to some extent. Some members of the finance department work in the head office in Toronto, doing company-wide financial analyses and reports, managing cash flows and overall company budgets, and handling payroll for the whole company. They are organized in a simple departmental structure.

Employing the matrix concept, an accounting supervisor and six accounting staff members are seconded on a relatively permanent basis to provide service directly to the European division. They do not work in Toronto, but are stationed in the central office for that division, which happens to be in Brussels. Similarly, an accounting supervisor and four staff members are seconded to the Asian operations, and are located in Singapore. The seconded accounting staff members are directly accountable to their respective supervisors. These supervisors are directly accountable to the vice president of the geographic division to which they are seconded. In effect, they are members of the European or Asian divisions. Their primary involvement with the central finance department is to implement company-wide policies and to forward to head office financial reports from the European or Asian division in the form and at the times required by the vice

**Exhibit 5-9**    *An Abbreviated Illustration of Matrix Organization*

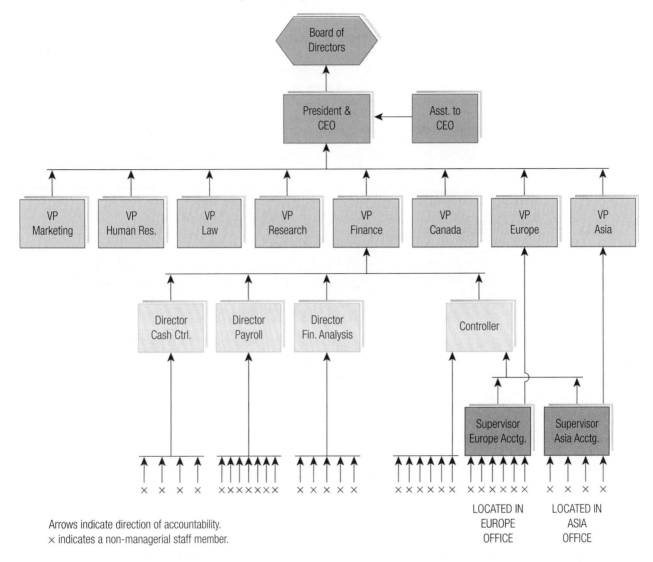

Arrows indicate direction of accountability.
× indicates a non-managerial staff member.

president of finance. In their work in Brussels or Singapore, the seconded staff members must satisfy the vice president, Europe or the vice president, Asia in terms of their accessibility, their usefulness, and their ability to function as contributing members of the geographical division. At the same time, they must meet the professional standards set by the vice president of finance and they must apply corporate policies and meet corporate schedules to that executive's satisfaction.

Exhibit 5-9 illustrates the matrix relationships for only one staff function, the finance division. To illustrate the relationships throughout the whole corporation, a similar chart would have to be drawn for each geographic (or product) division and for each staff department that chooses to operate on a matrix basis. Any attempt to portray all of these relationships in a two-dimensional chart would be unduly complicated, so it should be noted that Exhibit 5-9 is intended only to illustrate the principle, and not to reflect the situation within the whole corporation.

The matrix form appears to violate the basic premise of management that no individual should be accountable to two different superiors. When viewed in another way, however, the anomaly is resolved. In effect, the seconded members of the staff function consider the geographical vice presidents as their "customers." Just as in any department in which employees have contact with customers (or, for that matter, with suppliers or other members of the public), the seconded staff members must satisfy their customers—in this case, the line executives of the geographical divisions to which they are seconded. This responsibility is not at all in conflict with their accountability to the vice president of finance.

Within the organization, the matrix structure can be effective, as long as the vice presidents communicate effectively and frequently with each other. This cooperation must recognize that the Brussels-based and Singapore-based accountants have two "masters," and that each vice president is responsible for different aspects of the accountants' work—the vice president of finance for professional competence, and the geographical vice president for quality of service.

The matrix structure can lower the communication barriers between departments that otherwise may exist when the company adheres strictly to any of the "pure" forms of organization. It also facilitates daily on-site relationships between the seconded representatives of the staff functions and the members of the line functions. Like all of the forms of organization, it also has a hazard: that jealousy and possessiveness by vice presidents can create dissension. This form of tension at the level of the vice presidents places employees in an untenable position, as they effectively are caught between the vice presidents, not knowing which one to obey when they have different priorities.

Matrix organizational forms have increased in popularity as organizations have become more complex and more decentralized. Frigidaire Co., a subsidiary of Swedish-based Electrolux, has used a matrix organization for many years and attributes some of its success in increasing its competitiveness and flexibility to the matrix form.[32] Dow Chemical, on the other hand, found that adopting a matrix form of organization in the 1960s seemed to cause an increase in paperwork for internal communication and a proliferation of committees. Despite this reservation, Dow managers believe that some of the company's corporate successes would not have occurred had it not been for the cross-departmental communication that is encouraged by the matrix form.[33]

Each of the forms of departmentalization has its adherents and its detractors. The essential facts are that no form is perfect and that circumstances may dictate one or another format for the time being. It also should be noted that whatever format is adopted, interdepartmental communication is the key to its success.

## Span of Control

span of control
The number of people who are accountable to a single manager.

The number of people who report to one manager or supervisor is referred to as that person's **span of control**. Questions relating to span of control are the final decisions managers must make in designing organizational structure. The objective is to determine the optimal span of control, wide or narrow. A wide span of control (or flat organization) exists when a large number of employees report to one supervisor or manager. A narrow span (or tall organization) exists when one supervisor or manager is responsible for only a small number of employees, and consequently there are more layers of management.

There is no magic number of how many subordinates a manager can adequately supervise and coordinate. If those reporting to a manager are all doing similar kinds of work, the number can be larger than if the subordinates are doing widely different kinds

**Exhibit 5-10**

*Factors to Consider in Deciding the Span of Control*

1. *The competence of both the manager and the subordinates.* The more competent they are, the wider the span of control can be.

2. *The degree of interaction required among the units to be supervised.* The more the required interaction, the narrower the span of control must be.

3. *The extent to which the manager must carry out non-managerial tasks.* The more technical and job-related work the manager has to do, the less time is available to supervise others; thus the narrower the span of control must be.

4. *The relative similarity or dissimilarity of the jobs being supervised.* The more similar the jobs, the wider the span of control can be; the less similar the jobs, the narrower it must be.

5. *The extent of standardized procedures.* The more routine the subordinates' jobs are and the more each job is performed by standardized methods, the wider the span of control can be.

6. *The degree of physical dispersion.* If all the people assigned to a manager are located in one area and are within eyesight, the manager can supervise relatively more people than if people are dispersed throughout the plant or country at different locations.

of work and meeting different types of problems. Exhibit 5-10 sets out some of the factors that should be taken into account in deciding the optimum span of control for a particular manager. Consideration of these factors can result in different numbers being assigned to different managers at the same levels, depending on their experience or the nature of the jobs they are supervising.

Consistent with some of the current trends in organizational structure already discussed, including employee empowerment and group decision making, many organizations are widening their spans of control to develop a flatter organizational structure. In doing so, they allow decisions to be made without having to go through several levels of management, thus eliminating the need for large numbers of middle managers, whose positions are becoming redundant and who are being laid off in large numbers.

## The Workplace of Tomorrow

Many different terms have been used to describe changes in modern organizations. Among them are *reengineering, paradigm shifting,* and *reframing.* The emerging organizations of the future have been described as lean, flexible, responsive, and perhaps above all else, highly competitive. Many of these attributes are captured in what Philip Crosby calls *completeness,* as characterized by the following:

- Policy is made by leadership with the consent of the governed;
- Requirements are provided in a way that everyone understands;
- Everyone keeps learning due to the availability of information and freedom of choice;
- Performance is measured on the basis of a culture of consideration; and
- The organization's purpose is to help individuals be successful in every aspect of their lives.[34]

If used imaginatively, modern communication systems can help managers to keep in close touch with suppliers and customers to minimize misunderstandings. As pointed out at the beginning of this chapter, an effective organizational structure assists the employees to get the job done effectively. The successful organization has a responsive structure that is focused on accomplishing objectives and goals. As long as managers and

## Beyond Certainty: The Changing Worlds of Organizations

In this collection of 35 short essays, Handy draws on his experience as an oil company executive, an economist, a best-selling author, and a professor at the London Business School. He examines many of the myths that have been accepted at various times as panaceas for much of what is wrong with business organizations.

Typical of his willingness to take positions that are at odds with what might be called "accepted wisdom" is his quotation from Adam Smith, whom he correctly describes as "the high priest of market economies and of modern capitalism." The keynote essay in the collection begins by quoting with approval the warning that Adam Smith offered some 250 years ago, that *growth* is "… undirected and infinitely self-generating in the endless demand for all the useless things in the world."

Handy's thesis, as reflected in the title of the book, is that uncertainty is the only certainty in this age of rapid change. Again culling ancient wisdom, he reminds the reader that two millennia ago Heraclitus said that one can never step in the same river twice. The river is ever changing, just as life is, and, of course, just as organizations and their environ-

ments are. In another essay Handy describes a change in organizations that is seldom noticed but, in his view, is critical to an understanding of organizations. He states, "… companies used to be physical assets, run by families and their helpers. Nowadays they are largely people, helped by physical assets." He deplores the buying and selling of companies, and with them, of people. This practice, to Handy, is a source of the fear that pervades so many organizations today—a fear of stepping out of line. With such an atmosphere, how can any organization innovate or even adapt to meet changing conditions? He points to the greater freedom offered to managers and other employees in today's organizations. This freedom, he says, leads to choice, the responsibility of choosing, and the willingness to suffer the consequences of making the wrong choices.

Managers may find Handy's words somewhat troubling but, at the very least, thought-provoking.

Source: Charles Handy, *Beyond Certainty: The Changing Worlds of Organizations* (Boston, MA: Harvard Business School Press, 1996).

employees are human, no single form of organization will solve all of the problems. Many challenges remain. However, new forms of organization will be developed to meet them. Each new form will address some perceived weaknesses of the existing forms, but will, itself, have some weaknesses that must be addressed. So, questions of organizational form will continue to be dynamic, and the effective organization will continue to consider them and make adjustments as circumstances warrant.

## Summary of Learning Objectives

▷ **Define the terms** *organizing* **and** *organizational structure.*
Organizing is the process of structuring both human and physical resources to accomplish organizational objectives. Organizational structure is the framework of jobs and departments that directs the behaviour of individuals and of groups towards achieving the organization's objectives.

▷ **Determine when organizational structure is a problem.**
Whenever work is not being done well, organizational structure is likely to be one of the causes. Conflicts between departments or groups within an organization suggest a

structural problem. Difficulty in coordinating work between departments, slowness in adapting to change, and ambiguous job assignments also indicate problems with organizational structure.

▶ **Explain how managers decide on organizational structure.**

Managers decide on organizational structure by deciding the degree to which jobs are to be specialized, determining the extent to which authority is to be delegated, grouping jobs according to some logical arrangement (departmentalization), and determining the number of people who are to report to each manager (span of control).

▶ **Distinguish between the principles of scientific management and craftsmanship.**

Scientific management requires that tasks be broken down to the smallest element and that problem solving be left to managers. Taylor used time and motion studies to identify basic movements that minimize effort and maximize output. Craftsmanship is basically the opposite. Craftsmen are responsible for their own work, with management providing the means and facilities for the craftsmen to perform the entire operation. Most organizations function somewhere between the two forms of organization.

▶ **Discuss the significance of work teams and quality circles.**

Many organizations are modifying and restructuring jobs so that they can be performed by work teams. A work team is a group of employees who (1) work closely together to pursue common objectives and (2) can be directed by a manager or are self-managed. A quality circle is a small group of people who do similar work and meet regularly to discuss their work, identify problems, and present possible solutions.

▶ **Discuss how authority can be delegated.**

Authority can be delegated by decentralizing the organization, giving an individual (usually a manager) the right to make a decision without obtaining approval of a higher-level manager. Some organizations have begun to empower production workers to make decisions that typically have been made by managers.

▶ **Describe the most common bases for departmentalization and their respective strengths and weaknesses.**

The most common bases for departmentalization are by function, product, customer, and geographical area. Most organizations use some combination of these, operating in a mixed or hybrid form that combines features of more than one of the theoretically pure forms.

▶ **Describe the matrix form of organization, and discuss its advantages and disadvantages.**

In this form, members of staff departments are assigned on a semi-permanent basis to provide their specialized services to the line departments to which they are assigned. In effect, these staff members must perform to the satisfaction of both the manager of the staff function and the product, customer, or geographic line manager. The matrix form facilitates the provision of services to the line operations and helps to break down communication barriers among various functions. A potential disadvantage is the conflict that may arise if the managers of the staff and line departments do not agree on fundamentals and fail to collaborate to ensure that the services are provided at optimum levels.

▷ **Discuss how organizational structure can help or hinder an organization's quest to fulfil its mission and meet its goals and objectives.**

All managers and employees operate within a structure, whether formalized or not. The reporting and accountability relationships within the structure may help individuals to work towards common ends or, conversely, may hinder that effort.

▷ **Explain why there is no perfect form of organization.**

Like management styles and methods, organizational forms must be responsive to conditions within an organization and to factors from the external environment, all of which are changing constantly. Every form of organization has its weaknesses; the effective manager must remain aware of those weaknesses and, regardless of the form of organizational structure, attempt to compensate for them.

## KEY TERMS

centralization, p. 181
chain of command, p. 185
customer departmentalization, p. 189
decentralization, p. 181
departmentalization, p. 188
empowerment, p. 183

functional departmentalization, p. 188
geographical departmentalization, p. 190
line position, p. 185
matrix form of organization, p. 191
mixed departmentalization, p. 190

organizational structure, p. 174
product departmentalization, p. 188
quality circle, p. 180
span of control, p. 193
staff position, p. 186

## REVIEW AND DISCUSSION QUESTIONS

### Recall

1. What are some common myths about organizational structure?
2. What is the difference between teams and quality circles?
3. What are the advantages and disadvantages of decentralization?
4. Distinguish between line and staff positions.
5. Compare the different forms of departmentalization and explain the strengths and weaknesses of each.

### Understanding

6. Why is organizational structure so critical to the success of an organization?
7. What is empowerment and how does it relate to organizational effectiveness?
8. In terms of organizational structure and design, what are the apparent trends of the future? How do you think the organization of the future will look?

### Application

9. Think of recent purchases in which you, as the customer, were not satisfied. Did you hold the employee responsible? Could your dissatisfaction be attributed to problems with organizational structure and design? What specific steps could managers take to make sure that other customers do not experience the same problem?

**CASE 5-1**

## Johnson & Johnson Decentralizes

The 1980s became known in business as the decade of financial restructuring. Takeovers, mergers, and acquisitions dominated business during this period. The 1990s have seen a different kind of restructuring as corporations try to decentralize their organizations, giving people more freedom to be creative and eliminating inefficiencies that have plagued many large organizations. The problem is not size itself but the burden that size places on the job of managing. According to management consultant Peter Drucker, "The Fortune 500 is over." Drucker doesn't mean that large corporations will all go out of business, but he believes they will begin to divide their assets and other resources into smaller, more efficient, and more independent businesses. IBM is organizing into more autonomous units, GM is eliminating 74,000 jobs and closing 21 factories, and AT&T has not only spun off several corporate progeny, but is contracting out for services such as payroll, billing, and public relations.

Reflecting a change in philosophy, the 1990s were characterized by mergers and other less complete forms of intercorporate cooperation. Corel Corporation entered into what it called a "strategic partnership" with Samsung. For several months, SmithKline Beecham PLC and Glaxo Wellcome PLC negotiated terms for a megamerger only to call it off, apparently because of the differences in corporate culture between the two organizations. Two pairs of Canadian banks proudly announced plans for mergers, only to run into roadblocks with the federal government. These and other mergers and near-mergers mask some of the difficulties in bringing two corporate structures together. It has been suggested that a major stumbling block is wildly different organizational structures, which reflect differences in philosophy of operations that are either difficult or impossible to resolve.

Some companies have found what appears to be a happy medium between the move to expand and the move to decentralize. Johnson & Johnson (J&J), with annual revenues of $12.4 billion, is a large organization with some of the best features of a small organization: focus, flexibility, and speed. CEO Ralph Larsen oversees 166 highly decentralized businesses, each of which focuses on health care, with annual sales from $100,000 to $1 billion. Larsen not only encourages each company's president to act independently but he expects them to. Marvin Woodall, president of tiny startup Johnson & Johnson Interventional Systems Co., doesn't spend much time at his parent company's headquarters. He prefers to run his small staff from a separate office only an hour away. If he wants to go to Europe to check on operations there, he doesn't need to ask for anyone's approval. Larsen also decides whom to hire, what products to produce, and to whom to sell them. Ultimately Larsen and the other 165 presidents are accountable to executives at J&J headquarters, which some presidents visit as infrequently as four times a year. Only 1.5 percent of J&J's 82,700 employees work at headquarters, which doesn't manage but provides capital and selects people to run the 166 businesses.

J&J decentralized long before it became fashionable. Decentralization was pushed by Chairman Robert Johnson in the 1930s, when he encouraged Ethicon Inc. (manufacturer of sutures) and Personal Products Co. (specializing in feminine hygiene products) to operate independently. Since J&J has more than a half-century of practice, the company knows how to make decentralization work. But J&J also knows the importance of balancing autonomy and corporate structure—decentralization and centralization. Such a balance is difficult to achieve.

At the heart of J&J's management system is a diverse array of products ranging from familiar consumer goods like Band-Aids and baby powder to advanced care products for yeast infections and athlete's foot. Given all of these different products, Larsen compares his job to that of an orchestra conductor: providing inspiration and direction but assuring creative freedom. For instance, the company provided hundreds of millions of dollars to its Vistakon division to start a new business to manufacture and sell disposable contact lenses. Today this business generates $250 million a year in sales. Larsen's job is not only to fund such ventures but also to require that everyone in the organization focus on cutting costs sensibly and on generating an acceptable return on investment. Thus, each president has to think like an entrepreneur, counting every penny and spending only on projects that yield a satisfactory profit. Therefore, it is critical that Larsen select the right executives to run J&J's 166 companies.

Decentralization is not without risks. A multiplicity of businesses operating autonomously can result in duplication of function and increased overhead. It would not be unlikely for two divisions of a decentralized company to be actively competing with each other for the same customers. At J&J, overhead is 41 percent of sales, compared with only 30 percent for more centralized Merck and 28 percent for Bristol-Myers Squibb, another competitor. Sales functions also are duplicated, as dozens of J&J sales representatives from different units call on large retailers such as Wal-Mart and Kmart even though big retailers prefer to reduce the number of contacts from suppliers. To reduce duplication, Larsen has established employee teams called customer-support centres to work on-site with retailers to simplify distribution and ordering. Larsen also has pushed the different companies to reduce duplication in functions such as payroll, purchasing, distribution, and accounts payable. In addition, he presses hard to keep expansion of staff from getting out of hand, another problem with decentralization. In a sense, Larsen is introducing some of the aspects of a matrix organization.

Although decentralization does pose some problems, Larsen plans to stick with it. Since 1980 yearly returns on investment have averaged mare than 19 percent. As global competition intensifies, large organizations will have to be focused, stay close to the marketplace to come up with ideas, and encourage employees' creativity.

## Questions

1. How can organizational structure limit a large organization such as Johnson & Johnson?
2. In what ways does decentralization seem to be working at J&J? In what ways is it not working so well?
3. How does J&J balance centralization and decentralization?
4. What are some of the problems organizations are likely to face when decentralizing?
5. Could J&J be described as a multidivisional organization? Explain.
6. How may structure influence relationships between separate organizations?

Source: Adapted from Joseph Weber, "A Big Company That Works," *Business Week* (May 4, 1992): 124-32; Brian Dumaine, "Is Big Still Good?" *Fortune* (April 20, 1992): 50-60; Joseph Weber, "How J&J's Foresight Made Contact Lenses Pay," *Business Week* (May 4, 1992): 132; Mark Evans and Patrick Brethour, "Corel-Samsung Deal," *Globe and Mail* (June 17, 1998): B31; Elizabeth Church, "Alliances Tricky," *Globe and Mail* (June 23, 1998); Madelaine Drohan, "Culture Clash Wrecks Marriages," *Globe and Mail* (April 21, 1998).

*CASE* **5-2**

## Teamwork at Volvo

Volvo is trying to determine if the assembly line has become outdated as mass markets disappear. In 1974 the Swedish auto maker dismantled the assembly line at its plant in Kalmar, Sweden. The line was replaced with a system in which cars are built by small, decentralized work teams that produce sections of cars. Volvo officials believe strongly that teams and a return to craftsmanship will improve quality and increase employees' pride in their work. In fact, Volvo believes so strongly in teamwork that this system is also being put into place at the company's new plant in Uddevalla, Sweden.

The Uddevalla plant was completed in 1990 to build the 740 and 940 models. By the end of 1991 the plant was producing about 22,000 cars annually; at full capacity it will employ 1000 workers and produce 40,000 cars annually. At the Uddevalla facility, self-managed teams of eight to ten members assemble complete cars from start to finish. Cars being assembled are not moved on a conveyor line from worker to worker but rather are assembled in a stationary position. A special device tilts the car as needed so that workers can perform their tasks. Each team has a high degree of autonomy and responsibility; they set their own break times and vacation times and they reassign work when a team member is absent. Teams also participate in policy-making decisions and are responsible for a variety of tasks, including quality control, production planning, developing work procedures, servicing equipment, and ordering supplies.

Workers at the Uddevalla plant are paid for performance. In addition to wages, bonuses are paid for maintaining quality and productivity and for meeting weekly delivery targets. There are no supervisors or plant foremen. Each of six "production workshops" house 80 to 100 employees who are divided into assembly teams. Each assembly team has a coordinator (chosen on a rotating basis) who has direct contact with managers. To make sure the system works, employees are provided with abundant information. Volvo also goes to great lengths to ensure that all employees have an in-depth understanding of company history, tradition, and strategy. Free flow of information is encouraged and workers have input on everything from assembly processes to new-product innovations.

The new system at Uddevalla isn't completely successful. Although morale is up and absenteeism is down, productivity is not as high as at Volvo's plant in Ghent, Belgium, where building a car on an assembly line takes about half the time. Lennert Ericsson, president of the metal workers' union at the Uddevalla plant, thinks the approach there will work: "I am convinced that our ways [teams] will be successful and competitive. Our next goal is to be better than Kalmar, and when we get to that, our goal will be to get to Ghent."

Volvo has invested heavily in training workers at the Uddevalla plant. First, employees attend a 16-week initiation course as part of a 16-month training program in which workers learn about auto assembly. Workers are encouraged to share experiences with one another and exchange ideas.

Both union and management feel confident that the new system will improve the organization. But it will take time. The system puts heavy demands on everyone, and there has been some resistance. Only time will tell whether the structural changes introduced at the Uddevalla plant will survive the decrease in productivity as Volvo adapts to the pressures that arise from new relationships with North American auto makers.

### Questions

1. Can it be said that Volvo is returning to craftsmanship? Why does the company think that these changes will improve quality and competitiveness?

**2.** What is the difference between teams at the Kalmar plant and self-managed teams at Uddevalla?

**3.** How important is empowerment in Volvo's Uddevalla facility?

**4.** Why might there be resistance to the team approach at Uddevalla? How might Volvo overcome this resistance?

---

Source: Adapted from Charles Garfield, *Second to None* (Homewood, IL: Business One Irwin, 1992): 165-68; "Safe, Staid Volvo May Soon Be Burning Rubber," *Business Week* (January 27, 1992): 27; Stewart Toy, Mark Maremont, and John Rossant, "Gentlemen, Start Your Mergers," *Business Week* (May 25, 1992): 43-44.

## *APPLICATION EXERCISE* 5-1

### Starting a Quality Circle

Consider whether a quality team concept would be able to function effectively in a business management class. Using the following guidelines, design a program to implement a quality team: (1) participation as a team member is voluntary, (2) emphasis is on self-development and mutual development, (3) all individuals who decide to join the team will participate, and (4) the team will operate continuously throughout the semester or term.

Describe how you would complete each of the following steps.

- Step 1: Stimulate interest;
- Step 2: Identify the issues;
- Step 3: Identify the areas for improvement;
- Step 4: Select team leaders; and
- Step 5: Form teams.

Predict how successful the program will be at each step and predict the reasons for its success, partial success, or failure.

## *APPLICATION EXERCISE* 5-2

### Establishing a Matrix Form of Organization

Assume that you are the vice president, human resources of Reliable Manufacturing Company Ltd. Reliable has always had a product form of departmentalization. Of Reliable's 10,000 employees, only about 800 are in the plastic extrusion division (PED), which is located 480 kilometres from Reliable's head office. This division has been experiencing problems in employee morale and in rapid staff turnover. You would like to assign two of your human resource staff to work at the PED plant. There, they will recruit employees for the plant, explain health and personnel benefits to PED employees, help to resolve personnel conflicts, and provide training in health and safety matters. You envision retaining in Reliable's head office such matters as payroll preparation, union negotiations and grievance arbitration, and development of company-wide personnel policies. You have not discussed this plan with anyone except Reliable's CEO, who has given you full support to initiate this pilot program, to see if it ultimately would be feasible for several of Reliable's other nine divisions.

Write an action plan stating how you will enlist the support of those who will be affected, what the implementing steps will be, and when you will take each step.

## INTERNET APPLICATION  5-1

Enter Federal Express Canada's Web site (www.fedex.com/ca/ca_english). Click on "About FedEx"; then click on "FedEx Corporate Philosophy."

1. To what does FedEx attribute its success?
2. What policies does the company employ to ensure this success?
3. How easy would it be to institute FedEx's corporate structure at other organizations?

Search the Web for an organization that has a different corporate structure. For which organization would you prefer to work and why?

# CHAPTER

# 6

# Leading

After studying this chapter, you should be able to:

▶ Distinguish between leaders and managers;

▶ Explain the relationships between leadership and power;

▶ Compare the theories of trait, behavioural, and contingency or situational leadership;

▶ Explain the concept of transformational leadership;

▶ Define *self-leadership* and discuss the societal trends that contributed to its development;

▶ Describe the various behavioural and cognitive self-management strategies; and

▶ Explain how an organization can develop a self-leadership culture.

*IBM CEO Louis V. Gerstner, Jr.*

## Leadership in Transition

SUCCESSFUL ORGANIZATIONS ARE GUIDED BY PEOPLE
who have vision. Over time, IBM has been blessed with exactly that type
of leadership. Thomas Watson, Sr., built IBM's business by continually
developing punch card technology. With this technological innovation,
IBM (nicknamed Big Blue) became synonymous with successful big
business. But Watson's lack of vision about the influence of the next
technology—the computer—nearly cost IBM dearly. ▶

Fortunately, his son, Thomas Watson, Jr., had the youthful energy and foresight to envision the potential impact of the general-purpose computer in business applications. The passing of the reins from father to son was largely an internal decision at IBM. While not totally convinced of the computer's role in general-purpose data processing, Thomas Watson, Sr., stepped aside as chairman and CEO of IBM. Thomas Watson, Jr., quickly pushed for computer development based on the company's existing strength—punch card technology. His innovative coupling of punch card technology as a computer input medium gave IBM a competitive advantage in the early years of computing. One thing is sure: Thomas Watson, Jr., had a good understanding of the marketplace and the vision to interpret the computer's role in IBM's future.

For the next three decades IBM dominated the direction and technical standards in the computer industry. IBM frequently used its position in the industry to ward off the threat of competitive inroads into its market share. But over the past decade IBM's position as the industry leader has eroded. IBM's market share declined from 30 percent in 1985 to 19 percent in 1991. Its early 1990s market position worsened, with IBM reporting a $4.97 billion loss in the last quarter of 1992. Unlike earlier years when external threats were handled internally, IBM's CEO John Akers found board members and major shareholders pushing for his resignation. Akers finally was forced by the board of directors to step down as chairman and CEO of IBM.

Just as IBM's success can be attributed to leadership, so apparently can blame for failure be laid at the leader's feet. Who could lead IBM out of the dark period of loss towards renewed profit? After Akers' resignation, the IBM board of directors did the unthinkable (for IBM)—it went outside of IBM's executive ranks to select a new CEO. Louis V. Gerst-

ner, Jr., former RJR Nabisco CEO, was handed the reins of Big Blue. This move suggests that no longer can corporate executives expect to resolve their problems internally solely through managing better. Promoting from within wasn't the answer—new leadership from outside became essential.

In Gerstner's first year as CEO, IBM had a net profit of nearly $3 billion, its best in four years. But 68 percent of the profits came from high-end products such as mainframes and minicomputers—products for which demand had peaked and markets were dwindling. Recognizing the declining market segment, Gerstner announced in 1995 that IBM's new direction would be towards network computing and electronic commerce for businesses and individuals. In his vision, the key to success is communications rather than computing *per se*; this will involve everything from multimedia PCs to the Internet. In the fast-changing world of computers, any change entails risks and attracts criticism, but in this field, as in almost all fields, failing to change entails even greater risks.

In responding to critics, Gerstner made a cogent observation that would apply to all management decisions, and to all who aspire to be leaders: "There are no recipes. There are no certainties that what I am doing is going to work. You've got to go on instinct."[1]

Leaders realize that the world is always full of uncertainties, but this realization does not frighten them away from actually making decisions. ∎

Source: Stephen Baker and Maria Mallory, "IBM after Akers," *Business Week* (February 8, 1993): 22-24; "Akers Quits under Heavy Pressure; Dividend Is Slashed," *The Wall Street Journal* (January 27, 1993): A1-A3; Carole J. Loomis, "King John Wears an Uneasy Crown," *Fortune* (January 11, 1993): 44-46; George Anders, Eben Shapiro, Michael Miller, and Laurence Hooper, "IBM's Pick Is Talented but Some See Flaws in His Record at RJR," *The Wall Street Journal* (March 25, 1993): A1.

## Evolution of Leadership

Advocates of total quality management such as W. Edwards Deming, Philip B. Crosby, and J.M. Juran maintain that quality improvements are the responsibility of senior-level managers. The challenges of global competitiveness place a heavy emphasis on managers to encourage all employees to strive for continuous improvement and customer satisfaction. This requires leadership. Although profound changes—in training, statistical skills, and responsibility, for example—are needed among the workforce, these are not

**leadership**
The ability to influence people to act in ways the leader prefers—usually to achieve the organization's goals and objectives.

likely to occur without innovative and effective leadership. In this context, **leadership** refers to the process of influencing other people to attain organizational goals.[2] This chapter describes some of the many ways that effective leaders provide vision, direction, and meaning to organizational activities.

Our understanding of effective leadership has evolved and matured considerably over the years. A half-century ago, a common vision of leadership was that of General George Patton barking commands from a tank turret with the troops surrounding him eagerly awaiting orders, driven either by fear or by Patton's charisma to follow him into battle. Patton had a vision of the future, he mobilized resources, and he motivated people to join him in his quest. All too often this type of leadership is exemplified by corporate executives who attempt to rule by bombast and fear.[3] A more contemporary view of leadership is that of Mary Kay Ash awarding a pink Cadillac to top saleswomen. She, too, had a vision of the future, she mobilized resources, and she motivated people. Despite these similarities, her style of leadership is quite different from that of General Patton, even though she, too, can be tough when she has to be.[4]

*The Mary Kay signature pink Cadillac—long synonymous with the cosmetics and skin care leader—is the most recognizable of the many business incentives awarded by the company.*

As society, people, and situations change, so must leaders' actions change. Gone are the days of blind obedience to leaders (if indeed they ever existed). Contemporary leadership tends to be based more on participation. There has been a transformation from autocratic to more participative and democratic styles of leadership. But the overall purpose remains the same—to achieve the organization's goals and objectives.

## Leaders and Managers

Is there a difference between a "leader" and a "manager"? Noted Harvard psychologist Abraham Zaleznick thinks so.[5] He believes that managers focus on demands and constraints of the moment rather than on more far-reaching matters. Managers must deal with daily production concerns. Often managers seem more concerned with "getting things done" than with "getting the right things done." At its worst, managing may be reduced to little more than shepherding people and massaging materials. In the process, managers sometimes show little concern for the customer or for the product's final use. Unfortunately this may translate into getting the product out the door regardless of quality. This preoccupation with what Zaleznick calls *process* orientation leads to mediocrity. For the uninspired manager, the goal often becomes simply preserving the status quo.

**leader-manager**
An individual who is able both to exert leadership and to manage an operation.

Zaleznick believes that, unlike other managers, those who are both managers and leaders (the **leader-managers**) are bored with routine or, as Tom Peters puts it, they "thrive on chaos" and seek innovative and novel solutions. Rather than being concerned only with process, a leader-manager is concerned with *substance*. A manager asks, "What is the best way consistently to remain competitive and still meet production targets?" A leader-manager asks entirely different questions: "For a particular product, what is quality and how will the definition change in the future?" and "How can we become and remain competitive in the long run?" The difference between managers and leader-managers is reflected in what they do. Short-sighted managers deal with the pressures of the moment. They are concerned solely with the process surrounding work flow. The leader-manager is concerned with providing meaning or purpose in work for employees and creating meaning in the product for customers.[6]

Lee Iacocca's transformation of Chrysler is an example of how a leader-manager can create vision and meaning for both employees and customers. Under Iacocca's leadership, Chrysler workers believed that they could be part of the solution to problems facing the auto industry. They were creating the new Chrysler Corporation. With its minivan, Chrysler created a new alternative to the gas-guzzling station wagon—an alternative that fit the needs of families and the environment. Iacocca's strategic vision of new products, new markets, and new ways of creating quality and value for the consumer became a reality. Employees produced a better product—not just because of technology, but because they believed they could. The results were that both customer demand and profitability increased dramatically. Another result was the preservation of jobs for thousands of Chrysler employees who might otherwise have found themselves "downsized" by a declining Chrysler Corporation.

Another example, less well known but equally pertinent, is the transformation that J.E. (Ted) Newall created at Nova Corporation. This Alberta-based company specializes in effective ways to transmit natural gas and produces various plastic and other petro-chemical derivatives. One might expect the management of such a company to exhibit the classic management style—hard-driving, autocratic, idiosyncratic, heartless, and uncommunicative—that is often associated with what is known as the "oil patch." That description could have characterized Nova's management before Newall's arrival—and may have had some bearing on the company's loss of $937 million in 1991. Whatever miracles Newall accomplished, Nova reported sizeable profits in each of the next five years. Analysts attribute the turnaround almost entirely to Newall's *leadership*. How did Newall manage to earn the loyalty of Nova employees? He is described by his long-time friend Peter Lougheed as warm, friendly, and personable, but that is not enough. Doubtless there were many other reasons for his success, but one stands out. When he joined Nova in September 1991, he dramatically demonstrated to his employees and to the public at large his confidence in the future of the company by personally declining a cash salary, and instead taking only Nova shares and stock options as compensation. If Nova did well, Newall would do well; if Nova did poorly, Newall could find that he had worked for nothing. In fact, in 1996, under Newall's leadership, Nova did so well that Newall received compensation worth $6.3 million— the highest pay packet in Canada's petroleum sector.[7] And Newall puts into practice another prime characteristic of true leader-managers— he can admit publicly that he has changed his mind. In November 1997, despite his wish to keep the company together, he announced that since times had changed, he had to change his opinion and split Nova into two separate divisions.[8]

*An innovative, experienced, and charismatic leader, Ted Newall captured the loyalty of Nova employees when he joined the company as CEO by refusing a salary and accepting only stock options as remuneration—thus tying his own compensation directly to the company's operating results.*

Leadership is both an individual characteristic and a process. As an individual characteristic, leadership is a combination of personal attributes and abilities such as vision, energy, and knowledge. As a process, leadership is the individual's ability to create in others a shared vision of the future. Creating a shared vision requires the leader-manager to set goals, motivate employees, and create a supportive and productive culture in the organization. Indeed, in many instances it is difficult to separate the individual from the process. This is because, as can be seen in Ted Newall's personal commitment to the company he was to lead, the leadership process is an extension of the leader's personality and ideas. Collectively then, individual leadership characteristics and the leadership process influence employee behaviour.

Unfortunately, true leadership is not found as frequently as one might hope. Management consultants Charles Farkas and Suzy Wetlaufer told a *Globe and Mail* journalist that their interviews with 160 CEOs worldwide showed that "… some top executives simply do not lead." Farkas and Wetlaufer explain in an article in *Harvard Business Review*, "For some [top executives] their days are driven by whatever event appears on their calendars or whatever crises erupt. Others act according to their natural inclinations, doing what feels enjoyable and easy."[9]

A similarly depressing note was sounded by Sir Adrian Cadbury, the senior member of the Cadbury chocolate family and, not incidentally, a world-renowned expert on corporate organizations. His 1992 Cadbury Report on corporate governance was accepted by the London Stock Exchange as a definitive statement of what is good and bad about typical corporate governance. As examples of inadequate leadership, he pointed to the massive abuses in Robert Maxwell's stable of companies and to the

## What Managers Are Reading    6-1

### Moral Leadership: Facing Canada's Leadership Crisis

Robert Evans, a business consultant, observes that he has seen just about every style of leadership conceivable, including what he characterizes as "wretched behaviour." Yet, he says that he is comforted by his observation of the large number of managers who "behave with civility, exercise courage, and speak and act with clear moral voices." Evans castigates the media for an unrelenting portrayal of the worst examples of greed and excess that, even though true, are not representative of the great majority of managers.

Evans deplores the fact that in many cases the larger an organization is, the less effective is the influence that can be exerted on it by its leaders. In describing the leadership of a large organization as daunting, he points to the heavy work loads, the lack of security, the eroding financial rewards, and the inherent conflicts between middle and top management. Evans is not surprised that many well-qualified potential managers shun the role, and that many people who are currently managers wish they were not and are seeking ways to escape the responsibilities of being a manager.

Evans has little good to say about the sources from which future managers are selected (business schools, law schools, engineering and science faculties), nor about the way they are encouraged in-house by praise and promotions to work harder and longer, to quantify everything, and to "kiss the right people." In Evans' view, these two factors contribute to widespread leadership failure, because they emphasize and encourage attitudes and activities that are the antitheses of good leadership. Instead, says Evans, leaders have to curb their tendencies to exercise inflated egos, they have to accept ambiguity, and they have to communicate face to face. Above all, they have to make a commitment to themselves and to their ideas and their organizations. Evans leaves us with an unanswered question—how society today can change to ensure the development of future generations of leaders "who exemplify and demand of others the exercise of moral courage as the fundamental hallmark of a leader."

Source: Robert Evans, *Moral Leadership: Facing Canada's Leadership Crisis* (Toronto: McGraw-Hill Ryerson, 1997).

multibillion-dollar losses of Barings PLC for not properly supervising rogue trader Nick Leeson. In his view such problems could have been, and can be, prevented by improvements in leadership.[10] It is to these disturbing problems that this chapter is addressed.

## Power and Leadership

**power**
The capacity to influence people and accomplish desired objectives.

To influence others, leaders use their **power**, which is simply the ability to get people to do something they otherwise would not do.[11] For some people the very word *power* conjures up horrible images of autocratic, impersonal, selfish abuse of authority. While authority is one source of power, as will be discussed, it is neither the only nor the most important source. Furthermore, power in the sense of the ability to influence people always exists, whether it is acknowledged or not. If the centres of power are not identified and visible in a group, they are still there, but hidden and invisible. In an organization, what may appear to be an absence of power is in reality an abdication of legitimate power, and a resulting power vacuum. This power vacuum creates an opening for illegitimate, hidden, and often perverse uses of power in the form of unaccountable influence. At times this vacuum may provide an opportunity for a demagogue to sway large numbers of people. As Lord Acton is purported to have said, "Power tends *(sic)* to corrupt; absolute power corrupts absolutely." Those in positions of power may have a tendency to misuse it, although even Lord Acton did not suggest that misuse *necessarily* accompanies power, unless that power is absolute or free from control. Organizations must guard against the corruption that stems from absolute power. The best and perhaps the only way to prevent accumulation of absolute power is to make sure that the sources and holders of power are visible and recognized. In this way the organization can build in accountability and safeguards against misuse of power. Absolute power cannot exist in an organization in which leaders are visible and identified, their actions can be identified with them, and there are other balancing powers that act as checks and balances.

Responsible leader-managers recognize that they have the potential to wield enormous power, and that consequently they have the responsibility not only to use it wisely but to install systems to identify where power lies within their organizations and keep it visible and accountable. So, rather than decrying the existence of power, an organization is better served by examining its sources of power and taking whatever steps are required to make sure that it is used responsibly. The next section summarizes a number of sources of power within organizations.[12]

### Sources of Power

**reward power**
Power that stems from the ability to influence people through granting or withholding benefits that are of interest to them.

**Reward power.** One important source of power is **reward power**. It represents the manager's ability to allocate or to withhold organizational resources in exchange for cooperation. Reward power can be either positive or negative. It is positive when it involves promotion or salary increases; it is negative when it involves discipline such as critical personnel evaluations, withholding of pay increases, suspension, or severance. Negative reward power often is referred to as *coercive power,* but in many ways positive and negative reward power are two ends of a continuum. Both positive and negative reward power are potent motivational tools and are probably the most widely used forms of power in business organizations. Contrary to widespread assumption among managers, however, evidence shows that the use of reward power, especially negative reward power in the form of punishment, can generate fear, jealousy, and distrust among employees,

**Management in the Real World    6-1**

## The Use of Punishment Power at General Electric

When an employee is so troubled by a company's actions that he blows the whistle, will the employee be congratulated or condemned? How will society react? How will the employer react? Can a firm drive out distrust and fear by its leadership practices?

After several visible ethical scandals, including a 1985 conviction for altering time cards of engineers on a government project, General Electric made a concerted effort to increase employee awareness of ethical concerns. CEO Jack Welch became a strong advocate of voluntary disclosure of corporate wrongs. Welch, a globally admired leader of a firm with over $60 billion in annual sales and more than a quarter-million employees, found that his emphasis on profits had interfered with ethical compliance. To improve this situation, company-produced videos and seminars created an atmosphere that encouraged employees to identify and report wrongdoing by the company. But when employee Chester Walsh detected a $42 million fraud, GE's ethics policy came under scrutiny. On the one side, Walsh claimed that the real ethic at General Electric was to punish whistle-blowers (employees who find breaches of ethics and then report them), while on the other side, GE management pointed the finger at Walsh, saying he was motivated by a federal law that allows him (as the whistle-blower) to claim up to one-quarter of the $70 million settlement levied against GE. GE claimed the law encouraged Mr. Walsh to allow the corruption to grow so he could profit from the size of the settlement.

General Electric, a major supplier to the government and foreign trade, was big enough to merit its own investigation unit at the U.S. Justice and Defense departments. About 20 percent of 60 investigations of GE began with whistle-blowers. GE whistle-blowers say that GE's intense effort to be profitable was at the root of the problem. GE counters with the claim that a confidential toll-free phone number for reporting ethics violations, along with forms and alternative channels for letting management know where practices are questionable, provides a leadership culture of openness and receptiveness to whistle-blowers. Former GE employees, whistle-blowers themselves, claim otherwise. One woman, pointing out unfair billing practices to management, found herself ostracized rather than eliminated. Another employee, reporting time card fraud and overcharging on government work, claims he was dismissed for his effort.

One GE lawyer explained the pressure on GE to balance integrity with an emphasis on making its profit numbers: "To make sure that every time we give a performance message—make your number—we also give a compliance measure." In Philadelphia in 1985, in response to a threat that "heads would roll" if costs were not contained, GE managers illegally charged $800,000 in cost overruns to a phony research account to be paid by the U.S. Dept. of Defense. U.S. attorney Ed Zittlau said, "The managers feared for their jobs. From their point of view, the mischarging looked like the lesser of two evils."

Fear and greed drive some GE managers: fear of losing their jobs for below-par performance, greed for healthy bonuses for meeting goals. A manager can double a $200,000 annual salary if profit goals are met.

Is there any way out of this conflict of interest? General Motors attempted to drive out fear by shifting responsibility for measuring work from managers to workers, while keeping most of the other work mechanisms in place; by reducing the levels and numbers of white-collar, mid-level managers charged with inspection; and by encouraging innovation to improve work and save production jobs threatened by market failure. GM's California New United Motor Manufacturing Inc. (NUMMI) plant showed phenomenal success where once workers and management had witnessed only declining quality and profitability.

Source: Amal Kumar Naj, "Internal Suspicions: GE's Drive to Purge Fraud Is Hampered by Workers' Mistrust," *The Wall Street Journal* (July 22, 1992): A1, A4; Steven Pearlstein, "Contracting: Bringing a Breach of Ethics to Light," *Washington Post*, national weekly edition (July 27–August 2, 1992): 21–22; and "Manufacturing Management: Return of the Stopwatch," *The Economist* (January 23, 1993): 69.

and must be used carefully to ensure that the gains outweigh the possible damage to morale.

**expert power**
Power arising from expertise in a specific area, or from knowledge of specific circumstances or situations.

**Expert power.** This source of power, which is also called *knowledge power*, stems from an individual's technical or expert knowledge about a particular area. Expertise may be in the form of experience, information, or education that is more advanced or more relevant than that of peers within the group. Special knowledge may allow an individual to act in ways desired by the person having this kind of power. The person who has this kind of power may not be fully aware of it and may use the unacknowledged power responsibly. On the other hand, the use of expert power can cause two kinds of problems. It may lead to resentment on the part of people who lack the particular specialized knowledge. Also, some people bask in the knowledge that they have this power and want to preserve it by keeping the information to themselves, thus denying others the opportunity to grow and develop. It is a challenge for managers to ensure that knowledge is widely shared and does not become the personal property of any one person or small group of persons. The wise leader-manager sees that reward power can be used to encourage an atmosphere in which everyone is willing not only to share information, but also to serve as mentors to each other so that all grow and expand their horizons.[13] In this way, expert power is disseminated throughout the organization, and is used for the benefit of the whole organization.

**referent power**
Power that depends on the personal characteristics of the leader, as seen by those whom the leader seeks to influence.

**Referent power.** Personal characteristics that are esteemed by other people give rise to **referent power**. It is natural to attempt, consciously or unconsciously, to imitate and be loyal to those whom we admire. When they ask us to do something, or make suggestions as to how we might do it, we tend to follow their lead. This feature permits and facilitates the mentoring process, in which a more-experienced or better-informed person passes knowledge along to other people. Using their referent power, people, and especially leaders, can be role models and set standards of behaviour by their example.[14]

**personal power**
The combination of referent power and expert power.

**Personal power.** The combination of expert power and referent power constitutes **personal power**. A sense of personal power comes from the belief that one can reach predetermined goals. This sense is communicated by developing apparent authority, accessibility, assertiveness, a positive image, and effective communication skills.[15]

**hierarchical or position power**
Power that is the result of the leader's position in the organizational hierarchy.

**Hierarchical power.** This form of power, also known as *position power*, arises from the individual's position within an organization. The position itself carries express and implicit authority to make certain kinds of decisions. The purchasing agent has power to make contracts within specified limits; the shop floor supervisor has power to assign shop employees to various tasks and to compliment or reprimand them. The use of hierarchical power to direct, reward, discipline, and control workers is called the exercise of authority. As might be expected, hierarchical power is greatest for the CEO, less for vice presidents, still less for supervisors, and almost nonexistent for those in non-managerial positions. This is not to say that non-managers have no power, but only that the power they exercise, consciously or unconsciously, arises from other sources and not from position in the hierarchy.

The exercise of any one or more of these kinds of power constitutes the driving force behind leadership; without them, leadership is ineffectual.

# Models and Theories of Leadership

**trait**
An individual's personal attributes, including both physical and psychological aspects.

**contingency leadership model**
The analysis of leadership that assumes that different situations require different leadership actions and attitudes.

**trait theory of leadership**
The analysis of leadership that attempts to identify specific traits that indicate that a person will or will not be a successful leader.

Leadership is one of the most studied aspects of management. A tremendous variety of research underlies theories of leadership. Three widely accepted historical models have evolved through the twentieth century. Trait theory, the first attempt to describe effective leaders in a systematic fashion, focuses on **traits** such as physical or personality attributes of the leader. Studies of trait theory led to behavioural models, which focus on the work itself and on employee attitudes. Behavioural models, in turn, led to contingency models of leadership. **Contingency leadership models** state that the leader's behavioural style must be contingent on the situation if the leader is to be effective. Contingency models emerged as two different approaches: (1) fitting the leader to the situation, or (2) fitting the decision to the situation. Subsequent leadership theorists have sought alternative explanations for effective leadership, including visionary leadership and substitutes for leadership.

## Trait Theories of Leadership

A **trait theory of leadership** seeks to identify effective leaders in terms of various groupings of physical and psychological attributes such as intelligence, height, and articulateness. Trait-based leadership theories focus on the traits of those who emerged or assumed power as leaders and who are or were considered to be effective.

One review of 12 different leadership studies revealed that there was no consistency among the results obtained. Nine studies supported the idea that leaders were taller than followers, but two studies found the reverse to be true. The twelfth study concluded that leadership ability has nothing at all to do with physical height, but is primarily associated with the person's judgement and verbal skills.[16] (It should be noted that the term "verbal skills" applies to all skills that depend on the use of words—both oral and written.) Edwin Ghiselli notes that, within a certain range, intelligence is an accurate predictor of leadership effectiveness.[17] But, says Ghiselli, leaders who are much more intelligent or much less intelligent than their followers will not be effective. His findings also suggest that leader initiative, self-assurance, decisiveness, and maturity, among other traits, are important for leader success. A 1992 survey of 750 leading North American executives asked about the preferred skills or characteristics of an ideal MBA graduate. The qualities reported were oral and written communication skills (preferred by 83.5 percent of respondents), leadership skills (79.7 percent), analytical skills (75.3 percent), the ability to work in teams (71.4 percent), and the ability to manage rapid change (65.9 percent).[18]

A study of 21 less effective leaders suggested that leaders who were passed over for promotion (or who were fired or forced to retire) were more insensitive, abrasive, arrogant, intimidating, and excessively ambitious, and were unable to delegate, staff effectively, or adapt to bosses with different styles. By contrast, the more effective leaders were more direct yet diplomatic, and were flexible in dealing with others.[19] Another study found that specific technical skills and knowledge of the work group's task were related to leader success.[20] Flexibility is also a valuable leader trait.

Trait theory constitutes an important yet incomplete approach to leadership. Not all effective leaders have the same characteristics. In fact, some are markedly different from others. Differences exist between the cultures of different organizations. Some attributes that are seen as positive in some cultures are seen as negative in others. The differences are even greater when compared from country to country, or even from region to region. The leadership styles common in the "oil patch" in Calgary might be

## Management in the Real World    6-2

# Are Canadian Managers Different?

Since personality attributes arise from values and attitudes that have been nurtured from childhood and that in most individuals have been modified only slightly by experience, it is not surprising that management styles tend to differ from culture to culture. Of course, most countries contain several different cultures, but often mass communication and the mobility of populations within a country contribute to a lessening of the differences in management styles within a single country, or even within a region containing several countries. Even so, when working in the global environment it is important to recognize the differences that do exist.

As in many aspects of life, people often make the unexamined assumption that people in Canada behave in the same ways as those in the United States. Superficial similarities would seem to support this assumption, but a more careful examination reveals some marked differences. Certainly the wide distribution in Canada of U.S. mass media products contributes to a lessening of the differences. Even so, the few researchers who have tackled the question have concluded that, as a whole, management styles in Canada differ significantly from those in the United States.

Canadian Henry Mintzberg, who was mentioned in Chapter 1 and whose work is respected around the world, has studied some of these differences. His firsthand observations in Canada and the United States, as well as in several countries of the European Union and other areas, make him uniquely qualified to make such comparisons. It is, of course, dangerous and misleading to affix a stereotype to any diverse group of people, assuming that all will exhibit the same characteristics. In any broad group of managers, as has already been observed in this chapter, almost every conceivable management style and practice can be found. Nevertheless, Mintzberg confirms what some other observers have reported, that certain styles and characteristics are more likely to be reflected in the behaviour of Canadian managers than in managers who have learned their skills in the United States. Professor Mintzberg concludes that in Canada the management focus is primarily on *community*, whereas in the United States it is primarily on the *individual*. He suggests that Canadians tend to be less aggressive than managers in some other countries, including those in the U.S. He also observes that Canadian managers are much less likely than their counterparts in the United States to rush to follow the latest management fads, which he notes are continually being "offered up by consultants."[22]

Jacques Lamarre, president and CEO of SNC-Lavalin Group Inc., the Canadian-based multinational engineering company, says that "... we [Canadians] deal with human beings and they [Americans] deal with the system."[23] Another confirming view comes from Philippe de Gaspé Beaubien, chairman of Telemedia Inc, who is quoted as having said, "In general Americans work harder and they have more killer instinct. But this makes for a less human environment."[24]

Don McQuaig, president of MICA Management Resources, reports the results of a study of 3000 Canadian and 12,000 U.S. business leaders that was done by his company and its U.S. associate, Management Research Group of Portland, Maine. This massive study found that managers in the two countries were alike in some respects—both groups valued communication skills, innovation, strategic vision, and the ability to develop consensus within the organization. The two groups differed, however, in that they had contrasting views of the appropriate degree of *control* to be exerted over employee behaviour. Tight control was strongly favoured in the U.S. and much less so in Canada. As McQuaig says, "This suggests that our leaders [that is, Canadians] are further along in the process of empowerment than their American equivalents."[25] Again from Mintzberg, predominant Canadian and American styles tend to converge around the principle of openness, in marked contrast to the European styles that favour secrecy and closed systems.[26]

So what does this all mean for Canadian managers? Does it mean that one or the other predominant style is "better"? Not at all. Like any difference between two identifiable groups, these contrasts in style can be both a strength and a weakness. Canadians' tendency to avoid the bandwagon approach to new management theories may save them from costly and dramatic mistakes. At the same time it may cause them to postpone unduly the adoption of beneficial innovations and pursuit of new opportunities. The important thing is to recognize the differences, devise strategies to counteract their deleterious aspects, and make use of their creative aspects. If the Canadian style tends to be "soft," as is so often claimed, Canadian managers can guard themselves from yielding too easily and from preparing more thoroughly before commencing negotiations. In dealing with people from other countries, Canadians can self-cue themselves to state their wishes and negotiate points more freely, and to be assertive without being confrontational. Most of all, Canadian managers can be aware of the characteristics that are likely to be ingrained, as contrasted with the inherent practices likely to be found in managers from other countries, and particularly in those from Canada's major trading partner. In this area, as in so many others, knowledge is strength.

seen as inappropriate in Windsor, Nova Scotia; those effective in downtown Toronto might be unacceptable in La Ronge, Saskatchewan.

The trait approach is a simplistic method for trying to identify or predict effective leadership, but it only touches on the factors that separate effective and less effective leaders. Any trait that can be identified may be found in some successful leaders, but may be completely absent in other equally successful leaders.

The death knell for trait theories might have been rung by a comprehensive review of more than 100 trait studies carried out over the past half-century. It found that only 5 percent of the traits that were named in any study were even considered in three or more other studies. To put it another way, 95 percent of the traits that any one researcher identified as being part of the makeup of leader-managers seemed unimportant to the vast majority of other researchers.[21] Not only did this review cast doubt on the validity of trait theories, but it also pointed out the difficulty of measuring traits, and indeed of measuring success itself. So, since the early 1980s most researchers have given up trying to identify traits that might predict managerial abilities and prospects. This may seem to be bad news for people responsible for recruiting future managers, who might wish to mark off traits on a checklist and be able to predict infallibly whether the candidate would become a successful manager. But this lack of reliable predictability is probably good for society. How unfortunate it would be if all tall, assertive persons were inexorably destined to become leader-managers, while those shorter or quieter were doomed forever to be followers!

## Behavioural Models of Leadership

Dissatisfaction with the trait theories propelled scholars towards analysis of what leader-managers actually do, and how they do it. The outcome was the development of behavioural models of leadership. The focus shifted away from trying to identify leadership characteristics to the recognition that different leaders have or can develop different management styles that are equally successful. This approach, known as the behavioural model, defines leader effectiveness in terms of leader behaviours—what the leader *does* rather than what the leader *is* or seems to be.

**task-oriented behavioural style**
The type of management in which the leader is concerned primarily with accomplishing goals and objectives and concentrates on the task itself and only incidentally on the people doing it.

**people-oriented behavioural style**
The type of management in which the leader's primary focus is on relationships with and among people, with most emphasis placed on employee needs and morale.

**Task-oriented and people-oriented styles.** According to the behavioural models, effective leaders focus both on the work and on employees' attitudes and expectations. A **task-oriented behavioural style** consists of behaviours such as setting goals, giving directions, supervising employee performance, and applauding good work. Since Frederick Taylor's time, there has been considerable attention paid to the leader as a task-driven manager. Yet attention to task alone has been found to be insufficient. Thus, there evolved a **people-oriented behavioural style**, which consists of behaviours such as showing empathy for employee needs and feelings, being supportive of group needs, establishing trusting relationships with employees, and allowing employees to participate in work-related decisions.[27] Many managers have little training in people-oriented behavioural styles. According to Philip Crosby, "The future executive can go all the way through undergraduate business school and graduate business school without receiving a course on how to help the employee. It's always 'systems and programs analysis,' not how do we help the person do the job, how do we help people?"[28]

Some early research suggested that an employee-centred leader was most effective, but that study did not distinguish between cause and effect. Did an employee-centred leader produce good work, or did good work produce an employee-centred leader? Perhaps when managers are completely satisfied with the progress of the work, they feel they can devote time to employee morale, whereas when the work is going badly, they feel they have to be "tougher" and focus on the work, disregarding the feelings of the employees. If, indeed, this cause-and-effect relationship exists, any study that sought to predict work outcomes from examining whether the managers are task-oriented or people-oriented would be flawed by its circular reasoning.

Subsequently, research that was more carefully grounded found that while people-oriented leaders did create more positive employee attitudes, task-oriented leaders achieved higher employee productivity, at least in the short term.[29]

Other studies found that whichever style a manager chose, the success or failure of that style was difficult to predict. One crucial missing factor was the attitudes and reactions of non-managerial employees.[30] Some employees respond best to task-oriented leaders; others respond best to a more people-oriented style. As a consequence, it would appear that there are times when people-orientation enhances task performance and other times when it detracts from task performance.

**Measurement of behavioural styles.** As further studies were undertaken it became clear that one defect in all of the previous research was the lack of any accepted standard by which to judge whether a particular manager was task-oriented or people-oriented. In response to this need, Robert R. Blake and Anne Adams McCanse developed the Leadership Grid© as a vehicle for leader behaviour assessment and development. Using a series of questionnaires and structured seminars, the Leadership Grid technique assesses leadership orientation and incorporates both task-orientation and people-orientation into a two-dimensional matrix grid (see Exhibit 6-1). Concern for people and concern for production are measured on nine-point scales, one along the vertical axis, the other along the horizontal axis. A person with a high concern for people and a low concern for production would be represented by the (1,9) cell on the matrix. In the reverse situation, a person with a high degree of concern for production and a low concern for people would be represented in the (9,1) cell. In the midrange position is the person who is moderate on both dimensions, represented by the (5,5) cell. An individual rated highly on both dimensions would be in the (9,9) cell.

The Blake/McCanse technique reflects the fact that it is likely that both orientations are more or less present in all managers rather than there being distinctly different leader styles. Effective leaders must be able to demonstrate concern both for people and for pro-

**Exhibit 6-1**   *The Leadership Grid©*

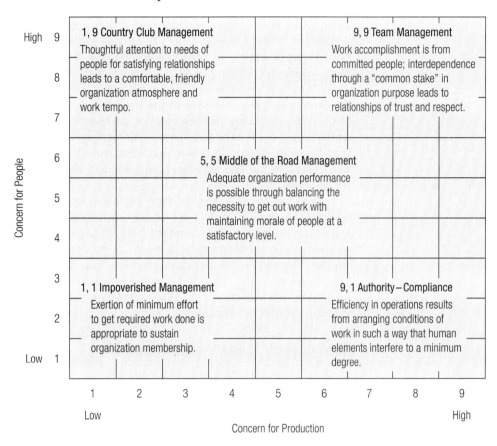

Source: The Leadership Grid© Figure from *Leadership Dilemmas–Grid Solutions*, by Robert R. Blake and Anne Adams McCanse (Houston: Grid Publishing Company) p. 29. Copyright © 1991, by Scientific Methods, Inc. Reproduced by permission of the owners.

duction. Not surprisingly, Blake and McCanse believe that the preferred style appears in the (9,9) cell, which represents high people-orientation and high task-orientation. The rationale for their belief is that a leader not only must support the employees but also must structure the work setting towards task achievement. Obviously, the organization will not progress if employees are completely happy but fail to produce the product or service for which the organization exists. Similarly, if employees are miserable, they are unlikely to work very effectively.

A positive feature of the Leadership Grid is the recognition that both types of leadership behaviours are important and that people have different orientations or predispositions that they bring to the management process. Blake and McCanse conduct a series of seminars to guide the participants/leaders towards the (9,9) orientation. These seminars reflect the assumption that leadership behaviours can be changed through seminar participation. Although this assumption may feel intuitively right, it needs further testing. In 1997, scholars from Queen's University and the University of Guelph completed a study that provides support for the assumption that managers can learn to change from a largely task-oriented to a more people-oriented style. Their study suggests that it may well be a good investment for an organization to invest the time and money necessary to sponsor workshop attendance for its managers. In this carefully controlled study, Julian Barling, Tom Weber, and Kevin Kelloway compared changes in leadership skills of the members of a group of managers who had participated in a one-day seminar on leadership with those of a control group of managers who had not done so. Over several months following the seminar the researchers conducted interviews, asking non-managerial employees for their perceptions of the qualities exhibited by the executives to whom they reported. The researchers then reported these perceptions to the executives. On conclusion of the study, they compared the employees' perceptions of the executives who had been part of the test group with those of the control group, who had had neither the seminar nor the feedback. The members of the test group were seen to be much more charismatic, considerate, and stimulating than the members of the control group. The researchers suggest that the crucial factor was the feedback that was provided.[31]

Of course, it can be argued that employee perceptions are one thing and that consistent improvement in productivity is another. Some scholars start from this point to argue that leadership styles cannot be taught in seminars, however well structured the seminars may be. More research needs to be done in this area. In the meantime, it appears that motivated managers can better see their own behaviours and learn new techniques or emphases if they participate in semi-formal training programs. This movement towards change is most likely to be possible if appropriate feedback is provided to the individual leader-managers.

## Contingency Models of Leadership

Dissatisfaction with the ability of behavioural theories to explain effective leadership led to the third phase in traditional leadership approaches, namely contingency or situational leadership effectiveness models. According to **contingency models of leadership** the appropriate leader behaviour is the one that best fits the constraints of a specific situation; in other words, it is contingent upon circumstances. In this context, contingency leadership theories (1) identify important leadership situations and (2) suggest various leadership behaviours that in those situations may lead to increased employee satisfaction and productivity.

Within this overall framework, two contrasting explanations of leadership effectiveness have emerged. In one, the *leader* is selected to fit the situation. In the other, the leader's *behaviour* or leadership style adapts to the situation as it exists. The first approach assumes that the leader's behavioural style is relatively fixed and not easily changed. In this approach the best advice is thought to be to find the situation in which the various leaders are most effective and to make sure that they are not assigned to situations in which they would be less effective. This may not always be possible, but the idea has some merit. If the organization can find the situation in which a manager's dominant leadership style is most effective, leaders, followers, and the organization are best served. An example of this approach to contingency leadership is Fiedler's LPC theory.

**Fiedler's LPC theory.**  This theory was one of the earliest of the popular contingency leadership theories.[32] **Fiedler's LPC theory** takes its name from "least preferred co-worker." In applying the theory, leaders are asked to describe the co-worker with whom they least like to work. The descriptions should focus on initiative, accomplishments, and other work-related characteristics. Then the leader's responses are analyzed. If the leader describes the LPC in positive terms, Fiedler would classify that leader as being relationship- or people-oriented. If the leader uses primarily negative terms in the

**contingency models of leadership**
Models that suggest that the most effective leaders are those whose leadership style best fits the situation within the organization.

**Fiedler's LPC theory**
An approach to leadership in which the leader's behaviour is first categorized on a scale from task orientation to people orientation, and then efforts are made to find a work situation to which that particular style is best suited.

*Effective leaders, such as Bill Gates, create a vision for the firm and establish corporate values, which are shared publicly.*

description, Fiedler would describe the leader as task-oriented. This method of assessing a leader's style has been questioned. It has been pointed out that in some circumstances, a particular co-worker actually may deserve a negative appraisal, so the description reflects the co-worker rather than the leader. Even so, Fiedler's research showed an improvement over noncontingent approaches to leadership.

After deciding whether particular leaders were task-oriented or people-oriented, Fiedler put the burden on the organization to place those leaders in positions where their respective leadership styles would be most effective. In making these job assignments, Fiedler advises that to be effective the leader needs to be task-oriented both for particularly difficult work situations (poor employee-manager relationships, little management power over employees, and an unstructured task) and for relatively undemanding work situations (good relationships with employees, high power over employees, and a clearly structured task). By way of contrast, Fiedler concludes that a people-oriented style works best in mixed (not easy, not difficult) situations. Exhibit 6-2 shows Fiedler's conclusions.

**Hersey-Blanchard situational leadership model.** Paul Hersey and Kenneth Blanchard suggest that the right mix of leadership styles is best found by focusing on the maturity level of the followers.[33] The concept is intuitively plausible because it is obvious but often overlooked that the effectiveness of a leader depends largely on the reactions of the followers. In the Hersey-Blanchard theory, leadership behaviour is composed of three independent parts: *directive* behaviour, *supportive* behaviour, and, in some cases, *coercive* behaviour.[34] As non-managerial employees become more mature and therefore willing to accept more responsibility for self-direction, the most effective management style

**Exhibit 6-2**    *Fiedler's Relationship of Situation to Optimum Leadership Style*

| Leader-member relations | Good | | | | Poor | | | |
|---|---|---|---|---|---|---|---|---|
| Task structure | Structured | | Unstructured | | Structured | | Unstructured | |
| Leader position power | High | Low | High | Low | High | Low | High | Low |
| | 1 | 2 | 3 | 4 | 5 | 6 | 7 | 8 |
| Favourable for leader → Unfavourable for leader | | | | | | | | |
| Type of leader most effective in the solution | Task-motivated | Task-motivated | Task-motivated | Relationship-motivated | Relationship-motivated | Relationship-motivated | Relationship-motivated | Task-motivated |

Source: D. Organ and R. Bateman, *Organizational Behavior*, 4th ed. (Homewood, IL: Richard D. Irwin, 1990): 558.

becomes less directive and reflects greater delegation, allowing further participation by non-managers. Although the theory has been both supported and refuted in various studies,[35] it has been used with apparent success at Xerox, Mobil Oil, and IBM.

**Vroom-Jago model**
A leadership theory that postulates that an effective leader is one who develops a variety of leadership styles, and in each situation applies the style that best fits the circumstances.

**Vroom-Jago model.** Another form of contingency theory makes the assumption that both the leader's decisions and the work situation are relatively fluid and subject to change. This perspective contradicts the assumption in the LPC approach that both the existing situation and the manager's leadership style are fixed and that neither will change. In work that built on the earlier Vroom/Yetton situational theories, Victor Vroom and Arthur Jago started with the assumption that managers are adaptive and able to respond effectively to different people and different situations.[36] In this view the ever-changing nature of work situations requires the leader to develop a variety of behavioural responses or decisions and apply them to the different situations as they occur. To Vroom and Jago, leadership requires a continuing series of assessments of the situation by the leader. They believe that the results of these assessments guide the leader towards the appropriate leadership style for the situation. As shown in Exhibit 6-3, the leadership styles range from autocratic through consultative to group-centred. Exhibit 6-4 lists the questions and decision rules Vroom and Jago used to determine which leadership style is appropriate for a given situation.

The autocratic decision is task-oriented and should be used when work conditions are simple or favourable to the leader. For example, when the information needed to make a decision is known to the leader and the decision must be made promptly, if the employees are almost sure to support the leader's decision the leader can be autocratic. In other situations, the leader also may be quite certain of the best response to the problem, but may have more time to make and implement the decision. Then the leader might profitably invest time in consulting with employees and developing their capacities to make later decisions themselves. But if the leader lacks important information, doubts the work group's likelihood of accepting an autocratic decision, and needs time to develop group commitment, a group-centred decision is indicated. Here the leader should act in a people-oriented fashion. When the conditions are unclear but not difficult, a consultative decision style is appropriate.

Although the research of Vroom and Yetton[37] and later of Vroom and Jago supported the theories they expressed, subsequent research has raised some questions. One difficulty is that it has been observed that one researcher might label as "autocratic" some behaviours that other researchers classify as "less autocratic" or even in some cases "consultative." As in many studies of human behaviour, the results are subject to two fundamental difficulties, neither of which can be eliminated entirely. One difficulty is that it

**Exhibit 6-3**

*Vroom-Jago Leadership Styles*

| Style | Explanation |
| --- | --- |
| AI | *Autocratic.* Solve the problem yourself using the information you have. |
| AII | *Less autocratic.* Obtain the needed information from workers; then solve the problem yourself. Workers provide information but not alternatives. |
| CI | *Consultative.* Share the problem with workers individually (but not as a group), seeking suggestions and possible alternatives. Solve the problem yourself. |
| CII | *More consultative.* Share the problem with workers as a group, seeking suggestions and possible alternatives. Solve the problem yourself. |
| GII | *Group decision.* Share the problem with workers as a group, seeking suggestions and possible alternatives. Attempt to reach a consensus and be willing to accept and implement the workers' solution. |

**Exhibit 6-4**

*Vroom-Jago Questions and Decision Rules*

| Question | Decision Rule |
|---|---|
| A | *Is there a quality standard that makes one alternative superior to another?*<br>If yes, go to B; if no, go to D. |
| B | *Do I have enough information to make a good decision?*<br>If yes, go to D; if no, go to C. |
| C | *Is the problem structured?*<br>If yes, go to D; if no, go to D. |
| D | *Must workers accept my decision if they are to implement it effectively?*<br>If A and D are no, choose Style AI.<br>If A is no and D is yes, go to E.<br>If A and B are yes, and D is no, choose Style AI.<br>If A, B, and D are yes, go to E.<br>If A is yes, B is no, C is yes, and D is no, choose Style AII.<br>If A is yes, B is no, C is yes, and D is yes, go to E.<br>If A is yes, B is no, C is no, and D is no, choose Style CII.<br>If A is yes, B is no, C is no, and D is yes, go to E. |
| E | *If you make the decision alone, are workers likely to accept your decision?*<br>If A is no and D and E are yes, choose Style AI.<br>If A is no, D is yes, and E is no, choose Style GII.<br>If A, B, D, and E are yes, choose Style AI.<br>If A, B, and D are yes and E is no, go to F.<br>If A is yes, B is no, C and D are yes, and E is no, go to F.<br>If A is yes, B is no, C and D are yes, and E is yes, choose Style AII.<br>If A is yes, B and C are no, and D and E are yes, choose Style CII.<br>If A is yes, B and C are no, D is yes, and E is no, go to F. |
| F | *Do workers share the firm's goals?*<br>If yes, choose Style GII.<br>If A is yes, B is no, C is yes, D is yes, and E and F are no, go to G.<br>If A is yes, B is no, C is no, D is yes, and E and F are no, choose Style CII. |
| G | *Is conflict among workers likely among preferred solutions?*<br>If yes, choose Style CII.<br>If no, choose Style CI. |

is almost impossible to isolate variables, that is, to identify which of the many factors that impinge on a person's behaviour are the primary causes of any particular result. The other difficulty is that different evaluators may apply somewhat different criteria in making their assessments, so results may not be consistent from evaluator to evaluator.

**Path-goal theory of leadership.** Robert House and Terrence Mitchell propose still another form of contingency theory that stems from the expectancy theory of motivation.[38] **Path-goal theory** is based on the assumption that people are motivated in proportion to two factors—the extent to which potential rewards are attractive to them and the degree to which they believe that their own actions can affect whether they receive or do not receive those rewards. For House and Mitchell, the role of the leader is twofold: (1) to clarify for the followers how they can achieve personal goals (for instance, salary increases and promotions) and organizational outcomes (increased productivity and profitability) and (2) to ensure that the rewards valued by the followers actually result

**path-goal theory**
A leadership theory, based on the expectancy theory of motivation, that suggests that the leader's role is to discover what rewards the workers value and to ensure that they realize that earning those rewards will depend on actions that meet the organization's goals and objectives.

from the desired behaviour. In essence, the leader motivates the follower towards outcomes valued by the individual as well as by the organization.

Path-goal theory identifies four types of leadership behaviours:

1. *Directive behaviour.* The leader makes task expectations clear by setting goals, structuring work flow, and providing feedback through regular performance feedback.
2. *Supportive behaviour.* The leader demonstrates concern for the follower and, when problems occur, is ready and willing to listen or, if requested, to offer advice.
3. *Participative behaviour.* The participative leader actively seeks ideas and information from non-managerial employees. Participative behaviour only occurs if followers actually participate in making decisions that affect them. For the participative style to be effective, employees must perceive that their participation is meaningful and that management will pay attention to their views, even if those views are not always adopted.
4. *Achievement behaviour.* Achievement leadership translates into setting expectations and task goals at a high level. This involves making the goals challenging but not impossible to accomplish.

These four behaviour patterns form a repertoire of meaningful actions that a leader might use under different work situations. This theory also depends on the leaders having the ability to increase rewards that are valued by the followers. Leaders are effective to the extent that they can motivate followers, influence their ability to perform, and increase their job satisfaction. The model postulates that a follower's attitudes and behaviours are influenced by two factors: leader behaviours and situational factors. Followers' attitudes and behaviours reflect their levels of job satisfaction and their abilities to perform their tasks. Situational factors (sometimes referred to as environmental factors) include task requirements, the composition and cohesiveness of the work group, and the formal authority structure. Personal characteristics include the extent to which the followers believe that they have the ability to perform well and that they have some control over the outcomes, rather than that control is totally vested in management or some external factor.

Path-goal theory prescribes which leader behaviours are likely to be effective within different situational constraints. Leaders are expected to change their behaviours towards the followers when situational changes occur. This theory suggests that leadership is most effective when there is an optimum match between leader behaviours and the situation. For example, directive behaviour is suggested for situations that require more task structuring, monitoring, and feedback. Directive behaviour may be particularly appropriate in connection with a new employee who has limited job experience. Supportive behaviour might be suitable in a situation where employees know the job well and are experiencing delays or "client conflict" and need to be reassured that they are doing the right thing. Participative behaviour is appropriate for employees who know their jobs well enough to make meaningful contributions to decisions that affect themselves and their department. Finally, achievement behaviour is suitable in situations where high performance is in the best interests of both the employee and the organization. A sales department compensated on a commission basis would be an ideal setting for achievement behaviour. This type of leader behaviour sets high sales expectations that,

*During a game, the coach of a professional sports team, like Pat Quinn above, must make autocratic decisions such as what strategy to follow and what players to field. But in other situations, even a coach must act in a more people-oriented and consultative fashion to gain the support of the team members and the owners.*

when they are met, yield greater financial rewards to the members of the sales department. Achievement-oriented leadership works best when the followers have a high need for achievement.

In summary, path-goal theory views the leader as the vital link between the organization and the individual. Leaders need to motivate employees to understand how their work efforts are tied to valued salary increases, promotions, praise, recognition, and respect.

**The present status of contingency models.** There is merit in all four of these approaches to contingency leadership. Research findings support all to some extent, but suggest that none of them, in itself, is a complete answer. As pointed out in the discussion of broad management theory in Chapter 1, however, this disappointing fact does not diminish the benefit that can be gained by studying and attempting to apply relevant aspects of several of the theories presented. It seems clear that managers will never find "the perfect solution" to questions of leadership, but each new theory offers some further insights and helps managers to devise their own personal approaches that may make them more effective leaders.

## Structural Limitations on Direct Leadership

In many work situations traditional approaches to leadership are ineffective or sometimes just not possible. Steven Kerr and John Jermier believe that situational characteristics can reduce the need for traditional leadership.[39] They identify three such situational characteristics: characteristics of the subordinate, of the task, and of the organization. These characteristics can act either as constraints on or as substitutes for leadership.

In certain situations, leader behaviour can be neutralized by a constraint that is inherent within the organization. In this context, a **constraint,** or as some scholars call it, a *neutralizer,* is any situation that prevents the leader from acting in a desired manner.[40] For example, a union contract may require that all employees in similar positions in the organization receive the same wage increase regardless of job performance. Sometimes an organization is forced to freeze wages, salaries, and promotions for an extended period for financial reasons. Both of these situations constrain or prevent the leader from using wage differentials to reward or reinforce positive behaviour or to sanction negative behaviour. If no one can be given a raise, obviously a leader-manager cannot use differential wage increases to reward superior performance and therefore is forced to forego an otherwise useful tool of leadership.

In other situations, an organization may have grown rapidly, or may have had substantial staff turnover. In these circumstances, the workforce may be largely inexperienced or at least unfamiliar with the culture of the organization. As has been pointed out, new employees often require more direct, task-oriented leader behaviours than do more experienced employees. Until training and education can take effect, leader-managers will have to act in a more task-oriented manner, even though they might prefer to be more people-oriented. In this context, the preponderance of new employees constitutes a constraint on the management styles that the leaders might wish to adopt if they were free to do so.

Leader-managers also may encounter constraints that arise from organizational culture. If all of the top managers of a particular organization exhibit a uniform style of management, whether task-oriented or people-oriented, those in middle management positions probably will be constrained to adopt the same management styles. If they act counter to the organizational culture, they likely will come into conflict with their

**constraint**
Any circumstance that limits freedom of action; in this context, a situation that hinders the leader from acting effectively to accomplish desired goals and objectives.

**Management in the Real World** 6-3

## Leadership and Quality: Reflections by Philip Crosby

When I was running my first production operation, I wanted very much to be a good leader. For this reason I read everything I could on the subject and watched closely how others handled their responsibilities. It wasn't long before I was certain that I knew a great deal about being a leader. We were running a three-shift operation six days a week, and I made certain that I was up to date on all data and personnel changes. I met with my staff each morning and spent a great deal of time with all the people.

One of my children became ill at this time and was forced to spend a few days in the hospital. We wanted to make certain that she was not alone, so the family divided the 24-hour day into segments. I visited during the day but my assigned segment was 8 p.m. to midnight. This let me do my office work while she dozed or watched TV, and I could still get some sleep before going to work.

The second night, when my uncle relieved me, I decided to drop by the plant on the way home to check in on our third shift. As I walked into the normally bustling plant I realized that things were different during that time period. It had been a long time since I worked that shift.

The people were delighted to see me, and I spent 30 minutes or so just wandering around seeing what was happening. One of the operators motioned me over to her work station and pointed out that they were out of components "again." The stockroom was locked on the third shift and not enough parts had been left.

"It happens all the time," she noted.

The superintendent grabbed me to have a cup of coffee with the members of the quality team who were having a 15-minute stand-up meeting. They were having a hard time obtaining customer information concerning new products that were being delivered. Requests to the quality engineering department were not gaining any response.

Before I left, I had picked up six different problems that were not being properly addressed by the rest of the operation. The next morning I brought these to the attention of my staff and asked them for action. No one knew anything about the problems I had brought them, but they agreed to respond more promptly. The quality engineering manager and the production control supervisor thought that the complaints were overstated. However, at my urging they agreed to get into the situation.

Two nights later I repeated my visit and found that a few things had been fixed, but that the people had no feeling that they were receiving much support. They also gave me five more assignments.

At the next morning's staff meeting I stated that I was tired of being an errand boy and that we needed to make the third shift, and the second one too, equal in all respects to the first. I handed them a schedule in which we would all take turns visiting these activities. I also brought the shift superintendents in so they could voice their discomfort. I told the quality engineering manager privately that he was going to wind up running the third shift if things did not improve quickly.

It all worked out for the best. Our output rose while our problems dropped to almost nothing. I heard later that they thought I was a great leader. But it was thanks to a sick child, not to proper leadership thinking. I'll never let my people get lonely again.

superior officers. Equally disturbing, they are also likely to find that their subordinates become confused by the two differing styles of management, and perhaps become distrustful of all leadership efforts.

It may be tempting for inexperienced leaders simply to accept existing constraints and limit their activities to stay within those constraints. Effective leaders, by way of contrast, seek to identify constraints and find ways to change or even remove those constraints that impede initiatives they believe are in the best interests of the organization.

# Transactional and Transformational Leadership

**transactional leadership**
A leadership style that focuses on activities, that is, the traditional management roles of planning, organizing, leading, and controlling.

Today it is generally recognized that *leading* entails more than just *managing*—important as management is. Several scholars have distinguished two approaches to leading by using the terms *transactional* and *transformational*. **Transactional leadership** refers to the more traditional managerial approach of concentrating on planning, organizing, and structuring the form of the enterprise and controlling activities within it. As the name implies, it is more concerned with transactions or activities than with broader, less concrete issues. Transactional leaders appeal to employees' rational exchange motive. They ensure that employees understand that in effect they are exchanging labour for wages. This is a simple concept, but often overlooked in the exigencies of daily work life. Another way of putting this exchange is that as employees work to further organizational goals, they are at the same time furthering their own personal goals. For the leader, it is a process of keeping workers focused on organizational goals.

**transformational leadership**
A leadership style designed to change (or transform) the culture of the organization by communicating to employees and others a new vision, and enlisting their support in moving towards it.

In contrast, **transformational leadership** focuses on changing or *transforming* the attitudes, beliefs, and ultimately the behaviours of employees.[41] It is primarily concerned with giving new enthusiasm to the organization by means of effective communication that conveys in positive terms the organization's vision for the future, and its goals and objectives to fulfil that vision. It stresses strategic planning and management of change as the organization works to achieve its plans.

Transformational leadership is typically manifested in three stages: (1) creating a vision for the future of the organization; (2) gathering support from people within the organization; and (3) leading and guiding key individuals into behaviours that facilitate the accomplishment of the new goals and objectives.[42]

Leaders such as Lee Iacocca of Chrysler, Ted Newall of Nova, and Pat Farrah of Home Depot instituted broad changes in the cultures of their respective companies, and those changes can be considered nothing less than transformations. That these and other transformational leaders have different backgrounds, different personal characteristics, and different management styles does not negate the principles of leadership. Instead, these differences illustrate the complexity of leadership and the variety of methods by which it can be exercised. In essence, an organization's culture seldom changes appreciably, either positively or negatively, unless there is a leader, or several leaders, who consciously or unconsciously wish the change to occur. Sometimes these leaders serve in a managerial capacity. At other times, the real leadership comes from one or more non-managers who are often not acknowledged but who nonetheless shape the course of the organization. Effective management consists in part of ensuring that this leadership comes, at least in the first instance, from top managers. If it does not, management may be allowing the organization's leadership to be hijacked by people who are not accountable for the outcomes and who may not share top managers' vision for the future.

Canadian society is undergoing massive changes, and there is little prospect that the pace of change will decrease. Leaders who have relied on transactional leadership will have to learn to think and act in terms of transformational change, or their organizations will fall behind in the competitive struggle.

## Self-leadership

Two other societal trends will have considerable impact on future leadership approaches.[43] First, a highly educated workforce in a democratic society will seek greater decision-making participation and other forms of power sharing.[44] Second, a highly competitive world economy has led to the necessity for intensified cost-cutting measures. For several decades, North American companies have had proportionately more middle managers than have most foreign competitors. To meet the competitive pressure, during the late 1980s and 1990s, Canadian companies eliminated many middle-management positions, causing what will doubtless prove to be a permanent reduction in the white-collar workforce. The goal is to have "a lean organization." These trends make a shift towards greater participation of non-managerial employees in decision making increasingly likely in the future.

As societal trends change, new leadership strategies emerge. For effective leadership in the future, two things must occur. First, leaders must engage in behaviours that actively encourage non-managerial employees to gain control over their work destinies.

### *Real World Reflection*   6-1

## Implementing Self-leadership Concepts

In the model of situational leadership, developed by Paul Hersey and Kenneth Blanchard, effective managers vary the amount of structure and support they provide based on the developmental level of the employee.

When an employee is new to the job, clear direction and instruction are needed. On the other hand, a highly experienced individual needs little direction or instruction to perform exceptionally on the job. This same employee may need only encouragement to take a chance in undertaking a new task.

According to Hersey and Blanchard, current skill level, amount of experience, and the degree of commitment exhibited by the individual determine the level of instruction and support required by the employee. An experienced person who disagrees with how the work should be done may require more direction than one who agrees with the method and goal.

Assess the following when delegating new work to an employee:

1. The employee's current skill level; and
2. The employee's level of commitment to the goal.

### SKILL TIPS

When the employee's skill level is low, provide direction and instruction. As the employee obtains the skills and experience to effectively complete the job, replace the direction with more encouragement and positive feedback.

As an effective manager you must work with employees to provide the appropriate amount of direction and support. Don't be afraid to ask for their feedback.

Contributed by Sydney Scott, British Columbia Institute of Technology.

*Some companies, such as Lincoln Electric Company, have eliminated almost all middle managers and supervisors, relying on employees to set the major parameters of their work.*

The trend towards telecommuting is an example of both cause and effect in this regard. This devolution of power requires confident, secure leaders as well as non-managers who are willing and able to accept responsibility. Second, non-managerial employees need to develop self-control strategies such as self-management and self-leadership. New leadership approaches to managing increasingly competitive markets will, of necessity, increase employee participation in the decision-making process.

To facilitate this change, some forward-looking companies such as the Lincoln Electric Company, assume that employees can be self-motivated. There is only one manager for each 100 or so employees, which is a remarkably low ratio. Employees are graded in part on their ability to work without a supervisor.[45] They can rearrange tasks, and any improvement in performance earns the employee more money, so both the employee and the company benefit from such an approach. Teamwork and reliability are rewarded, and some employees double their base pay through incentive compensation.

**self-leadership**
A strategy in which employees at all levels motivate themselves to accomplish not only the tasks that are interesting to them, but others as well that are required to meet the organization's goals and objectives.

**Self-leadership** reflects a management philosophy that encompasses a systematic set of behavioural and cognitive strategies that can lead to improved performance and effectiveness.[46] This philosophy encourages individual employees to develop their own work priorities that are consistent with organizational goals. What happens to the manager in the self-leadership process? Rather than abdicating control, the manager's role simply changes. Managers, as well as non-managerial employees, must learn new techniques. Managers must take active roles in encouraging subordinates to develop self-leadership capabilities. The role of the manager changes but does not decrease, and in some respects it becomes more demanding.

Employees who are given the freedom entailed in self-leadership tend to exhibit the human trait of gravitating towards tasks that they find enjoyable and personally rewarding, and neglecting tasks that they find boring or distasteful. The challenge for managers is to motivate employees to focus as well on tasks that may seem less attractive and rewarding, but that are equally important in meeting organizational goals and objectives.[47]

This change in emphasis is difficult to bring about. It is unduly optimistic to expect that all employees will jump at the chance for more personal control. Instead, some employees actively resist such a change. This resistance often stems from fear of the unknown. For many employees, throughout their careers they have been encouraged to complete their work according to procedures and standards designed by their managers or by specialists. With the self-leadership approach, employees are asked to assume new responsibilities, and with responsibilities come risks. Often they fear that they are not sufficiently trained and will be unable to fill this new role successfully. One way to increase employee self-control is to use empowerment to overcome worker resistance or fear. As discussed in other chapters of this text, *empowerment* is the process of providing employees with the skills, tools, information, and, above all, the authority and responsibility for their work. This gives employees direct control over many aspects of their work. Self-leadership transfers considerable control of individual work behaviour from the manager to the non-managerial employee. Leadership becomes an internal, personal process. Real empowerment involves the worker's commitment to **self-management**, which is the use of work strategies that help to control daily activities in order to achieve organizational goals.

**self-management**
A strategy that encourages all employees to arrange and control their personal activities and resources, with little input from external sources.

The manager's role in the self-leadership organization is to encourage other employees to develop the same kinds of self-control skills that managers must possess. By self-control is meant the ability to control one's own work destiny in both the short term and the long term. It means managing time well, setting and following priorities, and avoiding distractions. Self-leadership de-emphasizes external forms of control and requires complete rethinking of the role of the leader-manager. DuPont Canada has taken this change in role seriously. Most of its tens of thousands of employees have

## Real World Reflection    6-2

### Respecting Cultures in International Business— Dr. Rosalie Tung

Dr. Rosalie Tung's work encourages leaders from around the world to understand and respect each other's culture. As a professor at Simon Fraser University, Rosalie Tung has been hailed as one of the world's five most-cited authors in international business by the *Journal of International Business Studies*. Having written eight books to date, Dr. Tung is a pioneer in international business administration research, and her work on cross-cultural management is invaluable to companies facing globalization. She was recently appointed to the United Nations Task Force on Human Resource Management.

Dr. Tung's work is an invaluable tool for any individual working in a global arena. The concept of self-leadership inspires a sharing of information between the manager and employees that enhances future growth for employees and their organizations.

Discussing the concepts found in Dr. Tung's books, or making her books available to individuals working with international clients, is one way for managers to promote self-leadership in their workplaces.

Contributed by Marnie Wright, British Columbia Institute of Technology.

accepted greater responsibility for what they do, and for the outcomes. Front-line employees are empowered to deal directly with suppliers, avoiding misunderstandings and delays that used to occur when supplier contacts had to be filtered through the chain of command. As a result, DuPont has been able to eliminate five of the former eleven layers of management—increasing both efficiency and effectiveness.[48] At the same time, of course, these reductions in middle-management positions make redundant, perhaps permanently, the people whose positions have disappeared—a societal problem of dimensions only recently being recognized, and far beyond the scope of this book.

**role modelling**
Leadership by example, that is, demonstrating in daily work patterns the attitudes and behaviours wished for in the rest of the staff.

The primary vehicle leaders use to encourage self-leadership is **role modelling**, a process by which leaders exhibit behaviours that they expect and hope that other employees will follow. For example, leaders need to set goals for themselves in a manner that their employees can observe. If leader-managers wish their subordinates to use time effectively, they must manage their own time in ways that show the same responsibility. If they want employees to communicate positively with each other, they must be open themselves to suggestions and to constructive criticism. As pointed out in Chapter 2, employees soon emulate the actions of the managers to whom they are accountable, whether positively or negatively. Not surprisingly, for role modelling to have positive results the employee needs to see a connection between adopting the behaviour and achieving positive outcomes that the employee values. Research also suggests that employees are more likely to emulate the behaviour of the leader-managers they respect and see as being effective, rather than of those they see as ineffective or as not enjoying the favour of top management.[49]

## Behavioural Self-management

**behavioural self-management**
The use of activities such as self-set goals, self-observation, self-rewards, self-cueing, and self-designed jobs to help people gain greater control over their lives.

**Behavioural self-management** is the application of a set of strategies that help people gain greater control over their lives. Common behavioural self-management strategies include self-set goals, self-observation, self-rewards, self-cueing, and self-designed jobs.

**self-set goals**
Goals that are developed by the employee rather than by the manager.

With **self-set goals** the initiative for setting the goal and the level of the goal itself comes from the employee rather than from the manager. Self-set goals must be consistent with the organization's overall goals and are dependent on the employee's commitment to those goals. Self-set goals free the manager from a traditional supervisory duty and empower non-managerial employees with a greater measure of personal control. This autonomous approach to goal setting is recommended as a matter of ethics, not just as a matter of effectiveness.[50]

**self-observation**
Monitoring one's own behaviour, actions, and outcomes.

**Self-observation** is a process in which employees monitor their own behaviours and actions, events, and outcomes. Self-observation requires that performance records be kept. For example, a package delivery worker might keep a notebook recording the time of each delivery. A production employee might keep a record of time required to complete each item or batch, and also of the number of rejects or discards produced. An outside sales person might record the number of sales calls made, the time spent on each, and the amount of time lost between calls. Self-observation permits an increase in employment empowerment and autonomy.

**self-rewards**
Desired benefits, usually of a minor nature, that employees award to themselves for having reached pre-set goals or stages in their work.

Deming and other students of management urge the elimination of systems of payment on piecework incentive systems, and of inspectors and time clocks. Self-observation enables a person to answer the question "How am I doing?" without having to ask a supervisor. Of course, the organization still needs to know how individual employees are performing, so some external or management observation must be retained.

With **self-rewards** (also called *self-administered rewards*), employees monitor, evaluate, and give themselves small rewards for their own performance. Self-rewards enable

*Having achieved a goal of completing a particular stage of a task, employees take a self-administered reward—a few moments of relaxation before starting on the next task.*

the individual to recognize that a performance milestone has been surpassed. An example is rewarding oneself with a break only after completing a major stage of the assigned task. Another type of self-reward is consciously recognizing the naturally rewarding aspect of the work itself. With some guidance, almost all employees can appreciate that it feels good to have accomplished something worthwhile. While these ideas may appear simplistic, they get back to basics and are powerful motivators. The employee decides the measure and worth of an activity rather than adhering to a universal definition. Self-administered rewards can add meaning and purpose to work.

A mechanic who lays out the necessary tools prior to commencing work is practising **self-cueing.** This is defined as the process of planning or making arrangements for an activity prior to its performance, without having to depend on others to make these plans and arrangements. This practice helps to prevent delays and defects from occurring during the execution stage. One type of self-cueing, *behavioural rehearsal*, consists of practising an activity under simulated or controlled conditions. For example, the night before an important meeting with a customer, a sales team might enter into role play in which some members of the team play the role of the customer and ask appropriate questions, giving the sales team a chance to plan and rehearse their answers.

**Self-designed jobs** allow employees to propose and design work process changes, rather than have the changes originate only from management sources. This can result in a personal sense of competence, self-control, and purpose. At the central facility of Federal Express in Memphis, Tennessee, the company experienced serious problems due to late-arriving and mislabelled packages. To correct the problem, management implemented a system called minisort. But the minisort process was inefficient and unpopular among front-line workers. One observed, "If you got on someone's nerves, they sent you to minisort." So 12 front-line workers were appointed to a team to solve the problem. The team cut minisort staff from 150 to 80 workers, thus saving the wages of 70 employees. They were able to do this because they clarified minisort tasks and implemented prevention measures that cut from 10,000 to 4000 the number of packages sent to minisort each night. In four months the number of late packages dropped from 4300 to 432. The team's innovations resulted in a reduction in the number of employees, but as one member of the team said, "For management to listen to me, that's important."[51]

## Cognitive Self-management

Not all self-management strategies are observable and measurable, although their results usually are. In **cognitive self-management**, the individual employee creates mental images and thought patterns that are consistent with the organization's goals. Two cognitive self-management strategies are opportunity building and positive self-talk.

**Opportunity building** is the process of seeking out and, if circumstances permit, developing new possibilities for success. An oft-told marketing story involves two salespeople who were sent to a foreign country by a shoe manufacturer. The negative thinker told the company's headquarters, "Opportunities are nonexistent. Nobody here wears

**self-cueing**
Planning and making arrangements required to complete a task or project before embarking on it.

**self-designed job**
A job for which parameters and specifications have been established in whole or in part by the employee who will fill the job.

**cognitive self-management**
A mental process in which the employee creates images and aspirations that are consistent with achieving the organization's goals and objectives.

**opportunity building**
Seeking and developing possibilities for success, either as individuals or as an organization.

shoes." The positive thinker said, "Opportunities are unlimited. Nobody here wears shoes." Thus, an obstacle may be converted to an opportunity by the way managers and employees perceive and define the problem.

**positive self-talk**
Creative mental imagery that enhances the individual's sense of ability, capacity, and self-worth.

**Positive self-talk** is the process of creating mental imagery that reinforces one's sense of self-esteem and, in the process, enhances efficacy.[52] For example, customer service agents, when dealing with angry customers, can remind themselves that they have been successful in calming and satisfying angry customers in the past by listening for, and responding to, key words or phrases used by the customers. By maintaining self-confidence, the agents are using positive self-talk to help manage difficult situations. Although positive self-talk is an internal, personal matter, its positive benefits can be heightened if employees discuss it with each other, thus reinforcing each other's commitment to the process.

## Developing a Self-leadership Culture

The development of an effective self-leadership culture begins, like almost any major organizational change, with a commitment from the leaders in the top levels of management. Three keys to developing a self-leadership culture are sharing information, training, and positive reinforcement.

**Sharing information.**  Self-managed employees need more information than employees who are closely controlled by managers. Information that managers have not habitually divulged must be made available to everyone who is expected to become self-led. This information includes facts concerning costs and profits. When they are informed of these facts, non-managerial employees become more willing and better equipped to accept responsibility for their actions. In addition, open communication sends the message to employees that they are respected and trusted.

**Training.**  In preparing managers and non-managers alike for self-management strategies, organized training programs should focus on improving communication skills, team building, and developing the various self-management skills discussed in this chapter. Training helps to reinforce managerial policy statements at all levels of an organization. Managers may feel threatened by the idea of a self-managed workforce, so in addition to training in techniques they also need assurance that they will continue to have an important role in organizational success.

**Reinforcement.**  In addition to sharing information and providing training programs, administering performance rewards can help to reinforce the use of self-management behaviours. For instance, a "team player" or "star performer" award might be issued to an employee who demonstrates outstanding self-leadership ability. Like any reward that singles out one person or a few individuals, however, such recognition can trigger animosity and jealousy on the part of those who are not so recognized. "After all," they may think, "don't I deserve recognition for my work?" Some organizations have tried to avert this backlash effect by having all employees, or representative employees from the group, participate in selecting the individuals who will receive the awards. This may be successful if the panel making the selections changes frequently to avoid suggestions of favouritism. Perhaps the best way to handle an awards system is to institute it for a short period; after a few months or years, the organization can change to another awards system before problems become too ingrained and pronounced.

## Leadership Challenges

Critical global issues confront the economy and companies in the early years of the twenty-first century.[53] The most effective managers will be those who understand leadership as a broad, empowering tool, and who have a special capability to develop self-managed leadership in others.

The quest for quality and competitiveness implies a new kind of business leadership. Effective leadership in the future more likely than not will mean teaching others to lead themselves. Non-managerial employees will have to develop skills in self-management. Those who do will be better able to control the pace and flow of their work. To facilitate this process, effective leadership in the future must encourage employees to develop self-leadership skills.

Some of the challenges that future leaders and the country as a whole will face are:

- Increasing global competition;
- Emphasis on speed, service, and information;
- Lean and flexible work demands for more value-added labour and reduced indirect labour costs;
- The need to employ untrained, unskilled, and disenfranchised employees;
- Reduction in the number of low-skilled jobs at the same time as more inexperienced and low-skilled workers enter the market;
- Increasing gaps (1) between elite, skilled employees with long-term employment opportunities and a working underclass with limited skills and few employment options; and (2) between knowledge-intensive, highly educated employees and labour-intensive, unskilled employees;
- Employee demands for greater participation and a marked shift to teams, skill-based pay, and cooperation with the organization;
- Further expansion of information technologies; and
- Flatter, decentralized organizations with greater need for employee self-management.

## Managing Cultural Diversity

Another major challenge facing leaders today is managing a diverse workforce. In some areas of Toronto, racial minorities predominate. In Richmond, Delta, and some other areas of Greater Vancouver, a large majority of secondary-school students are first- or second-generation Hong Kong Chinese. These students will soon enter the workforce, bringing a strong work ethic that is rare among longer-term Canadians. Furthermore, the percentage of Canadian women engaged in the paid workforce has increased steadily since the 1960s. For instance, in 1971 only 44 percent of women aged 25 to 34 were in the paid workforce. Two decades later (the most recent Statistics Canada figures have not yet been released on this subject) these same women, then aged 45 to 54, reported a 76 percent participation rate.[54] It is generally thought, although not as well documented in published statistics, that the number of women who advance beyond entry-level jobs is also increasing, albeit not as rapidly as might

*As the workforce becomes increasingly diverse, managers constantly must be aware of cultural differences.*

## Management in the Real World  6-4

### Are Women Good Leader-managers?

As more women reach positions in top management, a question often asked (and unfortunately almost as often answered with little thought) is whether men or women are more effective as leader-managers. A widely held stereotype is that men are task-oriented, and that as a consequence they tend to deal more harshly with subordinates than do women, who are thought to be more relationship-oriented or people-oriented.[55] It is often said that men measure their success by win/lose standards, as in sports, while women do so by a combination of indicators that lead to overall satisfaction.[56] These stereotypes may be valid to some degree because, indeed, socialization has tended to push men towards more aggressive behaviours and women towards more noncompetitive behaviours.[57] Perhaps equally important is the effect of the self-fulfilling prophecy: if men are expected to act aggressively, they are likely to do so; similarly, if women are *expected* to act in a complaisant manner, they are likely to do so.[58]

Even if these contrasts were universally true (which of course they are not, given differences from person to person), this would still beg the question of whether men or women are better as leader-managers. As this chapter points out, some styles of management are more successful in some environments, while other styles are more successful in other environments.

Furthermore, even if despite all evidence to the contrary a central tendency could be found to divide leadership styles along gender lines, there are women leader-managers who are as tough and hard-driving as any man. Examples include Peggy Witte of Giant Mines, Anita Roddick of the Body Shop, and Carly Fiorina of Hewlett-Packard.[59] One has only to consider Maureen Kempston Darkes, president and general manager of General Motors of Canada Ltd., to realize that women as well as men can be phenomenally successful in the rough-and-tumble world of huge corporations without having to adopt the persona of the task-oriented, cigar-chewing, whip-wielding tycoon.

So, as might be expected but is often overlooked, leadership styles differ from one manager to another, *regardless of gender*. The answer to the question posed in the title of this vignette is quite clear: *Some* men are more successful leader-managers than *most* women, and *some* women are more successful leader-managers than *most* men.

The central point is that gender is not the determining factor in whether the leadership style of a particular leader-manager is most appropriate for a given situation. Therefore, the question posed in the title of this box reveals an unfortunate inherent bias. It could be argued that even asking the question implies that there *must* be gender-related characteristics deep within a person that make that person a successful or unsuccessful leader. It is a contradiction of terms to realize on the one hand that the trait theories of leadership have failed to identify "leader traits," while to assume on the other hand that "female traits" are more or less conducive to success as a leader. If an organization has no Sudanese tribesmen, Borneo hunter-gatherers, or gauchos from the Argentine pampas, it costs that organization nothing to assert that it would welcome them on equal terms if they appeared, and that it would celebrate the diversity they would bring to the organization. Right now, however, both women and men work in most organizations, so it is not enough to give lip service to equal opportunity for both genders. Instead, the leader-managers who truly recognize diversity will serve their organizations well not by asking, "Is this *woman* (or *man*) ready for a management position?" but rather, "Is this *person* ready for a management position?" As in all things, leaders are the ones who lead. If an organization is to benefit from the recently expanded pool of potential managers, that is, one that includes candidates from both genders, its leader-managers must strive to abandon their gender biases and convey a gender-neutral attitude throughout the organization.

be hoped.[60] When the same week sees the appointments of a woman as president and general manager of General Motors Canada,[61] and of another woman as vice president for marketing of Canadian Air,[62] it is clear that the workplace is changing. This is not to say that equality is even close to being achieved, since a survey in late 1998 shows that in Fortune 500 companies only 3 percent of the senior managers are women. Nevertheless, the glass ceiling obviously has some cracks in it, and managers must take this into account or they will fail their organizations.[63]

Whatever the reasons for these increases in workforce diversity, employers will have to train, manage, and motivate a workforce composed of individuals with widely varying backgrounds and perspectives.[64] A few decades ago, managers had only to manage a predominantly white, male workforce. Diversity is more than a question of race and gender—it requires transparency to characteristics of religion, culture, sexual orientation, values, and educational and skill qualifications.[65] Managing diversity requires changes in recruiting, hiring, training, and effective use of people from different cultural backgrounds.[66] Programs must be developed to promote both awareness of cultural differences and positive attitudes towards those differences. Tolerance is not enough; acceptance must be complete or the organization not only will fail to be competitive, but it may run afoul of the law. Work itself also will have to be restructured to remove the factors that arose from the prevalence of the largely male workforce.[67] For instance, this restructuring will have to include more flextime so women can rear children and still advance in their careers. Changes in family relationships will require provisions for parental leaves, for fathers as well as for mothers. As more people are living longer, adult children are taking more responsibility for aging parents, often at the same time that they are caring for their own children,[68] so other forms of flexibility will be required. Managers will have to recognize that elder care not only will require the time and attention of employees but may drain them emotionally.[69]

Any leader who sincerely values cultural diversity must make it safe for everyone in the organization to talk about differences. This means a change for those organizations that have been denying that differences exist while at the same time adjusting to accommodate what they consider to be unwelcome affirmative action guidelines. Valuing diversity means viewing the multicultural workforce from a positive perspective, recognizing that all people are entitled to equal opportunity, and encouraging open discussion of these differences of gender, age, ethnicity and language, sexual orientation, physical ability, and other attributes.[70] Training programs in diversity awareness can help bring these differences out into the open, and identify the unique characteristics and talents of diverse individuals that are valuable resources for the organization.

Actively managing diversity offers the potential for increasing an organization's competitiveness, but it requires commitment on the part of the organization. Like restructuring in other respects, managing diversity requires changing the culture of the organization. In this, as in all things, how leader-managers think and act communicate the organizational culture far better than published statements or other exhortations. Good leaders will first examine their own biases, take steps to correct any limitations they find, and *then* prepare to lead non-managerial employees to the desired attitudes and behaviours in regard to diversity.

While cultural diversity brings stimulation, challenge, and energy, it does not always lead to harmony.[71] A mix of genders, cultures, and alternative lifestyles can lead to conflict and misunderstanding. The job of the manager is to create an environment in which differences are appreciated and a group of diverse individuals work productively together. This is a formidable challenge, but organizations that meet this challenge will be those led by forward-looking leaders.

## The Workplace of Tomorrow

Frank Loscavio's crew rebuilt a Jamaican power plant in 6 months rather than the normal 22. Nickelodeon's Gerry Laybourne helps nourish creativity with one new idea after another, such as redesigning the work space to stimulate creativity. Richard Semler has made Semco the ultimate flexible company; six people share his title of CEO. Jack Stack, head of engine manufacturing company SRC, teaches factory workers everything he knows about the financial workings of the company.[72] While each may be unique in a particular way, these leaders share at least one common characteristic—they are unconventional. And unconventional leadership styles may work best as organizations embrace the concepts of reengineering, teamwork, and empowerment.

Effective leaders in the future will be employee-centred, putting people first without losing sight of organizational goals. By placing the interests of their employees on a par with their own, leaders earn loyalty and motivate workers. True leaders listen to subordinates, and consequently will be properly informed, enabling them to make effective decisions. As noted at the beginning of this chapter, leading and managing are different roles.

Managers ensure that the organization functions effectively. Effective leaders stress relationships with others, values, and commitment; articulate a vision for what the organization can be in the long run; move the organization in new directions, rejecting the status quo; communicate why things are done; favour calculated risk and change; and generate a feeling of value and importance in work.[73] These characteristics will be the indicators of leaders in the workplace of the future.

## Summary of Learning Objectives

▷ **Distinguish between leaders and managers.**

Managers are primarily concerned with the pressures of the moment. For the manager, efficient use of resources may be of greatest immediate concern. Leaders are more concerned with long-term visionary concepts, and how they will affect people as well as the organization. The ideal is a combination—the leader-manager.

▷ **Explain the relationships between leadership and power.**

Leadership requires the exercise of power. Every leader has a base of power, but for any two leaders the sources of power may be quite different. This chapter outlined several of the most common sources of power: (1) power based on the ability to reward or punish employees for their performance; (2) power based on knowledge, whether expertise in a particular area of competence, or information relating to a specific circumstance; (3) power based on respect that comes from personal characteristics, style of management, or personality; and (4) power based on position in the organization.

▷ **Compare the theories of trait, behavioural, and contingency or situational leadership.**

Trait theories of leadership tried to identify personal characteristics or management styles that characterized effective leaders. The attempts were largely unsuccessful, not only because of differences in organizational culture in which different leaders functioned but because there seem to be no common threads exhibited by any large sample of successful leader-managers. Behavioural leadership theorists looked for the behavioural indicators that successful managers might exhibit. Early research identified two types of behaviours: task-centred leadership and people-centred leadership. Contingency or situational leadership theory postulates that it is the situation in which a leader functions that determines what leadership method will be most successful. Key attributes of the situation in this context are the characteristics of subordinates, the culture of the organization, and the urgency and importance of the decisions to be made. Each of these theories can contribute to an understanding of leadership, but none, or even the combination of all three types, can explain satisfactorily what makes some leaders successful and others less so.

▶ **Explain the concept of transformational leadership.**

Transformational leadership refers to an inspirational form of leadership behaviour that modifies (or "transforms") the followers' beliefs, values, and ultimately their behaviours.

▶ **Define** *self-leadership* **and discuss the societal trends that contributed to its development.**

Self-leadership is an approach to management that encompasses a systematic set of strategies that gives to both managerial and non-managerial employees more control over their work. Two societal trends have made self-leadership more appropriate in work settings. First, today's employees at all levels are better educated and tend to have higher skills than those of previous generations. Second, increased competition requires greater efficiency and effectiveness, and it has been found that self-leadership often results in greater employee motivation and satisfaction, which in turn result in increased competitiveness.

▶ **Describe the various behavioural and cognitive self-management strategies.**

Behavioural self-management includes self-set goals, self-observation, self-rewards, self-cueing, and self-designed jobs. Behavioural self-management is designed to condition employees to use their observational skills to find ways to provide greater job satisfaction and enhance their productivity. Cognitive self-management includes opportunity building and positive self-talk. Cognitive self-management strategies foster mental self-images and thought patterns that can facilitate goal attainment.

▶ **Explain how an organization can develop a self-leadership culture.**

The commitment of top management is essential to build a successful self-management culture. In addition, to encourage the growth of self-management throughout the organization, management at all levels must share information and ideas. All employees must be involved in continual training, and the reward system must recognize positive gains derived from self-management.

## KEY TERMS

behavioural self-management, p. 229
cognitive self-management, p. 230
constraint, p. 223
contingency leadership model, p. 213
contingency models of leadership, p. 218
expert power, p. 212
Fiedler's LPC theory, p. 218

hierarchical or position power, p. 212
leader-manager, p. 207
leadership, p. 207
opportunity building, p. 230
path-goal theory, p. 221
people-oriented behavioural style, p. 216
personal power, p. 212

positive self-talk, p. 231
power, p. 210
referent power, p. 212
reward power, p. 210
role modelling, p. 229
self-cueing, p. 230
self-designed job, p. 230
self-leadership, p. 227
self-management, p. 228

## REVIEW AND DISCUSSION QUESTIONS

### Recall

1. What are the major differences between a leader and a manager?
2. What sources of power may be available to a manager? Which sources do most managers consciously employ?
3. Is the existence of power always a result of deliberate effort on the part of managers? Is power, by its nature, necessarily a bad thing?

### Understanding

4. Why do Blake and McCanse argue that the most effective leaders exhibit styles that are high in both people-orientation and task-orientation?
5. What is the underlying rationale for the path-goal theory of leadership?
6. What are some of the situations in which leadership is neutralized?
7. How can a manager help to develop self-leadership in subordinates?

### Application

8. Assume that you are a furniture department manager who has just been transferred from the Toronto branch of a large retail chain to its branch in Edmonton. You find that the 20 employees in your new Edmonton department are used to arriving at work late, taking long lunch hours, and making careless mistakes in paperwork. You observe that several of them often ignore customers in order to carry on personal conversations with their fellow employees. You are charged with leading the department to better work habits, and consequently with changing its long history of losses to a profit. What will your first steps in exercising transformational leadership be?

## CASE 6-1

### SAS: Business Class Means Quality

Jan Carlzon built SAS, the Scandinavian-based airline, into a world-class airline favoured among business people. Yet as the world evolved, SAS found itself in an awkward position. It was once protected by a generous government subsidy and fare protection in the highly regulated Western European market. But in the early 1990s Western European airlines united, rationalized, and privatized. The same business pressures that bankrupted Pan American, TWA, and Eastern (once the most recognized American air carriers around the world) brought airlines such as Air Canada, Canadian Air, Cathay Pacific, American, and Qantas into Europe. Thus, SAS faced new competitive pressures from airlines based in Canada, Hong Kong, the United States, Australia, and other countries.

In the price-regulated era, SAS had carved itself a solid niche among the favoured business travellers, for whom price is less important than service, meals, and scheduling. And SAS employees earned outstanding working conditions as well, leading to high labour costs. For example, although wages among SAS technical people were competitive with those in North America, SAS could count on only 1300 to 1400 hours of work from its mechanics each year (20 percent less on the night shift) versus almost 2000 hours for the typical North American airline. This provided a more than 30 percent cost advantage for the airlines that were now competing with SAS.

Driven by the need to serve customers best, SAS provided first-line workers with an unusually high level of freedom to make decisions. Carlzon often described SAS as an inverted pyramid, with customers on top, followed by front-line workers, and with Carlzon working for all of them at the bottom. But changing airline competition, with new players and reduced regulations, called for a new response to keep market share.

SAS responded with a twofold strategy. First, it continued to focus on the business traveller. Second, it built bridges by developing partnerships with similar carriers around the world. SAS also adopted the "hub and spoke" strategy. The North American domestic market had grown by use of a system in which planes are sent to hubs—massive centres for transferring passengers—and then sent out again through one of the hub's spokes. Vancouver's and Toronto's airports function as hubs in Canada; in the United States, airports in Atlanta, Chicago, and Minneapolis are hubs. SAS found it necessary to use the hub-and-spoke method on a global basis. Previously cut off from the North American domestic markets because it was not allowed connections through the international airports in Toronto, Montreal, or New York, SAS worked around that blockage through a partnership with Continental, only to see that carrier forced into bankruptcy. Nonetheless Carlzon defended having entered that partnership on the basis of increased revenues and reduced costs for SAS. "The Continental deal is worth $20 million a year net. What would have been the downside if we didn't do it?"

Partnerships also meant turning cost centres such as mechanical services into profit centres, where partner airlines could pool services, personnel, and other costs, while providing opportunities for both partners to benefit from increased customer service and scheduling. The European Quality Alliance (EQA) included SAS, Finnair, and Austrian. Later links were negotiated with Nippon Air (Japan), Canadian Airlines, and Spanair (a Spanish charter carrier).

SAS also employed sophisticated monitoring systems to alert pilots to developing problems. When pilots learned of a minor malfunction while in flight, they could radio ahead to mechanics, who could begin the repair process by assembling parts before the plane reached the repair facility. As a result, morning readiness for all of their fleet was over 99 percent and the availability of planes after unscheduled maintenance exceeded SAS's goal of 95 percent by 1.5 percentage points. At most cities, flight regularity reached 100 percent, meaning no cancelled revenue-generating flights.

At the same time SAS achieved efficiency with the mechanical staff. The number of technical employees per plane was reduced from 42 to 32, with a target of 30, while better scheduling increased productive flight times per employee from 57 to 71 hours per month, with a target of 75 flight hours per employee.

Carlzon believes firmly in doing 100 things each 1 percent better, rather than trying to do 1 thing 100 percent better, meaning continuous improvement. To achieve this, SAS leaders were expected to share information and then responsibility with employees. According to Carlzon, this results in empowered employees. "An employee without information can't take responsibility. With information, he (sic) cannot avoid taking it."

## Questions

**1.** What is Jan Carlzon's vision or strategy for SAS?
**2.** Why is cost cutting such a big part of SAS's strategy?
**3.** In what ways has SAS used self-leadership concepts to empower employees?

Source: Adapted from Ken Shelton, "People Power," *Executive Excellence* (December 1991): 7-8; Henry Lefer, "How SAS Keeps 'Em Flyin'," *Transport World* (November 1991): 68-74; Joan M. Feldman, "SAS: Playing Partners," *Air Transport World*: 102-6.

## CASE 6-2

# Aftech, Inc.

In 1969 two young, eager computer buffs began a computer software consulting business, long before this was considered a "safe" thing to do. Lloyd Milner and Bill Guiney scrambled to find customers wherever they could find them. They planned to develop a niche that would distinguish them from other consultants in the field, but as in most startup businesses, they had to take work as it appeared. From the first, they concentrated on providing not only accurate information but timely service. They made themselves available for effectively 24 hours every day. Their clients soon learned that they could get help when they needed it, rather than at the convenience of the consultants. Milner and Guiney devoted countless hours and considerable energy to developing specialized systems to meet the regulatory and tax requirements of credit unions and hospitals.

Personal lives were truncated as they devoted their energies to building their business in what was becoming a highly competitive industry. As described by Milner, there were good days and bad days, financial successes and financial disappointments. By 1973, Milner's and Guiney's reputations for competence and service had brought them to the attention of Sharad Medical Systems, a company about a decade old that had grown to $12 million in annual revenues. Partly for the security it offered them, Milner and Guiney accepted Sharad's offer to buy out their business and employ both of them as key employees.

Expanding their contacts through this new connection, during the next seven years the hospital side of Sharad's business reached a record $100 million in annual revenues, while the credit union side languished at $1 million. Both Milner and Guiney found that they really enjoyed the people with whom they worked in credit unions, and realized that they were itching to return to their earlier roles as entrepreneurs rather than employees—no matter how respected and well remunerated they were.

In 1980 Milner and Guiney left Sharad with two former employees and started a new company. As is usual, upon joining Sharad they had executed noncompetition clauses that prevented them from doing business with any of Sharad's customers except for one credit union that had been expressly excluded from the prohibition. With this restriction, the four specialists spent nearly a full year perfecting an online software system for credit unions. During this period, as Milner puts it, "We had expenses, but no revenues. It was an interesting time!" Finally, in 1981 they reentered the market, contracting with five large credit unions, and Aftech, Inc. (for Automated Financial Technologies) was fully launched. Then followed what Milner describes as a series of business cycles, with a great year followed by a poor year and then another great year. All possible revenues were put back into the business because of the rapid obsolescence of their technological products.

The key to their ultimate success was their keen desire to differentiate themselves from all other companies that could offer roughly the same capabilities. Accurate, user-friendly systems were essential, but the primary differentiation came in the level of service they offered. Milner and Guiney worked at knowing their clients and their clients' needs, but most of all they went back to their early practice of being completely available.

At this point, growth began to be both a benefit and a hazard. They found that in order to continue to provide outstanding service, they had to control growth, not only because of the strain growth places on working capital but because they could not stretch themselves too thin or they would lose contact both with the business and with the clients. They took a working motto from one of the many articles Milner had read in a management journal: "Growth for growth's sake is the ideology of cancer." As a result of this far-sighted leadership, Aftech has achieved the remarkable record of *never* having lost a client, except one that decided to do the same work in-house. In a field that then had 12 major vendors and about 100 smaller ones, Aftech thrived, becoming the sixth largest in North America, generating more than $13 million in sales in 1995, and providing stable employment for approximately 100 employees in six widely dispersed offices.

Then disaster struck. On a Monday morning in January 1996 the roof of their main building collapsed from the weight of snow. Because of the Herculean efforts of the company's principals and all employees, some $300,000 of computer equipment was salvaged, the staff was relocated, and the company was back in business only four days later. Not a single client suffered, because of the effective backup equipment and software that the leader-managers had prudently provided at considerable cost over the years. Because facilities could not be completely restored for several months, potential customers could not be brought in for demonstrations, so the previously uninterrupted pattern of growth was stalled through 1996, but now has resumed.

Looking back over his experiences, Milner remembers the long hours, financial drain, and risks of the early years, but comments that *security* can only come from being responsible for one's own destiny. With some nostalgia he recalls that when Aftech had only eight or ten employees, he was involved in everything and it was great fun. Now that the company is so much larger, he finds it somewhat less satisfying, in part because he spends more time on personality problems and broad policy issues, which formerly lent themselves to immediate hands-on solutions and now have to be handled through the organizational structure. He summarizes this change by commenting that the transition from "doer" to "manager" is difficult. From the success of the company, however, and from the enthusiasm with which he describes Aftech, it is clear that Milner has been able to exercise leadership skills successfully, earning the loyalty of employees and their personal dedication to the welfare of the company and its clients.

After many years, in 1998 the principals sold Aftech to Fiserve, a major software developer. It will be interesting to see how the business functions after the departure of the guiding leader-managers.

## Questions

1. How does Lloyd Milner's history as a leader-manager differ from that of a typical leader-manager in a large corporation?
2. Why does Milner say that it is difficult to change from a "doer" to a "manager"? How were Milner and Guiney able to be doers themselves at the same time that they had to be leaders of others?
3. Without knowing further details, what kinds of leadership styles is it likely that Milner and Guiney exhibited at the time of the roof collapse?

Source: Adapted from personal interviews with Lloyd Milner, May 1996, August 1997, and May 1998.

*APPLICATION EXERCISE* **6-1**

## Personnel and Production

For the past three years you have been the manager of the Sarnia plant of the Consumer Products Division of Dallinc Corporation. During your tenure, despite having found an aging physical plant, you have shown a profit increase each year that exceeded the corporate average.

One technique you brought to the Sarnia plant from your previous job at another company is self-managed goal setting. You believe that it has worked to your advantage at Sarnia. Although it took time to develop this system throughout the plant, the effort appears to have been worth it. Despite initial resistance from some managers (especially senior, autocratic types), you have found a general acceptance by most managers.

Carole Samson was hired as your personnel director three months ago, moving from another city and another corporation. As a matter of courtesy and practice, you delayed asking Carole for formal goals for herself and her department until she had time to learn more about the job and to hear about your self-managed goal system. Last week, in a brief note to Carole, you suggested that she think about setting goals for the coming six-month budget period. Carole wrote back:

> While I will be at corporate headquarters in Edmonton this week, I want to respond to your request for goals for myself and my department. While I see a need for goals in production and sales, I do not see how they apply to a cost centre like personnel. Last week, for instance, my staff was busy studying the new federal regulations and also collecting an attitude survey of team leaders. There seems to be a strong interest in a day-care centre and more training in computer software, so I'll have to attend to these issues shortly. And next week we begin work with the controller's office preparing for the upcoming contract negotiations; the new high-performing team concept has greatly complicated our negotiating strategy, especially since no one fully understands how it fits into our bargaining agreement. We have to schedule a meeting to explain the new fringe benefits to the exempt (non-union) staff. And the monthly safety inspection keeps things hectic, especially with the new federal requirements.
>
> So, you see, I think we are too busy putting out fires and coping with the new "diverse" workforce to consider setting goals. The old rules of union and management, of traditional personnel practices, have all changed. We have a tough enough time getting things done without spending more time setting goals. Take a close look at our department and I think you'll agree.
>
> If you check the personnel department, you'll probably also agree with my request for two new staff assistants at the C-II level to help us keep up with these new demands. My goal is to staff the department adequately and increase our budget to respond to the changing demands on personnel. I'd be happy to discuss these goals when I return. I hope you find my response to be helpful, given the unique problems facing the department.

In the same batch of mail was a note from Ann Rodwick, your production manager. The note was attached to a goal-setting statement from one of her team leaders, Paul Aguilar. Paul's goal statement said simply:

> For the six-month period, produce 80,000 finished units within budgeted costs of $1,525,000.

Ann's note said:

Paul is ambitious (he has reduced costs by 3 percent), but unless he gets a handle on quality control, he'll be in trouble on this one. And he has been having a tough time with the new computerized record-keeping system. Worse, unless he has the new Pace line installed by the third month of the six-month period, he'll never make this goal. And his staff turnover is getting worse; maybe he's been pushing his team too hard to meet these goals. But, bottom line, this is the level of output we are pushing Paul to achieve. Any ideas?

You have meetings with Carole and Ann scheduled for tomorrow morning.

### Questions

1. What do you plan to say to them?
2. Will you meet with them together or separately? Why?
3. Do you have any specific constructive advice?
4. Prepare some notes to outline your thinking. Then be ready to discuss this thinking with a small group of classmates for 20 minutes. Specifically discuss the following issues: (1) Are goal-setting concepts applicable to all departments, with particular reference to the personnel department? (2) What specific directions do you intend to set for the personnel department and the production department?

Source: This exercise was adapted from one originally written by Henry P. Sims, Jr. as "The Bill Minder Case."

## APPLICATION EXERCISE 6-2

### If You Were a Manager, Would You Be Comfortable with Self-leadership?

For each action described, score yourself between 0 and 10, where 10 means you would be completely comfortable, and 0 means you would not be comfortable at all. Total your scores and compare your results with those of your classmates.

_____ 1. Propose specific goals for your activities.
_____ 2. Reward yourself for doing a good job.
_____ 3. Refuse to punish yourself for doing a poor job.
_____ 4. Make lists of things to do that day, week, or month.
_____ 5. Check off completed items on the daily, weekly, or monthly list.
_____ 6. Keep an after-the-fact record of your daily activities.
_____ 7. Organize your day or week in your head while doing some other activity.
_____ 8. Rehearse the steps and sequence of an activity before you do it.
_____ 9. Ask people you work with to set goals for themselves.
_____ 10. Find great pleasure in simply knowing that you've done a good job.

Your Total Score: _____

*INTERNET APPLICATION*  **6-1**

Visit the Web site for Mary Kay Cosmetics (www.marykay.com), focusing on the section entitled The Company.

1. What are the qualities that Mary Kay Ash brought to her business that made her a successful leader?
2. What are the "principles" the company is governed by?

Visit the Web site of another visionary leader and describe what qualities appear to have contributed to success.

CHAPTER

# 7

# Controlling

After studying this chapter, you should be able to:

▶ Describe the red bead experiment and explain its message to managers;

▶ Describe the three elements of the control process;

▶ Define *total quality control*;

▶ Explain the role of non-managerial employees in total quality management;

▶ Explain management's role in total quality management;

▶ Contrast statistical process control with total quality control; and

▶ Discuss the approach taken by the ISO 9000 program, why it is attracting the attention of many Canadian companies, and what benefits a company might gain from participating in the program.

## The Red Bead Experiment

FOR MANY YEARS BEFORE W. EDWARDS DEMING'S DEATH in 1993, in his presentations to managers he used a vivid exercise to illustrate the use and misuse of controls in managing quality. The so-called "red bead experiment" was designed to show that worker inability to meet performance objectives is often a function of the system, not of their laziness or lack of skill or dedication.  ▶

The exercise began with a large container of 4000 beads—800 red and 3200 white. Deming would choose approximately six participants. He provided each with a paddle that contained 50 holes for collecting beads. The participants were intended to represent workers, and the paddles were to represent their tools. The workers' task was to dip the paddle into the container of beads and then to remove it with each hole containing a bead, some of which would be red and the others white.

Each worker, in turn, dipped the paddle into the container and withdrew 50 beads. This action represented production. It was very simple, but results were very frustrating. Deming had set a production quality standard of "4 percent, or no more than 2 red beads per 50 beads produced." That is, of course, eight beads fewer than the ten that would be expected from the respective proportions of the two colours of beads. Deming's standard was the basis for the quality control system for the demonstration.

Deming then served as the foreman, inspecting the results of each "production run." The demonstration thus had a production process, a standard, and a supervisory review process.

As one might predict, few of the workers' attempts to meet the production goal were "satisfactory." Since 20 percent of the beads in the large container were red, random samples of beads would, on average, contain 20 percent red beads. Workers occasionally could produce a paddle with two or fewer red beads, but the average expected would be ten red beads (20 percent of 50 beads) per production run. Over the long run, no worker could consistently produce fewer than ten red bead "defects" and therefore no worker could achieve the standard on a regular basis.

Acting in the role of foreman, Deming evaluated each worker according to the quality control standard of no more than 4 percent red beads (that is, 2 out of 50) among the white beads on the paddle. He proceeded to reward, promote, reprimand, and even ridicule and terminate workers based on their conformance or failure to conform to this standard. Deming lavishly praised any worker who succeeded

in meeting the goal. At times he offered the lucky worker a raise or a promotion. On the other hand, he harshly criticized every worker who produced more than 2 red beads per 50, because the control standard had not been met.

In this fashion, Deming illustrated the pointlessness of a merit system in which workers' performance is due to normal variation within management's system, not to the workers' individual abilities. He pointed out that it would be a waste of management time to find out why Worker X produced more beads than Worker Y. The difference between their performance was simply normal variation within the system created by management. In other words, it was sheer luck.

The important point is that any process can be looked at in the same way. Although workers usually have more control over the outcome of their work than in this demonstration, any process is subject to normal variation that affects even the best workers. People involved in this exercise soon realized both its futility and its parallels with actual work situations in the setting of goals, the chance that trying hard still will not produce "satisfactory" results, and the possible misdirection of motivating and reprimanding employees. In the demonstration, the only way to lower defect rates was to lower the number of red beads in the bowl. "Workers" knew the number of red beads was the problem, but they couldn't change the process. As a result of this exercise, most of those participating or observing realized that exhorting workers to try harder may not be the answer to making an organization more effective. They learned that it is often the system that needs improvement. ■

Source: Adapted from W. Edwards Deming, *Out of the Crisis* (Cambridge, MA: Center for Advanced Engineering Study, Massachusetts Institute of Technology, 1986): 109-12; Ronald Yates, "Prophet of Boom," *Chicago Tribune* (February 16, 1992): 14-22; Rafael Aguayo, *Dr. Deming: The Man Who Taught the Japanese about Quality* (New York: Fireside Books, 1990): 53-58; Ellen Earle Chaffee and Lawrence A. Sherr, *Quality: Transforming Postsecondary Education* (Washington, DC: ERIC Clearinghouse on Higher Education, 1992).

# Controlling—The Fourth Element of Management

The red bead experiment described in the opening vignette illustrates that the production system must be designed and managed to improve quality, rather than to create difficult or impossible expectations for workers. It is the managers' responsibility to design the system so that other employees can succeed.

Control is a fundamental management responsibility, closely linked with the planning and organizing processes. It also has an important impact on motivation and team behaviour. Control is both a process (for instance, working to keep things on schedule) and an outcome (for instance, ensuring that the product has met standards). The controlling function includes all activities the manager undertakes in attempting to ensure that actual results conform with the results predicted in the planning process (which was described in Chapter 4). Like many management terms, *control* has different meanings for different people so to some extent an individual's concept of control inevitably reflects a personal perspective. Statisticians may think of control in terms of numbers (variances, means, errors, and control limits); engineers may think of control primarily in terms of specifications, monitoring, and feedback; and general managers may think of controlling the activities, attitudes, and performance of subordinates. Despite these differing approaches to control, there are some aspects of all organizations that must be controlled. They include production and operations, financial resources, human resources, and organizational change and development (see Exhibit 7-1).

After planning or making a decision, managers must deploy organizational resources to achieve specific goals or objectives. (Chapters 3 and 4 discuss models of decision making and of planning, respectively.) Even though decision making and planning are conducted systematically and with accurate information, unexpected circumstances may yet arise in the social, economic, political, or natural environments. Thus, managers must be prepared to redirect organizational activities towards desired ends. To do this, they need an understanding of the elements of control.

## Elements of Control

**control**
The processes involved in maintaining conformance of the system with standards, objectives, and goals.

**Control** is a process used (1) to evaluate actual performance; (2) to compare actual performance with goals; and then (3) to take action to resolve any differences between performance and goals.[1] Quality statistician Walter Shewhart described these three elements within the control process using the terms *specification*, *production*, and *inspection*.[2] Exhibit 7-2 on page 248 illustrates the steps in the control process as described by Shewhart.

*Specification* is the statement of the intended outcome. Control requires the specification of a standard. A *standard* is an operationally defined measure used as a basis for comparison. Specification fully describes the preferred condition, which may take the

**Exhibit 7-1**  *Managers Must Control Four Aspects of Organization*

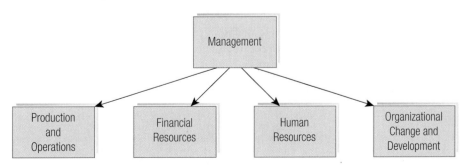

**Exhibit 7-2**   *Steps in the Control Process*

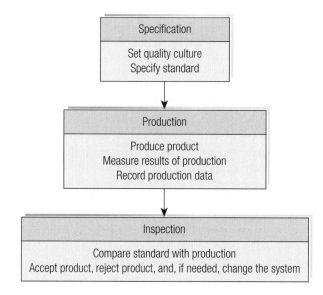

form of a goal, a standard, or another carefully determined quantitative statement of conditions.

*Production* means making the product or delivering the service. Shewhart defines this element as the work required to achieve objectives. This concept applies as much to the provision of services as it does to manufacturing.

*Inspection* is an evaluation of the products produced or the services provided, and a judgement concerning whether they meet the specifications. Inspection determines whether corrective action needs to be taken.

Clear specification of a performance standard requires an operational definition. An operational definition converts a concept into measurable, objective units.[3] For example, "weight" can be operationally defined in terms of grams, ounces, tonnes, or another

---

**Real World Reflection    7-1**

### Dated Control Indicators

In the early 1990s, Miranda's Coffee House, located in Prince Albert, Saskatchewan, counted its paper coffee cups to determine the number of cups of coffee sold in each size. It was an easy control method that allowed staff to check the number of cups for which payment was entered in the till against the cups actually taken.

When a local McDonald's opened down the street, offering free refills, Miranda's Coffee House found that its control method would have to be sacrificed in order to offer a bottomless cup to its clients.

Control methods change as consumer trends and competition alter the way that business is done.

Contributed by Marnie Wright, British Columbia Institute of Technology.

*Diamond cutters must use their professional judgement to decide how to cut each gem, but these decisions must fall within the parameters dictated by the managers who are responsible for the organization's output.*

standard measure. These measures are not subject to personal interpretation. In contrast, the concept "heavy" can be interpreted differently by different people or even by the same people in different situations. Almost everyone would agree that 100 grams would be heavy for a diamond, but light for a notebook computer. A strong warehouse employee might refer to a ten-kilogram carton as "light," while a clerical worker who was required to lift it to a high shelf might consider it unreasonably "heavy." According to Deming, "An operational definition puts communicable meaning into a concept. Adjectives like 'good,' 'reliable,' 'uniform,' 'round,' 'safe,' and 'unemployed' have no communicable meaning until they are expressed in operational terms. An operational definition is one that reasonable men (*sic*) agree on."[4]

To illustrate the importance of operational definitions, Deming told the story of the "wrinkled" auto instrument panel. A manager of an auto manufacturing plant told him that the reported defect rate in an auto instrument panel was 35 to 50 percent. The defect in question was "wrinkles" in the panel. When Deming examined this rate, he found that each inspector applied a personally derived standard of what constituted a wrinkle. Deming resolved the defect rate problem by working with the inspectors to develop an operational definition of wrinkle. Less than one week after the standard began to be uniformly applied, the reported defect rate dropped from the earlier range of 35 to 50 percent, a variation of 15 percent, to only 10 percent in total, which was consistent across inspectors.[5] In that case the quality of the product shipped became much more consistent, and was independent of which inspector happened to make the determination.

The process of setting performance standards must begin with a strategy, conveyed in terms of operationally defined measures. Operationally defined measures underlie the control process. Not only do they control operations through finished-product or after-service inspections, they also enable workers to evaluate processes as they are occurring.

Production and operations are controlled by performance standards, whether in manufacturing, resource processing, or the delivery of services. Standards determine the activity or outcome to be measured,[6] and the means of measurement to identify deviations from standards. Through measurement and assessment, employees often can find possible improvements within the product or process and indicate where to initiate change.[7] The simple act of calling attention to managers' interest in errors and defects often has an immediate, direct effect on reducing their number.

In service industries, and especially in not-for-profit organizations, it is difficult to establish measurable standards. A college's effectiveness cannot be measured solely by the number of students enrolled. The effectiveness of a shelter for battered women cannot be measured solely by the number of residents processed nor by the unit cost of meals served. Yet, in such organizations, standards are just as important as in a manufacturing enterprise. One of the principal ways in which service organizations control performance is through employee training, to give employees the knowledge and information they need to serve customers. Home Depot, the hardware and home repair discounter, has made an art of empowering employees to exceed each customer's expectations. As a result, the company has established a service reputation that prompted Wal-Mart CEO David Glass to remark, "They're running the best retail organization in America today."[8] Home Depot doesn't conduct extensive marketing surveys, but relies on its associates, who are trained to ask customers what they want and expect and to listen to their answers.

For many years, inspection typically occurred only at the end of the production process in manufacturing or, in the case of services, after complaints had been received. It is now widely recognized that to defer inspection to the end of the process is costly because it fails to catch defects at an early stage, when correction is relatively easy and inexpensive. Instead of this end-of-the-line inspection, an effective control system provides for "mini-inspections" at every stage of production. If a defective item is identified early in the process, the defect can be corrected or the item can be scrapped before further expenditure is wasted on it.

As might be expected, inspecting every item produced or monitoring every service encounter would be hugely expensive. For products such as T-shirts, dog collars, and magazines, no serious consequences would arise if an occasional item were faulty and had to be replaced. For items such as these, inspection costs can be kept within reasonable bounds by inspecting only a sample of the whole production run or a number of service encounters. Care must be exercised in deciding on the size of the sample and in ensuring that the items to be inspected are selected in a truly random manner. Then, within limits of accuracy that can be calculated using standard statistical methods, it can be assumed that the results shown in the sample are representative of the whole production run or of all service encounters.

*At Home Depot, because employees have been empowered, they can assist customers without close supervision or control by managers.*

The organization sets a standard consisting of the maximum proportion of defective items or encounters that will be considered acceptable. The inspected samples are then checked to see if their results fall within the established limits. If they do, it can be assumed that the overall defect rate is acceptable. If they fall outside the established standards, it is a signal that there are problems that must be corrected.

Because of statistical variation in any sampling process, even if all items in the sample meet the desired standard, there may be a few substandard items in the overall total that simply were not caught in the sample. This would not be satisfactory for some especially sensitive products, for which it is important that every item released to the public meet the standard. For example, it could be disastrous if a defective regulator for scuba diving, a defective heart pacemaker, or a defective smoke detector happened to slip through a sampling inspection. For such sensitive products, every item produced must be inspected because sampling alone would not give adequate protection.

## Types of Control

Managers have a large number of control methods at their disposal. Each has strengths and limitations. A manager must decide what type of control system to employ in each situation. Some control techniques have very specific, limited application; others are of more general application. Whatever control techniques are chosen, they must be economical, accurate, and understandable.

## *What Managers Are Reading*    **7-1**

### The Last Word on Power: Re-Invention for Leaders and Anyone Who Must Make the Impossible Happen

A consultant much in demand for lectures and seminars, Tracy Goss is noted for challenging popular ideas on what she calls "transformational leadership." She argues that the absence of the "power to consistently make the impossible happen" is why so many attempts at organizational re-invention fail. She makes the reasonable, but oft-ignored, caution that the first step towards re-invention is for leaders to re-invent themselves. In Goss' view, personal re-invention is not an accomplishment but, rather, a career choice.

She points out that the leaders are those who have shaped the organization as it is. If they want change, that is another way of saying that they want the organization to be something that it is not at present. If we acknowledge that employee behaviour is to a large extent a mirror of senior management behaviour, then it follows that the organization will change when and only when the senior managers change. And for them to change, or re-invent themselves, they must learn new skills. They have achieved their senior positions by exercising many elements of control, both personal and organizational. A master plumber could not be transformed overnight into a master carpenter. Different skills would have to be learned. Similarly, the forms of control that were effective a few years ago, and at lower levels in the hierarchy, no longer will

suffice, and may be inappropriate for higher levels of management.

In approaching re-invention, both for the individual and for the organization, it is natural to follow a misleading paradigm—to decide what should be and what shouldn't be, and then to try to act in such ways as to enhance what should be and to diminish the effects of what shouldn't be. Goss says that this approach is fatal to the success of re-invention. Instead, she says that it is first necessary to accept the fact that, in all probability, the "company's future won't turn out the way it should...." Once they accept that there inevitably will be disappointments and that perfection will not be achieved, the leaders will be free to accomplish the most that can be accomplished, without falling into despair and resignation.

Power is implicit in the concept of control. Even though *The Last Word on Power* is not likely to be really the last word, it may stimulate some reexamination of personal assumptions and attitudes. And if Tracy Goss is right, this reexamination is essential for anyone who wishes to grow in organizational stature and responsibility.

*Source: Tracy Goss, The Last Word on Power: Re-Invention for Leaders and Anyone Who Must Make the Impossible Happen (Toronto: Doubleday, 1996).*

Exhibit 7-3 on page 252 illustrates that for purposes of discussion control may be divided into three categories—preliminary, concurrent, and feedback—depending on when it occurs.

## Preliminary Control

**preliminary control** Control that focuses on preventing deviation in the quantity and quality of resources used in the operations of the organization.

There are several different groups of techniques that managers can use to control organizational behaviour and performance. They apply in three different time frames that are described as preliminary, concurrent, and feedback. **Preliminary control** focuses on preventing deviations in the quality and quantity of resources used in the organization. For example, human resources must meet the job requirements as defined by the organization. This means that employees must have the physical, emotional, and intellectual capabilities to perform assigned tasks.[9] There must be neither too many nor too few

**Exhibit 7-3**    *The Controlling Function*

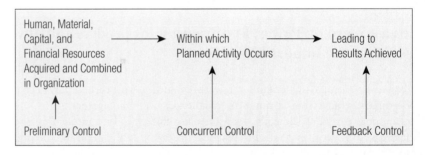

Source: James H. Donnelly, Jr., James L. Gibson, and John M. Ivancevich, *Fundamentals of Management,* 9th ed. (Burr Ridge, IL: Richard D. Irwin, 1995): 273.

employees for the objectives to be met. Materials used in production must meet acceptable levels of quality and must be available in the right quantities at the required times and places. Food purchased for a restaurant must be of the desired type and quality. Financial resources must be on hand to ensure an adequate supply of raw materials and components and appropriate plant space and equipment. There also must be sufficient working capital to function.

It is important to distinguish between *setting* policies and *implementing* them.[10] Setting policy is included in the planning function, which is discussed in Chapter 4. Implementing policy, on the other hand, falls within the control function.[11] Similarly, job descriptions are aspects of the control function because they tend to predetermine the activity of the jobholder.[12] At the same time, however, we must distinguish between defining and staffing jobs. Defining jobs is part of the organizing function, as discussed in Chapter 5. Staffing jobs is part of the controlling function.

Management is concerned with preliminary control of processes in three areas. These are human resources, materials, and capital or financial resources.

**Human resources.**  Defining the skill and knowledge requirements of a job is part of the preliminary control process. These requirements vary in degree of specificity, depending on the nature of the task. Preliminary control of human resources is further achieved through the selection and placement of managerial and non-managerial personnel.[13] Each step in the employment process, from initial screening of applicants to orientation and initial training after an applicant is appointed, is a preliminary control step. During this step the potential employee's skills, abilities, and attitudes are assessed in terms of fitness for the position in question.

Candidates for positions may be recruited from either inside or outside the organization, and the most promising applicants must be selected by matching their skills and personal characteristics to the job requirements. The successful candidate must be trained in methods and procedures appropriate for the job. Most successful organizations have elaborate procedures for providing training on a continual basis.

Appropriate attention to preliminary control of human resources ensures that the organization will have a match between its needs and the individual skills, abilities, and attitudes of its managers and other employees. This subject will be discussed further in Chapter 8.

**Materials.**  The raw materials and components that are converted into or incorporated into the finished product must conform to quality standards and specifications *before*

*Fresh fruit is inspected and graded by government inspectors, and can bear the designation allotted to it by the inspectors.*

they are used in the production process. At the same time, a sufficient inventory or delivery system must be maintained to ensure a continuous and timely inflow of raw materials and components so that production schedules can be met in order to meet customer demand. The techniques of inventory control are discussed in Chapter 11. The present discussion will be limited to the control of incoming materials.

Inspection methods may vary from item to item and from organization to organization. Depending on their value and importance, all items in an incoming shipment may be inspected or only a statistical sample may be inspected. As already mentioned, statistical methods are less costly and less time-consuming, but they entail the risk of accepting defective material if the sample is non-random or if by chance it contains none of the defective items. In some businesses, such as those involving fresh fruit or dimensional lumber, there are industry-wide standards that require that only specified percentages of items fully meet the specification, and that the remaining items meet only a less rigorous specification. Even in those instances, inspection is important to ensure that the required percentages of delivered goods fall within the prescribed ranges.

**Financial resources.** Every organization needs working capital—that is, funds that can be used to pay operating expenses until receipts from sales replenish the expended funds. The need for working capital becomes especially acute during periods of rapid expansion. During such periods the expenditures for raw materials and perhaps for labour must increase, but sales revenues may not be received for at least a few days, and perhaps for as long as several weeks, after these expenditures are made. The longer the gap between payment for raw materials and components and salaries and wages on the one hand and receipts from customers on the other hand, the greater is the need for working capital.[14] In addition, an organization needs to provide for increases in or replacement of existing equipment and facilities. This need, too, requires that managers plan the allocation of available cash.

The control tools most often used for this purpose are the budget—a prediction of revenues and expenditures—and the cash flow statement—a report of receipts and disbursements. Revenues are those items, such as sales, that affect the bottom line positively, whereas receipts are the actual cash and cheques physically received. The timing of receipts will differ from that of sales revenues if customers do not pay cash at the time of the sale. A parallel distinction is made between expenditures and disbursements. Expenditures are those items, such as purchases, that affect the bottom line, while disbursements are the actual payments by cash or cheque, which may occur at other times. From another standpoint, receipts and disbursements immediately affect the organization's bank account; revenues and expenditures do not do so until they result in receipts or disbursements.

**concurrent control**
Monitoring ongoing operations to ensure that standards are met and objectives are pursued.

## Concurrent Control

Unlike preliminary control, with its focus on activities that precede production or service operations, **concurrent control** monitors *ongoing* operations to ensure that objectives are being pursued. The standards guiding ongoing activity are set out in job descriptions and in policies that are created in the planning function. Through personal, on-the-spot observation and statistical reports, managers determine whether the work of others is proceeding in the manner defined by policies and procedures.[15] Delegation of authority provides managers with the power to use financial and non-financial incentives to effect concurrent control.

**direction**
Communication from managers to subordinates, whether managerial or non-managerial, to instruct how, when, or to what standards work is to be performed.

Concurrent control consists primarily of the actions of supervisors who direct the work of their subordinates. **Direction** refers to the acts of managers when they (1) instruct subordinates in proper methods and procedures; and (2) oversee subordinates' work to ensure that it is done properly and effectively.

Direction follows the formal chain of command, since a responsibility of each superior is to interpret for subordinates the orders received from higher levels. The relative importance of direction depends on the nature of the tasks performed by subordinates. The supervisor of an assembly line that produces a component part requiring relatively simple manual operations may need to give direction only occasionally. On the other hand, the manager of an operation that is installing a new process must devote considerable time to direction.

Directing is the primary function of the first-line supervisor, but at some point every manager in an organization engages in directing employees. As a manager's responsibilities grow, the relative time spent directing subordinates diminishes, while other functions take more time.

The scope and content of directing vary according to the nature of the work being supervised, and also depend on a number of other factors. For example, direction relies on personal communications, both written and oral. Subordinates must receive sufficient information to carry out their tasks and they must understand the information they receive. On the other hand, too much information and detail can be distracting. The tests of effective direction are similar to the tests of effective communication, which will be discussed in Chapter 10. To be effective, a directive must be reasonable, understandable, appropriately worded, and consistent with the organization's overall goals. Its effectiveness depends on whether the subordinate understands it, wishes to follow it, and is provided with the facilities, materials, and time to do so. Many managers have assumed that their directives were straightforward and to the point only to discover that their subordinates failed to understand or to accept them as legitimate.

## Feedback Control

**feedback control**
In terms of control, communication back to the originator of a process that is intended to indicate whether the process is functioning according to the established standards or whether some adjustments should be made.

The next phase in a complete control system is **feedback control.** Its methods focus on end results, and use actual results as the stimulus to guide future actions. A simple illustration of feedback control is the thermostat in a house or a room (see Exhibit 7-4). The thermostat constantly measures the actual temperature. It then sends signals—that is, feedback—to controls on a heating or cooling unit. Those signals direct the unit to take corrective action to adjust the room temperature to the predetermined standard. The feedback control methods employed in business organizations include comparisons of actual results with budgets, comparisons of actual costs with predetermined costs, analyses of financial statements, and other forms of performance evaluations.

Two feedback control methods widely used in business are financial statement analysis and standard cost analysis. (In the discussion that follows, it is assumed that the reader has at least a general understanding of basic accounting.)

**Financial statement analysis.**  An organization's accounting system is a principal source of information that managers can use to evaluate historical results and to fore-

**Exhibit 7-4** *Illustration of Feedback Control*

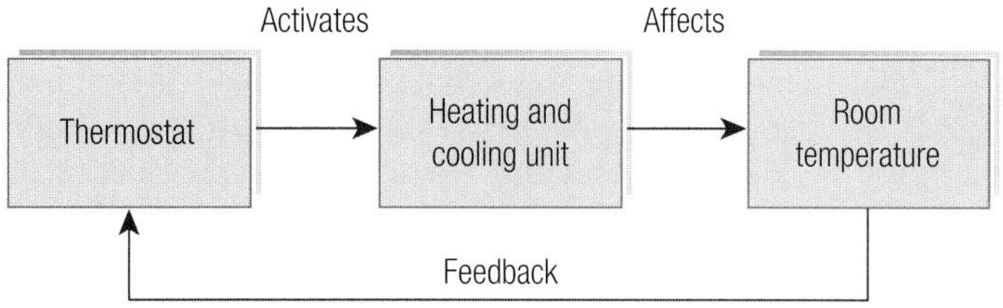


**balance sheet**
A financial statement that reports the organization's assets, liabilities, and equity (including retained earnings) at a particular time, usually at the end of a fiscal period.

**income statement**
A financial statement that reports the organization's revenues and expenditures during a stated fiscal period.

**rate of return**
A control ratio calculated by dividing net income (that is, profit) by the value of sales, owner's equity, or total assets invested in the enterprise.

**liquidity**
The extent to which an organization's assets could quickly and without material loss be converted into cash.

**current ratio**
Current assets divided by current liabilities.

**acid test ratio**
Liquid current assets (such as cash and near-cash items, but not including less liquid items such as inventories and prepaid expenses) divided by current liabilities.

**accounts receivable turnover**
The total of annual sales for credit, divided by the average accounts receivable balance (the inverse of which, when multiplied by 360 or 365, expresses the average number of days that elapse between a sale and payment by the credit customer).

cast future results. Of course, forecasts require the application of judgement and cannot be simply extrapolations of past trends. Periodically, the manager receives a set of financial statements that includes at least a balance sheet and an income statement. These financial statements summarize and classify the effects of transactions in assets, liabilities, equity, revenues, and expenditures—the principal components of the financial structure of the business.[16] (The financial statements for a not-for-profit organization are comparable, except, of course, that there is no personal ownership reflected in equity.)

The **balance sheet** describes an organization's financial condition at a specified time. The **income statement** is a summary of an organization's financial performance over a given time period and reports revenues and expenditures during that period.

A detailed analysis of the financial statement's figures permits management to determine the adequacy of the company's earning power and its ability to meet current and long-term obligations. Managers must have measures of and standards for profitability, liquidity, and solvency. A manager may prefer to use the **rate of return** on sales, on owner's equity, on total assets, or on all three. Whichever ratio is most relied upon, the manager must establish a meaningful norm, one that is appropriate to the particular organization given its industry and stage of growth. An inadequate rate of return will make it difficult to attract lenders or investors to provide funds for expansion, particularly if there is an apparent downward trend over time.

Measures of **liquidity** reflect the organization's ability to meet current obligations as they become due.[17] One of the most frequently used measures is the **current ratio**, which is the ratio of current assets to current liabilities. The standard of acceptability depends on the particular company's operating characteristics. Bases for comparison are available from trade associations that publish industry averages. A tougher test of liquidity is the **acid test ratio**, which is the ratio of only cash and near-cash items (current assets excluding inventories and prepaid expenses) to current liabilities.

Equally important are measures of financial activity. One such ratio is known as the **accounts receivable turnover** rate. Calculating this rate requires figures from both the balance sheet and the income statement. It is arrived at by dividing the total sales for credit during the year by the average accounts receivable. For example, if a company's annual credit sales total $100,000 and the average accounts receivable balance is $25,000, the turnover rate is four times per year. This is often spoken of in terms of days—in this example, one-quarter of a year, or 90 days. This means that, on average, credit customers are taking 90 days to pay their accounts. In most businesses a rate at that level would spell disaster, because it means that, in effect, at all times the business is making interest-free loans totalling $25,000 to its customers. This puts a strain on the company's working capital needs. Appropriate corrective action—that is, control measures—might be to tighten credit standards or to make prompter and more vigorous efforts to collect outstanding accounts. If these measures are not successful, it also might mean dropping some of the customers who take the longest time to pay their accounts.

**inventory turnover**
The total cost of goods taken out of inventory for sale or to be incorporated as a component into a product for sale, divided by the average inventory levels.

Analyzing **inventory turnover** also facilitates effective management of the company's financial resources. It is calculated by dividing the cost of goods sold during a year by the average inventory value. Cost of goods sold means the cost to the organization of acquiring the items that are later sold to customers or incorporated into products that are, in turn, sold to customers. An unusually high ratio could indicate that the company is keeping on hand a dangerously low level of inventory, which could disappoint customers who find items out of stock or could result in internal production slowdowns while staff members wait for goods. Conversely, a low ratio might indicate an overinvestment in inventory to the exclusion of other, more profitable assets. The "appropriate" ratio varies considerably from industry to industry. Companies selling slow-moving items such as furniture and jewellery must maintain comparatively high inventories to satisfy customers' demands for choice. These companies must be content with relatively low turnover ratios, despite the cost to them. At the other extreme, companies that sell fast-moving items such as dairy products will keep much lower inventories on hand relative to sales. They will have turnover rates measured in days or even in hours.

*Car dealerships must maintain high inventories to be able to satisfy customers' demand for choice.*

In not-for-profit organizations, inventory turnover is also a crucial factor. A hospital that recycles its bed linens every three days needs only half of the investment in linens that it would need if its recycle time were six days. Whatever the case, the appropriate ratio for the particular business must be established by the managers, based on the company's experience within its industry and market. Inventory control methods will be discussed in Chapter 11.

Another financial measure is **solvency**, which is the ability of the organization to meet its financial obligations—scheduled payments on its debts, such as loans, bonds, and mortgages, as well as timely payments to landlords and suppliers. An appropriate balance must be maintained between preserving cash and keeping suppliers sufficiently happy with the rate of payment that they will continue to provide the goods and services needed. A commonly used measure of solvency is the relationship of net income before interest and taxes to interest expense. This indicates the margin of safety. The higher the ratio, the higher the degree of solvency. However, a very high ratio combined with a low debt/equity ratio could indicate that management hasn't taken sufficient advantage of debt as a source of funds. The appropriate balance between debt and equity depends on many factors, but as a general rule, the proportion of debt should vary directly with the stability of the company's earnings.

**solvency**
The organization's ability to meet its financial obligations when they are due.

**debt/equity ratio**
The total of long-term and short-term debt divided by the total of owner's equity plus retained earnings.

**debt/asset ratio**
The total of long-term and short-term debt divided by total assets.

**standard cost system**
A control system based on setting the desired cost of each step or activity in the operation, in terms of the unit of output product or service.

Companies also use debt ratios to assess the amount of financing being provided by creditors. Two commonly used debt ratios are the debt/equity ratio and the debt/asset ratio. The **debt/equity ratio** is a measure of the amount of assets financed by debt compared with the amount financed by profits retained by the company plus the investments by the owners (including shareholders). The **debt/asset ratio** is the relationship of the company's total debts to its total assets.

**Standard cost analysis.** Standard cost accounting systems are considered a major contribution of the scientific management era. A **standard cost system** provides information that enables management to compare actual costs with predetermined (standard) costs. Management can then take appropriate corrective action or delegate to others the authority to take action. The first use of standard costing was to control manufacturing costs. Then as its benefits became better known, it began to be applied to selling, general, and administrative expenses.[18]

The three elements of manufacturing costs are direct labour, direct materials, and overhead. For each of these, an estimate must be made of cost per unit of output. For example, the direct labour cost per unit of output consists of the standard number of hours required per unit of production multiplied by the standard hourly cost of labour. The standard usage derives from time studies that fix the expected output per labour hour. The standard price of labour is fixed by the wage and salary schedule that applies for the kind of work necessary to produce the output. A similar determination is made for direct materials. Thus, in a hypothetical case, the standard labour and standard materials costs might be as follows:

| | | |
|---|---|---|
| Standard labour usage per unit | 2 hours | |
| Standard wage rate per hour | $15.00 | |
| Standard labour cost (2 × $15.00) | | $30.00 |
| Standard material usage per unit | 6 kilograms | |
| Standard material price per kilogram | $0.50 | |
| Standard material cost per unit (6 × $0.50) | | $ 3.00 |
| TOTAL DIRECT PRODUCTION COST | | $33.00 per unit |

The accounting system enables the manager to compare incurred costs with predetermined standard costs. Today, cost accounting practices are undergoing significant changes to keep pace with the rapidly evolving manufacturing environment. **Activity-based accounting**, a system of cost accounting based on activity, has been advocated by a number of academics and practitioners. Its underlying principle is that products consume activities, and that activities consume resources. The concept is that labour costs of supporting departments can be traced to activities by assessing the portion of each person's time spent on each activity. This, then, allows for restatement of departmental costs in terms of activities and their associated costs. Activity costs then are traced to the various products or services, based on the amount of activity volume each product consumes.

**activity-based accounting**
A control system based on the allocation of all costs, including those not directly related to production or the provision of service, to each unit of product or service.

An example would be the allocation of the costs of a single marketing executive. First there would be an analysis of all of the costs associated with that executive—salary and personnel benefits; travel, communication, and supplies costs; the cost of maintaining that person's office and secretary; and all other costs that can be identified. Then, the executive would complete a time log for a reasonable period showing how much time is devoted to Product A, Product B, and so forth. The total cost for that executive then would be allocated among the various products in proportion to the time that person spends promoting each product. In this way, all company costs are distributed to the final products, which is said to give an accurate picture of the true cost of that product, allowing management to decide whether it is really profitable or not.

The accuracy of this approach depends on the extent to which it is possible to allocate accurately each individual's time to various endeavours and activities. Some employees are engaged in work such as packaging, shipping, and billing in which it is relatively easy to measure the amount of time committed to each item produced. The process becomes more problematic when it is applied to general managers. When the manager is engaged in overall company planning, organizing, leading, or even controlling, the allocation of time to a particular product is at best an informed guess. Thus, to some extent, all of the calculations are subject to interpretation, and cannot be said to represent mathematically accurate results. Despite not being precisely accurate, activity-based accounting helps to focus the attention of managers on important issues. When the method is used in conjunction with other managerial tools, it can lead to closer control and improved results.

## Quality Control Techniques

The total quality movement has brought with it a set of tools and techniques for controlling organizational processes. The three basic approaches are described by the terms *statistical process control*, *total quality control*, and *total quality management*. These approaches are similar in that they focus on trying to exceed customer expectations. They are also alike in that they tend to focus the attention of management on seeking improvements in the system rather than on perceived inadequacies in the workforce. Applying some of these measures has helped North American automobile manufacturers to regain some of their competitive standing in the global marketplace.[19]

### *Management in the Real World*    7-1

## Control and Quality: Reflections by Philip Crosby

A football coach carefully planned and then studied the statistics of the games his team had played. In each of the past three contests, he noted, they had scored the same number of touchdowns as the opposing team but had lost the game because two extra point attempts had been blocked. As a result of this data, he decided that they should spend more time learning how to block the kicks the opponents attempted after they scored touchdowns.

Most of the practice that week was spent on this effort and the team was rewarded in the following game by being able to block three extra points. Even though they lost the game 18 to 7, they were encouraged by their success and began to devote all of their time to kick blocking. Soon they were denying their opponents that one point seven and eight times a game. They scored no touchdowns of their own but were brilliant in accomplishing their chosen goal. They never won another game or made another point, and the coach was fired. This is an example of being carried away by the concepts of containment and measurement.

It was some time later, and in a new profession, before it began to dawn on the coach that the best system for containing extra points was to keep the other team from scoring touchdowns. A defence

based on prevention achieved more than one focused on a single point.

This sort of discovery happens regularly. A city commission found that improved street lighting reduced crime rates more than extra police; a person with a weight problem found that a new, much more accurate scale had no effect on the weight loss program. We must be careful not to confuse the systems of measurement with the setting of goals. Keeping neat records of overspending is not the way to manage money.

The instruments on a car's dashboard are examples of control charts. Their purpose is to assist the operator in managing the vehicle. They control nothing in themselves; they just display what's happening, and they haven't changed much in 50 years. This is also true of statistical control charting.

Just as automobile drivers are successful when they are carefully trained, understand the requirements of operation, and are responsible for their own actions—so workers are successful when the same conditions exist. When they are directed to do useless work, or are limited in their communications, they fail.

All that comes from management. When management depends on focused systems rather than people, it pays the price.

Exhibit 7-5 contrasts the traditional model of control and a quality-based control model. The traditional approach provides only limited training for production-line workers. Control is exercised by managers, who inspect the results of production and issue reprimands or other sanctions if production specifications are not met. In contrast, the quality-based control model allows for considerable worker training. Inspection primarily is exercised by production-line workers at every stage during the production process, and consistent failures to meet production specifications are seen as an indication of the need for further training, for a revision of the system, or for both.

Any comprehensive quality control program includes the use of statistics. Whether an organization's primary focus is service, commerce, or manufacturing, statistical tools can provide insights that lead to process improvements.

**statistical process control**
A control system that uses statistical analyses to detect and correct variations from plan.

## Statistical Process Control

The use of **statistical process control** has long played an important role in business and industry.[20] It is based on two assumptions: (1) that nature is imperfect; and (2) that variability exists everywhere in systems. Therefore, probability and statistics play a major

**Exhibit 7-5**  *Models of Traditional and Quality-based Control*

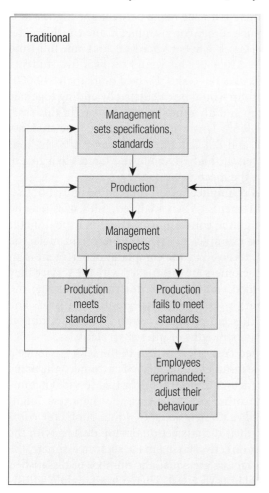
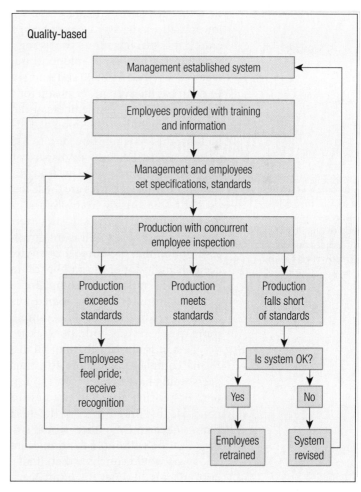

role in understanding and controlling complex systems. Charts, diagrams, and graphs are conceptual tools managers can use to summarize and report statistical data, measure and understand variation, assess risk, and make decisions. One definition of the term *statistics* is "that branch of applied mathematics which describes and analyzes empirical observations for the purpose of predicting certain events as a basis for decision making in the face of uncertainty."[21]

Statistical process control has long been employed in manufacturing environments. For instance, LaRoche Industries, a producer of low-density ammonium nitrate for industrial explosives, faced operating problems that threatened a plant shutdown. Before embarking on capital-intensive overhauls, the company used a system of statistical process control to gain a better understanding of plant operations and to assess the impact of possible changes in various process parameters. LaRoche found a way to make process improvements that saved nearly $300,000 a year by reducing raw material consumption and improving production yields.[22] Statistical process control also can be applied outside the classic manufacturing environments in such areas as project office functions.[23]

**descriptive statistics**
Statistics that directly state measured facts.

Statistics may be either descriptive or inferential. **Descriptive statistics** are, as the name indicates, those that describe a situation in numerical terms. An example of a descriptive statistic is the average (or "mean") time it takes to answer the telephone in the customer service department. Usually a more meaningful statistic is the median, that is, the figure in the middle of the range. Of all of the recorded times, one-half are greater than the median, one-half are less. When there is a wide range between the highest and lowest figures, the average may be highly misleading. For example, if one considers the annual incomes of a group consisting of Bill Gates, CEO of Microsoft, and nine full-time students, the median or midpoint might be $10,000. This would result if five students received less than $10,000 and four students plus Bill Gates received more than $10,000. In contrast, the average, or mean, for the group would be calculated by adding together the incomes of all ten members of the group and dividing this sum by ten. In this case, the result might be something like $500 million. This would result if the nine students had incomes ranging from zero to $15,000, and Bill Gates had an income of $5 billion. Clearly, where there is wide disparity between the highest and lowest figures in a group, the median is much more meaningful than the mean or average.

**inferential statistics**
Statistics that, when subjected to analysis, lead to conclusions or inferences but do not directly reveal them.

**Inferential statistics** are those that may be implied by certain relationships, but that do not result directly from physical measurements. When analyzed, inferences may be drawn from descriptive statistics even though the conclusions reached may be difficult or even impossible to measure directly. For example, an organization might make the assumption that the number of complaints received by the complaint department is an accurate indicator of the number of times customers are dissatisfied with the service they receive. The number of complaints recorded would be the descriptive statistic; the assumed number of dissatisfied customers would be the inferential statistic. The assumed relationship in this example might seem intuitively sound, but examining it more closely reveals both the weaknesses and strengths of inferential statistics.

First, it is obvious that not all dissatisfied customers will go to the effort to lodge a formal complaint. Therefore, to estimate the number of dissatisfied customers, the managers would have to apply some multiplier factor. After sampling actual service encounters, or reading academic studies done in other organizations, the managers might conclude that only 1 in 20 of the dissatisfied customers actually would phone the complaints department. Others would swallow their dissatisfaction or stop dealing with the organization without making any comment directly. Having made such an estimate, the managers would conclude that, if all other factors are equal, the number of dissatisfied customers is 20 times the number of complaints received. Then a less tangible adjustment might have to be made. Perhaps the complaints department staff members respond to complaints in an abrupt or rude manner, or perhaps the complaint department's phone line is often busy. In that case, many customers who might otherwise complain might not bother to do so. This would invalidate the presumed relationship between the number of complaints and the dissatisfactions of the customers in general, as the ratio might be 30 or 40 to 1, rather than the assumed 20 to 1.

This example illustrates some of the difficulties in using inferential statistics. Despite these difficulties, however, inferential statistics can be highly informative. Pursuing this simple example, managers might observe a sudden decrease in the number of formal complaints made. That should trigger them to try to discover whether the decrease resulted from markedly improved customer service (perhaps from increased clerk training) or happened because the complaints department altered its procedures in ways that discouraged complaints. Thus, it may be seen that inferential statistics can be very useful, but that their use requires judgement and managerial skill.

**Inherent variation.** Variation exists in any process, but especially in service industries, because no two service encounters are exactly alike. Even in carefully controlled manufacturing, unless the product is quite simple there is likely to be variation from unit to unit. In an extremely complicated product, such as an installation of an upgraded Windows software program, it is not surprising that despite very tight manufacturing controls, there will be some minute variations, resulting in malfunctions that are sometimes exceedingly difficult to resolve. The control of quality is largely the control of variation. The job of statistical process control is to limit this variation to within an acceptable range. So, managers must determine what is acceptable variation.

There are two general types of variation, often described as common and special cause variation. **Common cause variation** is the random variation in a system that may result from occasional human error, from equipment breakdown because of delayed maintenance, or from other unforeseen circumstances for which the system has failed to provide protection. As part of their continuous improvement process, managers should work continuously to improve the system in order to minimize the *range* of common cause variation. In this usage, *range* refers to the whole panoply of instances between the extreme upper and lower measures of the variables.

Since the perfect system cannot ever be reasonably achieved, some common cause variation will remain, despite managers' attention and care. In fact, it even can be said that if common cause variation were to be completely eliminated, it would be a signal that far too much time and money had been expended in preventing every possible source of this type of variation. Absolute perfection is extremely costly, and might severely reduce competitiveness, so the manager's challenge is to find the middle ground between perfection and sufficient quality.

**Special cause variation**, on the other hand, is due to some influence that comes from outside the system itself. This could be anything from the receipt from a supplier of poor quality materials or components to error by suppliers' employees to floods or earthquakes. It also might result from late delivery by a trucker, absence from work of a key employee because of illness, or an unpredictable breakdown of an instrument or machine. Managers must seek to eliminate special cause variations to the extent feasible. In these examples, the special cause variation might be reduced by more thorough inspection of materials received or by changing suppliers, by locating in areas less prone to floods or earthquakes, or by providing additional health care training and preventive measures for employees. In addition, the effect of employee absences might be guarded against by having more than one person learn each task. Loss of production because of instrument or machine failure might be made less likely by regular inspection and

**common cause variation**
A random variation from planned outcomes that results from occasional and often unpredictable causes.

**special cause variation**
A variation from planned outcomes that results from identifiable causes that are external to the system.

**stable system**
A system in which special cause variation has been almost entirely eliminated (for the time being) and the effects of common cause variation have been minimized, so that results are reasonably predictable.

**control chart**
A graphical display of statistics, often used to highlight variation.

maintenance, or its effect could be reduced by keeping essential spare parts on hand. A **stable system** is one that has largely eliminated special cause variation and is subject only to unavoidable (yet perhaps still reducible) common cause variation.

Statistical process control also may involve sophisticated statistical sampling and the use of graphs to determine acceptable variation. Samples of an important variable within a process are collected. The values are plotted on a graph, usually a **control chart**. In almost all graphs of data, the points will fall along a "normal curve," with most points falling near the middle and only a few falling near either extreme. Using established statistical tools that are beyond the scope of this discussion, upper and lower control limits can be established. Any event that falls outside of these limits would indicate the existence of a special cause that should demand attention and probably require corrective action. Exhibit 7-6 shows a normal curve (also called a *bell-shaped curve*), which is a convenient statistical artifact or tool. It shows the mean and upper and lower control limits based on mathematical calculations of what statisticians refer to as "three standard deviations." Although it may not be obvious from the chart, the area under the curve between these limits accounts for 99 percent of figures taken from almost any collection of data in which there is not some independent influence that skews the results.

Statistical measures such as these, coupled with changes in management styles, have facilitated the widely publicized transformation in approach to quality that has been taken in recent years by Motorola. This company calls its quality program its "six sigma" program. The term comes from a statistical term that expresses its company-wide goal of less than three defects per million for each product it produces. This rate compares very favourably with that of the average North American company, which may operate at four sigma, that is, about 6200 parts per million, or even at three sigma, about 67,000 defects per million (each lower sigma representing exponentially higher numbers of defects). Motorola employees train at "Motorola University," where they learn statistical process control, or how to use statistical tools to control their processes. The company conducted a survey of 100,000 of its employees to determine whether they felt the quality tools and training were useful. They found that most employees thought that it was useful, but that it wasn't happening fast enough. This from a group that management had traditionally thought to be resistant to change[24] and disinterested in improvement.

*"Motorola University" provides a wide spectrum of learning opportunities for its employees, helping them to perform within the parameters established by the company.*

Almost any type of organization—whether in service, manufacturing, retail, not-for-profit, finance, or some other industry—can benefit from applying statistical methods to organizational processes and customer expectations. Although statistical techniques are in widespread use, managers must decide how best to apply these techniques to their own organizations.

Statistical process control is the most narrowly focused of the approaches to quality control. It is concerned primarily with quantitative measures of performance, and does not address the issue of how to achieve performance improvements. In recent years there has been much discussion of two terms: total quality control and total quality management. These approaches to management focus on the behaviour of managers and other employees as well as on techniques for controlling organizational performance through their activities.

**Exhibit 7-6**  *The Normal Curve*

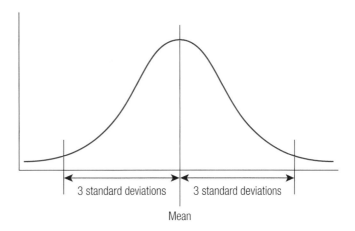

3 standard deviations | 3 standard deviations

Mean

### What Do Hits on a Web Site Communicate?

The Web has become an important source of statistical information for many companies. Knowing who is visiting their site, what they are looking at, how long they stop at each page, and how often they return provides detailed feedback on the value of their Web site and the interest in various products.

There are three key tools used to gather statistical data: counters, tracking services, and log analysis.

- *Counters:* This most commonly used tool keeps a tally of the number of times a page is loaded.
- *Tracking services:* A number of third-party companies provide statistical analysis by installing software to measure traffic in a variety of ways.
- *Log analysis:* Some companies ask for information when a first-time user logs on to a site. This detailed information creates a log entry and can be analyzed and categorized to give the company detailed demographic information.

As more and more business is done on the Web, the ability to gather detailed information very quickly and effortlessly changes statistical information-gathering methods. As marketing and merchandising becomes increasingly popular on the Internet, Web audits help paint a truer picture of where consumers are pausing and buying.

Contributed by Marnie Wright, British Columbia Institute of Technology.

## Total Quality Control

In times past, quality control in manufacturing usually consisted of assigning someone at the end of the assembly line to be responsible for ensuring that the product met the prescribed standards. Today, in forward-looking organizations, quality control begins at the beginning. That is, quality control is maintained from the design process through manufacturing, sale, and use of the product. The sum of all of these efforts is described

**total quality control**
A system that focuses on customer satisfaction by applying methods to improve and maintain quality of product or service.

by the term coined by Armand Feigenbaum—**total quality control**.[25] This term represents a more comprehensive form of quality control than statistical process control, although it also uses statistics to improve quality.

The principles of total quality control can be applied equally well to products or services. Most customers tend to seek products and services of consistent quality. To meet this demand, each individual in an organization provides a product or service for some other individual in the process, and that product or service can be evaluated using the tools of total quality control.[26] The emphasis of total quality control is on customer satisfaction.

According to Feigenbaum, "Total quality control is an effective system for integrating the quality-development, quality-maintenance, and quality-improvement efforts of the various groups in an organization so as to enable marketing, engineering, production, and service [to function] at the most economical levels which allow for full customer satisfaction."[27] To practise total quality control is to develop, design, produce, and service a quality product that is economical, useful, and always satisfactory to the customer.[28] Feigenbaum identifies several total quality control benchmarks:

- Quality is what the customer says it is;
- Quality is a way of managing;
- Quality and innovation are mutually dependent;
- Quality requires continuous improvement; and
- Quality is implemented with a total system connected with customers and suppliers.[29]

According to Feigenbaum, there is no such thing as a permanent quality standard. Demands and expectations for quality are constantly changing. Today we take for granted quality standards that were not even dreamed of 100, 50, or 20 years ago, or in some high-tech fields, even more recently than that. When cars were first introduced, a complete tool kit was an essential part of every vehicle, and any 50-kilometre trip that was not marked by at least one breakdown or flat tire was considered a remarkable achievement. Now we confidently expect cars to take us wherever we want to go without mechanical malfunction, and if tires do not give us trouble-free service for at least 60,000 kilometres we return them to the supplier for a refund.

One mark of good management is personal leadership in mobilizing the knowledge, skill, and positive attitudes of everyone in the organization to recognize that their efforts to improve quality help to make everything in the organization better and consequently help to make the organization competitive. Quality is also essential for successful innovation because of the rapid rate at which new products are developed. When a product design is likely to be manufactured globally, where international suppliers must be involved in every stage of development and production, it may be particularly important for the entire process to be clearly structured.[30]

In a quality-based system, control is a conscious, positive, preventive stance created in the system. Total quality control begins with planning that is designed to prevent quality problems from arising rather than to correct them after they arise. The concerns addressed by quality planning include:

1. Establishment of quality guidelines;
2. Building quality into the design;
3. Procurement quality;
4. In-process and finished product quality;
5. Inspection and test planning;
6. Control of nonconforming material;

7. Handling and following up on customer complaints; and
8. Education and training for quality.[31]

## Total Quality Management

**total quality management**
A system of control that focuses on improvements in the system rather than on the way that employees perform to accomplish improvement and maintenance of quality of a product or service.

Total quality management is similar to total quality control in its customer-focused approach to control. **Total quality management** uses the techniques and ideas of both statistical process control and total quality control, but goes further in its involvement of all employees in the quality process. The originator of the term *total quality management*, the late W. Edwards Deming, wrote and lectured extensively on issues relating to quality. According to Deming, total quality management treats the *system* as the primary source of error or defects in manufacturing or service work. Deming's management philosophy, summarized in his 14 points, was discussed in Chapter 1. Additionally, this chapter's opening vignette describes how Deming's red bead exercise demonstrated the folly of issuing reprimands or rewards to employees when they are operating within normal system variation.

Although total quality management techniques use a myriad of statistical techniques to control processes, there are also some fundamental lessons for control from a human psychology perspective. Deming stressed in his 14 points such things as "pride of workmanship," "self-improvement," and "driving out fear." These are all elements of the "softer" side of management (the non-quantitative side) but are equally important for managers to master. Managers who use only statistical process control are likely to ignore the need for pride in workmanship that most employees develop if they are encouraged to do so. Thus, the *total* in total quality management requires managers to be intimately familiar with a wide range of factors about the workplace, both those that can be described mathematically and those that cannot. Exhibit 7-7 on page 266 illustrates the benefits that are expected to accrue to an organization from paying attention to these non-quantitative aspects of a total quality management approach.

*Personal Environment Modules™ allow individuals to control their personal work spaces by setting temperature, light level, sound level, and even fragrance without affecting the work spaces of their neighbours.*

### The employee's role in total quality management.
In their book *In Search of Excellence*, consultants Thomas Peters and Robert Waterman illustrate the importance of personal employee control in the search for quality.[32] They describe an experiment designed to determine the effect of loud, disturbing noise on performing a mental task. The members of the experimental group were provided with buttons that they could press to eliminate the annoying noise. The control group members had no such button. In performing the mental task, the experimental group achieved five times the productivity rate and only 20 percent of the error rate of the control group. Questions have been raised about the exact figures reported, but there is little doubt that the hypothesis seems reasonable even if other factors such as the Hawthorne effect might have contributed to the apparently startling increases in productivity. The important finding of this experiment is that, while the experimental group performed significantly better, no one in the experimental group ever touched the button! Subjects who knew that they had personal control over their working conditions achieved higher productivity and greatly reduced error rates compared with those who didn't believe they had control. A personal sense of control, not reduced noise, explained the difference between the two groups.

To enhance employees' sense of personal control, Johnson Controls has developed an office product it calls Personal Environments

**Exhibit 7-7**   *Total Quality Management Model*

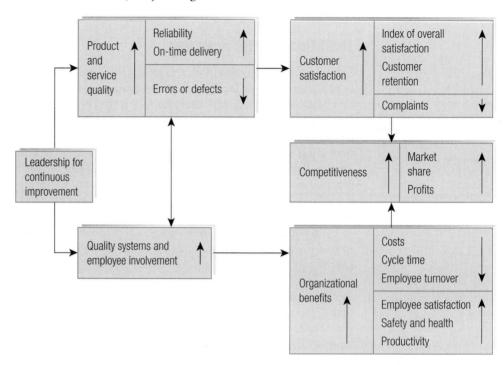

Source: U.S. General Accounting Office, *Management Practices: U.S. Companies Improve Performance through Quality Efforts*, GAO/NSIAD–90–190, May 1991, p. 15.

RH Modules (PEMs). These modules enable workers to control the temperature, light level, sound level, and even fragrance at their work stations. Independent investigators studied the effect of PEM work stations used by 500 employees at the West Bend Mutual Insurance Company. They found a measurable 2 percent increase in the productivity of workers who were placed in PEMs. West Bend executives think that the increase in productivity attributable to the work stations is more likely in the range of 6 to 8 percent. Terry Weaver, vice president at Johnson Controls, remarked, "The groundbreaking aspect of this study is that for the first time there is hard evidence that workers are more productive when they can control their environment."[33]

Japanese management expert Mikio Katano also recommends that managers place a high value on employees' sense of control. A production engineer with Toyota Motor Corporation's Motomachi factory, Kitano has been counselling factory managers not to rush in their application of automation. Kitano is not opposed to technology, but he does oppose machines that needlessly overcomplicate processes. "The key to productivity is simplicity," he says. "Men (*sic*) control machines, not the other way around." Kitano emphasizes that when employees feel they have control over a discrete section of the assembly line, they develop a sense of pride and autonomy.[34]

It is not only in Japan and North America that managers are discovering the virtues of allowing employees to control the processes for which they are responsible. In some Mexican factories, assembly-line workers also have achieved higher quality and productivity levels through increased personal control of work processes.

Deming provided an example of successful employee quality control in the production of stockings. Managers at a stocking company first recognized a problem in production costs when they faced a situation where costs were soon to exceed revenues. Management hired a statistician to help them diagnose their problem. The statistician recommended that the company send 20 supervisors on a 10-week training course to learn techniques for charting the number of defective stockings. When the supervisors returned, they were asked to apply some of the principles they had learned.

In all but two cases, defects fell to within statistically established control limits—a mean defect rate of 4.8 percent per production worker (called "loopers" in the stocking business). Next, the defect rates of individual loopers were charted. Management identified for the first time (1) an excellent looper whose skills were passed on to others by training them, (2) a looper whose performance improved markedly when fitted with eyeglasses, and (3) a looper whose performance changed dramatically after charting. One of the loopers remarked, "This is the first time that anybody ever told me that care mattered." Within seven months, the mean number of defects dropped from the original 4.8 percent to 0.8 percent, or one-sixth of its previous rate. Instead of 11,500 stockings being rejected each week, only 2000 were rejected.[35]

A quality-based system of control must be built on employee trust and pride of workmanship, which provides a basis for employee self-control. In this quality-based view, control must be seen as an internal, individual process before it can result in an external process. Control becomes an internal quality guide practised by all employees rather than an external set of rules applied by managers. A writer on quality issues, Joseph Juran, defines self-control as "A means of knowing what the goals are ... a means of knowing what the actual performance is ... a means for changing the performance in the event that performance does not conform to goals and standards."[36]

Applying standards, employees are provided with a strategy for determining the activities necessary for, and those harmful to, quality. Activities are built around the standards. Irrelevant, redundant, and non-value-added activities are eliminated.

**Management's role in total quality management.** While production workers play an important role in implementing a total quality management approach, management is responsible for leadership. In most organizations, non-managerial workers are unlikely to lead a revolution in organizational philosophy. It is up to management to plot the course and steer the ship. Managers must create the vision for the organization. This is no different in a quality-oriented environment than in an organization that operates in ways that pay less attention to customer satisfaction. What is different is the behaviour of managers.

Quality-based management operates on the belief that work processes are controlled first by the workforce, then by automation, then by managers, and finally by upper managers. Upper management is responsible for creating the system; other employees are trained to maintain control. Thus, a quality-based approach locates control at the lowest feasible levels of the organization. This is often at the level of the production or service workers on the line who produce the goods or provide the services.[37]

For managers, the traditional managerial control function focused on supervision during the production process. The emphasis was on watching for mistakes. Some managers resorted to using information technologies to eavesdrop on employees. Procter & Gamble, for example, examined employees' phone records to search for possible leaks of sensitive information. This type of practice has debilitating effects on morale and performance and invites criticism from an ethical standpoint. In some cases, the corporate trend towards downsizing and "rightsizing" has led employees from all levels in the corporate hierarchy to tell bosses only what they think the bosses want to hear, with-holding bad news and at times resorting to lies to cover up problems. Extreme pressure to perform can lead to improper behaviour. When jobs are hard to find and employees feel that their jobs are in jeopardy, they are more likely to take chances with unethical behaviour than if they feel their efforts will continue to be rewarded even if their productivity occasionally may fall below the prescribed standard.

The responsibility for instilling a culture of quality control ultimately rests with management. However, managers also must promote employee self-management or "quality-mindedness" practices, as Armand Feigenbaum refers to it.[38] To further employee self-management, managers must develop employee participation programs and policies. With knowledge of the company's costs and goals, almost all employees can practise control with minimal supervision. Management's job is to ensure that everyone has the knowledge, tools, and power to prevent problems from arising in their particular areas. Managers also must encourage employee suggestions and cost consciousness by recognizing and implementing quality improvement decisions. And when problems do arise, management should give the employees closest to those problems the first opportunity to solve them.

Managers need patience to transform their organization to one committed to the principles and tools of total quality management. If managers grow frustrated too soon with the lack of employee understanding or motivation to become involved in the new philosophy, they may not give it a chance to work.[39] As an Ernst & Young survey found, organizations that fail in their efforts to implement the philosophies of total quality management are usually those that did not provide their employees with the information and training they needed to be effective.[40] Most reliable employees want responsibility and control over their work. Most will understand and accept a new approach to their work if management demonstrates commitment to improving the system. This means that managers and other employees need to be trained in, and committed to, the applicable tools and techniques. They need to be empowered to control their work processes. And they need to be encouraged constantly to develop pride in their work and their organization. These elements of quality are the least quantifiable, but perhaps the most important.

## The ISO 9000 Standard

**ISO 9000**
A worldwide system of registration of an organization's operating sites that have been shown by independent audit to meet specified levels of quality and that continue to make effective efforts towards further quality improvement.

One measure of quality performance—the **ISO 9000** rating—is recognized worldwide. It is described as "… a structured process through which companies can raise the quality of products and services that they provide and maintain that level of quality which they achieve."[41] It was launched in Europe by the International Organization for Standardization (the initials of which in French are, not surprisingly, I.S.O.). The original impetus for the program was provided by the European Union, as it sought to standardize quality standards in order to eliminate international trade barriers within the EU based on allegations of quality defects.

It became widely known in Canada in the late 1980s, and has become a benchmark for quality performance. Separate standards and qualification techniques are provided for three segments. Designation 9001 covers services and service industries. Manufacturing industries are covered by the designation 9002. A third designation, 9003, relates to the computer hardware and software industries. Number 9004 refers to the system's Quality Management Guideline, which describes the program in detail.[42] A more recent designation, which was first published in 1996 and named ISO 14,000, covers environ-

*This Pioneer plant in Chatham, Ontario, has gone through the difficult steps to acquire ISO 9002 certification.*

mental standards.[43] In the first year, 1491 certifications were issued for ISO 14,000 in 45 different countries.

To be certified, an organization must apply and then undergo an extensive pre-audit. The company then describes its compliance plan and documents the processes being considered. The systems are modified as required, and employee training programs are designed and offered. When all of these steps are successfully completed, a separate independent audit is performed to permit registration as an ISO certified organization, under the appropriate 9000 or 14,000 number. To continue to use the ISO designation the company must submit to semi-annual audits to ensure that the established quality levels are being maintained.

The thrust of the ISO 9000 and 14,000 programs is not only to achieve high quality standards, but also to improve on them continuously. According to Norm Bush, general manager of MacMillan Bloedel's pulp plant in Powell River, B.C., "The process of getting ready for registration [in accordance with the manufacturing guidelines] prompted us to put in place new methods of training staff and conducting business."[44]

As early as 1966, 162,707 ISO registrations were issued in 121 different countries.[45] This number was triple what it had been only three years earlier.[46] Although the program got a late start in North America, according to the Canada Standards Council survey published in 1998, by 1996 there were 3955 completed registrations in Canada, 12,613 in the United States, and 412 in Mexico. These figures compare with the 109,961 sites in 41 countries of Europe, making up more than two-thirds of all registrations worldwide. Since those surveys were taken, the numbers have been growing rapidly; if trends continue, the number will double or triple again in only a few years.

Like any program of quality improvement, it is time-consuming and costly to gear up for ISO 9000 or 14,000 certification. Nevertheless, as global competition becomes ever more intense it is likely that more and more Canadian companies will take this important step.

## The Workplace of Tomorrow

The control process is becoming increasingly important in the global economy, where long-term survival depends on quality and competitiveness. Some companies adopt statistical process control because they recognize that it is a powerful tool for improving quality and hence competitiveness. Other companies institute statistical process control or qualify for ISO 9000 or 14,000 ratings because their customers require it of them. The Big Three auto companies require their suppliers to show proof that they use statistical process control methods in their manufacturing operations, or they will not be awarded contracts.[47] Driven by tougher customer standards, more steel makers are investing heavily in statistical process control.[48] Companies that provide services are increasingly investing the time and cost in earning and maintaining certification.[49] This trend is expected to continue in the years ahead as companies strive to improve quality and tailor production capabilities to customer requirements, if only to remain competitive.

In today's competitive environment, it is difficult to determine how extensive a company's control system should be. Managers are faced with a dilemma. They are under intense pressure to cut costs and be more competitive, yet they are expected to implement total quality control systems, and perhaps to qualify for ISO 9000 or ISO 14,000 ratings. Managers must strike a balance, recognizing that there are costs if an organization has too much or too little control. The key to the future will lie in finding this balance.

## Summary of Learning Objectives

▶ **Describe the red bead experiment and explain its message to managers.**

The red bead experiment illustrates the problems associated with attempts to control employee behaviour primarily with rewards and disciplinary actions. A high defect rate may be attributable to defects in the system rather than to failures of the employees. The experiment demonstrates that the system must be designed and managed to bring about quality, rather than to create difficult or impossible expectations for employee performance.

▶ **Describe the three elements of the control process.**

The three elements of control are specification, production, and inspection. Specification fully describes the preferred condition, a goal, a standard, or a carefully determined quantitative statement of conditions. Production is the action taken to meet the specifications (that is, making the product or providing the service). Inspection leads to evaluation as to whether the product or service meets the specifications. Appropriate follow-up actions then must be taken, based on the findings of the inspection.

▶ **Define** *total quality control.*

Total quality control is a system for integrating the quality-development, quality-maintenance, and quality-improvement efforts of the various groups in an organization in order to enable marketing, engineering, production, and service to function at the most economical levels that allow for the desired level of customer satisfaction.

▶ **Explain the role of non-managerial employees in total quality management.**

Primary control should be in the hands of the front-line employees, not in the hands of supervisors or outside or final inspectors. Management's job is to ensure that non-managerial employees have the knowledge, tools, and power to prevent problems from arising. A quality-based system of control must be built on employee trust and pride of workmanship, which provides a basis for employee self-control. In this quality-based view, control must be an internal process before it can result in an external process. Responsibility for planning, implementing, and maintaining control ultimately rests with management. The effective application of control and of achieving quality depends largely on the effective use of self-management practices. Control becomes an internal quality guide practised by all employees, rather than an external set of rules applied *by* managers *to* employees. Successful control must be recognized and rewarded.

▶ **Explain management's role in total quality management.**

The traditional managerial control function has focused on supervision during the production process. Supervision has been practised widely as a traditional method of keeping an eye on production or service employees and looking for special causes of variation. Traditional management has used technology to monitor and perhaps even to intimidate employees. In contrast, quality-based management believes that control is effected first by the workforce, then by automation, then by managers, and finally by upper managers. Upper management is responsible for the system; other employees are then judged capable of effecting control. Thus, a quality-based approach locates a large element of control at the lowest feasible levels of the organization—with information technology and in the hands of production or service employees.

▷ **Contrast statistical process control with total quality control.**

Statistical process control focuses on the use of statistics to identify and understand production and operations. It is little concerned with how to resolve problems in systems. Total quality control focuses on customer expectations to control production and operations. Although it recognizes the importance of statistics, it also sees the importance of employee involvement with the quality improvement process.

▷ **Discuss the approach taken by the ISO 9000 program, why it is attracting the attention of many Canadian companies, and what benefits a company might gain from participating in the program.**

The ISO 9000 program is a structured process through which companies can raise and maintain the quality of their products and services. Large corporate customers are starting to require that their suppliers have ISO 9000 certification. Companies often find that the steps required for certification lead to improved quality and hence to improved competitiveness.

## KEY TERMS

accounts receivable turnover, p. 255
acid test ratio, p. 255
activity-based accounting, p. 257
balance sheet, p. 255
common cause variation, p. 261
concurrent control, p. 253
control, p. 247
control chart, p. 262
current ratio, p. 255
debt/asset ratio, p. 256

debt/equity ratio, p. 256
descriptive statistics, p. 260
direction, p. 254
feedback control, p. 254
income statement, p. 255
inferential statistics, p. 260
inventory turnover, p. 256
ISO 9000, p. 268
liquidity, p. 255

preliminary control, p. 251
rate of return, p. 255
solvency, p. 256
special cause variation, p. 261
stable system, p. 262
standard cost system, p. 256
statistical process control, p. 259
total quality control, p. 264
total quality management, p. 265

## REVIEW AND DISCUSSION QUESTIONS

### Recall

1. What is a stable system? Who is responsible for creating and maintaining a stable system?
2. Describe the differences among preliminary, concurrent, and feedback control.
3. What are the differences between traditional control and quality control?

### Understanding

4. Explain the role of statistics in quality control.

5. How does the red bead experiment highlight the system as the source of error in work processes?
6. Who is responsible for achieving and maintaining control in an organization?
7. Can all variation within a system be eliminated by comprehensive preliminary control?
8. Why do most employees perform at higher levels when they have personal control of their work processes?
9. Why would a company be willing to commit the time and money necessary to qualify for an ISO 9000 or ISO 14,000 designation?

## Application

10. Design and implement a statistical measure to assess your arrival time for class each day.
11. Describe ineffective controls that you have experienced in school, at work, or in other aspects of your life. How were they ineffective? How might they have been improved?

# CASE 7-1

## Whirlpool Lets Customers Control Product Design

Manufacturing consultant Earl Hall has remarked that "The global markets of the 21st century will demand the ability to quickly and globally deliver a high variety of customized products." Futurist Alvin Toffler has coined the term *prosumer* (an amalgamation of *pro*ducer and con*sumer*) to signify the consumer's increasingly important role in the design of products and services. Some writers have projected that the time is rapidly approaching when consumers will play a role in the design of all of the major items they consume. Some companies are already riding this wave of change.

Whirlpool is a familiar name in the home appliance business. But the industry giant found itself faced with a dilemma even senior managers couldn't resolve. On the surface, the issue seemed simple enough—company surveys had determined that consumers wanted a cooking range with controls that were easy to clean. Whirlpool engineers responded to the survey, proposing that the company use modern touch-pad controls like those on microwave ovens. Touch-pad controls can be cleaned with one swipe of a damp cloth. The problem was that the idea of touch-pad controls flew in the face of industry wisdom. Earlier models with touch-pad controls had not sold well in stores; consumers chose ovens with knobs they could grasp and turn.

Rather than reject the results of its consumer study, the company decided to follow consumers' wishes to the letter. It designed a range with touch-pad controls and, during roll-out, monitored consumer reaction every step of the way. At the company's headquarters, consumer volunteers played with computer simulations of the new controls and marketers tested prototypes with passersby in nearby shopping malls.

The result of all this effort is a range with a touch-pad control system so easy to use it doesn't require a manual. The user simply turns on the oven in a simple series of steps. The new range hit the sales floor in 1992 and became one of Whirlpool's hottest-selling models.

This example of bringing the customer into the design process is one of the ways in which Whirlpool involves the consumer in controlling corporate behaviour. Each year the company sends its Standardized Appliance Measurement Satisfaction (SAMS) survey to 180,000 households, asking people to rate all of their appliances on a number of attributes. If the survey finds that a competitor's product ranks higher, Whirlpool engineers tear it apart to find out why.

In addition to the survey, the company pays hundreds of consumers to "use" computer simulations of potential products at the company's Usability Laboratory. Engineers record consumer reactions on videotape.

Vice President John Hamann explained that consumers' expectations aren't immediately clear. For example, one SAMS survey showed that people want clean refrigerators. After analyzing this and asking more questions, Whirlpool found that consumers aren't thinking of refrigerators that are easy to clean, but rather refrigerators that *look* clean. The company promptly designed refrigerators with stucco-like fronts that hide fingerprints.

Whirlpool uses consumer data to differentiate its products from the products of its chief competitors (Maytag and Electrolux). Since 1982, Whirlpool has nearly tripled in size to become the world's largest major appliance manufacturer. And it has plans for continued expansion. CEO David Whitwam is confident that consumer research methods will lead to big gains overseas. This confidence already has been justified in European microwave oven sales. Until recently, fewer than one-third of European households had microwaves. But Whirlpool's consumer research showed that more families would buy them if they performed more like conventional ovens. In late 1991, Whirlpool introduced the VIP Crisp, a microwave model produced strictly for European markets. It contains a broiler coil for top browning and a unique dish that sizzles the underside of the food. The VIP Crisp is now Europe's best-selling microwave.

Bringing the customer into the process of product design is another fundamental element of total quality control. Determining what customers are willing to purchase before developing a product or service helps to ensure that there is a market. However, consumer demand is constantly shifting, and companies such as Whirlpool that use sophisticated techniques to involve the consumer in new product design on a continuous basis will stay competitive in the global economy.

### Questions

1. What type of control is displayed by the Whirlpool SAMS survey?
2. Whirlpool managers are interested in controlling product design. What kind of questions might the SAMS survey ask? List ten questions that might help in the design of new home appliances.
3. Develop a means for measuring and assessing responses to the ten questions you developed. What type of statistics would help the most? Will descriptive or inferential statistics be used?

Source: Adapted from Sally Solo, "How to Listen to Consumers," *Fortune* (January 11, 1993): 77; William H. Davidow and Michael S. Malone, *The Virtual Corporation* (New York: HarperCollins, 1992); Alvin S. Toffler, *The Third Wave* (New York: William Morrow, 1980).

## CASE 7-2

# Tenneco's New Chief Controls by Setting High Standards

When Michael Walsh joined Tenneco in 1991, the board of directors had decided that since he was new to the company's many businesses, he should serve a seven-month apprenticeship as president before taking over as CEO. Tenneco is a $13 billion per year company that is engaged in several industries—chemicals, automotive parts, shipbuilding, natural gas pipelines, packaging, and the manufacture of agricultural and construction equipment.

In September 1991, a month before his official start date, Walsh let people know that he was in control. Presidents of the company's six divisions were invited to what was expected to be a casual dinner, in which Walsh would be introduced by outgoing CEO James Ketelsen. During the course of the evening, Walsh learned that one of Tenneco's subsidiaries, Case Corporation, would be reporting a third-quarter operating loss of $83 million—double what financial analysts had been expecting. When Walsh heard this, he took over the meeting, demanding explanations and giving orders. Objecting to Walsh's assertiveness, Case president Edward Campbell asked Ketelsen, "What the hell is going on here?" But Ketelsen deferred to Walsh and, in effect, Walsh's tenure began at that moment.

Before the evening was over, Walsh proceeded through farm equipment, natural gas, shipbuilding, and auto parts, raising tough questions and obviously expecting solid answers. He soon realized why earnings had been falling for three years in a row, and why in 1991 the company as a whole would post a net loss of $732 million.

Walsh discovered that Tenneco's auto parts and chemicals divisions—both profitable—didn't strive as hard as they might for higher earnings because the surplus they generated was dumped into the money-losing farm equipment division. He discovered bloated inventories of finished products that resulted because some managers kept production lines rolling despite slackening customer demand. He even found instances of such obvious carelessness that no manager should have been unaware of them. For example, shipping documents on some packages destined for industrial customers were so illegible that customers didn't know what the packages contained and didn't feel moved to make prompt payment, let alone place further orders. In short, Walsh found that quality control at Tenneco was little more than a joke.

After 18 months, not only was Walsh able to restore profitability to Tenneco's overall operations, but he was able to do so without massive layoffs or closing major operations. Walsh—who officially became CEO in April 1992—sought out inefficiencies wherever he could find them. For example, as a result of quality-oriented teams that he inaugurated, the welds on certain car parts were shortened without losing strength and scrap metal previously discarded was now recycled. He required managers to consider their factory layouts, resulting in the relocation of production equipment. With the new layouts, some products that formerly had been trundled around so much from process to process that they had travelled an incredible 179 miles *within the factory* were now moving much more directly and covering only a fraction of that distance while being processed.

These and other innovations resulted in a $250 million reduction in 1992 operating costs, and a dramatic turnaround from a serious loss to a respectable profit.

The secret, if it can be called that, was attention to quality of performance. Walsh insisted on setting high targets on every measure of performance, and was not hesitant to call a manager on the carpet if those targets were not met. Because of control measures such as weekly "flash reports," Walsh and other senior managers were able to detect whenever an operation was beginning to fall behind its agreed-upon objectives and goals.

Walsh's innovations could not have succeeded as they did had he and the managers he led not been able to instill in the vast majority of Tenneco employees the desire to perform more effectively in order to make the company competitive. Walsh's videotaped messages calling for innovation at all levels of the company encouraged one employee to refine a 30-year-old formula for making liner board. The result: fewer defects and an annual savings of $350,000.

Michael Walsh's Tenneco turnaround was made possible in large part because of his insistence on knowing facts concurrently with operations, his ability to inspire innovation, and his insistence on quality control. In Walsh's case, these factors constitute effective management.

## Questions

1. Why does Walsh make videotapes of his messages available to all Tenneco employees? How do you think the employees might have reacted to them?
2. From the standpoint of control, what are the advantages of the weekly "flash reports" from all divisions, and how can Walsh and other managers use them?
3. How do Walsh's actions reflect the role of leadership in transforming a company?
4. What would have been the reactions of the divisional presidents to Walsh's actions at the introductory dinner?

## APPLICATION EXERCISE  7-1

### Developing Performance Standards for Retail Sales Asscociates

Hibson's is a department store in a large, suburban mall. In the store, sales associates (SAs) are responsible for providing customer service, ensuring customer satisfaction, and making sales. Observations, anecdotal information, and a review of industry standards of sales dollars generated per SA have convinced management and the SAs that they are underperforming. You have been asked to assist management to develop a program that sets performance standards for 19 full-time SAs in one section of the store. Management and the SAs are looking to you for help in finding solutions.

Local market conditions are stable, with competition from a variety of retail stores. Advertising, pricing, and other marketing issues are outside the domain of your work. All of you agree that SA performance, not marketing, is the issue. SAs receive above-industry-average base compensation. An individual-based commission plan was attempted six months ago. The SAs asked management to drop the commission plan when they decided that it caused dysfunctional competition among them. They recognized the need for a more fluid team approach to sales, sales support, and customer satisfaction. That led to a behavioural survey.

In the survey, assistant managers and SAs collected observational measures, carefully recording and then classifying SA behaviours. Measures were taken over all shifts throughout a representative sales month. Management and the SAs agree that the measures are fair and accurate. Behaviour was classified as (1) selling (conversing with customers, assisting with selection and fitting, registering sales, and completing charge slips); (2) stock support work (arranging and displaying merchandise, tagging and replenishing stock, and packing and unpacking stock); (3) other work-related activities (giving directions, taking returns, checking credit, answering questions, etc.); (4) idle time (socializing and not working); and (5) absence from the work area. Sales figures for each SA have been recorded for each shift. Direct measures of customer satisfaction were not collected. Management will provide you with the full records of these measures shortly. You are not familiar with the specific results of the survey.

Outline your basic plan for effecting change. Include a problem definition, standards, measures, controls, an action plan, and recommended follow-up. Include timing for each step, how the plan will be communicated, and by whom.

Source: Fred Luthans, *Journal of Applied Psychology,* 66 (1981): 314-23; Fred Luthans, *Journal of Organizational Behavior Management,* 7 (1985): 23-35.

# INTERNET APPLICATION 7-1

Visit the Web site of W. Edwards Deming (www.deming.org). Click on "Teachings."

1. What are Deming's 14 Points for Management?
2. Which do you feel are the five most important points and why?

Search the Web for an organization that incorporates some of Deming's points in its corporate philosophy, although probably without referring to Deming or his listing of points. How has this philosophy contributed to the organization's success?

# Human Resource Management

After studying this chapter, you should be able to:

▶ Describe the usual scope of human resource management (HRM);

▶ Discuss the purpose of and explain some of the practices involved in job analysis;

▶ Discuss how job specialization relates to its opposites, job enlargement and job enrichment;

▶ Explain the importance of each of the steps in recruitment;

▶ Identify the sources of the rules against discrimination;

▶ Describe what constitutes sexual harassment and criminal harassment, and discuss why they are of concern to managers;

▶ Differentiate between equal pay and pay equity, and discuss their respective effects, benefits, and difficulties;

▶ Describe several bases used to determine compensation rates;

▶ Discuss why personnel benefits are important, and describe some of the most commonly provided forms;

▶ Discuss some of the implications of flextime and telecommuting; and

▶ Explain the nature of progressive discipline, and its place in a comprehensive program of performance evaluation.

## Hiring Right Makes Sense

TOP-PERFORMING ORGANIZATIONS INVEST MUCH energy, time, and attention in the hiring and selection process. Fairfield Inn puts a potential job candidate through an average of 14 interviews. Finding the right person for the job is considered essential to perpetuate the best culture at Thomas Interior Systems, an office furnishings designer and reseller. This small company has only 75 employees, but prides itself on having every employee become part of the company's competitive culture. At least two purposes are served by careful, intensive recruitment and selection practices such as those of Fairfield Inn and Thomas Interiors Systems. First, the organization gains a close look at candidates' suitability, and especially their fit with the culture. Second, attention to detail gives candidates plenty of opportunity to eliminate themselves if the culture doesn't feel right for them. Being rigorous, fair, and accurate in recruitment and selection minimizes the chance that the wrong person will be attracted to and accept the job. ▶

Rigorous screening is expensive, but hiring the wrong people—who do not fit the corporate culture, or who do not perform satisfactorily—is probably even more costly. Recruiting, screening, selecting, orienting, and initial training for a single mid-level management position can cost more than $50,000. Even for simple clerical or maintenance positions, a mistake in hiring is inevitably costly. One of the worst hidden costs in human relations management is to hire someone who, in the words of the old adage, is not good enough to keep but not bad enough to fire.

In part because of the high cost of making a mistake, some organizations are hiring temporary employees instead of adding to their full-time ranks. Largely in response to the downsizing of previous years, more than 20 percent of the increase in employment in 1994 was in temporary jobs. For example, KLA Instruments hires highly trained engineers on a project-by-project basis. Previous experience, specific skills appropriate to each project, and a willingness to undergo concentrated project-specific training are important as KLA screens applicants. Since KLA needs engineers to start being productive when they are first assigned to a project, it is important for them to select the correct person.

A company that is working hard to find and hire international leaders for the twenty-first century is Molex, Inc., a technology company. Molex generates more than half of its approximately $1 billion annual sales outside North America. It searches for applicants for entry-level positions who are fluent in at least one foreign language. The language requirement is an important part of the screening process, because of the company's international business and plans for further international growth. Molex career paths are developed for incoming professionals based on many factors, including an understanding of international issues and an ability to deal with other cultures.

Insurance company American General reduced annual turnover of its agents by more than 20 percent with the use of a carefully constructed questionnaire that was used to screen applicants. Younkers, a department store, cut staff turnover rates by 25 percent by applying a similar test. Hiring correctly, hiring the best people, and following up on the hiring itself are essential tools in good management. Hiring well just doesn't happen. It requires time, energy, and a commitment to recruitment and selection. ■

Sources: Adapted from Janet McFarland, "Renewable Contracts Fill Permanent Jobs," *Globe and Mail* (March 26, 1996); Gallian Flynn, "Contingent Staffing Requires Serious Strategy," *Personnel Journal* (April 1995): 50-59; Charlene Marmer Solomon, "Navigating Your Search for Global Talent," *Personnel Journal* (May 1995): 84-101; Suzanne Oliver, "Slouches Make Better Operators," *Forbes* (August 16, 1993): 104-105; Jim Clemner, *Firing on All Cylinders* (Homewood, IL: Business One Irwin, 1992): 148-49, 154-56; Michael Barrier, "Small Firms Put Quality First," *Nation's Business* (May 1992): 22-32; Barbara Levin, "Chevron's HR Conference: Strategic Planning to Meet Corporate Goals," *HR Focus* (May 1992): 9; and Jay W. Spechler, *When America Does It Right* (Norcross, GA: Industrial Engineering and Management Press, 1988): 541.

## Human Resource Management in Organizations

Human resource solutions are among the key factors in creating an organization that can function effectively. This is obvious in companies such as Fairfield Inn, KLA Instruments, Molex, Inc., and American General. Being recognized as an important person who is needed, respected, and listened to is an important factor in helping employees to feel that they belong to an organization, a work team, or even an occupation group.[1] Peters and Waterman's *In Search of Excellence* expressed a fundamental lesson about the importance of human resources:

> Treat people as adults. Treat them as partners; treat them with dignity; treat them with respect. Treat them—not capital spending and automation—as the primary sources of productivity gains.... If you want productivity and the

**Exhibit 8-1**    *A Model of the Human Resource Function*

| External Environmental Influences | Internal Environmental Influences |
|---|---|
| Competitive Organizations | Strategy |
| Economic Conditions/Domestic and International | Goals |
| | Organizational Culture |
| Government Requirements, Regulations, and Laws | Job Design |
| | Work Group |
| Composition of the Labour Force | Leader's Style and Experience |
| Unions | Communication |
| Location of the Organization | Control Systems |

**Human Resource Management Programs**

| HMR Activities | People | Outcomes |
|---|---|---|
| Pay Equity | Abilities | Enhanced Competitiveness |
| Planning | Attitudes | |
| Recruitment | Preferences | |
| Selection | Motivation | |
| Training and Development | Personality | |
| Performance Evaluation | | |
| Compensation | | |
| Benefits and Services | | |
| Job Analysis | | |
| Discipline | | |
| Labour Relations | | |
| Safety and Health | | |
| Work Schedules | | |

Feedback

financial reward that goes with it, you must treat your workers as the most important asset.[2]

This chapter addresses human resource practices, principles, and programs. It suggests that to improve quality and competitiveness, people must be the driving force. As the opening vignette suggests, managers must pay attention to people from the start. If they do not hire wisely, it will be almost impossible to instil the corporate culture that is needed for the organization to compete effectively, or perhaps even to survive. A study of 136 non-financial companies by Theresa Welbourne and Alice Owens showed that 92 percent of the companies that provide pay incentives and a "high regard for their workers" survived for at least five years after going public, while only 34 percent of those who did not were able to last that long.[3]

In large, formal organizations such as General Motors Canada and BCE, Inc., a specialized department usually guides the human resource program. But even in a small organization, managers must adopt an action-oriented approach to people and their needs, goals, expectations, skills, knowledge, and abilities. This chapter discusses human resource management in terms of the function, department, and activities that are required for an organization to achieve increased competitiveness by acquiring, retaining, developing, and properly using its human resources, both managerial and non-managerial.

## Human Resource Management Background

**human resource management (HRM)**
In an organization, the management of people and systems that pertain directly to employees.

The term **human resource management (HRM)** refers to the development and application of employees' skills and energies to accomplish the goals and objectives of the organization. It encompasses the planning of needs and requirements; recruitment, selection and training; measures to improve employee morale, and administration of compensation and personnel benefits plans. Exhibit 8-1 on page 281 illustrates the activities that usually fall under the heading of HRM, and shows that they depend on influences from the interactions of the external and internal environments. It also illustrates that the results of HRM are reflected in people and in enhanced competitiveness.

The importance of HRM has been increasingly recognized as the population has become more mobile, and as the expectations of employees have increased. In the days when the owner of a business could choose employees from a large pool of eager applicants, and could fire them at will, there seemed to be no pressing need to take much care in making the selection. If an error was made, it was easy to correct it by simply firing one employee and hiring another. During that period, employees did not receive health or other insurance benefits, employees were prevented or at least discouraged from organizing unions, and employees' interests and needs were of little concern to employers. Maintenance of payroll records was a relatively simple task, consisting of recording hours worked, rates of pay, and amounts paid. There were few obligations to report information to governments for tax purposes and none at all for unemployment and pension benefits. It is little wonder, then, that HR executives and departments were late in arriving on the business scene.

All of these factors have changed, creating a pressing need to consolidate many of the functions that we now label as HRM. As collective bargaining and other relationships with unions became more important, it was logical to assign responsibilities for these activities to the same individuals already involved in HRM.[4] Today any medium-sized or large organization that does not have an active HR officer or department would be failing to provide a basic support function. It also would be burdening managers at several levels, because they would have to discharge the functions that probably could be more efficiently provided by a consolidated HR department.

In a small business that has only a handful of employees, there probably will not be a single individual who is responsible for all HR functions. Nevertheless, regardless of the size of the organization, the HR functions should be recognized as distinct from other management functions, even though they are closely related. Some HR functions that are basically clerical in nature can be safely delegated to one or more office employees, often in conjunction with related tasks such as bookkeeping and other record-keeping activities. Other aspects of HRM are so important and potentially hazardous that they must remain a primary concern of the owners or at least of responsible managers who can give them proper attention. These include final recruiting decisions, establishment of wage and salary ranges, disciplinary actions, and monitoring operations to prevent harassment.

## Human Resource Planning

**human resource planning**
Forecasting the numbers and qualifications of employees and support services that will be required by the organization, and determining how those sources will be made available.

As thinking about the HR function matured, it became clear that a major aspect of organizational planning always must be questions of staffing and training. **Human resource planning** is a two-step process that involves forecasting future human resource needs and then planning how to meet and manage these needs. Exhibit 8-2 on page 284 outlines some of the activities involved in needs forecasting and program planning. The major objective of HR planning is to determine the best use of the talent and skills available to accomplish what is best for the individual and for the organization.[5]

As Exhibit 8-2 shows, needs forecasting involves four specific activities. The external market conditions must be studied, as well as the organization's future human resource requirements. It must be decided whether talented and skilled human resources are available. Decisions must be made as to the ways in which HR activities will contribute to reward systems.

Human resource planning also may involve considering the effectiveness of the performance of the organization and individuals. As discussed in Chapter 6, it may be desirable to move some individuals from positions where they are not very effective to others where they may be able to function more effectively. Thus, evaluation, developing compensation and reward programs, and coaching are important planning activities. There is also the need to guide, assign, develop, and manage the careers of individuals.

Human resource planning techniques include the use of some or all of the following:

1. *Human resource inventories*: gathering information about the skills, abilities, and knowledge that exist within the organization already;
2. *Human resource forecasts*: predicting the organization's future requirements in terms of numbers available, skill mixes, and external labour supply;
3. *Action plans*: designing the recruitment, selection, training, orientation, promotion, development, and compensation plans used; and
4. *Control and evaluation*: creating the monitoring system used to determine the extent to which human resource goals have been attained.

## Job Analysis

**job analysis**
Systematically gathering and analyzing the duties and skills required for a job.

One of the first steps in HR planning is to decide what jobs need to be done. **Job analysis** is the process of gathering, analyzing and synthesizing information about the jobs that are being done and any new jobs that are envisaged.[6] This procedure (1) specifies the tasks that must be accomplished to complete a job, and (2) describes the skills and knowledge necessary to perform the tasks.[7] Exhibit 8-3 on page 285 illustrates some of the questions that may be answered through job analysis.

To be effective, job analysis is an ongoing process. Organizations adapt to innovative technology, changes in the external environment, and other competitive pressures, requiring missions and objectives to be changed. By analyzing and redesigning existing jobs, organizations can adapt to those changes and remain competitive. Managers are learning that an organization is a collection of human beings that need to be developed and nurtured, not a collection of "assets" to be traded, manipulated, and motivated by fear. In one recent study of 1500 employees, Dr. Gerald Graham investigated 65 potential tools designed to enhance employee motivation. He found that personal congratulations from managers had the greatest impact on employee satisfaction.[8]

**Exhibit 8-2**   *The Human Resource Planning Process*

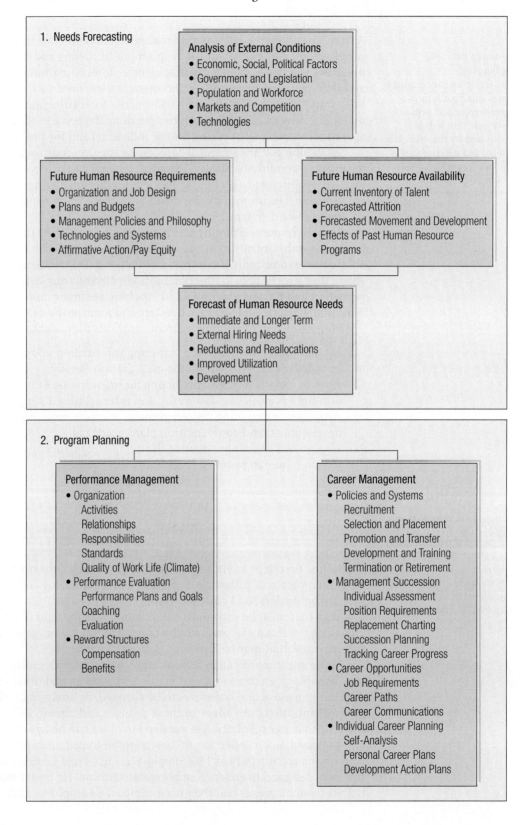

*Job analysis for a firefighter includes attention to organization and authority, priorities, methods, and how best to handle certain situations. Effective job analysis may well include life and death questions.*

Historically, job analysis began with factory jobs, as an integral part of the scientific management movement described in Chapter 1. By mid-century, job analysis began to be used in some organizations for office and clerical jobs. Today this tool is widely used for management jobs as well. Job analysis is used to help design work that enhances employee performance, rather than limit employees by enforcing the single best way to do things, as was proposed by Frederick W. Taylor. Often, those directly involved in doing the work are asked to participate in the job analysis, because they are closest to the task and often are best able to describe how the task is accomplished and what skills and knowledge they actually apply in performing their work.

## Steps in Job Analysis

A typical job analysis involves several steps, as illustrated in Exhibit 8-4 on page 286. First, the job analyst must examine how each job fits into the overall organization, as reflected in interrelationships of departments, units, and jobs. During this step, organization charts may be used to illustrate the formal relationships among the various segments of the organization, but informal relationships are more difficult to discover and describe. The interrelationships among jobs also must be discovered. The basic questions are, "Whose work precedes and has an impact on this job?" and "Whose work follows and is affected by this job?" For example, when analyzing an assembly line job, the analyst would investigate the flow of work to and from it. When analyzing a clerical job, the investigation would focus both on the flow of paper and on its impact on other jobs.

Analyzing every job in detail would be time-consuming and costly. To reduce cost, the second step consists of deciding which jobs are sufficiently similar to be considered as a group, so that one job can be analyzed in detail to represent the whole group.

The third step consists of collecting detailed information on the characteristics of the job, the behaviours and activities required by the job, and the employee skills needed to perform the job satisfactorily. Actual job performance is observed for the types of jobs that require manual or standardized activities such as assembly line work, crating and shipping, and warehouse materials handling. Workers are interviewed, and

**Exhibit 8-3**

*Questions That May Be Answered Through Job Analysis*

| Question | Possible Answers |
| --- | --- |
| What activities are required in a job? | Hand and body motions, use of equipment, services, communication with others. |
| What skills are needed to perform the activities? | Education, previous experience, licences, degrees, or other personal characteristics. |
| What are the working conditions of the job? | Physical demands, degree of accountability and responsibility, extent of supervision, and other job environment factors. |

**Exhibit 8-4**    *Steps in a Typical Job Analysis*

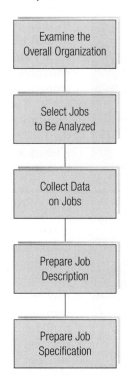

Examine the
Overall Organization

Select Jobs
to Be Analyzed

Collect Data
on Jobs

Prepare Job
Description

Prepare Job
Specification

**job description**
A written statement of
the job's activities, the
equipment required for
it, and the working con-
ditions in which it exists.

**job specification**
A written statement of
the skills, knowledge,
abilities, and other characteristics needed to perform a job effectively.

questionnaires or log entries may be prepared and analyzed. A typical questionnaire
appears as Exhibit 8-5.

## Job Descriptions and Job Specifications

The results of the job analyses are then incorporated into job descriptions. A **job description** is a written summary of a job, its activities,
the equipment required to perform it, and the
working conditions that surround it. It helps
the organization to clarify the job and its relationships to other positions. It also helps the
employees understand what the job entails and
what other jobs might fit their personal characteristics, skills, and interests. Exhibit 8-6 on
page 288 shows a typical job description for a
human resource manager. To achieve some uniformity and to make use of special HR skills,
the HR manager coordinates the preparation of
job descriptions, relying heavily on the knowledge and experience of the people doing the
jobs and their supervisors.

A **job specification** is a written statement
of the skills, knowledge, abilities, and other
characteristics needed to perform a particular

*To prepare a job description, it is necessary to observe how the job is
being performed, as well as to deduce how it might be performed better.*

**Exhibit 8-5**  *Job Analysis Questionnaire*

Your Job Title _____  Code _____ Date _____

Class Title _____  Department _____

Your Name _____  Facility _____

Supervisor's Title _____  Prepared by _____

Superior's Name _____  Hours Worked _____ AM/PM _____ to AM/PM _____

1. What is the general purpose of your job?
2. What was your last job? If it was in another organization, please name it.
3. To what job would you normally expect to be promoted?
4. If you regularly supervise others, list them by name and job title.
5. If you supervise others, please check those activities that are part of your supervisory duties.

____ Hiring          ____ Coaching               ____ Promoting
____ Orienting       ____ Counselling            ____ Compensating
____ Training        ____ Budgeting              ____ Disciplining
____ Scheduling      ____ Directing              ____ Terminating
____ Developing      ____ Measuring performance  ____ Other _____

6. How would you describe the successful completion and results of your work?
7. *Job duties* – Please briefly describe what you do and, if possible, *how* you do it. Indicate those duties you consider to be most important and those that are the most difficult.
   a. *Daily duties* –
   b. *Periodic duties* (Please indicate whether weekly, monthly, quarterly, etc.) –
   c. *Duties performed at irregular intervals* –
   d. How long have you been performing these duties?
   e. Are you now performing unnecessary duties? If yes, please describe.
   f. Should you be performing duties not now included in your job? If yes, please describe.
8. *Education.* Please check the blank that indicates the educational *requirements* for the job, not your *own* educational background.
   a. ____ No formal education required.          d. ____ Two-year college or university certificate or equivalent.
   b. ____ Less than high school diploma.          e. ____ University degree.
   c. ____ High school diploma or equivalent.       f. ____ Education beyond undergraduate degree
                                                    g. ____ Professional licence.
   List advanced degrees or specific professional licence or certificate required.
   Please indicate the education you had when you were placed on the job.
9. *Experience.* Please check the amount needed to perform the job.
   a. ____ None.                    d. ____ Six months to a year.    g. ____ Five to ten years.
   b. ____ Less than one month.      e. ____ One to three years.      h. ____ Over ten years.
   c. ____ One month to less than six months.    f. ____ Three to five years.
   Please indicate the experience you had when you were placed on this job.
10. *Skill.* Please list any skills required in the performance of your job. (For example, amount of accuracy, alertness, precision in working with described tools, methods, systems, etc.)
    Please list skills you possessed when you were placed on this job.
11. *Equipment.* Does your work require the use of any equipment? Yes/No. If yes, please list the equipment and check whether you use it rarely, occasionally, or frequently.

| Equipment | Rarely | Occasionally | Frequently |
|---|---|---|---|
| a. _____ | _____ | _____ | _____ |
| b. _____ | _____ | _____ | _____ |
| c. _____ | _____ | _____ | _____ |
| d. _____ | _____ | _____ | _____ |

**Exhibit 8-6**

*Typical Job Description*

---

JOB TITLE: HUMAN RESOURCE MANAGER

*General Description of the Job*

Performs responsible administrative work managing personnel activities of a large agency or institution. Work involves responsibility for the planning and administration of an HRM program that includes recruitment, examination, selection, evaluation, appointment, promotion, transfer, and recommended change of status of agency employees, and a system of communication for disseminating necessary information to workers. Works under general supervision, exercising initiative and independent judgement in the performance of assigned tasks.

*Job Activities*

Participates in overall planning and policy making to provide effective and uniform personnel services.
Communicates policy through organizational level by bulletins, meetings, and personal contact.
Interviews applicants, evaluates qualifications, classifies applications.
Recruits and screens applicants to fill vacancies and reviews applications of qualified persons.
Confers with supervisors on personnel matters, including placement problems, retention or release of probationary employees, transfers, demotions, and dismissals of permanent employees.
Supervises administration of tests.
Initiates personnel training activities and coordinates these activities with work of officials and supervisors.
Establishes effective service rating system, trains unit supervisors in making employee evaluations.
Maintains employee personnel files.
Supervises a group of employees directly and through subordinates.
Performs related work as assigned.

*General Qualifications and Requirements*

Experience and Training
    Should have considerable experience in area of HRM administration. Six-year minimum.
Education
    Graduation from a four-year college or university program with major work in human resources, business administration, or industrial psychology.
Knowledge, Skills, and Abilities
    Considerable knowledge of principles and practices of HRM selection and assignment of personnel; job evaluation.
Responsibility
    Supervises a department of three HRM professionals, one clerk, and one administrative assistant.

---

job effectively. It evolves from the job description. The key difference is that the job description describes factors about the job itself, while the job specification describes factors about the person who might best fit the job. The job specification helps to provide focus for the recruiting and selection of new employees. It is also useful for making job assignments for current employees, and for designing training programs.

In preparing a job specification it is necessary to resist the temptation to draft it as if it were describing the present incumbent. If the person presently doing the job has a degree in civil engineering, it is natural, but may be entirely wrong, to require that specific degree for future employees. Sober reflection may reveal that another field of engineering, or even a natural science, might prepare someone to do the job just as well.

The second hazard to be avoided is to specify a longer period of experience than may be justified. If the present incumbent has had ten years of experience, it might seem that it would take ten years for someone else to perform as well. The fallacy of this assumption is shown when it is realized that the present incumbent did not have that much experience when first on that job, yet apparently was able to perform satisfactorily. It even might be found that someone with only two years of experience, and consequently with a more recent formal education, would be more up to date on recent developments in the field than the present incumbent.

The third potential pitfall is to make the job specification too rigid. It is often better to state that certain levels of education, experience, and skills are *desirable* rather than required. Where appropriate, individual assessment of the candidate may indicate that a lesser level is acceptable if other attributes compensate for the apparent lack. The penalty for overspecification, and for rigid adherence to "paper" qualifications, is that the organization unwittingly may reject candidates who otherwise would be perfectly competent but whose résumés lack the specified qualifications.

## Job Design

**job design**
The tasks required to complete the job, including how it relates to other jobs.

After job analyses have been conducted and job descriptions and job specifications have been prepared, an organization can use this information to design and redesign jobs. **Job design** is the process of describing jobs and arranging their interrelationships. Its purpose is to structure each job element and task in ways that increase both efficiency and effectiveness. One function of job design is to attempt to differentiate essential tasks from tasks that may have been added in the past but are no longer essential. Over time, almost all jobs will acquire by accretion some minor tasks that need not be done, but that are done because of habit or because of the particular interests of the person who holds the job. A common example is the reports that are generated within certain jobs and then circulated widely, but that are of interest only to the persons who generate the reports.

Any change in one job likely will require complementary changes in other jobs. Consequently, it is seldom effective to consider the design of a single job without concurrently considering the design of several related jobs. Job design may entail any or all of several related concepts: job specialization, job rotation, job enlargement, and job enrichment, each of which will be described in the following sections.

### Job Specialization

**job specialization**
Assigning to one job a small number of different tasks, which will be repeated.

**Job specialization** is a logical outgrowth of the theories advanced nearly a century ago by Frederick W. Taylor. Jobs are designed so that each employee becomes a specialist in performing a limited number of different tasks. According to Taylor, this should permit the employee to learn and practise the most efficient way to do those few tasks, without having to learn any other tasks. The ultimate in job specialization would be that of a worker on an assembly line who tightens one particular screw on each of thousands of items produced each day.

The disadvantage of job specialization, even when not carried to such an extreme, is that there is no variety in the work and little opportunity for discretion or innovation. In such a situation, employees are likely to become bored and careless, leading to decreased productivity and quality.

## Management in the Real World    8-1

### Job Design: Reflections by Philip Crosby

My first job that let me move around the building was as a reliability engineer in a missile assembly area where I learned that the way to enjoy a job, and be considered useful at the same time, was to adjust the job so I would be comfortable with the things that interested me and I would be of the most value to the organization. I had discovered that most jobs are described by people who never actually perform them and have no idea of the reality involved. The layout of my job was to investigate problems found by the inspection and test functions during assembly and then classify the incidents as to seriousness, cause, and responsibility. With a code system I filled out these determinations on the bottom of a defect report. Then I was supposed to feed it to my IBM punch card system (obviously, this was a while ago) and go find another problem. However, I soon determined that nothing happened to this information after it went into the system except to be produced as a long, very heavy report for management to ignore.

So I began going to see the department I had determined to be responsible for causing the problem. This was pretty much limited to engineering, production, purchasing, marketing, and quality. Now and then the navy, our customer, was the villain. There was always enough blame to go around.

When I visited them at the senior levels (although I certainly was not senior), I showed them the problem and asked what they wanted to do about it. I offered to help them gather information or take action or both. They were always pleased with the offer and usually were surprised that the situation existed after all. I learned a great deal by participating in their analysis and evaluation. They assumed that I already knew as much as they did so they let me in on everything.

The result of all this was that we routinely began to get rapid corrective action that actually eliminated the problems. I began to publish a regular list of problems and the actions taken. Everyone wanted to be listed on the page that said the action was completed. The part of my job involved with causing this action to happen probably took 5 percent of my time. However, without that time investment, I would have just been another in a long line of frustrated trouble shooters. No action ever came out of that list of problems published by the card machine.

The result of it all was that I was promoted to another job where I could help others work in the same way. I immediately redesigned that job to make it more effective and interesting. All this was done by doing; there were no corrections made on paper.

Jobs need not be defined so that they are limited as soon as they brush up against something else. It is reasonable to encourage overlap and innovation as long as the effect is to help the process move towards success. Most jobs are laid out to be too small; none that I ever saw were too big. The more unimportant they are, the longer the description of their content.

## Job Rotation

**job rotation**
Systematically moving employees from job to job.

In an effort to reduce employee boredom, some organizations practise systematic, planned **job rotation**.[9] In this plan, employees are moved from one job to another, sometimes on a fixed schedule and at other times as work loads and employee preferences dictate. Job rotation increases job range by introducing employees to more different jobs and consequently to more tasks. For instance, in a machine shop an employee may work on a turret lathe one week, conduct stress tests the next week, and operate a drill press in the third week.

The major limitation with this form of job rotation is that it does little to change the nature of the work itself. In the example given, the employee works on different machines that require different technical skills. Nevertheless, those skills are closely

*Job rotation helps this retail clerk avoid boredom, and also ensures that several employees are trained for each job to cover for emergencies and vacancies.*

related and the thought processes involved are quite similar. Rotation among a broader range of tasks may reduce the boredom factor, but probably will increase the time and cost required for training. These disadvantages may be offset by the gains derived from ensuring that more than one person is completely familiar with every task so that the organization does not face a crisis when a specialized employee is absent or leaves the job entirely. This advantage is especially important in a small organization, where the departure of a single individual may leave a gap in tasks with which no one else is completely familiar.

Because of its possible disadvantages and the difficulty of coordinating the rotations of several employees, job rotation is not used widely by itself, but is often coupled with other approaches or applied only when a particular employee shows signs of needing a change.

## Job Enlargement

In a study of mass production jobs in auto assembly plants, researchers found that employees were dissatisfied with their highly specialized and repetitive tasks.[10] Reflecting this fact, employers started experimenting with **job enlargement**. In this approach, the number of tasks assigned to an employee is increased, broadening the range of the job and offering variety. For example, if there are eight tasks to be applied to 100 items a day, the original job design might provide that each of eight employees would perform one of the tasks for all 100 items. Job enlargement might change the assignment so that the eight employees are divided into four pairs, with each pair performing all eight tasks on 25 items a day. While job rotation involves moving employees from one job or task to another, job enlargement seeks to increase job satisfaction by increasing the number of tasks each employee performs. Job enlargement offers most of the same advantages and disadvantages as job rotation. However, if job enlargement simply results in an employee doing four boring jobs instead of one, there will be little benefit. But if job enlargement is carefully planned, it can show positive results.

**job enlargement**
Increasing the number and variety of tasks assigned to a job.

## Job Enrichment

Much attention has been directed towards changing jobs in more meaningful ways than is accomplished by job rotation or job enlargement. The basic idea is that employees are motivated by jobs that increase their responsibility and feelings of self-worth.[11] **Job enrichment** attempts to give non-managerial employees more control of their activities, thus addressing their needs for growth, recognition, and responsibility. This broadening of responsibility is often described as employee empowerment, which is helpful in some circumstances and in other situations less so.[12] Empowerment will be discussed in greater detail in Chapter 9.

Job enrichment may increase not only the job range or number of tasks performed, but also the job depth by giving employees more opportunity to exercise discretion over their work. In an effort to make the work as interesting as possible, managers should look at the design of jobs from the standpoint of the non-managerial employees, rather than solely from their own perspective.[13] Usually when thought is given to the question, managers find that they can provide learning opportunities, give employees more control over resources and tasks, and let them schedule their own work within broad

**job enrichment**
Giving employees more control over their work to make it more interesting and address their needs for growth, recognition, and a sense of achievement.

parameters. These are all facets of job redesign. Attention can be focused on these goals by measures such as that taken by Abitibi-Price, which announced in a recent annual report that one of its goals was to achieve a superior level of employee relations through just such means.

In any approach to job enrichment, managers should think first of the personal and work outcomes that they hope would result from the enrichment. Then they should consider the psychological and emotional states that are most likely to cause the employees to reach those outcomes. The third step, working backwards, is to review the core dimensions of the jobs and consider what might be done to provide the desirable results. These important core dimensions are reflected in Exhibit 8-7 and include:

- *Skill variety*: The extent to which the job requires a variety of different activities in carrying out the work, involving a number of an individual's skills and talents;
- *Task identity*: The extent to which the job requires completion of a "whole" and identifiable piece of work, that is, by doing a job from beginning to end with an identifiable outcome;
- *Task significance*: The extent to which the job is seen to have a substantial impact on other people's lives or work, whether in the immediate organization or in the external environment;

**Exhibit 8-7**   *Job Characteristics and Expected Outcomes*

| Core Job Dimensions | Critical Psychological States | Personal and Work Outcomes |
|---|---|---|
| Skill Variety<br>Task Identity<br>Task Significance | Experienced Meaningfulness of Work | High Internal Work Motivation |
| Autonomy | Experienced Responsibility for Outcomes of Work | High-Quality Work Performance<br><br>High Satisfaction with Work |
| Feedback | Knowledge of Actual Results of Work Activities | Low Absenteeism and Turnover |
| | Strength of Employees' Need for Growth | |

Source: Adapted from J. Richard Hackman and R. G. Oldham, "Motivation through the Design of Work: Test of a Theory." *Organizational Behavior and Human Performance,* August 1976, p. 256.

- *Autonomy*: The extent to which the job provides substantial freedom, independence, and discretion to the individual in scheduling work and in determining the procedures to be used in carrying it out; and
- *Feedback*: The extent to which carrying out work activities required by the job results in individuals obtaining direct and clear information about the effectiveness of their performance.

As these core dimensions are reflected in a job Richard Hackman and Greg Oldham predict that employees will experience three critical psychological states that are necessary for motivation and satisfaction:[14]

1. *Experienced meaningfulness*: The extent to which jobholders experience work as important, valuable, and worthwhile;
2. *Experienced responsibility*: The extent to which jobholders feel personally responsible and accountable for the results of their work; and
3. *Knowledge of results*: Jobholders' understanding of how effectively they are performing their jobs.

To the extent that these three perceptions are encouraged, the organization is likely to find higher motivation, improved performance, and enhanced satisfaction. When these factors improve, absenteeism and turnover probably will decrease.[15]

The final part of the Hackman-Oldham model, called employee growth-need strength, suggests that people with a strong need to grow and expand their potential are expected to respond more strongly to the core job dimensions than those with low growth-need strength. For example, job enrichment probably will have less effect on a person who does not have a strong need for personal growth than on a person who values personal growth.

Job enrichment may require that the employee have and use a higher level of skills than before. Thus, some employees may not be able to perform the enriched job, especially without additional training. And the organization may need to adjust its compensation rates for the enriched job because of the higher skill levels required.[16]

Before beginning a job enrichment effort, managers should gain a thorough understanding of the job in question. Accurate job descriptions and job specifications can facilitate greatly in this process. After studying them it may be found that enrichment is not feasible due to costs or other technological constraints. Second, individual preferences about enriched work should be considered. Managers have to ascertain whether employees want their work to be enriched. If they do not, whatever the reasons, any attempt to force enrichment on them will be met with resistance.

## Flextime

**flextime**
A plan in which employees can set their own work hours, within limits set by management.

Another approach to redesigning jobs lets employees have input in establishing their work schedules. **Flextime** is a practice that allows employees to select starting and quitting times within parameters set by management.[17] These parameters typically provide that everyone must work during peak periods of the work day, such as between 10 a.m. and 3 p.m. As long as those core times are covered, one person might choose a work day that begins at 8 a.m. and ends at 4 p.m., while another might start working at 10 a.m. and finish at 6 p.m. Such flexibility permits employees to fit their working hours to their other personal commitments. It may provide the organization with a collateral benefit. It many cases it results in the organization being staffed from an earlier to a later hour than would be feasible if all employees worked the same hours. Flextime is most often authorized for positions such as bank tellers, data entry clerks, lab technicians, scientists and engineers, and nurses. The policy is difficult to implement in organizations in which

*Communicating by computer and modem with the office, employees can avoid commuter time and stress by working at home.*

employees work as teams if the work of the group depends on a specific individual working at a coordinated time. In other situations, even if employees are organized in teams, it may be possible for the various members of a team to work at slightly different hours, as long as the temporary absence of one member does not impede the work of others.

Although extensive research on the effects of flextime has not been done, preliminary findings suggest that usually it is well received by employees, and that most employers who have experimented with it intend to continue to offer it. In one study, more than half of the companies surveyed reported improvements such as increased productivity, lower labour costs, and higher morale.[18] Another study found that flextime reduces paid absences, idle time, and overtime pay.[19] Yet another study reported that satisfaction with work schedules and interactions improved significantly for both managers and non-managers.[20] Furthermore, companies are finding that flextime builds loyalty, and that employees are committed to making flextime work.[21]

One disadvantage is that, with the institution of flextime, managers and supervisors must extend their work day at both ends; otherwise, some employees who start early or leave late will be working with less or even no supervision for part of the work day. This difficulty may be alleviated at least in part by employees assuming greater personal responsibility in order to make the flextime system work.

## Telecommuting

**telecommuting**
Doing work at home or in other locations but staying in communication with the workplace and other employees through networks, computers, and modems.

A recent development, made possible by the widespread availability of personal computers and modems, is **telecommuting**.[22] Telecommuting employees work part-time or even full-time at home or on the road, using computers and modems to connect with data banks in the office and to communicate with their colleagues, wherever they may be.[23] Full-time telecommuting generally is limited to a few positions within the computing industry and to other jobs where work output can be monitored readily. In other work situations, many managers are finding that an imaginative mix of telecommuting, flextime, and regular working hours can provide desirable flexibility, with positive effects on employee morale and productivity, leading to greater competitiveness for the organization. There has been increasing recognition that organizations' increasing dependence on the talents and efforts of women will result in some new competitive pressures. The demand for flextime schedules inevitably will increase to allow for child care, elder care, and other family responsibilities[24] that, despite relatively recent changes in family roles, still fall more heavily on women than on men.

## Recruitment

**recruitment**
Searching for and selecting suitably qualified and motivated candidates for positions within the organization.

In a large organization, recruiting new employees is an ongoing task. Even in a small organization new employees may have to be recruited from time to time, if only to meet the demands of growth in work volume. In addition, there is usually some turnover among existing staff, so new employees have to be recruited as replacements. In any organization, then, managers periodically are required to seek, select, attract and orient new employees. The strength of the organization and its ability to function competitively are dependent to a large extent on the quality of its employees. Consequently, **recruitment** is a critical aspect of almost any managerial task. Even in an organization that maintains a professional HR manager or department, other managers still must take part in the selection process and are primarily responsible for orientation and some aspects of training. In an organization in which recruitment is decentralized, each manager must carry the whole burden of recruiting. In these cases, because of the pressures of routine day-to-day responsibilities and the desire not to be distracted from what the managers see as their primary duties, many functional managers tend to spend too little time and energy on employee selection, hurrying the process in order to fill perceived vacancies. It is a common fallacy for functional managers to hope to put behind them what they see as intrusions in their "real" work. The folly of this approach is often evident later, when it becomes apparent that the employees who were chosen were not best for the jobs.

**recruitment plan**
A systematic description of the need for recruitment and how, when, and by whom it will be accomplished.

When new employees must be recruited, either to replace departing employees or to fill newly created positions, the first step is to create a **recruitment plan.** This plan starts with job analysis and the creation of, or review of, a job description. If there is no collective agreement that mandates a certain wage or salary level, the range of compensation for the position must be determined. This is an ideal time to consider job redesign. Any change in job scope or depth that seems desirable is obviously easier to implement at the time a new employee takes the position than when someone who is already in the position has to be persuaded to support the change and then be trained in new ways. Furthermore, if the job is to be changed materially, this may mean that managers should seek new employees who have different skills and characteristics than present employees.

The next step in the recruitment plan is to consider from what sources suitable applicants might be attracted, and how to reach those sources. The recruitment plan next sets out what steps will be taken in the search process, who will screen and interview, and who will make the final selection. It is crucial at this time also to make a tentative decision about the expected need for job training, what its purposes will be, and who will conduct it. Finally, start dates and completion dates should be assigned to each planned step. The timetable must allow for the fact that in most cases some of these steps will depend on managers who will have to find time within what are already full-time duties.

Experience has shown that these steps, which seem so obvious on an intellectual basis, are often carried out hurriedly and casually, if not omitted altogether. The result of this inattention is that often inappropriate employees are recruited, and management fails to inculcate in them the job requirements and the culture of the organization. All too often the result is recurring dissatisfaction with new employees and the need for considerable disciplinary action and even dismissal, so that the cycle has to be repeated once again, perhaps with no better results.

## Sources of Candidates

After completion of the recruitment plan, a critical first step in the recruitment process is to decide where and how suitable candidates might be found. In a small organization, it is often fruitful to ask current employees for suggestions as to potential candidates. This has the merit of reassuring employees that are they seen by managers as valuable parts of the organization. Equally important, current employees know the organization's culture, and are likely to suggest acquaintances who would fit the culture. A disadvantage is that if too many friends form a clique within the organization, that clique may become a self-supporting pressure group. If that occurs, discipline applied to one member of the group may affect the others adversely. There also is a temptation for members of the tightly knit group to cover for each other's mistakes and inadequacies. Being aware of these possibilities helps the manager to counteract their potentially negative effects and to develop a responsible culture in which the informal groups function in positive rather than negative ways.

job posting
Making available to all employees written notice of job vacancies within the organization to permit those interested to apply for the positions.

Another internal source is tapped by **job posting**. An increasing number of organizations follow a policy that every vacancy that management intends to fill be described in a notice that is posted where employees can see it. This permits current employees to apply for the vacant position before the competition is opened to outsiders. Employees see this as giving them a fair opportunity for advancement, or for change if they are beginning to get bored with their present job assignments. Managers recognize this element of fairness, and also recognize that current employees may have untapped talents that are not being used in their current positions.

If the position requires special skills or education, the institutions that provide those skills or education may be good sources of potential candidates. Wise HR managers, and many forward-looking functional managers, make it a point to maintain good personal relations with instructors and administrators in the colleges, institutes, and universities that produce graduates of particular interest to the organization. Some organizations volunteer to employ students enrolled in cooperative programs on their work terms. This is a socially responsible act on the part of the organization, as it facilitates the education and training of young people. Moreover, it gives the organization an opportunity to screen potential candidates for the future, because they can observe their performance in the actual workplace.

Although professional journals and magazines have fairly long lead times between placing an ad and its publication, those ads can be productive sources of candidates in some relatively specialized or narrow fields of interest. Professional organizations in most major Canadian cities keep rosters of their members who may be seeking other employment, and some employment agencies specialize in specific types of positions. Recruitment through the Internet has been widely touted as a panacea but as yet has not fulfilled its potential. Tapping more widespread sources may include placing advertisements in local newspapers and listing vacancies with Canada Employment offices.

In published ads, a decision must be made as to whether to identify the company or to provide only a box number to which applicants are invited to send their résumés. Some organizations only use "blind ads" because an ad identified with the organization may attract hundreds of applicants, and it will be time-consuming to respond to each

*To fill key positions, organizations often retain executive search firms such as KPMG to broaden their areas of search and to screen potential candidates.*

applicant. It is believed that there is no need to respond if the company is not known to the applicant. On the other hand, if the organization has a reputation as being a good place to work, its identity may attract responses from highly qualified applicants who routinely disregard blind ads.

Commercial employment agencies and Canada Employment offices may be useful sources for some kinds of jobs, especially those requiring little skill or experience. At the other end of the spectrum are executive search agencies, who specialize in high-level managerial positions. The success of their efforts depends in large part on how well they have been familiarized with the culture of the recruiting organization and its expectations for the jobs in question. Executive search agencies, jocularly known as "headhunters," charge substantial fees, often in the neighbourhood of one year's salary for the targeted position. Used wisely, however, the cost may be a worthwhile investment.

In today's employment climate, a large number of fully qualified people are either unemployed or underemployed. Those seeking to better their prospects often deliver unsolicited résumés to employers who do not have any vacancies at the time. If the organization finds that it frequently recruits new employees, it is useful for each unsolicited résumé to be scanned briefly and, if it looks at all promising, retained for future reference when vacancies do occur.

## Selection

**Preliminary screening.**  There are two steps in the selection process: **screening**, and making the decision. In a well-planned recruitment process, the managers involved will screen résumés, weeding out applicants who are clearly unqualified or unsuitable for other reasons. For screening to be meaningful, it is essential for managers to have clearly in mind the criteria being sought, in terms of education and training, experience, personality characteristics, and particular skills. If the position under consideration involves communication skills, a number of résumés may be discarded because they are physically sloppy or show either carelessness or an inability to communicate effectively. Also, many managers will disregard résumés that appear to be designed for all-purpose use and that have not been tailored to the particular position or organization. Managers reason that they are not interested in an applicant who is not sufficiently motivated to find out about the position and the organization and adapt a résumé accordingly.

**screening**
Analyzing résumés and associated information to sort applicants and select those who appear most suitable for employment in the organization.

**Short list.**  After one or more cycles of screening, the bundle of résumés should have been reduced to a **short list**. This is a listing of the handful of applicants who appear most likely to be worth pursuing, bearing in mind that going further involves considerable time and management effort. At this point, it is a courtesy and good business practice to send letters to all who have submitted résumés but have not made the short list. The few organizations that take the time and effort to send a personalized but standard letter to all such applicants find that their reputation as a good place to work spreads, and may be of significant value in future recruiting efforts.

**short list**
The small number of preferred applicants who remain of interest to the organization after various stages of screening.

**Detailed analysis of résumés.**  The next step is careful analysis of the résumés remaining on the short list. These résumés are studied carefully in an attempt to learn salient

## What Managers Are Reading    8-1

### Working with Emotional Intelligence

In his trend-setting best-seller published in 1995, Daniel Goleman coined the term "emotional intelligence." Since then, several other authors have jumped on the bandwagon created by Goleman. Now Goleman has sought to reclaim recognition for his concept by expanding on his original theories. His first book focused primarily on students, but now he has applied the concepts to the workplace.

So, what is "emotional intelligence," or EQ? According to Goleman, it is the bundle of personal characteristics and behaviours that are commonly referred to as "people skills." Goleman lists self-awareness, self-confidence, and self-control as important qualities. He stresses the necessity of communicating effectively. A leader must demonstrate personal integrity and a high degree of commitment to what Goleman calls "organizational citizenship." A true leader, says Goleman, inspires and guides individuals and groups. To achieve top performance, a person cannot just excel in one or two of these skills, but must excel in a mix of them. Successful managers must work well with people, and with teams.

In arriving at the application of his EQ theories to the workplace, Goleman conducted studies at 121 companies, collecting job profiles that executives and other managers provided to describe qualities they believed were essential for excellence. He found that EQ skills were always predominant, and that technical and cognitive skills were much less important. Goleman's book contains enough anecdotal evidence from the companies that he identifies to lift EQ from the realm of the theoretical to the pragmatic and demonstrable.

The book makes an insightful analysis of the respective characteristics of women and men. Contrary to popular assumptions, Goleman finds that neither gender is superior to the other in terms of EQ. Instead, he identifies gender-specific areas within EQ, saying that women tend to be more adept in interpersonal relations, to be more self-aware, and to show more empathy. To balance these attributes, he finds that men tend to be more self-confident, to handle stress better, and to adapt to change more readily. He wisely avoids the nurture vs. nature controversy, and says that on balance, as far as EQ is concerned, there are far more similarities than differences between the genders.

Goleman argues that a high EQ contributes more to success than a high IQ. He illustrates this point even with such intellectually demanding positions as computer programming. There he says that the people who are ranked in the top 10 percent of EQ actually produce effective computer programs at a rate 320 percent greater than the average. Partly as a result of Goleman's original work, it is now widely recognized that, unlike IQ, which is thought not to change appreciably after adolescence, an individual's EQ may be greatly enhanced through conscious learning and experience—that is, through acquiring maturity. This finding provides encouragement to managers who aspire to succeed and to grow. It also may contribute to another of Goleman's requirements for outstanding success—optimism. If Goleman is correct that higher EQ can be learned and developed (and there is no reason to think that he is wrong), then why should anyone not do so?

Source: Daniel Goleman, *Working with Emotional Intelligence* (Toronto: Bantam Books, 1998).

features about the as-yet-unknown individuals who have submitted them. An attempt should be made to see how closely the applicant's qualifications fit those that are desired. Unexplained gaps in time should be highlighted for further investigation. After all, if a year is not accounted for, it would be useful to know why. The applicant may have been unemployed, backpacking around Southeast Asia, recovering from some personal trauma, working at a job before being fired for cause, or serving time in prison for embezzlement! Clearly, the explanation can affect the organization's decision. An unexplained time period is not necessarily a reason to eliminate the applicant from further consideration, but if left unexplained it could be a source of considerable embarrassment in the future.

**Checking references.** Opinion is divided as to whether references should be checked at this stage or only later in the recruiting process. One advantage of checking references at this stage is that, if they reveal disqualifying facts, an applicant can be dropped before further time is invested in interviews. And it should be noted that checking references at some stage is imperative in the light of many studies that have found that a large proportion of résumés contain some exaggerations, and that many include actual falsehoods.[25]

When checking references, specific facts may be verified, such as dates employed, titles held, and the wage or salary received. Because many people contacted fear potential lawsuits for defamation, they may decline to give much more than these bare facts. Although this may be a real risk in the United States, Canadian courts have recognized the benefit to the public of protecting those who give honest references that are not motivated by malice.

Even if the person contacted is reluctant to be forthcoming, a perceptive questioner can elicit valuable insights into an applicant's previous work habits, emotional stability, and ability to get along with co-workers and supervisors.[26] For instance, an applicant's former supervisor may hesitate to say that the applicant lacks skills, but the same information can be gained by asking open-ended questions that are not threatening. For example, a manager might ask: "If you were hiring this person for the position I have described, what kinds of training would you suggest?" Such a question is more likely to elicit an informative response than if the person was asked to comment directly on the applicant's weaknesses or deficiencies. Another useful question, even with a relatively cautious reference source, is, "Would *you* hire this person for the position I have described?" Even if they don't want to explain their reasons, most referees will answer this question frankly.

Often the current employer does not know of the applicant's intention to look for another job, and great embarrassment would result if that fact were to be revealed prematurely. Whether general reference checking is done at this stage or later, it is neither ethical nor fair to make any contact with an applicant's current employer without first warning the applicant. Also, any reference checking should be done on a confidential basis, after having warned the person of whom inquiries are being made that the applicant's name is to be held in strict confidence.

**Pre-interview contact.** Another useful screening device is pre-interview communication. The manager can telephone each person whose application has survived preliminary screenings. This is a good time to inquire about any gaps in the résumé, and to resolve any points that require clarification. This seemingly casual conversation, springing from one or more items in the résumé, will help the interviewer to infer some of the applicant's personal as well as work-related characteristics.

If the phone discussion reveals factors that diminish the attractiveness of the applicant, the contact can be closed with a polite statement such as, "We are pursuing several other attractive candidates and will get back to you within X days." The promised date for further communication should be chosen with care to ensure that it can be met. And, of course, that further communication must take place when promised.

If the phone discussion is fruitful, an appointment can be made for a face-to-face interview, which should be scheduled within a few days. If the applicant is employed, it is thoughtful to offer an appointment outside of normal business hours.

**Interview.** The interview should be held in the manager's office, not in a social setting. This emphasizes that the interview is a serious business activity, and not just a social occasion "to get to know each other better." If the interview is to be held outside of normal business hours, at least one responsible manager other than the interviewer should be very much in evidence, perhaps in an adjacent office with the door open. This precaution helps the applicant feel at ease, particularly if the applicant and interviewer are of opposite genders. It also helps to prevent later recriminations and false accusations alleging harassment.

The success of an interview is to a large extent dependent on the care with which the interviewer has prepared for it. It is essential to be completely familiar with the details of the job, the applicant's résumé, and the results of any pre-interview reference checking. Questions should be carefully planned and tailored to each applicant, although the interview itself should flow naturally rather than following a rigid format. It is the interviewer's responsibility to make sure that the interview elicits as much relevant information as possible. Within this constraint, the applicant's comments and responses to the interviewer's questions largely will determine the *order* of topics covered and the emphasis given to each. The most skilled interviewers are at all times in unobtrusive but definite control of events. Although the most informative interviews are those in which the tone is friendly and welcoming, it always must be remembered that the purpose of the interview is to provide the basis for a *decision* (hire or not hire) that can have a serious impact on the applicant as well as the organization, perhaps for many years to come. And since the immediate purpose is to find out as much relevant information as possible, the interviewer should talk less than half as much as the applicant, guiding the interview by occasional questions and non-judgemental responses but concentrating on listening closely.

If the interview goes well, it should end with the interviewer briefly providing further details about the job. These details include what will be expected if the applicant is hired, a description of the organization's history and culture, and a realistic prediction of the future prospects both for the job and for the organization. In closing, the interviewer should explain the next steps in the selection process and their expected timing. It is important for the manager to curb any tendency to oversell, as any material misrepresentation may give rise to a later lawsuit. Furthermore, if the applicant needs to be enticed by distorting facts, it is not in the interest of either the applicant or the organization to proceed further.

As in all stages of the recruitment process, immediately after the interview closes, the interviewer should make detailed notes of the information elicited. It is particularly important to make note of any commitments made, as well as points that should be followed up. The notes should include the impressions the interviewer had of the applicant's suitability for the job, together with the reasons for these impressions.

**Group interviews.** Some organizations arrange for applicants to be interviewed in a single session by several managers (and possibly by some employees who would be working with the applicant if chosen). The rationale for this procedure is that various viewpoints will be represented. The hazard, however, is that, as with any exercise in group dynamics, one member of the interviewing group may dominate the session and the outcome will reflect that person's views rather than a true consensus of the group. A second difficulty is that since the group as a whole is supposed to make the hiring decision, no one individual is accountable, and each may take a somewhat casual attitude towards following up on any areas of discomfort. Third, in a group there is a tendency to take the "least common denominator" approach. When this occurs, a particular applicant may offend or at least appear inadequate to one member of the group. A second applicant may have the same effect on another member of the group, and so on, until one applicant is found who doesn't offend any of interviewers. In such a circumstance, all too often the group will settle for the applicant who has managed to avoid having a negative effect on any of the interviewers. The outcome may be that the group settles for a colourless, unassertive person and rejects other applicants who might have been less complaisant but a superior choice overall.

The tension between the need for group involvement and acceptance and the hazards of group interviewing may be partially resolved by having the short-list applicants go through a second round of interviews after having had an initial screening interview with a single interviewer. In this second round, the applicant meets in a series of one-on-one interviews with several of the organization's members. Each of the interviewers writes a report on the applicant and these reports are consolidated and reflected as appropriate in the final decision, which is made by the lead interviewer.

## Discrimination

**discrimination**
Making decisions or taking actions based on an individual's personal characteristics that do not directly impinge on fitness for a job.

Selection, hiring, and management of personnel must be free from **discrimination** on certain prohibited grounds. The Canadian Human Rights Act (which governs federally regulated organizations such as banks and airlines) and the various provincial and territorial human rights codes list the prohibited grounds for activities within their respective jurisdictions. All prohibit discrimination on the grounds of race or colour, marital status, or sex. Most prohibit discrimination on the basis of national origin, religion, or creed, or because of mental or physical disabilities that do not relate to job requirements. (For example, it would not be a violation of the law to reject an applicant confined to a wheelchair if the job required the employee to run up and down ladders, but it would be a violation if the job were one that could be done at a desk, even though it might mean that the employer would have to expend money to provide wheelchair access.) An increasing number of jurisdictions prohibit discrimination on the grounds of sexual orientation. Discrimination on the basis of age is prohibited in most jurisdictions. For this purpose, the definitions of age differ considerably, with typical legislation prohibiting discrimination only against those between the ages of 18 or 19 and 65.

Part of the HR manager's responsibility is to become and remain conversant with the exact provisions of the act or acts that pertain to the particular organization. Then care must be taken to ensure that application forms and other documentation comply with the relevant statutes. No application or other pre-employment form can ask questions that might reveal whether the applicant falls within a group against whose members discrimination is prohibited.

More difficult, but equally important, is monitoring matters such as wage and salary levels and promotions and job assignments to ensure that other managers' actions do not contravene the legal requirements. Training programs for managers and supervisors are almost essential to ensure that they understand the requirements and are committed to adhering to

*With the increasing diversity in the workforce, old patterns of segregation are being replaced not only because of federal, provincial, and territorial human rights codes, but also because managers are learning that is good business.*

them precisely. Of course, the thrust of such programs is to create and sustain the realization that the statutory provisions only set a threshold below which the organization cannot trespass, but that in the interests of having a harmonious and productive workplace, discrimination of any sort must be avoided.

## Sexual Harassment

**sexual harassment**
Any act, word, gesture, or situation that diminishes an individual's sexual dignity or integrity.

Of increasing concern to managers is the issue of **sexual harassment.** Canadian courts, up to and including the Supreme Court of Canada, have struggled for a number of years to arrive at a satisfactory definition of sexual harassment that protects the interests both of the alleged harasser and of the person alleging harassment. One definition that is coming to be applied frequently, either expressly or implicitly, is that sexual harassment consists of any words, acts, gestures, or situations that diminish the sexual dignity or integrity of any person. Although most sexual harassment is by males of females, the reverse can be true, as can that of males by males and females by females. The extent to which sexual harassment is a ground for dismissal of the offending employee(s) is a matter still not clearly settled by the courts. There is no question, however, that when sexual harassment has been condoned or overlooked, the employer and often the managers involved may be the subject of civil suits.[27]

An aspect of sexual harassment that has been more prevalent than originally suspected is what was formerly described by the term *stalking*, a term that is still in common usage. Since a 1994 amendment to the Canadian Criminal Code, this offence has been properly referred to as *criminal harassment.* Criminal penalties are provided for anyone convicted of persistent, pressing, and unwanted attention to an individual, whether through letters, phone calls, following, or other physical presence. The dividing line between acceptable attention and criminal harassment occurs when the person being pursued becomes frightened.[28] Experts report that although some 4200 cases were reported in Canada in 1995, the number is "just the tip of the iceberg." They also report that stalking reflects an obsession on the part of the stalker, and that even a prison sentence does not change the stalker's behaviour.[29]

Often it is at work that the stalker first became aware of the targeted person, and the stalking commenced thereafter. Even though the stalking takes place outside of working hours and away from the workplace, the employer may be held liable if there was any way that the unwanted attention could have been noticed and corrective action could have been taken. This is particularly true if the person being stalked made even an informal complaint and the managers did little to correct the situation.

Some observers have suggested that normal social relations are inhibited by the everpresent threat of sexual harassment complaints. Whether this concern is valid may depend largely on one's definition of what constitutes "normal." The essence of the sexual harassment offence is that the alleged harasser *knew* or *ought to have known* that the behaviour was *unwelcome.* If the person offended by the behaviour has previously made it known that it is unwelcome, then clearly the alleged harasser *knew* that it should not occur. The courts have also held that if the behaviour is such that anyone in the situation *should* have realized that it would be unwelcome, then it also constitutes harassment.

There are at least three reasons why managers should be alert to possible situations that might constitute harassment, whether of a sexual nature or otherwise. One is that any harassment can be highly damaging to employee morale, and as has been discussed, lowered morale can seriously impair the organization's competitiveness, and even its chances for survival in the competitive marketplace. A second reason is that if harassment occurs in the workplace or as a result of contacts that were made in the workplace, the employer may be held liable vicariously. Fines, judgments in civil suits, orders to reinstate and recompense harassment victims, and highly unfavourable publicity all may follow an organization's inattention to harassment situations. In addition, as was discussed in Chapter 2, an organization and its employees have an ethical obligation to promote working conditions, and conditions in society as a whole, that are conducive to quality of life for everyone.

## Training and Development

**employee training**
An organized program in which employees are provided with information, concepts, and skills that the organization believes will help them to become more effective in their jobs, or in jobs to which they may later be assigned.

Training and development of human resources involve change: change in skills, knowledge, attitudes, and behaviour. To remain competitive, changes in these areas are needed. In some fields such as computer technology, the need for almost constant change seems obvious, just to keep up with innovations constantly being announced. In areas such as the relationships within an organization, the need for change is not as widely publicized, but is nonetheless equally important. Chapter 9 is devoted to managing change, but an important element falls within the purview of HRM—the need for training and development. Little change is likely to occur if employees simply continue to think and act as they have always done. Leading them to adopt new attitudes and new ways of thinking, as well as new ways of acting, usually requires not only skilled leadership but also intentional training.

The responsibility for planning and coordinating training programs within an organization often falls to the HR managers. Managers of functional departments are usually best qualified to train employees in the tasks and technical skills required within their respective departments. Even in these areas, however, HR staff members can be helpful in designing and presenting training programs. In the more general areas, such as problem solving, team building, and interpersonal relations, the special expertise of HR professionals is needed. In a large corporation these skills probably can be found within the corporation. For a smaller organization, much the same result can be obtained by sending employees to seminars and short courses offered by educational institutions and commercial ventures.

A well-designed training program reflects four fundamental decisions. First, decisions must be made about the program's objectives. These objectives will be based either on perceived inadequacies in the present situation or on further needs that will arise with the implementation of changes that are planned.[30] Part of this decision includes identifying the employees who may profit from the proposed training. Obviously, even the best-designed training program will fail if the employees involved participate only because they are ordered to do so. Therefore, if employees do not show an active interest in training pro-

*In an effective organization, people who have many years of experience welcome the opportunity, and are encouraged by management, to offer mentoring to younger people, helping them to expand their knowledge and enhance their jobs.*

grams, it is first necessary to explain to them how the programs will benefit them. This may take the form of opportunities for advancement or wage increases, or may be more indirect in the form of enhancing satisfaction for jobs well done.

The second decision is determining what training techniques and approaches might be the most effective, given the trainees who will be involved and topics to be covered. The third decision is who will best be able to provide the training. Often the ideal is a cooperative blend of specialists in the functional field, assisted and guided by training specialists whose skills lie in the disciplines of course design, presentation, and group dynamics. Finally, the training plan should include definite decisions as to how results will be evaluated and how feedback will be provided to assist in the design and presentation of future training programs.

**career development plan**
An individualized outline of training, experience, and possibly education designed to facilitate an employee's growth and enhance opportunities for advancement.

Closely allied with training programs is the development of **career development plans** for key individuals. As has been discussed in several other parts of this text, employee boredom almost inevitably reduces productivity, and the boredom usually comes from having had little change in tasks or other dimensions of work. It is in the employer's interest, as well as that of the employees, to provide opportunities for change and growth. A systematic career development plan may contribute to this desirable objective.[31]

## *Management in the Real World*   8-2

### Human Resource Development in Japan

Human resource development in Japan consists of four principal elements. Managers in many Japanese companies believe that the most important element is on-the-job training (OJT).

The second element is a focus on intellectual skills—the know-how to deal with unusual situations such as changes in or problems with production. For example, if a machine is producing defective parts, workers must have sufficient reasoning skills and knowledge to rectify the problem. Japanese manufacturing efficiency is based on production workers with intellectual skills similar to those of production engineers.

Nissan Motors, for example, has gained a reputation for having the most customer-oriented dealers of all auto manufacturers. The company not only trains longer than any other car maker, but insists that every dealer employee—including clerks and secretaries—attend its training. The company's six-day "boot camp" for dealers is heavy on preparing people intellectually for the challenges of selling cars.

The third element of Japanese human resource development is the use of a variety of OJT experiences coupled with short, intensive, off-the-job training (off-JT) to develop necessary skills. Workers gain experience in two to three dozen positions within a cluster of related workshops or work sites.

This broad OJT allows workers to become familiar with a variety of machinery and production methods, and it provides a basis for developing vital intellectual skills.

Theory-oriented off-JT helps workers develop the ability to theorize about and systematize their on-the-job experiences. Japanese workers participate in short (two days to one week) off-JT experiences inserted between OJT every few years.

On a special test track in its training boot camp, Nissan puts everyone behind the wheel of the Infiniti cars they will be selling. For three days participants swoop around the track. They also drive competitors' cars, giving them a chance to learn the difference between how the cars "feel."

The fourth element of human resource development in Japan is fair assessment of skill development and fair compensation. If two workers are doing the same job but one is better at problem solving, that person is compensated accordingly.

Source: Adapted from Kazuo Koike, "Human Resource Development in the Private Sector in Japan," *Workforce Quality: Perspectives from the U.S. and Japan* (International Symposium Report, U.S. Dept. of Labor, 1991): 12-13; and Larry Armstrong, "The Customer as Honored Guest," *Business Week* (October 25, 1991): 104.

Career development plans assess an individual's present skills and abilities and compare them with those required for the job. Then consideration is given to the areas of growth that might be indicated by this assessment. A tentative plan is prepared, listing steps that might be taken to offer growth in various areas, and the timing that might be involved. Various aspects may be included: job enlargement, job rotation, reassignment, in-house training, and external training. Then the tentative plan is discussed with the employee. It is stressed that the plan is only a suggestion, but that it is one that the employer is prepared to support financially and through paid time off if the employee wishes to pursue all or part of it. As a result of these discussions, the employee and employer enter into an informal compact that whatever plan has been agreed upon between them will be commenced, but that at any time the employee may elect to defer or cancel any remaining part of the plan.

Preparing and particularly implementing career development plans requires a heavy commitment of time, cost, and likely disruption of work schedules. Consequently, most organizations that prepare detailed formal plans limit their availability to middle and upper managers. On a scaled-down model, however, similar plans should be effective in regard to non-managerial employees, even in small organizations.

## Performance Evaluation

**performance evaluation**
A formal, systematic appraisal of the qualitative and quantitative aspects of an employee's performance.

**Performance evaluation** is the systematic review of individual job-relevant strengths and weaknesses, as shown by the individual's performance on the job. It is important that the evaluation be related solely to performance, rather than to irrelevant personal characteristics, real or imagined. It is tempting for managers to rate highly those whose lifestyles and personal attributes mirror those of the manager, and to rate less highly those who are seen as being *different*. The possibility of personal bias has caused some researchers, and many employees and employee representatives, to oppose any form of performance evaluation.[32] If that opposition were to be carried to its ultimate conclusion, it would be impossible to reward performance that managers see as good, or to sanction performance that they see as unacceptable. This could remove most of the incentive to perform well, to everyone's ultimate disadvantage.

Another approach has been to try to reduce the extent to which subjectivity enters the appraisal process, and to substitute an objective measure as well. Some organizations have substituted appraisal by a committee consisting of the employee's immediate supervisor and two or three other supervisors at the same level who have had an opportunity to observe the performance being evaluated.[33] Others have combined managerial evaluation with some form of peer evaluation. And still others have provided for employees to evaluate their supervisors' performance. In a study published by Royal Bank and York University, it was reported that four-fifths of the 193 employees surveyed said that they believed their employers cared about customers, but that only half thought they cared about their employees.[34]

**graphic rating scale**
A listing of performance characteristics and behaviours that is used to evaluate numerically the performance of an employee and arrive at a total that is intended to rate that performance in terms of value to the organization.

Some organizations have used a matrix of desired performances, such as quality and quantity of work output, the extent to which supervision is required, reliability of attendance, and ability to get along well with managers and co-workers. These qualities are listed on a **graphic rating scale** and raters are asked to assign numbers, perhaps ranging from one to five, for each of the aspects on the form. The employee's total is compared with totals for other employees, and the employees' performance ratings are ranked.

The numeric ratings suggest an objectivity that may be illusory.[35] First, a rater's biases are just as likely to be reflected in the numbers that rater assigns as in any other form of evaluation. Perhaps more importantly, the weighting assigned to each category of performance may predetermine the outcome for an employee, without necessarily reflecting the employee's value to the organization. For example, one employee might do excellent work and be rated 5 (high) on quality of work, but having missed one day every month receive only 1 (low) on attendance. In contrast, another employee may consistently turn out work that has to be rejected, so is rated 1 on quality, but has never missed a day of work so rates 5 on attendance. They will have identical totals of 6 (considering only these two qualities for the purposes of this example). Clearly, their value to the organization is not equal, so the "objective" measure fails to accomplish its purpose. Nevertheless, this type of rating is probably the most commonly used in Canadian organizations today.

Another approach is to have the raters for a group of employees apply a priority **ranking** that is intended to reveal which employees are the best performers and which are the least satisfactory. Experience has shown, however, that different raters subconsciously apply different values to different aspects of performance. This is further complicated by the fact that the performance of an employee is a composite of a large number of factors, which the raters have difficulty in evaluating and keeping in mind while doing the ranking.

Some evaluation plans make use of the **descriptive essay**. In this method, each rater writes a brief statement of each employee's strengths and weaknesses. Some organizations require each rater to comment on a specified list of qualities; others leave the choice of topics to the raters. The essays are difficult to compare because their usefulness depends so much on the rater's writing skill and style. They also may differ because different raters use the same words to convey different meanings. Some raters will use the term *average* to describe the level of behaviour that is generally expected, while others will use the term in a critical sense, as being less than completely satisfactory. Another difficulty with the descriptive essay method is that raters tend to fall into habits, using the same words for each employee and failing to make clear distinctions between employees.

This tendency is reflected in a slightly different way in what is known as *halo error*. This term is used to describe a common rater failing—the tendency to give all characteristics of a particular employee much the same rating. In effect, the rating assigned to the first characteristic tends to creep into the ratings assigned to all other characteristics. For example, if the rater assigns a value of 5 to the first characteristic, the tendency is to assign a 3, 4, or 5 to all other characteristics. If the characteristics had been listed in a different order, and the first one had been assigned a value of 2, the halo effect might have caused the other characteristics to be rated near that figure.

**Managers' judgement.** Despite numerous imaginative attempts to devise performance rating methods to replace subjectivity with objectivity, none has yet surfaced that completely accomplishes this desirable objective. Managers must consciously employ a combination of the decision-making tools described in Chapter 2, including the use of intuition, and work constantly to improve their skills and identify and counteract their inherent biases. Once again, it has to be recognized that there is no substitute for conscientious, courageous, and honest managerial judgement.

## Compensation

**Compensation** includes every type of monetary reward provided by the employer to the employee in exchange for the employee's work. It may be both direct and indirect. Direct compensation consists of the pay an employee receives in the form of wages, salary,

**ranking**
Comparing the performances of employees by listing them in rank order of their contribution to the organization's effectiveness.

**descriptive essay**
A brief statement describing a manager's evaluation of an employee's job performance.

**compensation**
The total of all rewards having a monetary value that are received by an employee in exchange for working for the employer.

bonuses, and commissions. Indirect compensation (also called *personnel benefits*) consists of all financial rewards that are not included in direct financial compensation. Examples are vacation allowances, parental and maternity leave, and employer-paid insurance. Non-financial rewards such as praise, self-esteem, recognition, and opportunities for growth are not part of compensation, as the term is usually used, but they do affect employees' satisfaction with the compensation system.[36]

Compensation is an important element in an organization's financial plans. In a manufacturing company, it may equal 50 percent or more of total expenditures; in a service company it may range upwards to 90 percent or even more. It may be the major method used to attract employees, as well as the primary way to try to motivate employees towards more effective performance. Compensation is significant to the economy. For the past 30 years salaries and wages have equalled about 60 percent of Canada's total GNP, and as the service sector of the economy grows, this proportion is likely to increase.

## Compensation Objectives

The objective of a compensation plan is to ensure that it is equitable to employer and employee alike. The desired outcome is an employee who is attracted to the work and motivated to do a good job for the employer. Thomas Patton, who has studied compensation policy extensively, says that an effective compensation policy will have seven qualities:

- *Adequate:* It will at least meet minimum government, union, and competitive requirements;
- *Equitable:* Everyone should be paid fairly, in line with their efforts, abilities, and training;
- *Balanced:* The compensation package should not emphasize any one of pay, benefits, and other rewards over the others;
- *Cost-effective:* Total compensation should not be excessive, considering what the organization can afford to pay;
- *Secure:* Compensation should be enough, and distributed in ways that will help employees feel secure and satisfy their needs;
- *Incentive-providing:* Compensation should motivate effective, productive work; and
- *Accepted by the employees:* Employees should understand the pay system and feel that it is reasonable for the enterprise and for themselves.[37]

Compensation plans should provide three aspects of comparability. Positions that are roughly comparable within the organization should have compensation levels that are also comparable. This does not preclude individual differences based on performance, but the ranges for the positions should not differ markedly. The level set for a position should recognize its relation to other positions, reflecting such factors as the levels of education and experience required, responsibility and managerial risk, working conditions, and other relevant factors. Finally, the compensation level established for a position has to take into account what competitors are paying people in similar positions. If the compensation level is substantially less than what potential applicants are offered elsewhere, not only are the organization's current employees being underpaid, but it will be difficult or even impossible to attract desirable candidates to fill any vacancies. Compensation policy, therefore, is a major factor in the ability of an organization to attract and retain the kind of employees who will contribute most to the ongoing welfare of the organization.

> ## Real World Reflection   8-1
>
> ### Outsourcing in a Union Environment
>
> One of the hot topics in union negotiations across Canada these days is the issue of outsourcing typical duties performed by unionized workers to non-union employees.
>
> On one side of the issue are long-term employees who believe that their jobs are undermined by bringing in "outsiders" who may be willing to work for less money or endure lower standards to get the job done.
>
> On the other side of the issue, management is faced with increased pressure to "do more with less." Stretching financial resources to the limit and pressure to turn around work in a pinch often leads managers to look for services outside of their union work pool, if tasks can be done more efficiently or less expensively.
>
> _____
> Contributed by Marnie Wright, British Columbia Institute of Technology.

## Compensation and Performance

Increasing payroll costs and competition in the global marketplace have caused managers throughout the world to search for ways to increase productivity by linking compensation to employee performance.[38] High performance requires much more than employee motivation. The provision of suitable facilities and equipment, good physical working conditions, effective leadership and management, safety, and other conditions all help raise employee performance levels. Employee health and fitness are often direct contributors to employee performance. Companies such as Husky Oil and British Columbia Telephone Company believe that productivity is directly related to employee fitness. Acting on this logic, they provide their employees with complete fitness facilities, and encourage them to exercise and work out during lunch breaks and after working hours.[39]

A number of studies indicate that if pay is tied directly to performance, employees produce a higher quality and quantity of work.[40] However, there is some disagreement on this seemingly self-evident connection.[41] Some researchers argue that if you tie pay to performance, you destroy the intrinsic rewards a person gets from doing the job well.[42] Intrinsic rewards are powerful motivators, too, but research on this subject has been limited to only a few studies. The importance of money varies from individual to individual. If the organization claims to have an incentive pay system but most pay increases actually are based on seniority, the motivational effects of pay will be minimal. The key to making compensation systems more effective is to ensure that they are directly connected to expected behaviours.[43]

In sum, theorists disagree over whether pay is a useful mechanism to encourage better performance. Further definitive research is needed to examine (1) the range of behaviours that can be affected by pay; (2) the amount of change in employee behaviour that can be caused by changes in pay; (3) the characteristics of employees who will be influenced positively or negatively by changes in pay; and (4) the environmental conditions that may make pay changes more or less effective.

Different managers view performance-based compensation programs as anything from almost miraculous cost-reallocation processes to ineffectual misallocation of

*Some progressive organizations, like British Columbia Telephone Company, invest substantial sums in employee benefits such as fitness facilities, recognizing that good physical health complements good mental health, and that both lead to happier, more productive employees.*

resources.[44] Many of these views have some merit, but their contradictions illustrate once again the complexity of human behaviour. To implement a performance-based compensation system, managers must keep in mind that the objective is to develop a productive, efficient, effective organization that enhances both employee performance and motivation.[45] The pay-for-performance program, therefore, must be driven by performance-oriented systems and processes rather than by the organization's existing compensation system and processes.

Developing a system that shows employees that pay is actually tied to performance requires a number of circumstances and managerial skills. First, managers must have the actual authority to allocate pay on the basis of merit. Second, managers must be willing to discriminate specifically in terms of rating and rewarding performance. They cannot reward all employees the same. Furthermore, if it is to be motivational, the merit pay increase must be meaningful and not just a token. Third, managers must communicate the pay system at the time of employment in terms of initial pay, expected long-term pay progressions, and pay adjustments.[46] The manager also must inform the employee that specified performance levels are required to obtain the pay increases. Finally, managers must have the will and the ability to discuss meaningfully with subordinates the linkage of pay to performance, and the confidence to discuss the situation with any employees who are dissatisfied with their raises.

A pay-for-performance work culture requires the development of performance evaluation systems that are considered equitable, meaningful, and comprehensive by both managers and other employees. If performance measures are poorly developed, employees will have difficulty perceiving the connection between pay and performance. Thus, if compensation is to have any influence on motivation, it is crucial to develop acceptable measures of performance.

Linking pay to performance may seem to have become simpler because of the availability of computer technology.[47] Readily available spreadsheet programs used on personal computers enable managers to transform performance evaluations directly into projected pay increases. These pay increases can be costed out accurately and subsequently tied to the company's overall financial strategy. The problem, however, as discussed earlier, is that performance evaluation is anything but an exact science, so the compensation linkage depends on a potentially faulty evaluation process.

## Selected Methods of Compensation

Employees can be paid for the time they work (flat wage rates), the output they produce (individual incentives or piecework pay), or a combination of these two factors.

**Flat wage rates.** In a company that has a collective agreement, wage rates are established by collective bargaining. Unions often insist that wages must be established for each position and then varied only on the basis of seniority or length of service, without regard to performance evaluation.

**Individual incentives.** Under an individual incentive plan, the employee is paid for the number of units satisfactorily produced. Individual incentive plans take several forms: piecework, production bonuses, and commissions. These methods seek to achieve the incentive goal of compensation.[48]

In Canada, with straight piecework an employee is guaranteed an hourly rate (often the minimum wage) for performing an expected minimum output (the standard). For production over the standard, the employee receives an agreed amount per additional piece produced. The standard is set through work measurement studies as modified by collective bargaining. The base rate and piece rate may emerge from data collected by pay surveys.

A variation of straight piecework is the differential piece rate plan. In this plan, the employer pays a smaller piece rate up to the standard and then a higher piece rate above the standard. Research indicates that the differential piece rate is more effective in encouraging incentive than is the straight piece rate, although it is used much less frequently.[49]

Sales employees may be paid on the basis of commissions, calculated on the volume of sales. Straight commission is the equivalent of straight piecework and is typically a percentage of the item's price. In other plans, the salesperson receives a base salary that may be topped up with a commission or bonus when the budgeted sales goal is exceeded.

Individual incentives are used more frequently in some industries (such as clothing and textiles and the steel industry) than in others (such as the forestry, beverage, and bakery industries), and in some types of jobs (sales and production) than in other types (such as maintenance and clerical jobs). Individual incentives are possible only in situations where performance can be measured in terms of output, such as sales dollars generated or the number of items produced. In addition, employees must work independently of each other so that individual incentives can be applied equitably.

Research results are mixed as to whether individual incentives produce the results expected.[50] Most studies indicate that they do increase output, though other performance criteria may suffer. For example, in sales, straight commissions can lead to salespersons paying less attention to servicing accounts. Working on hard-to-sell customers may be neglected because the salesperson will prefer to use the time to sell to easy customers. Also, unless the commission is based on sales for which the customer eventually pays, the salesperson, intent on earning a commission, may eagerly sell to a customer who has a bad credit rating, not actually caring whether the customer ever pays for the purchase. Individual incentives also may create internal dissension, as employees compete with each other for the more lucrative accounts or the tasks that have the greater

## Management in the Real World    8-3

### Human Resources Management: Reflections by Philip Crosby

Unfortunately even the best intended human resource functions and programs usually turn out to have some negative impact; people just do not like to be regulated. Even such helpful things as pension programs, ESOPs (employee stock option plans), and savings programs can affect people the wrong way. Most folks do not peer into the future too well when it comes to their work life. They like things now, not later. Many of those who work in HR discover that trying to help people is the most frustrating mission of all.

All of this relates to quality since we all know that one of the main supporting legs of that effort is employees' morale and cooperative spirit. Traditional benefit programs are supposed to help bolster that spirit and yet often do not, no matter how often or how well they are explained. It has always seemed to me that this is because they are not personal enough. I know that nothing should seem more personal than a pension or health care program, but people look at them as entitlements. They think the company is not going out of its way in providing them. So you get no points for doing, but lose points for not doing.

However there is at least one program that is always taken personally, is viewed as a great and much appreciated benefit, and does not cost much. That is assistance with child care for both male and female employees.

I set up a child-care funding program in our company, over the objections of HR and the executive committee. It cost us about $100 per month per child. The employees who were directly affected were more thrilled than I have ever seen employees be thrilled. They would seek me out when I walked through the company to shake my hand or give me a hug, or both. Even those who had no eligible children thought the program was wonderful, and that is a rare thing. Usually those who do not benefit from something are upset about it.

The aspect of all this that I never shared with anyone was that the program began when I had a conversation with our receptionist. She told me that half her calls in the afternoon were from children or babysitters checking in with parents. From that I figured that the child-care program would gain the company a lot more work output and a lot less time settling sibling arguments. And it worked out that way. Her parent-child calls dropped to a dribble, with most concerning someone being sick.

So I gained a reputation for being altruistic when in reality I was being a money-grubbing opportunist.

---

potential for a bonus.[51] There is also evidence of individual differences in the effect of incentives on performance.

**gainsharing incentive plan**
A compensation system in which the remuneration paid to employees is calculated on the basis of a pre-announced formula the results of which are dependent at least in part on the financial success of the employer, usually as a result of increased competitiveness arising from improved productivity or cost reduction.

**Gainsharing incentive plans.**  Gainsharing plans are company-wide group incentive plans. Their goal is to unite diverse organizational elements behind the common pursuit of improved organizational effectiveness by allowing employees to share in the proceeds.[52] Gainsharing rewards usually are distributed on a monthly or quarterly basis,[53] although in some plans the period covered is a year or even more. In some business organizations the system has proven to be exceptionally effective in enhancing organization-wide teamwork. Gainsharing plans that use cash awards and that have been in place for at least five years have reported productivity improvements resulting in labour cost reductions of as much as 29 percent.[54]

The factors that seem to be indicators that a gainsharing plan will succeed include (1) being in a large company, (2) having been in effect for several years, (3) reflecting financial stability in the company, and (4) being in a unionized company. One of the more critical factors is that it is essential for managers to support and discuss the plan, and for employees to understand and support it as well. A gainsharing plan is expensive to administer, so projected benefits must be weighed against costs. Linking pay to group performance and the creation of team spirit are two reasons cited for gainsharing's rising popularity.[55] These potential benefits for the organization may explain why jeans maker Levi Strauss &. Co. announced in 1996 a gainsharing plan that may provide all 37,500 employees, located in Canada and 59 other countries, with bonuses equal to as much as one year's pay if the company meets its cash flow targets by the year 2001. If the company achieves two-thirds of the plan, the bonuses will be half a year's pay; if the targets are exceeded, the bonuses will be prorated upward.[56] Because of the reported successes, coupled with increasing pressure from employees and unions, it is likely that gainsharing will increase in popularity both with managers and with non-managerial employees.

## Equal Pay and Pay Equity

It is a much-publicized fact that women receive substantially less pay than men. According to Statistics Canada figures, the differential was 40 percent in 1971 ($21,920 versus $36,743, in constant 1995 dollars). The gap has narrowed so that in 1995 the differential was "only" 26.9 percent ($29,700 versus $40,610).[57] A number of reasons are offered as to why this difference exists. Many women leave the paid labour force for a period to raise young children, thus losing their places in the career ladder. Many women are engaged in the helping professions, where pay is typically quite low.[58] (One might ask whether this is cause or effect—Is the pay in those professions low because women predominate there or would it be just as low if men predominated?) Many managers assume that women are not interested in promotion, so often they are not considered when openings arise. Women are assumed by some people not to be "management material"—a myth the fallacy of which has been discussed in Chapter 6. Women only recently have entered middle management positions, so only a few have served long enough on those rungs of the ladder to be considered ready for top management positions, where their executive-level pay would raise the salary averages for women as a group. Even after all of these factors are taken into account, however, it is clear that there is still systemic discrimination, in which women are paid less than men even when all other factors are equal. To adjust for this historical fact, all of the provinces and the federal government have enacted **equal pay** laws. These laws require, with substantial penalties for noncompliance, that female and male employees doing identical work be paid the same wage rates.[59] Several large companies, and even branches of the federal government, have been required by the courts and by human rights boards to pay millions of dollars in back pay to women who were underpaid in relation to men who held identical positions. To maintain an equitable workplace and to comply with the law and protect their organizations from legal penalties, managers at all levels must ensure that women and men who do identical work are paid at the same rates, and that the same adjustments are applied to both genders for such factors as seniority and experience.

**Pay equity** is a different concept from that of equal pay for equal work. It refers to paying equal amounts, regardless of the gender of the employees, for *work of equal value*. This concept requires equal pay rates for jobs that are different, but that contribute equal worth to the organization.[60] The federal legislation, and several provincial pay equity acts, provide no specific guidelines for job evaluation, but they do require that any evaluations made must be on a gender-neutral basis.[61] Managers are experiencing some difficulty in making valid comparisons of disparate jobs, so administration of pay equity plans is not simple. Constitutional challenges and political pressures are shaping pay equity thinking and legislation. For several years the federal government resisted orders

**equal pay**
Wage or salary schedules based on the concept of paying the same amounts for identical jobs, regardless of the gender of the employees doing those jobs.

**pay equity**
The concept of setting wage and salary rates that are identical for jobs of equal value or equal worth to the employer, regardless of the gender of the employees doing those jobs.

from investigating bodies that mandated the payment of several billions of dollars in back pay to women who had been paid less than men in comparable positions.

Given the emotional nature of these complex issues, the prudent manager will keep informed on a current basis. It will be necessary to seek current and informed legal guidance to ensure that the organization's policies comply with the ever-changing law.

## Benefits and Services

**personnel benefits**
Forms of employee compensation that are measurable in dollars but that are not part of wages or salaries.

Indirect financial compensation, called **personnel benefits** and services, consists of all financial rewards that are not included in direct financial compensation. Most benefits and services programs include vacations and statutory holidays, insurance to extend benefits beyond provincial health plans, dental plans, pensions that are intended to supplement Canada Pension Plan (or Quebec Pension Plan) and Old Age Security, and services such as child care, employee discounts on purchases, psychological and financial counselling, and reimbursement for tuition paid for educational courses.

Every Canadian province and territory has its own act that sets minimum standards for matters such as statutory holidays and paid vacations, hours of work and overtime provisions, minimum wage rates (usually for all except farm and domestic employees), and severance pay for dismissed employees. In many cases, collective agreements and the organization's own practices provide for benefits in excess of those required by the statute. Even so, managers must be aware of these provisions, and as a minimum be sure to comply with them to the letter. For example, an employee or group of employees may request that they be allowed to work four ten-hour days in a week rather than five eight-hour days. If the provincial statute provides, as most do, that wages must be paid at the overtime rate (for instance, one-and-one-half times the regular rate) for all hours worked in excess of eight in a day, it does not matter that the employees were the ones who requested this arrangement. Complying with their request would be an offence if the organization did not receive express prior approval in writing from the appropriate government official, whose title typically might be Director of Wages and Standards. Failure to get this prior approval would leave the employer subject to possible fines, as well as to an order to pay the employees back wages at the overtime rate, if in the future one of the employees becomes disaffected and files a complaint. As in regard to any statutory requirement, a manager cannot afford to take casually the specific provisions of the governing statute.

Just as direct compensation must keep abreast of (or preferably slightly ahead of) the competition, the personnel benefits offered must meet employees' expectations. Surveys suggest that a large majority of employees say that personnel benefits are crucial to job choice.

**flex benefits plans**
Benefits plans in which employees are assigned a certain amount and can allocate that amount to the benefits that best suit their own personal circumstances.

Like the introduction of flextime, described earlier in this chapter, some employers have initiated **flex benefits plans**. In these plans, a total dollar figure is allotted to each employee, for allocation among the various benefits that are available. Employees choose those benefits that they think are most appropriate for their own interests and family circumstances. For example, one employee may prefer to allot most of the allowance to extended medical and dental coverage for the family, while another employee who is covered under a spouse's medical plan may allocate the whole amount to extra vacation or to more life insurance coverage. Flex benefits plans are popular with employees in companies such as Cominco, IMC, and Pepsi-Cola Canada, where they have been inaugurated.[62] In KPMG Canada and in Canada Life Assurance Company, employees even have the option of taking their allotted amounts in cash instead of in benefits.[63] Managers contemplating this type of program should restrict the cash option to amounts after allowance for medical and long-term disability coverage. Otherwise, if an employee opts for cash instead of these protections and later becomes seriously ill or disabled, the employer may be subjected to intense pressure from other employees to provide financial support for their ill colleague.

## Discipline and Dismissal

Managers have an obligation to their organizations to act on instances of employee misbehaviour, incompetence, insubordination, or other breaches of the employer's legitimate expectations. The ultimate discipline is, of course, dismissal from the job. This may be supportable if the employee is still within a three-month or six-month probationary period. But for longer-term employees, it is unfair to the employee, and hazardous for the employer, to jump to this ultimate sanction for a single breach of rules.[64] Summary dismissal is probably only justified after the probationary period if the breach is of such magnitude that it constitutes a danger to people or, in an extreme instance, to the organization. In such a case, dismissal might be held on any appeal to have been for *just cause.*

**progressive discipline**
A connected series of escalating disciplinary measures applied to an employee who is failing to meet the organization's standards and policies.

For less serious infractions, however, under the labour relations acts or codes of the provinces and federal government, employees are entitled to warnings and to the application of **progressive discipline**. This means that the manager must advise the employee of the offending behaviour and apply disciplinary measures that escalate as infractions are repeated. These might take the form of an oral warning for the first offence, a written reprimand for the second, a one-day suspension without pay for the third, and a three-day suspension for the fourth. Each of the infractions and the discipline meted out should be described in a memo and discussed with the employee, who should be asked to sign the memo acknowledging that it is accurate and has been discussed. Only after this, or perhaps a more extended series of progressive disciplines, and the continued failure of the employee to correct the problem should the manager dismiss the employee.[65]

Even then, in provinces such as British Columbia, the employee is automatically entitled to take the matter to arbitration or to a panel of the Labour Board. Experience has shown that in such appeals there is a strong possibility that the discipline will be judged to have been too harsh, and the employee will be reinstated and perhaps awarded some or all of the back pay that was lost.[66] Therefore, before taking action that appears likely to lead to serious penalties or to ultimate dismissal, managers should consult a labour relations professional. In doing so, the organization may be able to avoid the embarrassment and the cost of having failed to take all appropriate steps to protect both the employee and the organization.

Some managers attempt to circumvent the difficulties that are likely to be experienced in dismissing for just cause by declaring that the employment is being terminated as a layoff rather than as a dismissal. They even may fill out the federally mandated Record of Employment (ROE) indicating that it has been a layoff, perhaps for "lack of work." Sometimes this is done to be kind by helping the dismissed employee in applying for employment insurance benefits. Aside from the dishonesty involved in misstating the facts on the ROE, the practice, while commonplace, may backfire. Under most labour legislation, an employee who has been laid off is entitled for a stated period, often six months, to be recalled ahead of any new employees being hired. If the ROE indicates that the dismissal was a layoff, the employee may take advantage of this provision and insist on being reinstated in the job before any replacement is hired—completely defeating the purpose of the dismissal. The employer hardly could argue that the manager had been dishonest in filling out the ROE, and that the employee really had been dismissed rather than laid off, as was reported!

# The Workplace of Tomorrow

Throughout this book, the changing nature of the employer-employee relationship has been stressed. Employees are much less accepting of dictatorial styles of management than they used to be. They expect, and in many organizations are receiving, recognition as individuals and information and decision making are being shared with them. Hiring practices, performance evaluation systems, compensation and benefits plans, provisions to prevent discrimination and harassment, and all other aspects of HRM must keep up with, and in many ways lead, these changes. Business cycles may come and go, but while the trends already seen in HR practices may at times be slowed down, they are unlikely to be reversed. To remain competitive, an organization must keep informed of new practices and innovations, and adopt or adapt those that seem appropriate to their own organizational cultures and goals.

# Summary of Learning Objectives

▷ **Describe the usual scope of human resource management (HRM).**

Human resource management (HRM) is the collection of functions within organizations that facilitates effective relations with and use of employees to achieve organizational goals.

▷ **Discuss the purpose of and explain some of the practices involved in job analysis.**

Job analysis is designed to shape individual jobs to be the most effective in helping to achieve organizational objectives. The process starts with the collection of detailed data about the reasons for the job, how it is done, and what skills are necessary to do it. It examines how each job relates to those around it. It leads to the preparation of *job descriptions* and *job specifications.*

▷ **Discuss how job specialization relates to its opposites, job enlargement and job enrichment.**

Harking back to Frederick W. Taylor's theories of scientific management, job specialization permits an employee to be trained in a few narrowly defined tasks, which are to be repeated frequently, in an effort to increase efficiency. Experience has shown, however, that employee boredom arising from repetitive work may offset any gains in efficiency. Job enlargement broadens the scope of a job in an attempt to regain employee satisfaction by providing more variety and interest. Job enrichment plans are designed to add different dimensions to a job, often by allowing the employee more latitude in decision making. In designing jobs, managers have to balance specialization, enlargement, and enrichment to arrive at the optimum mix of the three in the particular circumstance.

▷ **Explain the importance of each of the steps in recruitment.**

The first step is to decide what sources might produce the best candidates, and to make use of those sources. Unless sources are well selected, the field of candidates will be restricted. Then résumés are solicited and screened. Screening permits the managers to reduce the number of applicants on whom time will be spent. Next, or perhaps later in the sequence, information is gathered from all references. Experience has shown that many résumés contain inaccurate or inflated information. Unless references are checked carefully, these distortions may go unrecognized. Also, checking references can uncover information that will not surface either in résumés or in interviews. Then, usually a pre-interview telephone conversation helps to refine the short list further, after which the most appropriate candidates are interviewed. The interview can complete the screening process and lead to the final selection. Finally, terms of the job are discussed with the best candidate, and arrangements are made for a start date and orientation.

▶ **Identify the sources of the rules against discrimination.**

Provincial or territorial acts, codes, or ordinances (or in the case of federally regulated organizations, the Canada Human Rights Act) prescribe the grounds of discrimination that are prohibited in the particular jurisdiction. Since the acts vary in detail, it is necessary to consult either the relevant act or a reliable secondary source to know exactly what is prohibited. In general, however, it is safe to assume that it is illegal to discriminate on any basis that is not directly job-related.

▶ **Describe what constitutes sexual harassment and criminal harassment, and discuss why they are of concern to managers.**

Sexual harassment consists of any words, acts, gestures, or situations that diminish someone's sexual integrity or dignity. Criminal harassment, formerly known as *stalking*, is any unwanted and persistent attention paid to someone. Harassment creates an unwelcome work environment. Furthermore, if harassment is not checked, the organization and the managers may be subject to legal penalties.

▶ **Differentiate between equal pay and pay equity, and discuss their respective effects, benefits, and difficulties.**

Equal pay provides that pay rates will be the same for everyone doing the same work, regardless of gender or other differences that are not job-related. Pay equity refers to wage rates that are equal for different jobs that have the same worth to the employer, regardless of the gender of the employees doing the work.

▶ **Describe several bases used to determine compensation rates.**

Flat rate wage plans prescribe the same amount of wages or salaries per hour or day or month, regardless of the work output. In piecework or incentive pay systems, the amount an employee earns is dependent at least in part on the amount or quality of work output. Gainsharing provides that some of the profits earned by the company will be shared with employees on the basis of pre-announced formulas.

▶ **Discuss why personnel benefits are important, and describe some of the most commonly provided forms.**

Surveys show that employees consider the benefits to be provided in deciding whether to accept employment with a particular employer. Most common forms are extended medical plans, pensions, paid vacations, and leaves for personal matters. Less common but growing in importance are such family-related benefits as child care and time off for parental obligations.

▶ **Discuss some of the implications of flextime and telecommuting.**

Flextime, or allowing employees to set their own hours within certain parameters, makes it easier for employees to balance work and family obligations or perhaps recreational opportunities. Disadvantages include some degree of lost supervision over the work, and difficulties in scheduling work by groups or teams whose individual schedules may not coincide. Telecommuting intensifies the diminution of supervision but, for jobs that can be done by computer and modem, provides greater flexibility for the employees, and consequently potentially heightened morale.

▶ **Explain the nature of progressive discipline, and its place in a comprehensive program of performance evaluation.**

Employees are entitled to receive feedback as to their performance. If performance is unsatisfactory, the employee's attention to correction is greater if it is accompanied by some form of discipline. Progressive discipline describes a series of escalating levels of disciplinary sanctions, starting with admonitions, warnings, short and longer periods of suspension, and if necessary, ultimately dismissal. If dismissal becomes necessary and the employee files a complaint with an arbitrator, a labour board, or the court, the result is likely to be an order of reinstatement unless a record of progressive discipline has been kept.

## KEY TERMS

career development plan, p. 304
compensation, p. 307
descriptive essay, p. 306
discrimination, p. 301
employee training, p. 303
equal pay, p. 312
flex benefits plans, p. 313
flextime, p. 293
gainsharing incentive plan, p. 311
graphic rating scale, p. 305
human resource management
   (HRM), p. 282

human resource planning,
   p. 283
job analysis, p. 283
job description, p. 286
job design, p. 289
job enlargement, p. 291
job enrichment, p. 291
job posting, p. 296
job rotation, p. 290
job specialization, p. 289
job specification, p. 286
pay equity, p. 312

performance evaluation,
   p. 305
personnel benefits, p. 313
progressive discipline, p. 314
ranking, p. 306
recruitment, p. 295
recruitment plan, p. 295
screening, p. 297
sexual harassment, p. 302
short list, p. 297
telecommuting, p. 294

## REVIEW AND DISCUSSION QUESTIONS

### Recall

1. Why has HRM become a more important part of management in recent years? Do you expect HRM to remain a top priority in the next decade? Why?
2. What are some of the methods that can be used in job redesign?
3. What are some of the advantages and disadvantages of a systematic plan of job rotation?

### Understanding

4. In what ways is job specialization beneficial, and what are its disadvantages?
5. From the standpoint of society as a whole, why should laws be enacted to prevent discrimination?
6. Why should managers understand, be alert to signs of, and take action concerning sexual harassment?
7. In an organization with 1000 or more employees, what part should HR managers and functional managers play in recruitment?
8. What personnel benefits plans and compensation plans might be best suited for a small retail store that has six employees? For a printing plant that has 30 employees and specializes in the design and printing of certificates, wedding invitations, and similar products?

### Application

9. Outline a sound policy to educate managers and non-managers in issues of discrimination and sexual harassment, for an auto repair shop and for a telephone company.
10. Interview an HRM contact in a large company. Discuss the methods they use to interview professional and unskilled employees and what tests, if any, they use in the screening process.
11. Search the literature and determine what types of performance evaluation approaches are available. Critique at least two of these approaches in terms of their validity and their usefulness to managers.

## CASE 8-1

# The Mirage Hotel: A Human Resource Volcano

At the world-famous Mirage Hotel in Las Vegas, the management team values human resources. The concerns for people stand out in many areas. With 3054 rooms and 7000 employees, the Mirage is one of the largest hotels in the world. The 7000 employees are the key to the Mirage's image as a top-quality hotel. In the hotel industry, employee turnover reaches a staggering 60 percent annually. But the Mirage's turnover rate is only about 19 percent. Why is the turnover rate at the Mirage only one-third of the industry's average?

The answer appears to centre on employees who enjoy their work and on customers who like to be around pleasant, thoughtful, respectful people. Mirage employees, from the newest desk clerk or cleaner to the director of operations, display pride in their work and a commitment to it, as well as a sense of belonging. They like their employer, and they project warmth and spirit for their customers.

As a place of employment, the Mirage has an excellent reputation for concern about employees. When the hotel opened, an aggressive recruitment campaign generated 57,000 applications for the original 6500 jobs. Then followed a thorough screening process. Once people are hired at the Mirage, they go through an intensive training and orientation program. All new employees must successfully master the ten essential Mirage job tasks, which were developed by analyzing jobs, customer satisfaction, and service. The Mirage spends $2 million annually on the ten-task training program.

One innovation introduced by Arte Nathan, the vice president for human resources, is the Mirage Employee Services Center. There the employees can file health insurance claims, receive payroll information, deposit checks directly, and receive other services. The employee cafeteria serves the same food as is offered to the hotel guests, but it is free, and employees can have as many meals as they like. Nathan wants employees to feel that they, like the casino and hotel customers, receive service from the hotel.

Thousands of customers stream in and out of the Mirage each day. The 7000 employees could become lost in the hectic shuffle. To create a more cohesive feeling, Mirage management decided to create 20-person teams, each of which has its own leader. Each team wears a different coloured badge or lapel to emphasize a sense of identity and team spirit.

The Mirage has concluded that employees are the first link in the chain of creating a friendly, cooperative, and productive atmosphere for customers. Customers appear to like the Mirage, and people enjoy working in the hotel and casino, contributing to the organization's financial success.

Arte Nathan and other managers applied the "customer-is-a-top-priority" thinking to Mirage employees. It is a simple notion that most companies miss in developing programs. The Mirage makes it a top priority in a very competitive business in a city filled with competitors.

## Questions

1. How could the managers of a hotel such as the Mirage decide whether the cost of these employee benefits is justified in terms of overall profits?
2. What specific benefits accrue to the Mirage organization from its reduced turnover rate?
3. How could some of the Mirage employee programs be adapted to, for instance, a multi-branch credit union, an ethnic restaurant, or a central public library in a medium-sized Canadian city?

Source: Adapted from Bill Leonard, "HR Policies Ensure the Mirage Won't Vanish," *HR Magazine* (June 1992): 85, 87, 91.

## CASE 8-2

# Improving Productivity Through Job Design at Whirlpool

Whirlpool Corporation is the world's largest manufacturer of major appliances. It has factories or joint venture partners in ten countries throughout the world. The key to Whirlpool's success in the highly competitive global market is productivity—output per hour of work. Increasing productivity enables Whirlpool to reduce costs and boost profits. Customers benefit from lower prices, and employees receive higher wages.

Like most organizations, Whirlpool has found it hard to increase productivity. Nevertheless it has succeeded at its Benton Harbor plant, where metal rods are turned into parts for washers and dryers. Since 1988, productivity has increased by more than 19 percent, from 92.8 to 110.6 parts manufactured per labour-hour. Additionally, the number of parts rejected has fallen from 837 per million to 10 per million, making Benton Harbor a highly successful factory. As a result, employees' pay at the plant has increased about 12 percent during this period, outpacing the gains of the average North American manufacturing employee. And aided by these and other gains in productivity, the company has been able to keep the prices of its washing machines down while increasing their quality.

Boosting productivity at Benton Harbor wasn't easy. Productivity at the plant had been terrible. Workers took little pride in their work and hid mistakes. If a machine broke, they made no attempt to fix it. By the mid-1980s the plant was near closing. A Whirlpool assembly plant next door to the parts factory was closed and 1000 jobs were lost. Unless productivity improved, the parts plant also would have to close. But Whirlpool didn't invest in new machines and equipment for the factory. Instead, the firm invested in its employees, teaching them how to improve the company's competitiveness.

Jobs were redesigned. Managers believed that by teaching workers how to improve quality, less time would be wasted on bad parts and productivity would increase. An important part of this effort was to design jobs so workers could see how their products (parts) are put into the final products (washers and dryers). Informing workers about the entire process enabled them to make adjustments to help the process flow more smoothly. A new training centre was developed, in which an interactive computer teaches employees everything from general math to skills needed to use tools and gauges. The objective is to design jobs that let employees use their heads, and then give them the knowledge and skills needed to do just that.

The turnaround at Benton Harbor will never be finished because Whirlpool has learned that improvement is a never-ending process. One group of employees is trying to find a way to recycle oil used to cool and lubricate the machines. Some employees admit they're working much harder than they ever did. But competition has only intensified, and major appliance prices have not kept pace with inflation. Also, major appliance sales have dropped in North America due to changing demographics and never fully recovered after recent recessions. The industry continues to suffer from overcapacity and price competition, which will mean continuing pressure to improve productivity.

### Questions

1. Why is productivity so important for Whirlpool?
2. What does job design have to do with productivity and competitiveness?
3. How did Whirlpool empower its employees, and how did this benefit them and the company?
4. Do you think Whirlpool could improve its situation even more by moving the Benton Harbor factory to another country with cheaper labour?

---

Source: Adapted from Rick Wartzman, "A Whirlpool Factory Raises Productivity—and Pay of Workers," *The Wall Street Journal* (May 4, 1992): A1, A4; Thomas Jaffe, "Brazilian Whirlpool," *Forbes* (June 8, 1992): 165; and David Woodruff and Fred Kapner, "Whirlpool Goes Off on a World Tour," *Business Week* (June 3, 1991): 98-100.

## CASE 8-3

## Personal Conflicts at HLP Telecommunications

All people are complicated and multifaceted. Interpersonal relations between any two people are dependent on many factors, including the personalities and experiences of the two people; their respective goals, objectives, and values; and the hierarchical or functional relationships, all of which are coloured by past contacts between the two. Furthermore, how one's personality and performance are described depends in large measure on the person doing the describing. Finally, if a manager seeks information from a co-worker about other employees, the responses will vary depending on the extent to which the employees feel safe in reporting frankly, rather than holding back and trying to give the responses they think the manager expects. For all of these reasons and many others, a manager receiving informal evaluations of an employee must expect that the comments seldom will be uniform, and may run the gamut from harsh criticism to unstinting praise. All managers must sift through both formal and informal comments about the employees who are accountable to them, weighing how much value to place on each comment but being careful not to disregard any completely. A critical comment may not be indicative of a problem about the person about whom the comment is made, nor indeed about the person who is making the comment. But a critical comment does indicate that there is a problem—perhaps with one or the other of the people involved, but equally often with the interrelationship between them.

Within the head office of HLP Telecommunications Limited, there are widely different perceptions of the performance of Markus Nelson, Director of Sales. Jamie Wilson, the CEO of the corporation, recognizes that tensions seem to be building up around Nelson, and that there may be some potential problems. Wilson has found that when she has vague feelings of discomfort, she can start to resolve them by putting in writing some of her perceptions. In this case, she jotted down her own perceptions, and then in intentionally casual conversations sought reactions from managers and staff whom she knows and trusts.

After collecting information for a few days in seemingly random encounters, Wilson reviewed her notes. They read as follows:

### Jamie Wilson, CEO

Markus is a real pro. He has managed to turn around that sales department in record time. He has an amazing ability to network with industry insiders. I suspect that is how he has improved sales so drastically. He serves on boards and committees all over the city, and it really expands his profile as a leader. He is a little high strung, and seems to handle internal processes differently than many of my managers. But he's so productive that I give him plenty of latitude. If I try to change everyone's management style to mimic my own, we'll have a company of clones. We all have to find our own best methods to manage.

### Markus Nelson, Director of Sales

Tuesday, Markus and I had a sandwich lunch in my office, ostensibly to go over sales projections. After reviewing the numbers I asked Markus how he sees his career. He made quite a point of saying that he has been a professional manager for over 15 years. He takes pride in the fact that in the two years since joining HLP he has increased sales by 27 percent. He sees himself as a highly effective change agent, concentrating on the low-performing departments and individuals.

### Andrea Wilson, Director of Marketing

Tuesday, on my usual "walking-around" tour of the office, I saw that Andrea was alone in her office, reviewing some sketches of a marketing ad, so I dropped in casually. Her take on Markus is that he is, in her words, "a very directive manager." She seemed to open up, saying, "He often loses his temper when we meet to coordinate marketing and sales. I understand he does that, too, in his sales meetings. I respect that he has a strong vision for upping sales. That gives him a good record on paper. But I don't know how his staff are surviving. His personal assistant produces more documents in one week than most departments submit in a month." Then Andrea told me that she had met with Markus several times to ask him to "take it easy on my marketing staff—but he never backs off."

Andrea seemed uncomfortable when she said, "Look, Jamie, I know that he is producing what you want. But could you just talk with him and help him to ease off a bit on people?"

### Jim McCready, Sales Associate

Wednesday at noon, Jim and I happened to be the only ones in the fitness centre. I got on the exercise bike next to the one Jim was riding and we chatted. Then I asked him point-blank how he gets along with Markus. He seemed comfortable, saying, "Markus definitely gets things done. He doesn't accept failure at any level. In our weekly sales meetings, if you haven't met your quotas, he humiliates you in front of everyone. Two weeks ago I had an impacted wisdom tooth yanked, and I missed a day of work. I made up most of it on the other days, but was about 6 percent under my quota. Markus called me a wimp—'Only wimps lie around for little toothaches.' Bill and Al and I can take it, but Jennifer and Sarah have left in tears more than once. That doesn't ease the pressure at all. Markus is abusive, but I am making more money than I ever did, and it's probably because he's on my tail all the time, so I guess it's worth it. Incidentally, what I said about Jennifer and Sarah—he's just as hard on men as on women, if you are worried about that."

### Sarah Lamont, Sales Associate

Thursday evening about 9 p.m. I bumped into Sarah in the parking lot. I asked her why she was working so late. She said, "Tomorrow is our weekly sales meeting, and if I don't have all of my customer analyses done, Markus will jump all over me." I said, "Is he really tough?" Sarah started to cry, and said, "He is a monster. For the year to date I am the top seller of all of the sales associates, but last week both Jim and Al beat my numbers. In front of the whole group Markus sneered and said, 'What's the matter, isn't sex appeal working this week?' I don't use sex appeal. I know the products we can deliver, when we can deliver them, and what they will do. I am the top performer because I work harder. I know he's hard on all of us, but he singles out the women in the meetings. I just don't know how much longer I can take it. And Jennifer feels the same. She is talking about going to a lawyer about it. I don't know—what can I do?" I calmed her and told her I would look into it and see what can be done to help the sales meetings go better.

**Summary**

I'm glad I did this scouting around. Markus is too valuable to alienate, but we can't have all of the others upset or their work will fall off—or they'll quit. Obviously he produces good figures, but he is tough on almost everyone. Maybe I'll just have a quiet chat with Markus, but I'll be careful not to make him so mad that he will think he is unappreciated. I guess it's a case of "You can't make an omelette without breaking some eggs."

**Questions**

1. How would you characterize Wilson's approach to the people with whom she discussed this issue? (You might use terms such as empathic, autocratic, judgemental, sneaky, benevolent, prejudiced, inquiring, responsible, etc.) What indications are given that the terms you chose are appropriate?

2. From her notes, what do you think that Wilson will do in regard to Nelson? Will her actions improve the situation?

3. What steps do you think Wilson should take? What might be the outcomes—both positive and negative—of the actions you propose?

4. How would you describe the atmosphere in HLP Telecommunications in regard to Markus Nelson?

5. Was it ethical for Wilson to act as she did, inviting comments from one employee about another? If it was ethical, what might be the limits on such inquiries? If it was not ethical, what other methods could Wilson have used on which to base an opinion and take corrective action if it is needed?

6. Is there a potential claim for sexual harassment? How would you characterize the actions of Markus Nelson towards Sarah Lamont and Jennifer? How can Wilson weigh the validity of McCready's assurance that there is no gender bias against the validity of Lamont's statement that Nelson exhibits gender bias? What specific clues might help you (or Wilson) come to a conclusion on this question?

7. Would training be of any value in these circumstances? If not, why not? If so, training for whom and what kinds of training? How would you structure it?

Adapted from a case written by Marnie Wright, British Columbia Institute of Technology.

## APPLICATION EXERCISE  8-1

### Developing a Job Description

The purpose of this exercise is to develop a job description for a job of your choice. Since the job description is the output of a systematic job analysis, you must select a job and obtain the needed information before developing the job description. You can select any job, perhaps one you have held, are holding now, or would like to hold. Some suggestions follow:

| | | |
|---|---|---|
| Airline pilot | Talk show host | Buyer for a department store |
| Computer operator or technician | Teacher | Tour or convention organizer |
| Golf coach | Retail clerk | Accountant for house builder |
| Police constable | Intensive care nurse | Newspaper photographer |
| Machine operator | Auto mechanic | Advertising salesperson |

Once you have selected a job, reread the material on job analysis. How can you obtain the information needed to write the job description? Try calling an organization and talking with someone in that job or in the HR department. Once you have all the information you need, use the following format to write the job description.

1. *Job title:* Give the job's title and other identifying information, such as its salary or wage range and benefits classification.
2. *Summary:* In a brief one- or two-sentence statement, describe the job's purpose and what outputs are expected from someone holding it.
3. *Equipment:* List and describe the tools, equipment, and information required to effectively perform the job.
4. *Environment:* Give the job's working conditions, location, and other relevant characteristics of the immediate work environment, such as hazards, radiation and noise levels, the need for travel or physical strain, and the degree of personal stress.
5. *Activities:* Describe job duties, behaviours required for the job, and social interactions associated with the work; for example, the size of the work group and the amount of interdependency in the work.

## APPLICATION EXERCISE  8-2

### Understanding Competencies

There is a trend in human resource management for organizations to use competencies as a basis for performance management. Competencies are characteristics of behaviours that are needed to be effective in a given job, association, or organization. They tend to package knowledge, skills, and behaviours. These blocks allow the person to perform multiple tasks using the given competence. For example, communicating effectively, initiating or managing change, customer service, and teamwork are examples of the titles one might use to define a competency. Organizations often will define appropriate measurements for different positions or levels.

Prepare a list of the competencies you would expect for two different positions—a computer repair technician and a member of a provincial forest service department who manages public campgrounds and gives presentations on local animals and plant life. Distinguish among the three categories of knowledge, skills, and behaviour, and explain why they differ for the two positions.

Contributed by Sherry Campbell, British Columbia Institute of Technology.

## INTERNET APPLICATION  8-1

Many organizations take active steps to recruit and retain valuable employees. One such company is Molex. Scan Molex's Web site to learn more about this company (www.molex.com).

1. What steps is Molex taking to recruit and retain employees? Do you think such an approach is effective? Why or why not?

Find Web sites of two organizations that try to recruit new employees by means of the World Wide Web. Are their approaches similar or different? What are the advantages and disadvantages of each approach?

# Managing Organizational Change

After studying this chapter, you should be able to:

▶ Explain why individuals often resist change in organizational settings;

▶ Describe the different types of change agents;

▶ Define *survey feedback* and explain how it is used;

▶ Explain how managers can use the six steps described as constituting the framework for managing change;

▶ Discuss why it is often difficult to reshape an organization's culture;

▶ Explain the types of diagnostic techniques available to managers;

▶ Explain the technique of *force field analysis*;

▶ Explain the term *foresight-led change*; and

▶ Describe what is meant by a *stretch target*, and how managers can use it to achieve greater competitiveness.

## Honda Changes Design Tactics to Create New Civic

IT SHOULD HAVE BEEN A TIME OF TRIUMPH FOR ROB Shriver. The Honda engineer, then only 33 years old, had just helped launch the all-new Civic at the company's East Liberty factory. Already car magazines and enthusiastic buyers were showering praise on the spunky subcompact. *Car & Driver* magazine said, "Honda has achieved the pole position in the small car sweepstakes." ▶

But instead of celebrating, Shriver was worried. Slick new features on the Civic such as rear-seat heater vents and a beefier engine had hiked costs just as increased prices were causing auto sales to slump in both the North American and Japanese markets. Honda Motor Company's profit margins, already razor thin, looked as if they would disappear altogether. So, even as the first 1992 Civics were hitting the road, Shriver put together a 12-member team that would spend the next 18 months scouring Honda's North American suppliers and its employees for ideas to make the next Civic less expensive to build.

Shriver didn't know it at the time, but back in Japan, Honda executives from president Nobuhiko Kawamoto on down had reached the same conclusion: that the rising yen meant that Honda could no longer afford to overengineer its cars. Kawamoto assigned Hiroyuki Itoh, the Civic's chief engineer, to the task of putting together his own team—one that within a few months would merge with Shriver's North American crew to collaborate on an all-out battle to wring costs out of the manufacture of the Civic.

It was a new experience for most of those involved. For the first time, North American engineers and marketers were given the opportunity to have a say in shaping a new model from its earliest designs. The Japanese engineers, breaking with tradition, used an unprecedented number of money-saving suggestions from factory workers and suppliers on both sides of the Pacific. Honda's renowned engineers had always dictated new designs without "interference" from those outside their group. Sales and manufacturing executives were consulted only after designs were nearly set. When disagreements did arise, the engineers had the final word. And Honda's North American employees had no say except for minor cosmetic changes. "We always did what we wanted, thinking it was the right thing," said Kawamoto, a 27-year-old engineer who took over Honda's top job in 1990. "But we had to see that profits wouldn't keep growing."

So, soon after the fifth-generation Civic had its debut in 1992, Kawamoto ordered Itoh to begin revamping Honda's design *process* itself. Because previously Honda's R&D specialists hadn't sought input early enough from manufacturing specialists, Honda's factories rarely had had the time to test designs to minimize capital investment in machine tools and other facilities. Kawamoto also recognized

that Honda would have to work earlier with suppliers to eke out production efficiencies.

Itoh's first step was to end the autocracy formally exercised by the engineering department. Early that year, he put together a seven-member redesign team that united Japanese executives from engineering, manufacturing, purchasing, quality control, and sales—and all had an equal say. Shriver and a group of his North American employees flew to Tokyo to outline their plans to ferret out cost savings in their operations. "We received input from the factory much earlier," Itoh said. "We wanted to get sales thinking, 'How can we sell this?' and the factory thinking, 'How can we make this?'"

The result was a host of money-saving manufacturing changes that Honda fully expects that customers will not notice, or at least not find objectionable. Although no one change resulted in a major saving, in the aggregate they made up substantial cost economies. Whereas the older Civic sported a complicated trunk hinge that made it slightly easier to retrieve luggage, the new model returns to a simpler hinge that is cheaper to make, without sacrificing too much convenience. The dashboard and the inner door trim are each made from one moulded piece, instead of two or more, simplifying manufacture. And the upholstery on the rear seats, which get much less wear than the front seats, has 30 percent fewer threads per centimetre than that on the front seats.

Still, the Japanese designers and engineers sometimes resisted long and hard some of the new ideas. Often they reacted as they did to a suggestion concerning the front bumper. One East Liberty paint shop employee pointed out that the front bumper covers, or fascias, had two separate air inlets and a bottom section, all three of which had to be masked before painting. She suggested that the air inlets be fitted with removable grilles that could be installed after painting, thus eliminating the need for masking. This innovation was shown to Itoh and ten Japanese executives. They considered and then rejected it on the ground that Japanese customers are very picky about paint jobs. Unfazed, the employee persisted, and presented several alternatives, which, in turn, were presented to the executives. Finally, Itoh accepted a compromise: The front fascia would have only one easily masked opening rather than two and a bottom section. From this one innovation Honda saved $1.2 million in the North

American operations alone. As the paint shop employee said, "They weren't accustomed to hearing from the factory so early on, and they had to get over the shock."

With the intense competition in the automobile industry, Honda has to continue to innovate, to improve cost efficiency, and to market effectively. But the Civic perhaps would not have survived had its executives not seen the need for organizational change—reducing the autonomy of the design and engineering department and increasing the input from other divisions. ■

Sources: Adapted from Edith Hill Updike, David Woodruff, and Larry Armstrong, "Honda's Civic Lesson," *Business Week* (September 18, 1995): 71, 73, 76; and Larry Armstrong, Kathleen Kerwin, and Bill Spindle, "Trying to Rev Up: Can Japan's Carmakers Regain Lost Ground?" *Business Week* (January 24, 1994): 32-33.

## The Climate of Change

Change is a topic very much on the minds of managers today. Most would agree that the pace of change is forever increasing, leaving less and less time to think about decisions before they have to be made. Claims that we are in a period uniquely characterized by change, however, are overstated. These claims betray a common human failing to assume that *our* lives, *our* thoughts, and *our* times are different from any that have gone before or that are likely to come in the future. Even in early historic times, humans almost always have had to deal with more change than they could comfortably handle. In many ways we are better prepared to cope with change than, for instance, the residents of the cities overrun by Tamerlane or Genghis Khan (who usually massacred all who survived their attacks), the Scots who were forced off their lands by the Enclosure Acts, the Irish peasants whose main source of food was destroyed by the potato blight, or the craftsmen who were displaced by the Industrial Revolution. All of which is not to say that it is easy to accommodate to today's changes, but only that today's rate of change, fast as it is, should not be a cause for panic.

As the opening vignette illustrates, in modern, competitive organizations it is no longer acceptable just to try to adapt to change when it occurs. Today, managers must try to determine what the future is going to be like, and then change their organization in the present to prepare it for that future. Active foresight is required to help managers position their organizations to be competitive in the global marketplace of five, ten, or even twenty-five years in the future.[1]

In the past decade, managers have led the following organizational changes:

- The workforce has changed significantly; with many organizations being downsized to become leaner, reducing middle management numbers and the number of layers of corporate hierarchy;
- Networking technologies have been introduced to increase employee productivity;
- Flexible work systems have enabled a number of companies to meet the needs and expectations of an increasingly professionalized workforce;
- Employee training has helped employees to adapt to and thrive in new work environments that are increasingly diverse;
- Reengineering in organizations has reduced steps in work processes and forced organizations to focus on their core competencies; and
- Modern management has given non-managerial employees more power in the workplace, including involvement in decision making and planning and in achieving customer satisfaction.

**Real World Reflection    9-1**

### How Do You React to Change?

In *Managing Transitions: Making the Most of Change*, William Bridges suggests that when preparing for change one should "experiment a little every day." The ultimate goal is to be flexible and positively responsive to change.

In the next three days, focus on doing things differently than you usually would. In order to test this point, you might:

- Have a new cereal for breakfast or, better yet, have soup for breakfast.
- Do something new at lunch (e.g., go for a walk or take a fitness class lunch with colleagues), something you do not usually do.
- Ask someone a question you have been dying to ask.
- Ask "why?" to yourself and others, especially when it applies to doing things in the manner one always does them.
- Try new food.
- Learn something—focus on acquiring new information, perspectives, or skills.

Contributed by Sherry Campbell, British Columbia Institute of Technology.

Traditional ways of doing business are fast fading or gone entirely, along with many comfortable relationships, but if organizations are going to achieve and maintain competitiveness (which is another description for business success), they must reinvent themselves continually.[2]

In the past decade, many companies have tried to remake themselves into better competitors. Their efforts have gone under many banners: total quality management, reengineering, rightsizing, restructuring, and cultural change, among others. In almost every case, the goal has been the same: to cope with a new, more competitive market by changing the way business is conducted. A few of these change programs have been very successful. A few have been utter failures. Most fall somewhere in between these two extremes, with perhaps a tilt towards the failure end of the scale. The lessons learned from these failures will be relevant to more and more organizations as the business environment becomes ever more competitive. One lesson that has been illustrated is that change involves numerous phases that, together, usually take a long time to complete. A second lesson is that critical mistakes in the management of any of the phases can have a devastating impact on the success of the entire change effort.[3]

This chapter discusses some forces for change. It also presents frameworks and models that can serve as blueprints for ordering managerial thinking about change. They serve as a guide first for diagnosing and then for managing change. In addition, various intervention methods are discussed in terms of change. Finally, there is a discussion of the ever-present cultural and structural factors that make or break change interventions.

## Change Forces

Today, perhaps more than ever, the manager's time and energy are demanded by fast-breaking developments in mergers and acquisitions, regulation, privatization, downsiz-

*Managers must lead change to remain competitive. However, as occurred when Coca-Cola tried unsuccessfully to introduce a change in its product, sometimes the planned changes are not accepted by the market and must be reversed.*

ing, and union-management collaboration or strife; threatened or actual plant closings; technological reengineering; the management of culturally diverse workers; and the need for environmental protection. These and many other forces from outside and inside the organization demand attention.

Exhibit 9-1 reflects three strategies for managing change that managers can choose in their quest for competitiveness. Restructuring may lead to a smaller organization, reengineering and continual improvement to a better organization, and transformation or reinvention to a different organization.

For organizations to survive relatively unscathed while undergoing major change, there have to be some factors that bind people together. Sometimes a unifying factor is the change itself; in other cases, change has destroyed any feeling of unity that previously had existed. Which result will occur depends on the skill with which the change is managed. For example, American Express made a significant change when it created a comprehensive delivery system designed to meet external customer requests. Motorola is another example of an exceptional company whose success is largely a result of its systematic approach to implementing change. In Motorola's case, the unifying factor wasn't individual customer transactions, but rather the use of a common language to help unify its people.[4]

**Exhibit 9-1**   *The Quest for Competitiveness*

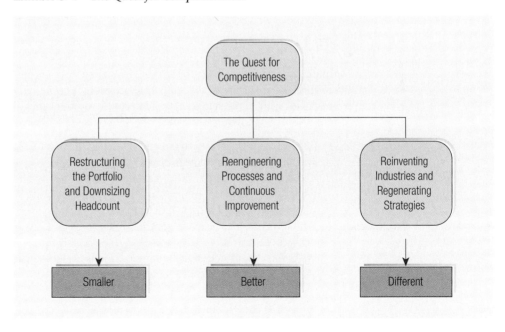

Source: Gary Hamel and C. K. Prahalad, *Competing for the Future* (Boston, Mass.: Harvard Business School Press, 1994), p. 15.

## Internal Change Forces

**internal change forces**
Forces for change that
arise within the organization, such as problems in
communication, morale,
and decision making,
and including financial
stresses and changes in
key personnel.

**Internal change forces** are pressures that come from within the organization. Sometimes the forces arise from inadequate communication. Sometimes the pressure is the cost of producing the product or service. If the unit cost increases, then to remain financially sound the price may have to be increased, threatening to make the organization less competitive. In some instances, turnover of key personnel may require that efforts be made in active change management.

Poor employee morale over some perceived inequity in the reward system could be an internal pressure point that a manager must become aware of and address. Although employee attitudes may be difficult to measure directly, any increase in grievance rates, absenteeism, or turnover may suggest poor or decreasing morale. It is essential to try to determine whether the poor morale is caused by the organizational culture, by its structure, or perhaps by the actions and attitudes of one or more managers.

The poor morale also may come from other employees bringing this attitude to work from outside influences and situations. Perhaps one or more employees are experiencing considerable personal stress, from financial, health, or family problems, or from relationship problems within the organization. Whatever the reason, the causes for the low morale must be searched for and identified. One effective tool a manager has for understanding and diagnosing the issues involved is the organizational survey. Surveys can be done through questionnaires or interviews. They help managers to stay in touch with the forces of change that are at work among employees. Staying in touch with these forces may allow them to be managed and turned to positive outcomes.[5]

### Real World Reflection  9-2

#### Inspiring Employees to Welcome Change

For many managers, *implementing* the planned change is the most complex task in the change management process. By inspiring others to welcome change the manager provides the focus for the conscious effort required to move the change process forward. Presented with change, many people will resist it altogether or backslide into a pre-change state. To keep the momentum going, effective managers consider the following strategies:

- Celebrate the successes made and regularly discuss the contributions of people at all levels of the change process.
- Avoid the tendency to "shoot the messenger," making sure that you understand the problem and all of its sources prior to selecting an appropriate action. Choose to respond rather than to react.
- Find a way to measure the work being done so that improvement and backsliding can be charted.
- Welcome others' ideas and change initiatives. Demonstrate the acceptance to change that you would like to see in others.

Contributed by Sherry Campbell, British Columbia Institute of Technology.

## External Forces

External (outside-the-organization) forces can make some change necessary. Government regulations, such as provincial and federal human rights acts and laws requiring affirmative action, could suggest the need to change an organization's physical facilities, its recruitment and selection programs, its organizational culture, or all three. Market competitors and how they reward employees, distribute products, service customers, or form alliances with other enterprises may signal the need for change. Foreign competitors often play by different rules that Canadian companies must recognize and learn to cope with, to decide whether to make internal changes to compete. Integrating and using the talents of a more diverse workforce, and effectively rewarding this culturally diverse workforce, will require changes in attitude, interpersonal interaction, and the perceptions of managers and, taking their cues from managers, of all other employees within the organization.

## Resistance to Change

Any change, no matter how beneficial to employees and to the organization as a whole, will meet with and often be sabotaged by employee resistance. The failure of many recent large-scale efforts at corporate change can be traced directly to active or passive resistance. This resistance may have arisen from several possible causes, including self-interest, habit or personal inertia, fear, peer pressure, and bureaucratic inertia.

### Self-interest

Even though we usually think of *ourselves* as being objective and free from self-interest, we can recognize that self-interest cannot be eliminated completely *in other people*. Some individuals resist change because they have a personal self-interest in the way things are done. They enjoy the work flow, or their position, or the power that comes from their specialized knowledge of the way things now are. They may feel that change threatens these sources of personal satisfaction, and indeed it probably does. Some companies have moved strongly into telecommuting (which is discussed in other portions of this text). When the employees begin to work primarily from their homes rather than from a centralized office, they lose much of the former opportunity to interact socially, compare work situations, and examine problems with their colleagues. Recognizing this potential for personal loss, despite the flexibility that telecommuting offers, employees may resist the move from the office to the home-based operation.

*Forward-looking employers are providing day-care facilities to benefit not only their employees, but themselves as well.*

### Habit and Personal Inertia

The comfort of working the same way day after day has a certain appeal to many people. They find unsettling any changes in personnel, work flow, structure, or technology, and resist pressures to make adjustments to their comfortable, habitual ways. It is also recognized that, at least initially, accommodating to any change will doubtless require more effort than just continuing in the same old ways.

## Fear

Change introduces uncertainty and an element of fear. People fear that they may have to become accustomed to a new leader. They also may fear that they will be unable to learn quickly the new tasks that will fall to them as a result of change. When employees are offered the opportunity to relocate and take a different, better-paying job in the same organization, they may consider such a change risky and prefer to retain their current jobs and relationships, thus blocking the change desired by their managers.

## Peer Pressure

An employee's peers may resist the introduction of automation because they assume it will result in a reduction in the workforce. These peers can pressure the employee who otherwise might support automation and its potential to improve productivity. Most people need the reassurance of belonging to a group. If other members of the group announce their opposition to automation, or indeed to any change, it takes considerable courage to risk being excluded from full "membership" in the group by stating publicly any disagreement with positions taken by influential members of the group. Thus, peer pressure can be very strong, and at times almost insurmountable.

## Bureaucratic Inertia

As discussed in earlier chapters, organizations must function through bureaucracies. Whatever the kind of organization, it is likely to have a built-in resistance because of the traditional rules, policies, and procedures. The refrain is "This is how we've done things for years. Why change?" During the 1980s and 1990s this sort of ostrich-like attitude seemed to prevail in retail department stores such as Eaton's, Woodward's, and Kmart. The intransigence of the senior managers led eventually to these stores' collapse or fundamental restructuring.

Inflexible rules, policies, and procedures preclude the use of adaptive changes in any organization, yet they are difficult to counteract. Often managers realize that they are in a bureaucratic maze, and they become discouraged because it is difficult to struggle through the barriers, delays, and stonewalling that they encounter.

# Reducing Resistance to Change

Recognizing that some resistance to change is almost universal, managers must seek to overcome or reduce the resistance, to encourage acceptance of the proposed changes, and to build support for them. There are no simple, universal, perfect prescriptions for reducing resistance, but in any situation, one or more of the following options may prove useful (see Exhibit 9-2).

## Education and Communication

Explaining why change is needed, in meetings, through memos, or in reports, can be especially helpful because a lack of information almost inevitably breeds resistance.

**Exhibit 9-2**

*Methods for Reducing Resistance to Change*

| Approach | Involves | Commonly Used When... | Advantages | Disadvantages |
|---|---|---|---|---|
| 1. Education and communication | Explaining the need for and logic of change to individuals, groups, and even entire organizations. | There is a lack of information or inaccurate information and analysis. | Once persuaded, people will often help implement the change. | Can be very time consuming if many people are involved. |
| 2. Participation and involvement | Asking members of organization to help design the change. | The initiators do not have all the information they need to design the change, and others have considerable power to resist. | People who participate may be committed to implementing change, and any relevant information they have will be integrated into the change plan. | Can be very time consuming if participants design an inappropriate change. |
| 3. Facilitation and support | Offering retraining programs, time off, emotional support, and understanding to people affected by the change. | People are resisting because of adjustment problems. | No other approach works as well with adjustment problems. | Can be time consuming and expensive, and still fail. |
| 4. Negotiation and agreement | Negotiating with potential resisters; even soliciting written letters of understanding. | Some person or group with considerable power to resist will clearly lose out in a change. | Sometimes it is a relatively easy way to avoid major resistance. | Can be too expensive if it alerts others to negotiate for compliance. |
| 5. Manipulation and co-optation | Giving key persons a desirable role in designing or implementing change process. | Other tactics will not work or are too expensive. | It can be a relatively quick and inexpensive solution to resistance problems. | Can lead to future problems if people feel manipulated. |
| 6. Explicit and implicit coercion | Threatening job loss or transfer, lack of promotion, etc. | Speed is essential, and the change initiators possess considerable power. | It is speedy and can overcome any kind of resistance. | Can be risky if it leaves people angry with the initiators. |

Source: Reprinted by permission of the *Harvard Business Review*. An exhibit from "Choosing Strategies for Change," by John P. Kotter and Leonard A. Schlesinger (March-April 1979). Copyright © 1979 by the President and Fellows of Harvard College; all rights reserved.

Open communication helps people prepare for the change. Resistance may be lowered by responding to people's fears, showing the logic of the change, and keeping everyone informed throughout the process. This option is usually time-consuming, not only because of the actual contact time, but also because the form and substance of the communication must be carefully and skilfully planned and transmitted. Communication techniques will be discussed in Chapter 10.

## Participation and Involvement

If those to be affected are asked to help design and implement the change, this involvement may reduce their resistance and, if their involvement is genuinely respected, probably will increase their commitment to and support for the change. Conversely, if the non-management employees feel that their participation is being treated lightly or that their involvement is only cosmetic, then their suspicion and resistance are almost certain to increase dramatically.[6] The management challenge is to listen positively, accept readily the useful ideas that come out of the involvement, and find ways to meet the disappointment felt by employees who make inappropriate or uninformed suggestions that cannot feasibly be incorporated in the plan.

## Facilitation and Support

Being supportive is always an important management attribute, especially when change is implemented. Managers must show genuine concern for subordinates, be good listeners, go to bat for subordinates on important issues, and provide training opportunities. Behaviours exhibited by leaders and managers can have a profound effect on employees' attitudes and perceptions about their work and their organization. Research conducted during a change effort in the marketing and sales division of an international pharmaceutical company showed that employee attitudes and perceptions were significantly related to different types of behaviours by managers.[7] Managers need to behave in ways that show commitment to the change and support for employees while they are learning to cope with change. Again, this approach is time-consuming, but essential if change is to be successfully administered.

## Negotiation and Agreement

Resistance can be reduced through negotiation. Discussion and analysis can help managers to identify points of negotiation and agreement and to meet employees' objections. For example, convincing a person to move to a less desirable work location may require offering to pay a bonus or to increase salary or perquisites. This tradeoff should not be imposed by the manager, but arrived at through negotiation between the manager and the employee. A disadvantage is that once this negotiated agreement is reached, other employees are likely to expect the manager to grant similar concessions to them, either now or at some time in the near future. Thus, in such a negotiation, the manager always must keep in mind the possibility of setting a precedent that may not be desirable over time.

## Concerns About Co-optation

Co-opting an individual involves offering a major role in the design, or perhaps only in the implementation, of the change. If the person chosen for this role is an opinion leader among other employees and is truly listened to and respected by the managers, the effect may be to help other employees accept the change. If, on the other hand, the person chosen enjoys little respect from other non-managerial employees, at best the effect will be minimal. Worse, if the co-optation is not sincerely meant by management, the co-opted person and other employees will recognize the exercise as a sham, and the result will be an erosion of trust and an escalation of resistance to the change.

## Unethical (and Ineffective) Methods of Seeking Agreement

### Manipulation

Another method that is often used to reduce resistance to change is manipulation. By this is meant the use of devious tactics to convince others that a change is in their best interests, when in fact its benefits are at best doubtful. Holding back information, playing one person against another, and providing slanted information are examples of manipulative behaviour. It is also a form of manipulation to announce one reason for the proposed change, when in fact another reason is driving the change. At times manipulation works. However, it is not only dishonest and unethical, but it often backfires. Usually employees discover that they have been used and then lose trust and respect for their managers, without which an organization cannot be truly effective.

An ill-advised manager may try to manipulate, thinking that the other employees would be upset if they knew the real reasons for the proposed change. Employees soon see through such subterfuge, and then often jump to conclusions that are more damaging to morale and support than if they had been told the real reasons in the first place. Despite these obvious disadvantages, many managers who do not credit their employees with common sense or intelligence seem to believe that manipulation is the easiest way to bring about change in employee attitudes and beliefs. When they do, they should not be surprised that other employees, in turn, use manipulative tactics in dealing with their managers and even with their fellow employees.

### Implicit and Explicit Coercion

In using coercion, managers promise rewards or threaten punishment to bring about what is often only superficial support for a proposed change. In the past, managers relied heavily on this method. Even today many still do, despite evidence that when used alone it seldom changes anyone's mind, and will at best engender only grudging acceptance of the change. Promises may include wage raises, promotions, and broader participation in management decisions. If the promises are kept, those who benefit may accept the change. Threats often include dire predictions of job losses, wage cuts, poor job assignments, and the loss of privileges. If the threats are not implemented, employees discover that they need not pay attention to any future idle threats; if the threats are implemented, the resentments may outweigh any temporary benefit gained from having employees give at least lip service to the change. Coercive behaviour, whether explicit (stated directly) or implicit (only implied), is risky because it often generates hard feelings, distrust, and hostility.

## Making Effective Use of Resistance to Change

Although it is natural and reasonable for managers to concentrate on winning other employees over to acceptance and ultimate support of change, there are some positive elements that may flow from resistance to change.[8] Managers who have been involved in planning the change naturally have a personal investment in it, and may have overlooked problems inherent in the plan, either through misplaced enthusiasm or because

## Management in the Real World   9-1

### Managing Organizational Change: Reflections by Philip Crosby

"I had this idea," I remarked at a staff meeting back in 1961. "We spend a lot of time and money checking and finding and fixing. Why don't we concentrate on getting things done right the first time? Then we won't have to check, find, and fix?"

As I looked around the room, expecting to see an enthusiastic response to this marvellous thought, I experienced instant disappointment. They gave me that "poor soul" look as if I had suggested we pop in for lunch on Saturn. Instantly I knew how Galileo had felt.

"That would cost a fortune, Phil," said the engineering director.

"People would be very upset if we demanded they do everything right every time. We would have psychos on our hands and a strike too," said the personnel director.

"I can't believe you're serious," said our quality expert. "Our acceptable quality levels are at 1 percent now, and that's very rigid. I'd need more inspectors if we're going to not have any defects."

"The employees are just not capable of doing that kind of work," said the production manager. "The school systems don't teach them good hand skills."

"I was thinking that we could train people more than we do. As far as I can see they're capable of doing great work," I replied. "I think the problem is that we've set up a process of doing work and then doing it over."

"That's the way everyone does it," replied the marketing manager. "It has been that way because that's the best way to work."

There was a finality to the statement and everyone seemed to nod at that moment for emphasis. Later I realized that each of them was thinking of the drastic revisions that would be necessary in their personal professional lives if these ground rules changed. Doing it right means that requirements must be clear; it means that people must be trained; it means that responsibility must be dropped down the organization chart; it means that some departments won't be as large as they were before; it means going against the conventional wisdom.

I was thinking that such a policy would make things easier. Everyone else was thinking it would be harder.

From this I learned in the final consideration that people aren't against change just because it's change. After all, they alter their own lives regularly. They change personal suppliers, such as restaurants; they change friends; they move; they get new clothes; they do all these things and more without even thinking of them as change. But in these cases they're the ones who are instigating the action.

In business life, when others start making things different, change is much more threatening. We may not understand the limits of what's going to happen. We may not have strings on it. We may, well, feel threatened. After realizing this I began taking care to explain the concepts of zero defects in a less terminal way, sort of easing into it until the group began to come up with the idea themselves. That way they could see how it would affect them and determine that it would make their lives easier, not harder.

of a lack of familiarity with details of operations. Front-line production or service employees, being intimately familiar with operations, may identify issues that have not been properly addressed in planning. The managers who are charged with managing the change must sort out the kernel of genuine objection from the chaff of personal resistance that has little to do with the details of the change. After all, if employees are kept informed, allowed to participate, engaged in negotiation of the terms, and above all *listened to*, the real inadequacies and errors in the plan probably will come to light. It is far better to learn of inadequacies and gaps before implementation starts, and to have the opportunity to correct them, than to find out what was wrong after the change has been implemented, when corrective action is more difficult and creates more confusion.

*Resistance to change or impatience with lack of change may be exhibited in many forms – here, in a strike by employees.*

## A Framework for Managing Change in Organizations

It has been said that, by its very nature, change cannot be managed.[9] If by this is meant that change cannot be completely controlled, then the statement is certainly true. But if the statement means that it is fruitless even to try to manage change, then it would be like saying that no one should ever try to look ahead, because at best the future is somewhat unpredictable. Instead of feeling caught in events that are inescapable, the successful manager addresses change head on and concentrates on finding ways to shape its effects and to deal productively with it.

Several different frameworks can be useful for thinking about change and change processes. Exhibit 9-3 on page 338 provides a process-oriented model that suggests six distinct stages at which managers can make decisions about managing change. Stage 1, the combination of forces for change, has been discussed already in terms of internal and external factors.

Distinguished psychologist Kurt Lewin introduced the notion of three stages in the change process: unfreezing, changing, and refreezing. Lewin argues that constant change is unsettling and inefficient. Instead, he advises holding on to the status quo until change is fully planned, then "unfreezing" and making the change as a concerted effort. When the change has been implemented, the next step is "refreezing," or holding back on further change until the first change has been fully digested. Other scholars argue that to remain competitive, change must be almost a constant.[10] In this view, frequent incremental changes are less disruptive than occasional massive changes. Which approach to take may depend on the urgency of the problems identified, the personality of the managers, and the morale and culture of the organization.

### Recognizing that Change Is Needed

In stage 2, managers must recognize when change is needed—that is, that the present state is unsatisfactory. For example, a manager might observe that there are few female

**Exhibit 9-3**    *Framework for Managing Change*

```
┌─────────────────┐      ┌─────────────────┐      ┌─────────────────┐
│ Forces for change│      │   Management    │      │  Diagnosis of   │
│ • Internal      │ ───▶ │  recognition of │ ───▶ │   problem and   │
│ • External      │      │ need for change │      │points of resistance│
│                 │      │                 │      │                 │
│        1        │      │        2        │      │        3        │
└─────────────────┘      └─────────────────┘      └─────────────────┘
        ▲                                                   │
        │                                                   ▼
┌─────────────────┐      ┌─────────────────┐      ┌─────────────────┐
│  Evaluation of  │      │  Selection of   │      │ Consideration of│
│ change and start of│◀──│intervention change│◀── │   alternative   │
│  change process │      │   methods and   │      │intervention methods│
│                 │      │ implementation  │      │ to initiate change│
│        6        │      │        5        │      │        4        │
└─────────────────┘      └─────────────────┘      └─────────────────┘
```

job applicants for middle management positions, even though the company proclaims its support for equal opportunity. A change in the organization's affirmative action program could initiate an increased flow of female job applicants. The need for change is more easily recognized if significant problems manifest themselves. Examples might be an increase in complaints about harassment, pay equity violations or other human rights questions, loss of market share, an acceleration of employee turnover, declining profit margins, or other serious problems.

The need for change will be overlooked if the indicators are less measurable or dramatic. A loss here and there, a complaining customer, a disgruntled technician, or a lost contract is not always an indicator that change is necessary. The effective manager distinguishes between those incidents that reflect isolated causes and those that are symptoms of wider problems. Recognition of this distinction can be made easier by benchmarking, or comparing how the organization is doing when compared with others in the same or a similar field.[11] For instance, Clayton Appleton, vice president of Toronto Hospital, initiated a survey that gathered performance on 26 different indicators from 28 Canadian hospitals, ranging from the 7000-employee Bloorville Macmillan Centre in Ontario to the much smaller Health Care Corp. of St. John's, Newfoundland. The results of this benchmarking helped the participants to compare their operations with those of other institutions in their own field, and thus to identify soft spots in their own systems.[12]

*Managers must identify when established ways of doing business need to be replaced. The success of Federal Express resulted from its innovation in bringing all shipments to one centralized facility and redirecting them from there.*

## Diagnosis of the Problem

Stage 3 emphasizes diagnosis. As in medicine, a diagnosis begins with identifying the symptoms, and then applying knowledge and experience to deduce what the causes of those symptoms might be. A sound diagnosis can clarify the problem and lead to the means to cure it. Diagnosis may use a variety of techniques. Exhibit 9-4 presents four techniques that are currently used by many managers, either alone or in combination.

As pointed out in Exhibit 9-4, a properly structured series of *interviews* can reveal much information. Like almost any method, interviewing has some drawbacks, including the time and cost required. The other most critical disadvantages are the possibility of misinterpretation of responses and the bias that both the interviewer and the interviewees bring to the process.

*Questionnaires* can cover a much larger number of people than *interviews.* Unless there is extensive follow-up, many of the people to whom the questionnaires are sent will neglect to respond. If the sample is small, the results may reflect a skewed result, because those who respond may have a particular gripe or in other ways be unrepresentative of the larger numbers of those who do not respond. In either case, it would be misleading to assume that the survey results actually represent broadly held views. Like responses to interviews, questionnaire answers are also subject to misinterpretation, and to the natural tendency of employees to want to provide the answers that they think the managers want to receive. Designing questionnaires is a task requiring a high degree of skill and experience, to ensure that the questions are clear and easily answered and that they actually address the issues for which information is desired.

*Observation* requires that those seeking information attend the work site and observe operations for a long enough period to get a clear picture of what is happening. The observer must be sufficiently familiar with the production or service processes to be able to evaluate the performance and identify possible problems. There is the ever-present danger of observer bias. Furthermore, the very presence of the observer will

**Exhibit 9-4**

*Examples of Methods for Diagnosing a Problem*

| Method | Major Advantages | Major Potential Problems |
|---|---|---|
| Interviews | 1. Adaptive—allow data collection on a range of possible subjects.<br>2. Source of "rich" data.<br>3. Emphatic.<br>4. Process of interviewing can build rapport. | 1. Expense.<br>2. Bias in interviewer responses.<br>3. Coding and interpretation difficulties.<br>4. Self-report bias. |
| Questionnaires | 1. Responses can be quantified and easily summarized.<br>2. Easy to use with large samples.<br>3. Relatively inexpensive.<br>4. Can obtain large volume of data. | 1. Nonempathic.<br>2. Predetermined questions miss issues.<br>3. Overinterpretation of data.<br>4. Response bias. |
| Observations | 1. Collect data on behaviour rather than report behaviour.<br>2. Real time, not retrospective.<br>3. Adaptive. | 1. Coding and interpretation difficulties.<br>2. Sampling inconsistencies.<br>3. Observer bias and questionable reliability.<br>4. Expense. |
| Unobtrusive measures | 1. Nonreactive—no response bias.<br>2. High face validity.<br>3. Easily quantified. | 1. Access and retrieval difficulties.<br>2. Validity concerns.<br>3. Coding and interpretation difficulties. |

Source: D. Nadler. *Feedback and Organization Development: Using Data-Based Methods* (Reading, MA: Addison-Wesley, 1977): 119.

affect the outcomes, as it did in the Hawthorne studies. If carelessness is causing an unacceptably high rate of defects, it is not surprising that the operators will become much more careful as soon as they become aware that they are being observed. The defect rate may drop precipitously while the observation is going on, only to rise again as soon as the observer leaves the area.

There are other measures that are reasonably unobtrusive, and consequently that have less effect on the outcomes. An example is the interpretation of statistics that have been gathered for other purposes, or that are gathered as a routine part of the production process. Some problems can be identified just by analyzing these figures, and by identifying trends and changes in trends. Astute managers can choose other unobtrusive measures, tailor-made to suit the circumstances. Managers generally use some combination of several of these and other available methods.

## Diagnosis of the Chance for Success of the Change Program

In addition to diagnosing the causes of the problem itself, in stage 3 managers considering a program of change should conscientiously attempt to diagnose the climate within the organization.

**force field analysis**
Analysis of the forces that might have a positive or negative effect on change.

**driving forces**
Forces, either internal or external, that would facilitate change.

**restraining forces**
Forces that would inhibit, delay, or prevent change.

**Force field analysis.** Once managers have determined that there is a gap between what is happening and what they would like to have happen, they are saying, in essence, that change would be desirable. Before undertaking any change strategy, it is useful to know what the opposing forces are. Those that would work in favour of change are known as **driving forces**; those that would work against change are known as **restraining forces**. This analysis, first described by Lewin, is known as force field analysis, because it is directed to an evaluation of forces. Driving forces might include words of praise from a manager, effective reward systems, and a high level of involvement from non-managerial employees. Common examples of restraining forces are low morale, unpleasant working conditions, financial insecurity (either of the individual or of the organization), and interpersonal conflict. When the driving forces are stronger than the restraining forces, change is likely to be implemented without great difficulty, as long as the implementation of change itself does not inaugurate more restraining forces. Conversely, when the restraining forces are greater than the driving forces, if possible the change should be deferred until the balance is redressed. If it is not feasible to defer the change, managers have to analyze which driving forces can be augmented and which restraining forces can be diminished in their impact. Then an effective program must be mounted to bring about an improvement in the balance of the force fields, before or simultaneously with the inauguration of the major change itself.[13]

**industry foresight**
Predicting the future of an industry in order to shape the present so that the organization will function effectively and competitively in the future.

**Foresight-led change.** In their book *Competing for the Future*, Gary Hamel and C.K. Prahalad argue that most organizations don't spend enough time thinking about the future of their industry and their business. They state that organizations typically exhibit what they call the "40/30/20 rule." Their study found that about 40 percent of senior executive time is spent looking outward, that is, outside the business. Of the time spent looking outward, only 30 percent is spent peering three or more years into the future. And of that time, only about 20 percent is spent attempting to build a collective view of the future. Thus, Hamel and Prahalad say that, on average, senior managers spend less than 3 percent of their time and energy (40% × 30% × 20% = 2.4%) building an organizational perspective of the future.[14]

To compete effectively for the future, organizations must develop what Hamel and Prahalad call **industry foresight**. According to them, "... industry foresight is based on deep insights into the trends in technology, demographics, regulation, and lifestyles that can be harnessed to rewrite industry rules and create new competitive space."[15] They distinguish this term from the more commonly used "vision," a term they don't like because it may connote unreality and intangibility.

**Introducing stretch targets.** Foresight-led change involves looking into the future, determining what the future is likely to be like, and then using that insight to change the organization in the present. Then managers set what may be called **stretch targets**, or objectives that are achievable, but only by dint of sustained and cooperative effort. The use of stretch targets reflects a major shift in the thinking of top management. Executives are recognizing that incremental goals invite managers and other employees to perform the same comfortable processes a little better each year. The all-too-frequent result is mediocrity. Stretch targets require big leaps of progress on such measures as inventory turnover, product development time, and manufacturing cycles. Adopting such imperatives can force companies to reinvent the way they conceive, make, and distribute products and services. Exhibit 9-5 provides guidelines for setting stretch targets.

**stretch target**
A goal or objective that is achievable, but only by the application of considerable effort and energy, and that exceeds the change that would come from a series of small incremental changes.

For CEO John Snow of CSX, the $9.5-billion-a-year railroad and shipping company, stretch targets were a natural extension of his business approach. In 1991, CSX's return on capital hovered well below the full cost of capital. Snow announced a bold goal: to ensure that CSX would earn the full cost of capital by 1993 and to continue to do so thereafter. As Snow predicted, the stretch target that he established forced managers to look hard at the railroad's core problem—the fact that much of the time the company's fleet of locomotives and railcars sat unproductively at loading docks and seaport terminals. Achieving faster turnaround for the massive fleet would greatly reduce unproductive costs, and thus improve the return on capital.

Having set the target, Snow then got out of the way. The strategy proved to be a winner. Since 1991, while handling a surge of business, CSX has eliminated from its rolling stock 20,000 of its 125,000 cars—enough to form a train stretching from Montreal nearly to Toronto—

*John Snow brought about the turnaround at CSX by setting stretch targets.*

but still has the capacity to carry the same amount of freight. As a result of this reduction, annual capital expenditures for supporting the fleet shrank by more than 20 percent—from more than $1 million to $800,000. CSX is now earning its full cost of capital.

**Exhibit 9-5**

*Guidelines for Setting Stretch Targets*

- Set a clear, convincing, long-term corporate goal. Example: Earning the full cost of capital.
- Translate it into one or two specific stretch targets for managers, such as doubling inventory turns.
- Use benchmarking to prove that the goal—though tough—isn't impossible and to enlist employees in the crusade.
- Get out of the way: Let the people in the plants and labs find ways to meet the goals.

## Consideration of Alternatives

It is always tempting to rush into a change program because of a feeling of urgency to correct the problems that have been identified. As a consequence, change may be initiated without proper preparation, and sometimes even with ill-conceived objectives. Even if a feasible solution seems to have presented itself, unless care is taken to seek out alternative solutions (stage 4), it is possible to overlook a much better solution that might have been found if more thought had been given to the process. As described in Chapter 3, decision making may degenerate into satisficing—accepting an *adequate* solution rather than taking the time and energy to find an even better solution. In most cases, the better management technique is to use the methods described in Chapter 3 to ensure that all feasible alternatives have been unearthed. Then, and only then, should the managers decide which alternative to choose.

## Selection of Intervention Change Methods and Implementation

After evaluating the pros and cons of various change techniques, one or some combination of alternatives should be selected and then implemented, as shown in stage 5. Implementation often isn't given enough consideration in attempts to bring about lasting change. It is just as important to plan carefully how, when, and by whom each step in the change program is to be done, as it is to plan the framework of the change itself. Just as in the planning stage, employee participation can help to reduce the resistance that is otherwise likely to arise even if the original announcement of the change was accepted by employees. It is in the implementation stage that people become disoriented, confused, and often fearful and resentful. If they did not pay much attention to the impending change when it was first announced, as soon as the implementation begins the impacts are not only visible but are keenly felt. All of the techniques described to reduce initial resistance must be exercised throughout the implementation stage, or the best-laid plans may well fail.

## Evaluation of Change and Feedback

Managers who have been involved in planning and implementing change often will breathe a sigh of relief as soon as the implementation stage seems to be complete. For days, weeks, or months they have been carrying work overloads from the pressures of the change program. Now, they think, they can get back to their "real work," and begin to clear up the backlogs that have accumulated while they were diverted by the change program. This is a dangerous, but all-too-common misconception. The final stage in the change program is as vital to its success as were the first five stages.

It is axiomatic that no change program designed by human beings is perfect. It is impossible for even the best-informed and most conscientious planning group to have foreseen every possible contingency. And some of those contingencies that were overlooked or deemed too remote to be worth bothering with are sure to occur. It is essential to realize this fact, and to make a concerted effort to identify those glitches in the new system for which answers have not been devised. It is not easy to measure the effects of change, but managers must do the best they can in this endeavour.[16] Keeping in mind the general guidelines that follow will help to make the measurement of effects more accurate and useful.

1. Measurements should be conducted over an extended period of time. Soon after change has occurred, participants are generally excited and interested because they

## Fad Surfing in the Boardroom

The message in this timely and thought-provoking book is twofold. First, Shapiro, the president of management consultant The Hillcrest Group, Inc., says that in her experience CEOs often commit themselves to the latest management fad, and risk everything on its effectiveness. The failures that she recounts are disappointing to any student of management who hopes to find in a new theory something approaching a panacea for the problems that beset managers. In analyzing the failures, Shapiro concludes that they usually stem from the tendency of some executives who are in a hurry to disregard the culture of the organization they are trying to transform. She points out the hazards that arise from trying to institute, for instance, empowerment of non-managerial employees without first having changed the attitudes of middle managers who are likely to resent and resist any attempt to curb their power.

Shapiro's second major theme appears when she decries what she sees as a failure of courage in managers, who look to instant solutions instead of slogging through the hard work of assessing situations, thinking through and choosing among possible options, and developing plans and implementing them. In one of her more trenchant observations, Shapiro says: "The hard truth is that there are no panaceas."

Shapiro's witty yet penetrating observations serve as a useful counterbalance to the spate of books that recommend single-focus solutions to all management problems.

Source: Eileen C. Shapiro, *Fad Surfing in the Boardroom* (Toronto: Addison-Wesley, 1997).

are being asked for their responses. Conducting measurements over a relatively long period of time will help to identify and eliminate distortions caused either by early enthusiasm and novelty, or conversely by inefficiencies that result from the need for employees to learn new methods.

2. When possible, the performance of groups that have undergone change should be compared with those that have not. These comparisons are a form of internal benchmarking, and help to isolate the effects of the change from effects that have arisen from other causes.

3. Quantitative measures such as cost, profit, units produced in a given time, or defect rates should not be the only criteria for evaluation. Managers should attempt to identify subjective measures. These measures might include what participants and non-participants say about the change and about work life in general, how they behave in respect to the work, and how they behave in respect to each other and to managers—all of which may contribute to positive or negative changes in morale.

When even minor loopholes are found, managers must feed them back into the system as new problems that deserve attention, starting again at the first stage of the framework. Pursuing the succeeding stages just as was done in the first cycle, the newly discovered problems will be addressed and solutions will be found and implemented. Presumably this second round will be considerably easier, quicker, and less trauma-inducing than the first round, simply because the new problems are at least an order of magnitude smaller. And so it goes, until after several rounds the new problems are so insignificant that they deserve only quick and simple correction. Only by this application of evaluation and feedback can a change program succeed to its fullest potential.

## Control in a Change Program

Since change disrupts the normal routine of events, existing control mechanisms are inevitably involved. (Chapter 7 explores the controlling function of management, the principles of which are applicable here.) During the transitional period, and sometimes after the change has been implemented, normal control and monitoring may be disrupted or not possible. Control is just as essential, or perhaps even more essential, during a change than during static operations. Consequently, control and monitoring, too, require attention in the same way as the original problems. Part of the stage in which alternatives are devised and considered must relate to the control mechanisms that will be changed and those that will be needed during the transition period. Failure to take account of control questions will lead to the very problems that control mechanisms are designed to alleviate, and may well cause the change program to fail in its entirety.

## Power in a Change Program

The balance of power among groups and the power wielded by individuals will be upset or altered by change. Since change introduces some uncertainty, it creates ambiguity. Uncertainty and ambiguity are breeding grounds for political manoeuvring and power brokering. It is essential, therefore, to include in the planning process an analysis of the changes in power structure, both formal and informal, and to take them into account. Anyone or any group that is destined to lose some power, or that perceives that it will do so, will need special care and handling. Everyone must be told, and understand, what the new power relationships will be, and when and how they are expected to react individually.

## Change Agents

**change agent**
An individual or group of individuals whose intention is to initiate and manage change within an organization.

A **change agent** is an individual or group that initiates and manages change. All managers have the responsibility to be change agents. Sometimes the changes they initiate are only incremental, that is they modify or expand current practice. At other times the changes are dramatic and have widespread and usually long-lasting effects on the organization. The most visible change agents are often the CEOs, because their visions and actions are given wide publicity to people within the organization, through published reports to the shareholders, and often, through the media, to the public at large.

Change is almost a constant in the Canadian business scene. In one reasonably typical week, Canadian newspapers carried lengthy articles on three senior executives who appeared to have been appointed to fill the role of change agent. One was Potash Corp's Charles Childers. In 1987, when he was appointed chairman and CEO of Potash Corp. of Saskatchewan, the company had just reported an annual loss of more than $100 million. Almost immediately after his arrival in the position, he began changing the corporate culture. His leadership as a change agent transformed a company that, to say the least, was not known for its innovative attitudes. He encouraged initiative, sought acquisitions, and, most evident to shareholders, led the company to a large annual profit. As business analyst Janet McFarland wrote in 1996, after nearly a decade of Childers' management: "Mr. Childers has quickly become a star in the unglamorous world of fertilizer, credited with turning around Saskatchewan-based Potash Corp. and making it the dominant world player...."[17]

The way of the high-profile change agent is not always an easy one. After serving 30 years in the ranks at Hydro-Québec, Benoit Michel lasted only seven months after his promotion to president and CEO. The appointment of Andre Delisle to the post was seen to reflect the board's desire to effect change in the corporate culture, and to bring to the huge utility profits that are at least equal to, and preferably better than, the average interest rate on its debt. With the typical utility's huge and apparently entrenched bureaucracy, the task was a formidable one.[18]

Another approach often taken is to retain professional change agents from outside the company. When senior executives of Labatt Breweries Ltd. decided that a major restructuring was necessary, they retained People Tech Consulting to act as change agents. People Tech representatives worked with the Labatt executives to change their focus to one that is more people-oriented than had previously been the case. The consulting group organized and led employee workshops on change, and the company president took a tour of all of the company's regions to explain the plans and how they would affect employees.[19] Subsequent events have shown that the change program was a success.

Although major change usually reflects the vision of senior management, the implementation and management of change necessarily falls to middle managers and supervisors. If they are not fully committed to change, the enthusiasm and even the basic message fails to reach the front-line employees, and the change process is doomed at best to have a minor effect, and at worst, a seriously negative effect.

## Intervention Methods

**intervention method**
The technique or means used to effect change within an organization.

The term **intervention method** is used to describe a method, technique, or means to manage change effectively. An intervention can respond to forces for change or can create forces that provide the impetus for employees to accept change more readily. The type of intervention selected depends on the diagnosis, cost, time available, organizational culture, management's confidence in the expected results, and depth preferred. **Depth of intervention** refers to the extent to which the change agents intend to become involved in people's attitudes and feelings, which is usually related to the degree of change that the intervention is intended to bring about.[20] A shallow intervention seeks mainly to provide information that is helpful to encourage improvements. A manager coaching a subordinate is an example of shallow intervention. Moderate-depth interventions, such as team building and exploring new means of communication, are intended to alter attitudes and perceptions. A deep intervention, such as sensitivity training for managers, is intended to bring about psychological and behavioural changes that will be reflected in improved job performance. With deep interventions, to avoid severe traumas and unpleasant repercussions, managers must exercise extreme caution in selecting change agents to ensure that they have the necessary credentials and experience to conduct this sort of highly sensitive activity.

**depth of intervention**
The extent to which the intended intervention involves changing employee attitudes and behaviours.

Many intervention methods are available for use in stimulating changes in people, structure, and technology. Four will be discussed in the following pages. As might be expected, there is no single method that is perfectly suited to or effective in every situation or case.

## Survey Feedback

**survey feedback**
A shallow intervention method that reports the results of a survey, usually including analysis of the implications of the information.

**Survey feedback** is an organizationally focused, shallow intervention method. This method is typically conducted in four stages.[21] First, a change agent works with top management to design the questions to be used in the survey to elicit the information being sought. Second, information is collected from a sample of managers and non-managers, or from everyone in an entire unit population (department, division, or in rare cases the whole organization). Data may be collected using a questionnaire, a series of structured interviews, a review of historical records, or some combination of these methods. Third, the change agent categorizes, summarizes, and interprets the information received from the survey and prepares reports. Fourth, employees are given feedback, meetings are held to discuss the findings, and implementation is begun on action plans for overcoming the identified problems.

Survey feedback is a popular intervention method. It can be efficient and participatory and provide much job-relevant information. As is usually the case, top management's endorsement and involvement are needed to help survey feedback achieve its goals.[22]

## Coaching and Mentoring

A shallow intervention that is crucial to the ongoing health of an organization is the mentoring done by experienced employees and managers, to assist in a gentle way the learning that all new and inexperienced employees must undergo. Sometimes this mentoring is part of the more experienced employee's job assignment; more often it is unscheduled, unplanned, and, regrettably, unrecognized and unrewarded by the mentor's managers. Experienced employees who naturally take to the mentoring role, and who can mentor without offending the less experienced, should be nurtured and, to the extent possible within organizational policies, rewarded by reducing their work loads, providing merit increases, and, when appropriate, promoting them. Such informal training is inexpensive, timely, and most effective because it is offered in small bites, rather than the huge gulps that formal training programs often require of the trainees.

## Team Building

**team building**
A moderate-depth intervention that is designed to create a sense of belonging to a "team" and, consequently, a willingness to work cooperatively to achieve the established goals.

**Team building** is a moderate-depth intervention that attempts to improve diagnosis, communication, cooperation, and the performance of members and the overall team. The team-building process should not be confused with the use of teams in problem solving that was described in Chapter 5. Unlike those teams, the purpose of team building is not so much to solve identified problems but rather to focus on the team itself. Its primary purpose is to develop a sense of *belonging* to the team, which it is hoped will lead to a desire to cooperate within the team to achieve common goals.

Team building involves setting goals and priorities, analyzing the group's work methods, examining the group's communication and decision-making processes, and examining interpersonal relationships within the group.[23] As each of these aims is undertaken, the group is placed in the position of having to recognize explicitly each group member's contributions, both positive and negative.[24]

The process by which these aims are achieved begins with diagnostic meetings. Often lasting an entire day, the meetings enable all team members to share with other members their perceptions of problems. If the team is large enough, subgroups engage in discussion and report their ideas to the total group. These sessions are designed for the sharing of all members' views. In this context, diagnosis emphasizes the value of open airing of issues and problems that were previously only the topics of gossip.

Next, a *plan of action* must be agreed upon. The plan should call on each group member, individually or as part of a subgroup, to act specifically to alleviate at least one problem that has been identified within the team. If, for example, it is agreed that there is a lack of understanding of and commitment to goals, a subgroup can be appointed to recommend goals to the total group at a subsequent meeting. At the same time, if problems

*Some organizations encourage their employees to engage in strenuous outdoor experiences to build teamwork and trust.*

are found in the relationships among the members, a second subgroup can initiate a process for examining each member's role in this respect.

Team building is particularly effective when new groups are being formed. There are often relationship problems when new organizational units, project teams, or task forces are created. Typically, members of such groups have technical expertise, but there is ambiguity about roles and relationships. Furthermore, because the group members are task-oriented, they often pay more attention to the team's assigned tasks than to relationships among team members. By the time relationship problems begin to surface, the patterns of behaviours have been firmly established and the group cannot deal with the problems. Performance then begins to deteriorate.

To combat these tendencies, a new group should schedule team-building meetings during the first weeks of its life. Meetings should take place away from the work site, so that members will not be distracted by the intrusion of day-to-day problems. Sometimes a half-day session may suffice, but one- or two-day sessions are often more successful. The format of such meetings varies, but their purpose is to enable the group to work through its timetable and members' roles in reaching the group's objectives.[25] Reports on team building indicate mixed results, but some evidence suggests that group processes often improve through team-building efforts.[26] This record of success accounts for the increasing use of team building as an organizational development method.[27] However, not all companies are rushing ahead to manage their business through the use of employee teams. Teams are probably not more widely used because a team is not easy to manage, and the results of team building are not easily measurable.[28]

## Empowerment

Another method that involves deeper intervention is to empower managers and other employees. As noted earlier, empowerment is a process that is designed to increase people's involvement in their work, including design of the job, work flow, interactions, and decision making. Empowerment can occur for individuals or for groups. It involves far more than giving employees greater decision-making power. In a true empowerment scenario, employees at all levels of the organization are involved in planning and problem solving in areas related to their work.[29] At its most practical level, empowerment uncovers and recognizes the wealth of useful knowledge and internal motivation that people will apply if given a chance.

As described by Margaret Houston and John Talbott in *CMA Magazine*:

Empowerment means self-direction, allowing people to participate in the decisions that affect them. It is a move from the conventional form of management to a transformational form of leadership.

1) Employees feel responsible not just for doing a job, but also for making the whole organization work better. They own rather than rent their jobs.
2) Teams work together to improve their performance continually, achieving higher levels of productivity.
3) Organizations are structured in such a way that people feel that they are able to achieve the results they want, that they can do what needs to be done, not just what is required of them, and be rewarded for doing so.[30]

Research has shown that there are three organizational ingredients for successful employee empowerment:

1. Open and candid sharing of information on business performance with all employees;
2. More structure (rather than less), as teams and employee groups move into self-management; and
3. Replacement of the organizational hierarchy with teams.[31]

Ultimately, achieving competitive success through people involves fundamentally altering how one thinks about the workforce and the employment relationship. It means achieving success by working with people, not by replacing them or limiting the scope of their activities. It entails seeing the workforce as a source of strategic strength and opportunity, not just as a cost to be minimized or avoided if possible. Organizations that take this different perspective are often able to outperform their rivals.[32]

Over the long term, the most productive employees are motivated by a sense of achievement, recognition, enjoyment of the job, promotion opportunities, responsibility, and the chance for personal growth. Employee motivation and performance are tied to the style of management that is applied and to the principles of positive or negative reinforcement.

Today, top-level managers at some of the most successful organizations are creating organizational change by increasing their face-to-face contacts with the people that make the organization run on a daily basis. Leaders such as Percy Barnevik of Asea Brown Boveri are beginning to articulate management's challenge to engage the unique knowledge, skills, and abilities of every individual in the organization. Their management philosophy is based on a personalized approach that encourages a diversity of points of view and empowers employees to contribute their own ideas.[33]

## Identifying and Coping with Employee Stress

Life itself is a constant source of stress, and without some degree of stress individuals would not function at all. On the other hand, an undue amount of stress can have severe effects on behaviour. Stress arises from many personal sources that are completely unrelated to the job. Research shows that people's stress levels often rise most when they experience the death of a family member or a close friend, when they undergo the breakup of a marriage or personal relationship, or when they face particularly difficult financial problems. Managers can do little about these external factors except to make allowances and be particularly understanding to all for a reasonable period of recovery. Other major sources of stress, however, are very much within the scope of the manager's responsibilities. Many employees experience high levels of stress when their job responsibilities change, when they feel unsure of what is expected of them, when they have to become accustomed to a different immediate supervisor, or when they feel that their work load is excessive.[34]

Recent studies have confirmed some earlier conjectures that the employees who are most subject to stress-related illness are not the high-tension CEOs or managers, but the employees who feel that they are not in control of their work and can do nothing about it. For instance, bus drivers and other mass transit operators find their work extremely stressful because they are required to meet precise timetables. They must maintain schedules despite traffic conditions, weather, and the vagaries of passengers, all of which are largely beyond their control.[35] In the office environment, the hard-driving manager has considerable latitude in determining what to do and when, while the manager's per-

*Too much stress can lead to employee burnout.*

sonal assistant has virtually no personal discretion, but must fit tasks into the schedule set by the manager—a recipe for stress.

The existence of any of these stressors may result in decreased production, absenteeism, carelessness, and accidents. Frequently they also lead to a tendency to anger or to psychological withdrawal and sulking. Consequently, the wise manager tries not to institute organizational change when one or more key employees are known to be suffering unduly from stress, and also tries to recognize that whatever change is contemplated is likely to result in some degree of increased stress for everyone involved. To maximize acceptance of change, then, the effective manager seeks to understand the causes of stress and to alleviate them by providing employees with more opportunity to participate in decisions that affect them and to have more influence on the timing and methods of their own work.

As is the case with other forms of health, prevention of employee stress is preferable to curing it after it occurs. The first line of defence is to be careful in selecting employees in the hope of avoiding those applicants who are unusually subject to ill effects from stress. Then, when considering organizational change, managers must be prepared for the effects of the stress that probably will be manifested, and should not become either discouraged or punitive. Instead the manager should use the techniques discussed in the section on reducing resistance to change and exhibit more than usual patience during and for a reasonable period after the change takes place.

As managers pay more attention to organizational culture, they need to have some insight into how it can be shaped and managed. The next section explores some ways to do this.

## Reshaping Culture and Structure

There are several intervention methods available to managers for successfully implementing change. But their impact is often limited by the culture and structure of the organization. Although interventions can be attempted at either a shallow or a deep level, ultimately both culture and structure may have to be altered to effect significant change.

### Cultural Reshaping

As described in Chapter 2, organizational culture consists of an unwritten code of behaviours and values that make up the belief system that prevails in an organization. It determines how things "should" be done and what behaviour is not acceptable. Consequently, any material change may be interpreted as an assault on the accepted norms. The culture of an organization is rooted in the national cultures of its country of origin.[36] As Canadian companies expanded overseas, the national cultures of the host nations, a diverse workforce, and new competitors helped shape internal company cultures back in Canada. Making a sudden, drastic change in the internal organizational culture of a domestic or international organization is extremely difficult, but in some circumstances the situation is such that it is not feasible to wait for an accumulation of unobtrusive, incremental changes.

As Compaq Computer learned from its reshaping in the early 1990s, there are five keys to creating a culture change:

1. *Provide a clear vision and decisive leadership.* When Eckhard Pfeiffer took over as CEO of Compaq in 1991, he exhorted people "to compete for market share across the entire spectrum" of the PC industry. "That was a simple change," he recalls. But, he continues, such a strategic shift is so radical that "you have to communicate it a hundred times or more. It doesn't sink in the first few times."

2. *Change the old guard.* Six senior Compaq executives quit soon after Pfeiffer became CEO. He trimmed nearly 20 percent of the total workforce during his first year.

3. *Tackle many problems at the same time.* During his first year Pfeiffer unveiled a new line of bargain-priced computers and also mounted an assault on the small-business and home-PC markets. In addition, he overhauled the manufacturing process and, as if that weren't enough change, he expanded abroad. In the "freeze-unfreeze and change-freeze again" sequence, Pfeiffer made clear his determination to "unfreeze and change."

4. *Change how the company's employees are judged and rewarded.* Especially, make sure that the compensation of management is tied to fulfilment of the new corporate goals.

**Exhibit 9-6**

*Juran's Breakthrough Sequence*

1. (Urge a) *breakthrough in attitudes.* Managers must first prove that a breakthrough is needed and then create a climate conducive to change. Information is collected to show the extent of the problem.

2. *Identify the vital few projects.* Managers must focus on a few vital projects, based on the frequency with which they occur and their impact, giving them priority over the multiplicity of trivial problems that always exist.

3. *Organize for breakthrough in knowledge.* A steering group and a diagnostic group are established. The steering group, composed of people from several departments, defines the program, suggests possible problem causes, gives authority to experiment, helps overcome resistance to change, and implements the solution. The diagnostic group, composed of quality professionals and sometimes line managers, analyzes the problem.

4. *Conduct the analysis.* The diagnostic group studies symptoms, develops hypotheses, and experiments to find the problem's true causes. It also determines whether defects are primarily operator or management controllable. The diagnostic group then proposes solutions to the problem.

5. *Determine how to overcome resistance to change.* The need for change is established in appropriate terms for people involved. Logical arguments alone are insufficient. Participation is required in both the technical and social aspects of change.

6. *Institute the change.* Departments that must take corrective action must be convinced to cooperate. These departments need to know the size of the problem, alternative solutions, the cost of recommended change, expected benefits, and efforts taken to anticipate the change's impact on employees. Time for reflection and adequate training are important.

7. *Institute controls.* Controls are set up to monitor the solution and keep abreast of unforeseen developments. The control sequence provides follow-up to monitor and correct sporadic problems.

Source: Adapted from V. Daniel Hunt, *Managing Quality: Integrating Quality and Business Strategy* (Homewood, IL: Business One Irwin, 1993): 79.

5. *Have full backing from the board, along with full accountability.* Board support is absolutely essential in a turnaround because, as Pfeiffer says, "You don't have a guarantee that it is going to be a winner. We have seen too many attempts that didn't work out."[37]

Employees are socialized into an organization's culture by a wide variety of practices, some subtle, some not so subtle. Shared meals, rituals, dress codes, and group membership result in socialization. By encouraging extensive interaction among employees, organizations help them become more attuned to the culture. In Exhibit 9-6 Joseph Juran suggests a seven-step process for identifying the need for change, and for implementing and monitoring it.

To reshape cultures to fit employees' mood and thinking, managers have moved towards a reward system that focuses on individual and group contributions to productivity rather than on seniority, loyalty, and friendships. To counter the jealousy and negative consequences that often accompany individually based merit pay rewards, an increasing number of companies are using company-wide or group-based profit sharing and bonus plans, as were discussed in Chapter 8.

Changes in society and in perceptions among employees have pointed out some significant inequities in the distribution of rewards, opportunities to learn new skills, and power within organizations.[38] Many employees have been alienated by the widely publicized golden parachutes that are often awarded to senior managers involved in mergers and acquisitions. They also notice and are often offended by the reports of senior managers' large paycheques and bonus packages. These reactions intensify the feelings that individual employees are not respected, with the predictable negative effects on morale, commitment, and productivity. Encouraging and practising more equity within the culture can, if done effectively, result in positive attitudes and feelings being transmitted in the course of employees' socialization.

Where cultural features support past ineffective or failed strategies, they can constrain change. Generating change involves (1) understanding the powerful force of culture, (2) aligning culture with positive ethical and equitable values, and (3) devising sound reward, education, and socialization systems. In a growing number of organizations, managers realize that reshaping culture requires reshaping structures.

## Structural Reshaping

Structural reshaping requires an understanding of power, authority, and personal interactions in organizational settings. The organization chart is intended to reflect how the organization works. Unfortunately, it seldom does so. The preparation of an organization chart may help to identify and define lines of accountability, but once it is prepared, it may mislead rather than enlighten. Many informal, but nonetheless important, relationships help to shape operations, yet are not shown on the organization charts and in many cases are not even known about by people other than those directly involved. Furthermore, communication goes on every day that cuts across organizational lines of authority yet, as a practical matter, helps to get the work done.

Another problem with organization charts is that they present an organization's structure as fixed and rigid. This, of course, isn't how most real interactions occur. Managers must use a dynamic approach to structure so that they can respond to changing conditions. Viewing the structure as a fluid and flexible blueprint is more compatible with today's world than establishing a set structure and trying to adhere rigidly to it for an extended period of time.

As changes become more far-reaching and as competition becomes more innovative, managers must be more responsive to the need to modify their structures. In recent years, restructuring has often entailed the splitting up of major corporations to permit each segment to focus more clearly on narrowly defined objectives. It was for this reason that Frank Stronach, chairman and founder of Magna International Inc., announced in December 1997 that the company would spin off its nearly billion-dollar Decoma division.[39] The restructuring of large, tightly centralized bureaucratic structures continues. Large organizations still exist, but with reshaped structures. This reshaping reflects the thinking of progressive managers, who are eliminating layers of administrators, decentralizing decision making, encouraging employee involvement, and improving communication. These processes are easy to state but often difficult to implement because of old fixed cultural norms, policies, rituals, and ideology. The productivity loss due to fixed, rigid, and culturally bound structures is incalculable in terms of lost efficiency, disaffected and lost customers, and failure to achieve global competitiveness.[40]

## The Challenge for Top Management

To achieve effective change, there must be organization-wide changes in attitudes, communication, employee involvement, and commitment. This is a large undertaking for any organization. Too often managers recognize the enormity of the task and hesitate to initiate change because it seems so overwhelming that it will be sure to fail. The power to make substantial change is largely vested in senior management. These few people must show the way, articulate the vision, and show by example that the quest for competitiveness is a matter of survival and that participation in the change process is mandatory for everyone in the organization.

Improved communications initiated by management must be a top priority. Merely inundating non-managerial employees with information is not enough. Communication must be a two-way process. Everyone must have an opportunity to provide input on the change and the strategy for change and, most of all, to be sincerely heard by managers. Through effective communication, management must explain why change is needed, how and when it will be accomplished, and what benefits accrue to *everyone involved.*

Managers must maintain overall control of the change process to avoid chaos. At the same time, managers must guide with a sufficiently loose rein that everyone's influence can be felt and acted on.

Management must be prepared for resistance to a change in culture, and recognize that it may take several years for it to become completely ingrained and effective. Unfortunately, many companies that have embarked on restructuring and cultural change have given up during the early stages of implementation. A McKinsey and Company survey found that two out of every three such programs stall and fail to deliver tangible improvements in performance.[41] The reasons for these dropouts vary: Initiators may have failed to carry their fellow managers with them; companies may be disappointed with early results and abandon the project prematurely; change programs may have unleashed forces that top managers view as uncontrollable and potentially destructive; and when there is a change in top management, incoming CEOs may regard current improvement programs as constraints on their authority[42] to make other changes that for them have a higher priority.

Nonetheless, the potential effectiveness of restructuring techniques is evident from the remarkable business turnarounds that companies such as Motorola, Saskatchewan Potash, Magna, and Ford Motor of Canada have achieved. In these companies and many others, change programs have been successful not just in improving product and service quality, but also in improving competitive and financial performance, enriching the jobs of employees, and transforming corporate cultures. The effectiveness of change programs is also evident in the fact that most colleges, universities, hospitals, and other victims of government cutbacks are still functioning despite what a few years ago would have been thought to be fatal reductions in support. In some cases, restructuring has achieved efficiencies; in other cases, the changes have doubtless resulted in limiting the availability of services, and perhaps the quality of those services. Whatever one concludes about the results of these changes, few would doubt that the institutions had no choice if they were to survive. These organizations had changes forced on them, just as all organizations have changes forced on them by circumstances beyond their immediate control.

## The Workplace of Tomorrow

The job of restructuring, reshaping, and implementing change is never done. Once a goal has been achieved, the organization must shift its focus to the next priority. Even though the first program has been successfully implemented, for the company to remain competitive, it is necessary for top management to initiate the next in the series of improvements. This building block approach has produced concrete results for some companies, and many are now adopting it. At Hewlett-Packard, CEO John Young promoted a single goal of a tenfold reduction in the expense of fulfilling warranties. This goal was structured to be reached in a series of steps. A similar one-at-a-time, sequential goal approach is central to Motorola's improvement program, in which quality targets are constantly updated with new standards as the old standards are met and surpassed.[43] Achieving and maintaining competitiveness is a never-ending challenge for managers in any type of organization. But, in the words of Deutsche Telekom's CEO, Ron Sommer, "It's not magic. You just have to do it."[44]

## Summary of Learning Objectives

▷ **Explain why individuals often resist change in organizational settings.**
Some individuals resist change because they are suffering from undue stress, either from causes within the organization or from situations within their personal lives. Others resist change for reasons of self-interest, because of fear, or because they are being subjected to peer pressure. Change is also stifled by bureaucratic inertia that reflects the tendency of people to hold on to habitual ways of acting.

▷ **Describe the different types of change agents.**
Outside pressure comes from an individual, group, or situation that is not within the organization, but that exercises influence over how the organization operates. Change agents employing people-change technology attempt to bring about change by altering people's behaviour directly through behaviourally oriented techniques. Organizational development change agents attempt to change behaviours of the entire organization through intervention methods that affect most individuals in the organization.

▷ **Define** *survey feedback* **and explain how it is used.**
Survey feedback is an organizationally focused, shallow intervention method that typically follows a four-step sequence. First, a questionnaire is designed after consulting with top

management. Second, data are collected from a sample or from a whole population. Third, survey data are categorized, summarized, interpreted, and gathered in a report. Fourth, informational feedback is given and action plans for solving problems are developed.

▷ **Explain how managers can use the six steps described as constituting the framework for managing change.**

A framework that can be used to manage change includes six steps: identifying forces for change, recognizing the need for change, diagnosing the problem(s) and points of resistance, considering possible alternative intervention methods, selecting methods of intervention and implementation, and evaluating change and then restarting the process.

▷ **Discuss why it is often difficult to reshape an organization's culture.**

Culture is so embedded and pervasive that it has become the basis for the behaviour that is "expected." Individuals hesitate to deviate from that behaviour because they instinctively fear rejection by the group. Furthermore, many individuals within the organization enjoy their present status and the comfort of knowing what is expected, so they prefer that the underlying culture remain unchanged.

▷ **Explain the types of diagnostic techniques available to managers.**

Tools of diagnosis include interviews, questionnaires, observations, and unobtrusive measures, such as observing the increase in noise level from a malfunctioning machine or analyzing statistics that are gathered routinely as part of normal operations. Each method has advantages and disadvantages.

▷ **Explain the technique of** *force field analysis.*

Force field analysis is a technique by which a manager defines the driving and restraining forces of change and assigns a value to each based on the degree to which it can influence the change process.

▷ **Explain the term** *foresight-led change.*

Foresight-led change helps managers prepare for the future. It involves attempting to predict what the future will be like and then using that insight to change the organization in the present to prepare to be competitive in that future.

▷ **Describe what is meant by a** *stretch target,* **and how managers can use it to achieve greater competitiveness.**

Stretch targets are those that involve major changes in quality, competitiveness, and effectiveness. They require transformation of the organization and, as a consequence, also require far-reaching shifts in thinking by individuals at all levels of the organization. A stretch target is contrasted with an incremental target, which requires only minor adjustment in thinking, attitudes, and actions.

## KEY TERMS

## REVIEW AND DISCUSSION QUESTIONS

### Recall

1. What do employees fear when a change is being considered?
2. Explain how force field analysis may help a manager to decide whether a change can be effectively managed at the present time.
3. What are the hazards of superficial involvement of non-managerial employees in the change process?

### Understanding

4. Why is survey feedback considered a shallow change intervention?
5. Why do many employees resist change even though the outcomes of the change may be beneficial to them?

### Application

6. Conduct your own diagnosis of a situation among your classmates, at home, or at work. Based on your diagnosis, what kind of change is needed? What methods might make that change more readily accepted by those affected?
7. Review some organizational development and training literature. Look at the most recent five years of a journal such as *Training, Training and Development,* or *Organizational Dynamics.* How many articles or pages in the most recent five-year period are directed to evaluating change programs? Why do you think this is the case?
8. Interview two or three human resource managers. Ask what framework or method their organizations use to manage change.
9. Use force field analysis to analyze the potential for changing your major field of study. What are the driving forces? What are the restraining forces?
10. Set a stretch target in your own life. What steps can you begin to take now to achieve that stretch target?

## CASE 9-1

### Volkswagen: A Return to Proven Methods

The consolidation of the European Union (EU) has created a sense of urgency in the European business community. How will business need to adapt? What opportunities and threats does the new, expanded market hold? Who will win? Who will lose?

Volkswagen AG has been a leader in European auto manufacturing since the 1930s. In the last decade, since Carl H. Hahn became chairman of the board of management, a rapid pace of expansion has been set with manufacturing plants now located in Mexico, China, Spain, the Czech Republic, and Germany, and strategic alliances functioning in Canada and the United States.

Hahn believes that the EU will become a new platform for global competition rather than an economic fortress, as some Western economists fear. Within this new platform, he hopes to convert Volkswagen into a "federated" community. That is, each of the various plants and operating units will be granted autonomy to achieve excellence. Hahn points out that smaller operating units enable the company to satisfy narrower and narrower groups of customers. He says, "We want integrated factories and design centers to offer customers the touches they really want. We want a network of various dealer organizations, in various locations, selling makes of various character, addressing various markets."

At the same time, it is important to Volkswagen's overall success to maintain the traditional quality standards customers have come to expect. On this point Hahn points to the company's failed effort to manufacture in the United States:

> Our U.S. manufacturing venture proved to be quite problematic. Our basic mistake was to entrust the design adaptation of the Golf—you knew it as the Rabbit—to "American" thinking: too much attention to outward appearances, too little to engineering detail. … We gave American customers a car with all the handling characteristics—one might say, the smell—of a U.S. car. We should have restricted ourselves to our traditional appeal, aiming at customers who were looking not for an American style but for a European feel.

The secret to success in the new European market, Hahn believes, is to be more aggressive about offering and learning to cope with variety. Niche marketing and increasingly individualized customer-manufacturer relationships will be critical to success. Hahn thinks that Volkswagen and other EU businesses can learn much from the Japanese. He laments that, for years, Western business leaders have complained that Japanese success in manufacturing was due to unfair trade practices or, from a Western point of view, an uneasy alliance between government and business. In reality, he says:

> The Japanese have simply re-examined the rules of manufacturing. They have had to overcome a reputation they have had for making junk, so they applied the lessons of certain American experts that most everybody else was ignoring. We have to realize their achievement, grapple with it, and change our attitudes. We have to go and learn, we Germans, we Europeans.

Hahn's federated vision for Volkswagen mirrors the transformation that Europe itself is going through. Although the EU is one large market with its member countries closely allied economically, the thrust is towards the individual, or at least towards small ethnic or racial enclaves. Volkswagen's goal is to grow along with a united Europe and create in its burgeoning, integrated market a base of operations for global competition. Hahn plans to do this by playing to the unique tastes of the various enclaves that are sure to remain a part of the European landscape despite economic unity. He envisions smaller plants capable of turning out 1000 to 1500 cars per day instead of the typical 4000. "The point" he says, "is to de-emphasize capital and automation and reemphasize the flexibility of the human being."

## Questions

1. Volkswagen's effort to build cars in the United States failed because its cars became too "American." Explain what this means.
2. Has Volkswagen conducted what you consider to be a thorough diagnosis to determine what changes needed to be made? Explain.
3. What structural reshaping is Hahn using to return Volkswagen to better performance?

Source: Adapted from Bernard Avashai, "A European Platform for Global Competition: An Interview with VW's Carl Hahn," *Harvard Business Review*, 69 (July-August 1991): 113; *and* William Dunn, "The Move Toward Ethnic Marketing," *Nation's Business*, 80 (July 1992): 39-41.

**CASE 9-2**

## Marks & Spencer

Michael Marks arrived in England in 1882 and began work as a peddler in Leeds. Within two years he had opened a stall that did business on Tuesdays and Saturdays. Above one section of his small table was a sign that said, "Don't ask the price. It's a penny."

Marks developed his small market and began to expand until Marks & Spencer, the successor to that tiny stall, had captured 20 percent of retail sales and service in the United Kingdom. Not content, Marks & Spencer opened retail outlets in Canada, Hong Kong, other Commonwealth countries, and nearly 30 other countries as well. In a decade ending in the early 1990s, Marks & Spencer achieved annual sales of about £5.6 billion (Cdn$13 billion) and tripled its annual profits to £680 million (Cdn$1.6 billion).

From the first, Marks & Spencer's success has been built on paying attention to people. According to an article in *The Economist*, "Marks & Spencer started being nice to its employees, customers, suppliers and neighbors decades before it was fashionable to do so. In the 1890s Michael Marks, the firm's founder, put wooden platforms behind his market stalls to keep salesgirls' feet warm; these days the company pays for everything from in-house dentists to local community projects."

In a recent survey of 1800 British business people, Marks & Spencer placed in the top three in six of the eight categories. It ranked number one in the ability to attract and retain the best employees. It also ranked number one in value as a long-term investment and in community responsibility, number two in quality of management and in quality of products and services, and number three in financial soundness.

M&S long ago asked, "What does the customer really want?" Its decision to focus on the customer led it to define its business as supplying targeted customers with a range of affordable, good-quality products. M&S has always viewed itself as the interpreter to industry of a burgeoning consumer market. M&S quickly moved to using its "St. Michael" brand to simplify its product line, build a brand image, and, they thought, make extensive advertising unnecessary.

As competition intensified from such discounters as Wal-Mart and Costco, Marks & Spencer needed to find new ways to remain competitive, or at least find better ways of doing what it has done so well for more than a century. Marks & Spencer has undergone countless restructurings and other changes as its markets have grown and its countries of operation have been extended. Apparently the M&S name was so well known in the U.K. that widespread advertising was not necessary. Company managers made the mistake of assuming that the same situation would apply in Canada. Events have shown that the brand was not a household name in Canada, and that the policy that was successful in the home country was a recipe for failure in Canada because of the different circumstances. The most recent restructuring for M&S was to bow to the inevitable and withdraw from Canada.

### Questions

1. Based only on the facts that appear in this case study, what do you think were the points in its history at which the most dramatic changes had to be instituted by managers of Marks & Spencer?
2. What strengths have been described in the Marks & Spencer policy and philosophy that would make future changes more readily accepted than otherwise?
3. What inherent characteristics of the company would make it difficult to institute major changes?

4. What changes in the Canadian environment suggested that Marks & Spencer would have to make major changes in its ways of doing business?

_____

Source: K.K. Tse, *Marks & Spencer: Anatomy of Britain's Most Efficiently Managed Company* (Oxford: Pergamon, 1985); Staff, "Britain's Most Admired Companies," *The Economist* (January 26, 1991): 66-67.

## ▶ *APPLICATION EXERCISE* 9-1

### The Beacon Aircraft Co.

The marketing division of the Beacon Aircraft Co. has gone through two reorganizations in the past two years. Initially its structure changed from a functional form to a matrix form. But the matrix structure didn't satisfy some functional managers. They complained that the structure confused the authority and responsibility relationships.

In reaction to these complaints, the marketing manager revised the structure back to the functional form. This new structure maintained market and project groups, which were managed by project managers with a few general staff personnel. But no functional specialists were assigned to these groups.

After the most recent change some problems began to surface. Project managers complained that they couldn't obtain adequate assistance from functional staff. The new structure not only resulted in more time being necessary to obtain necessary assistance, it also created problems in establishing stable relationships with functional staff members. Since these problems affected their services to customers, project managers demanded a change in the organizational structure—probably again towards a matrix structure. Faced with these complaints and demands from project managers, the vice president is pondering another reorganization. He has requested an outside consultant to help him with the reorganization plan.

1. Divide into groups of five to seven students. The members of your group will take the role of consultants to Beacon Aircraft.
2. With the other members of your group, identify and list Beacon Aircraft's driving and resisting forces.
3. Develop a set of strategies for increasing the driving forces and another set for reducing the resisting forces.
4. Prepare a list of changes Beacon Aircraft should introduce.
5. When the class reassembles, discuss each group's recommendations.

_____

Source: Adapted from K.H. Chung and L.C. Megginson, *Organizational Behavior* (New York: Harper & Row, 1981): 498-99. Reproduced with permission.

## ▶ *APPLICATION EXERCISE* 9-2      ACTIVITY

### Flexibility Evaluation

To manage changes we need to develop our own flexibility. We need to develop the skills to see things from many points of view and to respond to things in different ways. *On a scale of 1 to 10 rate yourself in the following behaviours.*

1. I handle multiple assignments and commitments well.
2. I constantly need to juggle my work to fit in new priorities and realities.
3. I can work in an ambiguous context, and when given an ambiguous assignment I make it work best for me and my priorities.
4. In emergencies I can prioritize my commitments and proceed, addressing the most critical issue first.
5. I am able to make compromises in order to move an assignment forward.
6. I am able to juggle the payoff between "perfect," "well done," and "good enough" to meet the needs, and will do so as required.
7. I am able to look at conflict in areas related to accomplishing a task and I deal with the issues in a nonpersonal, proactive manner.
8. I am able to address my own behaviours or performance and do so when I receive feedback that indicates this is needed.
9. I am able to deal with the same issue in different ways, depending on the personality and relationship of the other person concerned.
10. I work well with all personality types.
11. I constantly search for new and better ways to fulfil my responsibilities.
12. I ask for feedback from many sources. *Flexibility Evaluation Scoring Summary*

Total your score. 110-120: You wish! Look at your answers again. 100-110: A very high score. Make sure you solicit feedback to evaluate your answers against. 80-100: Excellent work. You are on the right path. 60 to 80: Keep up the good work. Make commitments to work on your flexibility in little steps. Be sure to celebrate success. Under 60: Our constantly changing world will be a challenge for you. Work on making yourself comfortable with little changes one at a time and you will be more accepting of the change around you.

Analyze those areas on which you have scored yourself high or low. Share this information and ask for feedback from classmates or other colleagues. Do their perspectives match your own? How are their perspectives different? Is it possible that you may intend things, but that others do not see or experience them as you would wish? What can you do to enhance your flexibility?

---

Contributed by Sydney Scott, British Columbia Institute of Technology.

## INTERNET APPLICATION   9-1

Enter the Web site of the Potash Corporation (www.potashcorp.com). Read about the company under the Overview heading and then check out the Profile section to read about how the company has evolved.

1. What is the company's main reason for success?
2. What is the company's strategy for growth?

Search for a Web site that tells the story of how an organization changed its structure in some way to increase efficiency and effectiveness. List details of how the organization achieved its goal.

# Interpersonal and Organizational Communication

After studying this chapter, you should be able to:

▶ Describe the communica-
tion process;

▶ Discuss the role of communication in organizations;

▶ Describe some of the
barriers to organizational
communication;

▶ Contrast the different
types of interpersonal
communication;

▶ Explain the importance of
informal communication;
and

▶ Discuss how organizations
can facilitate communication.

## Words May Mean Different Things to Different People

WHILE A FATHER RELAXED ON THE CHESTERFIELD watching the Grey Cup, his four-year-old son and two-year-old daughter asked him if they could wash their fire truck in the family room. He answered, "Sure, just put a towel under the truck and be sure to keep the water on the towel," and went back to watching the game. But when he got up at half-time, he heard gales of laughter from the family room. Checking on the kids, he found the carpet completely drenched with water. His question: "What do you think you're doing?" Their answer: "You said to keep the water on the towel and we did." Unfortunately they had poured dozens of buckets of water on the towel. It took a week to dry the carpet, the floor, and the room on the storey below. The father had intended to convey one meaning; the children had understood something quite different. Both the father and the children were well-intentioned, but through miscommunication the damage was done. ▶

It is not just in parent-child communications that problems can arise because of the different perspectives of those who say something and those to whom it is said. Few people would suggest that managers and non-managers have the same outlook and therefore the same bases for interpreting messages they send or receive. Yet, they communicate frequently on the tacit assumption that they do think alike. Their backgrounds, which may be different, their breadth of vision, which is likely to be different, and their motives (that is, what is important to them), which are almost certain to be different, will lead them to interpret the same message differently.

Communication errors also may arise when one person takes for granted that the other has all of the same information. If a manager tells a subordinate employee, "I need that report as soon as possible," the statement is open to such differing interpretations that two employees may react quite differently. One may work along at a normal pace, thinking that there is no urgency and that the boss simply wants to know when the report is finished, so that the employee should concentrate on that task to the exclusion of others. Another employee, hearing the same words, especially if they have been uttered in a gruff or impatient tone, may work all night without a break in order to place the report on the boss's desk the following morning. Which did the manager intend? The words were not precise, so either interpretation is valid. How much better it would have been if the manager had said, "I need that report no later than 9 a.m. Wednesday, in order to review it and summarize it for the board meeting that afternoon." That communication likely would have told the employee exactly what the manager needed, when, and why the deadline was inflexible. Both the manager and the other employee would have had the same understanding of the request, and would have felt comfortable that they were thinking alike on the subject.

In most organizations vague requests and orders, generalized statements, and misinterpreted communications cause constant conflict and ill will. With some attention and effort, communication skills can be improved markedly. Only when managers and non-managers alike work to perfect their communication skills—not only "sending messages" but accurate listening as well—will these problems be reduced.  ■

## Communication: A Management Essential

Some students of management say that communication is the single most important factor in ensuring that an organization becomes and remains competitive.[1] The view that communication is critical to organizational excellence dates back at least to 1938, when Chester Barnard wrote his influential book, *The Functions of the Executive*.[2] In it, Barnard described one of executives' major responsibilities as developing and maintaining a system of communication. Organization members must solve increasingly complex problems. Through effective communication, individuals can overcome barriers, work through problems, and achieve the organization's goals.

Whether one is in the role of parent, child, student, manager, non-managerial employee, or consumer, communication breakdowns can have negative consequences. Problems between spouses, among families, within organizations, and among nations often can be traced to communication failures.

Communication is an important part of the leadership function; managers cannot be effective leaders if they do not communicate effectively. Leaders don't just create budgets, they set direction.[3] Throughout this book, and especially in Chapters 1 and 6, it is emphasized that managers and leaders must function through effective communication. That is, they must have a clear picture of what they want the organization to be and then communicate that vision to other members of the organization. The effectiveness of their communication efforts is often the key to the behaviour of everyone in the organization. This chapter discusses interpersonal and organizational communication. First, it examines the nature and scope of communication and then explores various types of interpersonal and organizational communication. Finally, it looks at some of the barriers to organizational communication and strategies for facilitating communication.

# The Nature and Scope of Communication

**communication**
The exchange of information between a sender (the source) and a receiver (the audience or reader).

The term **communication** is in common usage. TV, radio, and newspapers are referred to as communications *media* (the plural of *medium*); the telephone and the computer are called communication devices. Unfortunately, communication is often taken for granted, though in fact it is a complex activity.[4] Failure to understand this complexity often leads to problems with communication.

Communication is defined as the exchange of information between a sender (the source) and a receiver (the audience or reader). To be effective, communication must transmit meaning accurately from one person to another. Poor communication leads to reduced productivity and to anger, lack of trust, and cynicism.[5] Despite the importance of communication, most CEOs of top North American companies acknowledge that they are not spending enough time on employee communication.[6]

## The Communication Process

Communication is a process in which a message is encoded and transmitted through some medium to a receiver who decodes the message and then may transmit some sort of response back to the sender. It is through the communication process that the sharing of a common meaning takes place. Exhibit 10-1 illustrates this process.

In organizations, the executives, managers, and non-managerial employees all can be the sources of messages. Executives must communicate with the board of directors and with groups and individuals outside of the organization, such as shareholders, regulatory authorities, and customers. Managers must communicate with managers in

**Exhibit 10-1**   *The Communication Process*

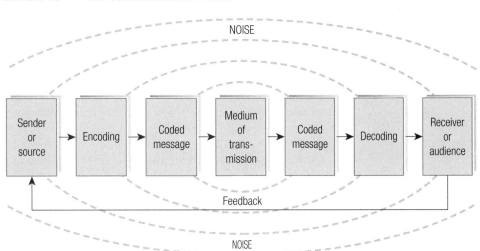

**message**
The content of the communication.

**encode**
To convert a message into groups of words, symbols, gestures, or sounds that represent ideas or concepts.

other departments and with superiors, subordinates, customers, and suppliers. All employees must communicate with superiors, customers, and each other. In fact, every organization member is a potential source with a message to communicate to internal and external parties and is also a potential receiver of messages.

The term **message** refers to the content of the idea that the sender wants to communicate. Messages can be communicated through many different means and at many different levels. The first step in effective communication is to consider who is the intended audience. The questions are: "To whom do I want the message to go?" and "What is the background information that will permit them to understand it?" A message to a skilled carpenter will be in a different form and at a different level of detail than one to a householder who has little experience with tools. A doctor's message to a patient who has a cold will be quite different from the same doctor's message that conveys detailed instructions to a technician who will perform a brain scan. A message to a dissatisfied customer will require more careful crafting than a message that asks a spouse to pick up a litre of milk on the way home from work.

*Messages between pilots and air traffic controllers must be clear, complete, and concise.*

To convey the idea that constitutes the message, the sender must **encode** it, that is, put it into words, symbols, or sounds (or in some cases, gestures) that mean the same thing to the sender as to the receiver. People who work together often develop a language of their own, in which they communicate effectively. A construction worker may direct a crane operator who is too far away to hear a spoken voice by using a language of hand signals that both understand. The Forestry Museum in Duncan, B.C., has a display that shows a standardized system of whistle blasts that were used in the forestry industry to give instructions to operators of locomotives and donkey engines, who were operating in such a noisy environment that they could not have heard oral messages. A doctor writes a prescription using abbreviations that a pharmacist understands. The antithesis of these examples of effective communication, however, occurs when the sender falls into the trap of using **jargon**. Perhaps one of the most common examples in BusinessSpeak is "*to finalize.*" When applied to a report, the sender may intend it to mean 1) completing a reasonably polished draft, 2) editing the report, 3) submitting it to the preparer's supervisor for review, 4) having it approved by senior management, or 5) having it printed, bound, and wrapped for distribution, or any variation of these different meanings. The lazy manager who uses this kind of jargon to give instructions should not be surprised if the subordinate understands something quite different from the manager's intended message.

**jargon**
Words or terms that sound superficially as if they had precise meanings but, in fact, do not. Often used by people within particular groups, kinds of work, or professions, and relatively unintelligible to people not in those groups.

**medium of transmission**
A means of carrying an encoded message from the source or sender to the receiver.

To relay the message, the sender must select and use a **medium of transmission** (a means of carrying an encoded message from the source to the receiver). Words and symbols on paper, sounds, and electronically produced signals by telephone, radio, or TV are all examples of transmission media, as are the systems of hand signals and whistle signals mentioned above. Organizations use memos, discussions at meetings, reward systems, policy statements, production schedules, and many other forms of media to communicate with members. Some forms may be appropriate in some situations and not in others. If a sender sends a message through an inappropriate medium of transmission, it may not reach the correct receivers intact.

**Decoding** is the process by which the receiver interprets the symbols (coded message) sent by the source and converts them into concepts and ideas. Seldom does the

**decoding**
The process by which the receiver interprets the symbols used by the source of the message by converting them into concepts and ideas.

**noise**
Interference that reduces the possibility that the receiver will receive the same message as the sender sends or that makes it more difficult to interpret and understand.

**feedback**
The receiver's response to the sender's message, communicated back to the sender.

**communication medium**
The channel through which a message is transmitted. The term includes face-to-face discussions; oral presentations to groups; telephoned messages; written memos, letters, notices, and instructions; printed matter; radio and television broadcasts; and electronic media such as e-mail, teleconferencing, and Web sites.

**media richness**
The extent to which media convey all of the message, including not only the express words but also the associated characteristics such as tone of voice, volume and speed, body language, and other attitudinal factors.

receiver decode exactly the same meaning that a sender intended to encode. When the receiver interprets the message differently from what the sender intended, the cause may be **noise** (interference that affects any or all stages of the communication process). Noise has many sources, such as competing messages, misinterpretation, radio static, faulty printing, or use of ambiguous or unfamiliar symbols. Sometimes noise exists because the receiver of the message feels so antagonistic either to the sender or to the content of the message that the receiver cannot possibly understand the message that was intended by the sender.

**Feedback** is the receiver's response to the sender's message. In feedback, the original receiver becomes the source of a new message that is directed back to the original sender, who then becomes a receiver. Thus, communication can be viewed as a circular process, as Exhibit 10-1 shows. It is only when feedback is received that the original sender can know whether the original message was received and how it was interpreted. Furthermore, there is a tendency for a receiver to indicate that the message has been received and understood, when at best it is only half understood but the receiver hesitates to ask questions out of a sense of pride, "to avoid looking dumb."

## Selecting a Communication Medium

A **communication medium** is a conduit or channel by means of which the message is conveyed.[7] Communications media include face-to-face oral exchanges, telephone conversations, and written and electronic communication. Managers must determine which medium or media to use in sending and receiving information. Suppose, for instance, that a sales manager wants to communicate a new compensation plan to the selling force. How should the new plan be communicated? What media should be used? Would letters, memos, oral presentations, telephone calls, or some other medium work best? Or should the managers use more than one medium, so that different employees receive the message in the manner that each finds most comfortable? The answers to these questions likely will affect the success of the new compensation program. Exhibit 10-2 illustrates some of the most commonly used media options.

In choosing the medium for a particular message, the manager must consider **media richness**. By this term is meant the extent to which a particular medium will carry all of the meaning of the message.[8] Depending on the message and the receivers, one medium may be richer than another; that is, one medium may have a greater capacity to convey the whole message than another.[9] Several criteria affect a medium's richness: the medium's capacity for timely feedback; its capacity for multiple uses, such as audio and visual; the extent to which the message can be personalized; and the variety of language that can be used, such as natural and body language.[10] Face-to-face oral communication is the richest medium. Tone of voice, pitch, facial expression, and the attitude and

**Exhibit 10-2**

*Alternative Communication Media*

| Oral | Written | Nonverbal |
|---|---|---|
| Face-to-face | Letters | Touch |
| Telephone | Computer printouts | Eye contact |
| Speeches | Electronic mail | Body language |
| Video conferencing | Memos | Time |
| Intercom | Bulletin boards | Space |

*As electronic communications media have become more reliable and more affordable, video conferencing has become commonplace, saving great amounts of travel time and inconvenience.*

movements of the body are all part of the message. Some feedback is instantaneous, as the receiver physically reacts to the message, and oral feedback is often almost immediate. Conversely, tables of figures such as computer printouts are the least rich because feedback is slow or nonexistent, data-carrying capacity is limited to visual information, and the major import of the message usually requires interpretation of figures.

Cost, both in dollars and in time, also must be considered. If a message is to be sent to sales personnel located all over Canada or in other countries, only the most sensitive and important messages would warrant the sales manager travelling to all of the locations, or having all of the representatives come to a central point for face-to-face communication. Instead, the choice would usually depend on finding a balance between the richest means, that is, face-to-face contact, and the additional cost this method would require.

One choice would be teleconferencing, in which all of the representatives, regardless of location, would be connected so they can see and hear each other on television screens. Often the cost is prohibitive, and in some locations the technology may not be available. Instead, the sales manager might choose individual telephone calls, or a conference telephone call linking all of the representatives. Tone of voice and instant feedback are still available to help convey the full message. Still further away from the theoretical "ideal" of face-to-face contact would be a conference by e-mail. If that is not feasible, the sales manager could send individual e-mail or fax messages or, as a final resort, trust the message to couriers or the postal service. In this final level of communication, most of the richness is lost, and the receivers of the message have only the written words to help with interpretation. There are no clues available from facial expression, tone of voice, or body language, and there is only limited opportunity for feedback. Yet because of factors of time and cost, most communication within, to, and from organizations is by memo, letter, or e-mail.

## *What Managers Are Reading*  10-1

### The 7 Habits of Highly Effective People

For a decade, Stephen R. Covey's *The 7 Habits of Highly Effective People* has remained a best-seller. In it Covey presents an integrated approach for solving personal and professional problems. Covey believes these habits distinguish the happy, healthy, and successful from those who fail or must sacrifice happiness for success. He outlines a step-by-step process for living with fairness, integrity, honesty, and human dignity. He maintains that these principles give an individual the security needed to adapt to change and the wisdom to take advantage of the opportunities that change creates.

Covey's Habit 1 is to be proactive, or to take responsibility for your own life. Habit 2 is to begin with the end in mind, or to start with a clear understanding of your destination. Habit 3 is to put first things first, meaning to organize and execute around priorities. Habit 4 is to think win/win, which means to seek mutual benefits in human interactions. Habit 5 is to seek first to understand, then to be understood. This habit involves empathic communication, or listening with the intent to understand. Habit 6 is to synergize, or use all of our skills in concert to reach greater heights. Habit 7 is to "sharpen the saw," or to practise and renew all habits. These seven habits, according to Covey, build on each other; that is, one cannot achieve Habit 2 until Habit 1 is mastered, and so on.

Source: Stephen R. Covey, *The 7 Habits of Highly Effective People* (New York: Fireside, 1990).

## The Role of Communication in Organizations

The whole thrust of this textbook is management in organizations. By its very nature, most management tasks depend on communication. It is clear that, in the words of a well-known writer on management topics, "The job of the manager is, ultimately, communication, regardless of how varied or specialized the activity of the moment might be."[11]

Many managers stress open communication as a means of improving organization effectiveness and quality. Open communication requires more than a manager announcing that "my door is always open." It depends on managers' actual accessibility to workers, day-to-day interaction between managers and other employees, and the elimination of traditional hierarchical barriers and resistance to change. In short, communication pervades every aspect of every organization, every individual, team, or department, and each external relationship with customers, suppliers, and competitors. The organization cannot achieve its goals and will not be competitive without open, two-way communication.

## Interpersonal Communication

**interpersonal communication**
Communication between two people or among a relatively small group of people.

Individuals spend much of their time in organizations interacting with each other. **Interpersonal communication** is communication between two people or among several people. The term is usually used to refer to face-to-face contact, but many of the principles are equally applicable to all media of personally directed communication,[12] as contrasted with communication aimed at groups of people. Other communication media (such as the telephone or e-mail) also can be used to communicate interpersonally. Through

**Management in the Real World    10-1**

## Interpersonal and Organizational Communication: Reflections by Philip Crosby

One Monday morning, while taking a break at a conference, I wandered over to the golf practice range. I realized that the man hitting balls out of the practice sand trap was one of the world's premier golfers. He had just won the previous PGA tournament, in fact. I edged over and stood watching in awe as he pounded ball after ball up near the pin.

Then he decided to rest for a few moments and climbed out of the bunker. He walked over to me and we shook hands and chatted. He asked about my game.

"Inconsistent is the word," I said. "I get six or seven pars in a round and the rest are not worth mentioning. Do you have any suggestions?"

"Hit a thousand balls a day," he said. "I haven't found any other way."

"Don't you have something you could sell me?" I asked. "How about some new clubs, or a pair of pants, or a ball warmer, or a magic glove?"

He laughed and patted me on the shoulder.

"You left out motivation classes for the caddies," he said. "You know as well as I do that you are responsible for your own game. If you can par six or seven holes, you can par them all." He went back to work.

The truest form of communication is participation. I have noticed that many managers try to tell their people something without being an example of it themselves. This is particularly true of quality. Executives in particular think that they can spend some money and buy what is called TQM. This consists of a bunch of techniques, tools, and classes intended to change the way people work. But the communication is not real. Management commitment cannot be demonstrated by anything else except the management being committed, in person.

I decided to take the advice of this obviously dedicated professional. Hitting a thousand balls a day is a little past my activity level, but I did take some lessons and began to work on what I was taught. I began to take the game more seriously, to make certain that I was lined up and set up properly. I thought about things. All of this didn't take any more time, but it certainly had an effect on my game. My handicap now is the lowest it has been in 25 years.

Communication is getting the message to the areas that need it in a way that will be accepted and implemented. That requires both credibility of presentation and integrity of content.

Don't try to sell something you don't believe.

interpersonal communication we develop and maintain human relationships—the basic social units of any organization. Thus, interpersonal communication is the fundamental building block of organizational communication.

It is extremely difficult for one individual alone to accomplish much within an organization.[13] The power to influence others is essential to enlisting cooperation, without which little change can be inaugurated. In its broadest sense, effective communication is the key to influencing the behaviour of others.

**verbal communication**
Any communication that conveys a message by means of words. Often mistakenly used to mean *oral communication.*

**oral communication**
Communication using the spoken word to convey a message.

## Oral Communication

**Verbal communication** uses words to convey a message. There are two levels—oral and written or printed. **Oral communication** (often mistakenly called *verbal communication*) takes place when the spoken word is used to transmit a message. Conversations can take place in person, via telephone, or through some other mechanism that allows individuals to speak with one another. Oral communication permits prompt, two-way interaction between parties, whether it is conducted face to face or by conference telephone or video conferencing. Questions can be addressed, positions and issues debated, and a

*Speaking on the telephone requires even more precise communication because there are few nonverbal clues in the message.*

**written communication**
Communication using written words, symbols, or designs to convey a message.

**nonverbal communication**
Conveying a message by means other than words, and including factors such as tone of voice, facial expression, and body language.

plan for action or resolution established. As pointed out earlier, all forms of oral communication offer the advantage of communication richness. Yet because of its immediacy, oral communication can result in poor communication. If, for instance, a person becomes angry, noise enters the communication process. Messages that are not clearly encoded also may fail to communicate the intended idea. A hurried manager may give an oral instruction or initiative without thinking about the outcome. While feedback is immediate, it also may be done with little thought, reducing the communication's effectiveness. Individuals often feel the need to respond immediately in a face-to-face meeting, when in some circumstances it might be better if they were to take time to prepare a well-thought-out response.

An even greater hazard of oral communication is that when time has passed after the communication, the sender and receiver may have quite different memories of what transpired. Everyone is subject to imperfect memory, which can lead to miscommunication and even to the perception by each party that the other has purposely altered position. Thus, despite all of its benefits, oral communication can, of itself, create problems.

## Written Communication

**Written communication** has the merit that there is a record of what has been said. Thus, imperfect memories do not later affect written communication, at least until the written record is discarded. Some interoffice memos are dashed off with little thought, and this tendency is even further pronounced with the breathless immediacy that often seems to accompany e-mail. Nevertheless, for important and sensitive issues a written message allows the sender to think about the message, reread it several times, and perhaps get others to review the message before it is transmitted. The receiver can take time to read the message carefully and accurately before a response is required.

Despite the advantages of written communication, managers generally prefer to communicate orally, when feasible. Written communication takes more time to prepare and does not allow interaction or immediate feedback. Managers rely on two-way oral communication to resolve problems quickly. It takes much longer to get ideas on paper, to distribute them to others, and to receive written responses; a telephone call or meeting is quicker. Written communication, by its formal nature, also may discourage open communication.

## Nonverbal Communication

All intentional or unintentional messages that are not framed in words, either spoken or written, are referred to as **nonverbal communication**.[14] Examples include tone of voice, the volume or rapidity of speech, body movements, facial expressions, personal appearance, and interpersonal distance or space. A certain look or glance, seating arrangements at a meeting, or a sudden change in voice tone can communicate a strong message. Even a period of silence can convey a powerful message. Nonverbal communication may be intentional on the part of the sender, but more often it is unintentional. In those cases, nonverbal communication may convey a message that is different from what the sender intends, and effectively may contradict the verbal message.

For example, if an employee is reporting a concern to a manager, and the manager appears to be thinking of something else or is looking past the employee to something happening elsewhere, the manager is conveying negative feedback, even though that was not the intention. The nonverbal message is saying, "I am not interested in your concerns, and probably I am not interested in you, either." To the employee the message is unequivocally negative. Other examples relate to body posture. Leaning towards a speaker and making eye contact says, "I am interested in what you are saying, and by inference, in you as a person." Leaning back and looking away conveys disinterest, boredom, and perhaps rejection of what is being said. It is important for managers to learn some of the physical postures and movements that are almost universally read as conveying particular messages, and to avoid those that give unintended impressions and messages.

Nonverbal communication is of particular importance to multinational companies operating in a foreign country. People in different countries and cultures have different sets of nonverbal symbols and meanings. Nonverbal cues such as touch, body language, and personal distance are used differently across cultures. For instance, a study of how often couples in coffee shops touched each other during their conversations reported that couples in San Juan, Puerto Rico, touched 180 times an hour; couples in Paris, France, touched 110 times; those in Gainesville, Florida, touched twice per hour; and in London, England, touched only once each hour.[15] It is probably safe to assume that similar differences would be found among different regions of Canada, and among people from different ethnic backgrounds or cultures even though they may live in the same cities. Someone unfamiliar with the local norms who touches "too much" or "too little" can offend without knowing why. Managers working in an unfamiliar culture may not only send unintended messages, but are likely to find it difficult to interpret nonverbal communication from foreign associates. Likewise, they are uncertain what nonverbal

## Real World Reflection    10-1

### E-mail Privacy Issues

Many managers log on to their password-protected e-mail program with a false sense of security. E-mail messages have replaced the use of oral communications, internal memos, and policy manuals because it is a fast and efficient medium. While e-mail does have many advantages, it also has limitations and potential pitfalls. The following guidelines should be considered prior to sending a message:

1. Consider the level of privacy required by the subject at hand. The ability of the recipient to attach and re-send documents to a broader audience than intended by the sender should always be a consideration prior to sending a message.
2. Don't use e-mail to communicate personal or potentially upsetting information to individuals. There are still issues that require face-to-face communication.
3. Make sure that you check and re-check the recipient box of the e-mail, especially if the material is sensitive in nature. You don't want to broadcast highly sensitive material to the wrong people.

Contributed by Marnie Wright, British Columbia Institute of Technology.

messages they may be transmitting. A business deal in Japan can collapse if a foreign executive gives offence by refusing a cup of green tea during a visit to a Japanese company.[16] Some of these problems will be explored in further detail in Chapter 14.

## Empathic Listening

**empathic listening**
Listening from the standpoint of the sender of a message to receive the full message that the sender intends without distorting it because of personal interests, biases, or inattention.

Everyone has considerable experience in *speaking* but, unfortunately, much less experience in *listening*. In his best-selling book, *The 7 Habits of Highly Effective People*, Stephen Covey suggests that the key to effective listening is to seek first to understand, then to be understood.[17] Although Covey's book has attracted something of a cult following, this statement cannot be faulted. Covey describes **empathic listening** as listening with the intent to understand. This is not easy—it requires looking at an issue from another person's point of view. It requires listening not only with the ears, but with the eyes and the heart as well.

Studies have found that 70 to 80 percent of our waking life is spent communicating on some level. For many managers, less than half of this communicating time is spent listening.[18] Unless someone listens, communication cannot take place. Fortunately,

---

### *Real World Reflection*    10-2

#### Practising Your Listening Skills

Ask yourself: Do you want to listen? Are you open to be influenced by the person you are listening to? If the answers are negative then you are not open to effective listening and the effort it takes.

Ask yourself if you do the following:

Do you:

1. Spend more time talking than listening?
2. Interrupt? Your thought is too good to wait?
3. Solve the issue while someone is still describing it?
4. Think about your next point rather than the point the speaker is making?
5. Cross your arms, lean away, doodle?
6. Miss points completely because your mind wanders?

Or do you:

1. Maintain eye contact?
2. Read nonverbal signals?
3. Reflect content and feelings?
4. Ask open-ended questions to draw the person out?
5. Paraphrase and summarize what has been said, even if you disagree?
6. Look and be interested—really curious?

A good listener reacts to the message in sequence: 1) Hear, 2) Understand, 3) Interpret, and 4) Respond. Never go from Step 1 to 4 directly. Practise in situations in which you can focus on effective listening. It takes focus and effort.

Contributed by Sherry Campbell, British Columbia Institute of Technology.

listening is a skill that can be learned and improved. By avoiding barriers to effective listening and by developing good listening skills, anyone can become an empathic listener.

Distractions such as interruptions, telephone calls, and thinking about unfinished work are major barriers to effective listening. Selecting an environment free from such distractions will improve listening. Many listeners also take detours during a communication. For instance, if someone mentions a word that brings out strong emotions, listeners may become distracted and tune out the message. Many receivers also begin mentally to debate a point and start planning a response before the speaker has completed the message.

Listening is not easy, but improving listening effectiveness helps a person to relax, close out other distractions, and give full attention to the other person. Assuming a non-threatening listening posture, maintaining eye contact, and maintaining an accepting and interested facial expression all help to demonstrate that the listener is interested in the other person's message. Effective listening is not a passive exercise; it is an active skill that requires full participation. Good listeners take notes, ask questions, and are totally attentive to what is being said.[19] Effective listeners focus on the message's meaning, postpone judgements until the communication is complete, actively respond to the speaker, and avoid focusing on emotionally charged words.[20]

Communication also can be improved by giving and requesting constructive feedback. If receivers of a message say what they think the sender wants to hear, feedback is of little value, and may even be misleading and destructive. Honest feedback can be used to determine whether the listener understood the intended message. It is unlikely to occur, however, unless the receivers of messages not only are encouraged to give it but feel safe in doing so. Thus, an important element of a manager's responsibility in communication is to create the climate in which honest feedback is most likely to occur.

## Organizational Communication

Some important communication in an organization occurs through formal, established, and recognized channels. Other equally important communication flows along informal and often unrecognized channels. The formal channels are the official paths prescribed by management. They usually follow the organization's chain of command.

### Formal Channels of Communication

Formal channels of communication are designed to communicate information downward, upward, or horizontally, and can be oral, written, or nonverbal.

**downward communication**
Messages that flow from those farther up to those more subordinate in the organizational hierarchy.

**Downward communication.**   Information that flows from a more senior to a more junior level in the organizational hierarchy is referred to as **downward communication**. Downward communication generally involves job instructions, manuals, policy statements, memos, motivational appeals, criticism and correction, and other forms of formal instruction or feedback. Downward communication is not always sufficient because non-managerial employees need more information than just job instructions. They also need to know, for instance, what other members of the organization are doing. Nevertheless, downward communication is important because lack of communication from superiors can leave workers misinformed, feeling disconnected, and less satisfied with their jobs. The trend in today's organizations is to provide non-managerial employees with information that was formerly shared only with managers, or even kept secret from all but the most senior managers.

This trend, while basically positive, requires managers to decide which information and how much of it to communicate to subordinates. Too much information, especially if it is irrelevant, is likely to be ignored, and often causes essential information to be lost in the deluge. The sender may have made every effort to communicate important information, and consequently assumes that it has been received. Yet the subordinates actually have not received it, because they have been so much in the habit of ignoring irrelevant messages that they have not sorted out those that are important from those that are not. Here, again, feedback may help to identify the problem and to permit managers to learn where they should strike a balance between too much and too little information.

**Upward communication.** Information that flows upward in the structure of the organization from subordinates to supervisors and managers is called **upward communication**. This type of communication is necessary for managers to evaluate the effectiveness of the organization's activities. It also may consist of feedback from downward communication. If it is encouraged, it helps non-managers to feel that they are a meaningful part of the organization. Many types of messages are communicated upward, including suggestions for improvements, feelings about the job or the organization, problems or grievances, and requests for action or information. Many employees are uncertain as to what they should communicate to superiors. It is the manager's responsibility to encourage upward communication, while guiding employees as to how they can distinguish important messages from those that are relatively trivial or routine.

upward communication
Messages that flow from those more subordinate to those farther up in the organizational hierarchy.

Obviously information is not effective unless it is accurate. Upward communication is often distorted in one way or another in the hope that the sanitized version will be more acceptable to managers. Employees may be reluctant to report problems if they think those higher in the organization will blame them. Managers must create an environment in which everyone feels comfortable reporting bad news as well as good. Managers can demonstrate that upward communication is valued by replying or acting promptly and positively. It is also crucial for everyone to be aware that "whistle-blowers" will not be punished, and instead will be respected and even rewarded in the long run.

Former Chief Justice of Ontario Charles Dubin completed a comprehensive study of the effects on employees who report violations of the Competition Act. As an outcome of his study, he prepared an analysis of legislation and other measures to protect whistle-blowers. That outline may be found on the Competition Bureau's Web site.[21]

**Horizontal communication.** Messages flow between persons at the same level of the organization through **horizontal communication**. This aspect of communication includes staff meetings, face-to-face interactions, and sharing of information through memos and reports. Horizontal communication is needed to coordinate the activities of diverse but independent units or departments. For instance, the manager of marketing and sales needs to communicate sales figures so the manager of production can avoid stocking too much or too little of a product and can schedule production runs appropriately in order to satisfy customers.

horizontal communication
Messages that flow, either formally or informally, between or among peers, that is, those who are not in positions of subordinate/superior to each other.

Many organizations are placing increasing emphasis on horizontal communication. In their influential book, *Re-inventing the Corporation*, John Naisbitt and Patricia Aburdene observe, "The top-down authoritarian management style is yielding to a networking style of management, where people learn from one another horizontally, where everyone is a resource for everyone else, and where each person gets support and assistance from many different directions."[22]

## Informal Channels of Communication

In addition to the formally authorized and recognized channels of communication, even more communication occurs informally. This communication, along casual channels, often is not fully recognized by the managers. Many managers are perplexed by the speed with which the **grapevine** conveys "news"—often inaccurately. Attention to this phenomenon is essential if an organization is to function effectively.

grapevine
An informal and unstructured communication channel that cuts across formal channels of communication in almost all organizations and that usually is characterized by rumour, gossip, and even outright fabrication, but that sometimes conveys factual information that has not been officially released.

While grapevine communications don't always have negative consequences, they are frequently troublesome to managers. A middle manager once learned of an impending transfer when she received a telephone call from a real estate agent in another part of the country. She eventually found that the real estate agent's contact at corporate headquarters learned about the transfer and passed it on to the realtor. Unfortunately, the woman's supervisor had yet to tell her about the transfer. As this example illustrates, news often travels faster by the grapevine than by established channels. As a consequence, managers who plan to distribute important information must do so promptly before leaks and rumours pre-empt the official communication. The grapevine may put an unwelcome spin on the information that can never be fully counteracted by the more accurate official version that is received by employees only after they have already formed opinions based on the earlier unofficial version.

The grapevine also can be the source of harmful rumours and gossip. This is particularly true when it relates to matters affecting personnel policies or interrelationships. Although the water cooler used to be the symbol of office gossip, this role has been assumed by e-mail.[23] With e-mail, rumours can be circulated instantaneously to large numbers of people, accelerating the spread of gossip. Also, e-mail gossip can be anonymous and consequently at best it may be completely irresponsible and, at worst, intentionally false and destructive. Managers can control to some extent the hazardous effects of gossip by communicating accurate, timely information, by maintaining and cultivating open channels of

*The grapevine is a remarkably efficient, albeit often inaccurate, manner in which information is communicated within the office.*

communication in all directions, and by moving quickly to dispel rumours and correct inaccurate information. If the managers truly practise open communication, the grapevine becomes less important. Non-managerial employees learn to rely less on the grapevine if they realize that through formal communication channels they are receiving accurate and complete information.

## Barriers to Organizational Communication

Communication isn't always effective. Breakdowns occur for many reasons. Some breakdowns result from poor habits—lack of preparation or vague directions. Barriers such as these can be overcome without too much difficulty if the communicator is willing to work at it. Other barriers can be much more difficult to overcome. For instance, a survey conducted at General Motors' Saginaw division found that lack of trust between management and labour was resulting in poor communication throughout the division.

General Motors started a new two-way communication program to share information and rebuild trust. The program was eventually a huge success, but took several years to get results.[24] This experience illustrates the fact that communication must be an ongoing concern of managers, because it is much easier to demonstrate good communication practices than to repair the damage done by a long period of poor organizational communication.

## Personal Characteristics

One major barrier to organizational communication is the personal makeup of the parties involved. People have attitudes about work-related matters, conditions in the world, their personal lives, and communication in general. Some individuals have defensive attitudes and interpret messages as an order or threat. Some people simply have incompatible personalities. Others feel inadequate or threatened, become defensive in an attempt to cover up their feelings, and respond aggressively. Constantly being on the offensive is an obstacle to communication.

**source credibility**
The degree of confidence and trust the receiver has in the sender or the source of the message.

Another problem involves the credibility of the sender. **Source credibility** refers to the receiver's confidence and trust in the source of the message. If the receiver has little or no faith in the source, it will be difficult for the two parties to communicate. Individuals lose credibility when they pass along inaccurate information or fail to follow through with directives or initiatives. New leaders are often greeted with a sense of excitement and hope by other members of the organization, but if they make promises they don't keep—pay raises, new offices, lower taxes, and so on—they lose their credibility and their ability to communicate effectively.[25]

Several other personal characteristics can inhibit communication. Some individuals tend to be disorganized, which carries over to their communication efforts. As emphasized earlier in this chapter, poor listening habits on the part of the receiver are often a communication barrier. Receivers also may have certain predispositions and tune out the communicator because the message is not consistent with their beliefs. This is a common problem in organizations where there is an employee-management split and the accompanying distinction between "us" and "them." Finally, communication may be inhibited because of bias on the basis of age, gender, looks, language, economic situation or class, or some other factor. Unless great care is taken, as the workforce becomes more diverse such biases may become even more of a threat to good communication and to the overall functioning of organizations.

## Frame of Reference

Individuals have different backgrounds and have had many different experiences that shape the meanings they assign to words. There is literally a world of difference in the meanings of the statement "I'm starving" when uttered by a middle-class Canadian reading the menu in a gourmet restaurant and when spoken by a refugee child who has been walking for days to escape from a civil war. There may be a similar difference in understanding within an organization when a 10 percent across-the-board salary cut is announced. All employees may understand the message in the same way, but each will feel its impact differently. The president may regret that it will delay the purchase of a new BMW, while the receptionist may be wondering how the next month's rent or day-care fees will be paid. The same message causes minor disappointment to one individual and creates havoc in the personal life of the other.

A related problem in communication concerns people blocking out information with which they are not comfortable or that does not agree with things they believe.

**selective perception**
The subconscious process through which receivers screen out all or some parts of a message that are inconsistent with their assumptions, beliefs, or background, or that they particularly do not want to hear.

**Selective perception** is the term used to describe when people screen out information that is not consistent with their beliefs or background. When people receive information that conflicts with what they believe, they tend to ignore it or to reinterpret it to make it conform to their beliefs.

Another form of selective perception occurs when two individuals apparently receive the same message but, because of their differing interests, pay attention to different parts and implications of the message. A corporation's financial officer, an environmentalist within or outside of the organization, a production employee, and a marketing executive all may learn at the same time and through the same medium that the organization is planning to open a new plant. The financial officer may think of the message in terms of the plant's cost and indicated rate of return. The environmentalist may think of the new plant only in terms of possible pollution and environmental controls. The production employee may see it as an opportunity for a new job or, conversely, as a threat to existing jobs. The marketing executive may think of it in terms of proximity to potential customers. Probably each person has *heard* the whole message, but has *listened to* only selected parts of it. Ideally, the initial announcement and follow-up communications will take into account these and many other perceptions, attempt to allay suspicions and fears, and provide sufficient information to encourage support for the project.

## Facilitating Organizational Communication

Although some barriers to communication cannot be completely removed, organizational communication can be facilitated in several ways. An individual can improve the effectiveness of communication by understanding the barriers and striving to be a better communicator. In some cases this may be relatively simple, perhaps accomplished by breaking a few bad habits. In other ways this can be a long, ongoing, demanding process.

### Developing Communication Skills

Contrary to what seems to be a widely held assumption, good communicators are made, not born. Communication, like any skill, can be learned. It takes concerted effort, skilled leadership, and the desire to improve. As non-managerial employees are given more individual responsibility, it becomes increasingly important for them, as well as managers, to improve these skills.[26] Many organizations are recognizing this fact and offering training programs in effective communication to employees at all levels in the organization.

### Elements of Effective Verbal Communication

**gender-exclusive language**
Masculine words or terms that are used to encompass both men and women or that inappropriately disregard the inclusion of one of the genders. An example is the use of the male singular pronoun (*he* or *him*) to signify all people regardless of gender.

In many organizations, both written and oral communications often illustrate easily correctable faults that inhibit communication. Long sentences tend to confuse rather than to clarify. A sentence in the passive voice (such as "The report will be prepared") lacks an important specific—who is to prepare the report. Archaic forms label the sender as either self-conscious or just plain old-fashioned. (An example is the use of the term "the writer" instead of the simpler "I" or "me"). Technical terms should be used only when the intended audience consists of specialists who, themselves, use the same terms. All four of these communication errors are woefully common in business correspondence.[27]

**Gender-exclusive language** is becoming less and less acceptable in all forms of communication.[28] Its use tends to alienate women, and many men as well. Some of the conventions that were formerly taught in schools are no longer valid. Among these are the use of the masculine pronoun "he" to represent both men and women—a convention that was created in the seventeenth century by (male) English grammarians who reflected the relationships that then existed between the sexes.[29] Some writers have attempted to avoid this old-fashioned usage with the clumsy "he/she" combination, the artificial "s/he," or by alternating the use of "he" and "she." More modern usage recognizes that these formulations give an appearance of self-consciousness, and distract the reader from the import of the message. Instead, the careful writer usually can recast a sentence to avoid the use of the third person singular pronoun entirely, and instead switch to plurals (the non-gender-specific "they" or "them") or the use of a noun such as "the manager" or "the employee."[30] Examples of rewordings that convert gender-exclusive language to gender-neutral language appear in Exhibit 10-3.

**Exhibit 10-3**

*Examples of Gender-Neutral Language*

| Instead of: | Consider Using: |
| --- | --- |
| My girl will let you know the time. | My secretary will let you know the time, *or, if known to the other party,* Anne (*or* Ms. Wilson) will let you know the time. |
| Ask the lady engineer. | Ask the engineer at the third desk. |
| Our negotiating team will have one lady and one man. | Our negotiating team will have two members, *or, if there is a real reason to make the distinction,* Our negotiating team will have one woman and one man. |
| Saleslady; salesgirl | Sales clerk |
| Managers and their wives | Managers and their spouses (*unless all managers happen to be male*) |
| Mrs. David Warren | Mrs. (or Ms.) Joanna Warren |
| Mr. & Mrs. David Warren | David and Joanna Warren |
| Dear Sirs: | Dear Colleagues (*or* Fellow Managers, *etc.*): |
| Each manager must forward his budget request form by June 15 if he wishes it to be considered. | To be considered, managers must forward their budget request forms by June 15. |
| This project will require a lot of manpower. | This project will require a large staff. |
| Each applicant must submit his résumé. | Each applicant must submit a résumé. |
| The security desk will be manned 24 hours a day. | The security desk will be staffed 24 hours a day. |
| Every team must select its chairman. He should be someone with experience in chairing a meeting. | Every team must select its chair (*or* moderator, *etc.*), who should be someone with experience in chairing a meeting. |

## Communicating with a Diverse Workforce

Managers increasingly face the prospect of communicating with a diverse workforce, which makes communication more difficult.[31] To facilitate communication in such an environment, managers must be aware of diversity and understand its value to the organization and to society.[32] Differences in gender, race, culture, and other characteristics influence how people interpret (decode) messages. A good communicator has to be aware of an individual's background and experiences and anticipate the meaning that will be attached to different messages.

*When an organization has many employees for whom English is a second language, as in this factory, managers have to communicate in simple terms and avoid slang and analogies that may not be understood.*

## Functional Illiteracy

A communication problem that generally is not recognized is that of **functional illiteracy**—the inability of a person to grasp the meaning of fairly simple, straightforward writing. In most organizations, much important communication is transmitted in writing. Yet reliable studies have shown that nearly one in six adult Canadians is not capable of reading and understanding a typical memo that is designed to instruct or inform on any but the simplest topics.[33]

**functional illiteracy** Inability to read and understand relatively simple written communications such as memos, instructions, and descriptions and to understand and complete typical business forms.

In the International Adult Literacy Survey, conducted in 1994 by Statistics Canada, it was found, not surprisingly, that reading and comprehending abilities are closely linked to the highest level of formal education attained. The survey found that 89 percent of those who had completed less than grade eight had difficulty in understanding newspaper articles and written instructions at work. One in eight secondary school graduates could not do so effectively. It may be difficult because of personal sensitivities for managers to test employee reading and comprehension levels directly. But it is possible to discover the educational levels attained by new employees by reading their résumés and application forms. If a significant proportion of the organization's employees have minimum educational levels, effective managers will adjust their communication methods to accommodate for the probability that some in the group will not understand written messages.

Despite widespread criticism of the present-day school systems, these functionally illiterate people are not concentrated in young age groups, but rather appear disproportionately in the two cohorts of ages 55 to 65 and over 65. These people are not stupid. They live seemingly normal lives. But perhaps when they were young they did not have access to much formal schooling, or perhaps for some reason their reading skills have deteriorated from lack of use. Understandably, because of pride they fiercely resist admitting their disability, even to themselves. They have learned to compensate in many ways, and most of their peers are not even aware of their limitation. Their ways of coping, however, are not up to the task of understanding written directions or policy.

When these functional illiterates are joined by those whose mother tongue is not English (or French, if that is the language of the workplace), it is clear that a manager

*Those who are functionally illiterate, especially among older workers, cope in ways that hide their disability so that only managers who are especially alert are likely to modify their communication to get past the hidden barrier.*

who relies solely on written statements for communication may be puzzled as to why the message is not getting across.

Regardless of employees' levels of education, managers must accept some of the blame for communication failures. They are the ones who often draft memos and instructions using jargon, convoluted sentences, and confused sentence construction. Even if all managers were to correct these needless errors, however, in most organizations there would still be an appreciable number of employees who would be unable to read well enough to understand a memo. The unfortunate fact of functional illiteracy only serves to reinforce the basic principle of good communication that the sender of an important concept should not rest until the receiver has provided feedback that reflects sufficient understanding of the message.

## Communication Audit

The **communication audit** is a helpful tool for managers to use in understanding and improving organizational communication. A communication audit is a systematic method of collecting and evaluating information about an organization's communication efforts, with the purpose of determining how effective communication is within the organization. Such an audit can:

- Provide information about communication behaviour in the organization;
- Offer a means for diagnosing discontent or for revealing problems in communication;
- Provide a clear picture of current communication patterns and determine those aspects that may be most affected by change; and
- Permit a before-and-after picture of organizational communication in relation to change.[34]

**communication audit**
A systematic program for collecting and evaluating information about the effectiveness of an organization's communication efforts.

Organizations use many different formats when conducting a communication audit. Information can be collected from both managers and non-managers by means of surveys, interviews, observations of operations, and reviews of formal and informal reports and procedures used to communicate. A pragmatic approach can follow individual communications as they travel through the organization to see whether they have achieved their desired purposes. Almost invariably, whatever the form of the audit, it will reveal some weaknesses in the communication practices and suggest means of improving their effectiveness. As many leaders have observed, communication is the indispensable link between strategy and performance.[35] Improvement in the communication process requires continual attention, but will reap rewards that more than repay the time and cost of the efforts.

## The Workplace of Tomorrow

From as far back as we can know how people lived, the ability to communicate has been fundamental to human relationships. Cooperation, learning new skills, sharing ideas—all have depended on communication, whether oral, written, or nonverbal. Consequently, it is probably illogical to say that communication is becoming even more important than in times past. Yet when put in the context of organizational management, it can be said that new demands are being made on the communication skills of managers. As organizations increase in size and complexity the chance for misunderstanding and confusion grows. Concurrently, as non-managers escape from the intimidation of the early years of industrialization they expect to participate more and more in planning and decision making. As both the internal and external environments change with increasing rapidity it becomes less safe to rely on traditional ways and habits of behaviour. All of these factors contribute to the need for managers to develop and perfect their communication skills. If someone in 1900 were to have listed the desired qualities for a manager, communication skills might not even have made the list. In mid-century, such a list certainly would have included communication skills, but it might have been near the middle of the list. At the beginning of the twenty-first century, most students of management would place communication skills in at least the second or third position, if not the first. Managers who are effective communicators will find that they are among the more successful practitioners of the craft of management. Those whose communication skills are deficient will find that their effectiveness and their career advancement will lag behind their peers. Fortunately, communication skills can be learned and honed with insight and practice. That is the message of this chapter for the years that lie ahead.

## Summary of Learning Objectives

▷ **Describe the communication process.**

Communication is a process in which a message is encoded by a sender and transmitted to a receiver through some medium. The receiver decodes and interprets the coded message. Because of interference or noise in the communication process, the receiver seldom decodes the exact meaning that the sender intended.

▷ **Discuss the role of communication in organizations.**

Communication is an essential part of all management activities. Managers largely function by communicating with people. Most managers profess open communication, but may fail to achieve it because of various barriers to communication.

▷ **Describe some of the barriers to organizational communication.**

Barriers include the personal characteristics of the parties involved, conflicting frames of reference and selective perception (screening out information that people are not comfortable with), lack of skill in framing and delivering the message, and failure to listen to oral messages or attend to written messages. The use of jargon, sexist language, or inappropriate terms that reflect bias also may impede good communication.

▷ **Contrast the different types of interpersonal communication.**

Interpersonal communication is communication between two people or among a relatively small group of people. It can be oral, written, or nonverbal. Oral communication makes use of the spoken word and permits prompt, two-way interaction between parties. Transmitting a message via written word allows the manager to think about the message before it is sent, and gives the receiver a chance to read the message carefully. Written messages also provide a permanent record. Nonverbal communication includes vocal cues and body movements. Nonverbal messages can be powerful but are often difficult to interpret. They also may send contradictory messages if they reflect moods or intentions that differ from the words actually spoken or written.

▷ **Explain the importance of informal communication.**

Informal communication does not follow the organization's official chain of command. Informal channels such as the grapevine communicate facts, opinions, rumours, and other information. Although they do not always have negative consequences, they can be the source of misinformation and harmful gossip.

▷ **Discuss how organizations can facilitate communication.**

An organization can facilitate communication by helping members develop important communication skills, including listening, empathy, feedback, and the use of simple language. Managers also must learn to communicate with a diverse workforce. Finally, a communication audit can identify problems with and suggest improvements in the communication process.

## *KEY TERMS*

communication, p. 363
communication audit, p. 379
communication medium, p. 365
decoding, p. 365
downward communication, p. 372
empathic listening, p. 371
encode, p. 364
feedback, p. 365
functional illiteracy, p. 378

gender-exclusive language, p. 376
grapevine, p. 374
horizontal communication, p. 373
interpersonal communication, p. 367
jargon, p. 364
media richness, p. 365
medium of transmission, p. 364
message, p. 364

noise, p. 365
nonverbal communication, p. 369
oral communication, p. 368
selective perception, p. 376
source credibility, p. 375
upward communication, p. 373
verbal communication, p. 368
written communication, p. 369

## *REVIEW AND DISCUSSION QUESTIONS*

### Recall

1. Why is it important for managers to be skilful in communication?
2. What are the advantages and disadvantages of oral, written, and nonverbal communication?
3. How can managers reduce the potentially damaging effects of informal communication, especially as it takes place through the grapevine?
4. Why does communication sometimes break down? What are some common barriers to communication?
5. What skills are necessary for effective communication?
6. How can managers cope with functional illiteracy, which may occur, especially among older workers?

## Understanding

**7.** Describe the communication process, providing an example of each component in a workplace environment.

**8.** How does communication within an organization relate to its competitiveness?

**9.** What are the major reasons why communication may be unsuccessful, and what can managers do to reduce these negative effects?

## Application

**10.** Select an advertisement with which you are familiar. Discuss it in relation to the communication process. Who is the source? What is the message? What is the medium of transmission? Who were the targets of the message? How did you decode the message? What was your response or feedback to the message? What noise do you believe was present in the communication process?

**11.** From the library, choose a popular magazine or journal that is more than ten years old and select two or three paragraphs that use language that reflects the insensitivity of that period to sexist language. Rewrite the sentences, using gender-neutral language but conveying the same basic message as the original author intended. Then search through a current issue of the same publication to see if the language has changed in this respect.

**12.** Select a business journal or government publication and find examples of jargon, unusually long or confusing sentences, or ambiguous descriptions. Rewrite the offending sentences in easily understood language.

## CASE 10-1

## Matsushita Communication Practices When It Acquired MCA

When a company is acquired by foreign ownership, the new culture must be communicated to employees. Managers and non-managers alike need to know about the new company's history, culture, portfolio, and business strategy. Any merger or acquisition can be potentially troublesome for employees, who are often fearful and uncertain of changes taking place. But when a foreign company acquires a domestic company, the potential for change is even greater. During the transition, which typically includes layoffs and restructuring, clashes due to cultural differences are also likely to occur. Damage to employee morale and productivity can be extensive.

Many companies fail to communicate to employees the new company's culture and the changes taking place. Managers may be spending their time dealing with the details of the merger or acquisition and simply fail to take time to communicate with employees. Some companies actually decide on a policy to wait to communicate with employees until all details are settled. Because of a lack of communication through formal channels, the grapevine becomes the source for employees to learn about the new parent company. Not surprisingly, much of this information can be inaccurate and result in more fear and uncertainty.

When Matsushita Electric Industrial Co. Ltd. of Japan purchased MCA Inc., employee communication became a priority. The new parent company assured everyone that it would be business as usual at MCA. The presidents of both MCA and Matsushita wrote letters to all employees with this reassurance. A communication plan also was developed to integrate the MCA companies, which included Spencer Gifts, Putnam Publishing, Curry Co., and Universal Studios. Up until this point, MCA did not have a formal communication program.

The communication program developed at MCA included several aspects. A team was created to manage communication concerning the transition. The team was made up of executives from human resources, personnel benefits, finance, legal, and corporate communications departments. The team's goal was to make the employee the receiver of transition communication. Employees were interviewed to determine their information needs and wishes. A newsletter, video presentations, and programs were developed to communicate to employees what MCA and Matsushita were about. Company meetings were held so employees could have their questions answered in person and be reassured about their jobs. Employees also learned that they were an important part of a team working all over the world.

### Questions

1. What are the roles of communication when one company is acquired by another company, especially if the acquiring company has a considerably different culture?
2. What can be done to minimize employee's reliance on the grapevine when one organization is acquired by another?
3. Why did MCA need a formal communication program after being purchased by Matsushita?
4. What were the benefits of the communication plan developed by MCA?

Source: Adapted from Neil Gross, "Matsushita's Urgent Quest for Leadership," *Business Week* (March 8, 1993): 52; Karin Ireland, "Marketing a Foreign Acquisition," *Personnel Journal* (November 1991): 96–102; and Karin Ireland, "Communication after the Foreign Acquisition of MCA," *Personnel Journal* (November 1991): 99.

## APPLICATION EXERCISE 10-1

### Communicating Big News Painlessly?

A large manufacturing corporation, which may be called "Altapak Manufacturing Ltd.," has decided to open a new plant in Halifax. The president wishes to inform all Altapak employees at the company's existing operations in Ontario, Alberta, and British Columbia of this development, and to enlist their support for the plan. She recognizes that this first communication is critical in getting the program off on the right foot and in generating enthusiasm and support throughout the organization.

With the help of her administrative assistant, she developed the following message:

While our company has done a good job, it simply hasn't been good enough. Faced with increasing competition from foreign companies, we have to reduce our costs and increase our output. The company has decided to open a new plant in Halifax to provide better nationwide coverage, to reduce shipping costs to eastern Canada, and to take advantage of lower costs in the Maritime provinces. Some managerial staff will be offered the opportunity to move to the Halifax plant to get it up and running. No one will be forced to go, although I expect that most who are offered the chance will seize it, since it will give them broader experience and, in many cases, increased responsibility.

Although product decisions have not been finalized, a few of the items now made in our other plants may be centralized in Halifax, but these should be only a small proportion of the capacity of the new plant.

The success of this new venture will require all of us to help in every way we can, with information, advice, and ideas. My door is always open, and I will welcome whatever input you can give. The division heads will be in touch with you shortly to provide more details as this new phase of the company jells.

With this new venture, we look forward to increasing our Canadian market share and our bottom line. This can only be of benefit to all of us, as our company grows ever stronger. We have had an 80-year record of strength, and this expansion should ensure that the next 80 years will be just as successful. I know that I can count on the wonderful loyalty and support that you have always given to Altapak.

## Questions

1. The first step in successful communication is to decide the audience to which a message is directed and to shape the message with that audience in mind. Did the president's draft seem to do this? What examples reflect this?
2. Did the president accomplish the objectives of the communication? Why?
3. Does the president demonstrate good communication skills?
4. Does this message encourage feedback?
5. Rewrite the message to meet the objectives of good communication and overcome any problems that you detected.

## ▶ APPLICATION EXERCISE  10-2

## Is Tone Important in English?

We recognize that many languages, such as Thai, Vietnamese, Burmese, and most of those indigenous to various areas of China, depend on the tone in which a syllable is spoken. In these tonal languages, an identical combination of consonants and vowels can be spoken in different tones and have entirely different meanings. When we consider means of communication in English or in most European languages, we may not realize how much meaning is lost when we move from oral to written form. This exercise is intended to demonstrate that loss of meaning when messages are sent by media that are less rich than oral communication.

The class will be divided into groups of four or five students, and the members of each group will be designated by the letters A through E. Student A says, "*Joan* is going to walk to town today," placing slightly greater emphasis on the italicized word than on the other words. The other members of the group listen carefully to intonation and emphasis. Student E takes a few moments to assemble thoughts and words, and then paraphrases Student A's statement using somewhat different words and word order and explaining the meaning of the different emphasis.

Next, Student B repeats the sentence with a different emphasis: "Joan *is* going to walk to town today." Student A paraphrases, paying attention to the difference in meaning that is conveyed by the emphasis.

Each student in turn repeats the sentence, emphasizing a different word, and in each case another student in the group paraphrases the sentence with words that reflect the emphasis given to the word chosen by the speaker.

## Questions

1. What implications does this exercise in emphasis have for communication by memo or by e-mail?
2. What conventions have appeared in e-mail to signify emphasis, surprise, joy, anger, and other emotions that might be reflected by vocal tone or emphasis in an oral message?
3. What wording might the writer of a memo or letter use to provide one or more of the emphases that otherwise would be lacking in a simple repetition of the words in the message used in this exercise?

## *APPLICATION EXERCISE* **10-3**

### Interpreting Nonverbal Cues

When watching for nonverbal cues, take note of facial expressions, hand gestures, posture, eye contact, cultural indicators such as space, positioning, and automatic responses.

During the next week, pick two one-hour situations and make note of the nonverbal communication you observe. This can be in casual situations such as people having coffee, hanging out with friends, or a bus ride, as well as more formal situations such as meetings and lectures. Place yourself in an observer-only role. Watch for nonverbal indicators of the listener's feelings and interest.

In one situation, concentrate on the nonverbal communication you are receiving while talking to others. In the other situation, concentrate on the nonverbal communication you are sending. Use the grid below to record your observations.

| Behaviour | Message communicated | Probable causes |
|-----------|----------------------|-----------------|
| • | | |
| • | | |
| • | | |

Contributed by Sydney Scott, British Columbia Institute of Technology.

## *INTERNET APPLICATION* **10-1**

Many companies around the world use the World Wide Web as a form of communication. Scan the Web site for British Airways (www.british-airways.com) to learn more about this company and the kinds of information it provides through its Web site.

1. What kinds of information does British Airways communicate to its customers through its Web site?
2. What kinds of information does British Airways communicate to prospective employees through its Web site?

Search the Web for an organization about which you know very little but would like to know more. Do you think its Web site effectively communicates important information about the organization? Why or why not? What additional information would you have found useful to have that was not available on the organization's Web site?

# CHAPTER

# 11

# Managing Production and Operations

After studying this chapter, you should be able to:

▶ Differentiate between *production* and *operations*;

▶ Discuss the evolution of modern manufacturing;

▶ Explain the typical roles of production and operations managers;

▶ Explain the factors that should be considered in selecting a site, and the impact of each;

▶ Explain the importance of productivity in achieving and maintaining competitiveness; and

▶ Discuss the ways in which safety can affect an organization's effectiveness and competitiveness.

## Flexible Manufacturing—The Next Frontier

IN THEIR BOOK *THE MACHINE THAT CHANGED THE WORLD*, a group from MIT's International Motor Vehicle Program showed how Japanese automobile companies were much leaner than North American auto manufacturers. The book's major message was that while North American car companies in the 1970s and 1980s were still using production techniques developed by Henry Ford in 1913, the Japanese were using a new system of *lean production*. This system involved using less of everything, including inventory, labour, factory space, and investment. Car company executives attributed the Japanese success to lower labour costs. But in 1982 Honda opened the first Japanese plant in North America and paid wages at the prevailing North American rates. Nevertheless, Honda still had lower overall labour costs than competitors in Canada and the U.S.  ▶

Since then, the world of auto making—and that of many other products—has changed. Canadian and American manufacturing firms have improved quality and competitiveness dramatically in recent years. In many instances, this has been accomplished by imitating ideas pioneered by the Japanese. Chrysler, for instance, after studying Honda, has cut $1 billion a year in costs. Many North American companies are manufacturing better-quality products with fewer workers and less inventory in less time. In many industries Japanese companies are no longer far ahead of Canadian and U.S. companies. But while the quality gap has been reduced, the world's best companies are gearing up for the next frontier—flexible manufacturing.

Through a flexible manufacturing system (FMS), a single factory turns out a wide variety of products with computer-controlled production equipment and robots. The idea behind this system is fairly simple. By reading the market more quickly, manufacturing many different products on the same line, and switching from one to another quickly and at lower costs, a company can respond to customers promptly and economically. New products reach markets faster, product improvements are made faster, and competitors are left to catch up. Many experts feel that flexibility will be the key to competitiveness in the coming decade. Japanese and North American companies are racing once again, and the Japanese are ahead. According to Aleda Roth, a manufacturing expert at Duke University, "Most American companies are a generation behind—as far behind as they were on quality." The Japanese take product quality as a given. Without durability, conformance to customer specifications and on-time delivery, a company can't survive. The Japanese focus is on more and better product features, flexible factories, expanded customer service, and more new product introductions.

Many leading North American companies (including Nortel, General Electric, and Motorola) are working hard to develop FMS. General Motors has upgraded some of its plants for flexible manufacturing. The accompanying photo of a General Motors assembly plant shows the bewildering mass of robotic devices now used widely in auto manufacturing. Robots and other machinery can be reprogrammed easily to build a wide mix of cars to meet changing demand. Employees also have been retrained to handle a variety of tasks instead of repeating a few rote tasks over and over. ∎

Source: Adapted from Erle Norton, "Small, Flexible Plants May Play Crucial Role in U.S. Manufacturing," *The Wall Street Journal* (January 13, 1993): A1-A2; Thomas A. Stewart, "Brace for Japan's Hot New Strategy," *Fortune* (September 21, 1992): 62-74; Bradley A. Steitz, "Detroit's New Strategy to Beat Back Japanese Is to Copy Their Ideas," *The Wall Street Journal* (October 1, 1993): A1, A10; and James B. Treece and Patrick Oster, "General Motors: Open All Night," *Business Week* (June 1, 1992): 82-83.

## Operations: A Specialized Area of Management

Businesses strive for the perfect blend of management and machine. Creating and maintaining that balance is the production and operations manager's task. Top management requires production and operations managers to increase production, to improve quality, and to cut unit costs—all at the same time. It was, and still is, a question of compete or close. And technology, competition, products, and employee skill levels have changed so much in the past 20 years that the production and operations managers' job requires a wide range of analytical and communication skills. These managers must understand sophisticated technology, delegate more, and forfeit some decision-making power. Until relatively recently, everything was mechanical; now it is likely to be more sophisticated and often computerized.[1] As this chapter's opening vignette illustrates, flexible manufacturing will be a key to future competitiveness in manufacturing. Similar efficiencies must be found both in small businesses that cannot afford massive robotic systems and in service industries and not-for-profit organizations that face similar competitive pressures.

This chapter portrays how production and operations managers do their jobs. It starts by describing production and operations, and gives a brief history of manufacturing. It then discusses the production and operations manager's various responsibilities, including organizing the production process, planning site location and layout, controlling materials, purchasing, inventory, and production scheduling. Other topics covered include using technology such as computers and robots, increasing productivity while maintaining quality control, and maintaining safety for employees, consumers, and the environment.

## Differentiation Among the Terms *Production*, *Manufacturing*, and *Operations*

**production**
The total process by which an organization creates its finished goods, often applied to the divisions of a company that transform raw materials and components into finished products. Also, the output of a service organization.

Many people confuse the terms production, *manufacturing*, and *operations*. **Production** is the total process by which an enterprise produces finished goods or services. This process might involve the work, ideas, and plans of the design engineers as well as those of the production manager, plant manager, plant superintendent, and their crews, plus any other department actually involved with bringing forth the product. Exhibit 11-1 illustrates different types of businesses, products, and the processes involved. The term *production* isn't limited to manufacturing goods; it also may be applied to the service and commercial sectors of the economy. For example, a company might produce shampoo and hair conditioner, which are manufactured goods; another company might operate a chain of hair salons, which produce a service.

**Exhibit 11-1**

*Production Processes for Different Organizations*

| Organization | Inputs | Production Processes | Outputs or Products (Type) |
|---|---|---|---|
| Magazine publisher | Information in various forms (written, oral, and photo or art pictorials), labour, energy, capital, ink, paper, tools, equipment, technology | Planning, budgeting, scheduling, design and layout, writing, editing, typesetting, art and photo preparation, management control, printing, folding, durable cutting, binding, shipping on time | Magazines (non-durable goods) |
| Hair-styling salon | Clients, hair knowledge, skills, information, hair care supplies, tools, technology, equipment, labour, energy, capital, water | Planning, budgeting, scheduling, materials ordering and handling, design, hair preparation, washing, conditioning, colouring, styling, meeting schedules, maintaining customer satisfaction (quality control) care | Personal hair (service) |
| Steel conduit manufacturer | Steel, chemicals, labour, energy, capital, tools, technology, equipment, water, location | Planning, budgeting, scheduling, materials ordering and handling, metal processing, labour organization, employee relations and safety, quality control, forming, cooling, storage and distribution, meeting schedules | Steel wire and pipe products (durable goods) |

**manufacturing**
The physical process of making something tangible by hand, by machine, or by a combination of the two.

**operations**
All of the functions involved in producing and delivering goods or services, including all support functions.

**Manufacturing** refers only to the physical process of producing goods; services are not manufactured. The word *manufacturing* comes from the Latin words *manu* (hand) and *factus* (made)—in other words, handmade—but now the meaning of the term has expanded to embrace machine-made as well as handmade products. Manufacturing is distinguished from production because it is restricted to activities that produce a tangible product.

**Operations** are the activities that are conducted through which the organization produces and delivers goods or services. In diverse organizations such as DuPont Canada (an industrial and manufacturing company), Toronto's Hospital for Sick Children (a not-for-profit organization), Sun Life Assurance of Canada (an insurance company), and SaskPower (a public utility), operations usually include purchasing, materials management, production, inventory and quality control, maintenance and manufacturing, engineering, and plant management. The principles discussed in this chapter apply with only slight modifications to any organization, regardless of its purposes and functions. The activities involved in producing and delivering a product or service add value (whether monetary or social) and contribute to individual, corporate, social, and national well-being.[2] Exhibit 11-2 shows some of the activities managed by operations in a traditional plant.

## The Evolution of Modern Manufacturing

Until the nineteenth century manufacturing was done largely by hand. Modern manufacturing can be traced from its harnessing of the sources of energy and mass production to today's technological innovations being developed throughout the world.

**Exhibit 11-2**  *Activities Managed by Operations*

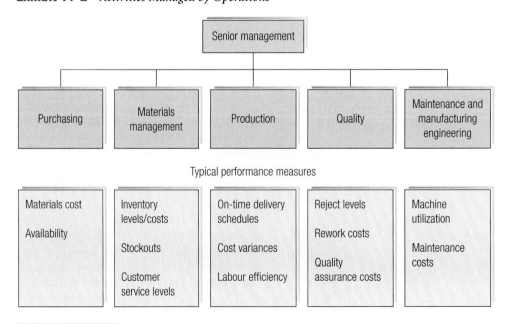

Source: Reprinted by permission of *Harvard Business Review*. An Exhibit from "Manufacturing's Crisis: New Technologies, Obsolete Organizations," by Robert H. Hayes and Ramchandran Jaikumar, September–October 1988. Copyright © 1988 by the President and Fellows of Harvard College; all rights reserved.

## Energy from Resources

*Harnessing the energy of water wheels, and later of the steam engine, provided sources of power that were much more concentrated than the former reliance on human and animal powers.*

For thousands of years in human history, energy was derived almost entirely from human or animal power. Later, water wheels that drove the early gristmills provided a great expansion of the energy available for manufacturing processes. Then, in 1769, the Scottish instrument maker James Watt received his first patent for the steam engine, applying the principles that other people had discovered but never commercialized. With its power and its freedom from dependence on locations with falling water, the steam engine opened new vistas for manufacturing. As the forests in Europe were almost wiped out to provide fuel for steam generation, discoveries of abundant coal in Canada and elsewhere made it possible for the steam revolution to continue and further expanded the sources of power available to manufacturing enterprises. Still later, in the late 1800s, the development of technology to use petroleum products provided yet another major source of energy. Then electricity began to be generated by the burning of coal and petroleum products, and by turbines in Canada's massive systems of hydro dams. Later developments have seen the advent of nuclear-generated energy. Now, in some large installations in Alberta, the Maritimes, and Denmark, wind power has been harnessed to generate electricity. Transmission lines made it possible to deliver to manufacturing plants the enormous amounts of power that modern manufacturing methods require. Without these innovations in the sources of power, manufacturing perhaps still would be limited to handcrafting, at high cost and extremely low productivity. But as in all developments, these changes were not without cost—pollution from coal-fired generating plants, inundation of agricultural land and injury to spawning fish by systems of dams, and as-yet-unknown long-range effects from the need to dispose of the waste of nuclear-energy plants.

## "Scientific" Approaches to Management of Operations

At the beginning of the twentieth century, as described in Chapter 1, building on the *scientific management* theories of Frederick Taylor, scholars, and eventually managers of organizations, began to recognize that management could be seen as an intellectual discipline, with fundamental principles, means of application, and skills that can be learned and practised. They also began to recognize that the application of selected management principles could increase productivity and permit an organization to function competitively.[3] Taylor's approach and the approaches of later proponents of management theory were not greeted with universal approval. Some unions feared these principles because many tended to be applied in a rigid manner and could be used to exploit employees. Also, until the advent of the human relations and behavioural approaches, unions played almost no role in the application of the principles, and employees' wishes and needs were largely ignored. The result of these early oversights was poorly designed production operations and overworked employees.[4] Despite critics and inept use, however, the movements initiated by Taylor helped shape work flow systems, incentive packages, and the design and arrangement of jobs, albeit in somewhat different manners than Taylor had expected.

## Mass Production

mass production
A system permitting the manufacture of large quantities of identical goods, using repetitive actions by people or machines.

assembly line
A conveyor belt or track that carries goods and materials that are being assembled or manufactured and moves the items from work station to work station.

repetitive strain injury
A physical injury suffered by individuals who repeatedly perform activities that require the same movements, postures, and muscle strains.

The use of assembly lines and the division of labour—each worker doing one small, specialized part of the work—characterizes **mass production,** which permits the manufacture of goods in large quantities. About 1913 a significant breakthrough occurred: the establishment of the moving **assembly line** for manufacturing Ford cars. In the mass production of early Fords the chassis moved forward from work station to work station. At one work station a worker attached the headlamps, at another work station someone else attached the hood, and so on. Each worker performed one function on each car as its chassis came down the moving conveyor belt or track. Ford's assembly line began at the entrance to a long shed-like building and emerged bearing finished cars at the other end.

Standardization of parts was another essential factor in the development of mass production. In the 1860s, Eli Whitney (who is better known as the inventor of the cotton gin) developed interchangeable parts for rifles. His innovation replaced the older system in which each rifle was essentially handmade, and if a part failed, a new one had to be crafted to fit the particular gun. Later, applying Whitney's innovation, at Ford each headlamp was exactly the same size and was connected to the same spot on identical car frames as they came down the assembly line. Thus, standardization permitted one worker to attach headlamps over and over rather quickly and easily with a standard level of quality.

Some workers and observers criticized the mass production system because it created "human machines" who moved their arms and hands over and over again, in the same motions, to the rhythms of the inescapable assembly line. We now know that these critics were right, as physicians have identified **repetitive strain injury**. But because of their efficiencies, mass production and the assembly line were here to stay. No significant manufacturer could afford to ignore their technological advances.

## The Management Challenge in Operations

During the economic expansion of the late 1950s and the 1960s, the pace of life—and the pace of production and consumption—escalated with unprecedented speed. Salaries rose, prices increased, production rates climbed. By the 1970s new and unexpected pressures appeared. Uneasiness and dissatisfaction began to spread. The public became disillusioned with leadership at national, local, institutional, and labour union levels. With disillusionment came cynicism. Manufacturers actually designed products with planned obsolescence—goods made to last only a short period of time so consumers would have to buy again. Consumers began to question both the quality and the prices of products and services. Critics also questioned the facilities being used for manufacturing, since many factories were outdated, inefficient, dirty, and in many cases unsafe.

Yet, the intensity of competition pressured companies to produce more products in less time. These pressures reduced the incentives for employees to take pride in their own accomplishments. Often quality declined and, with it, customer satisfaction. At the same time, competition to attract customers drove many companies to offer greater variety in models, colours, and specifications.

Henry Ford's oft-quoted comment, "The customer can have any colour as long as it's black," is often cited to illustrate that Ford didn't understand or care about his customers. But according to Peter Drucker, few people understand what Ford was actually saying: that flexibility costs time and money, and customers may not be willing to pay for it.[5] But in the early years of mass-produced automobiles, General Motors began to offer customers both some choice in colours and annual model changes, at prices that were competitive with Ford's. As a result, GM captured market share that has never been lost.

Today most manufacturers have learned to do what GM did in the mid-1920s, and some have gone even further in combining flexibility and standardization. Yet some manufacturing people continue to think, as did Henry Ford, that an organization has to choose between standardization at low cost and flexibility at high cost, and cannot do both. The successful factory of the future has no choice. It must find ways to be flexible, but at low cost. This is one of the biggest challenges for managers of operations, whether in large manufacturing or commercial corporations, in small businesses, or in not-for-profit organizations.

Nortel, Merck, Microsoft, Honda, and Toyota are known for their ability to develop, manufacture, and market what consumers want, when they want it, at an affordable price for a specific group of customers. Lucent Canada designed and built a nationwide cellular network from scratch in Argentina—in only 60 days. Because of their reputation for quality and particularly because of their proposed time frame (which they met), they won the contract over other global competitors, who had claimed that the project would take at least two years![6] Typically, innovative product developers such as Lucent are global in scope and outlook and one- to two-thirds of their sales come from outside their home markets.[7]

In the search for new and better manufacturing methods, production and operations managers are playing more significant roles in their organizations than ever before. As markets and technologies globalize, these managers increasingly need to understand foreign customers' needs, preferences, and price limitations. To be successful in global competition, Canadian businesses must be able to adapt their production and operations functions.

# The Role of the Production and Operations Manager

Production and operations managers are responsible for producing the goods or services that the organization intends to offer to its customers or constituents. There are many kinds of production and operations systems, just as there are many kinds of products in the marketplace. Production and operations staffs vary in size from a single person in a very small company to thousands of employees in a huge multinational corporation such as BCE.

## Functions of the Manager

The production goals of a successful business focus on producing products and services that are the best and the quickest, at the least cost. Thus, production and operations managers must produce with effectiveness and efficiency while maintaining quality control. It is production and operations managers' job to see that the operations necessary to achieve the company's production goals are carried out. To do this, these managers oversee a number of company operations. Typical functions include:

- Product planning;
- Site location and layout;
- Inventory control;
- Purchasing and materials management;
- Manufacturing and production;
- Production control;
- Quality control; and
- Plant management.

*Management in the Real World*    **11-1**

## Managing Production and Operations: Reflections by Philip Crosby

When people discuss quality and operations, a question that always arises concerns the cost of doing things right. Someone always asks about the situation where they would have to invest money in order to meet their current requirements. As it is now, people just toss out a portion of the output and feel they are making a sound economic decision. The way they describe the case, it always sounds like a fine management option. In reality the pain of trying to get money out of senior management justifies almost any action in their minds.

For many years I carried a bright shiny $100 bill in my wallet as preparation for this question. When anyone described such a situation, I would bring out the money and offer it to them if they could show me that what they were doing was financially correct. Forget ethical or quality policy: I would pay off on economics. Without exception, and in dozens of cases, it turned out that they were not counting the true cost of such a practice.

One questioner took me up on it and we journeyed out to the shop floor where he showed me the operation in question. The electronic component involved was programmed by a machine and then tested by another. The programming machine was not quite capable of meeting the full range necessary, but a new one would require a capital expenditure of several hundred thousand dollars. To get around this they had set up a checking operation where an operator tested each component and then returned those found wanting. These were processed through a special rework machine that had been built in the engineering laboratory, and then were tested again. About half of these passed; the rest were discarded.

"The cost of doing this is much lower than buying a new machine," said my host. "We've checked it out. You can hand over the $100 now if you wish."

I cautioned him about jumping to conclusions and asked the operator how many components were rejected on the first pass. He said that at least 20 percent failed and less than half of them responded to the rework. I suggested we agree that the process contained a 10 percent final scrap rate. Thanking the operator, we moved over to the quality engineering office and I asked the systems analyst about returns from the customers. It turns out that they amounted to another 10 percent, mostly due to marginal programming.

While we were mulling this over, the quality engineer volunteered that she had been drawing up a report on the failure rates in all of the operations. Technology was becoming more demanding, she noted, and the shop's instruments were not able to keep up with it. Therefore they were doing more evaluations that let them assume a rate of failure based on economic considerations. My host did not know about this and questioned the engineer sharply. She stood her ground.

"We know this is not in line with the quality policy, but it is the actual practice. We cannot ignore it, and apparently it makes sense from a cost standpoint."

"Do you know the cost of operating your whole shop?" I asked the manager. He nodded and gave me a large figure.

"If you are establishing a practice that is going to waste 20 percent of that cost in labour, materials, overhead, and customer returns also, then that is a lot of money down the chute," I noted. "That one operation we looked at is spending a great deal more money than proper machines would cost. But worse than that, the whole operation is being infected. It is like going back to 1958."

I still have my $100.

The idea of a well-designed operation is to have it proceed with its task without any special attention or interruption.

In moderate-sized organizations, the production and operations manager is often a vice president who reports directly to top management. Managers or supervisors representing the functions listed report to the production and operations manager. In managing these functions, production and operations managers usually are responsible for product planning such as preparing forecasts, schedules, and budgets in collaboration with top management, finance, and marketing. In startup operations, they oversee site location and layout. They are responsible for the hiring, training, and career development of personnel in the departments involved with production and operations. They also must work closely with all other departments in the company, and especially with marketing, physical distribution, warehousing, and shipping.

# Organizing for the Production Process

Chapter 5 discussed several different ways to organize, depending on needs, types of production, strengths and weaknesses of company managers, and other relevant factors. Job titles vary. The inventory control manager in one organization may be called the warehouse manager in another organization, or the purchasing and inventory control manager in still another.

**Traditional organizations.** The organization chart in Exhibit 11-3 follows the traditional form. It gives each manager a specific area of authority and responsibility; but it can also pit managers against each other. To illustrate, a purchasing manager may have budgeted $50,000 for a given quantity of a specific material, to be delivered several days later by truck. Suddenly, the production manager informs the purchasing manager that it is absolutely essential to have that material on hand immediately to meet an unexpected

**Exhibit 11-3**  *Traditional Manufacturing Organization*

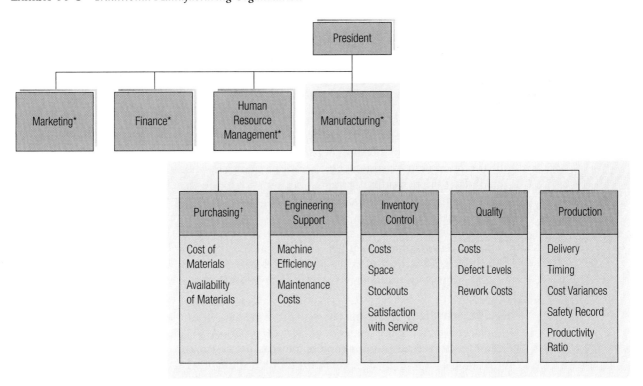

\* Each function would have a complete structure if chart were presented in full.
† Examples of performance measures are shown below each departmental grouping.

order. The purchasing manager knows that it will cost $10,000 more than the budget to expedite delivery of the material—perhaps by plane instead of truck. The purchasing manager's responsibility is to purchase at the lowest feasible cost, but the needs of the production manager prevent the purchasing manager from doing so. So, in this illustration, both the purchasing manager and the production manager have to consider foremost the overall goals of the organization. The traditional form of organization tends to compartmentalize managers, with each focusing solely on the objectives of one department. For the organization to thrive, the two managers in this illustration would have to decide together whether the additional cost is justified in order to meet a particular customer's demands.

Exhibit 11-3 also shows some of the factors that traditionally would be used to evaluate the effectiveness of the managers who are in charge of the various functions. Applying this traditional thinking, the purchasing agent would have little incentive to accommodate to the production managers' needs, and vice versa.

Some organizations have recognized this potential for departmental goals to get in the way of overall organizational goals. In an attempt to counteract this tendency, they have developed operational structures that focus on specific large projects.

**Project-based operations.**  These types of organizational structures are especially appropriate for very large projects for which materials and workers must be moved to other sites. There is no assembly line or work station layout within a factory or shop; the product is built in place, usually at the customer's site. Examples include building a mill or refinery, constructing and installing a large printing press or other piece of production equipment, or constructing a building. Companies such as SNC Lavalin (a Canadian engineering consulting and management company) and Cominco (a Canadian multinational mining and metals company) manage and operate these kinds of projects all over the world—from Greenland to Chile, from Uzbekistan to Papua New Guinea, and in Canada from Sydney, Nova Scotia, to Sidney, British Columbia.

## Planning Site Location and Layout

When a company opens a new branch or location, the production and operations manager is usually heavily involved in planning the site location and layout. Company officers, engineers, and heads of departments may be directed to channel their ideas and lists of requirements through the operations manager. Then the operations manager consolidates them, modifying them if necessary to fit the resources available. When an organization-wide list is agreed upon and approved by senior management, the operations manager may be assigned to coordinate detailed planning and negotiations. The list of requirements may be discussed with a real estate broker who specializes in industrial/commercial properties. Alternatively, the organization may retain other specialists to investigate possible sites and select design engineers. A list is prepared of suitable properties available in the area and within the price range planned.

**Site selection.**  A site may be bought or leased with or without a building already in place. The increasing tendency of large corporations to locate in industrial parks is a factor in the competition for good employees, because many prefer pleasant surroundings. But appearance may be less important than some other factors. Depending on the type of organization, more weight may have to be given to convenience to transportation facilities, availability of adequate utilities, or other production-linked factors. The Alcan Aluminium plant was located near Kitimat, B.C., because of its proximity to potential

*Site selection is dictated by many factors that vary in importance. For a logging operation, the availability of trees outweighs all other factors; for a shipping company, access to transportation facilities may be the crucial factor.*

hydro sources (massive amounts of electrical power being required in the smelting of aluminum). Service sector businesses often seek to locate in heavy-traffic areas convenient to customers or where parking is available.

A production and operations manager's plan for site location considers most if not all of the following factors:

- Economies of cost or other economic advantages for land, buildings, or units;
- Taxes, insurance, and other costs;
- Proximity to related industries and suppliers, warehouses, and service operations;
- Availability of a suitably trained workforce, at reasonable cost;
- Availability of economical transportation for materials and supplies, for finished goods, and also for employees travelling to and from work;
- Accessibility to markets for goods;
- Air and water conditions, including adequacy and reliability of supply;
- Proximity to plentiful, economical, and reliable energy sources;
- Climate and environment;
- Ample space for the organization's possible expansion;
- Proximity to employee needs such as housing, schools, mass transportation, religious facilities, day care, shopping, and recreational facilities;
- Conformance with appropriate zoning and other regulatory factors; and
- Community receptiveness.

**infrastructure**
The facilities that support operations, including utilities, transportation, and communication facilities, and controls of the working environment.

All of these and other similar factors in the external environment constitute the **infrastructure** that may dictate the decision as to where an operation can be located to the greatest advantage.

Seldom does one single factor dictate the choice of plant location. In the last quarter of the twentieth century, however, some managers were attracted by the lure of what appeared to be cheap labour. They located textile, clothing, shoe, and other types of plants in Korea and Taiwan because of the apparent abundance of cheap labour. The

*The Alcan Aluminium plant was located in Kitimat, B.C., because of its proximity to an abundant supply of water, which is required for the processing of aluminum.*

labour rates in the countries first targeted escalated rapidly, and the initial advantage soon dissipated. Next they moved to countries such as Malaysia and mainland China, and again encountered rising costs, not only in labour but in other areas as well.

Canadian auto parts manufacturer Magna International, for instance, reports that when all costs are factored in, total unit costs of their products produced in Mexico are roughly equal to those produced in Ontario, even though Mexican wage rates are a fraction of those in Canada. Magna International explains its decision to build an auto parts plant in Mexico not on the basis of wage rates but to be close to Mexican auto assembly plants, just as their Ontario parts plants are located near to Windsor, Oakville, and Detroit auto assembly plants.[8]

**Site layout.** Just as it dictates the kind and location of the facility, the type of business will determine the layout of the site selected. For different businesses, production and operations managers must meet different needs. Different kinds of production require varying space for assembly lines, work stations, warehousing, or other specific arrangements for work layouts.

The layout should be planned in detail *before* the site is chosen, because once the site is selected, its size, shape, or contours may preclude some favourable internal layouts. A huge one-floor assembly line would require a plant site that is reasonably level; an odd-shaped parcel might squeeze operating and related facilities into inefficient relationships to each other. The layout plan must account for the needed production and shipping areas, storage areas, office and conference areas, space for parking, and often for attractive landscaping. To draw up specific plans, managers use templates, models, drawings, and the latest computer techniques. Layout that effectively facilitates work flow can contribute greatly to keeping operating costs competitive.

One helpful tool for layout planning is the use of small wooden blocks that serve as three-dimensional models. Each block represents a scale model of a piece of equipment or furniture. These simple models can be moved around on a plan of the future space drawn on paper and mounted on a board. This permits the manager to try various configurations and interrelationships much easier than if each different arrangement required drawing a new set of plans. The method also helps to make appropriate allowances for physical movement of people and materials, remembering, for instance, that file drawers will be opened into passageways and that operators will be standing at the controls of machinery, thus closing off parts of areas that would appear on a paper plan to have been left for circulation.

Without this use of easily movable blocks, many planners fall into the traps that occur when preliminary plans are committed to lines on paper. Once lines are drawn, to change the location or orientation of any one piece of equipment or furniture requires adjustment of other pieces, which in turn requires still further adjustments. With blocks, this inherent rigidity can be eliminated to a large extent, because final locations remain completely flexible until all of the blocks have been satisfactorily placed in relation to the others.

A difficulty often encountered in site layout is that the production manager, having a primary interest in production facilities, neglects to consult sufficiently with those who work in other departments. Paper flow should determine the location and interrelationships of offices and segments of offices, just as material flow determines the location of production equipment. It is costly and time-consuming if an inefficient office layout (or assignment of offices by seniority instead of by function) requires that a single document criss-cross its own path several times in its travels within the organization. The prudent planner will plot on paper the paths of frequently encountered documents; for instance, following a document from receipt of an order, to purchasing, to warehouse, to production, to shipping, to billing and collection, and to final archives. If this route doubles back on itself to any great extent, a better layout may improve the work flow, reduce costs, and minimize delays. The cost of inefficient paper flow is hidden and often completely overlooked, but it impedes the organization's competitiveness nonetheless. Productivity standards apply in support functions just as much as they do in production.

Innovative answers to the needs of a changing workforce and changing management styles are beginning to be reflected in such seemingly mundane factors as office layout and design. Nortel, for instance, has gone one step further than the celebrated office layout at Lucent Technology's head offices. Nortel has brought together 1300 head office employees from various conventional offices scattered around Mississauga and Etobicoke, Ontario. They were relocated to a 600,000-square-foot space in Brampton, Ontario, formerly occupied by a Nortel manufacturing facility. But the head office personnel were not condemned to exist on an unused factory floor. Instead, they moved into what resembles a small city under one roof, with a main street and crossroads, attractive piazzas and parks with real trees, a bank, a travel agency, a fitness centre, and even a Zen garden. In the words of Ray Lopinski, director of real estate for Nortel's corporate headquarters, "This is not an office; it is an environment."[9] The high-tech employees of Nortel are reported to thrive in this environment. Although it is difficult to make accurate measurements of their productivity, it

*Nortel's Brampton, Ontario, headquarters is described not as an "office" but as an "environment."*

can be surmised from experience in other situations that heightened morale will translate into increased productivity.

## Managing Materials, Purchasing, and Inventory

Materials management, purchasing, and inventory control involve the planning, ordering, and internal storage and distribution of supplies and materials needed for production. Other names used for these functions include *material handling, procurement, supply room or warehouse management*, and *inventory control and management*.

Some variations occur in the ways that authority and responsibility are organized. In some companies the purchasing department contracts for everything purchased from outside sources. In others the purchasing function covers only those materials and supplies used in the actual production process, while other supplies are purchased by their end users in the organization.

In large companies the materials manager may oversee the functions of purchasing and inventory control, or inventory control may be part of production management, depending on its scope. The inventory control unit may handle only the inventories of components and subassemblies, or it may cover all inventories—of supplies, raw materials, components, subassemblies, and finished products.

### Just-in-time Inventory Control

**materials requirements planning (MRP)**
A computer-driven system for analyzing and projecting materials needs and then scheduling their arrival at the work station at the right time.

**just-in-time (JIT) inventory control**
A system that coordinates procurement and delivery of materials so that items are delivered by suppliers at the precise time that they are needed by production.

In recent years two important innovations have occurred in materials management and inventory control. **Just-in-time (JIT) inventory control** and **materials requirements planning (MRP)** have greatly improved the ways in which materials and inventory are managed and scheduled.[10] MRP is dependent on the master production schedule (which will be discussed later in this chapter) and takes into account such variables as lead time in ordering. MRP is only a shorthand method of referring to the analysis and management of all materials within a production facility—what is needed, when it is needed, and what the consequences would be if various items are not available when they are needed. In an enterprise that has only a few items to be controlled, MRP can be done by a combination of observation and handwritten notes. In a large organization or in any enterprise that has a large number of items, such as a retail hardware store, it is almost essential to employ a computer system tailored to the particular operation. Such a system would properly track receipts of orders from customers, issuing production work orders and listing inventory and materials requirements, signalling the need to replace inventory used, accounting for the inventory of work in progress, and recording and preparing documents for shipping, billing and collections. MRP leads logically to the JIT inventory concept.

The JIT approach was developed by Taiichi Ohno at Toyota Motor Company of Japan.[11] The first step in applying the JIT system is to try to match the output of manufacturing with market demand, making it possible to minimize inventories of finished products.[12] Then the application of MRP makes it possible to know within very narrow limits what quantities of raw materials, parts, and subassemblies are needed and when. Continuing orders are placed with suppliers, who are required to meet these schedules, delivering in the exact quantities specified and at the precise times specified—neither too early nor too late. Often it is possible to arrange for the suppliers to deliver directly to the specific location within the buyer's factory where the particular material will be used. This eliminates the double handling of more conventional methods, in which suppliers deliver to a warehouse area, the materials are shelved or stocked in inventory, and then handled again when they are called for to meet production needs.

Installing an efficient JIT system can result in lower inventories of purchased parts and raw materials, of work in process, and of finished goods. It saves warehouse and work area space. It reduces the amount of capital tied up in inventory, freeing funds for other purposes. The lower inventory levels result in reduced insurance premiums. Because items are not held for long periods in inventory, there is less likelihood of obsolescence, deterioration, and inventory loss from theft—a major concern in most organizations.

In today's economy, it is common for many customers to expect next-day delivery, even on hard-to-locate parts and materials.[13] National Semiconductor is reported to have reduced its delivery time by 47 percent, cut distribution costs by 2.5 percent, and increased sales by 34 percent, in large part by using a JIT system.[14]

Although the advantages of a JIT system are manifest, it also entails risks because it can only be successful if suppliers are almost perfectly reliable. If an item is required on Tuesday and it does not appear until Friday, the delay may cause production to falter or even halt. In an organization that carries unduly large inventories, a tardy supplier's failures may be overlooked and no correction may be sought. In a JIT system, a delinquent supplier will be required to mend its ways or be replaced. It also may be seen that the success of a JIT system depends not only on the reliability of suppliers but also on their proximity to the production facility; a manufacturer that is located at a considerable distance from key suppliers effectively may be precluded from initiating rigorous JIT inventory control. Even so, the concept of tailoring both production and ordering to expected sales can help make any organization more competitive.

## Zero Defects

**zero defects**
The concept of producing goods or providing services, all of which conform 100 percent with specifications and plans.

Because JIT systems leave little margin for error, both upstream work stations and suppliers outside of the organization must deliver on time in the right quantity, and with no defects. Defective parts, like late deliveries, defeat the very purpose of JIT. **Zero defects** is a term developed by Philip B. Crosby for a performance standard that responds to the attitude in some organizations that mistakes are human and acceptable.[15] By committing themselves to avoiding errors entirely, people can move closer to the goal of zero defects. The aim of a zero defects program is to build quality into a product and eliminate costly inspections after production. Jaguar, for instance, is reported to have reduced assembly line defects by 80 percent in two years[16] by instilling in its employees a commitment to the concept of zero defects.

## Inventory Control by Category

It is not easy to decide how much of any one item should be carried in inventory. One approach is to place all inventory items in one of three categories. Category A would be those items that, if not available when needed, would cause a critical work stoppage. An example would be a critical part for an essential production machine, or the supply of payroll

*Jaguar's emphasis on zero defects has not only saved the company money, but has enhanced the reputation of its products.*

cheques (the absence of which would not improve employee morale!). If an item in category A would not be available immediately from a reliable supplier, it must be carried in inventory to avoid unacceptably costly delays.

Category B would be those items that are essential to smooth functioning and that cannot be restocked quickly. Examples would be raw materials or standard production components. Category B items also should be carried in inventory, but only in sufficient quantities to cover the periods required to restock, plus a slight margin for safety.

Category C items would include machine parts that are routinely replaced before they fail in a program of preventive maintenance. However, if replacement of these parts

## What Managers Are Reading    11-1

### Strategy Safari: A Guided Tour Through the Wilds of Strategic Management

Once again, Henry Mintzberg, teamed this time with a fellow Canadian and a Scottish colleague, has analyzed some of the best-loved strategic management fads and offered insightful critiques and suggestions for rational interpretations. The authors start with the fable of the blind men of Indostan. The first man touches an elephant's side and declares that the elephant is a wall. The second man feels the elephant's tail and asserts that the elephant is a rope. The third man touches the elephant's leg and declares that the elephant is a tree. In the words of the original poem, "... each was partly in the right and all were in the wrong." The authors suggest that on questions of strategic management, business writers tend to act like the men in the poem, with rather myopic visions of strategic management as a whole.

In this engaging book the authors take a light-hearted approach that belies the seriousness of their subject. They attempt to survey the whole field of strategic management and conscientiously describe what they consider to be ten different schools of strategic management, clustered into three groupings. The first grouping consists of three schools that are prescriptive, that is, that attempt to prescribe the ideal. Then six schools are grouped together because they try to describe how strategies are actually made, rather than what should be the ideal case. The final group is not a group at all, consisting as it does of only one school. This school is described by the term *configuration*, based on the observation that it attempts to integrate the other nine schools and focuses largely on what has been termed strategic change.

Drawing heavily from writers who seem to exemplify each of the various schools, Mintzberg and his colleagues describe in relatively objective terms the components of each of their somewhat arbitrarily defined schools. Throughout each sketch runs a thread of argument that most theories of strategic management tend to oversimplify and to attribute much more validity to themselves than is warranted.

In the final chapter, the authors present a graph that purports to show the volume of publication in each of their ten schools from 1965 to about 1997. In another table, which covers six pages, the authors attempt to summarize for each of the schools the leading writers and champions, the messages conveyed, the leaders and environments, and even the homilies that fit—from "Look before you leap" to "To everything there is a season." For the serious student of strategic management, this table is a handy compendium and explanatory framework.

The humorous approach taken in this book makes reading it a delight, but might obscure the very real message it conveys—that strategic management is an extremely complex subject and, partly for that reason, is in a state of flux, with confusing and contradictory literature. This book may help its readers wend their way through the thicket of competing claims, contradictory analyses, and partly correct theories.

Source: Henry Mintzberg, Bruce Ahlstrand, and Joseph Lampel, *Strategy Safari: A Guided Tour Through the Wilds of Strategic Management* (New York: The Free Press, 1998).

is delayed a few days, no serious harm would be caused. This category also would include items that are critical but that can be replaced almost immediately if required, even at extra expense, such as requiring delivery by overnight air express instead of by the usual less-expensive truck freight. Category C items should be carried only in small quantities, if at all. Yet, studies have shown that a large proportion of most company inventories—often as high as 85 percent of the total value—are represented by items that should be in category C. In such cases, thoughtful analysis of inventory levels can offer large savings without disrupting operations.

Obviously, location is a factor in deciding inventory levels. If the plant is in Grande Prairie, Alberta, and the only supplier of an item is in Moncton, New Brunswick, a higher inventory level will have to be carried than if plant and supplier are located within a few blocks of each other, say, in Hamilton.

One rule of thumb, whether relating to a JIT system or not, is that if a category B or C item *never* runs out, the inventory level must be too high. Conversely, if an item in any category is subject to frequent stockouts, consideration should be given to increasing the carrying level for that item.

Together, JIT and MRP can save time and dollars. They also make it possible to meet delivery promises that have been made to customers—a critical component of competitiveness. Many observers believe that Wal-Mart's competitive gains over Zellers in Canada can be attributed to Wal-Mart's low-cost and efficient distribution system that, in the words of one analyst, "... ensures merchandise is on the store shelf in time to meet customer demand."[17]

JIT and MRP have had profound effects on suppliers as well. They are held much more accountable with JIT and MRP systems than with less demanding inventory systems. At the same time, suppliers of corporations that have adopted JIT and MRP can plan their own operations much more accurately. In very large operations, such as the Detroit and Windsor auto assembliers, nearby suppliers are connected to their corporate customers by modem and computer to follow the progress of assembly line work. From this vantage point, their delivery trucks can arrive at almost the moment the materials are needed. Lead times on orders are greatly reduced and costs of storing inventory drop sharply for everyone.

## Scheduling in Operations Management

Like all managers, the production manager's role includes all four elements—planning, organizing, leading, and controlling. The planning, organizing, and controlling functions can be coordinated using methods that are particularly adapted to production. Planning the use of labour, facilities, and materials for fulfilling the production schedule is a complex, ongoing task. The manager usually will have more than one product to plan for, with the resultant need for continual changes in materials, production processes, uses of space, calls for energy, and allocation of labour.

A *master production schedule* should be created. It will show when the manager plans to produce each product and in what quantities. The production manager is responsible for meeting the dates, quantities, and cost commitments on the schedule. The master schedule will affect the efforts and success of every department in the company. To be useful it must reflect the needs of the finance, sales and marketing, shipping, and all other departments.

Production managers must plan for flexibility—to be able to change from one process to another on short notice. They may use a number of tactics to meet emergencies or make changes in the plan. Requesting overtime, hiring temporary workers, cross-training workers so they can do more than one job, and many other methods are available.

## PERT Charts

PERT chart
A graphical display of all of the steps required to complete a project, showing the interrelationships among the steps, the order in which they must occur, and the times required to complete each.

Flexibility as well as adherence to schedule can be assisted with the use of the *program evaluation and review technique*, or **PERT chart**. This method was developed to manage and operate complex research, design, and manufacturing processes, such as those used for the production and deployment of missiles. It is based on constructing graphs to track events that must take place to accomplish a task. Its benefits include helping managers predict time requirements to complete projects, change methods in ways that actually will reduce overall times, and monitor and control multiple activities that feed into a complex project. There are five steps in creating a PERT chart:

1. Break the project to be accomplished into events or actions, labelling each with the amount of time needed to complete it.
2. List the first event of the task.
3. List the event that follows the first one, drawing an arrow from the first event to the next one, showing the sequence. (If two parallel events follow and depend on the first one, arrows are drawn to both events to show that one event leads to or permits work on two, or even more, events.)
4. In the same way, chart all of the events needed to complete the project.
5. Label the arrows with the amount of time it takes to complete each activity.

Exhibit 11-4 presents a typical PERT chart for the replacement of a machine in a manufacturing plant. The letters represent the activities necessary to replace the machine. The numbers in the circles represent completed activities, called *events*. Number 1 is the origin of the project. In this example, before anything else can be done, specifications for the new machine must be prepared and approved. This is represented by task A. Task B represents securing bids and awarding contracts. Number 3 reflects the point at which bids have been secured and contracts have been awarded. Each activity is also assigned an expected time for completion. In the example, for instance, Task C is the removal of existing equipment and is expected to take two working days. It will be completed on day 10 (8 + 2). The chart also shows that the whole process is expected to take 20 working days (8 + 5 + 4 + 2 + 1), which is the longest of the three paths to the concluding point (that is, tasks A + B + D + H + I).

A major advantage of the PERT chart is that it identifies bottlenecks. In the example given, if the managers wish to expedite the whole process, their focus should be on the longest route, the one that takes 20 days, because the other two routes take only 19 and 14 days. If task D, training, could be accomplished in two days instead of the expected four, that route would be reduced from 20 days to 18 days. This task could be expedited, for example, by paying overtime to provide the four days of training on two weekend days as well as two normal work days instead of on four normal work days. The manager would have to evaluate whether the extra cost would be warranted by the benefit of decreasing the overall time required for the project.

However, if task D, training, were reduced by two working days, the total time would be reduced by only one working day, because the next-longest path, now the longest (A + C + E + G + H + I), is 19 working days. The next step would be for the managers to evaluate each of these tasks to see if the time required for any of them could be reduced. As can be seen, the PERT chart highlights where the critical events are, and thus where modifications could reduce the total time required. It also makes clear that any reduction in task F, painting, for instance, would not reduce the overall time, because path A

**Exhibit 11-4**   *Example of a PERT Chart*

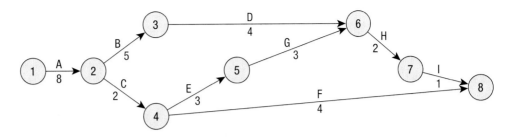

| Activity | Description | Completion Time (days) | Prerequisites |
|---|---|---|---|
| A | Prepare specifications | 8 | None |
| B | Secure bids and award contracts | 5 | A |
| C | Remove existing equipment | 2 | A |
| D | Train operators for new machine | 4 | A, B |
| E | Electrical modifications | 3 | A, C |
| F | Paint | 4 | A, C |
| G | Install machine | 3 | A, C, E |
| H | Test machine | 2 | A, B, D |
| I | Reschedule production | 1 | A, B, D, H |

+ C + F totals only 14 days, so completion of the project still would have to await completion of the tasks that lie on the other two paths. The PERT chart, therefore, calls attention to the critical paths, which leads to the method's other name—the *critical path method (CPM)*.

For a relatively simple application, such as the one shown in the example, a good manager might be able to keep in mind all of the components and the times for each, without resorting to PERT charts or CPM. For a more complex project or when a manager has several projects underway at the same time, it would be almost impossible to keep in mind all of this information and make appropriate decisions, especially as the project progresses and actual times differ from those that were expected. As managers become ever more sophisticated, the use of PERT charts or CPM will become almost routine whenever a manager approaches a complex task or project.

## Production Technology

**Computer-aided design (CAD).**  Increased production is achieved not only through efficient planning. Computers have added flexibility and speed to the production process. **Computer-aided design (CAD)** is the use of computers to draw plans for a product or service. CAD programs offer *smart analysis* functions that can speed up the development cycle for new products.[18]

**computer-aided design (CAD)**
The use of computers to draw plans for a product or service applying pre-programmed parameters that describe the desired finished product.

CAD has been used to design products ranging from buildings to potato chips. Dimension Measurement System Inc. has developed a technology that uses CAD to produce men's and women's suits made to measure. Light is projected onto a prospective buyer from three different angles and digital cameras capture the images. A computer processes these inputs to create three-dimensional contours of the body. These measurements are sent to a CAD pattern maker. The pattern maker modifies standard patterns to reflect the individual measurements, the CAD data are downloaded to an automatic fabric cutter, and finally, as the last stage, workers sew the precut pieces into the final garment.[19]

More than 80 percent of large North American manufacturers responding to a survey by the U.S. National Association of Manufacturers indicated that they employ CAD.[20] Although as yet no comparable study has been done of Canadian manufacturers, it is safe to assume that results would be similar.

**computer-aided engineering (CAE)**
The use of computers to plan engineering processes and test designs, permitting managers to forecast the changes that would occur if various parameters were varied.

**Computer-aided engineering (CAE).** **Computer-aided engineering (CAE)** is the use of computers to plan engineering processes and test designs. Many large corporations are using CAE in the early stages of design to compress product development cycles and save on both the cost and the time to develop models and prototypes.[21] CAE, when combined with CAD, has enabled the development of millions of new designs. Designs can be drawn, extended, contracted, added to, or taken from—all within the computer. Engineers can test designs for function and stress and try out variations without the cost or risk of building models or samples. Drafters using CAE can perform many of these tasks once the initial design is developed. The computer does much of the calculation and the drawing in two or three dimensions as needed.

**computer-aided manufacturing (CAM)**
The use of computer systems to monitor and control manufacturing processes.

**Computer-aided manufacturing (CAM).** The use of computers to control the operation of production processes is known as **computer-aided manufacturing (CAM)**. The combination of CAD and CAM systems make it easier for plants to make a wide variety of products and undertake production-line changeovers quickly.[22] Using CAD/CAM, the Marlboro Mercedes Formula One racing team designed a car in only three months,[23] which without these systems would have taken many months or even years to accomplish.

CAM also is used in continuous process manufacturing.[24] The mill at Cominco's Polaris mine in the Canadian Arctic uses CAM to monitor the various stages of the processes that convert raw ore into concentrate. Sensors are located at various points in the material flow to monitor factors such as water content, temperature, particle size, and even metals content. The information is then fed automatically into a bank of computers that have the capability to change parameters in the control equipment. The result is much closer tolerance of the output product and, consequently, a better product.

## Robotics

**robot**
A reprogrammable, computer-controlled machine that can function without direct moment-by-moment control by an operator to manipulate objects and materials and perform specified functions in accordance with detailed instructions.

One application of CAE and CAM is the programming and use of robots. The auto industry is the best-known user of robots for manufacture, although usage in the electronics industry is fast growing. A **robot** is a computerized, reprogrammable, multifunctional machine that can manipulate materials and objects in performing particular tasks. Robots paint, sand, test, and weld car parts; robots track individual cars on the assembly line and perform dozens of repetitive, exacting, unwieldy, or dangerous tasks.[25] The Fujitsu plant in Akashi, Japan, was using robots effectively in the 1980s. The plant specializes in sheet metal manufacture, producing more than 100,000 parts each month for 1500 different products. The production order, specifying the parts, the number, and

*Using computer-aided manufacturing, highly technical operations, such as at Cominco's mine and mill in the Canadian Arctic, can produce products of consistent quality at less cost than would otherwise be possible.*

the materials to be used, is given to the main computer. The computer then selects the most efficient way to make the parts and creates a layout for the automated shear machines and punch presses to follow. Use of CAM in the Fujitsu plant is estimated to have improved productivity by 40 percent, saving approximately $10,000 worth of material a month.

Robots not only relieve employees of tedious, repetitive tasks but they can work in environments such as nuclear power plants, areas contaminated by toxic gases or subject to very high temperatures, deep under the sea, or any other location where human activity either would be unsafe or would require so much protective equipment as to make the operations unwieldy and very costly. Despite their obvious benefits, fears have been expressed that robots will displace employees, thus contributing to Canada's growing body of unemployed or unemployable unskilled workers. It is not within the purview of this book to examine this growing phenomenon, but the issue cannot be overlooked as a social responsibility question that faces managers as they contemplate CAM and the use of robots.

As yet, the greatest use of robots is in heavy manufacturing. As robots become ever more sophisticated and plant designers become more familiar with their capabilities, they will be used more frequently in the service sector as well. For instance, it is not difficult to imagine a robot in a hospital laundry, removing linens from the dryers, sorting and folding them, and placing them on the correct shelves in the storeroom.

Given the exponential growth rate of the use of CAD, CAE, CAM, and robots, a word of caution is in order. No matter how sophisticated computers and their software become, their applications require careful planning and the selection of appropriate tasks to which they are to be assigned. As award-winning Edmonton architect Vivian Manasc has warned: "Technology is not a product problem, but a design problem. Buying technology won't solve a problem any more than buying two-by-fours will build a house."[26]

## Flexible Manufacturing Systems

**flexible manufacturing system (FMS)**
A system in which computerized controls, and often robots, can be programmed to permit rapid changes in production to accommodate frequent changes in specifications of the products being manufactured.

Robots and other computerized machines programmed to switch fairly easily from producing one kind of product to another can be grouped in a **flexible manufacturing system (FMS)**. Automated equipment controls the flow of parts and materials and automatically removes the finished products to storage or to shipping operations, as directed. Its flexibility allows FMS to be used for just-in-time inventory control projects as well as for manufacturing small batches of customized parts or products without raising costs drastically. The type of flexibility a company should emphasize in its planning depends largely on the competitive environment of the industry.[27]

The National Bicycle Industrial Co., a subsidiary of Japanese electronics giant Matsushita, has used FMS with great success. Robots, computers, and people work together to make production flexible and responsive.[28] With 20 employees and a design-smart computer, the firm can produce any of 11,231,862 variations of 18 models of racing, road, and mountain bikes in 199 colour patterns. National Bicycle designs and manufactures the bicycle to fit the customer's size, shape, and strength.

FMS extends beyond the confines of the manufacturing facility. Production doesn't start until an order is placed. The retail bicycle store makes a sale and then forwards the customer's specifications by e-mail to the National Bicycle plant. A computer operator inputs the data into a microcomputer. A bar code is created for each customer. The bar code is fed into the computer with details of the order. A robot is instructed as to exactly what specifications to apply, including the size, weight, and strength of components, the model number, the colour the bicycle should be painted, and all other details. The customer's name is imprinted on the frame. Within two weeks, the personalized bike is delivered to the customer. Personalized, flexibly manufactured bicycles sell for six times the cost of most other upscale bicycles, but for cycling aficionados, the difference is worth it. This kind of service would not be possible without FMS.

## Managing Quality Control

The quality control manager may be responsible for defining standards with exact specifications or for issuing guidelines regarding exact specifications set by an outside agency. Standards are set by hundreds of regulating agencies, some governmental and some private, such as the Canadian Standards Association and the Canadian Gas Association. These standards prescribe contents, colour, size, shape, taste, texture, durability, chemical or physical composition, safety standards, and many other properties of goods produced or sold in Canada. Government contracts can be lost and consumer purchasing can fall rapidly if standards are not met.

The quality control manager must select or devise procedures to test the quality of products, establish trouble-shooting procedures, pinpoint causes of any defects, and direct corrective action to minimize losses. Customer complaints or returns of defective products may indicate that some changes should be made.

Complaints and returns from customers can build up and result in lost customers and sales. Therefore, a quality control expert must develop a system that reduces the chances that low-quality products or services get to the customers. A four-step program can help ensure quality control.

**Step 1: Define quality characteristics.** The first step is to find out what customers or clients want. Necessary information comes from examining customer preferences, technical specifications, marketing suggestions, and competitive products. Customer pref-

*This quality control officer will inspect every item produced where a defect would create serious problems, or just a representative sample of those items where defects would be inconvenient but not disastrous.*

erences are extremely significant since repeat sales are likely to depend on a reasonable degree of customer satisfaction. A Rolex watch customer wants extreme accuracy, long service life, style, and, most of all, the social cachet of wearing a Rolex! In contrast, a Timex watch customer is looking for different characteristics. The Timex may not keep time quite as accurately as the Rolex, it is not expected to last as long, and it does not attract admiring looks, but it sells at a much lower price. The quality characteristics of the Rolex watches meet different customer preferences than those of the Timex watches.

**Step 2: Establish quality standards.** Once the quality characteristics have been defined, the next step is to establish the desired quality levels. Standards for factors such as size, colour, weight, texture, accuracy, reliability, time of delivery, and after-sale support are set by management.

The cost of achieving and sustaining a specific level of quality must be estimated and compared with the cost of potential rejections. The closer to the start of the production process a defect is discovered, the lower the cost of rejection. As the product or service progresses through the process, more resources are invested; the greater the amount of resources invested, the higher the cost of rejection. The greatest cost is incurred when the defect is not detected until the product is in the hands of the customer or the service has already been provided. In those cases the cost of processing the complaint and the cost of lost goodwill are added to the cost of resources. For example, complaints about Ford's Pinto were costly not only in the millions of dollars paid in response to customer lawsuits, but also in recalls to repair defective parts, lost repeat sales, and damage to the company's reputation.

In 1979, Philip Crosby's book *Quality Is Free* introduced the quality program he established at ITT.[29] He challenges the notion that achieving quality will reduce profits. Rather, he says, quality is *free*; that is, the cost of achieving quality is no greater and often is less than the cost of failing to do so. Unfortunately, however, the intangible costs of quality failure may be overlooked because they are difficult to measure. Crosby argues that the real costs that hurt profits are the costs of inspection and fixing problems, plus all other costs associated with not doing jobs right the first time.

**Step 3: Develop a comprehensive quality review program.** The methods for quality review, where and by whom reviews will be reported and analyzed, and other review procedures must be formalized to ensure that they are understood and will be followed. The requirements for an organization to qualify for an ISO 9000 designation were discussed in Chapter 7. The rapid growth in ISO-approved organizations attests to the growing realization that quality control is an important factor in competitiveness.

**Step 4: Build quality commitment.** A quality control program can be no more successful than the extent to which all members of the organization are committed to it and actually put it into practice. It has been suggested elsewhere in this book that participative management—that is, involving employees in important management decisions—may help to engender this commitment. According to Kenneth Bars, president of Lucent Canada's Business Communications Systems, "Involving your colleagues in making decisions instead of deciding for them, strengthens their dedication and allows us to serve customers more creatively."[30]

## Benchmarking

North American industry today is competing globally, as companies worldwide are eyeing global markets rather than relying on domestic markets. Given Canada's heavy reliance on foreign trade, Canadian companies must sell abroad to pay for the goods and services that Canadians purchase abroad and for the money that Canada has borrowed from abroad. To compete successfully in foreign markets, Canadian companies must explore foreign innovations such as those used in the Japanese auto industry and other manufacturing technologies being developed abroad. They must then decide which of these innovations would be desirable to them. Organizations that earn a competitive leadership role today set their standards to match those of their best competitors, whether Canadian or in other countries.[31] At Xerox, for example, every department is expected to conduct a global search for the company or organizational unit that performs its special function best. This performance level then is established as the target for the comparable Xerox function.

As discussed in Chapter 3, this comparative process is called **benchmarking.** It refers to the continuing process of measuring the organization's goods, practices, and services against those of its toughest competitors. The main themes of benchmarking are improving operations, including purchasing, production, and all aspects of service. Benchmarking is perfectly ethical, and enables an organization to establish operating goals and productivity objectives based on the best practices in the industry. Successful benchmarking requires three fundamental activities:

- Know your operation and assess its strengths and weaknesses by documenting work process steps and practices and defining the critical performance measurements used.
- Determine the industry leaders and most successful competitors, in part by evaluating the leaders' strengths and weaknesses.
- Incorporate the best practices and gain superiority by emulating and surpassing the strengths of the best.[32]

**benchmarking**
Studying operations in other organizations or other divisions of the company to learn what techniques are successful and to establish high standards for operations.

There are several different types of benchmarking, often described as *internal, functional*, and *competitive*. Internal benchmarking involves comparing divisions within an organization. The insurance, real estate, and banking divisions of Vancouver City Savings Credit Union might benchmark each other in terms of sick days lost by staff members. If one of the divisions shows a significantly lower ratio of sick days to the number of employees, the other two divisions might learn how the more favourable record is accomplished.

Functional benchmarking involves studying the best organizations for their operations of a particular function, regardless of their industry. For instance, a bank might select an office cleaning company to benchmark for the cleaning functions in the bank. Even though the two organizations are in different industries, they have a common interest in one group of activities—cleaning floors, walls, and counters efficiently and effectively.

Competitive benchmarking is the measurement of direct competitors' activities. Many companies use one or more of these benchmarking techniques. Manco, Inc., manufactures tape, weather stripping, and mailing supplies. Manco studies service leaders to learn their standards and emulate their strengths. Not only does Manco benchmark its major competitor (3M), but it also studies other service leaders such as Wal-Mart. And other leading companies, such as Procter & Gamble, in turn, benchmark their own operations against those of Manco.[33]

## Quality Circles

**Quality circles** are based on the concept that the people who work with the process are likely to be best able to identify, analyze, and correct the problems that arise in production. Popularized in Japan in 1962, quality circles were expanded into a highly developed system by Japanese companies. A quality circle usually consists of ten or fewer people working in a related area. They meet perhaps once a week and discuss the flow of work, problems, and potential solutions. Participation in the circle is voluntary, and employees select their own moderator or team leader to lead the discussion. The group's findings and proposals are forwarded to management.

Experience with quality circles suggests that several conditions are required for success. First, those involved must be intelligent and well informed. They must know how to use statistics and work design analyses, and they must know the technical aspects of the job. Second, management must trust the participants enough to provide them with confidential cost information, from the company itself as well as from competitors to the extent it is available. Third, participants must be dedicated to working together as a team. They must have a team spirit, since groups, not individuals, are rewarded for success. Fourth, quality circles work best as part of what is called *total quality control*. This philosophy applies three principles: (1) The goal is to achieve a constant and continual improvement in quality year after year; (2) The focus extends beyond the actual product or service that an organization provides, to every function in the organization, such as finance, accounting, and research and development; and (3) Every employee bears responsibility for quality improvement.

Quality is also important in the provision of services. If a hotel or cruise line serves mediocre food but charges a premium price, customer satisfaction and sales inevitably will fall. If a plastic surgeon performs a poor-quality surgical procedure on a patient's face, permanent disfigurement can result. In some respects, customer or client reaction may be more attuned to service quality than to product quality, so any service enterprise, whether a business or not-for-profit, requires constant monitoring and correction when needed. Once an organization gains a reputation for poor quality, it is difficult to reverse that reputation. How much better it is to have earned and kept a good reputation in the first place.

## Quality Control versus Quality Management

This section has discussed several techniques for controlling quality. It also has been noted that it is usually the job of the production and operations manager to manage and improve quality. Unfortunately, concepts of quality control and quality management are often confused, and this confusion leads to many problems that organizations encounter with quality programs or total quality management. Some organizations find that quality requires a long-run commitment and become so discouraged by slow results that they abandon quality initiatives. Plagued by poor earnings, McDonnell Douglas Corp. embraced so-called total quality management, only to drop the program in less than two years, declaring it a failure.[34] A study conducted by Ernst & Young found that many businesses waste millions of dollars on ill-conceived or poorly executed quality-improvement strategies that fail to improve performance.[35] In part, these failures can be attributed to the absence of quality management, despite the efforts being made to achieve quality control.

Quality *control* is based on statistical actions and techniques that contain or reduce the non-conformance of processes by applying a series of screening activities.[36] This often involves applying statistical techniques to control a process. This chapter's appendix summarizes seven commonly used statistical tools. The key issue in quality control is understanding the variability in key measures of a product or service. First, variability is controlled within specified limits; then it is reduced further.

In contrast, quality *management* is a commitment to operate the entire organization based on prevention, with the goal of allowing no failures that would have to be screened out.[37] Quality management includes quality control as one of its functions, but also includes other activities such as benchmarking, continuous improvement, and quality teams. While quality control uses statistical tools to contain non-conformance within a manufacturing process, quality management attempts to eliminate the non-conformance, that is, to achieve *zero defects*.

Quality control remains an effective way to reduce errors, but the essence of quality management is to create a culture of prevention in an organization—one that does not accept that any level of error is inevitable. This function cannot be delegated solely to technicians or non-management employees. Everyone in the organization must be helped to concentrate on doing their job right the first time. Without quality management, an organization's efforts to improve or control quality probably will fail to meet objectives.

## Improving Productivity

**productivity**
The measure of units of output, such as the number of items produced, against units of input, such as the hours of labour worked or dollars expended.

The rate at which goods and services are created (output per hour worked) is called **productivity.** For an economy to be healthy, productivity must be high and also steadily increasing. One common measure of productivity, *labour productivity*, is expressed in dollars of output (adjusted for inflation) per dollar of wages and associated personnel costs. Another important factor in output is technology and how employees use it. Labour and technology combined generate the outputs that are priced and sold to consumers.

Amid increasing labour, material, and opportunity costs, plus uncertain world events, fast technological change, and shifting investment policies, the productivity of a business must increase continually for it to remain competitive. This poses an enormous challenge to managers and non-managers in organizations of all kinds. Ignoring either quality improvements or productivity improvements is likely to result in lost markets, layoffs, foreclosures, and general business decay. From a manager's perspective, a motivated employee works hard, sustains that pace, and is self-directed towards meeting challenging goals. Productivity improvement can occur only through such motivated employees.

In their runaway best-seller, *In Search of Excellence*, Thomas Peters and Robert Waterman pointed to the success of companies that they said had put the responsibility for quality on every employee and backed it up with management commitment to job security, meaningful profit sharing, and recognition. They cited companies such as Dana Corporation, a manufacturer of propeller blades and gearboxes. Through the leadership of then-chairman Rene McPherson, Dana Corporation appeared in the *Fortune* 500 list as number two in terms of returns to investors. McPherson points out:

> Until we believe that the expert in any particular job is most often the person performing it, we shall forever limit the potential of that person, in terms of both his own contribution to the organization and his own development. Con-

sider a manufacturing setting: Within their 25-foot-square area, nobody knows more about how to operate a machine, maximize its output, improve its quality, optimize the material flow, and keep it operating efficiently than do the machine operators, materials handlers, and maintenance people responsible for it. Nobody.[38]

According to Peters and Waterman, this attitude is expressed in one way or another by the best of corporations. They define the attitude as "tough-minded respect for the individual and the willingness to train him (*sic*), to set reasonable and clear expectations … and to grant him practical autonomy to step out and contribute directly to his job."[39]

## Maintaining Safety for Employees, Products, and the Environment

The benefits from productivity gains can be lost if the organization shows too little regard for the environment or sacrifices safety for employees or others.

### Employee and Product Safety

Chapter 2 contains a detailed discussion of social responsibility. Here, this issue will be viewed in relation to the operations and production areas, where many of the potentially most hazardous materials, processes, and products are found. Although safety is part of every employee's responsibility, corporate responsibility for safety is most often delegated to the production and operations manager. Employee safety is mandated by a number of federal and provincial regulations and laws. The production and operations manager is responsible for implementing these regulations in the plant. Compliance requires the dedication of time, money, and constant attention, all of which must be provided for in schedules and budgets. Production and operations managers are learning that if they allow unsafe practices or contamination of the environment, they may be held personally liable.

Johnson & Johnson, makers of bandages and other health-care products, is intent on being known as the number one organization in terms of safety.[40] When any workplace accident causes death or injury resulting in at least one lost day of work, the head of the company unit involved must file a written report to top management within 24 hours. The head then must travel to company headquarters and personally explain what went wrong to a top-level committee. In the first eight years of this program (1981-89), Johnson & Johnson slashed its annual lost work day incidence per 1000 workers from 18.1 to 1.4.[41] Considering that wages and salaries constitute a large proportion of the expenses of almost any organization, regardless of size or type, it can be seen that even from a selfish financial standpoint alone, safety practices pay big dividends.

Not only must employees have safe working conditions, but the goods produced must be safe for the consumers who ultimately buy them. Product safety is the specific responsibility of the design and quality control departments. Growing consumer consciousness of the issue, and the resultant publicity and lawsuits, have increased organizations' efforts to make accident-proof products. Automatic testing devices tug and pull plastic eyes and noses on toy rabbits to ensure they won't come off in the mouths of eager two-year-olds. Medicine bottles are made tamper-proof, and sharp products such as paring knives bear brightly coloured labels to prevent consumers from cutting themselves accidentally. Even so, mistakes do occur. In December 1996 thousands of dolls were sold that were capable of chewing up the hair of young children who played with them. The recalls were costly, and the injury to several children was incalculable. The public

**Exhibit 11-5**

*The Monsanto Pledge*

- Reduce all toxic releases, working towards a goal of zero.

- Ensure that no Monsanto operation poses undue risk to employees and communities.

- Work to achieve sustainable agriculture through new technology and practices.

- Ensure groundwater safety—making our technical resources available to farmers dealing with contamination, even if our products are not involved.

- Keep our plants open to our communities, bringing the community into plant operations. Inform people of any significant hazard.

- Manage all corporate real estate to benefit nature.

- Search worldwide for technology to reduce and eliminate waste from our operations, with the top priority being not making it in the first place.

Source: *Business and Society Review* (Spring 1990): 66.

relations damage was (justifiably) severe, and the resulting lawsuits have the potential to cause staggeringly high costs. And all of this occurred because designers and managers did not conceive that a doll that is capable of "eating" plastic simulated food could take in other objects as well.

Safety is not something that just happens. It requires thoughtful analysis, foresight, rigorous management, and organization-wide vigilance. Monsanto, operating in the vulnerable chemical industry, has adopted a program to promote safety and help clean up the environment. Exhibit 11-5 reproduces that company's pledge. The wording of the pledge hardly could be faulted, but critics have questioned the ways in which Monsanto interprets it in action. In particular, criticism has been levelled at Monsanto's distribution of agricultural chemicals in less developed countries and its development of genetically engineered seeds. This controversy illustrates the difficulty of arriving at definitive positions on matters as complicated as environmental protection and social responsibility, as discussed in Chapter 2.

## Globalization of Environmental Pollution

It was not until 1992 that leaders from 170 countries met in Rio de Janeiro for the first meeting of the UN Conference on Environmental Development, which focused international concern on some alarming issues. A number of respected scientists reported that the atmosphere's ozone layer has been depleted by as much as 50 percent over some regions, including Antarctica and the northern parts of Canada, Europe, and Russia.[42] Sulphur dioxide pumped into the air by manufacturing and power plants has created rain with a high acid content (acid rain), which damages forests and lakes. Only about 40 percent of the original 6,750,000 square miles of the Earth's forests remains. Centuries ago, when metal smelting was first developed, the huge forests of Europe were progressively destroyed to provide fuel for charcoal burners and smelters. Forests in most of those areas have never come back. But the world has not learned from that lesson. Today the tropical forests of Brazil, Indonesia, and Malaysia are being devastated to provide lumber and pulp and to clear land for the grazing of cattle and sheep.[43] Millions of residents in the former Soviet Union breathe toxic air while factories pump sewage into lakes and pollutants into the air.[44] In today's megacities, such as Bangkok, Jakarta, and Mexico City, the pollution from automobiles is so bad that on several days each year, even their overly tolerant authorities warn people to stay indoors because the air is literally not safe to breathe. The pollution from one country often adversely affects conditions in several other countries. Canadian managers must deal with air that is polluted in countries as far away as the former Soviet Union. Environmental degradation, therefore, is not a localized problem, nor is it one that can be ignored.

Individuals, organizations, governments, and public-interest groups are discussing these problems, and there is hope that they might find some solutions. Throughout Canada, one source of pollution has been reduced by the mandatory use of lead-free gasoline in automobiles. Unfortunately, this initiative has not been followed in much of the rest of the world, but at least it is a start. Many companies are making products and containers that can be recycled, slowing the need for more and bigger landfills. Many Canadian municipalities operate "blue box" recycling programs, despite the fact that they often require subsidies to continue to function. Companies such as Canadian Tire welcome used motor oil, and feed it to other companies such as Lyondell Petrochemical, which has started making gasoline from it.[45] The United States and Mexican governments are working together on the pollution problem along their shared border, where some factories burn tires for fuel. The region along Mexico's northern border has been described by the American Medical Association as a "virtual cesspool."[46] Economists working for the United Nations and the Environmental Defense Fund arc trying to link countries with vastly different economies and environmental laws into a single pollution control system.[47] These are just a few examples, and the results may seem small in comparison with the enormity of the problem, but they are steps in the right direction. It will take the ongoing participation of every individual and organization together with cooperation from the governments of all nations to reverse the current threats to our environment.

*Blue box recycling programs are more costly than regular garbage disposal, but the benefits of a cleaner environment outweigh the costs.*

## The Workplace of Tomorrow

Tomorrow's production and operations environment will continue to benefit from innovation in assembly line techniques, lean manufacturing, and flexible manufacturing. For instance, Hotpoint Ltd., the United Kingdom's leading manufacturer of home laundry appliances, has integrated product verification and testing as the final step in its assembly line. By eliminating the intermediate shuttling of complete units to and from testing stations that are located some distance from production lines, Hotpoint reduces time and labour costs for work in process and lessens the potential for material handling damage.[48] Of course, as pointed out in this chapter, for optimum quality control this end-of-production inspection has to be combined with inspections at each stage of production, so that defects are caught at earlier stages of production.

As noted at the outset of this chapter, lean manufacturing and flexible manufacturing are changing the way that products are made. In the workplace of tomorrow, product development cycles will shorten. Lean manufacturing and JIT inventory systems will permit increased productivity, reduced costs, shortened lead times, and enhanced customer satisfaction. As managers apply an integrated approach to product develop-ment and manufacturing, they increasingly will apply lessons learned from bench-marking. The ways that people work will change as more organizations adopt innovative work spaces such as those at Nortel and as telecommuting gains in popularity.

All of these changes pose challenges to managers—challenges that can be met only by refining management skills, continually perfecting systems, creating opportunities for the career growth of all employees, and encouraging dedicated team effort. Canadian companies can either progress in competitiveness or regress in profits, numbers of jobs, and benefits to Canadian society. The direction in which Canadian industries go will have profound, long-term effects that, once started, will gain momentum and affect the lives of all Canadians.

## Summary of Learning Objectives

▷ **Differentiate between** *production* **and** *operations.*

*Production* refers to the process of manufacturing, transforming, or assembling parts or components to produce an end product. *Operations* is a broader term that encompasses all of the functions required to keep the organization operating. In some usages it is con-fined to the functions closely related to production; in other usages it includes almost all of the organization's activities.

▷ **Discuss the evolution of modern manufacturing.**

Natural and fossil fuel energy, principles of scientific management, and mass produc-tion were crucial to manufacturing's development. Mass production reduced costs and made possible the growth of large manufacturing corporations. Then the emphasis shifted to productivity and quality, combined with employee involvement. Domestic and global competition have forced companies to search for new and better production methods.

▷ **Explain the typical roles of production and operations managers.**

Production and operations managers are responsible for producing the products that a business intends to sell. Typical functions include product planning, site layout and loca-tion, inventory control, purchasing and materials management, manufacturing and production, production control, quality control, and plant management.

▷ **Explain the factors that should be considered in selecting a site, and the impact of each.**

Many factors should be considered, including cost of land or buildings; insurance and taxes; zoning and other restrictions; proximity to related industries and other important facilities or services; availability and cost of labour; availability of transportation; prox-imity to market for goods; air and water conditions; proximity to energy resources; cli-mate and environment consistent with needs; space for expansion; proximity to employees' needs, such as housing and schools; and receptiveness of the community.

▷ **Explain the importance of productivity in achieving and maintaining competitiveness.**

Improvements in productivity and quality have long-term effects on the success of the organization. Ignoring either quality improvements or productivity improvements is likely to result in lost markets, layoffs, foreclosures, and general business decay. Con-sumers are demanding more quality at reasonable cost, and companies need to improve the output per unit of labour and per unit of cost.

▶   **Discuss the ways in which safety can affect an organization's effectiveness and competitiveness.**

Corporate responsibility for safety is often delegated to the production and operations manager. Product safety is often the specific responsibility of the quality control department. Lapses in safety standards and practices not only may result in devastating the lives of those injured and their families, but may invite costly lawsuits and, at the very least, are likely to cause reduced productivity.

## KEY TERMS

assembly line, p. 392
benchmarking, p. 410
computer-aided design (CAD), p. 406
computer-aided engineering (CAE), p. 406
computer-aided manufacturing
    (CAM), p. 406
flexible manufacturing system
    (FMS), p. 408

infrastructure, p. 397
just-in-time (JIT) inventory
    control, p. 400
manufacturing, p. 390
mass production, p. 392
materials requirements planning
    (MRP), p. 400
operations, p. 390

PERT chart, p. 404
production, p. 389
productivity, p. 412
quality circle, p. 411
repetitive strain injury,
    p. 392
robot, p. 406
zero defects, p. 401

## REVIEW AND DISCUSSION QUESTIONS

### Recall

1. What are the functions of production and operations?
2. When is project manufacturing used? Give an example of project manufacturing.
3. What are the advantages and disadvantages of just-in-time inventory?
4. List some responsibilities of the production manager and the operations manager.
5. What is PERT? How is a PERT chart created?
6. What are some ways that quality and productivity can be improved?

### Understanding

7. In the evolution of modern manufacturing, what are the most significant events? How did they cause major changes?
8. If you were going to open a fast-food restaurant like McDonald's, what factors would be important in selecting a site and a site layout?
9. How have computers improved the production process? Give several examples of how computers are used in manufacturing.

### Application

10. Review a daily newspaper for one week. Cite examples of Canadian businesses that are concerned about environmental pollution and safety. Also cite examples of Canadian businesses that appear to have disregarded these factors.
11. Construct a PERT chart for a business operation of your choice, using your best estimate of the time required for each stage. (Examples you might wish to consider are (1) selecting and installing a new payroll system for a company of 20 people; (2) selecting, purchasing, and installing new filing cabinets for company records, transferring files from existing outdated filing cabinets, and disposing of the old filing cabinets; or (3) choosing, purchasing, and replacing an office's multiline telephone system without losing service, and informing interested parties of changed phone numbers.)

*CASE* **11-1**

## Kao Responds to Demand

Kao Corporation is Japan's largest soap and cosmetics company and the world's sixth largest, with annual sales exceeding $5 billion. According to James Abegglen, chairman of Gemini Consulting-Japan, no company can match the flexibility of Kao's distribution. Goods can be delivered within 24 hours to any of 280,000 shops, whose average order is only seven items. This capability is based on a comprehensive information system and a wholly owned network of wholesalers. This control enables Kao to get popular items on store shelves faster and to keep smaller inventories than competitors.

Kao's objective is to maximize the flexibility of the entire company's response to demand. This requires not only flexible manufacturing but also an information system that links all aspects of the business: sales and shipping, production and purchasing, accounting, R&D, marketing, stores' cash registers, and salespeople's hand-held computers.

Many companies in Canada and elsewhere rely on point-of-purchase data to determine production requirements. At Safeway and Save-On-Foods stores, customers are provided with Air Miles or "membership"cards, which provide rewards as long as customers identify themselves by handing over the cards to cashiers. Through modern cash registers, these cards enable managers to keep track of hour-by-hour sales that can trigger restocking orders, as well as monitor the items that various types of customers are buying.

At Kao this system is carried even further. In addition to sales, stock, and production figures, managers can learn about a competitor's sale within a day and make necessary adjustments. When introducing a new product, information from 216 retailers is combined with a test-marketing program called the Echo System. This system uses focus group interviews and consumer responses through calls and letters to measure customer satisfaction faster than surveys do. Within two weeks of the introduction of a new product, Kao knows if a product will be successful, who is buying it, whether the packaging is effective, and what needs to be changed. Response to the factory is immediate, and flexible manufacturing allows instant changes to be made.

Kao's system basically eliminates the lag between a purchase and feedback to the factory about the purchase. This makes Kao less dependent on keeping finished goods inventory. It also allows the company to smooth out production levels and increase variety without increasing stock. In 1987 Kao made 498 products, and inventory averaged 9.2 percent of sales. Today Kao makes 564 products, and inventory is down to 8.6 percent. This may not seem to be a significant reduction, but it amounts to savings of millions of dollars annually.

Flexibility at Kao comes not only from manufacturing but also from information. A flexible factory is of little use if it can't be fitted into an overall system of purchasing, marketing, and distribution. Kao knows what is selling and can respond to this information at the factory quickly.

### Questions

1. How does Kao stress flexibility?
2. Why is information so important to Kao?
3. How can Kao respond to customer demand more effectively than some manufacturing companies?

Source: Adapted from Thomas A. Stewart, "Brace for Japan's Hot New Strategy," *Fortune* (September 21, 1992): 62-74; Masayoshi Kanabayashi, "Japan's Top Soap Firm, Kao, Hopes to Clean Up Abroad," *The Wall Street Journal* (December 17, 1992): B4; and "A Time for Mutual Respect and Understanding," *Fortune* (July 27, 1992): S16-S17.

## INTERNET APPLICATION  11-1

Visit the Web site of Johnson & Johnson (www.johnsonandjohnson.com). Click on Background; then click on Environmental Health and Safety Report; then click on Safety and Industrial Hygiene.

1. What are the five strategic objectives Johnson & Johnson has set to achieve an injury-free workplace?
2. What is ERGO and why is it important at Johnson & Johnson?

Search the Web for an organization that has improved productivity by reducing accident rates. What steps has this organization instituted in order to make the workplace a safe environment for employees?

## Appendix: Seven Statistical Control Tools

The following seven basic tools—flow charts, run charts, control charts, fishbone diagrams, Pareto charts, histograms, and scatter diagrams—are used to communicate the results of statistical controls.

### Flow Charts

Flow charts are used to provide a visual description of the steps in a process or work activity. They show the sequence of events that make up the process. Generally, flow charts begin with inputs, show what takes place to transform those inputs, and end with outputs. Flow charts are especially helpful in visualizing and understanding how things are currently being done and how they can be done differently to improve the process. Exhibit 11-A1 on page 420 shows an example of a flow chart.

### Run Charts

Run charts are used to plot measurements taken over a specific time period, such as a day, a week, or a month. Usually the quantity measure is plotted on the vertical axis and time is plotted on the horizontal axis. The run chart can be used to determine how some factors are changing over time and whether problems are occurring at certain periods of time. For instance, the run chart in Exhibit 11-A2 on page 420 shows that the number of defective units produced increases as the day progresses. This might suggest that workers grow fatigued, bored, and careless as the day progresses. By plotting the incidence of defects as a function of time, the managers may be able to pinpoint the sources of the problems more effectively.

### Control Charts

Control charts show the results of statistical process control measures for a sample, batch, or some other unit. Such charts can be used to study variation in a process and to analyze the variation over time. The organization may decide that a specified level of variation is acceptable, but that deviation beyond this level is unacceptable. For instance, in Exhibit 11-A3 on page 421, lower and upper limits are specified for the diameter of a component used in manufacturing computers. Within those limits, the product is considered satisfactory; measurements above or below those limits for a sample of parts initiate a search for the cause of the variation.

**Exhibit 11-A1**   *Flow Chart*

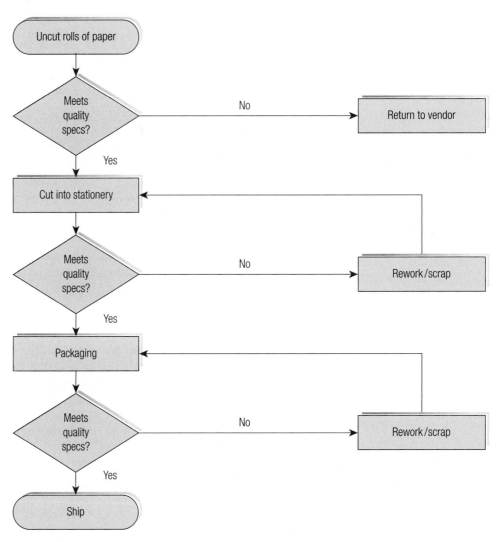

**Exhibit 11-A2**   *Run Chart*

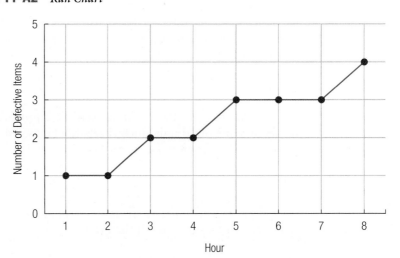

**Exhibit 11-A3** *Control Chart*

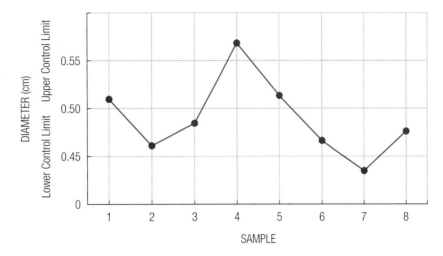

**Exhibit 11-A4** *Fishbone Diagram*

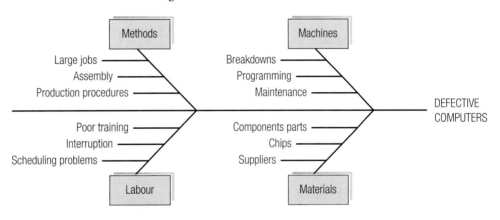

## Fishbone Diagrams

Fishbone diagrams are so named because they look something like a fishbone. They also are called cause-and-effect diagrams. The problem, such as a defect, is defined as the effect. Events that contribute to the problem are considered causes. The effect is the "head" of the fishbone, while the causes are the "bones" growing out of the spine (as seen in Exhibit 11-A4). The fishbone diagram can be used to see how different causes occur and lead to a problem. Once the causes are identified, corrective measures can be implemented.

## Pareto Charts

Pareto charts, named for their originator, are used to display the number of problems or defects in a product over time. Pareto charts are fairly simple to construct, displaying the results as bars of varying length. Exhibit 11-A5 on page 422 shows the number of defective cars for each type of error. The basic premise of the Pareto chart is that only a few causes account for most problems; the chart helps to identify those causes.

**Exhibit 11-A5**   *Pareto Chart*

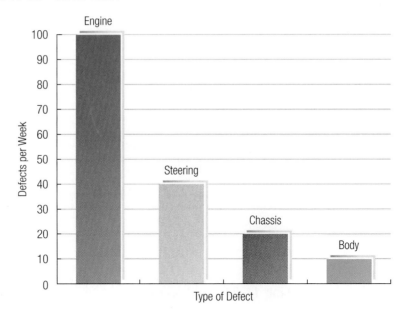

**Exhibit 11-A6**   *Histogram*

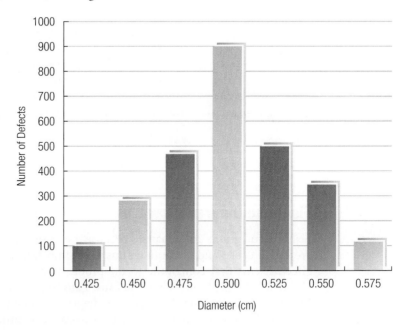

## Histograms

Histograms (also called bar charts) show the frequency of each particular measurement in a group of measurements. Exhibit 11-A6 shows the frequency of defects of a component part for varying diameters. This information is useful in analyzing the variability in a process.

**Exhibit 11-A7**   *Scatter Diagrams*

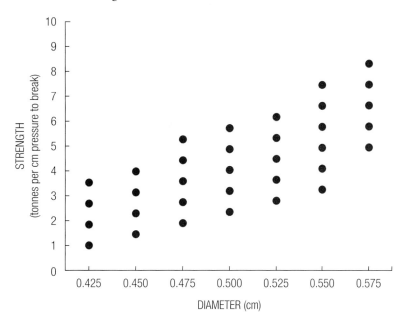

## Scatter Diagrams

Scatter diagrams show the relationship between two characteristics or events. Each point shows that at a particular value for the variable along the horizontal axis, a particular result occurred, which is plotted along the vertical axis. For instance, Exhibit 11-A7 shows the relationship between strength and diameter for samples of wires. By measuring these two variables and plotting the results, one can observe how one variable changes as the other changes. In this case, strength can be seen to increase with diameter.

# The Management of Services

After studying this chapter, you should be able to:

▶ Illustrate the meaning, in a management context, of the term *service*;

▶ Discuss the concept of tangibility as it relates to goods and services;

▶ List four characteristics that distinguish services from goods, and explain how these characteristics influence the emphases placed by managers in service organizations;

▶ Explain the significance of service quality and of service productivity;

▶ Discuss ways in which service organizations can improve quality and productivity;

▶ Describe conditions that indicate that an organization has a performance culture, and discuss the likely outcomes of having such a culture;

▶ Describe the components of peak performance; and

▶ Suggest ways in which managers can encourage peak performance.

## The High Cost of Poor Service

THE WORLD ECONOMY HAS BECOME HEAVILY dependent on the service sector. McDonald's actually has more employees worldwide than most major international companies that are seen as world leaders. In Canada, nearly three-quarters of total employment is in the service sector, including service businesses, not-for-profit organizations, and government. A trend began in about 1956, when white-collar workers outnumbered blue-collar workers for the first time. That trend continues today as the service sector sees the greatest job growth in fields such as transportation, communication, and public utilities; insurance, real estate, stock brokerage firms, and financial institutions; wholesale and retail trade; entertainment, publishing, and broadcast services; medical, legal, accounting, and other professional services; and not-for-profit organizations. ▶

Services are products that involve human effort and usually human contact, so they are somewhat different from goods. Quality services often require quality efforts from people, and there is a high cost for poor service. Research has shown that businesses and other organizations rarely hear from unhappy customers. More importantly, the average customer who has a problem with an organization tells an average of nine or ten people.[1] According to one expert, "It costs five times as much to get a new customer as to keep an old one." Thus, many organizations have turned their attention to service quality to become and remain competitive.

Until relatively recently, some service organizations have felt, often incorrectly, that they were sheltered from the ravages of competition. This naive notion may account in part for the fact that restaurant businesses (which combine service with product sales) are the most likely of all business segments to fail, and when they do, they have the quickest demise, from startup to insolvency.

Just as the resource industries and the large manufacturing companies underwent massive changes in the 1970s and 1980s, organizations in the service sector are destined to change or succumb in the next decade or two. And although many experts point to the creation of new jobs as one of the service economy's strengths, this is in fact a symptom of the inefficiencies that plague many service companies. With some notable exceptions, service companies have hired additional employees while neglecting technological innovations and economic efficiencies. As a result, they are especially vulnerable to competition, both from within Canada and from the United States and other foreign countries. Companies such as Wal-Mart have captured large volumes of Canadian retail business; chains have acquired Canadian hotels and motels; stock brokerages and real estate agencies have merged with foreign firms; and Canadian entrepre-

neurs have purchased franchises from multinational franchisors.

Even in businesses that sell products, the service component is increasingly important. Surveys have shown that when consumers select automobiles (after houses, their second-biggest purchases), their decisions are based as much as, or more, on the service they receive during their shopping phase as on what they know about the quality of the product itself. When one adds in the potential customer's perception of the dealer's reputation for after-sale service, it may be seen that even in this classic example of product sales, the service component is crucial. Infiniti and Toyota's Lexus division have established new industry standards for satisfying luxury car buyers. Now General Motors' Saturn division and other automobile companies are revising their approaches and redefining how buyers of lower-cost cars are to be treated. Saturn has attempted to eliminate the price haggling that many car buyers find so frustrating and offensive. Chrysler has invested more than $30 million in training to try to improve how their dealers handle customers. General Motors' Chevrolet division provides 24-hour roadside assistance to new car buyers.

All of these examples, and thousands more across Canada, illustrate that the service organizations that want to be competitive are recognizing a major change in consumer attitudes. They know that consumers will continue to demand ever-more satisfactory services, and that they will patronize the organizations that provide them. ∎

---

Sources: Adapted from Toddi Gutner, "Focus on the Customer," *Forbes* (August 2, 1993): 45-46; Raymond Serafin and Cleveland Horton, "Automakers Focus on Service," *Advertising Age* (July 6, 1992): 3, 33; Richard S. Teitelbaum, "Where Service Flies Right," *Fortune* (August 24, 1992): 115-16; and Scott Hume, "Fast-Food Chains Look Up Ways to Improve Service," *Advertising Age* (June 8, 1992): 3, 46.

## The Management of Services

Most organizations today are aware that the service they offer to their customers or clients is a significant source of competitive advantage. Even manufacturing companies, whose primary activity is the production of a tangible product, must be concerned with the way they interact with customers of that product. The measurement and the management of customer satisfaction has the overall objective of satisfying—

even delighting—the customers. Exceeding customer expectations is now widely recognized as an effective route to strategic, market-driven organizational behaviour.[2] The cost of failing to meet customers' expectations of service quality is high in terms of lost customers and bad publicity.

Managing services has become a critical issue as service organizations face many of the same challenges manufacturing companies have experienced—particularly increased competition and consumer demands for better quality. Some experts have pointed to parallels between the decline in manufacturing and the current challenges facing service organizations.[3] Management in the best service organizations is qualitatively different from that in their less-successful competitors.[4]

This chapter examines how services are managed. First, it discusses the nature and importance of services. Then it examines characteristics that distinguish services from other goods. Next a scheme for classifying services is presented. Then quality and productivity in service organizations and issues related to developing and managing services are discussed. Finally, the development of a performance culture is discussed.

## The Nature and Importance of Services

**service**
An intangible result of human or mechanical effort that is designed to meet the wants or needs of customers, clients, or other potential recipients.

A good is a tangible product that consumers can physically possess. A **service** is an intangible product that involves human or mechanical effort and does not have physical substance.[5] (Many services, from management consulting to car repairs, provide a tangible outcome—a written report by the consultants, a functioning car after the repairs—but the service itself is intangible, and the report or the repaired car is just its physical manifestation.) Another way to think about a service is that the receiver of the service "consumes" it simultaneously with its provision. In contrast, a manufactured product can be stored and used sometime after the transaction between buyer and seller. More than 70 percent of Canadian employees work in some type of service organization and this proportion is expected to grow. Exhibit 12-1 on page 428 shows Canada's largest service companies, listed in order of their reported numbers of employees. The table omits privately owned companies, such as General Motors Canada (all of whose shares are owned by General Motors, Inc.), because usually they do not make public their detailed statistics. It also disregards governments and governmental agencies, because while in one sense they are service organizations, their purposes and operations differ considerably from what is generally considered to be the service sector of the economy. Nonetheless, the principles discussed in this chapter are generally applicable both to private companies and to governmental bodies.

As illustrated in the opening vignette, few business transactions can be classified as consisting solely of sales of a product or solely of sales of a service; most transactions contain elements of both product and service. In ordering a meal, the customer orders a product—the meal—but also expects some element of service—complete service in a restaurant, and even in a self-service buffet, some tidying up at the buffet and removal of dirty dishes from the table. Which, then, is the transaction: purchase of a product or of a service? In many organizations, the answer is a combination.

Many businesses that traditionally had conceived of themselves solely as manufacturers or as miners are building competitive advantage around customer service. For example, according to William Toller, CEO of Witco Chemical Company, satisfying the customer is no longer the ultimate business virtue. He says that companies must go beyond satisfaction and create customer loyalty. To create loyalty among Witco customers, Toller says that his company looks for those things that customers perceive as adding value to their relationship with the company. This allows Witco to focus on the

**Exhibit 12-1**

*Canada's Largest Service Companies Ranked by Number of Employees (Companies Listed on a Canadian Stock Exchange)*

| Company | Industry | Head Office | Employees |
|---------|----------|-------------|-----------|
| BCE Inc. | Telephone utilities | Montreal | 122,000 |
| Laidlaw | Transportation and waste disposal | Burlington, ON | 80,000 |
| Nortel | Communications | Brampton, ON | 73,000 |
| AGF Management | Management | Toronto | 62,700 |
| Royal Bank of Canada | Financial services | Montreal | 58,133 |
| Canadian Imperial Bank of Commerce | Financial services | Toronto | 42,446 |
| Thomson Corp. | Newspapers, communications | Toronto | 40,000 |
| Bell Canada | Telephone utilities | Montreal | 39,328 |
| Bank of Nova Scotia | Financial services | Toronto | 38,648 |
| Bank of Montreal | Financial services | Toronto | 34,286 |
| Canadian Pacific | Transportation | Montreal | 33,600 |
| Toronto Dominion Bank | Financial services | Toronto | 28,001 |
| Quebecor Printing | Printing services | Montreal | 27,000 |
| Cara Operations | Food services et al. | Toronto | 26,000 |
| Imasco | Management services | Montreal | 23,060 |
| Canadian National Railway | Transportation | Montreal | 22,800 |
| Air Canada | Transportation | Saint-Laurent, PQ | 21,215 |
| Four Seasons Hotels | Hotel management et al. | Don Mills, ON | 21,000 |

Source: Adapted from *Report on Business Magazine* (July 1998): 89, 102-106.

few critical issues that affect both the company's performance for customers, and its profitability.

Exhibit 12-2 illustrates the concept of tangibility on a continuum ranging from pure goods to pure services. A pencil or some other simple object is an example of a pure good. A consultant provides an example of a pure service. Products falling in the middle have a mix of both tangible and intangible elements. In addition, when some products are purchased, even though the product itself does not contain a significant element of service, other services may be associated closely with its purchase. For example, in a full-service gas station, the purchase of gasoline represents a product transaction, but often services such as washing the windshield, checking the oil, and checking air in the tires will be associated with it. Since gasoline prices in a defined area tend to be uniform, and since most consumers do not expect quality to be different from one brand to another, the decision as to where to buy is often determined by the customer's perception of the service provided at a particular station.

**Exhibit 12-2**   *A Continuum of Product/Service Tangibility*

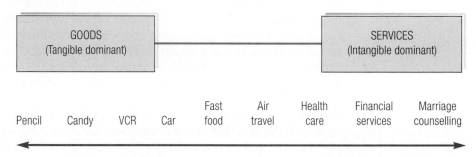

Although most products are neither a pure good nor a pure service, one element usually predominates, and this is the basis for classifying a product as a good or service. Air travel is considered a service because it is generally intangible. Pilots, airports, 767s, heli-jets, and AirBuses, however, are tangible. As will be discussed later, these tangible elements are important in managing services.

## Characteristics of Services

There are distinct differences between the provision of services and the sale of goods. These differences affect the manner in which services are produced and managed. Production and management of cars, for instance, is somewhat different from production and management of financial services. This is because financial and other similar services are distinguished by all or some of several characteristics: intangibility, inseparability of production and consumption, perishability and urgency in terms of time, and heterogeneity or variation. Each of these core characteristics influences the management of services.

### Intangibility

**intangibility**
Having no inherent physical substance.

One major feature that distinguishes the provision of services from the sale of products is that services cannot be physically possessed. **Intangibility** is the quality of not having physical substance, and usually of not being able to be assessed by the senses of sight, taste, touch, smell, or hearing. Because services are intangible, they are difficult for customers to evaluate. If the service is to clean a garment or trim a lawn, the result can be evaluated. If one has a physical exam, however, the situation is different. How does the patient know if it was a thorough and competent physical? A physical exam cannot be evaluated in the same manner as a tangible product or a service that produces a tangible result. Likewise, the client of a lawyer receives legal advice, and presumably acts on it. But the client is seldom able to evaluate the quality of the advice given. If the outcome is favourable, the client is likely to believe that the advice was good. However, other advice might have produced an even more favourable outcome, in which case the advice can properly be considered to have been bad. Equally, in the case of the unfavourable outcome, the advice may have been sound but the situation was so fraught with problems that there was no possible way of achieving what the client wished. This illustrates that it is difficult to evaluate services that are almost entirely intangible in form.

*Air travel is considered a service because it is intangible.*

Although it is difficult to evaluate most services, some clues are available. Before selecting a physician, one could visit the office, look at the facilities, talk to nurses and other doctors, and observe the clinic's atmosphere. These may provide *tangible clues* that are of some assistance in evaluating an intangible service. Even so, most clues as to the quality of service the customer or client can expect will come from word of mouth—sometimes ill-informed and the result of only a single experience, good or bad, that the source of information has experienced. This illustrates the vital importance to the service providers of maintaining consistently high levels of service, so that casual conversations among friends will not be spiced with horror stories that discourage other potential users of the services.

## Inseparability of Production and Consumption

**inseparability**
An identifying quality of a service, that the production and consumption of the service occur simultaneously, not at different times.

Most services also are characterized by the **inseparability** of production and consumption, meaning that they are produced and consumed at the same time. Goods can be designed and produced at one time and consumed at a later date. This is not the case for services. Inseparability has two important implications. First, the *service provider* plays a critical role in the delivery of services and to the customer may *be* the service. Insurance agents, flight attendants, hairstylists, bank tellers, postal clerks, and many other types of employees represent the organization to the customer and are indistinguishable from it. Many service organizations have implemented extensive training programs to ensure that their key front-line employees have the skills needed to deal effectively with customers. For example, the Canadian Airlines "Service Quality" program described earlier in this book was one of the most comprehensive training projects in North American business history.[6]

Another implication of inseparability is that because production and consumption occur simultaneously, the *customer* also has an important role in service delivery.[7] Many services cannot be performed unless the customer is present or directly involved in the production process. The customer must be present to get a haircut, to travel on a plane, or to see a movie. In some cases the customer actually shares part of the responsibility for delivering services. Many gas buyers pump their own gas, bank customers operate automatic teller machines (ATMs), and library patrons look up books in the library's computerized "card catalogue." Similarly, a sightseer who interacts with local residents, paddles a kayak down a river, or visits the National Gallery of Art, is involved in the production and consumption of a region's tourism services. Likewise, a patient often can assist a doctor in making a diagnosis by describing the symptoms of an illness.

**critical service encounter**
An element of the delivery of a service that likely will lead the recipient of the service to form an opinion as to its quality.

Because customers are so involved in service transactions, these **critical service encounters** are an excellent opportunity for businesses to gain feedback on their performance. A critical service encounter is one in which customers or other receivers of the service are likely to be forming opinions about the overall quality of the organization. Front-line service employees most often manage these critical service encounters and are a vital channel of communication about customers' reactions. Customer knowledge obtained by contact employees can be used to improve service in two ways: by facilitating the interaction with customers and by guiding the organization's planning and decision making. Employees who have frequent contact with customers or clients often have a better understanding of customer needs and problems than others in the organization who have less contact. Research has shown that open communication between managers and customer service employees can lead to improved customer service quality.[8]

Research has also shown that the warmth of communication style from the service provider to the customer can affect customer perception of service quality. Results from 83 participants in a simulated bank interview experiment indicated that the warmth of service personnel contributed to a high-quality service rating and increased the customer's future confidence in dealing with the bank.[9] This finding may be corroborated by the phenomenal growth of the Vancouver City Savings Credit Union, which is often attributed to the warmth of its service personnel.

Because customers often play an active role in producing services, the service customer must have the ability, skill, training, and motivation needed to engage in the production process. The service encounter cannot be completed unless the customer has the skills needed to participate in the transaction. This makes management of services even more complex. A VCR has poor quality because it is made that way; a bank may be providing poor quality or service to a particular customer because the customer never learned how to use an ATM card.

## Perishability

**perishability**
An identifying quality of many types of service, that they are time-sensitive and cannot be stored or deferred if not delivered at the relevant time.

The **perishability** of a service transaction results from the fact that production and consumption often cannot be separated. As a result, for many organizations unused service capacity cannot be stored and used at a later date. If a movie theatre is half empty for one showing, the empty seats cannot be stored and used for a later showing that is sold out. If an airplane or a cruise ship departs with seats or cabins unoccupied, that potential revenue is lost forever. For services that must be produced and consumed simultaneously, any unused capacity is wasted.

Many service organizations have tried to deal with this problem through pricing. Airlines offer deep discounts at certain low-traffic periods and through accumulators (who purchase large blocks of tickets and resell them). They know that unused capacity can never be recovered, and that even discounted ticket sales are better than no sales at all. Movie theatres drop prices for some low-traffic evenings. Restaurants offer "Early Bird Specials" at hours when customer traffic is usually low, but when staff will be on hand even if they have no one to serve. In some cases the bulk of a company's service activities must be performed in a predictably short period. Accounting firms are busiest in April when taxes are due. To the extent that they are able to do so, they schedule non-tax work at other times of year. Furnace repair companies are unable to handle all of the calls they get on the first cold day of fall. With the unpredictability of weather, they cannot predict when that day will occur, so the best they can do when it arrives is to be prepared to keep staff working for long shifts. Tourist agencies know that tours to the Caribbean, Hawaii, and Arizona will be heavily booked in February, but much less so in August. Because services cannot be stored, such fluctuations in demand present a challenge to managers to find ways to redirect some business from peak periods to slack periods.

## Heterogeneity

**heterogeneity**
The quality of services reflecting the fact that because they are delivered by different individuals at different times to different recipients, they will not be identical.

Robots are designed to be consistent in their performance, but services usually are performed by humans—and people are not always consistent. **Heterogeneity** refers to the inconsistency or variation found in human performance. Two different service providers inevitably will provide different kinds and levels of performance. Even a single service provider is likely to have varying levels of service, depending on mood, stress level, fatigue, or even inattention. Furthermore, the reaction of the service provider may be influenced by the attitude exhibited by the service recipient. A surly, impolite customer may receive less attentive service than one who is pleasant and appears cooperative. Because of these "human factors," services are more difficult to standardize than tangible goods.

To reduce the extent of service variability, managers develop standard procedures for the guidance of their staff members. Hotels issue to their desk clerks standardized procedures regarding reservations, registration, and checkout times and regulations. For a restaurant, standardized instructions may include the special favours that are to be given to a patron who has to wait an unduly long period for a table; who is to clear dirty dishes and pour water; and how drinks and dessert selections are to be promoted (because they have high markups, and sales depend on presentation). These procedures should be tailored to the kinds of patrons the restaurant hopes to attract, and will be quite different for one that caters to business people on a short lunch break and one that specializes in long, expensive, multi-course meals for customers who seek atmosphere and personalized service. Even with these firmly established rules, actual performance will vary from server to server. At the least, however, an organization that has established procedures has improved its competitiveness by narrowing the range of heterogeneity to help ensure that the service is closely aligned with the organization's goals and its customers' desires.[10]

# Classifying Services

For some purposes it is useful to develop a classification scheme for services. Not only do such schemes help managers understand customer needs, but they also provide insights into the management of services.[11] For instance, a categorization scheme for services may help address such questions as:

*ATMs and personal computer banking services bypass personal contact between customers and the staff of financial institutions. Forward-looking banks and credit unions are working hard to make the remaining contacts more personable and friendly.*

- Does the customer have to be present to initiate or terminate the service transaction?
- Does the customer have to be present for the service to be delivered?
- Does the customer participate in the service transaction?
- Is the customer or target of the service changed in some way after the service transaction is completed?
- Is there a high degree of labour intensiveness?
- How much skill is required of the service provider?

Answers to such questions help managers enhance service quality. When customers drop off their cars for service, their satisfaction with the service will be determined, to some extent, by their interactions with the personnel and their success in explaining the car's problems. On the other hand, using an ATM card requires little or no contact with bank personnel. The ATM must work and the transaction must be satisfactory, but how the money gets into the machine—the process—is of no interest to customers.

Exhibit 12-3 is a scheme for classifying services. Services are classified according to the type of market or customer to be served, whether consumer or organizational. This distinction is important because the way in which the buying decision is made differs between consumers and organizations. Consumers purchase (and consume) services to satisfy personal needs and wants. Industrial services are used (1) to produce other goods and services or (2) in the organization's ongoing operations. For example, both consumers and organizations need insurance, accounting services, and cleaning services. But the nature of these needs is usually quite different between the two groups. An accountant may help consumers prepare their income tax returns, while an organization must maintain a complex set of records for tax purposes.

Services also may be classified by their degree of labour intensiveness. Many services—including equipment repairs, education, and hairstyling—depend heavily on the knowledge and skills of the individual service providers. Other services such as telecom-

**Exhibit 12-3**

*Classifications of
Services*

| Category | Examples |
|---|---|
| **Type of market** | |
| Consumer | Home insurance, car repairs |
| Organizational | Management consulting, systems design |
| Consumer and organizational | Auto insurance, interior painting |
| **Labour intensiveness** | |
| Labour intensive | Appliance repair, executive recruiting, police |
| Equipment intensive | Transportation, excavation |
| Labour and equipment intensive | Dental practice |
| **Degree of customer contact** | |
| High contact | Hotel, health care, education |
| Low contact | Dry cleaning, movies, catalogue sales |
| **Skill of service provider** | |
| Professional | Lawyer, tax accountant, psychiatrist |
| Non-professional | Taxi, lawn mowing, house cleaning |
| **Degree of urgency in time** | |
| Highly urgent | Ambulance attendant, firefighter |
| Not usually urgent | Artist, bookbinder, picture framer |
| **Goal of service provider** | |
| Profit | Investment advice, courier service, retail sales |
| Not-for-profit | Government, education, hospice, food bank |

munications, fitness clubs, and public transportation rely more on equipment, even though all still have a personal element. Labour-intensive (people-based) services are generally more heterogeneous and consequently are more difficult to standardize than are equipment-based services. Teachers vary considerably in their teaching styles and even in the topics they choose to emphasize, while bus drivers follow predetermined routes at predetermined times. As noted, consumers tend to view the individuals who provide people-based services as the service itself. Consequently, managers of services must pay special attention to the selection, training, motivation, and control of employees.

Managers of labour-intensive services must be on guard against *employee burnout*. Customer service representatives are particularly susceptible to burnout because they often are required to deliver high levels of service quality while caught in the stressful position of perceiving that their organization cannot or will not meet a customer demand. Service representatives typically work long hours, lack autonomy, bear responsibility without equivalent authority, have insufficient resources at their disposal, do not have officially approved guidelines to help them resolve many common problems, and face demanding quotas. In addition to all of this, they have to remain calm and polite despite what are frequently unreasonable demands from customers and misunderstandings with managers. The results of a survey offer clear evidence of the consequences of burnout for customer service representatives. The higher the degree of burnout, the lower the employee's job satisfaction and organizational commitment. Burnout reduces the employee's energy level and leads to reduced effort at work. Managers should view burnout as a likely result of a stressful work environment. They can ameliorate the problem by creating a work culture that supports, recognizes, and rewards customer service representatives.[12]

A third way to classify services is by degree of customer contact. Health care, hotels, real estate agencies, and restaurants are examples of high-contact services. With high-contact services, actions generally are directed towards individuals. The consumer must be present during production; in fact, in most cases the consumer must go to the production facility. The service facility's physical appearance may be a major factor in the consumer's overall evaluation of a high-contact service. With low-contact services (such as repairs, dry cleaning, and courier services) customers generally do not need to be present during service delivery. (For example, consumers do not wait while their clothes are being cleaned and pressed at the dry cleaner, and they do not follow their packages as they are delivered by a courier.) As a result, the physical appearance of the facilities of the service organization is not as important for those categorized as low contact.

A fourth way to classify services is by the service provider's level of skill. Professional services tend to be more complex and more highly regulated than non-professional services. In the case of a doctor's physical exam to diagnose a medical problem, consumers often don't know what the actual service will be until it is completed because the final product is situation-specific. The same is true for lawyers, accountants in public practice, financial consultants, and marriage counsellors. In each of these types of service there is an additional uncertainty—the cost—since, unlike medical services, there is seldom any coverage by private or provincial insurance plans. All of these services, to a greater or lesser extent, are regulated by law and by professional societies, so while there is no guarantee of absolute quality, there is at least a modicum of protection for the consumer. By way of contrast, clerks in the concession stands at movie theatres, crossing guards, and window washers need lower skill levels to carry out their jobs, and there is no law or professional society to regulate their activities.

It is sometimes helpful as well to classify services in terms of their urgency in time. While on duty, ambulance attendants, firefighters, and emergency room personnel must be available for almost instant response. At the other end of the urgency scale are authors (unless there is an impending publisher's deadline), swimming instructors, and piano teachers, all of whom can usually defer their work for reasonable periods. This is not to say that low-urgency jobs are of less importance than those having a higher degree of urgency, only that there is a marked difference in the stress that arises from having to be constantly on the alert.

Finally, services can be classified according to the service provider's goal: profit or not-for-profit. There are several differences between profit and not-for-profit services. The major objectives of not-for-profit organizations cannot be stated in financial terms, although those organizations, too, must deal with financial accountability and constraints. The significant difference is not only that profit is not a goal, but that the overall success of the organization cannot be measured in financial terms, and in many cases cannot be meaningfully quantified. The success of a college cannot be measured solely in terms of the number of students it graduates, the percentage who complete their courses, the ratio of those who pass and fail, the number of classrooms occupied at slack hours, or the number of sporting events won or lost. Each of these statistics may provide some useful information, but even taken together they do not yield a definitive measure that is at all comparable to the profit and loss figures of a business that is organized for profit. In addition, not-for-profit organizations usually have two quite different stakeholders: clients who receive the services and donors

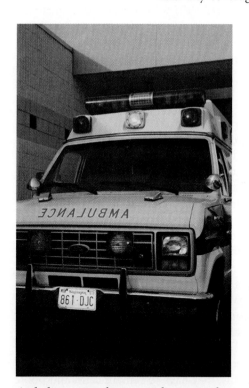

*Ambulance attendants must be prepared to provide an almost instant response.*

and other financial supporters. A public school system is targeted to families with school-age children but also relies on the general public for understanding and support through taxes. Many not-for-profit services, such as legal aid, are targeted to low-income individuals. Public perceptions of not-for-profit organizations affect their ability to raise funds, as the Canadian Red Cross found after the release of the Krever Report on the provision of tainted blood. So, although the methods needed to evaluate not-for-profit organizations are quite different from those used for organizations designed for profit, the need for evaluation is as great and the evaluation process is more difficult and requires more imaginative approaches. It is these differences, among others, that make it worthwhile to differentiate between the two types of organizations.

## Quality and Productivity in Service Organizations

Two major challenges facing service organizations are to improve quality and to improve productivity. The focus of quality improvement in a service organization is to exceed the expectations of the customer (or client, or recipient of service). It is essential to listen to customers with empathy, as described in Chapter 10, and to identify implicit needs and desires that are not expressly stated. For example, the most successful service organizations help customers decide what they want or need by providing options and examples of what will best meet their objectives. Service-oriented clothing stores do not just offer racks of clothing and fitting rooms, but in addition have knowledgeable and helpful staff members who can assist customers in making their choices. Some home improvement stores have experienced rapid growth in sales by providing sales staff who can help customers not only with their choices of products, but also with knowledgeable advice as to how various home repair tasks should be done, the tools required, the cautions to be observed, and even the approximate times required to complete specified tasks. As customers experience such examples of helpfulness, they come to expect either similar help from other stores and merchandise outlets or substantial cost reductions to reflect the "savings" made by the sellers who do not provide this level of service. In effect, more and more customers are coming to the conclusion that they are entitled either to advice and assistance or to significant price reductions. Businesses in the service industry will have to heed these trends and decide whether to offer super service or low prices. Businesses that try to offer only limited service at only medium-range prices may find that their customers have taken their business either to discount stores that offer low prices at the expense of service or to high-end service providers that provide outstanding service, but charge accordingly. These alternatives may leave a void in the middle, where customers are not attracted either by low prices or by outstanding service. Fear has been expressed that service in standard retail stores is deteriorating as a consequence of having inadvertently fallen into this void.[13]

*Cruise lines, which once catered almost exclusively to the well-to-do and retirees, have responded to competition by finding new markets among middle-income families and singles.*

### Service Quality

**Flexibility.** One aspect of service quality is the ability to adapt to changing conditions, and particularly to changing customer wants. Some cruise ship operators, who had long catered to the well-to-do retired customer, have found that there is a growing market for another approach. They provide all of the amenities that a land-based resort would, especially for families.[14] Still other businesses in the travel industry (one of Canada's largest industries) have stopped offering large-group bus tours that used to be most popular, and offer instead small group travel that is tailor-made to the explicit interests of specific customers.[15]

**service quality**
The extent to which a service meets the recipient's reasonable expectations.

**Customer perceptions.**  Only the customer can judge the quality of services. Thus, **service quality** is the conformance of the service to customer specifications and expectations.[16] To the administrators of a medical clinic, service quality often is viewed as being based on the credentials of the physicians. From the standpoint of the quality of medical care provided, there may well be a strong correlation. From the standpoint of the consumer, however, the credentials are often incomprehensible and carry little weight. Patients are more aware of the time they were required to wait, and of their personal interactions with staff and, finally, with doctors.[17]

We are moving into a time when service organizations do not merely *produce*, they *perform*, and customer-perceived value is the focus of competitive advantage.[18] Service organizations must determine what benefits customers expect to receive and then must develop service products that meet or exceed those expectations, as well as meet their own professional standards of performance that are little known to customers or clients.

True service quality rarely goes unnoticed. But providing service quality is easier said than done. Evidence of poor service is everywhere. Flights can be delayed unavoidably. How passengers react is largely determined by how much information they are given, yet often only the barest of explanations is given, and even those are provided only after long waits for the frustrated passengers. Restaurants can provide slow or inefficient service without offering meaningful apologies. Sales clerks can be rude or just uninformed. Such occurrences have led humorists to call poor service a growth industry.[19]

**Customer reactions.**  The typical customer of today is neither patient nor readily forgiving. When there was only one outlet for a particular kind of service in a community, and it was a time-consuming trip to the next town, people put up with what they had to accept. Now most communities have more than one provider of every conceivable kind of service, and customers who are not completely satisfied have no hesitancy in abandoning one provider and trying another. The result is intensified competition, and the need for every service transaction to meet the test of customer satisfaction.

In many service transactions, time of delivery is crucial. McDonald's capitalized on this customer demand for quick service and, by meeting it, forged a worldwide chain of outlets. Barrie Whittaker, general manager of AMP of Canada Ltd., tells of one of AMP's distributors who found that when potential customers phoned to inquire about price and delivery information, 80 percent placed an order *if and only if* that information could be given within two minutes. If the requested answers took longer than two minutes, the proportion of inquirers who placed orders dropped to less than 20 percent.[20] By carefully observing customer behaviour, that distributor identified a key aspect of their provision of service and, to the extent that they were able to streamline their systems for online data retrieval, opened a whole new area of sales improvement. Similar examples cited in earlier chapters are Federal Express, with its commitment to on-time delivery, and Wal-Mart, with its commitment to having what the customers want on the shelves ready for sale.

## *What Managers are Reading*    12-1

### JobShift and We Are All Self-Employed

Managers today are interested in the altered career paths available to them as a result of the wrenching changes that have occurred in the workplace. Two books, *Job Shift*, by William Bridges, a management consultant, and *We Are All Self-Employed*, by Cliff Hakim, a career consultant, point to the challenges facing managers today. It's not surprising that revolutionary changes in the economy should yield a wave of new insecurities. But what goes unnoticed amid the unsettling shifts are the many new opportunities that have been created as well. This upside is not yet apparent to most workers.

However it happens, the business of earning a living and planning for the future will require an attitude adjustment of monumental proportions. Bridges says, "Americans today are no better prepared for the new ways of earning a living in the emerging economy they face than 18th-century English yeomen were at the dawn of the Industrial Age." Hakim says that, at bottom, learning to combine the skills of being self-directed in your career and a savvy steward of your personal finances means being clear about your personal and occupational goals. The old career paradigm of signing on to a job right out of school and climbing a corporate ladder until retirement is no longer appropriate. The new paradigm requires that all workers—whether just getting started or nearing retirement—continually reassess where they stand occupationally and financially and be prepared to change direction as need or opportunity beckons.

Sources: William Bridges, *JobShift* (Reading, MA: Addison-Wesley, 1994); Cliff Hakim, *We Are All Self-Employed* (San Francisco: Berrett-Koehler Publishers, 1994). Adapted from Louis S. Richman, "Getting Past Economic Insecurity," *Fortune* (April 17, 1995):161-68.

**Complaints.** Another key aspect of service quality lies in the handling of complaints. No organization can safely assume that its employees will never make mistakes, and even if it could reach this standard of perfection, there would be circumstances in which customers would complain, if only because they had unrealistic expectations. In some organizations, complaints go virtually unheeded, or at best they trigger what the complainant recognizes is a nothing but a form letter designed to appease but not to satisfy. Other organizations, believing that front-line service staff cannot be trusted to make decisions, channel all complaints to a complaints department that is divorced from the usual customer contacts. The merit of such an organizational plan is that all complaints can be treated uniformly. This consistency, however, is at the cost of having the complainant shuttled from the original point of contact to a disembodied voice that asks the complainant to tell the whole tale of woe all over again. In most cases, the unhappy customer becomes further infuriated and even less likely to accept with grace any form of apology or redress.

The contrast with a more forward-looking competitor is obvious. The epitome of complaint management may be the program undertaken by Lexus when it had to recall some of its luxury cars to remedy a defect. The dealer who had sold the car phoned to make an appointment and sent an employee to pick up the car, leaving another car on loan for the customer's use. When the required adjustment was completed, the customer's car was returned—spotless (having been newly washed) and with a full tank of gas, a small gift, and a personally signed letter of apology. The cost of this extra service was appreciable, but it is not hard to guess where the customer who was treated this way will look first when it comes time to buy another car! All of the expensive advertising in the world could not buy the kind of customer loyalty, and the resulting future sales, that must have been created by going a bit beyond what was expected.[21] In the same vein, the Marriott Hotel chain took pride in advertising that one of their clerks had loaned his own cufflinks to a hotel guest. These companies recognize that having a reputation for excellent service is one of the most important factors in potential customers' choices of where to spend their money.

A perplexing problem, however, lies in the apparent reluctance of most customers to report their dissatisfaction with service. Those who have studied the subject report that perhaps only 1 in 10 or even 1 in 20 of those who are dissatisfied ever make that dissatisfaction known to the organization that has disappointed them.[22] They tell their friends, but not the offending organization. Instead, they "vote with their feet," moving their business to a competitor. In fact, some studies have shown that customers tell 10 or even 20 times as many people about bad service experiences as they do about good ones.[23]

One study of this hazard for service businesses suggests that there are four main reasons why many complaints go unreported. In order of frequency, these reasons are:

1. Customers believe that complaining will not accomplish anything because "the organization" does not care about them or their problems.
2. Whatever benefit they may receive will not be worth the time and trouble.
3. They don't know where they can complain, or how best to do it.
4. They fear that if they complain, they will encounter hostility, or that in some way vengeance will be wreaked upon them.[24]

**Exhibit 12-4**

*Criteria Used to Judge Service Quality*

| Criteria | Examples |
|---|---|
| Reliability: Consistency in performance and dependability | Accuracy in billing. Keeping records correctly. Performing the service at the designated time. |
| Tangibles: Physical evidence of the service. | Physical facilities. Appearance of personnel. Tools or equipment used to provide the service. |
| Responsiveness: Employees' willingness or readiness to provide services. | Mailing a transaction slip immediately. Calling the customer back quickly. Giving prompt service (e.g., setting up appointments quickly). |
| Assurance: Employee's knowledge and ability to convey trust and confidence. | Knowledge and skill of contact personnel. Company name or reputation. Personal characteristics of contact personnel. |
| Empathy: Caring and individualized attention to customer. | Learning customers' specific requirements. Providing specialized individual attention. Consideration for the customer. |

Source: Adapted from Leonard L. Berry and A. Parasuraman, *Marketing Services: Competing through Quality* (New York: Free Press, 1991): 16; A. Parasuraman, Valerie A. Zeithaml, and Leonard L. Berry, "A Conceptual Model of Service Quality and Its Implications for Future Research," *Journal of Marketing* (Fall 1985): 47; and A. Parasuraman, Valerie A. Zeithami, and Leonard L. Berry, "SERVQUAL: A Multiple-Item Scale for Measuring Consumer Perceptions of the Service Quality," *Journal of Retailing* (Spring 1988): 23.

The same study found that even when customers did complain, only one in three felt that they had received satisfaction—often because they were shunted around from one person to another and they had to spend inordinate amounts of time trying to have their complaint heard by someone who would or could do something about it. The outcome, not surprisingly, is that only 22 percent of those who felt their complaint was not handled well would repurchase, in contrast with the 51 percent who said they definitely would repurchase if they felt that their complaint had been handled satisfactorily.

**Improving quality.**  To improve the quality of its services, a service provider first must understand how consumers judge service quality. Several studies have reported that reliability is one of the most important determinants of customers' perceptions of service quality.[25] As shown in Exhibit 12-4 opposite, other important criteria include some tangible indicators, but otherwise depend almost entirely on the attitudes and behaviours of the service provider's employees.

## Improving Service Quality

**evaluative criteria**
The factors that the recipient of a service may use, either consciously or unconsciously, to judge the quality of the service.

Before embarking on a program to improve service quality, the organization must identify the **evaluative criteria** most likely to be used by customers, clients, or other receivers of the service. These are the aspects on which they judge service quality. It is the manager's task to find in what aspects the customers perceive the quality to be deficient. One frequently used source of this information is the survey. As pointed out in Chapter 3, for survey information to be useful, it is essential that the survey be carefully designed and tested before it is widely distributed. It is also necessary to select a statistically reliable sample of the customers to be surveyed. To the extent possible, the survey should include people who were once, but who are no longer, dealing with the organization. It is these people who are most likely to answer frankly and explain why they decided not to continue their association with the organization. It is also useful, although quite difficult, to get responses from people who are not customers or clients, but who might be if they could be convinced of the quality of the service available.[26]

To the customers, a rude flight attendant is a rude airline; a brusque, unaccommodating receptionist is a brusque, unaccommodating doctor. Unfortunately, in many organizations, these front-line employees are the least-trained and lowest-paid members of the staff. Recognizing this fact, airlines spend millions of dollars every year in training programs for flight attendants and ticket clerks, and McDonald's built and staffs what is known as Hamburger University. This recognition also explains the rush of service organizations to qualify for ISO 9002 qualifications, as was described in Chapter 7.[27]

Still another area of concern is the public's perception of the ethical standards of the organization. Again, as discussed in Chapter 2, this is an important factor in manufacturing and other businesses, but it is even more critical in regard to not-for-profit enterprises. When a customer buys a product, no personal relationship is established with the people who manufactured it; when the customer purchases a service, the relationship is with *people,* and they are seen as representing the ethical standards of the organization. With an ever-increasing number of charitable organizations and educational institutions seeking contributions from individuals and corporations, potential donors

*A flight attendant's demeanour in the face of difficulty contributes to the passengers' perception of the airline as a whole.*

are becoming more selective in their choices of recipients. Since the wide publicity given to the distribution of tainted blood by the Red Cross, the number of blood donors has declined precipitously, even though collection of blood has been taken over by another agency. In contrast, organizations such as Foster Parents Plan of Canada publish audited financial reports to their supporters, showing that they keep administrative costs lower than most similar organizations. As a result of earning a sterling reputation, Foster Parents Plan can boast more than a half-century of growth and of proud donors, as well as of grateful recipients of assistance in impoverished communities around the world. Not-for-profit organizations such as this have service responsibilities to at least two publics—those who provide financial and other forms of support and those who benefit from the assistance provided to them. If these not-for-profit organizations do not satisfy the expectations of the first group, their support dries up and they are unable to meet their stated purposes; if they do not satisfy at least a reasonable number of the expectations of the target groups, that information will filter back to the potential donors, with the same ultimate result. So, the not-for-profit segment of the economy has service quality and productivity goals that are little different from those of organizations that are organized for profit.

## Service Productivity

**service productivity**
The relationship between the services delivered and the resources used to produce them.

According to Peter Drucker, the single greatest challenge for managers is to raise the knowledge and productivity of service employees.[28] This involves getting the most out of people. Like manufacturing productivity, **service productivity** is the output per person per hour, per day, or per dollar of wages and benefits. Productivity improves in services when the volume or value of output increases relative to the volume or value of inputs. This can be accomplished by recruiting and training more productive employees, by reducing employee turnover, by buying and installing more efficient equipment, by automating the tasks performed by service employees, by eliminating bottlenecks in the production and delivery of services that lead to downtime, and by standardizing the process and the services output.[29] Demanding more work from employees is unlikely to be successful in the long term.

Productivity in the service sector has shown little growth in recent years.[30] Because it is more than twice as large as the manufacturing sector, the low productivity growth in services pulls down Canada's overall productivity figures. Nonetheless, capital spending in services has increased steadily for several years. Some economists suggest that service productivity is understated because statistics probably are not complete for service organizations that employ less than 25 people. True as this is, it cannot explain away the depressing figures completely.

The most effective way to improve service productivity is to invest in people.[31] Frederick Taylor used the term *working smarter* to describe a means for increasing productivity without working harder or longer. Working smarter is especially critical in service jobs. Productivity can be increased by defining the service task and eliminating unnecessary work. Service employees must be trained and retrained, with particular emphasis on people skills; continuous learning must be part of productivity improvements. The example set by Jacques Coté of Canadian Pacific may indicate that in most service enterprises there is room for some improvement in productivity. In two short but dramatic years, largely as a result of employee training and improving productivity so that trains ran on time, Coté converted CP's Eastern Division, now the St. Lawrence and Hudson Railway, from a money-losing drag on the parent company's profitability to a successful money-spinner.[32]

In another service industry, ServiceMaster completed its twenty-first consecutive year of record revenues and profits. Among other lines of business, the company contracts to mop floors, wash laundry, and operate lunch rooms for businesses and institutions. Its subsidiaries kill pests (Terminix), fertilize lawns (TruGreen), and clean homes (Merry Maids) for consumers. To increase productivity ServiceMaster invests in labour-saving tools such as a pump-oriented soap-dispensing sponge for washing walls. But the company's major investment is in its employees, who are thoroughly trained to perform what appear to outsiders to be routine tasks, such as washing windows, cleaning customers' ovens, and spreading fertilizer.[33] Not only do the employees learn better ways of performing their tasks, but the obvious interest managers show in the employees helps to instil a sense of pride in their work and leads to increased motivation and heightened productivity.

**critical success factors**
The elements involved in the delivery of a service that are essential to the success of the effort.

In the **critical success factors** approach to boosting productivity, managers try to ascertain those things that must go right if the organization is to succeed in attaining organizational goals. To do this, it is necessary to find ways in which the critical success factors are to be measured. Productivity measures taken from manufacturing are of little help. To illustrate, it is easy to count the number of pages inputted correctly by a keyboard operator, but the success of the relationship between a secretary and a manager, or between the secretary and a customer or visitor, are outcomes that are difficult to measure. To measure service productivity it is necessary to use more indirect measures, focusing on new standards of customer satisfaction. Then measurement becomes meaningful.[34]

To meet competition, some organizations have attempted to increase productivity by doing more with less. This involves trimming the number of employees and increasing the efficiency of those remaining through training and labour-saving technology. Grocery chains and other retailers eliminated thousands of positions by installing bar code readers and computerized cash registers. At the same time, customers benefited because of quicker checkout times. The availability of new technology will be discussed in Chapter 15, but the relevant point here is that one of the few ways to increase productivity in labour-intensive jobs is to apply technological aids selectively to extend the effectiveness of the employees.[35]

But technology alone does not immediately solve the problems of service productivity. Almost invariably, new technology requires extensive training that is costly in terms of employee time, and actually reduces productivity during the training period. A secondary benefit from the training, however, is that it may help to focus on unnecessary tasks that can and should be eliminated, and improve the flow of work resulting from the remaining tasks. Research reported by the National Center on the Educational Quality of the Workforce has shown that a 10 percent increase in investment in service employee training increases productivity by an average of 11 percent.[36] Since the original base of employee training is only a small fraction of the productivity numbers, the 10 percentage points applied to that small number may amount to only a fraction of 1 percent of total costs. Consequently, the small cost increase is repaid many times over by the 11 percentage points applied to the much larger number of productivity. Furthermore, it is probably safe to assume that the increased productivity often will be translated into time savings for customers, leading to heightened customer satisfaction and hence to increased sales, adding still further to the improvements achieved by the training of the service employees.

## Developing a Performance Culture

Because service businesses do not produce, but instead perform, they don't sell things, they sell performance. The human performance is the actual "product" that customers buy. The majority of complaints received by Bombardier (maker of snowmobiles and aircraft) or Black & Decker Canada (maker of tools and appliances) relate to the performance of products. In contrast, the majority of complaints received by Air Canada and Canada Trust relate to the performance of people.

In addition to careful selection and training of personnel, a service organization can invest time and money usefully in the development of a performance culture. An organization has a **performance culture** when it functions in ways that permit and encourage all employees to do their best work. Managers are responsible for developing a culture in which service employees have the training, knowledge, and freedom to meet customers' needs. Many organizations make the claim that they are "customer-driven," but it takes more than rhetoric or good intentions to develop a performance culture.

**performance culture**
In an organization, the internal environment in which there is widespread commitment to the effective and satisfactory delivery of service.

## The Components of Peak Performance

A customer walked into a downtown Victoria branch of a major Canadian bank with three transactions in mind. One was to deposit his business's receipts of $1650, the second was to buy a bank draft for 1300 Hong Kong dollars, the third was to buy another bank draft for 35,000 Canadian dollars, for which funds were being transmitted that day from a Vancouver branch of the same bank. He stood in line behind several customers, and when he finally got to the counter, the bank employee said that she could accept the deposit, but that another clerk would have to prepare the Hong Kong draft. The customer went to the second clerk, got the Hong Kong draft, and then was told that for the $35,000 transfer, he would have to wait to see a bank officer, who was busy at that time. He waited again and, when the officer was free, learned that the expected transfer had not yet arrived. He said that he would phone the Vancouver bank to see what was causing the delay. Instead of being offered a phone to do so, he was told that long-distance calls were not permitted on bank phones and that the direct interbranch line was reserved for the use of bank employees. He was directed across the street to a public pay phone in the lobby of the Eaton's Centre. He made the call from the pay phone, resolved the difficulty, returned to the bank, and got his draft. Before leaving the bank he closed his three business and two personal accounts in that bank and went down the street to another financial institution, where his accounts were warmly welcomed.

In this case, outmoded rules made by the bank's managers prevented the employees from providing what would seem to be a minimal level of customer service. Some of these rules subsequently have been relaxed at that bank, but the bank has lost that customer forever, and he is fond of relating his experience to friends, always giving the name of the bank that was involved. The outstanding service provided by Lexus dealers, described earlier in this chapter, may help to account for the booming sales of Lexus cars. Conversely, the kind of service experienced by this former customer of the bank may help to explain the transfer of business from some banks to other financial institutions.

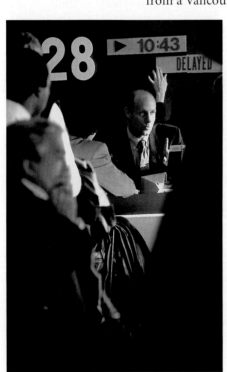

*One aspect of complaints that may frustrate service providers is that often the cause of the dissatisfaction is a factor beyond their control, such as delays caused by weather.*

Most of all, this example illustrates that even with sincere service orientations and the best training possible, service employees may be constrained from offering the kinds of service that customers expect if top management is not truly committed to the highest principles of service. Like any transformation or organizational

*Even within the curriculum requirements imposed by government agencies, a teacher's discretionary effort is quite high compared with that of a production or clerical worker.*

change, the first step in creating a performance culture is for top managers, and then middle managers, to become completely convinced that the success of their organizations, and even their continued existence, is dependent on creating and maintaining a culture of consistently exhibiting peak performance.

**discretionary effort**
The range in which an employee can decide to function with the minimum amount of effort and effectiveness required to avoid direct or indirect punishment, or with the maximum feasible effort and effectiveness.

The foundation of all peak performance and the development of a performance culture is **discretionary effort**, the difference between the minimum amount of effort a worker must expend to keep from being penalized (that is, barely acceptable performance) and the maximum amount a person can bring to the job.[37] Discretionary effort is that effort over which workers have the most control and over which managers have the least direct control. As Exhibit 12-5 on page 444 shows, jobs highest in discretionary effort are customer contact jobs and knowledge jobs. Moving from the manufacturing sector to the service sector, the discretionary content of jobs increases. Assembly line workers have comparatively little latitude for discretionary effort because the assembly line itself dictates the output of the employees and the time allotted to each task. In contrast, the jobs of teachers and consultants, and other similar occupations, include a large component of discretionary effort.

**peak performance**
The highest level of performance an employee or an organization can achieve.

**Peak performance** (the highest level of performance the employee can achieve) is the product of acceptable performance and discretionary effort.[38] Employees whose work involves discretionary effort become or fail to become peak performers depending on the extent to which their behaviour reflects the optional part of their job and not just the parts that are absolutely required to avoid being disciplined. Thus, discretionary effort is the common denominator of peak performance and the critical element for managers who are committed to developing a high-performance culture in their organizations.

## Achieving Peak Performance

It is not surprising that organizations whose managers recognize the concept of peak performance want to encourage it. But this is quite difficult because, as has been pointed

**Exhibit 12-5**    *Discretionary Effort Component in Various Types of Jobs*

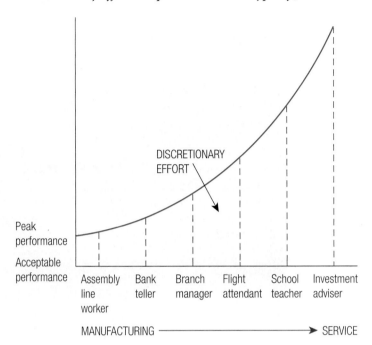

out, discretionary effort—the key to achieving peak performance—is not easily controlled by managers. Some service employees are satisfied with what is merely acceptable performance. But the reality of today's highly competitive economy is that *acceptable* performance is not enough. There may be little difference between the financial "products"—such as chequing accounts, auto loans, RRSPs, and term deposits—offered by various banks. But one bank may provide demonstrably better service than another. When the products being offered are the same, an organization wins or loses with the quality of its service. The challenge facing managers is to unleash employees' discretionary effort.

Empowering employees to make decisions and take action without management's item-by-item approval increases the likelihood that discretionary effort will be exercised. Employees who fear the consequences of making a mistake or who, because of the organization's policies, cannot make a decision on their own are less likely to exercise discretion. In the experience related above, the bank employees didn't provide satisfactory service to the customer, who promptly responded by withdrawing his accounts, because they either didn't care about the customer or (more likely) were afraid to violate or even bend the bank's policy. Service managers have begun to empower employees and to encourage them to exercise discretion, realizing that this may have a positive impact on service quality and customer satisfaction.

## Management Commitment

Not surprisingly, empowerment alone does not ensure that a performance culture is created.[39] Managers must be committed to developing a responsive organizational structure that encourages performance, and employees must be motivated and committed to the organization's goals. This means taking extra care in hiring service employees, paying close attention to matters of personality, social attitudes, and skill in handling inter-

## Management in the Real World  12-1

### Managing Services: Reflections by Philip Crosby

I had a chat with two hotel managers in an airplane. They were anxious to tell me about their service program that ensured that guests were getting what was needed. They worked for the same chain and were on their way to a corporate management meeting. They planned to present the results of their jointly developed program to this session.

The key to their program was an assistant manager at a desk in the hotel lobby. In each room was a tent card stating that the hotel had a "quality hotline." If guests had a problem they punched the hotline number on their telephone and the assistant manager answered. If she was off on a mission, the call would be transferred to the front desk. The call and its result were logged into the computer system and the resident manager could have an instant printout. They had some of these with them.

Guests' most common complaint referred to the time it took for room service. The second most common complaint had to do with items in the room, such as towels, being missing or inadequate. One hotel averaged 23 calls per day on the hotline; the other averaged 34. The number range was pretty standard over the six months that the program had been in effect.

"We're really giving our guests great service," said one manager. "They get their problem fixed within 20 minutes and we have a goal of 15 minutes by the end of this year."

I said it appeared to me that the same problems happened over and over. There didn't seem to be much effective corrective action. What they had was a very expensive way of fixing things temporarily. They were crestfallen and repeated the story to make certain that I had not misunderstood.

"How about installing that system on this airplane," I asked. "If we run out of gas, we can call a hotline and they'll send some up. I think I wouldn't like that."

"What would you suggest?" one said.

"Prevention, prevention, prevention. Use each problem as a way of learning how to never let it happen again. Guests really don't want to talk to the hotline. They would prefer to just go about their business."

They were disappointed.

"You're saying that what we call service is just another name for rework?" he asked.

"True," I said. "The best way to serve your customers is to not make them part of the problem."

personal relationships. It also means giving service employees adequate authority and providing them with more training and linking at least part of their pay to customer satisfaction.[40]

If managers aren't committed to customers, other employees are likely to behave in the same destructive manner. Thus, managers must identify performances that enhance the organization's efficiency and effectiveness. In many service organizations managers and non-managers alike spend an inordinate amount of their time, energy, and resources performing activities that aren't critical to achieving the organization's goals. Managers must identify those activities that are most critical and focus the organization's attention on being the best possible at these activities.[41]

Managers also should tie rewards directly to performance that enhances the efficiency and effectiveness of the overall work output. Recognition should be given to individuals who perform beyond the merely acceptable level. Non-managers should be encouraged to participate with management in defining goals and standards against which individual performance is to be judged. In short, if there is no incentive to perform beyond acceptable levels, individuals are likely to perform at bare minimum rather than at optimum levels.

Managers must be fully committed to a performance culture; their every action must demonstrate this commitment clearly to subordinates. Almost the worst thing a manager can do in this regard is to *talk* performance culture but to *take actions* that convey a much different message to other employees. Achieving competitive success through people involves fundamentally altering how everyone thinks about the workforce and the employment relationship.[42] It means achieving success by working with people, not by replacing them or by unduly limiting the scope of their activities. It entails seeing the workforce as a source of strategic advantage, not just as a cost to be minimized or avoided. Organizations that take this different perspective often are able to outmanoeuvre and outperform their competitors.[43]

## The Workplace of Tomorrow

With the introduction of technological tools in service industries, the interpersonal relationships between service employees and customers have been revolutionized. The customers of any modern bank or credit union can make deposits and get cash from ATMs, pay bills with bank cards tendered at stores, inquire about the status of accounts and make transfers among accounts by telephone or by computer and modem, have paycheques automatically deposited and utility bills automatically paid, and indeed perform almost all routine banking transactions without ever going near the premises of the financial institution. Consumers can dial listed numbers and receive from automated answering services the latest ferry schedules, theatre opening times and seat availability, and a summary of the latest news headlines. From this explosion of technology, some managers might be tempted to think that the personalized service given by service employees is almost a thing of the past, and that all they need to do is make sure that the recorded messages are delivered in a pleasant tone. In fact, almost the opposite is true. Now, when so many services are automated, the personal contacts that remain are much more likely than before to involve a high proportion of problem matters and nonroutine requests. In these circumstances, the way in which personal contacts are handled may be even more important than when most of them were routine and dealt with rather easily. Consequently, the advent of technological tools in the service sector probably has intensified the need for special care to be given to these interpersonal relations, and to how every customer or client is treated.

Whereas manufacturing and retailing enterprises often were forced to retrench in the 1980s and 1990s, service industries tended to burgeon both in number and in size and scope.[44] In the decades immediately ahead, service organizations face significant challenges. Those organizations that depend on voluntary donations are facing intensified competition from new not-for-profit organizations that are springing up almost daily, at the same time as potential donors are becoming more aware of their right to examine closely how effectively the organizations are operated. Those organizations that depend on government largesse have recently been feeling, and doubtless will continue to feel, an unaccustomed chill from municipal, provincial, and federal sources. Those service organizations that depend on sales to consumers are facing crucial demographic changes as the population ages and a higher percentage of Canadians enter their postretirement years. They must adapt to the fact that, in retirement, some people suffer greatly reduced discretionary income, while others are finally freed from mortgage payments and the expenses of children and so are able to spend more freely than they did when younger. At the same time, structural unemployment and the threat of further "downsizing" have done much to discourage nonessential purchases by those still employed in the workforce. In this era of new competitiveness, the service organizations that prosper and even survive will be those that apply some or all of the principles discussed in this chapter. Some service industries already are being proactive in these areas; others are seemingly content with "business as usual" and are beginning to show signs of deterioration and impending decline.[45]

In addition, there has been a marked escalation in the expectations of customers and clients. A study conducted by Xerox Canada revealed that as the business environment in the 1990s has become more complex, customers are demanding enhanced access to and responsiveness from those with whom they do business. According to this research, there must be an understanding on the part of the service organization that time and energy are seen by customers as valuable commodities[46] and that customers resent organizations that seem not to appreciate this fact.

It does not take great foresight to predict that, as has been discovered in the manufacturing, financial, and commercial industries, all service organizations and all governments will be facing more intense competition than ever before. It is certain that while outstanding management alone will not guarantee success, mediocre or inadequate management likely will lead to failure.

## Summary of Learning Objectives

▶ **Illustrate the meaning, in a management context, of the term** *service.*

A service is an intangible product that involves human or mechanical effort and fills some want or need of the recipient.

▶ **Discuss the concept of tangibility as it relates to goods and services.**

Consumers can physically possess a tangible good. A service cannot be physically possessed because it is intangible. Most products are neither a pure good nor a pure service, but a mix of tangible and intangible elements. One element usually predominates, which is the basis for classifying a product as a good or a service.

▶ **List four characteristics that distinguish services from goods, and explain how these characteristics influence the emphases placed by managers in service organizations.**

One distinguishing feature is intangibility (that is, most services, as distinct from the results of the services, cannot be assessed by senses of sight, taste, touch, smell, or hearing). Another difference is that in services, production and consumption are inseparable from each other, services being produced and consumed at the same time. Still another difference lies in the element of perishability, it being impossible to store unused services for use at a later date. Finally, services are characterized by heterogeneity, there being inconsistency or variation in the performance of the individuals providing the service. As a result of these differences, managers in service organizations place a higher priority on factors such as timeliness, atmosphere and ambiance, and the training of staff members in human relations.

▶ **Explain the significance of service quality and of service productivity.**

Service quality and productivity are at the heart of many service management strategies. Service quality is the conformance of the service to customer specifications and expectations. Only by meeting customer expectations on a consistent basis can an organization deliver service quality. Service productivity is the output per person per hour, per day, or per dollar of wages and benefits. A major challenge facing service organizations is to raise the productivity of service employees.

▶ **Discuss ways in which service organizations can improve quality and productivity.**

Service quality can be improved only when non-managerial employees as well as managers are committed to it. Organizations must develop specific guidelines that are communicated to employees and are both demonstrated and enforced by management. High-quality service must be recognized and rewarded. The major way to improve service productivity is to invest in people. Defining the service task, eliminating unnecessary work, and training service employees may contribute to productivity improvements.

▶ **Describe conditions that indicate that an organization has a performance culture, and discuss the likely outcomes of having such a culture.**

An organization has a performance culture when all employees are facilitated in doing their best work. Managers are responsible for developing a culture in which service employees have the training, knowledge, and freedom to meet customers' needs. An organization that has a performance culture will enhance the satisfaction of its customers, clients, or other recipients of its service, which will probably lead to an increase in its sales or other measures of the volume of its activities.

▶ **Describe the components of peak performance.**

Peak performance—the highest level of performance an employee can achieve—is the combination of acceptable performance and discretionary effort. Acceptable performance is the minimum amount of effort needed to avoid being penalized, either directly or indirectly (as in deferring raises or promotions). Discretionary effort is the additional effort that goes beyond acceptable performance and adds to customer satisfaction.

▶ **Suggest ways in which managers can encourage peak performance.**

Peak performance is more likely to be achieved when non-managerial employees are empowered to make decisions and take action without needing item-by-item approval from management. Managers must be committed to developing a responsive organization structure that encourages peak performance. All employees must be motivated and committed to the organization's goals.

## KEY TERMS

critical service encounter, p. 430
critical success factors, p. 441
discretionary effort, p. 443
evaluative criteria, p. 439
heterogeneity, p. 431

inseparability, p. 430
intangibility, p. 429
peak performance, p. 443
performance culture, p. 442

perishability, p. 431
service, p. 427
service productivity, p. 440
service quality, p. 436

## REVIEW AND DISCUSSION QUESTIONS

### Recall

**1.** What is a service? Name five different services that you have received within the past week.

**2.** What are the main characteristics that distinguish services from goods?

**3.** Describe a classification scheme for services, giving an example for each category.

4. What is service quality? How can it be improved?
5. What is meant by a critical service encounter? Give some examples that you have experienced recently.
6. What is meant by a performance culture?
7. What is a critical success factor?

### Understanding

8. Explain how a manager may use a classification of services.
9. Why is service productivity important to our economy? How can efforts to improve service productivity reduce service quality? Give an example.
10. What causes an individual to be likely to perform at the minimum acceptable level? What can an organization do to encourage employees to exhibit peak performance?

### Application

11. If the president of an airline that offers package charter vacations asked you to develop a program for improving service quality, how would you respond? Be sure to explain why your program would improve service quality and, consequently, competitiveness.

---

## *CASE* 12-1

## Carnival Cruise Lines

With 20 percent of the North American cruise market, Carnival Cruise Lines became the biggest line in the world through execution, not innovation. Carnival wasn't the first cruise line on network TV or the first to use the "fun" slogan. The company's success comes from delivering a consistent message and a consistently superior product. Says one major competitor, "Carnival's … approach has been brilliant. Nobody has been able to truly compete in their niche."

Carnival was founded in 1972 by Ted Arison, who decided to make the ship itself the product. Whereas most major cruise lines emphasized the ports of destination rather than the shipboard experience, Arison decided to make the ship the "destination." To achieve this, he instituted what was then an innovation. He made Carnival's ships into resorts on water, equipped with pools, casinos, and plenty of food. Passengers enjoy being on the ship as much as landing at some exotic Caribbean port. Ship names (like *Mardi Gras* and *Fantasy*) and everything else about Carnival connote fun.

To reinforce the idea that the ship is the destination, Carnival provides superior service. Whereas some competitors provide room service 16 hours a day, Carnival provides it around the clock. Three full meals, with two sittings for each, are served daily. In addition, there are two midnight buffets plus snacks available regularly beginning at 6:30 a.m. Room stewards are always around to keep cabins clean, help with luggage, and even turn down beds. Waiters who serve passengers on the pool deck learn individual passenger's beverage preferences and serve refills before being asked.

Carnival's cruises are priced competitively, many being 20 percent below those of competing lines. Its pricing has allowed Carnival to target people who previously could not afford to go on cruises. Surveys have shown that the average annual household income of Carnival's Canadian passengers is in the $40,000 to $75,000 range. Many passengers aboard the *Jubilee* are young, blue-collar entrepreneurs, who were not previously seen as typical cruise ship passengers.

The way in which cruises are sold is limited because of inseparability of production and consumption. Nevertheless, Carnival is the industry's most forceful cruise operator in this regard. By using travel agents to help facilitate sales, Carnival has established an effective marketing network. It encourages travel agents to let vacationers know that cruises are an alternative to a trip to a theme park like Disney World. To enlist travel agents' cooperation, Carnival employees pay personal calls on them. Carnival also gives cash awards to some agents who recommend Carnival. The company strategy works—most Carnival passengers say that a travel agent recommended the cruise line. Although the popularity of cruises is growing, only 5 percent of North Americans have taken a cruise. This leaves a huge potential market for the cruise industry. Carnival is currently building three of the largest passenger ships in the world (the *Fantasy*, the *Ecstasy*, and the *Sensation*) at a total cost of $600 million. Carnival hopes these three ships will tap into the huge potential market. The firm also has established a joint venture with Club Méditerranée, the French chain of vacation villages. The companies jointly operate a cruise ship in the Mediterranean, and will explore the idea of starting cruises in the Asian market.

### Questions

1. What does Carnival Cruise Lines sell?
2. What are some of the tangible elements associated with cruises?
3. Why is service quality critical to Carnival's strategy?
4. Does Carnival have a performance culture? Explain.

Source: Adapted from Bradley Johnson, "Carnival," *Advertising Age* (July 6, 1992): 5-22; Michael J. McCarthy, "Carnival Plans Europe Venture with Club Med," *The Wall Street Journal* (May 19, 1992): B1, B12; Faye Rice, "How Carnival Stacks the Decks," *Fortune* (January 16, 1989): 108-16; Fran Durbin, "Carnival Plans to Use Fantasy on Short Trips," *Travel Weekly* (October 27, 1988): 1-2; and Stephen Koepp, "All the Fun Is Getting There," *Time* (January 11, 1988): 54-56.

## CASE 12-2

## British Airways

The spirit of airline competition in the 1990s probably can be best described as service or else. In the words of Bob Ayling, British Airways' chief executive, "... it's not just that the competition is getting tougher, which certainly has a part to play. What really has changed is the expectations of our customers." Having lost billions of dollars in recent years, carriers are desperate to raise fares, and some feel that better service will make higher fares possible. So rather than competing on price, airline companies are focusing on service. At the top of the heap stands British Airways (BA), named in *Euromoney* magazine's annual poll of business travellers as the airline providing the best service.

In 1995 BA's profits were an industry-high of £452 million (more than Cdn$1 billion), which represented nearly one-half of the total profits of all major airlines. BA's average revenue per passenger was also among the best in the industry. In terms of passengers carried and passenger miles flown, BA has become the world's largest international airline. All of this from the airline that lost an industry-record $1 billion in 1982.

When Sir Colin Marshall took over as CEO of British Airways in early 1983, the company was the laughingstock of the industry. Comedians referred to the company, known by its initials BA, as "Bloody Awful." Employee morale had hit rock bottom; thousands of employees had just been laid off and those remaining were embarrassed to work for the worst airline in the world. Marshall's first challenge was to restore company pride. To send a clear message to both employees and potential customers, he ordered newly designed uniforms for all personnel. The fleet of planes was repainted with bright stripes and the motto "To fly, to serve." With this motto, the service era was born at BA.

Words alone do not guarantee service quality, so Marshall launched a major campaign to change employees' attitudes towards service. He surmised that many passengers, especially those travelling on business, desired better service from airlines. Marshall required that all BA employees attend a two-day seminar called "Putting People First." Its purpose was to put airline employees in the customers' shoes. Employees were asked to think about some of their own bad experiences with service. In subsequent years, all BA employees have attended other service-oriented seminars entitled "A Day in the Life" and, most successful of all, "To Be the Best."

Obvious problems—dull, tasteless food, poor cabin service, cramped leg room—were remedied immediately. But Marshall also scrutinized the less obvious details. For example, research had shown that passengers like to be called by name, so BA employees spent several months observing passengers on flights from London to Glasgow and Manchester. They saw that when ticket agents addressed passengers by name, customer satisfaction scores went up approximately 60 percent. Now BA agents call customers by name whenever possible. Trouble shooters who speak several languages were placed at London's Heathrow Airport to provide passenger assistance. Booths were set up at JFK Airport in New York for BA passengers to videotape comments about service. Flights were scheduled for the convenience of customers, not of the airline.

BA also changed its Concorde service. Marshall decided to treat the company's seven Concordes, which were losing money, as a symbol of a revitalized airline. The planes were redecorated and prices were raised substantially. The new price is 30 percent higher than first-class fares on a conventional jet. But because the Concorde can cross the Atlantic Ocean in half the time it takes other jets, BA developed a new advertising theme to emphasize the importance of time to business travellers. As a result, the Concorde began flying at over 60 percent occupancy (the breakeven point) on its transatlantic routes.

Then, starting in 1989, BA invested huge sums to improve first-class service. Video terminals were installed at each seat, and cabin interiors were redesigned. First-class "seats" convert into horizontal beds that are 6'6" long and are separated from each other by partitions to provide privacy and sound control. A new wine cellar offers an improved selection; first-class passengers may have their meals when they wish—a valuable attribute for those who are changing time zones. Business-class passengers can "raid the larder" and get fairly substantial snacks whenever they feel like it.

These changes are all part of Colin Marshall's service imperative, and managers from other service industries are taking note. Marshall himself likes to recall the famous Twentieth Century Limited, the train that ran from New York to Chicago. Conductors would pay passengers $1 for every minute the train was late, no matter who or what was to blame. With all of the air traffic delays and weather problems, it would be tough for airlines to make the same offer. But, as Marshall says, "We could promise to make the delays completely painless with concentrated service attention. Think how many customers you could acquire for life if and when the guarantee is cheerfully, quickly and easily paid."

Today British Airways' *market place performance unit* tracks some 350 measures of performance, including aircraft cleanliness, punctuality, technical defects on the aircraft, customer complaints, the time it takes for a customer to get through when telephoning a reservations agent, and customer satisfaction with in-flight and ground services. The unit's overreaching mission is to act as a surrogate for customers in assessing the airline's performance.

## Questions

1. Why did Colin Marshall have to change employees' attitudes towards service?
2. How did British Airways use research to help serve customers better?
3. Why would a passenger pay 30 percent more to fly on a Concorde than to fly first-class on a conventional jet? Is it all a matter of time saved?
4. How does the marketplace performance unit help ensure service quality, customer satisfaction, and competitiveness?

Sources: Adapted from Steven E. Prokesch, "Competing on Customer Service: An Interview with British Airways' Sir Colin Marshall," *Harvard Business Review* (November-December 1995): 110-112; Steven E. Prokesch, "Measuring Performance Through Customers' Eyes," *Harvard Business Review* (November-December 1995): 108-109; Paula Dwyer, "British Air: Not Cricket," *Business Week* (January 25, 1993): 50-51; "British Investment in USAir Approved," *Lexington Herald-Leader* (March 16, 1993): B3; Stewart Toy, Andrea Rothman, and Paul Dwyer, "Air Raid," *Business Week* (August 24, 1992): 54-61; Richard D. Hylton, "United to BA: Take Off," *Fortune* (September 7, 1992): 9; "Best and Worst in the Air," *Parade Magazine* (June 7, 1992): 8; Kenneth Labich, "The Big Comeback at British Airways," *Fortune* (December 5, 1988): 163-74.

## APPLICATION EXERCISE 12-1

### How Could *Your* Service Have Been Improved?

The purpose of this exercise is to evaluate the service you have received recently, and to consider how that service could have been improved. Select the service that you wish to use as your example (perhaps an airline flight, a meal in a restaurant, a haircut or styling, a medical or dental appointment, etc.). Then evaluate each of the criteria listed below, on a continuum from 1 to 10, where 1 represents impossibly bad service, 5 represents average or mediocre service, and 10 represents superlative service that made you feel cared for, respected, and valued.

### Criteria

1. Service performance and dependability.
2. Condition and appearance of the facilities, equipment, and other tangibles.
3. Appearance and interest in your concerns shown by the service providers and their support staff members.
4. Knowledge, skills, and ability of the service providers and their support staff members.
5. Degree of personal attention exhibited by the service providers and their support staff members.
6. Willingness of everyone to communicate what you would have liked to know about the service you were seeking.

Having recorded your evaluation of each of these criteria, consider specifically how each of the criteria could have been better met to increase your personal satisfaction. Then decide what the cost might have been to provide that increase in service acceptability. Finally, decide whether that additional cost, *if any*, would be justified in terms of the organization's effectiveness and competitiveness.

## APPLICATION EXERCISE 12-2

### Coping with the Quality of Perishability

Assume that you have just been hired as general manager of the Embassy Hotel, an upscale hotel in Cedarview, a city with a population of 80,000. You were hired to turn the Embassy around from showing a consistent loss to a profit position. The Embassy records show that dinner service results in a slight profit, but that the hotel loses money on both breakfast and lunch. It has been assumed that in order to accommodate overnight guests it is necessary to offer breakfast and lunch, despite the small numbers of patrons who use this service. You conclude that to bring the Embassy out of the red, you will have to find ways to increase lunch patronage.

The Riverview Inn is the only other hotel in the city that is a real competitor in terms of quality and ambiance. On investigation, you find that the Riverview has what amounts to a monopoly on the service club luncheon business, with a different service club luncheon meeting there on each of Monday, Tuesday, Wednesday, and Thursday. Each of these luncheons has about 40 members in attendance, and they pay about $9 each for their lunch. Your predecessor (the manager who presided over the consistent losses) refused to provide lunch for such a low price on the grounds that, when all costs are factored in, $9 would barely cover the costs and would return no profit. The employment laws in your province provide that the cooks and serving staff who are on duty for the lunch period have to be paid throughout the afternoon if they are to work the dinner hour as well. As a result, there is a slight surplus of staff during the lunch period, and then for at least two hours in the late afternoon the kitchen and serving staff have almost no work to occupy them, although they are being paid during this period.

Write a plan to present to the Embassy's board of directors that you think will help take up the slack at noon and provide some productive work for the late afternoon period.

## INTERNET APPLICATION 12-1

Visit the Web site of Four Seasons Hotels and Resorts (www.fourseasons.com). Concentrate in particular on the information found in its Press Gallery, News Releases section.

1. How does the corporation's mission statement reflect its focus on customer service?
2. What kind of innovative services does Four Seasons offer that sets it apart from other hotels?

Search the Web for an organization that makes customer service a priority. What kinds of things does it do in order to make the customer "number 1"?

# Entrepreneurship and Growth

After studying this chapter, you should be able to:

▶ Explain the meaning and application of the term *entrepreneur*, and distinguish it from the coined term *intrapreneur*;

▶ Explain some of the most common reasons why someone might decide to become an entrepreneur;

▶ Discuss how Canadian conditions have contributed to the kind of inventions that have been made by little-known but deserving Canadian inventors and entrepreneurs;

▶ Discuss some of the risks associated with becoming an entrepreneur;

▶ Describe the phases of the four-stage growth model;

▶ Explain why an entrepreneur should prepare a business plan, and discuss its uses;

▶ Describe the essential features of a business plan; and

▶ Discuss why a person might prefer to purchase a franchise instead of start up a new business venture.

## Outsourcing to Reduce Capital Requirements and to Focus on Core Activities

SMALL BUSINESSES TEND TO START WITH ONLY A SMALL amount of capital, but if they grow appreciably they soon need infusions of capital. Traditionally, acquiring the additional capital required resorting to loans and to giving up part of the enterprise to people willing to put up capital in exchange for part ownership or, more likely, a majority interest. The debt load resulting from the loans, or the loss of ownership, burdened the new enterprise and in many cases caused its failure. Today, entrepreneurs are finding that they are able to get new ventures started with much less need for capital by outsourcing many aspects of their work.  ▶

Outsourcing is defined as the selective, often short-term use of one or more outside contractors or consultants to assist in the accomplishment of a necessary business function. Payroll services, tax compliance, employee benefits, and claims administration are among the most commonly outsourced services. Other possibilities are equipment maintenance, cleaning, accounting, and marketing. Bryker Data Systems of Toronto has built a lucrative operation by providing specialized software applications to small businesses that do not have, and do not want to maintain, in-house capability for this purpose. Even corporate giants such as Crown Life Insurance Company and Stelco find it economically prudent to retain STM Systems Corp. (Canada's largest computer services company) to handle their computer networks and other applications.[1]

The term *outsourcing* also includes having other companies manufacture components, or even a large part or all of the product that the entrepreneur intends to market. This arrangement has been an established part of the automobile industry for many years, and has given rise to countless businesses whose sole customers are automobile assembly plants. Canada's Magna, to which reference is made in Chapter 11 and elsewhere in this book, illustrates the symbiotic relationship between such companies and their primary customers, as the suppliers tailor their daily production schedules to the immediate needs of their customers. Although a small business does not have as much of an impact on a supplier as a huge corporation such as the Ford Motor Company, Chrysler, or General Motors, more and more suppliers are recognizing their opportunity for growth may lie in developing similar relationships with a long list of entrepreneurial enterprises.

A good summary of the concept underlying outsourcing is given by Tom Asacker, of Innovative Medical Systems, Inc., a small New Hampshire company that sells devices for alleviating sleep apnea. Asacker says, "We practice outsourcing both strategically and by necessity. I believe I improve my quality and responsiveness to the market by outsourcing to experts the things that I'm not expert at. And if I can get to the market fast with the highest-quality products using outsourcing, I've won for the long term, too."

Small companies that do a lot of outsourcing tend to gain by being more flexible, and by being able to react to changes in the market more rapidly than their competitors who have committed themselves to doing everything in-house. International accounting firm Coopers & Lybrand studied 400 small companies that had median revenues of $6.5 million and median employment of 65 people. Two-thirds of the companies surveyed were actively engaged in outsourcing. The study also showed that the companies that used outsourcing enjoyed revenues, sales prospects, and growth rates that significantly exceeded those of the companies that did not use outsourcing. A study by Dun & Bradstreet in 1998 indicated that by early 1999 the practice of outsourcing in Canada would have grown by 21 percent over what it was a year earlier, to a total of nearly $23 billion.

"Initially, outsourcing was something that very large companies did that were in trouble; it was a controversial move," says Frank Casale, executive director of the Outsourcing Institute, a New York company that provides information and offers seminars on outsourcing. "Now it's more accepted as a strategic-management tool for use by businesses of all sizes as compared with a last-second maneuver by a company that has run out of choices."

Outsourcing can help small businesses to focus more on what they do best—their core competencies. It also enables them to have the other functions performed by companies for which those functions are core competencies. Many small businesses have moved from outsourcing solely peripheral tasks to contracting out multiple functions that are critical to their success. Thus, tasks from administrative paperwork to product design are likely to be performed at a higher level of quality and effectiveness and usually at less cost than if a single company tried to do them all.

Black Rock Ventures is a company that is nearly invisible, yet it generated roughly $10 million in sales in its first year of operations. One secret to its success is that the company, maker of the Killer Bee golf driver, is a prototype of a small "virtual company," that is, a company that is based on the concept of outsourcing. Black Rock principals had an idea, contracted with a company to design the Killer Bee, used five different marketing agencies around North America for its TV infomercials and other promotional activities, and had two Asian companies produce the club components and had two North American contractors assemble them. Still another company is contracted to handle telemarketing, order fulfilment, and customer service. Larry Hoffer, Black Rock's general manager (and one of the five full-time employees), explains, "We basically spend our time managing our vendors and planning our strategic direction." He admits that later they may find it desirable to bring some of the functions in-house, but "We don't want to grow beyond probably 20 employees. We'll leave the messy stuff to outside people."

Today's entrepreneurs still need ample skills, capital, and knowledge to start a successful new business venture. But, unlike a few years ago, they can get started without knowing how to do every step of the business process. Many small businesses have learned to focus on their strengths, and to contract with another company or companies to help them with other business functions. This trend seems likely to continue, and those entrepreneurs who are able to form alliances with other companies may be the ones most likely to succeed. ■

Source: Adapted from Diane McDougall, "News and Views," *CMA Magazine* (October 1998): 3; Dale D. Buss, "Growing More by Doing Less," *Nation's Business* (December 1995): 18-20; and "Virtual Companies, Real Profits," *Nation's Business* (December 1995): 21.

## The Entrepreneurship Ingredient

**entrepreneur**

A person who assumes the major risks of starting a new business by committing equity, time, and often career to the venture.

The word *entrepreneurship* is derived from a seventeenth-century French word, *entreprendre*, which referred to a person who *undertook* the risk of a new enterprise. A current definition of **entrepreneur** is a person who assumes the major risks of starting a new business by committing equity, time, and often career. The product or service itself may or may not be new or distinct, but value is added by an entrepreneur.[2] Although innovative and entrepreneurial activities usually occur in the startup phase of a small business, as will be discussed later in this chapter the entrepreneurial spirit and focus also can occur in large organizations, where it is often referred to as *intrapreneurial*, from *intra*, meaning "within."

Examples of entrepreneurs include Steven Wozniak and Stephen Jobs, who jointly founded Apple Computer, and Henry Ford, who originated the Ford Motor Company; both of these enterprises grew enormously. They also include Gabe Magnotta of Magnotta Winery Estates of Vaughan, Ontario, and Irvin Goodon of Irvin Goodon Industries of Boissevain, Manitoba; both of these enterprises also started on a shoestring and now enjoy several million dollars in annual sales, but they are hardly household names beyond a relatively small local following.[3] For each of these phenomenally successful entrepreneurs, there are thousands of other entrepreneurs who are making only a modest living and creating a few jobs for others, or perhaps who are struggling to make ends meet and laying off employees to keep from insolvency.

Many entrepreneurs took on this role out of necessity, after having been downsized or after having searched unsuccessfully for employment after finishing formal education. Major corporations are attempting to capture what is referred to as entrepreneurial spirit in the organization as a whole. Entrepreneurs are viewed by many as the individuals who can give the economy the boost it needs to compete globally, to create new products and jobs, as well as to initiate new forms of business.

Around the world, emerging economies also are relying on entrepreneurs to raise the standard of living. For generations, true entrepreneurs have existed in what are now known as emerging countries, in the form of the women who sell produce and handicrafts in local markets. They have been the mainstays of the economies of their countries, and often the sources of almost all of their families' cash income and sustenance. This phenomenon is expanding in its scope and effect in other emerging countries. An example is the growth of newly created small businesses in Estonia, where the government belatedly encourages the development of a private sector economy and recognizes that much of that growth will have to come through small businesses.[4]

**What Managers Are Reading    13-1**

## Innovation and Entrepreneurship

Although this book by the highly respected Peter Drucker was first published in 1985, it is still being read by managers throughout the industrialized world. The thrust of the book is that the United States was then moving from a managerial to an entrepreneurial economy. Drucker wonders whether other industrialized countries would move in the same direction. He provides the background that underlies his analysis of the transition in the United States, and the thoughtful reader will see close similarities in Canada. Drucker points out that despite the publicity given to high-tech companies, the great bulk of the job creation in recent years had been distributed throughout many other segments of the economy—notably manufacturing, commerce, and finance. He points to the public-private partnerships that are beginning to bloom throughout North America. Most of all, he stresses that the growth areas are, indeed, in new technology, but that this new technology is not in what are generally described as high-tech areas, but rather in entrepreneurial management.

In discussing entreprenuership, Drucker writes: "Innovation is the specific tool of entrepreneurs, the means by which they exploit change as an opportunity for a different business or a different service." He says that the sources of innovation can be categorized under seven headings:

- The unexpected;
- Incongruities;
- Process need;
- Industry and market structures;
- Demographics;
- Changes in perception; and
- New knowledge.

After illustrating each of these sources of innovation, Drucker concludes with a plea for two necessary social innovations. One is the creation of a policy to "take care of redundant workers" (the "throwaway people" spoken of by sociologists as they view the downsizing that has occurred since the mid-1980s). The second essential social innovation, according to Drucker, is ". . . to organize the systematic abandonment of outworn social policies and obsolete public-service institutions." This prescription, made nearly two decades ago, is just as relevant and, unfortunately, just as unfulfilled as it was on the day it was written. Managers and entrepreneurs, who well may have read this incisive book when it was first published, are again turning to it for, if the seeming irony may be excused, *innovative ideas* and means of fostering entrepreneurship.

Source: Peter F. Drucker, *Innovation and Entrepreneurship* (London: William Heinemann, 1985).

In Canada, it is generally accepted that small businesses have been the creators of most of the new jobs through the past decade or two. Layoffs and downsizing in large corporations certainly have decreased the numbers of employees in those companies, and those actions have been widely publicized. However, recent studies by Statistics Canada have called into question the emphasis given to some of this received wisdom about the relationship between small-company and large-company job creation. According to the analysis written by economists Garnett Picot and Richard Dupuy, "A few firms grew rapidly, while others either grew slowly or lost employment. This was true for both small and large firms, although job creation was more highly concentrated in the small-firm sector than in the large." Their study shows that only 5 percent of the small companies accounted for 43 percent of the new jobs created by small business, while an equally small proportion of small companies accounted for one-third of all jobs *lost* in the small company sector. From these statistics, the authors point out the misinterpretations that can arise from treating the "average" as typical of the other members of a group. The study showed that some large corporations also created large numbers of new jobs, while others contributed to the loss of jobs in the large company sector. Finally, the authors of this study show that whether jobs are created or lost over a period may depend entirely on what period is chosen for the comparison. For instance, in the recession and recovery years of 1981 through 1984, small companies that existed at the start of the period lost 14 percent of their employee numbers, while large companies lost only 11 percent. By way of contrast, in the business growth period from 1984 through 1988, paradoxically, the small businesses increased their employment numbers by a rather meagre 3 percent, but the large companies did even worse, showing no increase whatsoever.

Another factor that confounds the conclusions that can be drawn from statistics is that the jobs that are created may or may not survive past the first two or three years. They may have alleviated the unemployment of certain individuals for a brief period, but not have done much for the overall employment rate on a continuing scale. Statistics could be misleading because two new jobs would have been reported and one cancelled in the case of a single individual who started in a new job at one company, then left because of the collapse of that job and subsequently took another job in another small business. One person, but three numbers in the statistics! Going back to the figures for 1981 to 1984, Picot and Dupuy point out that if the numbers include the new jobs created in small companies that were *newly formed* during the four-year period, the small business sector would be shown to have *increased* its employment numbers by 12 percent, rather than showing the 14 percent *loss* in the companies that existed at the beginning of the period. Given the rapid rate of attrition of small business, as will be discussed later in this chapter, it may be questioned how many of the new jobs were still in existence five or ten years later.[5] Thus, job creation taken as a statistic in a vacuum may generate misleading conclusions.

This chapter looks at entrepreneurs and their growing role in business and management. It examines the uniqueness of entrepreneurship and entrepreneurs, and discusses how management principles are used by these individuals in ways that may differ from those usually used by managers who work in large organizations.

## The Entrepreneurial Environment

A nation's environment has a significant impact on the extent of its entrepreneurship.[6] As pointed out, the market women of the developing world are true entrepreneurs, but without access to capital, an efficient distribution system, and perhaps most of all a cultural inclination towards entrepreneurship, their broader entrepreneurial role will not progress rapidly. In contrast, immigrants who came to the New World were self-selected for qualities that led to entrepreneurship, whether in the sixteenth and seventeenth centuries in the Atlantic provinces and central Canada or in two waves in the early and later nineteenth century in the prairie provinces. In the rugged West, physical survival absolutely depended on self-reliance and a positive approach to what we now characterize as entrepreneurship. The prevailing mood of the day in the early nineteenth century was well expressed in the writings of the Unitarian social critic Ralph Waldo Emerson. In his famous essay, "On Self-Reliance," he emphasized concepts such as self-reliance, independence, and self-determination.[7] Nearly a century and a half later, a business scholar wrote: "[T]he controversy over what entrepreneurs are is far more than a debate about how to run a business. It is about how to lead and who is to lead."[8]

*In many countries of the developing world, women entrepreneurs are the mainstay of their families' income.*

New ideas spread globally, as was the case with solid state transistors. Researchers at the Western Electric Company invented the solid state transistor in 1947[9] but did not exploit it commercially. Six years later the company licensed the technology to Sony for a token $25,000. Immediately the transistor was transformed from a laboratory curiosity to a commercial necessity. A few years later RCA licensed several Japanese companies to make colour TVs—and that was the beginning of the end of colour TV production in North America. Going back nearly a century, Canadian Alexander Graham Bell invented a strange device that allowed the human voice to be carried over wires and then reconstituted at the other end. Unfortunately for possible Canadian investors, Bell was unable to raise enough capital in Canada to go into commercial production, so he founded the Bell Telephone Company in the United States, and it dominated telecommunications around the world for three-quarters of a century.

## Unsung Canadian Entrepreneurs

It is not always the inventor of a new product, the discoverer of a new concept, or the original entrepreneur who eventually profits from it or gets credit for it. Successful commercial exploitation requires more than just the idea. It requires capital, marketing expertise, and, in some cases, fortunate timing. Canadians have a long and illustrious history of innovation and invention, but often both Canadians and others have succumbed to the widespread assumption that, in general, inventions have originated either in the United States or in Japan. In some cases this assumption may be understandable because, like Alexander Graham Bell, Canadian entrepreneurs frequently have had to turn to the United States to finance the exploitation of their inventions because of the relative shortage of risk capital in Canada. In other cases the assumption is more difficult to understand.

Exhibit 13-1 lists a sampling of important Canadian inventors and their most notable inventions. Not surprisingly, the list reflects interests especially important to the Canadian economy over time, such as those involved in wheat drying, uranium mining, fog alarms, and the snowmobile. In many other cases, however, the inventions are worldwide in their impact, without any special reflection of Canadian emphases. Examples of these are the variable-pitch propeller, the development of insulin, the many inventions involving radio and broadcasting, and robotics technology, which was before its time when it was developed by Leaver more than a half-century ago, but which formed the basis of what is now nothing less than a revolution in manufacturing. For Canadian enterprises to remain competitive in the world economy, entrepreneurship and innovation must remain strong, and initiative must continue to be taken by Canadians who are willing to risk the hazards entailed in striking out on their own.

To help prepare those who lean towards entrepreneurship, or who are driven towards it by circumstances, Canadian colleges and universities offer courses in entrepreneurship, and some offer comprehensive year-long diploma programs.

**Exhibit 13-1**

*A Sampling of Unsung Canadian Inventors/Entrepreneurs*

| | | |
|---|---|---|
| Thomas Ahearn | 1899 | Electric cooking range |
| J. Armand Bombardier | 1937 | Snowmobile, steering vehicles by skis |
| Karl Adolf Clark | 1920s | Process for recovery of oil from oil sands |
| William Harrison Cook | 1950s | Process for drying wheat, saving wet crops |
| Georges-Édouard Desbarats | 1873 | Printing of half-tone photos; newspaper printing of photographic illustrations |
| Charles Fenerty | 1841 | Paper from wood pulp instead of only from rags |
| Ivan Graeme Ferguson | 1970 | Multiscreen projection, IMAX |
| John Bright Ferguson | 1950s | Inexpensive manufacture of optical glass |
| Reginal Aubrey Fessenden | 1906 | Superheterodyne principle, basis for all broadcasting |
| Robert Foulis | 1860 | Steam-operated automatic fog alarm and signal |
| Abraham Gesner | 1846, 1853 | Kerosene oil, coal oil lamp (foundation of the petroleum industry), wood preservative, method of making asphalt roads |
| William Wallace Gibson | 1910 | Twin engine airplane |
| Frederick Newton Gisborne | 1856, 1866 | First under water telegraph cable; first successful transatlantic cable |
| Sir Charles Frederick Goodeve | 1940 | Method to degauss ships to avoid magnetic mines |
| Uno Vilko Helava | 1963 | Analytic plotter to make maps from aerial photos, now basis for all mapping from satellites |
| George Klein | 1940s, 1970s | Effective wind tunnels; aiming methods for artillery; chief designer for Canadarm gears |
| Eric William Leaver | 1947 | Robotics technology of uranium mining and for manufacturing; later, portable Geiger counters |
| Lloyd William Pidgeon | 1941 | Previously unattainable high-purity magnesium |
| Frank Morse Robb | 1928 | Electronic organ based on photos of sound waves; cobalt "bomb" for cancer treatment |
| Edward Samuel Rogers | 1925 | Battery-powered home radios; later, method to reduce 60-cycle hum from power mains, making home radio reception practical |
| Sir William Samuel Stephenson | 1920s, 1940s | Radio facsimile (fax); wireless transmission of pictures; later, master spy "Intrepid" |
| Wallace Rupert Turnbull | 1927 | Variable-pitch airplane propeller |
| Thomas Leopold Willson | 1880s, 1892 | Dynamos in aluminum production; methods to produce bulk carbide and acetylene |

Sources: Thomas Carpenter, *Inventors: Profiles in Canadian Genius* (Willowdale, Ontario: Camden House, 1990); and Mel Hurtig (ed.), *The Canadian Encyclopedia* (Edmonton: Hurtig Publishers, 1985).

## Entrepreneurship in Organizations

There are countless examples of successful individual entrepreneurship, but for the truly revolutionary effects to be manifested quickly and make an impact in the increasingly competitive environment, often entrepreneurship eventually must have the support that only a larger organization can provide. Collective entrepreneurship involves close working relationships among many different people at all stages of the innovation, implementation, marketing, and later modification stages of an idea. Individual skills must be integrated into the group effort. The members of the group learn about each other, and the overall capacity of the group becomes greater than the sum of its parts.

Much publicity is given to the rags-to-riches stories of individuals such as Ray Kroc, the founder of McDonald's (who is reported to have suffered several cycles of personal bankruptcy from failed business ventures before acquiring his multimillion-dollar personal wealth). Obviously, these few examples are anything but the norm. Most individual entrepreneurship results in what may be a high degree of personal satisfaction, and often a comfortable income, but seldom makes headlines or changes the world. Although this chapter is devoted primarily to matters dealing with the individual entrepreneur, it would not be complete if it did not discuss the entrepreneurship spirit within large organizations. Some business authors use the term **intrapreneur** to describe someone who works in and for an organization, but who exhibits many of the same attitudes and approaches to life as entrepreneurs who are acting independently. This term may be used to describe any employee of an organization who is unusually innovative, and who uses that innovativeness to further the organization's goals and objectives.

As more organizations recognize the benefits they can gain from intrapreneurship, managers will have to challenge their own conventional thinking and develop new ways of organizing and managing. Human resource managers, in particular, must adjust their biases in order to employ and promote some employees who do not fit the conventional patterns. All managers also must reflect an orientation towards innovation and risk taking, apply flexibility in long-term planning, and emphasize overall flexibility, results over process, and active employee participation.[10]

**The skunkworks concept.**   Many of the conventional systems and concepts in modern corporations intentionally or unintentionally discourage innovation, and punish employees who act in ways that seem inimical to predictability and good order—the qualities that many managers seek but that drive many innovative people to distraction. Some large corporations have consciously addressed this problem by allowing the creation of **skunkworks**.[11] This term has been coined to describe an informal group of innovative employees who are permitted to digress temporarily from their regular tasks and "waste time" by dreaming of innovative ideas. They are encouraged to try out their innovations in pilot experiments, even if they have to use equipment and supplies that are "borrowed" from conventional operations. When an idea from a skunkworks shows promise, the denizens of the skunkworks turn it over to more conventional employees, who then develop it through normal channels of the organization. Members of a typical skunkworks spend most of their time and effort on what prove to be totally impractical ideas, but the few usable ideas that are developed are thought by management to be well worth the investment in people and money.[12]

## Intrapreneurship

Gifford Pinchot describes the intrapreneur as "a corporate commando who forms teams … that use company resources to work on their own pet projects."[13] It is true that intrapreneurs sometimes make things happen *in spite of* the organizational bureaucracy, but no organization can afford to have too many people who ignore or actively circumvent the organizational structure and lines of authority. Yet, any organization that wishes to be competitive must nurture and cherish those employees who show creative and productive imagination, and who constantly seek to improve how the organization func-

**intrapreneur**
An employee of an organization who exhibits the characteristics and actions of an entrepreneur.

**skunkworks**
An informal group of innovative employees who are permitted to digress temporarily from their regular tasks and "waste time" by dreaming of innovative ideas and trying them out in pilot experiments using equipment and supplies that may have been "borrowed" from conventional operations.

tions. Thus, the competitive challenge for managers is to find ways to encourage intrapreneurship, while at the same time applying sufficient control to ensure that the major thrust of the organization is directed to accomplishing its goals and objectives. As in most matters, the proverbial "Golden Mean" is the ideal, but is often elusive.

Art Fry, the 3M engineer who invented Post-it notes, is an example of a corporate entrepreneur, or intrapreneur. He first thought of semi-sticky paper as a church choir director, wanting to have page markers for hymnals that would neither damage the books nor slip out easily.[14] He worked on the idea during his spare time. After years of experimenting, he finally came upon a workable glue and a pad concept with tear-off edges. Today hundreds of millions of dollars worth of Post-it notes are sold. Fry's bent for innovation, and his perseverance, was of considerable benefit to his employer.

Research into the effectiveness of intrapreneurship such as this suggests that it may be a generally effective means for improving the organization's long-term organizational financial performance, especially when operating in unusually hostile environments.[15]

## Types of Intrapreneurship

Different types of entrepreneurships evolve within organizations.[16] There are at least five approaches to intrapreneurship: administrative, opportunistic, acquisitive, imitative, and incubative.

**champion**
A person who is highly committed and enthusiastic about an idea or innovation, who continues to present and defend it, and who authorizes or helps to secure needed resources to develop it and to move it from the laboratory to the market.

**Administrative intrapreneurship.** The use of a **champion**—someone who takes a leadership role and is positioned to help ensure the success of the idea or innovation—is almost essential for any intrapreneurial effort to succeed. The administrative champion may be in the R&D unit or may be a manager in another unit who views the idea or concept as important enough to invest time, energy, or creativity. Often the people who are most innovative are not especially adept at marshalling support within the organization, without which even the best of ideas can never come to fruition. For example, the Sony Walkman was invented by an R&D team at Sony, but a marketing team championed the Walkman system and pushed it to its current position as the industry standard. When an intrapreneur and a champion join forces, the combination often will be far more successful than if either individual acted without the other.

**Opportunistic intrapreneurship.** The thrust behind companies such as Tupperware and Mary Kay Cosmetics is to provide freedom for individuals to search for and seize opportunities. Representatives are encouraged not only to seek out new customers, and to develop loyal repeat customers, but also to find new ways to demonstrate their products. As they become more proficient and their personal innovations begin to bear fruit, their commissions increase commensurably. Other companies continually seek other outlets for their business, or new geographic areas into which expansion might be considered.

Mountain Equipment Co-op (MEC) has functioned on this theme since its founding in 1971 by a few inveterate hikers and mountaineers from the Varsity Outdoors Club of the University of British Columbia. In its first year it sold $12,000 of equipment solely for mountaineers. Now MEC sells all of the supplies and equipment that are coveted by skiers, cyclists, backpackers, kayakers, and canoeists, as well their original coterie of hikers and climbers. With stores in Vancouver, Calgary, Toronto, and Ottawa, and with a biennial catalogue (from which 12 percent of sales come), MEC's annual sales to its 648,000 members are approaching $100 million. This remarkable growth has come partly from MEC pursuing opportunities in ever-widening fields of outdoor sports, partly from its commitment to offer quality goods at reasonable prices, and partly from

*Optech, a high-tech company in North York, Ontario, was awarded the prestigious Canada Award for Business Excellence in Innovation. Allan Carswell, the company president, combines skills as an intrapreneur and as a champion to make innovation possible.*

its reputation for its support of environmentally aware projects, to which it contributes more than $250,000 in a typical year.[17]

**Acquisitive intrapreneurship.** Some companies encourage a strategy of courting other companies that have knowledge, ideas, or promising products. Magna International, BCE, Bombardier, and others have created joint ventures or new subsidiaries or have added innovative product lines to their portfolios through acquisitions. Acquiring other companies or establishing new joint ventures requires entrepreneurial thinking and action. First, the market must be scrutinized constantly to find promising targets. Then, after details of a target's operations are learned, intrapreneurs must imagine what differences the potential acquisition might make in the parent company. As a final step before launching into the acquisition, the intrapreneurs must decide how to integrate the acquisition into the parent company— who will be primarily responsible, how the organizational structure will be modified, and how the new acquisition will meld with the existing parts of the parent company.

**Imitative intrapreneurship.** In this form of intrapreneurship, the manager observes the ideas, products, and technology of another organization, adapts them for use, and then tries to improve on them incrementally. Sometimes the imitation takes the form of doing exactly what the other organization was doing, but doing so in a different geographic area. In other cases the intrapreneur simulates but does not exactly copy the other organization's activities. When the first franchised donut shop demonstrated that the idea was a success, a plethora of other donut shops promptly opened. The result exemplified the old adage that even if a little is good, a lot may not be better for anyone. After a relatively brief period, donut shops were facing so many competitors that only the best were making the kind of profits that were enjoyed early in the cycle. Soon donut shops found that to stay competitive they had to expand their lines, adding fancier donuts, muffins, cookies, and eventually items such as soup, sandwiches, and wraps.

Another old adage says that imitation is the sincerest form of flattery. Even so, many entrepreneurs would be happy to continue without this form of flattery. They do their utmost to make it difficult for competitors to imitate their successes. One company that does so is the maker of Slick 50, an oil additive that is touted by its devoted users as having amazing restorative properties for tired car engines. The ingredients in Slick 50 are a closely guarded secret—so closely guarded that even the company's CEO is said not to know them. Potential competitors have tried to analyze the product—after all, the concept of imitative intrapreneurship demands it—but so far have been unsuccessful.[18]

**Incubative intrapreneurship.** The incubative version of entrepreneurship involves subjecting a new idea, technology, or innovation to experimentation and testing. Does it really work? Is it good? What risks are involved? The incubative champions are considered a semiautonomous new venture development unit that can either take the product from development to market or abandon it if it appears unworkable.

The classification system used to describe corporate entrepreneurship, or intrapreneurship, shows that opportunities to be self-reliant and creative can exist in most organizations, whether in business or in not-for-profit organizations, regardless of their size.

## Real World Reflection  13-1

### The Roles of Internal Consultants in Organizations

The internal consultant can function in many roles, ranging from the expert at one end of the continuum to the process facilitator at the other end. At one phase of the consulting cycle, the internal consultant may be more of a technical expert. At another point, he or she may be more process-oriented. An opportunity for internal consulting may present itself through an organization, involving employees, past employees, or other external advocates for an organization.

There are multiple roles for the internal consultant. These include the advocate, the information specialist, the trainer and educator, the joint problem solver, the identifier of alternatives, the fact finder, and the process consultants.

Some organizations recognize the value of tapping internal entrepreneurial talent. To do this they either may create explicit positions or just make time available for innovative "consulting" by employees who occupy various positions.

Contributed by Sherry Campbell, British Columbia Institute of Technology.

The challenge for organizations is to attract, retain, reward, and support the individuals who can move products from the idea stage to commercial success. The entrepreneurial environonment of an organization will either encourage or discourage successful innovations. Large companies are becoming smaller or are being divided into smaller, cohesive units. They are becoming more responsive to change and more tolerant of champions who challenge the accepted routines and patterns of doing business. Global competition probably will encourage even more of all five types of intrapreneurship or corporate entrepreneurship.

Joseph Schumpeter, the classical economist, said that the job of the entrepreneur is "creative destruction." He meant, of course, that the entrepreneur is the one who challenges the status quo, disregards the naysayers, and transforms opportunity into success. Entrepreneurs and intrapreneurs seek to change the economic and organizational equilibrium. They are driven by a vision of success that propels them over obstacles, around dead ends, and on to success if it can possibly be achieved.

After discussing entrepreneurship, intrapreneurship, and the five categories of corporate entrepreneurship, we might conclude that there is no one best description of an entrepreneur. Peter Drucker described the entrepreneurial role as one of gathering and using resources, but he added that to produce results "resources" must be allocated to opportunities rather than to problems.[19] Redirection of resources is an important concept in illustrating how entrepreneurs differ from traditional managers.

## The Small Business Entrepreneur

Usually when one speaks of an entrepreneur one is referring to the proprietor of a small business. In this usage, the term describes a person who initiates a small business and sets its patterns of operation and growth. The entrepreneur in small business will have the satisfaction and perhaps the recognition that comes with success, and at the same

## Management in the Real World    13-1

### Entrepreneurship Provides Refuge for Outplaced Middle Manager

The decade of the 1990s has been indelibly marked by the pain and suffering of thousands of middle managers who suddenly found themselves without jobs. Corporate downsizing, along with outsourcing of many formerly in-house roles, has put a large number of talented managers out on the street. And while many of them were able to find new jobs with other companies, the vast majority have had to restructure their careers. Many have decided never again to be the victim of large corporation "cost saving." They have opted to regenerate new careers in the world of entrepreneurship.

This trend towards new careers as independent entrepreneurs has been studied by a number of people. Harvard professor John Kotter studied the careers of 115 members of the Harvard Business School 1974 graduating class. By most measures, this is a successful group. Their median 1994 income was $260,000 and median net worth was $1.2 million. How did they do it? Kotter found that the best off followed eight simple rules:

- Do not rely on convention; career paths that were winners for most of this century are often no longer providing much success.
- Keep your eyes on globalization and its consequences.
- Move towards the small and entrepreneurial and away from the big and bureaucratic.
- Help big business from the outside as well as on the inside.
- Do not just manage; now you must also lead.

- Wheel and deal if you can.
- Increase your competitive drive.
- Never stop trying to grow; lifelong learning is increasingly necessary for success.

When the organizing principle of many companies today seems to be ceaseless reorganization, it's hard to know what a career is, let alone how to keep yours on track. University of Southern California professor of leadership Warren Bennis counsels that careers today should focus on projects and competencies instead of on titles. He says, "People will be evaluated not vertically according to rank and status, but flexibly according to competence. Organizational charts will consist of project groups rather than stratified functional groups."

It's clear that career paths are changing. Time was when many business school students, when asked about their future careers, projected themselves into a comfortable middle management position in some major corporation. That option has become increasingly scarce, and many students are preparing themselves for the new, more entrepreneurial workplace of the future. What are you doing to be ready for a flexible, rapidly changing career track that will involve more risk, more creativity, and more tough decisions than those of the previous generation?

Sources: Adapted from John P. Kotter, *The New Rules* (Cambridge, MA: Harvard Business School Press, 1995); Thomas A. Stewart, "Planning a Career in a World Without Managers," *Fortune* (March 20, 1995): 72-80.

time takes the risk of failure. There is no universally accepted definition of the term small business. The agencies of the federal and provincial governments use slightly different definitions, depending perhaps on economic and political purposes and the uses to which the definition will be put. Some of these definitions are based on the number of employees—25 or less is typical—or on the number of owners combined with maximum levels of sales or assets. Revenue Canada applies a definition for Canadian small business tax rates and for assessing personal taxes on shareholders that is based on both maximum revenue and total assets. For some of its studies and reports, Statistics Canada uses one definition; for others, the definition is somewhat different. Various authors use still different definitions. But for the purposes of this text, it matters little what the exact definition might be as long as the term is used to describe a business that has something like 25 or fewer employees, perhaps $2 million or less in annual revenues, and no more than perhaps five owners.

It also should be noted that some entrepreneurs start businesses that are small but that outgrow any definition of "small." Ray Kroc of McDonald's, Bill Gates of Microsoft, and many others did just that, yet few would deny that they were always entrepreneurs, even though their scopes changed and in some respects so did their methods of operation, as well as their personal fortunes!

## Risks of Small Business Entrepreneurs

It is sometimes said that 75 or 80 percent of small businesses fail within the first five years. Like many widely quoted statistics, the accuracy of this statement is open to challenge. A number of studies have shown that only 25, or even only 20, percent of small businesses started still exist in the same form five years later. But does this mean that all of the other small businesses fail? Some entrepreneurs work hard and manage to survive but not to build enough net income to be worth the effort. After a few years, they will decide to close the business after paying off all of their creditors. In contrast, others make substantial profits and then merge with or sell out to another company, thus disappearing as an entity. Other entrepreneurs enjoy three or four years of what many would call success, and then just decide to try something else, perhaps selling their interest or just dropping the original venture entirely. Other entrepreneurs encounter bad health or just retire. One or two may have quit a thriving business when they win a large lottery or inherit more money than they knew what to do with. All of these businesses will be counted in the 75 or 80 percent statistic of "failures," yet they have had histories completely different from those small businesses that actually became bankrupt, with the entrepreneurs and creditors suffering losses as a result. Thus, it may be seen that in

*Sole proprietors have the satisfaction of running their own businesses, but in exchange, at least in the early years, usually must work long hours with little financial reward.*

this, as in many oft-quoted statistics, it is necessary to consider the definitions employed and whether the raw data really represent what may be inferred from a casual look at the numbers.

Despite these quibbles, it is undisputed that within their first few years of operation many small businesses fail, by even the most restrictive meaning of the word. Of those that actually fail (that is, closing while unable to meet their financial obligations) perhaps as many as 20 percent collapse within their first year of operation. Most of the other real failures occur within the first three years, but after that the annual failure rates fall dramatically. To state these figures another way, if a new small business manages to survive the first three years it is likely to be able to continue for a relatively long future.[20]

## Reasons for Failure

Whatever rate of failure one accepts as representative, it is high enough to serve as a caution to any entrepreneur who contemplates starting a small business. Interestingly, a number of studies and some of the statistics gathered by Statistics Canada suggest that small businesses that are started by female entrepreneurs have about twice the survival rates of those started by male entrepreneurs.[21] Various observers have suggested at least three differences that possibly may account for this striking gender-based disparity. One is that lending institutions traditionally have been more reluctant to lend to women than to men. While this discrimination is hardly a boon to women, in a perverse way it may account for some of the difference in failure rates. If one group, in this case female entrepreneurs, has more difficulty getting loans than another group, in this case male entrepreneurs, this may help prevent the female entrepreneurs from overborrowing. It is a well-established fact that one of the major reasons for small business failure is that the entrepreneurs have taken on an insupportable debt load. Perhaps the gender differential has had the beneficial effect of weeding out more of the shaky loans applied for by women than the equally shaky loans applied for by men.

Perhaps another explanation, which may arise in part from the first, is that women as entrepreneurs typically tend to be more cautious and conservative in their financial decisions than men as entrepreneurs. The tendency of entrepreneurs of both sexes is to

---

### Real World Reflection   13-2

#### The Role of Failure in Succeeding

Who would have thought that Walt Disney was fired from a newspaper for not being creative enough? Some of the biggest winners in life were also failures, especially among entrepreneurs, whose profile and strengths are often liabilities in highly structured environments. For most entrepreneurs failure is an early step towards success.

The way in which one deals with failure often will determine resilience and future success. Understanding how one views personal success or failure or one's "locus of control," is a powerful insight for many managers. Many individuals attribute luck (either good or bad) to the events in their life, rather than taking personal responsibility for both their success and failures.

Contributed by Marnie Wright, British Columbia Institute of Technology.

be optimistic, and indeed that is an essential ingredient for entrepreneurship. However, for women this optimism may be tempered somewhat by socialization not to "bet the farm"—as contrasted with the socialization of men to be more willing to take risks and be less concerned about consequences. Of course, this is not to say that all women are more cautious than all men, but only that fewer businesses owned by women have expensive new furniture and the latest in computer hardware and software than similar businesses owned by men.

Still another possible explanation is that several researchers have found that women tend to start up businesses in which they have already had some experience while employed by others, whereas men are more likely to start businesses in which they have enthusiasm and probably interest as consumers, but little or no experience in the business side of the industry. This difference between the genders may be changing, as more women are entering types of business previously occupied almost exclusively by men.[22]

*A woman who has worked for a nursery may take those skills and start up a business of her own.*

Whatever the gender differences may be, it is demonstrable that prudence, caution, and background knowledge are almost indispensable qualities for an entrepreneur to expect reasonable success in starting a small business. It behooves both men and women who are considering launching a new business venture to heed these warnings, and to consider how to benefit from the implications disclosed by the different failure rates of the two genders.

Studies of the reasons for small business failure tend to list a number of identified causes. A recent Statistics Canada study reported that most small business failures were the result of the entrepreneur having neglected the basics. Seven out of ten failures were linked to bad financial planning, including a failure to develop an adequate business plan.[23] Exhibit 13-2 on page 470 provides a more detailed list of 16 of the most common reasons for the failures of small business. Most of these reasons reflect one or more of three generalizations:

- Lack of management skills, including an inability to understand financial reports;
- Inadequate financing, especially if initial growth is relatively fast; and
- Gross overoptimism about sales potential, reflecting a lack of ability in forecasting markets and an underestimation of the competition.

Besides considerable business risk, entrepreneurs face significant *financial risk*, as they typically invest most if not all of their financial resources in the business. This commitment of personal funds may stem from their optimism and their personal commitment to the business. More often they have no choice because lending institutions almost invariably require that small business owners personally guarantee the lines of credit and other forms of loans that are made to the business. Thus, entrepreneurs usually have at risk not only the amounts they have directly invested in their businesses, but also their houses, cars, and other assets that likely will be seized by the banks if the businesses default on their loans.

In addition to the financial risks, entrepreneurs take a *career risk* when they leave a secure job for a venture with a highly uncertain future. They also incur *family and social risks*. In this connection, one study by Canadian think-tank Environics found that the median work week for entrepreneurs fell between 60 and 69 hours.[24] Such work loads

**Exhibit 13-2**

*Common Reasons for Small Business Failure*

- *Capital.* Businesses that start undercapitalized have a greater chance of failure than those with adequate capital.

- *Record Keeping and Financial Control.* Firms that do not keep updated accurate records and lack adequate financial controls have a greater chance of failure than those that do.

- *Industry Experience.* Startups managed by people without prior industry experience have a greater chance of failure than those managed by people with such experience.

- *Management Experience.* Startups managed by people without prior management experience have a greater chance of failure than those with experienced management.

- *Planning.* Startups that do not develop specific business plans have a greater chance of failure than those with such plans.

- *Professional Advisers.* Startups that do not use professional advisers have a greater chance of failure than those that use them.

- *Education.* People without any college education who start a business have a greater chance of failing than people with one or more years of college education.

- *Staffing.* Organizations that cannot attract and retain quality employees have a greater chance of failure than those that are more successful and retain quality in this regard.

- *Product/Service Timing.* Firms that select products or services that are too new or too old have a greater chance of failure than firms that select products or services that are in the growth stage.

- *Economic Timing.* Firms that start up during a recession are more apt to fail than those launched during an expansion period.

- *Stereotypical Gender Behaviour.* Men are more likely to fail than women.

- *Age.* Younger entrepreneurs are more likely to fail than older ones.

- *Partners.* A business started by one person has a greater chance of failure than a business started by more than one person.

- *Parents.* Startup owners whose parents did not own a business have a greater chance of failure than those whose parents owned a business.

- *Minority.* Minorities have a greater chance of failure than non-minorities.

- *Marketing.* Startup owners without marketing skills have a greater chance of failure than those with marketing skills.

place heavy strains on marriages and friendships. Entrepreneurs also assume *psychological risks*—the risks that arise from a deep sense of personal failure if the business doesn't beat the odds and succeed.[25] One highly successful entrepreneur succinctly summed up the considerable personal risks of entrepreneurship by describing the emotions of launching a business as "entrepreneurial terror."[26]

Given this intimidating list of reasons why a small business might fail, one might wonder why anyone would risk becoming an entrepreneur. The next section explores some of those reasons.

## Motivations of Entrepreneurs

While risks and potential costs are high, rewards also can be substantial. Entrepreneurs launch businesses because of one or more entrepreneurial motivations: for independence, for personal and professional growth, as a superior alternative to an unsatisfying job, for increased income, for expected security, or to "make a difference."

**Desire for independence.** "Being my own boss" is a powerful motivator for many entrepreneurs who seek the freedom to act independently in their work. As heads of businesses, they enjoy the autonomy of making their own decisions, setting their own work hours, and determining what they will do and when they will do it. It would be a mistake, however, to interpret this to mean that entrepreneurs allow themselves much leisure time. A Canadian Business Development Bank survey confirms the Statistics Canada figures mentioned above concerning work weeks, and adds that entrepreneurs averaged less than two weeks of vacation per year, which is substantially less than is found in almost any other segment of the workplace.[27]

In theory, sole owners of businesses are completely independent in that they can make whatever business decisions they wish—subject, of course, to very real practical controls from their bankers, suppliers, employees and unions, landlords, and customers. As one entrepreneur has said, "When I left my job and started my own company I traded one boss for a thousand bosses. But the trade was a good one because now if I want to, I can tell any one of my present thousand bosses to get lost!"

**Desire for personal or professional growth.** The challenges of building a business inevitably involve individual growth. To succeed, an entrepreneur must be able to cope with risk, uncertainty, and stress, to handle many different interpersonal relationships, and to manage a business with limited resources. Many individuals become entrepreneurs to experience this growth and the fulfilment gained from building a business into a purposeful, productive entity. At the end of a career, the typical successful entrepreneur can say with pride, "This business is my creation." The desire to feel that pride is another strong motivator, especially for the middle manager in a large organization who begins to feel that no single person's contribution makes much of a difference in the overall organization. One of the most crucial lessons of entrepreneurship is that one can develop a sense of purpose that propels one forward.[28] This sense of purpose can bring meaning to the entrepreneur's life outside of the business as well.

*One of the benefits of being an entrepreneur is setting your own schedule and being able to take care of family issues as needed.*

**As a preferable alternative to a routine job.** Many entrepreneurs establish businesses as an alternative that they perceive as being superior to unsatisfying jobs to which they otherwise feel condemned. A survey conducted more than a decade ago of the CEOs of the *Inc.* 500 (the 500 fastest-growing private companies) found that, for these executives, frustration with working in large companies was the primary motivator for starting a business.[29] The CEOs of the private companies to which they had jumped were dissatisfied with the situations in their earlier large corporations, with slow decision making, bureaucracy, and their limited autonomy as managers. Other entrepreneurs who felt that they had reached a plateau in their previous jobs have launched businesses as a second career, after taking early retirement.[30] These entrepreneurs bring to their new ventures many years of business experience and professional contacts.

Since that survey was taken, a relatively new phenomenon has emerged—the young entrepreneur, often just out of, or still within, college or university. These entrepreneurs, many of whose recent predecessors have experienced remarkable success, are reported

## *What Managers Are Reading*    13-2

### How to Think Like an Entrepreneur

This book provides valuable insight on how to become a successful entrepreneur. Written in a simple and straightforward manner, the book advises aspiring entrepreneurs on how to get needed information and how to use it. Relying on his experience and wisdom, Michael B. Shane tells his readers how to use information instead of money as the essential tool to build an entrepreneurial business. According to Shane, new business ventures today often don't revolve around money, but around information.

In addition, the book provides insights into negotiating, planning, evaluating the competition, and creating a business plan with the three fundamental "M"s of successful entrepreneurship—Marketing, Management, and Money. The decision-making process is identified by three categories of business decisions: (1) superficial decisions, (2) gut decisions, and (3) knowledge decisions.

The 140-page book also emphasizes that the customer is the source of success, security, and independence for the entrepreneur. Successful entrepreneurs must commit themselves to the customer above all else. Behind every successful entrepreneur there are happy, satisfied customers who are the driving force in the business.

Although the title of the book invites the attention of entrepreneurs, it contains lessons that carry a message to the management and CEOs of every large or small business operation.

Source: Adapted from Michael B. Shane, *How to Think Like an Entrepreneur* (White Plains, NY: Bret Publishing, 1995); "How to Think Like an Entrepreneur," *National Public Accountant* (April 1995): 13.

to have become entrepreneurs primarily for two reasons. One is the mirror image of the reasons stated by the CEOs of the new venture companies cited in the survey in the previous paragraph—that they do not want to become part of what they see as a massive, intractable, and inflexible bureaucracy in a large corporation. The other reason is more pragmatic and less philosophical. Many of today's graduates either have experienced or expect to experience great difficulty in finding a job in their chosen careers. Almost out of necessity, they have started small businesses, often as an interim measure while continuing to search for the "right" job. Many have found the experience satisfying, and now would not trade their present situations for the apparently greater security but lesser autonomy of working for someone else. The founders (and still principals) of Mountain Equipment Co-op, described earlier in this chapter, may fall into this category.

Many female entrepreneurs report poor advancement opportunities in conventional employment as their major reason for launching a business.[31] One-third of the female executives of the *Inc.* 500 companies cite their inability to move up as a major motivator for becoming an entrepreneur. This is twice the percentage of male managers who report this reason.[32] Hélène Boyer, a single mother, illustrates this point. She had finished an apprenticeship in auto mechanics, but found that on the job she was relegated to such tasks as sweeping floors. With another female auto mechanic, Renée Lapointe, she opened an auto repair business in Montreal called Les Femmes Mécanos, or The Women Mechanics. They promptly hired another woman as an apprentice, thus offering opportunity to another gender-blocked would-be mechanic. Like these three, an increasing number of women are challenging the traditional types of careers that are "socially approved" for women.[33]

Other women have tired of the "corporate grind" that can be exceptionally difficult for women managers with children. They view running a business as ultimately providing the flexibility needed to have children as well as a professional career. These trends have contributed to a boom in women entrepreneurship. According to Women Entrepreneurs of Canada, approximately one-fifth of medium-sized business in Canada are owned exclusively by women entrepreneurs, and another 27 percent have joint female and male ownership. The same organization reports that women-owned companies are growing at twice the rate of all businesses.[34]

**Desire for more income.**  Some entrepreneurs are enticed by the sizeable profits that a highly successful business can provide, although such outcomes are the exception rather than the rule. But many beginning entrepreneurs are more realistic and do not rate money as their primary motivation for starting a business. The surveyed *Inc.* 500 entrepreneurs ranked money fourth in importance, after frustration with working for traditional organizations, independence, and control of one's life.

**Need for security.**  Given the substantial risks and uncertainties of entrepreneurship, personal security may seem like an unlikely motivator. But in a time of much corporate downsizing and layoffs, some entrepreneurs, especially those in the middle and latter stages of their corporate careers, view running their own business as a more secure alternative. Often they take advantage of buy-out packages offered by their corporate employers to encourage them to take early retirement, and use the funds as startup investment for their own entrepreneurial businesses. These mid-career and later entrepreneurs are able to apply the lessons they have learned in their earlier careers and to make use of the business contacts they have made already. They do face a shock, however, as they discover that important but mundane tasks such as filing, photocopying, addressing envelopes, and making reservations for airline flights and restaurant meals— all of which were done invisibly by office staff members in the large corporation—are now the lot of the entrepreneurs, who cannot afford the support staff to which they had been accustomed.

**Desire to "make a difference."**  Another group of people who choose entrepreneurship over employment in larger organizations do so out of a desire to achieve something positive for society as a whole. The risk, of course, is that in trying to make a difference the managers may fall into the trap of thinking that good motives will make up for any failure to apply sound business practices. If they take a hard-headed business approach along with their commendable altruism, the additional dedication and positive outlook are good qualities that may help to ensure their success.

## Entrepreneurial Characteristics

A number of studies have been conducted to determine whether entrepreneurs differ in personality and other characteristics from managers and the public at large. It is difficult to draw generalizations from this research because the studies differ in their definitions of entrepreneur. In Chapter 1 it was pointed out that there was little uniformity in similar studies that attempted to discover common characteristics of managers. The studies of entrepreneurial characteristics show slightly more consistency than those of managers, probably because there are some fundamental issues that every entrepreneur must address, whereas the environments in which managers function vary more from one to another. Within their environments all entrepreneurs face a high degree of uncertainty and risk, a need for self-reliance, and situations in which the praise or blame cannot be avoided or even shared. For these environmental reasons, some evidence exists for a few characteristics that are shared by many entrepreneurs to a greater degree than by other types of managers and by the public at large.[35]

Several studies agree that entrepreneurs possess a significantly greater need for independence and autonomy than do managers. Other studies have pictured the entrepreneur as having a substantial need to achieve and a tolerance for ambiguity—the ability to handle uncertain situations. Many entrepreneurs also have high energy and endurance, substantial self-esteem, and a strong dominance thrust and need for power and influence. Several studies also found that entrepreneurs have a lower need for social support than do most managers. This characteristic is often revealed by their disinterest in joining non-business organizations and their discomfort in situations where they have to work in a team. Another common characteristic is that entrepreneurs who succeed usually have an internal locus of control—that is, that they feel that they are primarily in control of their lives, rather than thinking that external circumstances are the primary factors.[36] Exhibit 13-3 lists some of the personal characteristics that are often found in successful entrepreneurs. It should be emphasized that many successful entrepreneurs do not fit this profile; nor does a person who fits this profile necessarily find success as an entrepreneur.

The next section describes how many successful entrepreneurs use or adapt their personal characteristics to guide the formation and growth of their business ventures.

**Exhibit 13-3**

*Personal Characteristics Often Found in Successful Entrepreneurs*

| | |
|---|---|
| Self-confident and optimistic | Energetic and diligent |
| Able to take calculated risk | Creative, achievement-oriented |
| Responds positively to challenges | Dynamic leader |
| Flexible and able to adapt | Responsive to suggestions |
| Knowledgeable of markets | Uses initiative |
| Able to get along well with others | Resourceful and persevering |
| Independent-minded | Perceptive with foresight |
| Possesses versatile knowledge | Responsive to criticism |
| Assertive but not aggressive | |

Source: Adapted from John A. Hornaday. "Research about Living Entrepreneurs," in *Encyclopedia of Entrepreneurship*, ed. Calvin A. Kent, Donald L. Sexton, and Karl H. Vesper (Englewood Cliffs NJ: Prentice-Hall, 1982): 28. Adapted with permission.

## The Stages of Business Growth

Taking an idea, working with it, and eventually turning it into a business or product is seldom an orderly process. The steps through the process are often unplanned, are outside the entrepreneur's total control, and may occur haphazardly. The sequence of events is different for each product or service and for each entrepreneur. Yet, in general, the movement of an idea from its origination to its fruition in a functioning business follows a four-stage model. Exhibit 13-4 shows these four stages, as described by David Holt.

**Exhibit 13-4**   *Holt's Four-stage Growth Model*

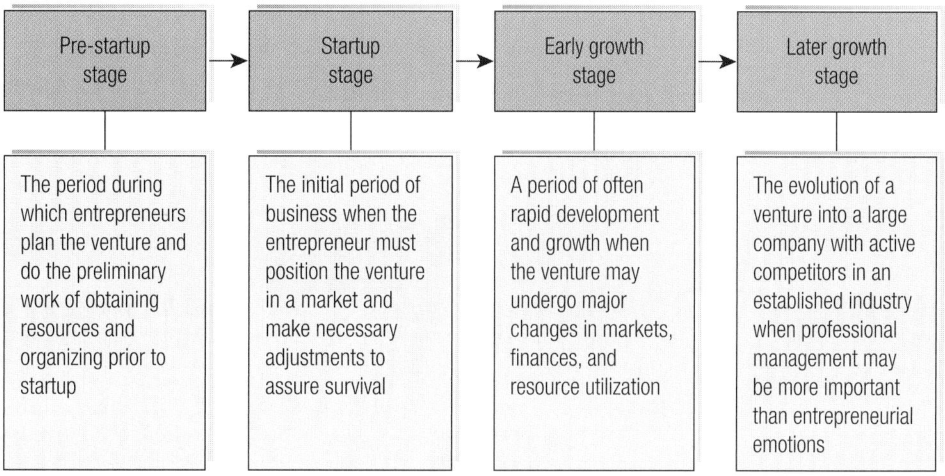

Source: Adapted from David H. Holt. *Entrepreneur* (Englewood Cliffs, NJ: Prentice Hall, 1992): 104.

## Pre-startup Stage

Exhibit 13-5 on page 476 presents four essential pre-startup activities: defining the business concept, analyzing the product market, planning the financing, and pre-startup implementation.

First, the entrepreneur must consider whether the product or service will be needed or wanted by its intended users. That entails determining whether it is an improvement on what is already available in the market. To be competitive, it must be better, more available, more attractive, or less expensive. Then the market must be analyzed, to determine whether, regardless of quality, availability, and price, there are enough people who will seek the product or service. All of this information must be reflected in realistic financial projections, break-even calculations, and assessments of the funds that will be available. Finally, if the indications are still positive, the entrepreneur must make detailed plans and commence initial contacts. These will include preliminary negotiations with suppliers, perhaps pilot production runs and test marketing, initial hiring, preparation of marketing and advertising programs, investigations of sites and facilities, and establishment of operating and management systems.

One of the key factors in a new-venture startup is the industry in which it will operate. The strengths, weaknesses, opportunities, and threats that exist in that industry will have profound impacts on the new business. A strategic position in a growing and dynamic industry is a positive sign. However, in an industry that is mature or declining, even the most able entrepreneur may find it impossible to succeed.[37] Equally important is an analysis of the existing competition, and of changes that are likely to occur in it. These and other vital facts and predictions will be reflected in the entrepreneur's business plan, which will be described in a later section of this chapter.

At this stage, the entrepreneur must curb the natural tendency to be unduly optimistic and, instead, heed all of the warning signs that appear but that it is tempting to disregard. Sound advice on this point appears in Philip B. Crosby's reminiscence (see Management in the Real World 13-2 on page 477).

**Exhibit 13-5**  *Four Essential Pre-startup Activities*

| Business concept defined | What is the purpose of the business? What does the entrepreneur want to accomplish with the business? |
|---|---|

| Product-market study | Product research: Is the product or service needed? Realistic? Market research: Who will buy? Where are they? What niche? What competitors exist? |
|---|---|

| Financial planning | Financial projections: What cash is needed? How will income be generated? What expenses are expected? What is invested? Borrowed? What is needed to meet operating requirements? |
|---|---|

| Pre-startup implementation | Getting ready to start: The entrepreneur must find resources, purchase beginning inventory, hire those needed at startup, and obtain necessary licences, permits, leases, facilities, and equipment. |
|---|---|

Source: Adapted from David H. Holt. *Entrepreneur* (Englewood Cliffs, NJ: Prentice Hall, 1992): 105.

## Startup Stage

This is the initial period of operations. During this stage the entrepreneur acts to meet the objectives set in the pre-startup stage. Examples of objectives in terms of sales, growth, and position might be:

- *Sales:* To attain monthly sales volume as forecasted in the pre-startup stage;
- *Growth:* To increase monthly sales by at least 5 percent each month during the first year of business; and
- *Position:* To capture at least 10 percent of the market share at the medium-priced end of the market within 15 months after starting the business.

Ideally, the predictions will have been sufficiently accurate and conservative that the business will meet its sales, growth, and position objectives. Meeting these objectives, however, may not mean that a profit will be earned. Most businesses post losses in the first year, or perhaps the first few years, of operations. Recognizing this probability, it is essential for the entrepreneur to have arranged at the outset for sufficient capital to cover expenses and not to have proceeded until adequate financial arrangements were in place.

**Management in the Real World   13-2**

## Entrepreneurship and Growth: Reflections by Philip Crosby

I had lunch with my old friend Herman Advent while I was in his city on business. Herman had worked in a big corporation and I had gotten to know him when I did some consulting with the firm a few years back. He was now out on his own and had set up a new business. I had assumed that he was doing well but it only took one look at his face to know that the sun wasn't shining everywhere.

After exchanging greetings and ordering lunch we sat quietly while I waited to hear his story. It's much better to just sit smiling rather than begin to interrogate the subject in cases like this. I wasn't disappointed.

"I always thought business wasn't too tough," he said, "but I've sure learned a lot the hard way since starting my own company."

"How are things going?" I asked.

"Not well at all. We're on the edge of going under. The bank isn't interested in extending the line of credit, and the payroll is getting harder to meet every week. We just need more time: I know the business is there, but I'm running out of money.

"You know," he remembered, "that the old man always said the worst thing to do was run out of money."

I nodded.

"Did you have enough money at the beginning?" I asked.

"Apparently not," he replied. "I thought, with my savings and with the money the bank loaned me using my home and stocks as security, that we'd have enough. But there were a lot of startup costs. A venture group is willing to give me some more but they want a big hunk of the operation. It's back-to-the-wall time."

He sighed.

"What did you spend the startup money on?" I asked. He looked surprised.

"Why, 'starting up,' of course. I needed an office, computers, marketing manager, production people, secretaries, and such. Why do you ask?"

"Well, most beginning companies use money for facilities and things they don't need rather than using it to buy time. The goal needs to be to create a cash flow that pays for stuff rather than trying to be five years old at the start."

He had a puzzled expression.

"But we had a business plan."

"And I suspect that you've met it in every spending aspect, but haven't met the revenue projections. Right?"

He nodded.

"That's what happens, particularly to those of us who come out of big corporations. We think it's just numbers, but it's really blood. Money is nourishment, not a scorekeeping device. Business plans use up all the time and money."

"So what should I do?"

"Get rid of everything that doesn't involve a customer. Sell out of the trunk of your car if necessary. All you need are customers, and when they force you to have an office and all those people, they'll be willing to pay for them.

"Don't give up your company to the venture people, and don't plan on increased revenues to save you. Cut the costs, do only what's absolutely necessary. Get real instead of conventional. First the pushcart, then the department store."

"Who said that?" he asked.

"I'm not certain," I replied, "but someone should."

"I feel better and I'm going to go back and do exactly that. We just might make it. As part of this new program I'm going to let you pay for lunch."

"Happily," I said, "happily."

After a brief startup period, the entrepreneur should reconsider the goals and objectives that were originally planned. Operating experience probably will have shown that some of the original thinking has not been borne out, and that some minor, or even major, adjustments would be desirable. Toronto's Sporting Life store is an example of the benefit of rethinking at an early stage. In 1979, when Sporting

Life opened its first store, the owners/entrepreneurs planned to have advertised sales perhaps only twice a year. Dr. Brian McGrath, one of the three partners in the firm, describes that decision as "a downright disaster." He explains that "No matter what else you're offering, that customer has got to feel like he's getting a great deal." As a consequence of their change of direction, Sporting Life began publishing frequent ads offering 20 to 50 percent off of regular prices on selected merchandise. David Russel, another of the three partners, describes an additional change of direction, from carrying run-of-the-mill sports clothing and accessories to carrying prestige lines. The third partner, Patti Russel, devotes her time and energy to keeping up with, and often ahead of, fashion trends. As a result of their flexibility and willingness to change from their original concepts, these three partners have created a highly successful, well-respected enterprise that never would have been possible had they stubbornly stuck with their original plans.[38]

*Sporting Life is one firm that reconsidered its original goals and objectives and became a great success.*

Another crucial feature of this stage is to reevaluate the whole concept, to ensure that it includes a clear definition of the **niche** the business intends to occupy. By niche is meant the special characteristics of the planned business that set it apart from all of the similar businesses that presently exist, and that, for a reasonable period, will set it apart from the new competitors that will enter the market. The niche may include the provision of a new product or service, its provision in a different geographical area, its provision in a form that is more acceptable to potential customers, its provision at a lower cost, or some other basic characteristic that will cause customers either to leave their present sources of supply or to decide to patronize the new venture for a product or service that they do not purchase from anyone currently.

**niche**
The special characteristics of the planned business that set it apart from all of the similar businesses that presently exist and that, for a reasonable period, will set it apart from the new competitors that will enter the market.

An example of the niche strategy is reflected in the history of Aftech Inc. (which stands for Automated Financial Technology), a company that was discussed in some detail in Case 6-2. Aftech choose a narrow niche, but one that is occupied by 12 major vendors and more than 100 smaller vendors—to design and provide software systems for credit unions. Since its modest founding in 1980 (with roots going back to 1969) Lloyd Milner and his partner, Bill Guisey, together with two employees, have built Aftech until it is sixth-largest in its field in the United States, employing 100 mostly high-tech people. A true entrepreneur, Lloyd Milner explains Aftech's success as the result of having been able to differentiate themselves from all of the other companies with similar capabilities. That differentiation, he explains, is based on service, on always being available online to its customer credit unions. Another example of service is Aftech's ability to install a new system without disrupting service, instead of requiring a period of downtime in which the credit union's customers would be unable to have access to their accounts on the system.

Milner points out that in the early years, he and his partner suffered a severe financial drain, worked incredibly long hours, and *had fun*.[39] It is this unquenchable enthusiasm at the early stages of a venture when money is tight and unforeseen problems are constantly cropping up, that, more than almost any other characteristic, may distinguish entrepreneurs from other managers.

## Early Growth Stage

Once the venture is positioned, successful businesses usually will have an early growth spurt. In some ventures the spurt is small and slow; other businesses' spurt is dramatic and rapid. Compaq Computer reached $1 billion in annual sales within five years after it was started, which is reported to be faster than any other company in history. On the other hand, Coca-Cola's growth was slow and steady. Atlanta pharmacist John J. Pemberton invented Coca-Cola in 1886. His bookkeeper, Frank Robinson, named the product after two of its ingredients: coca leaves and kola nuts. By 1891 another Atlanta pharmacist, Asa G. Chandler, bought the company for $2300, a sizeable but not astronomical sum in those days. Today, annual sales are over $6 billion.

Most entrepreneurs cannot predict exactly where or how big the growth spurt will be when they start the business. Although John Pemberton invented Coca-Cola, his unique product's success was harvested by those who bought him out. Similarly, when Ray Kroc bought out the McDonald brothers, from whom he got the idea for fast food, they received a sizeable payment, but it did not compare with the hundreds of millions of dollars they might have received if they had stayed in Kroc's company. Entrepreneurs do not always accurately assess market demand, market changes, and resource needs. Managing sales, costs, and resources carefully is important in the early growth stage.

## Later Growth Stage

In the later growth stage the growth rate is usually slower. In fact, in a number of successful entrepreneurships, growth tapers off and the business hits a plateau. Although Aftech apparently has not reached such a plateau, Lloyd Milner presciently remarks, "Growth for the sake of growth is the ideology of cancer." There may be an optimum size for a particular company, although the entrepreneurial spirit usually drives businesses to continue to seek continuous growth. The challenge for an entrepreneur is either to recognize that the business has reached an optimum size and that perhaps it is time to spin off a subsidiary or enter a new niche or, at the very least, to recognize that the personal qualities that were most successful in the early growth stage have to be adapted to the more mature later growth stage.

New factors inevitably will have arisen that must be taken into account; the external environment will have changed in significant ways, even if only because of the existence of the entrepreneur's business itself. Active domestic and international competitors are likely to have entered the market. After all, if the entrepreneur's business has demonstrated success, there will be imitators hoping to garner similar fruits of success. As a company grows, it needs more working capital, and often more capital for expansion in facilities. At this stage, possibly the only feasible way to acquire the needed capital is to sell shares to selected investors or to the general public. If shares are to be sold to more than a handful of investors, provincial securities regulations dictate the issuance of an extensive (and expensive) prospectus that divulges considerable information that the entrepreneur may have wished to keep confidential.

Also, as the business grows, of necessity the entrepreneur must become a manager, using different skills and applying different concepts. As Lloyd Milner describes this difficult transition, "When there were only eight to ten employees, I was involved in everything. Now I spend most of my time dealing with such things as broad marketing concepts and personality problems. The transition from 'doer' to 'manager' is difficult, but can't be avoided if growth is to continue."[40]

The four-stage growth model illustrates that greatest emphasis needs to be directed to different factors at each stage. During the pre-startup stage the primary attention should be on the business concept, the product or service, financial plans, and implementation activities. The start-up stage requires that the primary emphasis be on positioning. At the early growth stage, proper management of sales, costs, and resources is of primary importance. During the later growth stage, the primary focus of attention is to make the transition from an entrepreneur-driven business to a professionally managed business, although all of the earlier aspects must be kept in mind and not allowed to slip because of inattention.

## Entrepreneurship and the Business Plan

Creating and building a successful enterprise requires, above all, effectively performing all of the four management functions: planning, organizing, leading, and controlling. As research clearly indicates, poor management and management inexperience are the primary causes of new venture failure.[41] Of the four management functions, in most cases the one that is least well done is planning. Effective planning provides a well-thought-out blueprint for action, at least during the critical first months of a new business. In this period, finances are usually very tight, so even slight missteps can lead to financial disaster. Careful planning reduces the chance that major mistakes will be made.

**business plan**
A document that describes the business idea and how it is expected to be achieved, including primary aspects of the product or service, marketing and promotion, operations, management and staffing, and financing.

The planning should be reflected in a comprehensive **business plan**, often described as the most important tool of the entrepreneur.[42] A well-crafted business plan creates a form of self-discipline that forces the entrepreneur to examine rationally such crucial factors as the external environment, the extent and strength of competition, the potential for customers, and the overall strengths, weaknesses, opportunities, and threats that the new business may face.[43] But despite its importance in planning, and its reflection in the potential for success or failure, many entrepreneurs fail to prepare a comprehensive business plan. Various reasons are given for this surprising lack of preparation, but often it is less a conscious decision than just succumbing to the urgency to get the business up and running.[44]

Other entrepreneurs explain their failure to prepare a business plan on the ground that if they do so, they may find themselves frozen into an inflexible position.[45] The fallacy of this notion is seen when one considers that the only continuously effective business plan is one that is used to monitor progress and adapted periodically to reflect actual results.

### Purposes of the Business Plan

The business plan is a written description of the intended business. It covers the products or services to be provided, an analysis of the industry, how the business will be organized and will function, opportunities and strategies for marketing and promotion, the extent and strength of competition, the experience and skills of managers, staffing, expected sources of funds, and projected financial results as reflected in pro forma financial statements.

If properly prepared and periodically updated, it serves several functions. First, chronologically, it serves as a reality check. If all aspects are considered and their interrelationships are spelled out, the business plan may help the budding entrepreneurs to identify gaps in their thinking and planning. Disappointing as it may be to discover that the proposed plan will not fly, it is far better to learn this sad fact at the pre-planning stage than only after time, energy, and funds have been invested in a business venture that is not likely to succeed.

Second, the business plan charts a course, setting significant objectives for specific times. With a good business plan, after operations commence it is easy to see in what ways actual experience meets the planned results, and in what ways there is either a shortfall or a better-than-anticipated result. The sooner it is possible to identify any deviation from the plan, the sooner the entrepreneurs can adjust their thinking and their operations to meet the new conditions. For instance, when sales do not meet expectations, the entrepreneurs can make an early adjustment, perhaps by reducing expenditures, by dropping unprofitable lines, or by seeking more financing, and thus avert disaster that would have occurred if the shortfalls had not been identified until the problem had grown beyond correction.

Third, the business plan can be used to acquire financing, either by way of a bank loan or from private investors or government agencies. In most cases a business plan is absolutely required by any individuals or organizations that are considering whether to supply funds. Unfortunately some entrepreneurs discover this fact at a late stage in their planning, and then feel that they do not have the time to prepare as thoroughly as might be desirable. The result often is a business plan that contains internal inconsistencies or that omits critical information. It has been said that the best business plan in the world does not necessarily guarantee that funding will be forthcoming, but that an inadequate business plan will almost guarantee that it will *not* be.

## Preparing the Business Plan

As in many difficult tasks, probably the hardest part in preparing a business plan is getting started. To get over this hurdle, some entrepreneurs who do not see themselves as good at "paperwork" decide to retain consultants who offer to prepare their business plan for them for a fee. There are at least three distinct hazards in following this course. First, the outside consultant will be unlikely to understand fully the plans and thinking of the entrepreneurs, so the draft business plan will not represent those thoughts faithfully. Second, if the entrepreneurs themselves do not prepare at least a nearly final draft (perhaps subject only to final editing by a consultant or adviser), they will not have subjected themselves to the disciplined thinking that is entailed in putting their ideas to the test of expressing them in writing. Third, if the business plan is to be used, as most eventually are, to seek funding, the entrepreneurs may not be able to respond adequately to questions posed by bankers or potential investors because they are not as intimately familiar with the plan's details as they would be if they had prepared it themselves. So, entrepreneurs are well advised to face the hard work of preparing the business plan, even though they may elect to have an outsider serve as a reviewer and constructive critic of the final draft.

**executive summary**
An abstract or summary of all of the fundamental facts included in the business plan.

As for the approach to preparing the business plan, it is helpful to start by drafting the **executive summary**. This summary, no more than a page in length, includes a few words on each of the major topics, but provides little or no detail. Its purpose in the final form is to permit the reader to grasp the overall picture before becoming immersed in the details while reading the rest of the business plan. The executive summary should give a complete picture of what is intended, the opportunities and to some extent the threats, and the hoped-for outcomes. At the preliminary stage of drafting, having written the executive summary, the entrepreneurs have focused their minds on the big issues and in effect have identified the major points that should be highlighted in the body of the business plan.

As the full business plan takes shape it will become obvious that some revisions will be necessary, perhaps involving a complete rewrite of the executive summary when the body of the plan is completed. Even so, the first draft of the executive summary will have served its purposes even if the final version bears little resemblance to that first draft.

## Contents and Structure of the Business Plan

Many different outlines can be followed in preparing the business plan. Which to select will depend to some extent on the wishes of the entrepreneurs, but even more on the specifics of the proposed business. If the business is to build and market a technological invention, of course the details of that invention and matters such as patent protection will occupy a featured place in the business plan. If, on the other hand, the business plan describes a ski rental shop, internal operations will be of less importance, but competition, location, brand names, and other pertinent information will need to capture the attention of the reader.

Elements represented in a typical business plan will include most of those that follow.

**Cover page.**   This page will include the company name; address, phone and fax numbers, and e-mail addresses; and corporate logo if there is one. There should be a prominent statement that the business plan contains confidential information and is not to be copied. Since in Canada the authors of a work have an automatic copyright, the copyright symbol (©) followed by the year and the company name help to reinforce the confidentiality of the plan.

**Table of contents.**   This should be detailed, with page numbers provided. This helps the reader to find the portions of greatest interest, and to return to selected sections later for further consideration on subsequent readings.

**Executive summary.**   As explained above, this is an essential part of the business plan and should be written even more carefully than any other section to ensure that it emphasizes the most important points and states them clearly.

**Company history or profile.**   If the venture is to be started by the purchase of an existing business, a brief history of that business, with particular reference to its financial results, should be included. If it is to be a franchise operation, the history of the franchisor should be summarized. Whatever form the startup is to take, the business plan should include the mission statement, the broad goals, and more detailed measurable objectives with the dates on which they are expected to be achieved. The form of organization and the ways in which it will operate also appear in this segment of the business plan.

**The product or service.**   Expanding on the description in the executive summary, the product or service should be described in such detail as to convey all of the pertinent statistics and specifications. To be useful both in-house and for people outside the organization, it is best to write this information in terms that are easily understood by lay people. This segment of the business plan should include a conservative estimate of how the product or service will compare with those of competitors. It is tempting to believe, and to write, that *our* company will provide superior service at less cost than the competition, but on sober reflection it will be seen that this is an unlikely prospect.

**Business strategy.**   An important part of the plan is the description of the business strategy the entrepreneur plans to follow. An analysis of existing and projected future competition is essential to gauge the likelihood of success in meeting sales projections.

**Marketing and promotion.** A detailed promotion and marketing plan describes how the business will position itself in the market. This should reveal who will constitute the target market or markets, how they will be informed of the new company's existence, and what will bring them to it as customers.

**Operations.** It is desirable to include a description of the planned facility, whether it is to be leased or otherwise made available, and, if relevant, a layout of the facility and key pieces of equipment. If inventory is involved, a description of the planned control measures will ensure that these details have been considered thoroughly. Finally, the description should cover the planned methods of collections (if credit is to be granted), production scheduling, and other operating details. The description of equipment should include details such as model numbers, capacity, and useful life. If employees will be hired, it would be helpful to describe in some detail their qualifications and the training programs planned. Business licences, permits, and similar governmental involvement should be explained.

**Management and staffing.** Anyone who is evaluating the company's prospects for success will need to evaluate the management skills and potential that will be brought to bear on operations. The educational and work history of the principals may help in this evaluation, as will a description of how they plan to divide the responsibilities among themselves. Staffing plans will assist in an orderly progression and hiring sequence. Training plans will help to highlight, both for the entrepreneurs and to outsiders, the time and cost of these essential aspects of business that are often overlooked in planning until their need becomes urgent.

**Financial information.** This section has to be prepared after the rest of the planning is nearly complete, yet it is usually the first section, after the executive summary, to which bankers and potential investors will turn. A break-even analysis, a startup cost schedule, and cash flow statements must be added to the usual pro forma balance sheets and income and expense statements, which should cover at least three years.

**Appendices.** To avoid cluttering up the body of the business plan and to ensure that the flow of text can be followed easily by the reader, supplemental information should be presented in one or more appendices, tabbed and referred to as appropriate in the body of the text. Items that might be included are maps, layout sketches, lists of equipment, lists of suppliers, costs of individual items, and other information that the entrepreneurs have gathered before writing the text but that are not required to understand its basic thrust.

Each business plan will be tailored to the specific business it describes. The items to be included and their order will be determined by the importance of each. The important factor to keep in mind in preparing the business plan is that the more thorough its analyses, the more useful it will be both to the entrepreneurs and to other interested readers. Once the business plan has indicated that the project is feasible, it can establish the plan of action that will be followed for optimum results.

Writing a business plan is a difficult task. Whether it is 50 pages long or only 15, if it is comprehensive it will represent many hours of data gathering, analysis, and thought. But without it, the entrepreneur is sailing in uncharted waters and is likely to founder on a shoal about which the business plan might have given warning in time to take corrective action. Although time spent in preparing the business plan might seem to be nonproductive, in fact it could well be some of the most productive time the entrepreneur will ever spend.

## What Managers Are Reading  13-3

### The Complete Canadian Small Business Guide, 2nd edition

Although not a book aimed at the general reader, since the publication of its second edition in 1994 Douglas and Diana Gray's guide to small business deservedly has had a consistent and enthusiastic following among entrepreneurs and those who wish to become entrepreneurs. It presents in a comprehensive manner fundamental information that almost anyone would find helpful in starting and operating a small business.

Although it is not accompanied by Study Guides and Instructors' Manuals and it does not delve into management theory, this compendium is sufficiently complete and accurate that it could serve as a resource for a college or university course in entrepreneurship. Yet it is completely readable for the entrepreneur who seeks guidance in a specific aspect of small business or one who wants to upgrade knowledge and gain some new insights.

Early in the discussion, the authors offer an admonition that before embarking on entrepreneurship the would-be entrepreneur should make a self-assessment, to weigh the possible advantages and disadvantages of doing so. Considerable emphasis is placed on the need for adequate planning and for the development of a business plan. As one among scores of sample forms and checklists (that occupy nearly 200 pages, or one-third of the book's length), the authors provide a useful listing of topics that might be covered in a typical business plan.

Practical but mundane topics include a brief overview of financial statements and financial analysis, which would help to dispel some of the mystery that surrounds these documents in the minds of some entrepreneurs. A useful topic that is unusual in business books covers tips for selecting advisers such as lawyers, accountants, business consultants, and bankers. Use of these tips alone might save an entrepreneur many times the cost of the book.

In several areas the authors offer sound advice for the novice business buyer. An example is the counsel to flee from any seller of a business who claims to be skimming receipts and not reporting all for tax purposes. As the authors comment, such a claim means that the financial statements that have been provided are worthless, and also that the sellers cannot be trusted on any matter whatsoever. They must be dishonest—because either they are cheating on their taxes or they are lying about the skimming. Whichever is the case, a potential buyer should take the hint and find a better business to buy somewhere else.

Careful reading of this book would provide a good overview for the person contemplating entrepreneurship, as well as a good refresher (or, does one dare suggest, a useful addition to knowledge) for the person who already operates a small business.

Source: Douglas A. Gray and Diana L. Gray, *The Complete Canadian Small Business Guide*, 2nd edition (Whitby, ON: McGraw-Hill Ryerson, 1994).

## Getting Started

There are three methods most commonly used by entrepreneurs to start in business: buying an existing business, buying a franchise, and starting afresh (also known as a *greenfield* startup). Although the beginning entrepreneur should learn considerably more about all three methods before embarking on planning, this section provides an overview of each.

### Buying an Existing Business

There may be several advantages to buying a business that is already operating. Among other possible advantages, the cash flow not only is relatively predictable but already is coming into the business. The new owner may be able to retain many of the existing customers. In effect, even with the change of ownership, for a time, the reputation of the old business, whether it be good or bad, will carry over to the new business. Staff will be in place and will know their jobs, but they are there, whether they are competent or incompetent. Even if they are competent, however, they may resent the new owners who have replaced those with whom they had become friends. Furthermore, they may resist changes, responding negatively and obstructively that "this is not the way we have always done it." Also, by buying the shares of the business, the new owners will inherit any problems that remain from the old business—such as product liability suits, unpaid and unbooked debts, and unfulfilled promises to staff, customers, and suppliers.

One crucial question that must be answered to the best of the ability of the potential new owner is why the old owners want to sell. Perhaps the picture is not as rosy as is made out; perhaps there is something in the external environment that the old owners know about but do not divulge, and that will adversely affect the business in the future. Perhaps the old owners know that the return on investment is so low that if they can get cash and invest it elsewhere, it will produce greater returns for them. Any one of these or a myriad of other reasons should lead the potential purchaser to assess once again whether new ownership will be enough to make up for the apparent deficiencies. In other cases it even may be true that the old owners just want to retire and leave business entirely. Before accepting that assertion at face value, however, the prospective buyers should make an independent verification of this oft-given excuse that may turn out later to have been at best a half-truth.

One of the greatest difficulties is to determine how much should be paid for the business. The absolute minimum that the present owners are likely to accept is the amount they might raise by selling all of the assets in their present condition. The maximum that the purchaser should pay is the amount it would cost to replace all of the business assets if they were purchased on the open market, including appropriate allowances for such intangibles as customer lists. Between this minimum and this maximum, the sellers and the purchasers will have to negotiate. Evaluation of a business can be done in several different ways that are beyond the scope of this book, but any entrepreneur contemplating the purchase of a business would be well advised to seek professional help in setting a price. Many buyers of small businesses have discovered to their rue that they paid so much for the businesses that they are heavily burdened with debt, and that the prices that were negotiated were unreasonably high.

## Purchase of a Franchise

**franchise**
A contractual arrangement in which the entrepreneur, as franchisee, is permitted to use the name of the franchisor in business, the operations of which are controlled to some degree by the franchisor, in exchange for payment of royalties calculated as a percentage of the gross revenues of the business.

Another method of entering business for a quick startup is to purchase a **franchise**. According to a Dun & Bradstreet report, the failure rate of new franchises is less than 10 percent, as compared with the 60 percent rate they quote for greenfield startups. The franchise is based on a contract under which the franchisor agrees to provide specified management and operational advice and gives permission to use its name in the franchisee's business. The contract may provide for mandatory or optional training programs, operating manuals, and sometimes the purchase of products and supplies from the franchisor. In return the franchisee (entrepreneur) pays an initial fee and thereafter a specified percentage of gross revenues to the franchisor. This percentage, called a royalty, may range from a low of perhaps 3 percent to a high of 5 or 6 percent of revenue as a fee, plus another 3 or 4 percent that the franchisor intends to use for widespread advertising. In addition, usually the franchisee contracts to invest specified sums in facilities and equipment—as little as a few thousand dollars for the smallest Rent-A-Wreck franchise to well over $1 million for some fast-food franchises. Often franchisors such

*Purchasers of franchises often receive valuable guidance and are taught proven methods, in exchange for which they sacrifice some freedom of action as well as a share of the revenues.*

as McDonald's require that each franchisee undertake an extensive training program, and thereafter follow operating manuals to the letter. Other franchisors offer little or nothing in the way of training and operations guidance, so the franchisee must question what service is being provided in return for the substantial royalty (which must be paid whether the business is making or losing money).

As in any investment, the entrepreneur is wise to follow the advice "Investigate before you invest." One way to do this is to find out if the franchisor has any locations either in Alberta or in the United States. If it has franchisees in either of these jurisdictions, it will have been required by law to prepare a comprehensive prospectus, which a prospective franchisee can request and peruse carefully to learn exactly what the contract will require of both parties. Further information about franchises can be obtained by visiting the home page of the Canadian Franchise Association on the World Wide Web.[46]

## Greenfield Startup

**greenfield**
A colloquial term used to describe an operation that starts from little but an idea—as contrasted with the purchase of an existing business or a franchise.

The initial dream of most entrepreneurs is to start a **greenfield** business. An advantage is that in this method the entrepreneur is not burdened with the baggage that comes with the purchase of an existing business. Also the new business is not burdened with what may be onerous royalties in a franchise arrangement. Among the disadvantages, one that looms large is that there are no exact precedents to follow—predictions are based entirely on theory. If a business similar to the one planned by the entrepreneur has been successful in Etobicoke, is it safe to assume that the success will be duplicated in Kingston or in Brandon? These are three different communities, with different cultures. Even more important, the competition may be entirely different in the three communities, so the history in one may have little relevance to another.

Another major disadvantage of a greenfield startup is that since there is no history, and there are no facilities, it will be especially difficult to obtain financing. Bankers tend to be sceptical of ideas, preferring some tangible assets.

Whichever form of startup the entrepreneur chooses, it is essential not to be rushed into decisions. Gathering crucial information takes time; preparing a competent business plan takes time; assembling equipment, staff, and contacts takes time. If it appears that the business opportunity is going to be missed if decisions are not made immediately, there is a good chance that the opportunity is not only ephemeral but also illusory.

## The Special Challenges of a Home-based Business

Many, if not most, small business greenfield startups operate for a few years out of the entrepreneur's home. Basing the business in the home offers some distinct advantages. There is no rent to pay, and there even may be a tax saving from charging some expenses to the business that otherwise would have to be absorbed by the family budget. There is little or no initial cost for furniture and fixtures, and there is no commuting time and cost. In some cases, basing the business in the home may save on child-care costs.

The disadvantages are also real, but may not be quite as readily apparent. The biggest drawback of a home-based business is the very factor that offers the savings—a near-merger of home and business life. The entrepreneur whose business is home-based is likely to be "on call" almost 24 hours a day, 7 days a week. Elizabeth and Don Purser moved their freelance film office to their home from a downtown Toronto office tower. They enjoyed the proximity to their teenage daughters and the freedom from a time-consuming daily commute, but in exchange they increased their work schedules by some 10 hours a week.[47] Experience also has shown that someone trying to run a business in the home suffers from tensions that range from demands of children to self-imposed distractions arising from household chores that beg for attention. Anyone considering a home-based business, therefore, must be able to exert considerable self-discipline to keep a reasonable balance between home life and business life.

## Planning for Succession

Just as effective managers are always aware of the need to groom their successors, so there is an even greater need for entrepreneurs to prepare for their successors. A recent survey found that most family-owned businesses do not have any plan to deal with succession of their leadership.[48] In a family-owned business, it may appear that succession is assured. There are at least three difficulties with this assumption. First, the members of the next generation may not be interested enough in the parents' business to put in the time and effort that have built it and caused it to grow. Second, they just may not be capable. Henry Mintzberg, the Canadian management scholar and author, has called family succession "Russian roulette"—a gamble that the members of the second and third generation may be able to repeat the successes of their parents and grandparents. He points to the troubles at Toronto-based Dylex and to the Canada-wide retrenchments of the Eaton Company as illustrations of his concern,[49] and he might have included the Canadian Tire and McCain family enterprises.

Another problem with family succession is that all too often the "retired" parents just cannot keep from meddling, so the business ostensibly being run by the second generation is fettered by the older people's unwillingness to change. Of course, as in most generalizations, it is not difficult to find exceptions. One such exception is Terra Nova Shoes Limited, a boot manufacturer started in the 1970s in Harbour Grace, Newfoundland, and now having a second manufacturing plant in Markdale, Ontario. After the retirement in 1992 of its founder, Ab Aleven, not only nominal but actual control was given to his three adult children, Dan, Jackie, and Joan. They have continued to build the company by expanding their product lines and starting to export. They installed

*Carrying on the family tradition, the fourth-generation Alevens have surmounted the problems of family succession, expanding Terra Nova Shoes until annual revenues now approach $30 million.*

CAD/CAM systems, automated sewing machines, and even robotics. They are well on their way to Dan Aleven's dream of $100 million in annual sales, thus illustrating that family succession may not always be a bad thing.[50]

Even in situations where the initial entrepreneur has no children, or where the children are not interested in the business, it is desirable to have an active and current succession plan. No one can be sure whether the entrepreneur will be struck down by a physical disability or a serious accident. If no succession plan has been decided upon and made known to everyone involved, such an event can trigger chaos, infighting, and aimless drift, causing serious losses for the business. After it has been decided to whom the mantle will be passed, or how the responsibility will be divided and apportioned, the details should be set out in a legally sound document and copies should be distributed appropriately. Only with this degree of foresight can the entrepreneur ensure the successful continuation of the business into which so much time, effort, and dedication have been invested.

## The Workplace of Tomorrow

As downsizing in industry, commerce, and government proceed, more and more people will find themselves becoming entrepreneurs to avoid permanent unemployment or, at best, underemployment. If they blunder into entrepreneurship without adequate preparation, their chances of failure are high; if they prepare by studying principles of management, research their personal potentials and the potentials for markets, and prepare thorough business plans, their chances of success are greatly enhanced. Then they may find careers as entrepreneurs that are rewarding both personally and financially. The decades immediately ahead doubtless will see a continuation of the trend of the past two decades, in which small business formation considerably outpaced the growth in large enterprises. For this and other reasons that have been discussed in this chapter, entrepreneurship and intrapreneurship will become ever more important in Canadian society.

## Summary of Learning Objectives

▶ **Explain the meaning and application of the term** *entrepreneur,* **and distinguish it from the coined term** *intrapreneur.*

An entrepreneur is a person who assumes the major risks of creating incremental wealth by making a commitment of equity, time, and usually career to start and operate a small business. Intrapreneur is a term that has been coined to describe the person who applies the same thinking and approaches in a large organization as the entrepreneur does in the small business.

▶ **Explain some of the most common reasons why someone might decide to become an entrepreneur.**

Each entrepreneur has a different set of motivations, but many entrepreneurs are motivated by a desire for independence, control of their own lives, personal and professional growth, and more rewarding work. Some entrepreneurs follow this route because of disillusionment in finding appropriate jobs in the marketplace.

▶ **Discuss how Canadian conditions have contributed to the kind of inventions that have been made by little-known but deserving Canadian inventors and entrepreneurs.**

Canada's climate may have given impetus to Bombardier's invention of snowmobiles. Canada's industries led to the invention of the processes for drying wheat and recovering petroleum from the tar sands and to the manufacture of paper from wood pulp. Many of the other inventions that we now take for granted stemmed from Canadian entrepreneurial spirit and innovative genius.

▶ **Discuss some of the risks associated with becoming an entrepreneur.**

Risks may abound for entrepreneurs in small businesses. They risk interference with their personal lives, failure of their businesses with the loss of personal assets, psychological stress, and social and family pressures.

▶ **Describe the phases of the four-stage growth model.**

The first stage is the pre-startup stage, which involves planning, organizing, and obtaining resources. The second, or startup, stage focuses on positioning the venture. In the third, or early growth, stage the significant features are adjusting to changes and appropriately using resources. To remain competitive in the fourth, or later growth, stage the entrepreneur is required to change personal styles or perhaps to engage professional managers as the business grows too large to be controlled entirely by one person.

▶ **Explain why an entrepreneur should prepare a business plan, and discuss its uses.**

A comprehensive business plan disciplines the entrepreneur to think of all aspects of the proposed venture, and may help to determine whether it is feasible. It constitutes an important planning document and sets the course for the business, providing measurable objectives against which actual results can be measured. Comparison with these objectives may help to warn the entrepreneur of trends in variations early enough to permit corrective action to be taken. In many cases a business plan is required to attract financing.

▶ **Describe the essential features of a business plan.**

The executive summary provides a complete description of the proposed venture in capsule form. The body of the business plan contains more detailed descriptions of the product or service, organization, marketing and promotional plans, management and staffing, an evaluation of competition, financial projections, and all other information that is important to the particular venture.

▶ **Discuss why a person might prefer to purchase a franchise instead of start up a new business venture.**

The franchise contract may offer the person an established name, advertising, guidance, and training, allowing a relatively inexperienced person to benefit from the experience of others and perhaps get a faster start in business.

## KEY TERMS

business plan, p. 480

champion, p. 463

entrepreneur, p. 457

executive summary, p. 481

franchise, p. 485

greenfield, p. 486

intrapreneur, p. 462

niche, p. 478

skunkworks, p. 462

## REVIEW AND DISCUSSION QUESTIONS

### Recall

1. Describe the major sections of a typical business plan.
2. What are the uses to which a business plan can be put?
3. How do the growth model's four stages relate to each other?
4. What are some of the differences between owning a franchise and owning your own business?

### Understanding

5. How can the principles of entrepreneurship be applied in a large organization?
6. Why might people want to attempt to start their own businesses?
7. What are some of the risks associated with being an entrepreneur, and how can one reduce those risks?
8. What are some of the advantages of buying an existing business?

### Application

9. Make a list of several business ideas that you might want to pursue. Choose one and list the obstacles that you might face if you were to pursue it actively. With each obstacle, explain the steps that you might take either to overcome it or to reduce its impact.
10. Locate three entrepreneurs: one who is more than 50 years old, one younger person of the other sex, and one who is a relatively recent immigrant to Canada. Ask them why they became entrepreneurs. Prepare a report on their answers and your own interpretation.

## CASE 13-1

### Entrepreneurship and Bed and Breakfast Businesses

The Internet is providing a valuable resource for entrepreneurs. In addition to resources providing information on available franchises (see www.canadianfranchise.com), there are Web sites that provide the statistics and data to support the startup of new business ventures (see www.gdsourcing.com) along with a built-in interactive research consultant who will help you design and problem solve throughout your business planning process. There are magazines (see www.canbus.com and www.canadaone.com), and speakers willing to share in their experiences (see www.smallbizpro.com).

Check out Rita and Christopher and their Northern Island Adventure Bed and Breakfast business (see www.niacanada.com). The bed and breakfast industry is quickly growing as a very popular area for entrepreneurial activity for the domestic business owner. This is one of the fastest growing home-based businesses across Canada.

In British Columbia, the competition among bed and breakfast businesses is sharpening. In addition to books published on available lodgings, bed and breakfast owners are using the Internet to market their services. "Picturesque, private, luxurious, gourmet meals, spas and hot tubs, beaches and fireplaces"—these words adorn many of the Web-site business promotions for bed and breakfast locations.

Island Retreat Cottage is a bed and breakfast business located on a small island in the Gulf Islands chain. It is owned by anthropologists Robin and Jillian Ridington, who have written articles and books from this island habitat. The accommodation is a two-bedroom luxurious guest house, which they built in 1995 on a seven-acre private island and which is the only other structure on the island besides their own home. The site is a very short boating distance to the larger and more populated Galiano Island.

The owners arrange to transport guests by private boat to the island. Stays are a minimum of two days to one week in the summer. During your stay you may view other properties owned by this couple (e.g., Maui), each one serving a different niche, and they will provide guidance to the wildlife and culture of the main island, including boat transportation for the adventurous. The couple retired and invested in the island to enjoy the natural setting while continuing their writing careers. Their extended families live in the lower mainland area of British Columbia within ferry distance. They are active participants in island preservation issues and the study of island living.

### Questions

1. What forms of entrepreneurship are represented in this small community?
2. How have these entrepreneurs improved upon or carved out a niche for their businesses?
3. What career, family, or social risks do they face, and how have they prepared themselves for these risks?
4. How might the bed and breakfast business best serve the owners? What would be your recommendations for the development of skills for bed and breakfast owners generally? Would your recommendations be any different for Island Retreat Cottage?

---

Contributed by Sherry Campbell, British Columbia Institute of Technology.

## APPLICATION EXERCISE  13-1

### Evaluating Your Skills to Start and Operate a Business

Think about a business that you might like to start and operate. Any business can benefit from a person's skills and experience in a number of areas. This brief self-assessment exercise is intended to promote serious thinking about experience and skill. As the chapter suggests, many businesses fail due to lack of managerial know-how; that is, skills and experience are lacking and the consequence is not being prepared for the day-to-day challenges of starting and/or operating a business.

Circle or place an X on the spot on the scale that best describes your experience in each area. Place the number that's closest to indicating your experience in the last column.

| Skill | Much Experience | Some Experience | Little Experience | Rate Your Experience |
|---|---|---|---|---|
| Planning | 3 | 2 | 1 | |
| Accounting | 3 | 2 | 1 | |
| Establishing financial and accounting systems | 3 | 2 | 1 | |
| Selling | 3 | 2 | 1 | |
| Advertising | 3 | 2 | 1 | |
| Purchasing | 3 | 2 | 1 | |
| Recruiting and selecting human resources | 3 | 2 | 1 | |
| Coaching | 3 | 2 | 1 | |
| Motivating | 3 | 2 | 1 | |
| Evaluating human resources | 3 | 2 | 1 | |
| Organizing | 3 | 2 | 1 | |
| Production | 3 | 2 | 1 | |
| Quality control | 3 | 2 | 1 | |
| Quality improvement | 3 | 2 | 1 | |
| Quality assessment | 3 | 2 | 1 | |
| Computer use | 3 | 2 | 1 | |
| Other: | 3 | 2 | 1 | |

In which areas do you lack experience? Don't be discouraged if you lack experience in any of these areas. Various sources of information can help you become knowledgeable before you enter into a business. Sources include books, seminars, training programs, business people, business consultants, small business administration courses, college courses, and adult education courses.

## INTERNET APPLICATION  13-1

Read the story of Art Fry's invention of the Post-it note (www.3m.com/Post-it/artslab/story.html).

1. What is 3M's approach to innovation and product development?
2. How did the company turn an unknown product into an international bestseller?

Search the Web for an organization that encourages innovation and product development. What kinds of activities does the organization engage in and how does it manage its product development process?

# Canadian Business in the Global Economy

After studying this chapter, you should be able to:

▶ Discuss the nature and importance to Canada of the global environment;

▶ Describe the approaches that Canadian organizations can take to enter international business;

▶ Describe the environments for multinational or global business;

▶ Explain how laws and regulations influence international business;

▶ Discuss the roles played by some international organizations and their impact on management;

▶ Discuss the international trading blocs and their importance to Canadian business; and

▶ Discuss the major challenges facing Canadian organizations functioning in the global environment.

## The Shrinking World

THROUGHOUT THE WORLD, MANAGERS ARE FACING the same challenge—competitors appearing unexpectedly, often from foreign countries. Not only large corporations such as the automobile companies and Nortel, but also small businesses such as Spruceland Millworks Inc. of Edmonton and Skyjack, Inc. of Guelph, Ontario,[1] are fighting for customers by venturing beyond Canada's borders, spurred on by opportunities they see abroad, as well as by inroads made in Canada by foreign companies. A survey of 750 companies conducted by accounting and consulting firm Arthur Andersen & Co. and National Small Business United reports that 20 percent of companies with fewer than 500 employees exported products in 1994, which was an increase from 16 percent just one year earlier. From all appearances, the trend towards more exporting is continuing. Global fever has reached the ranks of Canadian entrepreneurs as well as the huge corporations.  ▶

As a result of the competitive scramble to enter foreign markets, companies around the world are in a business war. Makers of automobiles, CDs, and household appliances face intense competition from foreign manufacturers. Ontario and British Columbia vintners compete against wines from California, France, Chile, and even Hungary and Bulgaria. Quebec-made Fruit-of-the-Loom T-shirts hang in retail stores next to similar garments manufactured in South Korea, Hong Kong, China, Malaysia, and Tanzania. High-tech companies, in particular, fight a constant and costly battle against "pirates" who counterfeit CDs, books, and software programs in huge factories in countries such as China and Indonesia.[2]

Canadian telephone companies compete vigorously with Sprint, MCI, and several smaller providers of long-distance telephone service. Competing claims are confusing, and constantly being upgraded, making it difficult for the consumer to decide which carrier to choose. And this phenomenon is not unique to North America. In the consumer electronics markets in Thailand, Japanese companies Sony and Matsushita struggle against each other for market share. Around the world, even with the protectionist measures adopted by many countries, local monopolies are being faced with foreign competitors about whom they never used to worry. So, whether they are trying to free themselves from the stifling effects of saturated domestic markets or seeking growth to supplement Canadian opportunities, more and more Canadian companies of all sizes are looking to foreign markets for growth opportunities. With this change in outlook, Canadian managers have to redirect their thinking in a number of ways. ∎

Source: Adapted from Jaclyn Fierman, "When Genteel Rivals Become Mortal Enemies," *Fortune* (May 15, 1995): 90-100; and Amy Barrett, "It's a Small (Business) World," *Business Week* (April 17, 1995): 96-101.

## The New Borderless Economy

More than ever before, there are people throughout the world who want many of the same things. A single product or service may be attractive, perhaps with some modifications, to people of the same economic circumstances but in vastly different cultures. Assigning any particular "nationality" to a corporation may be misleading.[3] As recently as the 1980s, the world economy was the sum of the individual economies of many nations, but this is no longer the case. An export for one country is an import for another, so the totals of national figures will include some transactions twice. Thanks to international joint ventures, exchange of technology, the cross-fertilization of many cultures, and many other factors, a truly global economy has been created. This new global economy poses many new challenges for today's managers.

This chapter examines the global management environment in terms of (1) the nature and importance of the global economy; (2) types of organizations in the global economy; (3) the environment for global business; (4) regulation of international business; (5) multinational trading blocs; and, reflecting all of these factors, (6) the challenges facing the managers of organizations in the global environment.

## The Nature and Importance of the Global Economy

In the global economy, almost any product made anywhere has to compete with products made everywhere else. Steel produced in Hamilton competes with steel made in Japan; flowers grown in Victoria compete with flowers grown in Mexico; wine bottled in the Okanagan or the Niagara Peninsula competes with wine bottled in France, Chile, or Spain. The question facing companies in Canada and throughout the world is not *whether* they should compete with foreign companies, but rather *how* they can compete to survive in the global economy.

The answer to this question, of course, is complex. We know that customers are demanding better products, improved service, and lower prices. Global competition means that consumers have a better choice of products, often for less money than before. In the past decade the dominance of the Western industrialized nations has been severely challenged by businesses in what are often known as the less developed countries (LDCs) or the newly industrialized countries (NICs). The inescapable conclusion is that the economic status of Canadian businesses and of Canada as a whole in the new global economy will depend on Canadians' ability to meet new competitive standards.

## The New Form of the Global Economy

Throughout history there always has been a global economy. As is pointed out by Fernand Braudel, the renowned French economic historian/philosopher, it can be said that the Phoenicians had an early version of a world economy. A form of world trade was later the source of greatest strength for the civilizations, in succession, of the Carthaginians, the merchants of the Greek city states, the Romans, and later the leaders of the Islamic world. In Europe the practices of world economy began nearly 1000 years ago when Muscovy formed trading connections with the eastern nations, Siberia, China, and India.[4] Braudel traces the rise and fall of, successively, Bruges (in present-day Belgium), Venice, Portugal, Antwerp, Amsterdam and the rest of Holland, and England, all of which dominated world trade at one time but eventually succumbed to competition and sank to less-prominent positions.[5] So, a look at history tells us that what is now probably will not always be.

There is, however, a significant difference between the world economies of the past and those of today. In the past, even though the wealthy merchants were deeply involved in foreign trade, it had little impact on most of the population. Today, in Canada, as in other countries of the industrialized world, the average citizen (to the extent that there is such a person) lives constantly in a welter of foreign influences. Until the beginning of the nineteenth century, the average person could not afford luxury goods such as the silks, spices, and other items brought in from the Orient. Food and clothing that was not produced directly by the family seldom travelled more than a few kilometres from its point of origin. Now, much of the clothing worn in Canada is produced in Asia or Africa. In the huge array of different items on supermarket shelves, there are hundreds or thousands of varieties of tropical fruits, foreign-grown vegetables, and preserved, frozen, and tinned foods, all of which would have been inconceivable even 50 years ago. Canadian homes are filled with appliances, furniture, toys, electronic devices, carpets, glassware, and dishes—all of which are as likely or more likely to have been produced in another country as in Canada. So no longer is foreign trade the concern and interest of only a tiny segment of the population, but rather it is part of everyday living for the great majority of Canadians.

As for business, the impact of foreign trade is also direct and inescapable. For many reasons, Canada as a nation depends more on international trade and business than do many of the industrialized countries. Figure 14-1 on page 498 shows how Canada's dependence on foreign trade compares with that of other countries that have annual exports and imports that total more than US$100 billion. Statistics from some countries are notoriously difficult to acquire, and once gathered may be unreliable because of differences in data gathering methods. The governments of some countries intentionally distort figures to create desired political impacts at home and abroad. In addition, different situations may create erroneous impressions, even though the figures may be perfectly accurate. For instance, the statistics for Singapore and the Hong Kong Special Administrative Region of China are somewhat anomalous because large quantities of goods are shipped into them and promptly shipped onward to other countries, rather than being consumed within the country itself. Thus, while the so-called entrepôt function of trans-shipment provides local employment and business opportunities, the figures for imports and exports are not comparable to those in countries where imports are consumed within the country. Despite these defects in the data, however, the important fact to note in Exhibit 14-1 is that Canada's dependence on foreign trade is greater than that of either Japan or the United States, which in addition to being Canada's largest trading partners are also the two largest foreign traders in the world. In both of those countries, while their overall volumes of international trade exceed those of Canada, their much larger economies mean that their respective dependencies on foreign trade are substantially less than that of Canada. As a consequence, Canada always enters negotiations with its largest trading partners with more at stake than they have, and therefore is more vulnerable than they are.

It is also instructive to note with which countries Canada does most of its trade. Exhibit 14-2 shows this information, as gathered by Statistics Canada. The fact that more than 80 percent of the exports by Canadian organizations go to businesses, consumers, and governments in the United States clearly indicates that economic and social trends in that country have a profound impact on Canada. The next largest grouping of

**Exhibit 14-1**

*International Trade as a Percentage of GNP, in Countries Exporting More Than US$40 Million*

| Country | Exports—1995 ($US billion) | Imports—1995 ($US billion) | GDP—1997 ($US billion) | Exports + Imports ÷ GDP |
|---|---|---|---|---|
| Singapore | 125.0 | 132.4 | 66 | 389% |
| Hong Kong, SAR | 188.1 | 208.6 | 176 | 226% |
| Switzerland | 72.5 | 71.1 | 91 | 157% |
| Austria | 64.8 | 129.6 | 152 | 85% |
| Sweden | 82.7 | 65.5 | 177 | 84% |
| Malaysia | 78.7 | 78.6 | 193 | 83% |
| Taiwan | 121.3 | 113.9 | 290 | 81% |
| Germany | 512.4 | 401.7 | 1450 | 66% |
| Netherlands | 194.0 | 177.4 | 609 | 61% |
| **Canada** | **214.4** | **201.0** | **694** | **60%** |
| Belgium | 170.3 | 156.4 | 575 | 57% |
| France | 289.8 | 269.2 | 1008 | 55% |
| United Kingdom | 281.5 | 312.9 | 1140 | 52% |
| Korea | 136.6 | 144.6 | 591 | 48% |
| Italy | 238.2 | 208.3 | 1090 | 41% |
| Spain | 104.4 | 122.7 | 565 | 40% |
| Australia | 62.9 | 128.8 | 405 | 32% |
| Japan | 421.0 | 349.2 | 2680 | 29% |
| Thailand | 57.6 | 61.4 | 417 | 28% |
| United States | 688.7 | 899.0 | 7170 | 22% |
| Mexico | 65.3 | 142.0 | 721 | 20% |
| Russian Federation | 87.4 | 155.0 | 796 | 19% |

Sources: Adapted from *United Nations Statistical Yearbook, 1995* (New York: United Nations Secretariat, 1995): 153-195; *United States Statistical Abstract, 1996* (Washington: Bureau of the Census, 1996); *World Development Report 1994* (Washington: World Bank, 1994); and *World Almanac 1998.*

Canada's customers is the whole of Europe, accounting for less than 7 percent of Canada's total. Of course, no single European country constitutes more than a fraction of this total. Consequently, Japan, at 4 percent, is Canada's second-largest customer after the United States. China and South Korea are the only other countries that reach 1 percent.[6]

**Exhibit 14-2**

*Canada's Trading Partners, 1997*

| Country | Exports from Canada to— ($US billion) | Imports into Canada from— ($US billion) |
|---|---|---|
| United States | 210.1 | 157.3 |
| Europe, all countries | 17.5 | 28.2 |
| Japan | 10.4 | 10.4 |
| China | 2.7 | 4.9 |
| South Korea | 2.7 | 2.7 |
| Taiwan | 1.4 | 2.9 |
| Hong Kong | 1.1 | 1.1 |
| Indonesia | 0.8 | 0.6 |
| Singapore | 0.5 | 1.2 |
| Thailand | 0.5 | 1.0 |
| Malaysia | 0.5 | 1.6 |
| India | 0.3 | 0.6 |
| Approx. 100 others | 10.0 | 20.4 |
| TOTALS | 258.4 | 232.9 |

Sources: Adapted from *Globe and Mail* (April 26, 1997): D9, with statistics from Statistics Canada.

## The Global Boom

**international trade**
The exchange across national boundaries of goods for money or for other goods.

It is important to distinguish between the terms *international trade* and *international business*. **International trade** describes the exchange of goods for money, or for other goods, across national boundaries. **International business** refers to the conduct across national boundaries of business of all kinds, including financial transactions, the purchase of insurance from a foreign company, and even the expenditures of foreign tourists (provisions for which constitute a major industry segment in Canada).

**international business**
The conduct across national boundaries of business of all kinds, including financial transactions, expenditures by tourists, and transactions such as the purchase of insurance.

All nations, from Albania (which for half a century was the most tightly closed nation) to Zambia (which is one of the more backward of the LDCs), participate in international business. In addition, even if a Canadian business neither buys from nor sells directly to a foreign country, it is profoundly affected by international business. At the very least, some of its products, some of the components of its fixtures or machinery, or some of the parts in its vehicles certainly will have come from foreign sources. The costs quoted to it by its suppliers and the prices it charges to its customers are influenced, if not actually set, by foreign trade.

At the end of the Second World War the world's total international trade is estimated to have been about $50 billion, a formidable figure in itself. Now the total is nearing US$4 trillion (i.e., US$4000 billion)—an eightyfold increase. These figures overstate the actual growth somewhat because they include the effects of inflation. Much of this increase, however, is real—the result of negotiations within the General Agreement on Tariffs and Trade, which was superseded on January 1, 1995, by the World Trade Organization. These negotiations have led to substantial reductions in artificial barriers to international trade. Another factor has been both cause and effect. More open international trade has facilitated the rise of multinational corporations; the existence of multinational corporations has facilitated international trade.

**international management**
The process of management when conducted across national lines.

**International management** refers to the management process when conducted across national lines. International management reflects all of the challenges involved in domestic management, plus a host of other challenges. As in domestic management, international managers must exercise skills in planning, organizing, leading, and controlling. These skills, however, become more difficult when lines of communication and transportation are extended, when their exercise must be adapted to the culture of the host country or countries, and when managers must ensure that their organizations meet the requirements of the laws and regulations of the host country or countries in addition to those of the home country. Exhibit 14-3 lists examples of some of the complications faced by managers that result from engaging in international operations.

In its early years, Canada was forced by English law to conduct most of its international trade directly with Great Britain, so that at the time of Confederation approximately 45 percent of Canada's foreign trade was with Britain. An additional 45 percent was with Canada's neighbour, the United States, and only 10 percent was with the rest of the world. This contrasts with the current mix—in which about 3 percent of Canada's foreign trade is with Britain, 83 percent is with the United States, and 14 percent is with the rest of the world.

During Canada's early years, because transportation was so difficult, almost all domestic trade was confined to the geographic area in which the goods were produced. It was difficult and time-consuming to communicate beyond the local sphere, let alone transport people or goods. By the early nineteenth century, when the Hudson's Bay Company had expanded clear across the continent to Victoria, the only practical method

**Exhibit 14-3**

*Challenges Managers May Face in International Operations*

- Possibly unstable governments in host country
- Changes in host country laws regarding foreign ownership
- Changes in exchange rates to Canadian dollar
- Currency controls to prohibit taking profits to Canada
- Possibility of runaway inflation
- Threat of expropriation or confiscation
- Threat of kidnapping or terrorism
- Necessity to abide by laws of host country as well as laws of Canada
- Unreliability of utilities, transportation, and communications
- Possibility of shortages of skilled labour or professional staff
- Cultural differences in perceptions of authority, time, and motivation
- Cultural differences regarding bribery or "gift" giving
- Language barriers
- Inadequate communication with administrative offices in Canada
- Personal isolation from others in the organization
- Loss of visibility in promotion opportunities in the organization
- Dissatisfaction of spouse or children
- Unsatisfactory living conditions for family
- Pollution, substandard air quality, and noise
- Inadequate schooling for children
- Inability of spouse to find meaningful work
- Absence of amenities taken for granted in Canada (e.g., public libraries, etc.)
- Separation from members of extended family in Canada
- Unexpectedly heavy work load

of travelling from Montreal to Victoria was to sail down the St. Lawrence River and south in the Atlantic Ocean, then either struggle overland across the isthmus of Panama or brave the hazards of Cape Horn, and finally sail north along the Pacific Coast. Consequently, for the first three centuries of Canada's history most businesses had little competition from outside of their local areas, and other types of organizations functioned only locally as well. It was not until 1885, when the last spike was driven to complete the Canadian Pacific Railroad,[7] that most Canadian organizations could seriously contemplate operating nationwide. Companies in one region began to compete with others in distant parts of the country.

Starting as early as the 1950s, fibre optics, communications satellites, improved transistors and their applications in computers, and the development of efficient and relatively inexpensive air travel made geographic distance less relevant. With fax machines and e-mail readily available, businesses can now exchange detailed information instantaneously, bringing distant branches effectively next door to their respective home offices. In the twenty-first century, the organizations that adapt their thinking to a worldwide perspective will be those most likely to succeed.

## Global Opportunities

Without these technological innovations today's international business could not be what it is. Potential consumers in LDCs learned about lifestyles, or rather versions of lifestyles glamorized by television, in the industrialized countries. As a result, they developed new "wants," fuelling a consumer demand that growing corporations rushed to fill.

As the economy of an LDC grows, some of its consumers gain more disposable income. This allows them to purchase goods that are not being produced in their home country. As they are able to purchase more imported goods, a market opportunity develops, first for exporters from industrialized countries and a few importers in the LDC. Later, these new markets create opportunities for new businesses and industries in the LDC itself.

Related to these opportunities are many ethical questions, such as those discussed in Chapter 2. It must be recognized that the material gains from these global opportunities are not distributed evenly among the whole population, but tend to be captured by a select few. For instance, today there are probably more millionaires in the People's Republic of China than in Canada, but the great majority of the 1.1 billion Chinese people are still living in conditions that by Western standards would be classified as extreme poverty. Nevertheless, as the economies expand in countries such as China, India, Russia, members of the former Soviet Union, and parts of Latin America, the demands for food, clothing, appliances, vehicles, leisure items, medical care, and so on will offer burgeoning market opportunities for multinational corporations in the more industrialized world, as well as in those countries themselves.

Taking advantage of global opportunities will not be easy, nor will it be risk-free. As the

*As consumer income grows in developing countries, the demand for luxury goods and services also grows. When this demand is coupled with relaxing government restrictions on imports and "Western culture," new markets open for businesses.*

World Bank points out in its respected *1995 World Development Report*, it is not just the poor countries, but the rich countries as well, that must adapt to the global economy or suffer the consequences of "harsh reality."[8]

# Types of Organizations in the Global Economy

Any organization, large or small, can become involved in international business. While international companies are perceived to be large and well known (such as Sony and Royal Dutch/Shell), many small companies also buy or sell products in foreign markets. This section discusses multinational and global corporations and their approaches to becoming involved in international business.

## Multinational and Global Corporations

**multinational corporation (MNC)**
A company that conducts business in two or more countries. MNCs usually are based in one country, with some operations, production facilities, and perhaps marketing functions in one or more other countries.

A company engaged in operations in two or more countries is commonly referred to as a **multinational corporation (MNC).** These organizations usually are based in one country, with some operations, production facilities, and perhaps marketing functions in one or more other countries. Nortel is Canadian, Royal Dutch/Shell is Dutch, Deutsche Bank is German, yet all are MNCs because they carry on business in more than one country. *Multinational corporation* is a term often used as a pejorative, that is, meaning something evil and destructive. Some MNCs behave irresponsibly; others behave responsibly. Just as some irresponsible individuals throw trash in the street and drive cars that spew black smoke, so do some MNCs wreak havoc on the environment and devastate the living conditions of their neighbours. Similarly, some responsible individuals devote time and money to improving conditions around them, and some MNCs provide health, educational, and economic benefits to people with whom they come in contact. In fact, any single MNC is no better and no worse than the individuals who manage it. The form of an organization does not determine whether it is good or bad. The difference is that the larger the organization, the greater its impact, whether for good or ill. Exhibit 14-4 lists the world's largest MNCs. Although from year to year their respective rankings may change, for the past decade or more, the names on the list have changed very little.

**global corporation**
A company that operates as if the world were a single entity and that has corporate headquarters, manufacturing facilities, and marketing operations throughout much of the world. While similar to an MNC, it is not as directly anchored in a single country, and its operations in several countries are as important as in the country in which it originated.

Another term used to describe a type of organization emerging in the global economy is *global corporation*. In contrast to an MNC, a **global corporation** operates as if the world were a single entity. It has corporate headquarters, manufacturing facilities, and marketing operations throughout the world. While similar to an MNC, a global corporation is different in that it is not as directly anchored in a single country, and its operations in other countries are as important as those in the country in which it originated. An example is Baker & McKenzie, the world's largest law firm. Although it has an accounting office in Chicago, its more than 2400 lawyers are based in over 50 cities around the world. Its quarterly executive meetings and its annual partner meetings are held each time in a different city around the world. Although English is usually used for official communication within the firm, it is a second or third language for many of the firm's lawyers, who represent scores of different nationalities. Strategies and plans, while tailored to conditions in each of the offices, are decided on with their global impact in mind. Another example of a global corporation is the Canadian telecommunications giant, Nortel. Its huge telephone switching contract in China is just one example of its aggressive pursuit of worldwide operations regardless of national origins or locales.

Although there are a few examples such as these, global corporations are not yet common. Most international companies are MNCs that started in one country and have

**Exhibit 14-4**

*The World's Largest Multinational Corporations*

| Rank | Company | Country | Revenues (US$ billion) |
|------|---------|---------|------------------------|
| 1 | Mitsubishi | Japan | 175.8 |
| 2 | Mitsui | Japan | 171.5 |
| 3 | Itochu | Japan | 167.8 |
| 4 | Sumitomo | Japan | 162.5 |
| 5 | General Motors | U.S. | 155.0 |
| 6 | Marubeni | Japan | 150.2 |
| 7 | Ford Motor | U.S. | 128.4 |
| 8 | Exxon | U.S. | 101.5 |
| 9 | Nissho Iwai | Japan | 100.9 |
| 10 | Royal Dutch/Shell Group | Britain/Neth. | 94.9 |
| 11 | Toyota Motors | Japan | 88.2 |
| 12 | Wal-Mart Stores | U.S. | 83.4 |
| 13 | Hitachi | Japan | 76.4 |
| 14 | Nippon Life Insurance | Japan | 75.3 |
| 15 | AT&T | U.S. | 75.1 |
| 16 | Nippon Telegraph & Telephone | Japan | 70.8 |
| 17 | Matsushita Electric Industrial | Japan | 69.9 |
| 18 | Tomen | Japan | 69.9 |
| 19 | General Electric | U.S. | 64.7 |
| 20 | Daimler-Benz | Germany | 64.2 |

Source: "The World's Largest Corporations," *Fortune* (August 7, 1995): F1.

expanded their operations to other parts of the world. Honda, with a large automobile plant in Ontario, is correctly considered an Asian company. Honda cars built in Ontario still must incorporate at least 62.5 or 65 percent (depending on the type of vehicle) Canadian-made parts and labour in order to be classified as Canadian products, and enjoy the associated benefits. Within a decade or so, global corporations no longer will be the exception. Companies that fail to recognize their emerging presence face a serious competitive threat.

## Approaches Canadian Companies Can Take to Enter International Business

There are several approaches an organization can take to engage in international operations. They range from those that entail a low level of commitment to those that require a major, almost irreversible, commitment of resources and reputation. These approaches include at least three modes of exporting (direct, piggyback, and through trading companies), original equipment manufacture, licensing, franchising, countertrading, joint ventures, strategic alliances, and direct ownership.

## Exporting

The simplest way to enter international business is **exporting**, which is selling goods in a country other than the country of origin. (*Importing* is bringing goods into a country from another country.) Exporting requires the lowest level of resources and commitment, and consequently the lowest level of risk. More than half of the companies engaged in international trade export goods.[9] As may be seen from Exhibit 14-5, despite Canada's relatively small population, it is the seventh-largest exporting and importing country in the world.

Once the product has been exported from the home country and reaches the host country, it must be distributed there. The exporting company may establish its own marketing and distribution network in the host country. This method is called *direct exporting*.

**Piggyback distribution.** Another method of distribution is often termed **piggyback distribution.** In this method, the exporting company contracts with a company already active in marketing in the host country and arranges for that local company to distrib-

**Exhibit 14-5**

*Largest Exporting and Importing Countries*

| Country | Total Exports and Imports (US$ billion), 1997 |
|---|---|
| United States | $1588 |
| Japan | 770 |
| Germany | 754 |
| United Kingdom | 594 |
| France | 559 |
| Italy | 447 |
| **Canada** | **415** |
| Hong Kong SAR | 397 |
| Netherlands | 371 |
| Belgium | 327 |
| People's Republic of China | 325 |
| Korea | 281 |
| Singapore | 257 |
| Taiwan | 235 |
| Spain | 227 |
| Malaysia | 157 |
| Russian Federation | 155 |
| Sweden | 148 |
| Switzerland | 144 |
| Mexico | 142 |
| Austria | 130 |
| Australia | 129 |
| Brazil | 118 |

Source: Adapted from *United Nations Statistical Yearbook 1997*: 153-197.

*As North American corporations seek to expand their markets in other countries, they often find it necessary to work with and through local companies to facilitate their entry into the market and to take advantage of local connections.*

**trading company**
A company that purchases goods or products from a company that has produced them and then sells them for its own account, often in another country.

ute the product in addition to the products they already carry. In addition to reducing the investment and thus the risk, this method has the added advantage of being able to draw on the distributor's existing contacts and knowledge of the host country market.[10]

**Trading companies.** In contrast with the piggyback method, which makes use of a distribution network that already exists in the host country, the Canadian company may decide to deal with a **trading company**. A trading company serves as a link between buyers in one country and sellers in another. It is not involved in manufacturing products, but is simply an intermediary that takes title to products and undertakes all of the activities required to move the products from the country of origin to customers in the foreign country. In this way, a trading company assumes much of the manufacturer's risk in exporting. In addition, the trading company can provide sellers with valuable information about markets, product quality and preferences, and price expectations. Asian companies are aware of the strong local preferences for certain brands, knowledge of which can help build markets for Canadian companies whose managers do not have this crucial familiarity.[11] Because it is local, a trading company also may be favoured by the local government, and working through it may facilitate entry into the foreign market.

The best-known trading companies are the huge Japanese conglomerates such as Mitsubishi, C. Itoh, and Mitsui. These and six others together account for half of Japan's exports and two-thirds of its imports.[12] Although Canada's largest exporters are not comparable in size to the Japanese giants, Exhibit 14-6 on page 506 shows that some of Canada's best-known companies have large stakes in exports, and that in the aggregate their export activities have a marked impact on the Canadian economy.

## Original Equipment Manufacture (OEM)

**original equipment manufacture (OEM)**
A contractual arrangement in which one company produces goods and a second company markets those goods under its own name.

Sometimes a distributor or retailer wishes to sell products under its own brand or "house name," but it does not wish to own and operate manufacturing facilities. Sears Canada's "Kenmore" brand is well known, but Sears does not actually manufacture the appliances that carry this brand name. Instead, Sears may contract with Whirlpool to manufacture its automatic washers, and with Westinghouse to manufacture its refrigerators, yet both appliances carry the Kenmore brand. The customers place their reliance on the Kenmore brand without knowing the manufacturer's name. This type of arrangement, known as **original equipment manufacture (OEM)**, is especially useful for Canadian manufacturers who wish to enter a foreign market. The Canadian manufacturer has the benefit of the added sales volume, yet avoids the cost, risk, and management involvement that would be required to establish a distribution network in the host country. Furthermore, the use of a local brand name may allow quicker penetration into the foreign market because of its familiarity to the host country consumers.[13]

We often think of Canadian international business as being that which originates in Canada, but the reverse direction is also important to the Canadian economy. Most electronic appliances, such as CD players, television sets, and VCRs, are manufactured by a handful of large corporations, many of which are in Japan or Korea. Under OEM contracts, they may be sold in Canada through chains of local retailers, bearing a Canadian

**Exhibit 14-6**

*Canada's Largest Exporters*

| Company | Export Sales ($ million) |
|---|---|
| General Motors of Canada | 17,900 |
| Chrysler Canada | 13,500 |
| Ford Motor Co. of Canada | 10,800 |
| IBM Canada | 5380 |
| Canadian Wheat Board | 3500 |
| Noranda | 3000 |
| Bombardier | 2960 |
| Alcan Aluminium | 2800 |
| TransCanada Pipelines | 1857 |
| Avenor | 1590 |
| Magna International | 1515 |
| Honda Canada | 1419 |
| MacMillan Bloedel | 1362 |
| Inco | 1300 |
| Pratt & Whitney Canada | 1289 |
| Falconbridge | 1267 |
| XCAN Grain Pool | 1258 |
| Canadian Pacific | 1231 |
| Abitibi-Price | 1172 |
| Shell Canada | 1160 |

Source: Adapted from *Report on Business Magazine* (July 1996): 96.

house brand name. These arrangements not only furnish employment in import and in retailing companies, but they also provide the consumer with wider choice than if only Canadian sources were available.

## Licensing

**licensing**
A contractual arrangement in which one company, the licensor, grants to the licensee the rights to use specified technology or manufacturing processes or components in exchange for a fee, called a royalty, based on the volume of sales or usage.

A Canadian company may agree to grant certain rights to a foreign company for a fee, called a "royalty," which is usually based on the volume of the foreign company's sales under that agreement. The licence may grant the right to use specified technology or manufacturing processes, or components made by the Canadian parent company. Usually the subject matter of the licence is covered by patents, trademarks, or copyrights, but in some cases it consists of trade secrets. Licensing agreements are common in the brewing industry. For instance, Lowenbrau of Germany licenses the Miller Brewery in Milwaukee to produce and market Lowenbrau beer in the United States, while San Miguel of Macau and the Philippines licenses independent companies in several Southeast Asian countries to produce and market its beer in those countries.

**franchising**
A contractual arrangement in which one company, the franchisor, grants to the franchisee the right to use the franchisor's name, and its business and operating techniques, within a specified area in exchange for a fee based on the volume of sales generated.

**countertrading**
A bartering arrangement that provides for the exchange of goods for other goods, or the exchange of goods for other obligations that do not require direct payment.

**joint venture**
A form of business organization similar to a partnership, in which the co-venturers each agree to contribute funds, expertise, or other benefits or assets and to divide the products produced.

# Franchising

There are literally thousands of franchisors in Canada in many different kinds of business, ranging from fast-food outlets to beauty salons to car rental and houseboat rental agencies. Some franchisors operate internationally. Because a franchisor's investment in a foreign country is minimal, many franchisors expand into foreign markets soon after starting business, with varying degrees of success. McDonald's, for instance, is reported to have had instant financial returns from its restaurants in Hong Kong, but apparently has been less successful in some other foreign ventures.

# Countertrading

Arrangements called **countertrading** involve complex bartering agreements between two or more countries. (*Bartering* refers to the exchange of merchandise rather than having one party pay money for goods purchased from the other.) Countertrading allows a nation with limited funds to participate in international trade. Because LDCs typically have cash shortages but often have a surplus of commodities, this method may open opportunities both for the LDCs and for companies in the industrialized countries that seek to expand into new markets.

Some countertrading arrangements are quite complicated and involve several steps. For instance, McDonnell Douglas sold $25 million worth of commercial helicopters to Uganda in exchange for a commitment to provide financial support to a Ugandan business that catches and processes Nile perch and to another that produces pineapple concentrate. These businesses were then sold to buyers in Europe, providing Uganda with hard currency to pay for the helicopters. Through these arrangements, benefits were gained by the aircraft company in the U.S., by the Ugandan companies, and by the European buyers of the companies.

Nevertheless, countertrading poses some significant problems for the managers involved. First, it is often difficult to determine the true value of goods offered in a countertrade agreement. Second, it may be difficult to dispose of bartered goods after they have been acquired. These problems can be reduced or eliminated through adequate market analysis and negotiation. Despite the possible drawbacks, countertrading arrangements are expected to grow in the years immediately ahead.[14] Companies that disregard opportunities to countertrade, even if they are small, may lose out on significant benefits.

# Joint Ventures

A company also may conduct international business through a **joint venture**. This form of business organization is much like a partnership, although it is different in some financial and tax aspects. For ventures that require massive amounts of capital and entail considerable risk, such as mining and major construction projects, joint ventures may be the best way for Canadian managers to structure their international operations. Joint ventures also may be

*Recognizing the need for international managers to have special training, many multinational companies and organizations either have in-house training programs or contract with organizations such as Ann Carol Enterprises Ltd. to provide this training.*

**Management in the Real World**    14-1

## Global Catastrophe?

Donella and Dennis Meadows sparked intense debate in 1972 with the release of their book *Limits to Growth*. Through the use of computer models, the authors predicted that population growth would collide with the earth's ability to absorb pollution and regenerate itself. Some saw this as a serious warning of a potential global catastrophe; others passed it off as a false alarm. Twenty years later, leaders and negotiators from 170 countries met in Rio de Janeiro for the UN Conference on Environment and Development (UNCED). The major topic was a controversial agenda to protect the earth's atmosphere and inhabitants, attack poverty, and foster less destructive industrialization. A number of ecological trends are seen as likely to occur, resulting in increased levels of environmental regulation worldwide. The problems are far from simple:

- World population is expected to double, reaching 11 billion within 40 years. Industrial output would have to quintuple to meet the needs of all of these people.
- Industrialized nations make up only 25 percent of the world's population, yet they consume 70 percent of the resources. As more nations become developed and boost economic growth, resources will be scarce.

- Seven industrial countries, including Canada and the United States, are responsible for 45 percent of human-caused greenhouse gas emissions. As developing nations industrialize, worldwide pollution will skyrocket.
- Human activities are destroying the earth's soils, forests, wetlands, and grasslands. Over 40 million acres of tropical forests are destroyed each year, and the ozone layer is thinning, increasing the potential for global warming.
- Damage to the environment costs industrialized nations 1 to 5 percent of their GNP (gross national product). Forest damage in Western Europe is cutting GNP by $30 billion a year.
- In places like Mexico City and Eastern Europe, millions breathe toxic air. China will soon deplete all of its harvestable forests. The Baltic Sea is dying from sewage and other pollution.

Source: Adapted from Gene R. Laczniak, Anthony Pecotich, and Angela Spadaccini, "Toward 2000: A Tougher Future For Australian Businesses," *Asian Pacific Journal of Management* (April 1994): 67–90; Emily T. Smith, "Growth vs. Environment," *Business Week* (May 11, 1992): 66–75; and Peter Hong and Michele Galen, "The Toxic Mess Called Superfund," *Business Week* (May 11, 1992): 32–34.

created to gain access to distributors, suppliers, and technology. They also may facilitate connections with governments in the host countries.

Because of host government restrictions on foreign ownership, a joint venture with a local business may be the only way a corporation can acquire or operate a business in some foreign countries. In India, for instance, under regulations adopted in 1974, foreign-owned corporations were required to have at least 40 percent of their shares owned by Indian nationals. In 1991, that percentage was increased to 50, and with nationalistic fervour becoming a highly political issue, many foreign companies are concerned that there may be further increases in the local ownership levels required. In China, although a few companies have been allowed to establish foreign-owned branches, in most cases, a substantial proportion of the ownership is required to be held by Chinese nationals, who are often specifically chosen by the local authorities.

A major drawback to international joint ventures is that a company may lose control of its operations. For example, Coca-Cola entered a joint venture in India with an agency of the government. When India increased the required percentage of local ownership, which would have placed the government in a controlling position, Coca-Cola withdrew rather than risk losing its secret formula.

## Strategic Alliances

**strategic alliance**
An agreement between two businesses in which they share technology, market connections, or some other advantage that one has and the other lacks.

A **strategic alliance** exists when two independent companies agree to share technology, market connections, or some other asset that one has and the other lacks. Strategic alliances have been growing in the highly competitive global marketplace at an annual rate of 27 percent since 1985.[15] IBM alone has established more than 400 strategic alliances with other companies. To illustrate the complicated arrangements sometimes made, Goldstar, a Korean company, entered a strategic alliance under which its Irish subsidiary designed a refrigerator. The Italian company Iberna manufactures it, using many components made in Germany by Gepi. These arrangements are designed to facilitate entry into the markets of the European Union.[16] Another typical example is the August 1995 agreement in which the Ford Motor Company entered a strategic alliance with Jiangling Motors Corp in China. Jiangling was already in a joint venture with Japan's Isuzu Motor Corporation, so now three companies from three different countries will be collaborating to produce cars in Nanchang, Jiangxi Province.[17]

Strategic alliances are not all between large corporations, or between two corporations of the same size. Dynapro, a Vancouver company with only 160 employees, designs and markets computer-based industrial control systems. In 1983, Dynapro invited Allen-Bradley, a large MNC owned by the even-larger Rockwell Corporation, to purchase an equity share in Dynapro. Allen-Bradley gained access to Dynapro's unique technology and Dynapro gained access to Allen-Bradley's sizeable U.S. market. The arrangement is reported to have been profitable for both companies.[18]

## Direct Ownership

**direct ownership**
A form of entry into business by purchasing all or a portion of an existing business or by establishing and operating a new business.

Another approach to international business is **direct ownership.** This approach may consist either of purchasing all or a portion of a foreign business, or of building and operating a new business in the foreign country. Direct ownership typically involves a large investment in production facilities, research, personnel, and marketing activities. For instance, when the government of Hungary embarked on a program of divesting itself of industrial facilities, General Electric invested US$150 million to purchase 12 plants that manufacture light bulbs. GE planned to spend another US$140 million over a five-year period to modernize the plants, with no expectation of getting back its investment for several years.[19]

Companies invest in foreign subsidiaries for a number of reasons. In some countries, direct ownership may reduce manufacturing costs because labour and operating costs are lower than in Canada. Direct ownership enables a company to avoid paying tariffs that the host country otherwise would charge on products produced in another country and then imported. Additionally, by paying taxes in the host country and providing employment for local residents, a foreign company can build good relations with the host government. The greatest danger of direct ownership is that a company may lose a sizeable investment because of market failure or because the foreign government nationalizes the business and its assets. When problems arise in a foreign country, it is often very difficult and expensive, or even impossible, to move operations out of the country.

Nortel, Brascan, and MacMillan Bloedel are all examples of Canadian MNCs that have large investments in other countries. The converse is also true. Some of Canada's largest companies, such as General Motors Canada, Amoco Canada Petroleum Co., and

Mitsui and Co. (Canada) are owned by foreign companies. These cross-border connections illustrate the increasing globalization of the world's economies.

# The Environment for Global Business

There are significant differences between the business environments of domestic and foreign markets, even as between similar cultures such as those of Canada and the United States. A detailed analysis of these differences is critical in determining whether to enter a foreign market, and by what means. If a manager of an MNC or global corporation is to be effective in the global environment, differences in cultural, economic, social, and political-legal environments must be understood.

## Cultural Environment

**cultural diversity**
The differences in language, perceptions of time and authority, mannerisms, and attitudes that exist both within and among different societies.

Appreciating the differences among cultures is a basic requirement for successful international management.[20] **Cultural diversity** refers to the differences that exist both within and among cultures.[21] Different cultures attach different meanings to gestures and other aspects of body language, to perceptions of promptness and time, to manners of greeting, to the need for personal space, and to many other things that we tend to take for granted. These differences must be recognized and adapted to if managers of multinational corporations are to function effectively outside of the cultures to which they are accustomed.

For example, when planning a restaurant in Japan, McDonald's management recognized an aspect of Japanese culture that differs from that in North America. They located their first restaurant in Japan in a prestigious area of Tokyo, despite the high rents there. Based on the local culture, they reasoned that if it had been located in a less-costly and less-prestigious suburb, the Japanese would have considered it a second-class enterprise. Understanding how Japanese customers view locations helped McDonald's succeed in Japan,[22] where it now has twice as many restaurants as in Canada. (Yet despite its Japanese successes, McDonald's is experiencing disappointing returns in some of its foreign markets, often because of currency exchange rates over which it has no control.[23]) As another example, Yokohama Rubber Co., based in Tokyo, had to recall auto tires with a tread pattern that resembled the Arabic word for Allah, after Muslim customers protested. Yokohama apologized for its lack of knowledge of Islam, discontinued the tires, and replaced them free of charge in Islamic nations.[24]

Language differences, too, can cause difficulties. When General Motors introduced the Chevy *Nova* into Latin America, its failure seemed inexplicable until someone pointed out that the Spanish words "*No va*" can be translated as "It won't go"—hardly a selling point for young macho males, who otherwise might have been a target market!

How managers communicate in different countries varies greatly. For example, managers doing business in Asia have to be aware that Japanese and other Asians value saving face and achieving harmony. Thus, to be successful, managers never put an Asian business person in a position in which it is necessary to admit failure. Reflecting local cultures, direct communication about money is postponed as long as feasible, and then carried on rather indirectly, by North American standards. Finally, and perhaps most difficult of all, Western managers must wait patiently for Japanese and other Asian meetings to move beyond what seem to them to be time-wasting social amenities before serious negotiations can begin.

Even the extent to which employees prefer independence from close supervision differs from culture to culture. In Sweden, for instance, workers function best with a high degree of independence. In Greece, on the other hand, workers often will be very uncomfortable unless they are given detailed instructions.

**Women in international assignments.**  A question that has been given considerable press coverage is whether Canadian women can function effectively in foreign assignments. In a few countries, such as Saudi Arabia, the law prohibits women from driving a car or carrying on the simplest business transaction, such as buying groceries, from a man who is not a close relative. In Japan, much business is conducted during sake-soaked dinners at which women would not be welcome. But except for these and a few similar situations, it appears that much of the concern rests in the minds of executives in the organizations' Canadian head offices, who assume that women may not be respected by foreign executives. This assumption may help to account for the fact that for every 15 male expatriate executives, there is only one female. Actually, a number of companies have found that women are able to do very well in foreign postings. One female expatriate executive explains that in a meeting of a dozen people, if she is the only woman, everyone remembers her, even though they may forget the names of some of the men. Another female expatriate says that foreign executives respect her because they assume that she must be outstanding, or she never would have been given the appointment in the first place. Bell Canada International's Claire Lanctôt is an example of a woman who has been highly successful in an international assignment. As executive director of finance for BCI's affiliate in Colombia, she is highly regarded in that especially difficult country, where men are macho, corruption is rife, and physical danger is ever present.[25]

*There are relatively few Canadian women serving in international assignments, but reports indicate that in many foreign countries Canadian women executives are able to surmount local prejudices and function successfully.*

Business customs also play a major role in international management. In some countries, one major goal in business is to be accepted by others. Japanese workers, for instance, are usually more concerned with being accepted by their fellow employees than with excelling personally. A common saying is "The nail that sticks up will get pounded down." In the Middle Eastern oil markets, companies frequently have to do business with a "connector," who has access to the oil producers and receives a commission for this role.

**Ethical concerns in international operations.**  Ethical standards differ from culture to culture. In China, Indonesia, Malaysia, and many other countries, price fixing, payoffs, and bribes are frequently encountered and have become almost a way of life. But even those countries are beginning to feel international pressures to eliminate corruption. For executives of companies based in the United States or that have affiliates there, for several decades bribery anywhere in the world has attracted heavy fines and even prison terms for the executives involved. Vigorous lobbying through the Organization for Economic Cooperation and Development, especially by American representatives (who have been disadvantaged by the laxness of rules governing their competitors), finally resulted in Canada and 33 other countries agreeing to sign a Convention on Combating Bribery of Officials in International Business in December 1997.[26] In accord with this convention, on February 15, 1999, Canada brought into force a new law, the Corruption of

## What Managers Are Reading  14-1

### A Manager's Guide to Globalization

Stephen Rhinesmith is currently advising a dozen or more of North America's best-known global companies on how they can best function in the global economy in which they find themselves immersed. His cogent concepts and clarity of presentation commend this book to anyone engaged in, or even just interested in, international operations, whether in the field of business or in connection with governmental or not-for-profit enterprises that cross national borders.

He starts with the observation that in order to manage globally one must completely change one's mind set. By this he means how one looks at the world. The change in mind set to which he is referring includes a desire always to learn more, to welcome diversity, and to adapt quickly to the unforeseen and ambiguous. Acknowledging implicitly that management means operating in a climate of uncertainty, Rhinesmith stresses that the uncertainties found in international management are many times those in domestic management. He explores how the culture to which one is accustomed is a major determinant in how one thinks. In his

view, most managers have been trained to think in a reductionist manner, by analyzing, reasoning, and evaluating. Rhinesmith's advice for global management is not to abandon this method, but to apply it quite differently, in a holistic manner. His exposition concerning organizational structure and the authority-responsibility equation, differ little from principles of management on the domestic scene, but he translates these principles into formulae for effective action in a global corporate culture.

One of the more interesting segments of the book explores the management of multicultural teams. In view of the increasing diversity of the workforce in Canada, Rhinesmith's words on the subject would apply even within an organization that has no expectation of developing a global sense. Perhaps the best summary of Rhinesmith's contribution to the literature of management would be to say that in many ways global management is like domestic management, only more so.

Source: Stephen H. Rhinesmith, *A Manager's Guide to Globalization* (London: Irwin Professional Publishing, 1996).

---

Foreign Public Officials Act.[27] It is difficult to know what effect this Act will have, because it will be some years before prosecutions under it will work their way through the courts. However, there is reason to believe that Canadians who bribe foreign officials now will be subject to heavy fines and possible imprisonment. When (and if) domestic legislation is enacted in the other signatory countries, Canadian corporations no longer will face the devastating competition that has resulted when confronted by some of the actions of executives from other countries. Under German law, for example, bribery in Germany is illegal, but when operating in other countries, German nationals have been free to pay bribes and even to declare those bribes as tax-deductible expenses. It has been difficult for Canadians to compete in countries where business licences are dispensed only to companies that are willing to make deposits into foreign bank accounts of government officials.[28]

**Cross-cultural preparation.** An increasing number of MNCs are providing cross-cultural training to help managers prepare for assignments involving international business. One company that has profited from this awakening has been Victoria, BC's Protocol International, a company that sells cross-cultural training to executives who are destined for international postings.[29] Other companies provide similar training in-house. Coca-Cola, which operates in more than 200 countries, has its own formal International Service Program, in which approximately 500 senior managers and professionals are engaged.[30] This training typically covers language, culture, and history of the foreign country, as well as guidance on how to conduct business there. Candidates for international assignments are screened carefully to evaluate their adaptability, and often are required to have lived in a foreign country and to have some facility in one or more foreign languages.

Another precaution taken by a number of MNCs is to assign a mentor to each manager who is assigned to a foreign position. This relationship is considered a formal part of the mentor's work, and is taken seriously by both parties to it.[31]

Even with these precautions, there are difficult personal and business adjustments for the manager and family as well. Studies have found failure rates for international assignments that have ranged from 20 percent to as high as 66 percent.[32] Considering an international assignment's high cost, both in money and in personal and corporate disruption, any company that considers a foreign posting for any of its managers would do well to heed the cautions, and to do all that is feasible to prepare for and facilitate the transitions.

Another problem facing organizations that wish to assign managers to other countries is that the managers often perceive, with some reason, that if they spend a few years in a foreign posting they will be left out of the corporate politics that lead to recognition and promotions in the organization's mainstream.[33]

## Economic Environment

The process of international management is also influenced by a country's economic environment. Foreign economies are often unfamiliar and may fluctuate even when the domestic economy is relatively stable. Thus, the stability of a host nation's economy must be considered before managers can assess the market potential for their products. Developed nations such as Canada, the United States, Japan, and the countries of Western Europe tend to have more stable economies than LDCs such as Ethiopia, Vietnam, and Nigeria. Export markets are unreliable in countries experiencing hyperinflation that sometimes reaches rates exceeding several hundred percent per year, as has occurred in Brazil, Ecuador, and the former Yugoslavia, among others.[34]

The size of the foreign market is another economic factor that must be understood before engaging in international business. To be a feasible target, a country must have a large enough number of people able to afford the product in question. Together, China and India have perhaps 40 percent of the world's population, with a total of more than 2 billion people—or some 70 times the population of Canada. More important than overall size, however, is the economic potential. One frequently used indicator is the Gross Domestic Product (GDP) per capita. For the United States, Japan, and Canada, GDP per capita is at or above US$20,000. For China the comparable figure is thought to be approximately US$1300; for India it is about US$380.[35] Does this mean that Japan has 16 times the market for rice as does China, or that China has nearly 4 times the market for refrigerators as does India? Not at all. The important factor is the actual number of people in a country who can afford a product, and who would be interested in buying it. It has been suggested that China has more actual millionaires than Canada, although of course the percentage of the population is much smaller. If that is the case, for someone selling the most expensive luxury goods there may be more potential customers in China than there are in Canada, if those potential buyers can be reached and persuaded to buy the items in question and if the Chinese government will allow those items to be brought in. Whatever the figures, managers must exercise great care in interpreting them to ensure that they actually apply to the marketing questions involved.

**infrastructure**
Support facilities and capabilities within a country or geographic area, including transportation, communication, energy, and other similar services.

**Infrastructure.** A nation's **infrastructure** refers in part to its transportation, communication, and energy facilities that are needed for efficient business activity. The extent to which a company can successfully promote a product in a country depends in part on the communications media available. In a developed country, business is carried on through sophisticated systems that depend on reliable communication by telephone, fax, and e-mail. In many LDCs, communication has to depend primarily on face-to-face contact and the use of private messengers. Similarly, the quantity and quality of transportation facilities affects a company's ability to distribute its products. LDCs typically have rather primitive road systems by the standards of industrialized countries, and most freight is carried by rail, which limits the number of distribution points.

Energy consumption per capita is another measure of a country's infrastructure that is often used to gauge a country's economic strength. This statistic, like most, must be interpreted with care. A country with a large number of metals smelters, for instance, will consume large amounts of electricity, while at the same time lacking reliable electric power for much of its population, considerably limiting its potential as a consumer market for electric appliances.

## Social Environment

A major factor facing the managers of Canadian MNCs when they engage in international business is to reconcile social conditions in the host countries with those in Canada. It is a dilemma to know how much to expect Canadian practices to be engrafted onto social structures found in the host countries. In some LDCs there is widespread exploitation of children and female workers. In some LDCs environmental degradation is at best winked at by governmental officials, and at worst actively encouraged to improve profit margins. In some countries, land is expropriated from peasants to grant it to friends of the government for construction of factories, for factory farming, or for logging. In some countries (notably China) it is alleged that prison labour is a mainstay of much industrial production. Canadian managers who are contemplating a venture in any foreign country must try to determine in advance what conditions they may find there, and then decide whether they wish to accept the fact that they may be unable to make much change in those conditions or whether they should abandon plans to start business there.

*Negative publicity followed allegations that Kathie Lee Gifford's clothing line was manufactured in sweatshops.*

**demography**
The study of the people of a society, including factors such as education and literacy, age, ethnic and language preferences, and other distinguishing features.

**Demographic factors.** Other important social factors include literacy rates and the extent of training in aspects of modern technology. These factors tend to be unfavourable in developing countries, but in some countries, especially in Latin America and some countries of Southeast Asia, these factors are improving. Many LDCs in Africa and South Asia have low education levels, inadequate infrastructure, limited technology, and very low GDP per capita. Demographic projections show that in Canada the number of older people is increasing rapidly as a percentage of the population. This is in contrast with the situation in many LDCs, in which young people predominate and their proportion of the total is increasing. In contrast with the industrialized nations, whose population growth is relatively slow, the populations of LDCs in South Asia, and especially in Africa, are growing at very high rates, and in some countries are expected to double within 20 years. A question that has profound implications for international business is whether food production in the fast-growing countries can keep up with population growth. Although current business opportunities are limited in LDCs, long-term opportunities may be quite attractive in those countries that manage to keep their population growth within the limits of their economic growth.

## Political-legal Environment

Political and legal forces also help to determine a country's attractiveness for international business. Managers must consider the political stability of any country in which they wish to operate. This may be especially true for charitable organizations, because by their very nature they are likely to want to address needs in countries that have considerable poverty or that have experienced a natural disaster—both of which are breeding grounds for political instability. Countries with high levels of political unrest may change their policies towards foreign companies whenever there is a change of government, and even with changing political agendas in the same government. This risk creates an unfavourable environment for international business. In some political power struggles, production facilities have been destroyed, corporate assets have been seized, and the personal security of employees and their families has been jeopardized. Recent examples of this have occurred in Somalia, Bosnia, and Zaire.

A government's policies towards public and private enterprise, consumers, and foreign corporations influence a company's decisions as to whether to enter a particular foreign market. Some countries continually seek out foreign investors; others actively discourage them; still others oscillate between the two positions. Tax concessions may be offered and later withdrawn; foreign owners may be welcomed and later forced to sell their holdings to local companies at fire-sale prices. The government of an LDC may invite Canadian, Japanese, Taiwanese, U.S. or British investors to build facilities and then, when the facilities are built, change the rules to prohibit profits from being removed from the country, so that the original investment can never be repaid. These restrictions are called *exchange controls*, and the possibility that they may be invoked is a strong disincentive to invest in a country where this may occur.

In a number of countries, expatriate executives and their families face severe physical risks. Some anti-government groups actually finance their activities in large part by collecting ransom for the return of expatriate executives who have been kidnapped—often in broad daylight in the middle of cosmopolitan cities. Recent carjackings in Lima, Peru, by Tupac Amaru terrorists, and by a similar group in Nairobi, have put Noranda executives in jeopardy and resulted in the deaths of two British businessmen. Similar events have occurred in Columbia, Yemen, and the Philippines. The United Nations reports that it has had more than $1 million worth of vehicles stolen in the former Yugoslavia.[36] In Johannesburg, public authorities advise local residents to stop using anti-theft devices such as steering wheel and ignition locks, so that the prevalent car thieves do not become frustrated and do severe damage to the car when their theft does not go smoothly!

As a consequence of these and similar situations, several organizations have training programs for executives about to be posted to some countries. These sessions include how to be as inconspicuous as possible by using old, battered, dirty cars, how to avoid predictable daily routines by changing routes and times of going to and from work or clubs, and how to behave when kidnapped—keeping enough cash on hand to satisfy kidnappers, looking only at the ground so as not to be able to identify the kidnappers, and practising "determined cowardice."[37] These factors can have a dampening effect on the enthusiasm of prospective candidates for foreign postings.

## *What Managers Are Reading*   14-2

### How to Negotiate Anything with Anyone Anywhere Around the World

Some books that purport to instruct on the principles of negotiation place most of their emphasis on tricks that can be played to achieve gains at the expense of those on the other side of the bargaining table. Fortunately, Frank Acuff not only avoids this misleading advice but turns it around and provides a useful table of possible responses to use when The Other Side (TOS in Acuff's lexicon) tries some of those tricks.

Much of what Acuff has to say about negotiations in general would apply in Canada as well as in foreign lands—fulfilling the "anyone, anywhere" promise implicit in his title. But the real contribution of the book is that it provides a thumbnail sketch of background information on each of 60 countries, with brief comments on how nationals of

that country tend to view social and business relations and how business is conducted there. Since the book obviously is directed to business people in the United States, Acuff's comments about negotiating in Canada provide a handy checkpoint to see how accurate he may be with his analyses of other countries. In general, he is quite accurate about the Canadian psyche, so it would seem that he might be close to the mark for Kuwait, Poland, Turkey, or whatever other countries might be of special interest to a reader.

Source: Frank L. Acuff, *How to Negotiate Anything with Anyone Anywhere Around the World* (Toronto: American Management Association, 1997).

**expropriation**
The taking by a government of property that belongs to private individuals or companies in exchange for some form of compensation.

**confiscation**
Expropriation without payment of compensation.

Aside from terrorism, one of the greatest overt political risks is that of **expropriation**, which in the international context means the taking by the government of property or business rights that were owned by a foreign national. Sometimes the government pays an inadequate amount for what is taken; in other instances, nothing at all is paid, in which case it is called **confiscation.** In either case, what was hoped to be a source of financial return becomes a serious loss for the MNC. In the years immediately after the Second World War, Angola, Chile, China, Cuba, Libya, Ethiopia, and a number of countries in Eastern Europe expropriated almost all of the foreign companies within their borders. Between 1960 and 1980, 1535 companies were expropriated by governments in 76 different countries, according to statistics gathered by the World Bank.[38] Then the epidemic of expropriation tapered off, in part because most of the countries that had done the expropriating had no targets left in their countries. In some countries the government leaders began to realize that when they acted irresponsibly, investors from the industrialized world declined to risk more of their funds, so confiscation had a negative effect on the guilty countries themselves. In the 1980s and 1990s, expropriation has become a rarity, but the threat of a resurgence still must be considered.

**Evaluating political risk.** International banks and accounting firms, various kinds of consultants, and MNCs themselves try to evaluate the economic and political risks that might be encountered in doing business in different countries. Some publish periodic lists of these evaluations. An example is the annual listing published by the respected publication *Euromoney.*[39] In one of their recent listings, Japan was rated as having the least political and economic risk, having been assigned a rating of 99.55 on a scale of 100. Closely following in descending order, all with ratings above 97.4, were the Netherlands, Switzerland, Germany, France, the United States, and Austria. Next, in eighth place, was Canada with a rating of 97.14. At the bottom of the scale, in 169th place, was

Cambodia with a rating of 2.56. Only slightly better, all with ratings lower than 10, were Iraq, North Korea, Somalia, and Cuba. Of course, as conditions change the ratings will vary from year to year, but when a country has a bad rating in one year, it is unusual for it to improve appreciably in the succeeding few years. Although any such predictions can be fallible, it would seem foolhardy for an MNC contemplating investment in one of the low-rated countries to disregard the warnings implicit in these low ratings.

## Direct Barriers to International Trade

**tariffs**
Customs duties established by law that require payment of fees to the government to bring products into a country, with the payment being based on the value of the products, their number or physical amount, or a combination of the two.

**non-tariff barriers (NTBs)**
Legal methods other than tariffs that are used to discourage, delay, or prevent goods from entering a country.

**quota**
In international trade, a specified limit as to the amount or value of goods or products that can be brought into a country during a stated period.

**embargo**
A legal prohibition on bringing specified goods or products into a country.

**Tariffs** are one of the most direct governmentally imposed barriers to reduce the quantity of goods imported into a country. A tariff, or duty, is a tax on an import or export that has the effect of increasing the ultimate price of the product, thus discouraging its import or export. Since the Second World War, tariffs around the world have been reduced progressively, until now, especially with the North American Free Trade Agreement, they do not constitute a major factor for the importation of most goods into Canada.

There are many **non-tariff barriers (NTBs)** in use by various countries. A **quota** limits the amount, or the total value, of a product that can leave or enter the country. Some quotas are formal, such as the limitations placed by the U.S. on imports of cotton clothing from various Asian countries under the Multi-Fibre Agreement that was in effect for more than two decades. For many years, the importation of several kinds of fruit, dairy products, poultry, and eggs were subject to formal quotas set by the Canadian marketing boards. These quotas now have been replaced with tariffs as high as 299 percent of value, so importation of these items is still extremely restricted. Other quotas, such as those placed by several countries on imports of Japanese-made cars, are termed "voluntary" because the exporting country has assented to them, albeit under threat of trade sanctions being imposed by the importing country if they do not assent.

An **embargo** prohibits the import or export of certain goods. For instance, Muslim nations impose an embargo on the importation of alcoholic beverages because consumption of alcohol is a violation of Muslim values. For many years, Canada imposed an embargo on the importation of used cars, although that restriction has been removed, having the result of lowering the market prices of all used vehicles in Canada. For several years Canada, Australia, the United Kingdom, and the rest of the European Union have battled to introduce various embargoes on items such as Canadian or Australian beef, unpasteurized French cheese, and some German pharmaceutical products. Whenever an embargo is introduced by one country, the others introduce compensatory embargoes or punitive tariffs, stopping the flow of products and directly or indirectly penalizing businesses that are caught in these trade wars.

Technical and safety standards are sometimes used to restrict the ability of foreign producers to compete. For instance, each model of an electrical appliance must be approved by the Canadian Standards Association before it can be sold to consumers in Canada, and by the Underwriters' Laboratories before it can be sold in the U.S. These rules are explained on the basis that they are for the protection of the consumer. However, the standards of the two organizations are roughly the same, so it would seem sufficient protection for the consumer if a particular model were to be approved in both countries as long as either of the two testing organizations had passed it. Yet, for manufacturers in Canada to sell in the U.S., and *vice versa*, they must submit their models for lengthy and costly testing by the organization in the other country, even though those very models have already been approved in the country of origin. Similar duplication of effort in other realms tends to discourage cross-border trading.

## The Regulation of International Business

As business between nations grows, so does the volume of laws and organizations involved in regulating international trade. This section examines some of those constraints.

### Legislation

Canadian companies engaged in international business not only must comply with Canadian laws, as do their domestic counterparts, but also must comply with the laws of the various host countries within which they operate. This multiplicity of laws can lead to complications and, in some cases, to conflicting requirements.

In recent years, the Canadian government has intensified its interest in and support of Canadian companies engaged in international business. The Department of External Affairs has groupings of experts, called "desks," that are staffed by experts on regions and specific countries. It also maintains Trade Commissioners' offices in Canadian embassies and consulates abroad to assist Canadian business people to make contact with their counterparts in other countries. Several governmental programs offer financial assistance for companies that wish to export Canadian-made products. The Export Development Corporation offers credit insurance to provide some protection for Canadian companies involved in international trade. All of this assistance tends to ease the transition from domestic to international business, but risks still exist, and considerable effort and time are entailed in planning and implementing the change.

The Competition Act[40] prohibits price fixing, bid rigging, and several other forms of anti-competitive behaviour. It contains an express exception for actions that "… relate only to the export of products from Canada." On first reading this may seem to offer broad latitude for anti-competitive action in foreign operations. On reflection, however, it may be seen that, operating as companies do in the global market, almost any action relating to exports likely would have at least a minimal impact on domestic business. The safest course of action, therefore, is to structure business affairs in ways that comply with the requirements of the Competition Act even if they appear superficially only to affect exports.

Many foreign countries do not have, or do not enforce, strict laws governing environmental impact, child labour, or the exploitation of employees. Some Canadian companies have established operations in these permissive regimes on the assumption that costs will be lowered. In some cases this has occurred, but often infrastructure and other costs have made up for the saving that was expected from escaping Canadian regulation. It also must be remembered that the Canadian public is becoming increasingly aware of the unsavoury conditions in which some products are manufactured in countries with little regulation. This awareness has sometimes led to lasting damage to the image of the companies that permit these antisocial practices, and in some cases to the establishment of informal but effective boycotts of the offending companies' products.

### International Organizations and Agencies

Companies operating in the global business environment must recognize that economic integration among nations is increasing, and is likely to continue to increase. The second half of the twentieth century has seen the development of literally hundreds of binational and multinational agreements that affect international trade and business. The United Nations and its subsidiary organizations, such as the Food and Agricultural

Organization (FAO) and the United Nations Educational, Social and Cultural Organization (UNESCO), have had an impact on international trade, especially by providing a forum for exchange of information and technology.

International financial organizations have greatly facilitated cross-border investments and the movement of capital among countries. The Bank for International Settlements provides a clearing-house to facilitate payments among the central banks of its member countries, thus simplifying international payments. The International Monetary Fund (IMF), created at the end of the Second World War, was designed to help member countries dampen fluctuations in exchange rates among the currencies of various countries. Each member country subscribes to an assigned quota of the funds required by the IMF. To stabilize exchange rates, when a nation's currency is under pressure, the IMF may grant it a loan to provide support. Often the IMF sets conditions on its loans, requiring the nation to take steps to improve its financial accountability, reduce its operating deficits, curb inflation and corruption, and take similar steps to put its financial house in order. The IMF has been criticized, both for this interference with domestic financial policy of borrowing countries and, paradoxically, for not refusing to lend to countries headed by unsavoury dictatorships. In effect, the IMF has been criticized for interfering in some cases and for not interfering in others! Nevertheless, it generally is conceded that in recent years the IMF has had a beneficial effect on world economic stability.

The International Bank for Reconstruction and Development, usually referred to as the World Bank, also was established near the end of the Second World War. Its original purpose was primarily to administer the huge amounts of aid being sent, primarily by the U.S. under the Marshall Plan, to rebuild war-shattered Europe. Now its role is to lend money for development programs, primarily to governments of LDCs, for terms of up to 35 years. It is financed by member countries in proportion to their respective economic strengths. It has been criticized because in its first 40 years or so its loans were almost always for megaprojects such as massive dams, which aggrandized political leaders in the recipient countries but did little to help the impoverished. In recent years the World Bank has been emphasizing infrastructure such as clean water supplies and local roads that tend to provide considerably more benefit to local populaces.

## Forms of Economic Integration

**economic integration**
The situation that exists when two or more countries agree to reduce tariffs and non-tariff barriers on goods or products passing from one to another and, in some cases, including other forms of economic cooperation.

**Economic integration** is said to occur when two or more countries mutually agree to establish rules to facilitate trade and economic cooperation. Achieving economic integration requires long and skilful negotiation, because whenever any nation agrees to be bound by external rules, it necessarily gives up some of its own independence, or sovereignty. Each party has to decide whether the overall benefits it foresees will outweigh the freedom of action it must yield in exchange. Otherwise, it will walk away from negotiations and the economic integration will not occur.

Within the last four centuries, economic integration has gone through at least three major cycles. First was the colonialism that saw the rise of empires, with mother countries and subservient colonies. Often the terms of trade were exploitative and much resented by the colonists. This sense of being exploited was one of the causes of the American Revolution, and of the wars of independence and political upheavals that freed Indonesia from the Netherlands, Algeria and Vietnam from France, and Chechnya, Uzbekistan, Kazakhstan, and their neighbours in the Soviet Union from domination by Russia.

Now some LDCs are being exploited by MNCs that control host country production, exportation of products, and sometimes even governmental policies. This type of control is aptly called *neo-colonialism*. Perhaps the example best-known to Canadians is the control exerted by the United Fruit Company in Central America, but many other examples could be cited.

In a comparatively recent development, most countries active in international trade have aligned themselves in one or more trading blocs, many of which are or seek to be free trade areas. Unfortunately, critics of this trend often have confused this development with neo-colonialism. This confusion overlooks the fact that when a country negotiates entry into a formal trading bloc, it always has the choice of rejecting the association, unlike countries that became colonies by force of arms or the subjects of neo-colonial exploitation who succumbed to economic pressures. It can be argued that economic pressures almost force some countries to join free trade groups, but a more accurate perception may be that in each case the government of a country has decided that affiliation is better for the country than any of the available alternatives. Whether its decision is right or wrong, even if the country is the weakest member of the bloc it still would have the option of withdrawing from whatever group it may have joined, and indeed some groups have had members withdraw after joining.

The most significant direct impact on worldwide international trade, however, has come from the General Agreement on Tariffs and Trade (GATT) and its successor, the World Trade Organization (WTO), and from the formation of trading blocs for economic integration.

## World Trade Organization (WTO)

As the Second World War drew to a close, 23 industrialized nations decided to take concerted action to help make international trade more free than had been the case previously. They remembered that when the United States Congress enacted the Smoot-Hawley Act in the 1930s, raising U.S. tariffs to unprecedented levels, it triggered almost worldwide retaliatory measures and a precipitous drop in international trade that greatly aggravated the worldwide Great Depression. To avoid repeating that tragic era in history, these nations founded the General Agreement on Tariffs and Trade, or GATT. Its announced purposes were to encourage the growth of international trade, primarily through providing a forum for nations to agree to mutual reductions of tariffs and non-tariff barriers.

In pursuit of these goals, GATT established two basic principles. One was the Most Favored Nation (MFN) rule. This says that every nation that belongs to GATT/WTO is entitled to be treated as favourably as the most favoured member nation. The second principle is National Treatment (NT). It says that once the products of an exporting country have cleared the border of a host nation, the imported products must be treated in the same manner as similar products that have originated in the host country. Provision is made for specific exceptions to both rules when it seems desirable to do so in order to assist with development of an LDC.

Negotiations have taken place in a series of "rounds," with the estimated impact of each shown in Exhibit 14-7. The issues have been complicated and negotiations at times have been difficult. Negotiations during the last round extended over a period of seven years. The agreement signed at its conclusion in 1994 filled 26,000 pages, which, according to the *Globe and Mail* "… if bound in a single volume would be nearly two metres tall."[41]

GATT had no enforcement mechanism, and decisions under WTO, its successor since 1995, must rely almost entirely on an offending nation's desire not to be seen as an

**Exhibit 14-7**

*GATT Negotiating Rounds and Their Estimated Impacts*

| Round | Dates | Number of Countries | Value of Trade Covered | Average Tariff Reduction |
|---|---|---|---|---|
| Geneva | 1947 | 23 | US$10 billion | 35% |
| Annecy | 1949 | 33 | Unavailable | — |
| Torquay | 1950 | 34 | Unavailable | — |
| Geneva | 1956 | 22 | US$2.5 billion | — |
| Dillon | 1960-61 | 45 | US$4.9 billion | — |
| Kennedy | 1961-67 | 48 | US$40 billion | 35% |
| Tokyo | 1973-79 | 99 | US$155 billion | 34% |
| Uruguay | 1986-94 | 125 | US$235 billion | 40% |

Source: Adapted from John H. Jackson, *The World Trading System* (Cambridge, MA: MIT Press, 1989).

international pariah in the eyes of the world. Even so, what might be termed international social pressure under GATT/WTO has been a major factor in the subsequent reduction of tariffs (by what various scholars have estimated may be from 60 to 80 percent) and of countless NTBs. These liberalizations of trade rules have contributed significantly to the massive increase in international trade mentioned earlier in this chapter.

Another weakness of WTO is that it has 124 members, including scores of countries such as Vanuatu and Turks and Caicos that have only a few thousand inhabitants and little or no impact on world trade. These tiny nations have equal votes in the WTO as such economic powerhouses as the United States and Japan, and indeed Canada. As a result, several of the major countries around the Pacific Rim, including Canada, have been working to create strong ties through the Asia-Pacific Economic Co-operation forum. It would not be surprising if this and similar developments arising from the European Union ultimately would make the WTO relatively insignificant in the future, despite the massive effect that GATT has had in the past.

**free trade area**
A combination of countries that have agreed to reduce or eliminate tariffs and non-tariff barriers that apply to goods and products passing from one country to another.

**customs union**
Multinational agreement that goes beyond a free trade agreement and provides that the member nations will establish common trade policies with respect to non-member countries.

**common market**
In addition to the provisions of a customs union, the members of a common market provide for free movement among themselves of the factors of production, that is, labour, capital, and technology.

## Economic Integration Through Trading Blocs

Because more countries are aligning themselves into trading blocs, forward-looking managers include consideration of international trade agreements in their planning as they decide whether a particular country is an apt target for investment or operations. There are five ascending levels of economic integration through trading blocs. In practice, no two trading blocs are identical, even though they may be classified on the same level.

The least restrictive level is the **free trade area**. In this form, tariffs, quotas, and many other barriers to trade between or among the members are eliminated either immediately or over a specified period. Further economic integration is achieved in a **customs union**. In addition to free trade provisions, members of a customs union establish common trade policies with respect to non-members. Further integration may create a **common market**. The distinguishing feature is that in addition to the provisions of a customs union, in the common market there is free movement among the members of the so-called factors of production, that is, labour, capital, and technology. The final level of

**economic union**
An arrangement that combines the features of a common market and in addition covers harmonization among the members of economic policies relating to government spending, taxation, and monetary policy.

**political union**
A combination of what were formerly independent countries into a single country.

international economic integration is the establishment of an **economic union**, in which government spending, taxation, and monetary policy are all harmonized among the members. The only further step is **political union**, in which there is not only economic integration, but also cohesion as a single nation. For Canadians the obvious example is the establishment of the Dominion of Canada by confederation of the disparate colonies in 1867, the addition of other provinces subsequently, and finally the addition of Newfoundland in 1949.

## North American Free Trade Agreement (NAFTA)

An early example of a modern free trade agreement is the one that has existed between New Zealand and Australia since the 1960s. Under that agreement, tariffs between the two countries were reduced gradually, and now the two countries have a high degree of economic integration, although not to the level of a customs union.

The example that is of most interest to Canada is, of course, the North American Free Trade Agreement (NAFTA) among Canada, the United States, and Mexico, and its predecessor, the Free Trade Agreement (FTA) between Canada and the U.S. The impact of FTA/NAFTA is greater in Canada than in the U.S. because of Canada's much greater dependence on international trade, but since each country has the other as its largest trading partner, it is a major factor in both countries.

*Although there are unresolved arguments as to the impact of FTA and NAFTA on Canada, there is no doubt that these free trade agreements have caused a marked change in Canada's foreign trade and business.*

After five years of political policy reversals in Canada, and protracted negotiations between representatives of the two countries, FTA finally came into effect on January 1, 1989.[42] Opposition in Canada largely had centred around the issue of sovereignty, and the assumption that Canada would be driven into a "branch-plant" economy that could not compete with more-efficient companies in the United States. This line of reasoning said that FTA would eliminate thousands of Canadian jobs, creating massive unemployment. Support for the agreement, on the other hand, was based primarily on the assumption that it would open the large U.S. market to Canadian manufacturers and tend to provide more choice and lower prices for Canadian consumers. It also was argued that in light of the clear signs that the sentiment for protectionism was growing in the U.S., Canada would be best protected by negotiating some form of trade agreement before the U.S. Congress took further steps to stifle Canadian exports to the U.S. All of these arguments, both positive and negative, have proved to be partly correct and partly exaggerated. The intervening years have not seen either the disasters predicted by many of the opponents nor the panaceas predicted by many of the enthusiasts. NAFTA proponents can point to the fact that Canada now has tens of thousands of more jobs than pre-FTA, and that since FTA was enacted, according to figures from the Organization for Economic Co-operation and Development, North American job growth has exceeded 80 percent in the aggregate, while there has been no job growth in the same period in Europe.[43] On the other hand, NAFTA detractors can point out that Canada still has unemployment that hovers around 10 percent, and argue with equal sincerity that were it not for FTA/NAFTA there would have been even greater job growth. Trade between Canada and the U.S. has increased markedly, but whether the net effect is better or worse for Canada than other possible alternatives will have to await the judgement of history, and even then will depend largely on the point of view of the observer.

Mexico's inclusion in NAFTA in 1995 has had little practical effect on Canada because of the small amount of trade between Canada and Mexico. Plans for the addition of Chile and other Latin American countries have been stalled in domestic disputes between the U.S. Congress and the U.S. president, but Canada is proceeding to negotiate with some of those countries to create a wider free trade zone for Canada and its neighbours. Frustrated by the delay in NAFTA admission, Chile, too, has been negotiating independent free trade agreements with Canada, Mexico, other Latin American countries, and the European Union.[44]

The most direct impact of FTA/NAFTA on Canada-U.S. trade is in the area of tariffs. In the FTA, export goods were divided into three groups. For one group, tariffs were eliminated immediately. For the second group, tariffs were eliminated at the rate of one-fifth for each of the years 1989 through 1993. For the third and largest group, tariffs were eliminated at the rate of one-tenth for each of the years 1989 through 1998. The phasing out, rather than immediate elimination, of tariffs was designed to allow manufacturers and suppliers to adjust their marketing and buying processes to the new regime without tariff protection.

Many of the FTA/NAFTA provisions merely repeat GATT terms to which all three countries had been subscribing for many years. The major difference, however, is that now trade disputes between any two of the three countries are settled through the decisions of binational adjudicatory tribunals, instead of in the courts of either country. Since 1989 these tribunals have proved remarkably objective, with individual members apparently voting on principle rather than slavishly voting to advance the cause of their own country.

Sentiment has arisen in Canada for what was been dubbed TAFTA, for transatlantic free trade agreement. Arguments for such an agreement are that it would open much larger markets for the 15 members of the European Union and the 3 members of NAFTA. From this same assumption others argue that to have such an exclusive trading bloc would send an unmistakable message to LDCs that their interests are being ignored by North Americans and Europeans.[45] Because of Canada's strong and growing connections with Pacific Rim countries, this perception might seriously damage prospects for Canadian trade growth in these fast-growing areas.

## The European Union (EU)

Among several dozen other formal and informal trading blocs in the world, three are likely to have the most immediate impact on Canada. One is the European Union (EU), which is the outgrowth of a steel and coal consortium formed in 1957 by the Treaty of Rome and now has progressed into a customs union. Although the EU has a European Parliament, a European Court of Justice, a large bureaucracy, and several other structures of a federal government, individual countries still retain considerable political autonomy. Since March 1, 1986, there have been no tariffs between most of its members and NTBs gradually have been reduced or eliminated, creating one of the largest markets in the world, with over 340 million consumers who have high incomes by world standards. In July 1990 most EU countries eliminated barriers to the free movement of capital. Signed in 1991, the Maastricht Treaty was designed to create a single currency and central bank by 1999. Most EU countries have adopted the Euro as the denomination of currency, allowing for a period of transition. A few others, most important of which is the United Kingdom, have elected to retain their national currencies. Consequently, the prognosis for total financial integration in the near future is doubtful.

The elimination of trade barriers already has meant big gains for Europe in several industries, including airlines, telecommunications, and financial services. On the other hand, high wage levels combined with low productivity in some of the EU countries (notably France, the United Kingdom, Portugal, Spain, and Greece)[46] have created some internal strains within the EU and have reduced somewhat the competitive impact on Canadian companies that have been exporting to Europe. Even so, Canada's trade with EU member nations inevitably will suffer as trade from one EU member to another increases at the expense of trade with outsiders.

## The Association of Southeast Asian Nations (ASEAN)

The second trading bloc that may have considerable direct impact on Canada's trade is the Association of Southeast Asian Nations (ASEAN). Its members are Brunei, Indonesia, Malaysia, the Philippines, Singapore, and Thailand, with Vietnam a recent entry. Of greater impact than is made on Canada by these countries, Japan has entered cooperative agreements with ASEAN, which if pursued further could make the association extremely powerful. This organization has created a unique international stockpile of rice to reduce annual fluctuations in food supply, and its members have agreed on rationalization of industrial development, permitting one country to specialize in a particular industry and another country to specialize in another industry. Although Canada's trade with ASEAN members has not been large, some scholars have suggested that Canada must look to this area to replace the trade with EU members that will be lost. Because of the severe economic downtown in this area in 1998, the extent of ASEAN's impact on Canada is problematical.

## Asia-Pacific Economic Co-operation Forum (APEC)

The third bloc likely to have the greatest impact on Canadian international trade is APEC. For several years Canada, the United States, Japan, China, and 14 other Pacific Rim countries[47] have held annual meetings of the Asia-Pacific Economic Co-operation Forum to discuss various forms of cooperation in international trade matters. In 1994, at their meeting in Indonesia, they agreed in principle that the industrialized APEC members should eliminate intergroup trade barriers by 2010, and that by 2020 these barriers should be eliminated by the other members as well.[48] Although meeting this goal would create the largest free trade zone in the world, containing half of the world's foreign trade, little attention was paid in the Canadian press to the report of this loose agreement. In August 1995 an APEC task force recommended that tariff reductions agreed upon in the Uruguay Round of GATT negotiations should be accelerated within APEC to reach the GATT/WTO goals in half of the time allotted by WTO.[49] Decisions made at the APEC meetings in Osaka in November 1995 and in Vancouver in November 1997 are expected to result in even greater strengthening of the ties among these countries. Despite the importance of the agreements reached, in the minds of the public the publicity in Canada concerning security arrangements for the Vancouver conference has obscured the potential impact of those decisions. If commitments that were made in APEC are actually met, this trading bloc will be one of the most powerful in the realm of international trade.

## The Commonwealth of Independent States (CIS)

With the breakup of the Soviet Union on December 25, 1991, the former Soviet republics became independent countries. The most important of these is Russia, which includes a large proportion of the former Soviet Union's population, economic wealth, and land area, including the vast reaches of Siberia. The Ukraine is important to Canada because of its competition in the world wheat market; Kazakhstan, Uzbekistan, and other small countries are important because of several projects to develop mineral resources; and the Baltic states of Latvia, Lithuania, and Estonia may develop into consumer markets.

Most of the former Soviet republics have joined the newly formed Commonwealth of Independent States (CIS). It is a loose economic and political alliance, but falls short of being a classic trading bloc. The borders of CIS countries theoretically are open to each other, but there is no central government or coordinating body, and old animosities against Russia and among the other nations will take long to heal. In economic terms, the Slavic countries tend to be loosely affiliated in a zone that depends on the Russian ruble; the countries that speak a Turkic language are loosely affiliated with each other in dependence on the Turkish lira, although it does not have an official status.

Several companies from the Western world are establishing joint ventures in the CIS, but most are proceeding cautiously to see what will be the outcome of the political and economic tensions that are evident in the aftermath of the Soviet breakup. Canadian managers will need to keep informed about these developments in order to take advantage of opportunities as they present themselves within the fast-changing conditions.

## The Workplace of Tomorrow

The world will continue to change at a rapid pace. Change never comes easily—it brings problems and challenges—but it is inevitable. Companies risk failure if they don't acknowledge the changes that are taking place and in so doing fail to adapt to them. Although any prediction of the future is prone to error, it seems safe to expect that as competition becomes more intense on the world scene, various countries will continue to seek advantage by allying themselves with other countries in international trade and business. Free trade agreements and other forms of trading blocs are likely to proliferate, with their members changing allegiance as their interests seem to change. Economist Paul Krugman, writing in the *Report on Business*, scoffs at those who predicted that trading blocs were only the "flavour of the decade." He points out that in Canada, as in some other nations, "embittered voters" have tended to blame their woes on free trade, when in reality most of the economic and social gains and most of the difficulties have been caused by other factors.[50]

Nevertheless, it is clear that for the individual business, and hence for managers, it is essential to watch carefully all developments in the creation, growth, and possible decline of trading blocs. Markets will open, others will shut down, and the organization that wants to remain competitive will have to adapt to these changes. Whatever happens with trading blocs, the most successful managers will be those who can command several languages, operate comfortably in different cultures, and accurately forecast trends in attitudes, preferences, and economic strengths of various countries. Globalization, with all of its warts and blemishes, is here to stay and will continue to be a factor with which managers must cope.

The essence of the global challenge is threefold. To survive and prosper in the global economy, Canadian companies must

1. Recognize that competition and opportunity are no longer confined to domestic situations, but encompass almost the whole world; and
2. Adapt to constantly changing conditions, including the planned reductions of tariffs and non-tariff barriers; and
3. Develop international trading strategies that optimize benefits from trading blocs that include Canada and that counteract the loss of trade with those trading blocs that exclude Canada.

# Summary of Learning Objectives

▶ **Discuss the nature and importance to Canada of the global environment.**

Today, any product made anywhere has to compete with similar products made nearly anywhere else. Nearly $4 trillion is spent annually on trade between nations, illustrating this increase in competition. Both Canada as a nation and Canadian managers individually must recognize the impacts of international trade and take effective steps to participate effectively, while preventing as many of the excesses and deleterious effects as possible.

▶ **Describe the approaches that Canadian organizations can take to enter international business.**

A multinational corporation (MNC) can export—that is, sell in a foreign country—goods made in its home country. It can distribute through a piggyback arrangement, or enter original equipment manufacture (OEM) contracts. It can issue a licence or a franchise to a company in the host country, allowing that company to use the parent's technology, brand name, or operating techniques in exchange for a royalty. It can enter a joint venture or a strategic alliance, cooperating with a company in the host country. It can sell through a trading company. If the host country has currency limitations, the company may find it useful to make a countertrading arrangement. The deepest commitment exists if the MNC either purchases a business venture in the host country or establishes its own subsidiary there.

▶ **Describe the environments for multinational or global business.**

The environments include cultural, economic, social, political-legal, and technological forces, all of which differ among countries. Culture includes the learned values, attitudes, expectations, and behaviours that are shared by a society. Managers must adjust to cultural differences when doing business in a foreign country. International management is also influenced by economic factors, including a country's stability, market size, income, economic condition, and infrastructure. Consideration also must be given to a country's social environment, including demographic factors, working conditions, and technological and educational levels. Political stability and government regulations also influence a company's decisions to enter a foreign market. Some countries encourage foreign investors; others develop barriers to entry; others vacillate between the two extremes.

▶ **Explain how laws and regulations influence international business.**

An MNC must abide by the laws of its home country and also of the host country or countries. The Canadian laws that usually have the greatest impact on an MNC are the Competition Act, the new Corruption of Foreign Public Officials Act, and the special acts that govern the agencies that assist with economic development and particularly with exports.

▶ **Discuss the roles played by some international organizations and their impact on management.**

The World Trade Organization (WTO) and its predecessor organization, General Agreement on Tariffs and Trade (GATT), have been responsible for agreements that have caused massive reductions in tariffs and non-tariff barriers, thus opening opportunities for international trade. The International Monetary Fund (IMF) has helped to stabilize currency exchange rates; the Bank for International Settlements (BIS) has facilitated international payments, and the World Bank has made loans to developing nations that have been designed to hasten their development of business-oriented infrastructure. Since these organizations influence how various countries will function economically, Canadian managers must keep abreast of their changing plans and policies.

▷ **Discuss the international trading blocs and their importance to Canadian business.**
A trading bloc is a collection of countries that agree to freer trade and various forms of economic cooperation among themselves. These agreements effectively make competition more difficult for outsiders. The forms, in progressive order of integration, are a free trade area, a customs union, a common market, an economic union, and a political union. The North American Free Trade Agreement (NAFTA), linking Canada, the U.S., and Mexico, and potentially other Latin American countries, is of most direct impact on Canada. Because in effect it is exclusionary towards Canada, the European Union (EU) has an indirect but substantial negative effect. The Asia-Pacific Economic Co-operation Forum (APEC), which includes Canada, has the potential to create a free trade area encompassing half of the world's international trade.

▷ **Discuss the major challenges facing Canadian organizations functioning in the global environment.**
The major challenges include the need to maintain the quality of Canadian products and to maximize the benefits from trading blocs that include Canada, while minimizing the barriers that are put up by trading blocs that exclude Canada.

## KEY TERMS

common market, p. 521
confiscation, p. 516
countertrading, p. 507
cultural diversity, p. 510
customs union, p. 521
demography, p. 514
direct ownership, p. 509
economic integration, p. 519
economic union, p. 522
embargo, p. 517

exporting, p. 504
expropriation, p. 516
franchising, p. 507
free trade area, p. 521
global corporation, p. 502
infrastructure, p. 514
international business, p. 499
international management, p. 500
international trade, p. 499
joint venture, p. 507

licensing, p. 506
multinational corporation (MNC), p. 502
non-tariff barriers (NTBs), p. 517
original equipment manufacture (OEM), p. 505
piggyback distribution, p. 504
political union, p. 522
quota, p. 517
strategic alliance, p. 509
tariffs, p. 517
trading company, p. 505

## REVIEW AND DISCUSSION QUESTIONS

### Recall
1. What is international business? What is international management?
2. What are the different approaches a company can take to become involved in international business?
3. What types of trade barriers do some nations use to discourage entry of foreign companies or products?
4. How can international organizations facilitate world trade?

5. What effects on world trade can be attributed to the General Agreement on Tariffs and Trade/World Trade Organization?
6. What challenges face Canadian companies wishing to enter international trade?
7. What are some of Canada's largest exporters?

## Understanding

8. What is the difference between a multinational corporation and a global corporation?
9. What environments must a Canadian manager consider in deciding whether to enter a foreign market?
10. What is the significance of multinational trading blocs to Canadian companies?
11. What might be the impact on Canadian international trade of the European Union? NAFTA? The free trade bloc that might be established under the Asia-Pacific Economic Co-operation Forum?

## Application

12. In a recent business journal (e.g., *Canadian Business*, *Report on Business*, *Fortune*, *The Economist*, or *Far East Economic Review*) read an article that discusses international business, a trading bloc, or an international trade dispute. Discuss how the information in the article might affect Canadian international trade.

## CASE 14-1

### KFC's Recipe for Global Success

Since 1939, when Harlan Sanders developed a secret chicken recipe with 11 herbs and spices, KFC (formerly Kentucky Fried Chicken) has become known all over the world. KFC's chicken is sold throughout North America, Europe, the Middle East, Africa, Asia, the South Pacific, Latin America, and the Caribbean. World sales in 1991 totalled $6.2 billion, including $2.8 billion outside the United States.

Colonel Sanders first became involved in international business in 1956 by opening stores in Canada. Today KFC has 3424 international stores (562 owned by the company, 457 joint ventures, and 2405 franchises). Worldwide, KFC has 8480 stores. Its 70-restaurant operations in Mexico is expected to triple in five years. With 105 restaurants in Malaysia, KFC has 60 percent of the nation's fast-food market. And KFC's ten stores in China serve an average of 1 million customers a year, four times the average in the United States.

What's KFC's secret to global success? First and perhaps most important is the worldwide acceptance of chicken. In Malaysia, for instance, annual per capita consumption of chicken has doubled during the past decade. According to Allan Huston Jr., president of KFC International, "Chicken is probably the most universally accepted source of protein. There is not a country in the world where you won't find chicken." And unlike other meats, chicken isn't forbidden by religions or cultures except among vegetarians. This acceptance presented an excellent opportunity for KFC, but it didn't guarantee success.

KFC made some early mistakes in Latin America and Europe. The company learned that opening an American fast-food restaurant abroad isn't simple. Cultural differences between countries result in different eating habits. For instance, people eat their main meal of the day at different times throughout the world. Different menus also must be developed for specific cultures, while maintaining the core product, fried chicken. You can always find original recipe chicken, cole slaw, and fries at every KFC outlet, while restaurants in China feature

Chinese tea and French restaurants offer more desserts. Above all, KFC emphasizes consistency. Whether in Shanghai or Toronto, the product basically tastes the same.

KFC usually enters a new foreign market by opening a single store in a large urban area on the most visible piece of real estate available. If the project fails, the land can be sold. Usually foreign stores are eat-in restaurants, compared to the take-out style generally found in the United States and Canada. Prices are usually high at first to appeal to an upscale market.

International markets offer many opportunities and challenges for KFC. The company is growing outside of the United States at nearly five times the rate of its domestic growth. While many businesses complain about the inability to compete in Japan, KFC has nearly 1000 restaurants in Japan alone. The secret, according to Huston, is quality, such as using fresh chicken rather than frozen. Freezing chicken causes a discolouring of the bone, which bothers the Japanese. Eastern Europe also holds great promise for KFC. With two stores in Hungary, KFC is working on deals in Poland and the Czech Republic.

KFC faces several challenges. In some areas of the world, such as Malaysia and Indonesia, it's illegal to import poultry, which has led to product shortages. Another challenge is to adapt KFC's people perspective. The company has been most successful in foreign markets when stores are operated by people who understand the culture. The objective is to think like a local, not like an American company starting an American business in a foreign country.

### Questions

1. Why has KFC been successful globally?
2. What approaches to international business does KFC use? What are the advantages to each approach?
3. What are some of the cultural barriers encountered by KFC in its global operations?
4. Why do you think Kentucky Fried Chicken changed its name to KFC? Does this name change have any global implications?

Source: Adapted from Andrew Tanzer, "How Wings Take Off," *Forbes* (January 18, 1993): 74; Alan I. Kirschenbaum, "The 'Original Recipe' for International Success," *The Lane Report* (May 1992): 17-24; Sid Astbury, "KFC Malaysia: By No Means Chickenfeed," *Asian Business* (August 1992): 8; and Heidi Dawley, "Franchising: Mexico's Arms Are Wide Open," *Restaurant Business* (March 20, 1992): 74-77.

*CASE* **14-2**

## Nestlé Expands Globally

The Switzerland-based Nestlé corporation, once a Swiss chocolate maker, now is the world's biggest food company and the largest producer of coffee, powdered milk, and frozen dinners. The company also became number one in candy after passing Mars. And with the purchase of Perrier for $2.7 billion, Nestlé became the world's largest producer of mineral water with a 20 percent share of the world market. Nestlé achieved its success through intensive global expansion. Nestlé does only 2 percent of its business in Switzerland; the remaining 98 percent is in other countries.

One of the first multinational corporations, Nestlé now has production facilities in more than 60 countries. Its products can be found almost everywhere around the globe. In Europe, where Nestlé's success is greatest, sales of instant coffee, mineral water, yoghurt, frozen foods, cold cuts, candy, and cereal bars total roughly $10.2 billion. Sales in North America are approximately $6.7 billion for products such as Nescafé instant coffee, Carnation Coffeemate non-dairy creamer, Friskies pet food, Nestlé Crunch chocolates, and Stouffer frozen foods. Other big markets for Nestlé have been Asia ($3.1 billion in sales), Latin America ($2.4 billion in sales), and Oceania—Australia, New Zealand, and other islands of the Pacific Ocean—($0.6 billion in sales). The firm spends about $1.2 billion annually on advertising.

One secret to Nestlé's success is that many of its products—especially instant coffee, chocolates, and frozen foods—appeal to consumers all over the world. For example, coffee is closing in on tea as the favourite drink in Japan. Frozen dinners, long a hit in the United States, are catching on in Europe. And of course chocolate tastes the same in any language. Although these products have to be adapted slightly to local tastes, they generally can be sold worldwide. Because of high research and development costs as well as high costs of marketing, Nestlé benefits greatly by offering products with global appeal. After making large investments in its products, the company has been able to move brands from one country to another with relative ease.

Nestlé's Lean Cuisine dinners provide a good illustration of how the company expands internationally. Lean Cuisine was introduced in the United States in 1981 and became a huge success. In 1985 Nestlé chief executive Helmut Maucher endorsed a plan to sell Lean Cuisine in Britain. In the beginning, before the company's British frozen-food plant reached full production, products were imported from a plant in Canada. The cost of shipping frozen dinners in refrigerated ships, in addition to paying customs taxes, was extremely high. But Maucher was patient and the venture paid off. In 1989 sales of frozen dinners in Britain reached $100 million and Nestlé achieved a 33 percent share of the market. Lean Cuisine also has been successfully introduced in France.

Nestlé has several new projects in the works. Coca-Cola Nestlé Refreshment Company (CCNR), a joint venture between Coca-Cola and Nestlé, should dominate the ready-to-drink iced tea market with Nestea Iced Tea. Distribution will be handled through the Coke bottling system, while Nestlé provides the brand awareness. Nestlé also bought British confectioner Rowntree Mackintosh. Few brands have Rowntree's recognition or appeal throughout Europe, which should help Nestlé build brand awareness in national markets. Nestlé manages its own operations in Thailand, where it has 80 percent of the nation's instant coffee sales. Nestlé's most recent venture in Thailand is the launch of an iced coffee drink.

Now Nestlé is looking to what Maucher thinks is the market of the future, the Third World. Currently, 20 percent of the world's population consumes 80 percent of Nestlé's products. Maucer thinks his company's products will be seen soon in more parts of the world. The company also will look to what Maucher considers the food of the future—pasta. As he puts it, "We can't feed the world on beefsteak. So noodles will conquer the world."

Most industry experts agree that Nestlé is in the best position of any food company to expand internationally. Most of its competitors, which have been concentrating on their domestic markets, are scrambling to become involved in the profitable international trade.

## Questions

1. Would you classify Nestlé as a global corporation? Why or why not?
2. What are the advantages of Nestlé's joint venture with Coca-Cola?
3. Will competitors be able to follow Nestlé into foreign markets with the same degree of success?
4. Which environmental considerations are most important as Nestlé expands into Third World nations?

Source: Adapted from Bruce Crumley, "Nestlé Muscle May Pump Perrier," *Advertising Age* (March 30, 1992): 59; Greg W. Prince, "Coke-Nestlé Venture Finally Bears Tea," *Beverage World* (January 31, 1992): 1, 4; John Parry, "Nestlé's Name Plan," *International Management* (December 1991): 54-55; Joyce Raivat, "In Thailand, Nestlé Goes Direct to the People," *Asian Finance* (September 15, 1991): 14; and Shawn Tully, "Nestlé Shows How to Gobble Markets," *Fortune* (January 16, 1989): 74-78.

## APPLICATION EXERCISE   14-1

### Cultural Differences in Job Preferences

The first column below lists several characteristics of jobs in general. In the second column, record how you think you would rank the various characteristics when you are perhaps 35 and in middle management ranks. In the remaining columns, record how you believe these characteristics might be ranked in terms of importance by a middle management employee in each of the countries named. Assign rankings from 1 to 5, where 1 is assigned to those qualities of most importance, 2, 3, and 4 are assigned to those of consecutively decreasing importance, and 5 is assigned to those of little or no importance.

|  | Canada | U.S. | Japan | Malaysia |
|---|---|---|---|---|
| Opportunity for promotion | _____ | _____ | _____ | _____ |
| Variety in job | _____ | _____ | _____ | _____ |
| Independence, autonomy | _____ | _____ | _____ | _____ |
| Freedom to make choices | _____ | _____ | _____ | _____ |
| Approval of co-workers | _____ | _____ | _____ | _____ |
| Job security | _____ | _____ | _____ | _____ |
| Availability of mentor | _____ | _____ | _____ | _____ |
| Regular hours | _____ | _____ | _____ | _____ |
| Good pay | _____ | _____ | _____ | _____ |
| Interesting work | _____ | _____ | _____ | _____ |

Now take a look at what is important to you and your perceptions of what may be important to people in other cultures. There are probably some differences. Realizing that your rankings are based only on your perceptions, answer the following questions.

1. What cultural factors might explain some of the differences?
2. Do these differences say anything about the quality of work that might be expected from managers in each country? About global competitiveness?
3. Do you think that your parents and grandparents would rank the job characteristics differently than you did? Why? (You might ask them.) What might any generational differences say about changing cultures in Canada (or wherever they may have lived previously)?

## INTERNET APPLICATION   14-1

Explore the Web site for Noranda (www.noranda.ca).

1. What is Noranda's method of expanding into the global environment? What are some of the major events that occurred that transformed Noranda into an international organization?
2. How will declining barriers of distance and culture affect the way Noranda operates?

Search for the Web site of an organization with a strong global presence. What are the main forces in the global environment that affect the way this organization operates?

# Technology and Innovation

After studying this chapter, you should be able to:

▶ Distinguish between *technology* and *innovation* and describe *technology transfer*;

▶ Explain the value chain analysis procedure;

▶ Describe the managerial skills needed for managing technology;

▶ Discuss the differences among technology-driven transfer, market-driven transfer, and product-and-process-improvement transfer;

▶ Describe some important techniques that managers can use to encourage creativity; and

▶ Discuss why an organization might decide either to provide or not to provide creativity training for its employees.

*Sun Microsystems CEO Scott McNealy.*

## Sun Microsystems Keeps Creativity Flowing

THE COMPUTER AND TELECOMMUNICATIONS INDUS-tries worldwide are among the most competitive arenas in which to conduct business. New ventures are continuously entering with aggressive strategies, novel technologies, and brilliant leaders. Managers are finding that they can no longer rely on old strategies that depended on economies of scale. To be competitive an organization must focus on constant innovation, high quality and a guiding vision of the future. ▶

For more than a decade, Scott McNealy has led Sun Microsystems by preaching the gospel of network computing—the idea that the true value of computers is realized when they are hooked together in networks. For years that message has been known by high-end users on Toronto's Bay Street and in engineering firms. But for several years the mainstream business market with their desktop computers did not hear McNealy's message. That was before the explosion of the Internet and before its potential for business was realized.

In more recent years, businesses have been tripping over themselves to get on the Net. Now McNealy's mantra, "The Network Is the Computer," has begun to resonate and be heard around the world. Its Java programming language has created excitement among the cyberspace set. Java was officially released in January 1996, but word of what it might portend had been circulating for months before that. Java is a programming language that permits the creation of tiny applications called "applets" that race across the Internet's World Wide Web and run on any computer platform. Programmers already have created applets for everything from animation to transmitting electronic ticker tape.

McNealy is not the stereotypical leader of a Silicon Valley company. He does not bury himself in the arcane world of computer code. Nor is his history one of climbing corporate ladders through a series of engineering or computing jobs. After receiving his Harvard degree in economics, McNealy completed his MBA at Stanford. McNealy briefly held positions at FMC Corporation and at minicomputer maker Onyx Systems. In 1982 he got a call from former Stanford classmate Vinod Khosla, asking him to join Khosla and computer designer Andreas Bechtolsheim in starting Sun. McNealy's manufacturing skills enabled the young company to keep up with wild demand as sales soared from $9 million in 1983 to $39 million just one year later.

After Khosla left the company in a dispute with Sun's board, McNealy was named CEO at the age of 30. Although he says that he dislikes being labelled as brash, that is the adjective that follows him around. At Sun's California headquarters, he has built a corporate culture based on his own inelegant but forthright motto, "Kick butt and have fun." The company has become famous for its aggressive marketing, and equally so for the stories of juvenile antics around headquarters. Each April Fool's Day, scores of photographers and reporters converge on Sun Headquarters to record the elaborate pranks that engineers play on McNealy and other executives. Once, for example, the engineers built a golf course hole in golf-lover McNealy's office—compete with water hazard and green.

McNealy participates in their pranks. He has played the part of general in an intramural squirt-gun war. The humour has an important effect: It helps bind the company together and helps employees live with their demanding jobs. "His humour and ability to raise a crowd to its feet is in many respects exactly what you need in a CEO and in leaders in today's industry," says Thomas J. Meredith, a former Sun treasurer.

An example of how McNealy's style promotes innovation and creativity inside Sun is Java itself. Without McNealy's stubborn commitment to Java, it never would have gotten off the ground. The idea behind Java was introduced to McNealy in 1990 when he asked a departing engineer to write a memo on how Sun could improve itself. The engineer wrote that it should create a software system for portable devices. McNealy was so impressed that he persuaded the engineer to stay on at Sun and do it. McNealy gave the new project total independence and served as its champion. Once, when the team was burning out, he dropped in for a demonstration. The team only had a shaky prototype, but McNealy turned morale around when he exclaimed, "This is the greatest thing I've ever seen."

McNealy's style has led to a spirit of innovation and creativity at Sun that has suddenly vaulted the company into a competitive position that allowed it to take on industry leaders such as Microsoft and Intel. But McNealy knows that Sun's innovative Java language isn't the last word in computing and networking, and he continues to push Sun to its limits to be the first to create the next important technology. ∎

Sources: Adapted from Robert D. Hof, Kathy Rebello, and Peter Burrows, "Scott McNealy's Rising Sun," *Business Week* (January 22, 1996): 66-73; and Robert D. Hof and John Verity, *Business Week* (January 22, 1996): 73.

## The Technological World

Imagine a world where nearly everyone has access to the Internet, and to virtually unlimited cable television channels in their homes. Imagine a world where more than 50 percent of all employees work out of their homes. Imagine a world where the greatest art, music, literature, and scientific discoveries are available to everyone at the touch of a few buttons. Although that world doesn't exist in reality (and given the extreme poverty of most of the world probably will never exist), it does exist in the minds of leaders in technology, such as Microsoft's Bill Gates. He built his home of the future at a cost that rivals those of people such as the Sultan of Brunei and the oil-rich potentates of Saudi Arabia, Oman, and Kuwait. Gates's home features rooms that tailor themselves to the individuals who use them. As people enter a room, the technological marvels in the room identify them, show their chosen artworks, play their favourite music, and adjust the lighting to their personal preferences. Personal newspapers are displayed, with a selection of the types of stories they favour from publications around the world. The technology required for these marvels is available to everyone if, of course, they are willing and able to dedicate several tens of millions of dollars to the design and construction of their homes. As Gates predicts in his book *The Road Ahead*, advances in computing, telecommunications, and other technologies will continue to make radical changes to the ways in which we work, live, and play.[1]

*Assembly of computers, and many other high-tech operations, requires a degree of cleanliness that would have been inconceivable only a few years ago. In this "clean room," employees wear special clothing, air circulation and filter systems remove every speck of dust, and entry is possible only through a pressurized double door air lock similar to that of a space capsule.*

Even Gates, however, does not predict that homes such as his will ever reach the mass market. And some of his predictions, while exciting, may miss the mark by almost as much as the prediction contained in a 1949 issue of *Popular Mechanics*, that "Computers in the future may weigh no more than 1.5 tons." Or the assurance given in 1977 by Ken Olson, the president, chairman, and founder of Digital Equipment Corporation, that "There is no reason anyone would want a computer in their home." Or even the prediction attributed to Bill Gates himself in 1981, that "640 K ought to be enough for anybody."[2] Today, we can chortle at how much these predictions understated the real future. But they are instructive in that we should remind ourselves that whatever predictions we make based on today's knowledge may fall far short of what will be commonplace in another half-century or less. And that will be the time when many of today's college and university students will be enjoying the fruits and deploring the negative consequences of technologies that even our most far-sighted prognosticators cannot envision.

This chapter discusses technology and innovation in the context of current conditions and future expectations to the extent that they can be assessed today.

## Meanings of Technology and Innovation

The word *technology* is derived from the Greek words *techne* (meaning art or craft) and *logos* (meaning discourse or organized work). The practice of technology is an art or craft, as distinguished from the practice of a science, which is based on theoretical principles and depends on findings that can be verified or replicated. Technology is applied to achieve a practical outcome but it is not necessarily based on science, because in some instances the engineering technology may precede a true scientific understanding of the principles involved.[3]

**Technology** can be applied only through people. It is the totality of the means people employ to provide comfort and human sustenance and to accomplish desired tasks.[4] **Innovation** is defined as the generation of a new idea and its implementation into a new product, process, or service. It can lead to national economic growth, increased employment, and creation of profit. Innovation is a cumulative process of numerous decisions, ranging from the conception of the idea to the development of technology. No matter how significant technological invention may be, it is of no benefit to an organization if its use does not result in greater effectiveness in meeting the goals of that organization.

For example, video conferencing is an innovation that has become much more common in recent years as the technology has become more reliable and as costs have dropped. According to Peter Lee, a senior telecommunications specialist of Calgary-based Novacor Chemicals Ltd., the use of video conferencing has reduced travel costs and saved the time of Novacor's executives who previously shuttled among the company's 13 or more far-flung offices. He cites the example of Novacor's weekly production and planning meetings. Before video conferencing, one member of, for instance, the business group in Sarnia, Ontario, would devote the greatest part of three days each week to travelling to Calgary, attending the meeting, and then returning to Sarnia to brief colleagues on what took place at the meeting. Now, instead of only one member from Sarnia attending the meeting, several members participate through video conferencing. Only three hours each week is spent on the meeting, communication is improved, and more people can contribute to the decisions made. Lee says that the million-dollar investment to equip 13 geographically dispersed offices for video conferencing has been more than repaid by the cost savings it has generated.

Canadian Tire Corp. Ltd. has recently invested $150,000 in three room-sized video conferencing rooms and five personal computer-based systems. Robert Forneri, the executive responsible for all of Canadian Tire's voice communications, argues that face-to-face communication is essential for proper communication and permits senior executives to maintain close contact with the general managers of business units without having to invest immense amounts of time in travel. Now Canadian Tire Acceptance is starting to use video conferencing with major customers and suppliers, as well as within the company itself.[5]

Of course, video conferencing is not for everyone. A complete video conferencing room costs at least $75,000 to $100,000. This cost is prohibitive for many small organizations. For larger organizations, however, rather than having their executives spend great amounts of time and energy travelling from place to place, this innovation certainly pays dividends. As technology improves still further, and as costs continue to drop, this innovation will come within the reach of many more organizations.

Exhibit 15-1 presents a model of the innovation process. This model portrays innovation as a sequential process that can be divided into functionally separate but interacting stages. It involves bringing together various technological capabilities and market needs. Innovation includes the technical, design, manufacturing, management, and commercial activities involved in the marketing of a new (or improved) product or service or in the commercial use of a new (or improved) process or piece of equipment.

## Technology and Competitive Advantage

Since the early 1980s, newly industrialized countries such as Korea, Taiwan, Singapore, and Hong Kong have achieved spectacular national economic growth in part because

---

**technology**
The totality of the means people employ to accomplish desired tasks.

**innovation**
The generation of a new idea, and its implementation into a new product, process, or service.

**Exhibit 15-1**   *Interactive Model of the Innovation Process*

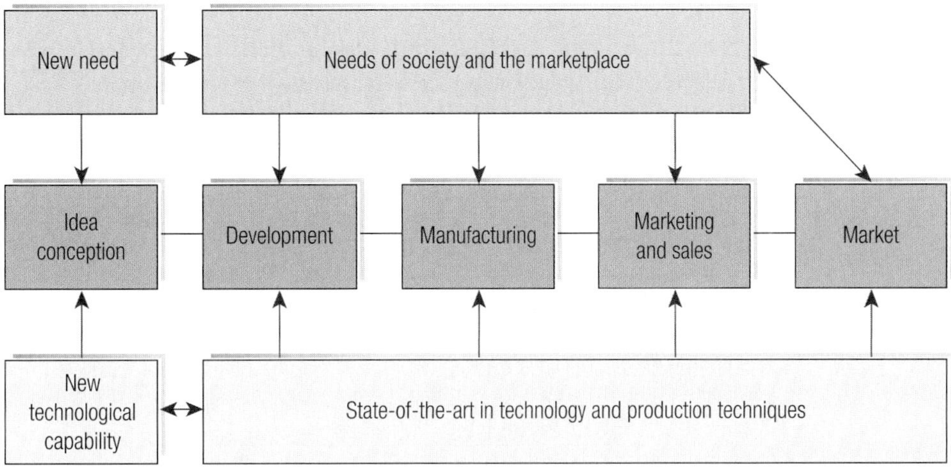

Source: Roy Rothwell and Walter Zegueld, *Reindustrialized and Technology* (Essex, England: Longman, 1985): 50.

they have made large investments in research and development and have developed infrastructures that facilitate the incorporation and use of new technologies. As discussed in Chapter 14, competition from these and other newly industrialized countries is expected to intensify in the next few decades.[6] Managers in Canada and other industrialized countries may experience increasing frustration as their international involvement increases and they find they have to adapt their ways of doing business to those of less-technologically advanced countries.

Some developing countries can be highly competitive with the countries that have been industrialized longer, because they offer abundant labour at low hourly rates. Often the only way that companies in the Western countries can compete is to redirect their resources towards the design, production, and manufacture of high-value, capital-intensive, technology-intensive goods and away from the more labour-intensive segments of the economy.

Another key to manufacturing success in the future for Canada and other similar countries is to deliver products or services more promptly than their competitors. Quick response manufacturing means reducing lead times, both in the time needed to bring new products to the market and in the time required actually to transform raw materials and components into finished products. Combining these attributes, usually a business can simultaneously achieve lower cost, higher quality, and greater customer satisfaction. All of these enhancements can be aided by the judicious application of technology and innovation.

Differences in macroeconomic conditions, as well as in government trade and technology policies, affect the use of technology and innovation. These are important factors. But this chapter focuses on the role that management can and should play in building and sustaining competitive advantages through the application of technology.

## Value Chain Analysis

**value chain analysis**
A system designed to analyze the sources of competitive advantage.

One concept that is useful for identifying opportunities for technology application is called **value chain analysis**. Harvard Business School professor Michael E. Porter

**Exhibit 15-2**    *The Value Chain and Representative Technologies*

| | Inbound logistics | Operations | Outbound logistics | Marketing and sales | Service | |
|---|---|---|---|---|---|---|
| **Infrastructure** | Information Systems, Planning, Budgeting, and Office Technologies | | | | | |
| **Human resources** | Training, Motivation Research, and Information Systems Technologies | | | | | |
| **Technology development** | CAD, Product, Pilot Plant, Software Development, and Information Systems Technologies | | | | | |
| **Procurement** | Transportation Systems, Communication Systems, and Information Systems Technologies | | | | | MARGIN |
| | Transportation, Material Handling, Testing, Storage, Preservation, Communications | Processing, Materials, Machine Tools, Packaging, Maintenance, Testing, Design | Transportation, Material Handling, Packaging, Communications | Media, Recording, Audio/Video, Communications | Diagnostics, Testing, Communications | |

SUPPORT ACTIVITIES (vertical axis, left)

PRIMARY ACTIVITIES (horizontal axis, bottom)

Source: Value chain concept by Michael E. Porter, © copyright 1985. Adapted from Michael E. Porter, *Competitive Advantage* (The Free Press, division of Macmillan, 1985).

designed this tool for analyzing the sources of competitive advantage in a company and how activities can be integrated.[7] Porter's analysis is shown in Exhibit 15-2. Each activity listed can contribute to the company's cost position and each is linked to other activities.

Activities in the value chain are divided into five primary and four support categories. Primary activities are those involved in the logistics of designing, then in physically creating, marketing, delivering the product, and providing after-sale support. Support activities provide inputs or the infrastructure necessary for primary activities. The four main support activities are:

1. The infrastructure of the company, including management overhead;
2. Human resource management in the form of training and motivation;
3. Technology development for performing the activity; and
4. Procurement of inputs, such as raw materials used to produce the product.

Information systems, planning, motivation, product, and other technologies must be coordinated into a complete system because every activity (generating a new idea, operating a robotics centre, purchasing raw materials, or servicing customer complaints) affects every other activity. Information is needed for the coordination of the separate but related activities.

To use value chain analysis effectively, Porter suggests examining internal and external activities for the value they contribute to customers. The value of a product or service to customers can be enhanced by incorporating advanced technologies in it, differentiating the company's offerings from those of its competitors. An example is the production of automobiles with computer interface units that allow for better diagnosis and maintenance.[8]

Some forward-looking credit unions and banks adopted automated teller machines (ATMs) before their competitors and thus gained a lead on them. Airlines that first installed automated flight reservation systems provided faster, more accurate service than was available before, so by this means they increased true competitiveness and their customer service levels. For a time, competitive advantage was gained by retail stores that first installed point-of-sale bar code scanners connected with cash registers that fed information to databases. In these, as in most technological innovations, the advantage was temporary because soon most of the innovators' competitors recognized that to keep up they had to install similar equipment. Despite the short-term nature of the initial boost to sales, the early innovators often tended to have a long-term advantage because customers who started patronizing them may have continued out of habit or inertia.

Similar but broader in purpose are the point-of-sale systems that are now found in many restaurants. Issam Rafie, the owner of Orgasmo, a European-style café in the Bloor and Bathurst area of Toronto, installed a computer-driven system that combines control of meal orders, billing, and product usage that enables him to place orders for foods that he needs to maintain inventory. At the end of each day, he is able to fax orders to suppliers, using their own classification and category codes. Rafie finds his system especially useful not only because it saves him time and reduces errors, but also because it is user-friendly for his serving staff.[9] In the highly competitive food business, any such enhancements can make the difference between profit and loss.

Porter emphasizes that a company's value chain must be managed as a system rather than as a collection of separate parts, just as the grocery chains and Issam Rafie do. A company can create competitive advantage by better optimizing or coordinating the activity linkages to the outside constituents. The value chain can provide managers with a tool for understanding the sources of cost advantage.[10] It is not enough to find ways to reduce costs in a single activity. Companies that are successful cost leaders usually excel in several areas, as low-cost developers, low-cost distributors, and low-cost service providers. In most cases cost leaders consider all nine of the activity categories so that optimal margins can be achieved.

*Cash registers that scan bar codes not only identify the price of the item purchased but may allow the retailer to accumulate information about the customer's shopping preferences, which can be used in marketing campaigns.*

**differentiation**
The ability to provide superior value to a buyer or user in ways that are different from competitors. These advantages may be in terms of the availability of the service or product, its special features, its quality, or the after-sale service.

**Differentiation** is the ability to provide unique and superior value to a buyer in terms of the availability of the service or product, its special features, its quality, and the after-sale service. Use of the value chain analysis highlights the areas in which there may be differentiation. There are many points of contact between an organization and its customers, clients, or other users, each of which represents a potential source of differentiation. The most obvious is how the product or service is used.

For example, a hand-held "personal navigator" tells users their geographical position within 2 metres, 15 metres, or 60 metres, depending on the sophistication of the instrument being used.[11] Not surprisingly, the instrument that gives the closer reading is considerably more expensive than the one that is slightly less accurate. But are the differentiation and the additional cost of value to customers? For the casual sailor or hiker, 60 metres is probably close enough. For the person staking mineral claims in Canada's North, the additional cost of the more accurate instrument could mean the difference between staking a bonanza and spending years in court trying to defend overlapping claims.

Competitive advantage arises from attention being paid both to cost and to other aspects of the differentiation concept. This attention is facilitated by the value chain analysis.

## Technology Forecasting: The S-Curve

A company's competitive position depends to some extent on its leadership in one or more applications of technology. Even for companies that are not leaders in technology, it is necessary to keep up on trends to avoid technological obsolescence and surprises. Uncertainty about the future effects of an innovation may come from several sources, and this uncertainty continues long after the new technology is introduced commercially. Some of the difficulty arises because new technologies often are marketed before they are fully perfected, and before anyone can predict their total impact. Their eventual uses emerge during an extended improvement process in which their applications may extend considerably beyond what was originally envisioned.[12]

**technology forecasting**
Predicting the direction and impact of a new technology.

**Technology forecasting** is designed to predict the direction and impact of a new technology. It provides valuable insights for companies that hope to create or sustain competitive advantage. A useful framework for technology forecasting is the S-curve, which graphs the relationship between effort put into improving a product or process and the company's results from making the investment.[13] The S-curve portrays the life cycle of a particular product or process. Exhibit 15-3 presents a pair of S-curves. It shows how one technology eventually outperforms another previously higher-performance technology. At the point of maturity in one curve, a discontinuity exists. It is at this point that opportunities or innovations become most important. For example, years ago IBM outpaced Smith Corona in the office by developing electric typewriters and computer-based word processors before Smith Corona was able to do so.

*Satellites not only permit the transmission of telecommunications, radio, and television to Canada's far North but allow anyone with a hand-held device to determine exact geographic location.*

As new technologies are developed, new demands are placed on industries. For example, to compete successfully in the future, hotels will have to invest heavily in telecommunications technologies.[14] The competition for business guests is heavy, because they are most likely to be repeat customers and, equally important, to pay cheerfully for special services. Hotel managers must plan how they can best accommodate the needs of their business guests of the future. In the 1970s and 1980s the leading-edge hotels provided "business service offices" that, for a fee, loaned typewriters, photocopiers, and fax machines and, in some cases, provided limited secretarial services. That level of service is no longer considered adequate by most business travellers. Now these same hotels have had to provide modem-ready network connections right in hotel rooms, so business people can connect directly with their offices and their business contacts. Some leading hotels offer in-room printers and, for a substantial fee, video conferencing facilities. Hotels that fail to accommodate to the technological innovations demanded by discriminating business travellers will lose this lucrative source of business.

Airlines have added satellite-linked telephones, even in economy sections. Automobile repair garages offer computer analyses. British Columbia Ferries provides work stations for passengers, complete with desk lights and power outlets for the connection of laptop computers. All of these innovations are being driven by the heightened expecta-

**Exhibit 15-3**   *Technological Discontinuities in the S-Curve*

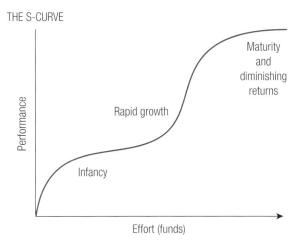

THE S-CURVE

The S-curve or maturity curve depicts the life cycle of a new technology. It is a useful tool for technology forecasting.

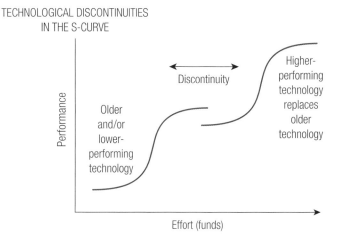

TECHNOLOGICAL DISCONTINUITIES IN THE S-CURVE

S-curves almost always appear in pairs. Together they represent a discontinuity — when one technology replaces another.

tions of customers and by the pressure of competition, as discontinuities appear in the respective S-curves.

Managers must decide how they will respond and defend their own advantages when competitors attempt to create discontinuities. That is, managers must decide what is the right technology and when is the right time to change to new technology or hold on to the old. As a technology approaches the top of its S-curve, it takes greater effort or more funds to produce even small positive incremental changes in product or process performance.

Retailers also are faced with a vast array of new technologies. One school of thought says that a retailer should replace technologies faster than is now occurring because each

*Consistent with its image as one of the most modern ferry systems in the world, B.C. Ferries has provided desks for business travellers, complete with power outlets for laptop computers.*

new technology has a quicker payback and becomes outmoded sooner. In many cases this is good business strategy because the purpose of technology, when it is implemented and managed correctly, is to continue to drive costs down and productivity up. According to retailers, it has become almost a necessity to have direct connections to vendors, and to use product imaging, document imaging, and executive information systems. There is now widespread use of hand-held radio frequency terminals connecting managers and clerks into the company's central data banks.[15] Retailers, often seen as slow to change, cannot afford to wait until they get to the top of the S-curve to implement the next technological change.

**data mining**
Drawing useful inferences from information that is available.

Another advance in the retail industry is what is called **data mining**. One example is the analysis of customer data to facilitate marketing. When a customer in a grocery chain hands the cashier a "membership card" to collect premium points or an Air Miles card to collect future airline credits, scanning of the card starts a chain of events of which the customer is usually unaware. First, items purchased by the customer are matched with the other items purchased by the customer in the same shopping expedition. From this matching the managers' computer system can tell them which items usually are purchased together. If pumpkin pie filling and frozen pie crusts usually are purchased at the same time, the managers might put one on sale, but certainly would not put the other on sale at the same time. Later, by matching the numbers and types of items purchased with the customers' postal codes, the marketing department can decide in what areas and to what income levels future marketing should be directed. The composite totals for an hour or a day reveal trends that help the manager place orders for resupply and schedule staff for restocking shelves. Mining the data so easily collected can give the retailer valuable insights into customer behaviour and add to competitive advantage.[16]

Richard Foster has provided the following managerial guidelines for assessing when a current technology is approaching its maturity limit or the top of the S-curve.

1. There is increasing discomfort about the productivity of system developers;
2. Development costs are increasing and delays are more common;
3. Innovation and creativity actively wane;
4. Disharmony and poor morale are evident among the developers;
5. Across-the-board improvements become rare;
6. There are wide differences in technology spending among competitors that use the same technology, with little or no apparent effect;
7. Frequent changes in the management team seem to have little impact on technology productivity; and
8. Smaller competitors in select niches, and even competitors who are thought to be weaker, start succeeding with radical approaches that everyone else thought couldn't work.[17]

Responses to these indicators of obsolescence require observation, interpretation, and questioning of customers, vendors, and competitors. The S-curve presents a framework for helping select the long-term technology portfolio a company needs to compete successfully. The management of discontinuities shown in the S-curve analysis can help identify areas where the company could take advantage of innovations and other changes in technology.

# An Integrated Technology Management Framework

The speed of technological change and the shifting competitive approaches in the global economy suggest that managers can benefit from a framework for considering the issues.

Managers have a crucial role to play in integrating competitive actions, considering value chain concepts, and understanding the opportunities associated with discontinuities. Fusing technological issues and management practice is important because these concepts cannot operate in isolation. Technology must be managed properly.

Exhibit 15-4 presents a framework that is driven by the need for product or service quality to meet customer demand. An organization deciding whether to introduce new technology should proceed with caution. Two studies, one by the Toronto office of management firm KPMG and the other by consulting firm Compas Inc. together with the London School of Economics, found similar results. They both discovered that only approximately one-third of investments made by organizations in new technology resulted in improved profitability. From another standpoint, fully two-thirds of the expenditures probably were wasted.[18] Prudent managers typically will follow the three phases described in Exhibit 15-4: assessment, position taking, and policy formation. The assessment phase includes evaluation of both the industry and the environment, noting when the organization's present technology was installed, assessing new and emerging technologies, and determining how the company conducts the transfer (or commercialization) of technology.

The second phase of the framework—position taking—involves the activities traditionally emphasized in management; that is, deciding what investments will be made

**Exhibit 15-4** *The Integrated Technology Management Framework*

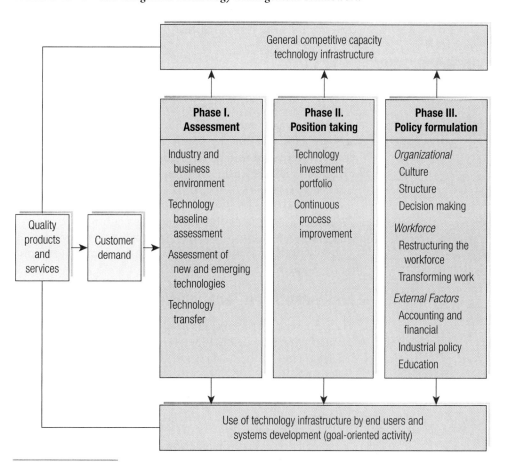

Source: Rod F. Monger, *Mastering Technology* (New York: Free Press, 1988): 38.

in various technologies. How many resources will be committed in the short and long terms? It is wise to heed the advice contained in the aphorism that "We don't have to accept all the things technology can give us just because it can be done."[19] At this stage decisions have to be made as to the extent of required improvement in the technological infrastructure. Since the effectiveness of technology, like that of all systems, erodes over time, continual improvement is crucial in the struggle to stay competitive.

The framework's third phase is the formulation of management policies relating both to internal and to external factors. They must be integrated so that a technology strategy can be formulated, implemented, and monitored. Organizational, workforce, and external environmental issues must be addressed. Perhaps one of the most crucial areas involves the managerial skills required.

## Managerial Skills Needed

Research has indicated that leadership, technical, and administrative skills are needed to operate effectively and competitively in today's technology-oriented companies.[20] Of course, a mix of skills is needed. The kinds of skills that are most important in high-tech situations are similar to the types of skills discussed in other chapters of this text, with the exception that technical skills are given a higher priority than in non-technical organizations. Studies have indicated that most high-tech managers learned their skills by experience rather than through formal educational programs. The corollary of this finding is that it is likely that because they have not studied management in general these same high-tech managers will not have learned the other management skills that are essential for peak performance.

## Technology Management

The failures of some businesses to meet technical challenges from domestic and global competitors have been largely the result of managerial failures. At various points managers of failing companies did not allocate resources needed to remain technologically competitive, failed to take timely advantage of S-curve-type discontinuities, and failed to support and reward an environment that encourages innovation. Meeting these needs is not easy. It requires a skilled individual who understands technology, innovation, and the interrelationships among organizational units and components. Prior to the early 1980s the management of technology concentrated on research and development (R&D) functions. Now a much broader, integrated view prevails. Manufacturing and process technology and the entire new-product development technology transfer processes are being studied.

## Implementing a Technology Strategy

There are several related concepts that underlie a successful program of technology management. Managing technology is widely recognized as essential, but too little attention has been paid to the concepts of the strategic use and implementation of technology. Together with the overall organizational strategy, the technology strategy defines how a company can most effectively invest its technology resources to achieve sustainable competitive advantage.[21] Planning the technology strategy of a company is most effective as a four-step process.

- Technology situation assessment (a scan of the internal and external environments beyond the depth of the traditional business portfolio mix);

- Technology portfolio development (determining the relative importance of the technology and the relative position of the company's investment in a technology);
- Integration of technology and overall company strategies; and
- Setting technology investment priorities.[22]

The significance of a technology strategy is that it links an organization's technology goals with its overall goals and business strategy. To plan the use of information technology, managers need a conceptual understanding of currently available information technology and how it relates to the strategic use of information within organizations. Business and organizational priorities must be set and communicated, because taking full advantage of information probably will restructure functional responsibilities within the organization. Global operations elevate information technology decisions to even more critical importance.[23]

As discussed in Chapter 14, competition in the global economy is intensifying. For example, steel companies in India, such as Tata Steel, face both domestic and international competition. Tata focused on its competitive strategy, research and development activities, and human relations management to boost its competitive position. In a three-phase modernization plan, new technology was introduced gradually. This has allowed Tata to become one of the least expensive steel companies in the world in terms of hot metal costs, giving it a clear advantage over other major integrated producers.[24]

Organizations not only must have clearly stated overall strategies, they also must possess technologies that are efficient, profitable, and effectively implemented. A survey of industry-leading companies reveals that they usually go through a five-step process to decide on technological commitments. The process includes:

- Examining the current position;
- Setting goals;
- Making a plan;
- Committing to the plan; and
- Implementing the plan in small steps.

Adherence to this sequence helps to identify areas in need of improvement before the organization makes capital investments or human resource changes or disrupts the existing situation in other ways. Following these steps can produce high-impact changes at minimal cost.[25]

*Process control is much more accurate than ever before, and can occur continuously so that instantaneous corrections can be made to ensure consistency of output.*

A number of commentators have attributed Japan's success in the consumer electronics industry to superior technology management practices. But a more compelling view is that in the late 1970s most North American companies considered television to be a mature business (at the top of the S-curve) whereas the Japanese viewed the whole associated industry to be at the high-tech growth stage, represented by discontinuity in the S-curve. This difference in strategic thinking could have led to different emphases and time horizons, investment priorities, and approaches to new product and process development—in essence, to entirely different technology strategies.[26]

Clarity of focus and consistency of strategic technology implementation seem vital for successfully transferring technology to the marketplace. Modesto Maidique and Robert Hayes say, "Even a superficial analysis of the most successful high technology firms leads one to conclude that they are highly focused."[27] Today's most innovative

## What Managers Are Reading    15-1

### Riding the Tiger

Harvey Gellman, who created the software for Canada's first computer in about 1952, teamed up with Alistair Davidson and Mary Chung, who, like Gellman, are now consultants, to write *Riding the Tiger*. Although their book could have profited from more rigorous editing, it does offer some insights into the dilemmas encountered by top managers when they are faced with major decisions involving technology.

Of course, the title comes from the Chinese aphorism that "He who rides the tiger may not dismount." The thesis is that once having entered the technological age it is impossible to disregard it. Inevitably, CEOs will have to decide which highly touted technological innovations will enhance the organization's strategic performance, and which merely will make it possible to do quicker something that is not worth doing at all.

Some of the best advice in the book's nine chapters is that CEOs and other top managers have no choice except to become reasonably computer-literate.

There is no suggestion that managers have to become hackers or computer buffs, but the warning is clear that it is dangerous to leave decisions concerning expansion of computer systems to the enthusiasts who are utterly fascinated by computers and what they can do. Sober heads are needed to avoid the all-too-common assumption that just because a certain technology is available that is sufficient reason to acquire it. As the authors point out, a bad system that is automated remains a bad system.

An interesting and useful analogy is that the introduction of any serious new technology must be treated with the same care and attention as a new product launch. If managers would keep this in mind, much unproductive investment in overcomputerization would be avoided.

Source: Alistair Davidson, Harvey Gellman, and Mary Chung, *Riding the Tiger* (New York: HarperBusiness, 1997).

companies focus resources by concentrating on fewer projects and spending more time on basic engineering and strategy. During the recession of 1990-91, sales at 3M were relatively flat. Although new products contributed 25 to 27 percent to the bottom line, management recognized that new initiatives were needed to remain competitive. To speed the time required to market new products, the company established what it called the Corporate Time Compression Committee. This committee was successful in reducing the time-to-market for new products by 50 percent, thus aiding considerably in 3M's efforts to remain competitive.[28]

Strategic application of information technology is helping businesses in a wide range of industries to gain competitive advantage through better knowledge of customer wants. For example, getting close to customers is an important issue today in the pharmaceuticals industry, which is undergoing massive changes as more of its drug patents are expiring. Eli Lilly & Company has taken an imaginative step in transfer of technology in recognition of the impending loss of patent protection on Prozac, the antidepressant that is prescribed for more than 20 million people in North America alone. Instead of waiting for generic drug manufacturers to pounce at the moment the patent expired, four months before the expiry date Lilly licensed Pharmascience to sell a generic version of the drug under the name "pms Fluoxetime." As a result of having this head start on the other generic drug manufacturers, within six months Pharmascience had captured a 60 percent share of the market for the drug and paid an undisclosed amount in royalties on its $23 million in sales.[29] Pursuing its technology strategy, Lilly believes that technology will help it play a broader role in disease management as it uses information technology to stay ahead of its competition.[30]

## Technology Transfer

**technology transfer**
A transfer of knowledge from a concept or even a prototype to some more tangible application. Also used to describe the situation in which the source of a concept or innovation makes it available to another person, unit, or organization.

Integrating the technology and the overall business strategy is at best a daunting task. As pointed out, possession of or knowledge about a technological innovation is of little value unless it is put to some use. The term **technology transfer** often is used to describe this transfer from a concept or even a prototype to some more tangible application.[31] The term also is used to describe the situation where the person or organization that originates a concept or innovation makes it available to another person or organization. Technology transfer can occur from one unit in an organization to another unit, from the lab to the marketplace, or from one organization or business to another. Transfers can occur from government, academic, and research organizations to private industry and vice versa. There are three broad reasons that a technology transfer may be desirable.

### Technology-driven Transfer

A *technology-driven* transfer is one in which the new technology is so revolutionary that it creates market opportunities. At the early stages of the development of a new product or service, there is often technological competition. A race develops between those pushing for improvements in existing technologies and others committed to developing a new technology. Usually in technology-driven development this change is evolutionary. When a new product isn't yet tried in the market, there are few competitors or supporters. Usually the only people or organizations that are willing to take the risks of supporting its development are those who have been closely connected with the creation of the new technology or who have some special reasons for seeing a bright future for it.

An example is the history of Joe Wilson and Sol Linowitz, who developed a product that made multimillionaires of both of them, and of several other early investors. The "Ditto" process (a trade name for a system of copying documents) had been developed in the early years of the twentieth century. This method required writing or typing on a special master sheet. It, in turn, was laid on a gelatin surface, contained in a metal tray. The ink from the master sheet was transferred to the surface of the gelatin. Sheets of paper were then laid on the gelatin one at a time and pressed with a roller. Some of the ink would be transferred, so the sheets picked up what had been written. The process was slow and messy, required some care and skill, and a single master sheet could be used only to prepare a maximum of perhaps 40 copies. It was, however, a significant improvement over having to type four or five copies with carbon sheets, and then having to retype the same material over again for more copies.

By the 1920s, this technological innovation was improved upon and replaced by a later technological innovation. Innovators developed a machine that replaced the gelatin surface with a rotating drum past which individual sheets were fed by an operator. The process ran the copies through a liquid bath, so they emerged quite damp and had to be dried. This technological improvement over the gelatin method was still messy, and the chemical fumes from the liquid bath were so unpleasant that under today's standards they would be unacceptable.

## Real World Reflection  15-1

### Letter Perfect

Advances in technology have raised standards, especially in the area of word processing and data entry. The quality of work that used to be achieved by professional editors, graphics designers, and desktop publishers is now often expected of most support people.

Expecting perfection from workers is a common pitfall experienced by many new managers. There is a difference between motivating staff to deliver high quality work and expecting perfect work. Consider the following guidelines:

- Take the time to demonstrate trust in the competence of the person reporting to you.
- Actions speak louder than words; don't hover over your employees while they work.
- Be sincere when you express confidence in your employee's abilities; choose a specific behaviour to comment on when delivering constructive criticism.
- Try not to impose your own way of doing things. Allow people to find their own way of managing their work.
- Don't impose perfectionist standards on your staff.

Contributed by Marnie Wright, British Columbia Institute of Technology.

Then, in the mid-1950s Linowitz, a lawyer, and Wilson, a photographic scientist, combined several different technologies into a new, dry electrostatic copying process. They needed funds to bring their new invention to the market, so they offered a few friends the opportunity to invest $5000 each in their tiny company, Haloid Inc. A few took the risk, but most were unsure that such an untried product would be able to break into the market for office copying. Those that provided modest investments in the Haloid company watched with interest, and considerable joy, as Linowitz and Wilson proceeded with their marketing plans, later changing the company name to Haloid-Xerox, and eventually to the Xerox Corporation. Thus, a technological advance that offered benefits previously unavailable grew from the tiny Haloid company to the huge copying industry that supplies a facility without which most managers would feel they could not function. The Research Center of the Xerox Corporation has continued to develop and move to market a huge number of innovations in the fields of printing, personal work stations, and related products. The Research Center's chief scientist and corporate vice president, John Seeley Brown, draws a distinction between invention and innovation. He says that one cannot manage invention, but that it is possible to create an environment in which inventions are more likely to occur. To be an innovator, he points out, one must carry the inventions to the marketplace.[32]

One invention that the Xerox Research Center did not transfer to the marketplace is the graphical user interface (GUI), which is a feature of many personal computers running today. When they created the first Apple computer in their garage, Steve Wozniak and Steve Jobs developed their own version of the GUI that they had seen at the Xerox Research Center. Apple went on to make GUI an essential part of the operating system for each computer it made. Within ten years, most IBM and compatible machines were

## Management in the Real World 15-1

### Technology and Innovation—The Basics Stay Basic: Reflections by Philip Crosby

When I first became a reliability engineer my assignment involved the manufacture and test of printed circuit boards, the advanced technology of that day. Components were stacked on the board at the unheard of concentration of 25 or 30 on an eight-inch-square piece of fibreglass. Two of the components were vacuum tubes, others were resistors, capacitors, and a few very new transistors. After the components were mounted the board was sent through the flow solder machine. When that was complete it went to a rework area where the inadequacies of flow soldering were repaired. Soldering was the largest single problem in our electronics operation.

One day I asked that area's supervisor if any books or manuals had come along with the flow solder machine. He rooted around and found a four-inch-high notebook in the back of a cabinet. At my insistence they read the book and calibrated the machine according to its instructions. They even began to operate it that way. In a few days there was hardly any rework for the rework station to accomplish. Within a month there was none. As a result of this effort we began to look at soldering systems used elsewhere in the shops and soon set up a solder training school. The problems began to disappear as soldering became consistent. We were soon producing a much more reliable product at a lower cost.

Recently I was in an electronics plant and looked at a new type of printed board. It held millions of components, most of which looked like little dots to the unaided eye. As I looked around it was apparent that there was a large area dedicated only to rework. The technicians there explained that their biggest problem was soldering. The new wave solder machines were inconsistent. I went back to the fabrication area and asked the supervisor of the machines if there had been an instruction book with the equipment. She rooted around and soon found a six-inch notebook in the back of a cabinet. It was written in four separate languages and had schematic drawings of the machine's circuitry. I suggested that we calibrate the machine to the information in the book. After they did this, solder irregularities dropped to almost nothing right away. In a few days they were gone all together.

When we looked at the hand soldering going on in the assembly area we learned that there was no consistent approach and very little training. We set up a school to teach proper soldering and sent everyone, including the supervisors and engineers, to it. The result was that soldering is not even on the list of problems.

These incidents took place 30 years apart. People get so involved with the great leaps of technology and innovation that they forget to put gas in the car. Never get away from the basics. Their importance lies in the fact that they are called *basics*.

using Microsoft's Windows, incorporating a GUI much like the Apple interface. Now the applications of GUI offer sophistication and expanded scope on the Internet and other computer applications.[33] The Xerox Research Center's failure to recognize the commercial potential of its GUI interface provides a good example of the importance of being able to move from invention to innovation.

Sometimes an invention fails to succeed in the market because it is before its time. An example was AT&T's attempt to bring video imaging to telephone service. The Bell system developed the Picturephone® in the late 1960s. It was introduced as a product in 1971 in Chicago, with a monthly price of $125, which would be the equivalent of at least triple that today. Market studies had suggested that it would be accepted and grow. It failed miserably, contrary to indications from the market surveys. The company had misjudged the extent to which businesses or the public would pay that much for the service. Now, many years later, organizations are investing large sums to make effective video conferencing possible. So Picturephone® was ready for the public before the public was ready for it.[34] In marketing new technology, timing is everything.

## Market-driven Transfer

In most cases the primary driver of transfer for commercialization is that a need exists.[35] In a *market-driven* transfer, customers express a need for a technology and the company finds the technology to meet that need. The task is to find the best technology to meet the need. A technology can be applied in several different markets. Sometimes the transfer from the lab or pilot phase to a new market can be dramatic. For example, application of the heart pacemaker, which was invented in 1928 but first used in 1960, brought dramatic hope to many heart patients.

An even more dramatic and socially conscious example of market-driven technology transfer is the use of telecommunications in connection with the provision of medical care. One of the first to realize its potential was Dr. William Feindel, a professor of neurosurgery at the University of Saskatchewan. In 1956 he started using closed-circuit television to transmit real-time tracings of electroencephalography. In the 1970s, Telesat Canada's Anik B satellite made possible the transmission of patients' graphs from remote areas in the Canadian Arctic to specialists in southern Canada, who were then able to make diagnoses and prescribe treatment. Dr. A. Maxwell House of Memorial University in St. John's, Newfoundland, inaugurated the first telemedicine clinic, which has blossomed into 14 advanced projects across Canada. The fibre optic link between Pembroke, Ontario, and the University of Ottawa Heart Institute can carry 5000 ultrasound pictures per second and transmit real-time angiograms while catheters are still inside the hearts of patients.[36] Thompson, Manitoba, did not have a radiologist to read X-rays, but a physician there was able to transmit X-rays to a qualified radiologist in Winkler, Manitoba, who read them and responded with instant diagnosis and advice. In the same province, a dozen practising physicians in Thompson, another dozen in St. Boniface, and some 75 physicians and medical students at the University of Manitoba "went on grand rounds" together by means of video conferencing facilities at the university.[37] Advances such as these show promise of revolutionizing the practice of medicine in small communities, giving immeasurable benefit to their residents. They also permit instantaneous consultations among specialists faced with unusual or difficult-to-diagnose cases—consultations that previously would have caused delay and required loss of crucial time in travel, at the very least, or, more likely, that never would have taken place.

## Product-and-process-improvement Transfer

In a *product-and-process-improvement* transfer, improvement in existing technology leads to a better product or to a process that meets customer needs. To remain competitive a company's business processes also must be more responsive and flexible than those of its competitors. Some companies have been able to improve their systems by giving travelling sales representatives small hand-held computers that can be connected by modem to the company's central database. The representatives can know exactly what items are in stock and instantly can make bids to potential customers and promise deliveries that can be fulfilled. In one study it was found that sales representatives could make bids in one-tenth the time that had been required previously, greatly enhancing the company's competitiveness. Innovative ways must be sought continually to provide technology to support motivated, adaptable employees dedicated to meeting or exceeding customers' requirements in the shortest feasible time.[38]

The pace at which technological change can be applied often depends on a variety of technological and economic factors not directly linked to the product or service. For example, the facsimile (fax) machine and Internet booms were possible because of telephone system technology; and the VCR was only successful because of the widespread use of TV sets.

The Internet and the emerging global telecommunication "infrastructure" pose new opportunities and threats to business. Some companies are finding that the Internet enhances sales; others have had considerably less success in selling in cyberspace. According to Don Ulsch, a senior vice president of O'Reilly & Associates, a company that specializes in providing Internet information, the shipping and handling problems and the fear of credit-card fraud are causing potential customers to hesitate to buy through Internet connections.[39] On the other hand, when the product is easily handled, and the amount of money involved is not great, Web sales can be a useful source of additional sales,[40] and even can provide international access. That has been the experience of The Cookbook Store in Toronto, at which Internet sales have been small but growing in its first year of online operation.[41]

Chapters Inc. reports a different experience. In October 1998 it launched its much-heralded online bookselling operation. Chapters Online registered a remarkable trebling of sales between its first and second quarters of operation and another doubling of sales in the third quarter. However, many observers were surprised when Chapters reported in a prospectus that Chapters Online is still operating at a substantial loss, and that company executives believe that it will continue to register operating losses "for the foreseeable future."[42]

Peter Todd of Queen's University and his collaborators found that marketing on the Internet requires a different approach from conventional marketing. Their study showed that Internet prices tended not to be very competitive, so Internet marketers should focus on products for which delivery and distribution costs can be saved, with the savings passed along in the form of lower prices.[43] It is predicted, therefore, that as the volume of business on the Internet increases, transaction costs will decrease, and this will lead to a growth in electronic commerce.[44] As illustrated, the retail industry is the most likely to benefit from Internet exposure.

One serious concern about Internet business is whether contracts that have been exchanged electronically can be enforced in court. Without expensive encryption systems, it is difficult to verify signatures and to preserve the security of documents. Landmark cases in the courts eventually will resolve those questions one way or another, but until then prudent managers still will require hard copy confirmation of any large contracts negotiated through the Internet.[45] Despite these unresolved questions, those retailers who recognize the opportunity and plan for the future may be the industry leaders of the future.[46]

As a product, process, or service approaches maturity, the market begins to be saturated and new markets and new applications replace older products or services. Demand for hotel services has reached this stage. There are still opportunities for innovation (e.g., bounce-back weekends, hotel-

*Customers can be connected with a supplier's online catalogue, which shows prices and availability of items and makes purchasing quick and easy.*

entertainment packages, hotel/tour packages), but the innovations come from pushing package improvements or modifying previous packages for hotel guests.

A troublesome mistake a manager can make is to conclude that no improvement—technological or otherwise—can be made in a particular product, service, or process. Industries that are thought to have reached their zenith can be revived if improvements can be introduced to make their products easier to use and more valuable to customers. Such is the case with the robotics industry. When robotics first appeared in commercial quantities (long after their invention by Eric Leaver in 1947), there was considerable hype about how they would revolutionize every industrial and commercial application. After an initial flurry of activity in the 1970s and 1980s, especially in the automobile industry, there was little further expansion of robotics. Then, to the apparent surprise of the robotics industry itself, in 1994 the decline seemed to have reversed itself, with North American robotics manufacturers reporting increases of 20 and 25 percent in sales over the previous year's figures. Guy Potok, president of the Robotics Industries Association, attributes this turnaround to the development of robots that are more functional, reliable, and user-friendly.[47]

Robots are even appearing in the service industries. At Good Samaritan Hospital in Cincinnati, when a patient missed a meal, a nurse used to have to rush down to the kitchen for the tray. Now the nurses can call the food service department and request that SAM bring it up. Short for Self-directed Automated Machine, SAM is a cordless, programmable robot courier that the hospital rents for $4500 a month.[48] Hospital administrators believe this is a bargain because of the saving of critically limited nurses' time.

Speed and quality of incremental innovations are critical to the success of product-and-process-improvement-driven market transfer. A vice president for science and technology at IBM concisely stated the importance of speed:

> Most development work is done just one step ahead of manufacturing. ... One cannot overestimate the importance of getting through each turn of the cycle more quickly than a competitor. It takes only a few turns for the company with the shortest cycle time to build up a commanding lead.[49]

Being first to market a new product or service, or to use a new process, may allow the company to participate in the most profitable portion of the product life cycle. As illustrated by the relationship between Eli Lilly and Pharmascience, the more often a company is first to introduce important incremental innovations, the greater its market share is likely to be in the industry.[50]

Continually improved products, processes, and services require management attention. They must be managed in a way that they become competitive advantages. Benchmarking (making comparisons with the technology and the costs of other organizations) is important in maintaining competitiveness.[51] Product, process, and service comparisons can point out strengths, weaknesses, and competitive advantages. As described earlier, the founders of Xerox invented what has become the standard process for photocopying. Japanese companies such as Ricoh and Epson focused on copiers and benchmarked Xerox during a period in which Xerox failed to make significant improvements. As a result Xerox's market share dropped from 90 percent in the early 1970s to about 20 percent in the late 1990s.

Benchmarking allows management to make comparisons in a real-time (current and most up-to-date) manner. Using benchmarking performance gaps, action plans to make improvements can be established, and management can monitor the adjustment and modification of standards and goals for the product, process, or service.

Technology-driven and market-driven transfers of commercial technology usually occur early in the life of new technologies. At this early point, value lies in the matching of technology and market needs and being early to market with a high-quality technology. Product-and-process-improvement challenges are more likely to occur later in the life cycle, when value comes from being the first to apply product, process, quality, or service improvements.

## International Technology Transfer

The increasing globalization of business has focused more attention on the concept of international technology transfer. *International technology transfer* occurs when concepts and ideas or specifications concerning products, processes, and services are originated in one country and then made use of in another. This is a common phenomenon, not only when the originators intend it, but also through benchmarking and outright piracy. In any international transfer, differences in national cultures,[52] economic infrastructures, political systems, laws, and social norms create challenges.[53]

International technology transfers sometimes occur without the intention of the transferor. This can occur when nationals of one country study in a host country, obtaining knowledge that they later take back to their home countries. There are also government-to-government agreements involving the dispatch of experts to the receiving country, but also including transactions such as Canada's sale of Candu reactors to China. These transactions have been deplored by many, but they are a clear example of the transfer of technology, because operating manuals are an essential part of any such sale. Other forms of transfer occur as a direct result of contracts to build plants in other countries, under which companies such as SNC-Lavalin are employed for their expertise, and by the very nature of their work display their special knowledge, which can be learned and copied by the receiving nation.

In recent years four modes of international technology transfer have grown in importance: licensing, joint ventures, strategic alliances, and industrial and commercial espionage. The first three have been discussed in previous chapters. Industrial espionage has a long history, going back at least as far as the thirteenth century when Marco Polo is supposed to have smuggled silk worms out of China to try to establish a silk industry in Venice. The advent of modern technology has opened new vulnerabilities.

**Industrial espionage.** As the stakes in global enterprise have risen, so have illicit efforts by some companies to obtain technological secrets from competitors.[54] For example, French intelligence agents conducted espionage operations against the overseas offices of IBM and Texas Instruments.[55] Two Koreans were arrested after allegedly paying $40,000 for blueprints of Dow Chemical's polymer plant in LaPorte, Texas.[56] A former Merck and Schering-Plough employee was sentenced to nine years in prison for attempting to steal the formulas for the medicines Ivernection and Interferon.[57]

The problem for companies with trade secrets has become even more pressing with the advent of the Internet. Hackers can penetrate company networks, where they can damage data banks or steal confidential information and sell it. Security companies are hard at work developing encryption programs to make access considerably more difficult for even the most sophisticated hacker.[58]

An organizational protective device may be employed within the organization itself that wishes to protect its technology. That is the erection of what are called "fire walls." In this practice, the company organizes its distribution of technical knowledge so that no one person has access to more than a modicum of the total. Then when that person leaves the company or engages in subversion, only a part of any process or design is lost.[59] Of course, any such organizational structure comes at a price because it impedes the free flow of information within the company. This disadvantage, however, is seen as preferable to the greater cost of unauthorized leakage of secret information. In the long run, any such precautions, while necessary, increase the cost of doing business, and ultimately will be passed along to the consumer.

## Creativity and Innovation

**creativity**
The ability to create new and useful ideas.

Organizations are finding that in order to become and remain competitive, it is necessary to foster innovation. The precursor to innovation is the elusive quality of creativity. A convenient definition of the term **creativity** is that it refers to the creation of new and useful ideas. To be successful, an organization must encourage, support, and harness the creative potential of every employee. Nearly a half-century ago, Alex F. Osborn, an early student of creativity, made the then-startling revelation that almost *everyone* has the capacity for creative thinking and actions. To support his claim, he cited studies done by the Human Engineering Laboratories of Stevens Institute. Their researchers had tried to analyze the various characteristics and talents of a large number of what they classified as "rank-and-file" mechanics. These were people who, for the most part, had never had any higher education and whose overall intelligence levels were thought to be about the same as those of the general population. The researchers found that two-thirds of those studied were *above average* in creative capacity. From the results it has to be concluded that for some reason the mechanics were not representative of the general population in all respects, because otherwise only half could be more creative than the median (which in this case would be roughly the same level as the average that was cited).[60] Even though one might quibble with the methodology of the study, Osborn's book in which it was cited had a considerable impact on both the scholarly community and the business community. It spawned a plethora of articles and books on attempts to unleash creative potential, such as formal employee suggestion systems and brainstorming.

Thirty years later, Teresa Amabile, a student of the subject, suggested that a product or a response to a problem or need can be considered creative to the extent that it is novel and appropriate, correct, and useful to the task at hand.[61] In her view the task is heuristic rather than algorithmic. Fixing a flat tire is an algorithmic task because it follows a specific pattern and sequence of events. Developing a new biomedical instrument is largely heuristic because it follows no set pattern and has not been done before, but it reflects disparate bits of knowledge from many disciplines.

Earlier in this chapter innovation was explained as the generation of a new idea and its implementation into a new product, process, or service. Innovation, therefore, is a process, whereas, in contrast, creativity is the generation of something new—an idea, a process, or even a technique or style.

### Creative Individuals

Managers hope to identify those employees who have the greatest potential for creativity. To do this successfully, it is necessary to try to identify attributes that creative people have to a greater degree than less creative people. It generally would be agreed that Albert Einstein, Wolfgang Mozart, Margaret Atwood, and members of the Group of Seven are or were all creative people. They possessed special traits and attributes. The paradox is that in many ways they differed considerably from each other. But there are some characteristics that seem to be essential for creativity to flower in an individual. Raudsepp stated that creative people seem to be flexible, self-motivated, and sensitive to problems; they are original thinkers and are able to concentrate; they can think in terms of images; and they have little fear of failure.[62] Other researchers have described creative people as nonconformists who enjoy problem solving. This formulation has intuitive support because the opposite of nonconformity is conventionality—obviously a poor source of creativity—and anyone who does not enjoy problem solving would not seek out problems and try to find solutions.

Another listing of the characteristics of typically creative people appears as Exhibit 15-5. Comparing these three formulations, it can be seen that there is nothing startling about any of them, or indeed about several other similar approaches to the identification of potentially creative people. Yet despite what may seem to be truisms, and incomplete truisms at that, these insights may help managers to pick out employees who might assist the organization through the application of creativity if they were encouraged to do so. And that observation leads to the question of how best to encourage creativity and to benefit from its application within the organization.

## Managing Creative People

Since the potential for creativity is difficult to isolate and pinpoint, one might conclude that it would be futile to attempt to identify and manage creative people in ways that

**Exhibit 15-5**

*Some Characteristics of Many Creative People*

| | | |
|---|---|---|
| 1. | *Knowledge.* | Creative people spend a great number of years mastering their chosen field. |
| 2. | *Education.* | Education doesn't increase creativity. Education that stresses logic tends to inhibit creativity. |
| 3. | *Intelligence.* | Creative people don't necessarily have high IQs. The threshold for IQ is around 130. After that, IQ doesn't really matter. Creative people have been found to possess the following intellectual abilities: sensitivity to problems, flexibility in forming associations between objects, thinking in images rather than words, and synthesizing information. |
| 4. | *Personality.* | Creative people are typically risk takers who are independent, persistent, highly motivated, sceptical, open to new ideas, able to tolerate ambiguity, self-confident, and able to tolerate isolation. They also have a strong sense of humour and are hard to get along with. |
| 5. | *Childhood.* | Creative people usually have had a childhood marked by diversity. Experiences such as family strains, financial ups and downs, and divorces are common occurrences. |
| 6. | *Social habits.* | Contrary to stereotypes, creative people aren't introverted nerds. Creative people tend to be outgoing and enjoy exchanging ideas with colleagues. |

Source: Based in part on Robert G. Godfrey, "Tapping Employees' Creativity," *Supervisory Management* (February 1986): 16-20; and "Mix Skepticism, Humor, a Rocky Childhood—and Presto! Creativity," *Business Week* (September 30, 1985): 81.

**Exhibit 15-6**

*Rosabeth Moss Kanter's Ten Rules for Stifling Innovation*

1.  Regard any new idea from below with suspicion because it's new, and because it's from below.

2.  Insist that people who need your approval to act first go through several other levels of management to get their signatures.

3.  Ask departments or individuals to challenge and criticize each other's proposals. (This saves you the job of deciding; you just pick the survivor.)

4.  Express your criticisms freely, and withhold your praise. (That keeps people on their toes.) Let them know they can be fired at any time.

5.  Treat identification of problems as signs of failure, to discourage people from letting you know when something in their area isn't working.

6.  Control everything carefully. Make sure people count anything that can be counted frequently.

7.  Make decisions to reorganize or change policies in secret, and spring them on people unexpectedly. (That also keeps people on their toes.)

8.  Make sure that requests for information are fully justified, and make sure that it is not given out to managers freely. (You don't want data to fall into the wrong hands.)

9.  Assign to lower-level managers, in the name of delegation and participation, responsibility for figuring out how to cut back, lay off, move people around, or otherwise implement threatening decisions you have made. And get them to do it quickly.

10. And above all, never forget that you, the higher-ups, already know everything important about this business.

Source: Rosabeth Moss Kanter, *The Change Masters* (New York: Simon & Schuster, 1983): 101.

differ from basic management principles. Yet, creativity is a resource that will not flourish unless it is nurtured, supported, and rewarded. Any evidence of creativity must be supported and given positive reinforcement. One of the best ways to give this reinforcement is to have an established practice that when a creative idea surfaces, resources will be assigned to it. On the contrary, some existing management practices effectively stifle creativity. Rosabeth Moss Kanter's tongue-in-cheek listing of the Ten Rules to Stifle Innovation are reproduced as Exhibit 15-6, and may serve as an "anti-checklist" for managers. Ted Pollock takes a more direct approach, offering some strategies that can foster creative thinking, both as managers attempting to enhance employees' potentials for creativity and as individuals trying to improve their own creative potentials. Pollock's strategies are:

1.  Use analogies;
2.  Ask provocative questions;
3.  Think in terms of possibilities;
4.  Reward original thinking (either as part of an organizational strategy or as self-administered rewards as discussed in Chapter 8);
5.  Become a creative *reader*;

6. Learn to listen carefully;
7. Study the process of innovation;
8. Be receptive to the unexpected; and
9. Resist falling into the "one right answer" trap.[63]

Exhibit 15-7 provides another listing of the ways in which managers can foster creativity. Which steps will be the most effective depend to some extent on the manager's style, the creative attributes and practices of the employees, and the overall culture of the organization.

Finally, it is essential for an organization seeking to create a culture of creativity to resist the temptation to punish failure, or even to stigmatize all failures as nonproductive and undesirable. Employees who have reason to fear these responses to failure will tend to be cautious and take few chances, and thus will stifle their own creativity. As James Burke, CEO of Johnson & Johnson said, "We won't grow unless you take risks. . . . Any successful company is riddled with failures. There's just no other way to do it."[64]

## Creativity Training

Just as there is debate as to whether management can be taught, so is there disagreement as to whether creativity can be taught. Although it is not possible to declare an end to

**Exhibit 15-7**

*Selected Prescriptions for Fostering Organizational Creativity*

1. *Develop an acceptance of change.* Organization members must believe that change will benefit them and the organization. This belief is more likely to arise if members participate with their managers in making decisions and if issues like job security are carefully handled when changes are planned and implemented.

2. *Encourage new ideas.* Organization managers, from the top to the lowest-level supervisors must make it clear in word and deed that they welcome new approaches. To encourage creativity, managers must be willing to listen to subordinates' suggestions and to implement promising ones or convey them to higher-level managers.

3. *Permit more interactions.* A permissive, creative climate is fostered by giving individuals the opportunity to interact with members of their own and other work groups. Such interaction encourages the exchange of useful information, the free flow of ideas, and fresh perspectives on problems.

4. *Tolerate failure.* Many new ideas prove impractical or useless. Effective managers accept and allow for the fact that time and resources will be invested in experimenting with new ideas that don't work out.

5. *Provide clear objectives and the freedom to achieve them.* Organization members must have a purpose and direction for their creativity. Supply guidelines and reasonable constraints will also give managers some control over the amount of time and money invested in creative behaviour.

6. *Offer recognition.* Creative individuals are motivated to work hard on tasks that interest them. But, like all individuals, they enjoy being rewarded for a task well done. By offering recognition in such tangible forms as bonuses and salary increases, managers demonstrate that creative behaviour is valued in their organization.

the disagreement, the preponderance of evidence seems to suggest that, at the very least, training can sensitize both managers and non-managerial employees to the need to identify and encourage creativity. Some companies, such as Frito-Lay, believe that training is an effective way to keep creativity alive. One survey suggests that about 25 percent of all North American companies employing over 100 people offer creativity training to employees. Of course, that statistic means that 75 percent do not do so, showing that most managers probably doubt the efficacy of such training. Yet in those organizations that do provide creativity training, there must be a conviction that the investment in time and money is worthwhile.

Most creativity training techniques fall into four categories: *fluency exercises*, which are designed to stimulate the generation of ideas; *excursion exercises*, which push the mind to illuminate ideas; *pattern breakers,* which are designed to cause thinkers to restate problems in novel ways; and *shake-up exercises*, which help to loosen up groups and make their members more receptive to unusual ideas.[65]

**fluency exercise**
An exercise that is designed to open participants' minds to new ideas.

**brainstorming**
A small group process designed to free participants from stereotypical thinking by having them uncritically express ideas, no matter how seemingly bizarre, and in which evaluation and judgement are deferred until the end of the process.

The purpose of **fluency exercises** is to generate ideas that might never surface in more conventional linear thinking. It is assumed that most of the ideas generated in a fluency exercise will be impractical and never pursued, but that a few will be valuable. The oldest fluency exercise is **brainstorming**, in which a group of people fire off as many ideas as possible, no matter how impractical or bizarre they may seem initially. The premise is that a group will produce a far greater number of ideas than an individual can. Judgement on every idea is deferred. Criticism is forbidden until ideas are evaluated later in the session, or even in a subsequent session.

A newer fluency exercise is *brainwriting*. Employees write down their ideas on slips of paper with no identification of the originator. Then they exchange the slips of paper and attempt to build on each other's insights. *Mindmapping* is a fluency exercise in which a representation of a primary idea is drawn at the centre of a large piece of paper. The group members are invited to suggest new or related ideas, which are then drawn as branches or vines growing in all directions from the centre.

An example of an excursion exercise is the *forced relationship.* This technique was used by Polaroid managers from several different departments, for example. A person designated the "creativity facilitator" asks the managers to look at a number of paintings and describe what they see. Managers are then asked to "force fit" their impressions about the paintings to the task of figuring out how to improve interdepartmental harmony.

**excursion exercise**
A technique designed to take participants' minds away from the problem at hand in order for them to approach possible solutions from different and unexpected directions.

**Excursion exercises** are intended to take a person's mind away from a problem so the unconscious mind can mull it over. *Pattern breakers* use a slight modification of this approach, by keeping the problem directly in focus, but in a different light. Synectics, a creativity consulting firm, asks selected groups of the client's employees to take a stroll snapping pictures with an instant film camera. The pictures then are used as prompts. One group returned with pictures of a glass jar, a household washing product, and a Federal Express package. Two of the photos did not generate any interest, but the photo of the glass jar triggered a productive discussion about ways to improve sales of a particular service.

**shake-up exercise**
A technique designed to break down barriers among participants and to develop a sense of cooperation and community among them.

**Shake-up exercises** use games or team activities to help individuals laugh or relax, and to overcome the distances created by organizational hierarchy. First Chicago Bank employs role-playing games—replete with funny costumes—and outdoor activities. Kodak uses a "humour room" stocked with games, objects such as balls for juggling, toy robots, and Monty Python movies. Groups of employees use the room to conduct meetings and also to relax.

Another approach that is intended both to unlock creativity and to foster intragroup bonding involves activities such as taking groups of executives wilderness camping, rock scaling, and cave crawling. Executives return exhausted, but proponents claim that they have learned respect for each other and in some ways have eliminated past stereotypes of individuals and of "acceptable" ways of thinking.

All of these types of exercises are designed to break down inhibitions and self-imposed restrictions that arise from past experiences and conditioning, and to unleash an acceptance of lateral thinking that lead to ideas that would otherwise never surface.

Despite the growing popularity of creativity training, some researchers, and many organization executives, believe that they are just flaky fads and that, like all fads, the creativity-training boom will soon pass.[66] A more serious concern is whether evidence derived using rigorous evaluation methods suggests that creativity training actually makes a difference. The question is whether employees who have experienced these exercises are more creative than those who have not. To date, there is little solid evidence that creativity training improves performance, innovation development, or technological development. Yet, considerably more research must be done on the subject before it is relegated to the dustbin of past enthusiasms.

## Dilemmas for Managers

There is little doubt in the minds of almost everyone who gives thought to technology that most of the technological innovations now in use are here to stay. But there is equally wide consensus that some of these innovations pose significant challenges for managers.

### The Elusive Productivity Gains

Tom Healey, general manager of Andersen Consulting Canada, reports the results of a survey conducted jointly by Gallup Canada and Goldfarb Consultants. It showed that by mid-1996 an astonishing 29 percent of adult Canadians had used the Internet. That was two-and-a-half times the proportion reported by a survey taken just one year earlier.[67] Since that time, many similar, although perhaps less reliable, figures have indicated that this remarkable growth rate is continuing. A Compas Inc. survey reported that 40 percent of Canadian companies have some Internet connections, up from half that percentage only six months earlier.[68] Cultural anthropologists report that as soon as a particular technology has been adopted by 15 percent of the population, the rate of adoption rises rapidly.[69] The explosion in the numbers of Internet connections seems to bear out that contention. Even though as the proportion goes higher the rate of growth necessarily must decrease, within only a few more years, the penetration of Internet use may rival or exceed that of automobiles.

But there is an apparent paradox. As stated in an insightful article in the *Globe and Mail* in 1997: "Millions invested in technology have failed to spark growth in output."[70] One reason that has been advanced is that there is always a lag in time between when a technology is introduced and when it begins to show benefits. As just noted, the growth in Internet connections has been recent, so greater benefits should come in the future. Andrew Sharpe, executive director of the Centre for the Study of Living Standards, a respected Ottawa-based organization, suggests that some of this apparent paradox exists because much of Canada's economic activity that is counted in the statistical study is in the service industry. This segment of the economy, as already noted, does not lend itself readily to this type of productivity measurement or innovation,[71] so while productivity gains may be occurring, they are not measurable. It seems to make intuitive sense that often when a computer system is introduced in a business, errors are reduced and managers are able to get quicker, more accurate, and more comprehensive information, but these marked improvements do not show up in productivity measures. Whatever the reasons for it, the apparent paradox will be studied with interest and will spawn countless scholarly papers, and probably will not impede the continued growth of computers, networks, and the use of the Internet.

## Employees' Personal Use of the Internet

One of the challenges that technology poses for managers arises from the widespread access to the Internet from office computers. On the plus side, the Internet greatly simplifies communication, and searches for information needed by the organization will be quicker and will tap more sources. On the minus side, some employees become so fascinated with the new technology that they waste untold hours surfing the Internet and using their office computers to play computer games. In 1996, Nielsen Media Research Inc. conducted a computer log analysis at IBM, Apple Computers, and AT&T. Their study showed that employees of these three companies alone visited the Web site of *Penthouse* magazine 12,823 times in a single month. The average visit to the *Penthouse* site consumed 13 minutes of the companies' time, for a total equivalent of 347 eight-hour days for which employees were paid but seem to have been contributing little value to their organizations.[72]

As a result of what is widely acknowledged, but often-overlooked, frivolous use of business computers, some entrepreneurial companies have developed software that allows managers to monitor what is happening in their employees' cyberspace. Tinwald Networking Technologies Inc. and Sequel Technology LLC, both of Toronto, offer tracking software that can monitor improper usage. Some people consider that this constitutes an indefensible breach of employee privacy. In response, other people argue that it is no different in substance than observing employees to ensure that they take 15 minutes instead of an hour for a coffee break.

On a happier note, this same software makes it possible for managers to identify those employees who fail to use valuable sources of information that would make their work easier and more useful.[73] When these laggard Internet users are identified, special training programs can encourage greater legitimate use, and thus enhance productivity.

## E-mail: Useful Tool and Uncontrolled Toy

With e-mail, faxes, voicemail, and electronic transmission of databases, there is no shortage of information in circulation. A serious challenge facing managers is the sheer volume of e-mail messages that circulate in their companies and that they receive personally. There are undoubted benefits from electronic communications, but these benefits are accompanied by this growing problem. Douglas Stewart, a consultant on personal productivity at the Institute for Business Technology in Unionville, Ontario, suggests that people tend to send more information and to send it in ways that duplicate each other because they are insecure—unsure whether their messages are being read and unsure whether they may be criticized for failing to share information. As for savings, Stewart points out that studies have shown that fully 60 percent of e-mail messages are now copied onto paper, usually at both ends of the communication.[74]

One study showed that the 1800 employees of Netscape Communications Corp. send and receive a staggering 45,000 pieces of e-mail *each day,* or an average of 25 messages per person per day.[75] It is no wonder that often managers complain that their con-

**Management in the Real World    15-2**

## Coping with the Deluge of E-mail

As Judith H. Dobrzynsk says in a syndicated article from the New York Times Service, quoted in the *Globe and Mail* on May 2, 1996, "It takes a push of a button to send everyone conceivably interested a copy of that E-mail memo, so why not? And why waste time with a conversation? Just send E-mail. . . . In fact, the use of E-mail and voice mail has become so incessant that it is gumming up the works of some companies. . . . It seems that people are so busy wading through the overload and responding that they don't have time for real work. . . . And E-mail presents another problem because it indiscriminately mixes the trivial with the monumental."

She relates the sad plight of one company executive who returned from a week's holiday to find 2000 e-mail messages awaiting him. He solved the problem in an imaginative way. He blithely erased all of them, presumably on the assumption that if any had been important, their originators would communicate again. But this hardly solved the problem he must have encountered the next week, when he received another 2000 messages.

What are companies doing about the problem of too much use of e-mail? According to Dobrzynsk, Computer Associates of Islandia, N.Y.—a computer company, no less—actually shuts down its e-mail for four hours a day, two hours in the morning and two in the afternoon. Another, SmithKline Beecham, "charges business divisions what amounts to user fees, based on the number and the length of each unit's e-mail messages."

Clearly, the problem constitutes a serious challenge for managers. So far, there seem to be no totally satisfactory answers.

cern is not a shortage of information, but an overload. It is so easy for anyone to send e-mail messages to a long list of addressees that the manager is often overwhelmed by the volume of "mail" that requires some time to scan, even if the manager does not answer all of it or even read beyond the "subject" line. Similarly, it is so easy to produce voluminous reports on a computer that often the manager is deluged with printouts that are so detailed that they obscure the broader issues. Prior to the computer age, the manager often was hampered by having inadequate access to information; now the manager is faced with such a volume of information that the problem becomes one of having to select which information to heed and which to disregard.

*A few years ago some optimists predicted that the computer would permit a "paperless office." In fact, with the proliferation of copies of reports and e-mail messages, the opposite may well have occurred, with more paper being consumed than ever before.*

### The Deluge of "E-junk"

Enormous as the in-house problem is, it is at least matched by what Beppi Crosariol, writing in the *Report on Business Magazine*, has called "insidious e-junk"—a term that is self-explanatory. Whenever anyone posts a message on a bulletin board or joins a chat group, that person's e-mail address becomes available to anyone who wishes to use it to post e-junk.[76] The same article quotes Eric Arnum, editor of *Electronic Mail and Messaging Systems*, as saying that he wouldn't be surprised if one-quarter of the 15 million plus people connected to the

Internet are spending at least five minutes every day digging through unwanted junk e-mail. As Crosariol points out, if that time is allotted a salary rate of $20 per hour, in a year that wasted time would generate $6.5 billion—or more than the GDP of Prince Edward Island. Prohibition at the source of e-junk not only would be difficult to police, but would offend most Canadians who cherish freedom of speech. Crosariol has a suggestion that may work for some people to curb the deluge at the receiving end. A personal or business computer, or an intranet server, can have two different e-mail addresses. One is reserved for communications to and from a selected list of people who have been given the address. The other is used for chat lines and bulletin boards, and is thus susceptible to being picked up by the direct e-mailers of junk. This permits the recipient to ignore all of the messages received at the second address, on the assumption that it is sure to be junk. Messages that have any importance would be presumed to be received at the other address, to which access has been restricted to selected sources. Short of widespread use of such a solution, the flood of e-junk is likely to continue.

## The Threat of Viruses

One of the more publicized challenges facing managers is the threat of viruses. When an employee loads a pirated copy of any kind of software or any of the widely available shareware, there is a chance that it will contain a virus. A virus also may be introduced by any connection with external networks such as the Internet and the company-supplier and company-customer links that are becoming common. If the personal computer is connected in an intranet, the whole system may be infected, corrupting programs and destroying information that is vital and costly or even impossible to replicate. According to a survey conducted by accounting firm Ernst & Young, more than three-quarters of North American companies surveyed reported that they had lost information to viruses or to hackers in the preceding two years.[77] Some virus detectors are quite sophisticated, but must be updated continually in order to identify new viruses that are created almost daily. Some other virus detectors look for and identify any odd lines of code that seem out of place or inexplicable. But any virus detector is only as helpful as the frequency with which it is used. Some organizations require that the virus detector be run every time a computer is booted, but they have found that, to save the few seconds this procedure requires, some employees have gone to great lengths to disable the virus detectors that the information officers have installed. Probably the only way to meet the virus problem is to educate all employees who have access to computers, and to enlist their support and vigilance.

## Internal Sabotage

Nearly one-third of the instances of data loss discovered in the Ernst & Young survey resulted from intentional and malicious actions of employees. Employees who are severely disciplined or dismissed, or even those who feel unappreciated, create potential threats to the organization's computer security and protection of information. As John Kearns, a director of Ernst & Young in Toronto, says, "When they [companies dependent on computerized systems] have a disaster, the impact can be quite devastating." He found that many companies would not discuss the losses they had suffered, but that of the 30 percent who did provide information, 14 percent had lost between $250,000 and $1 million and 2 percent had lost more than $1 million. The magnitude of the threat certainly requires attention from managers to attempt not only to prevent these losses but at the very least to ameliorate their effects by routinely providing daily off-site backups of all important information.[78]

## The Workplace of Tomorrow

It hardly can be doubted that Canadians are in an age of rapid change, and that much of that change will have profound effects on how everyone lives in this country, whether connected to the Internet or living in the remotest community without a dish to receive satellite signals. The question that faces Canadians, and indeed everyone in at least the industrialized world, is how society will cope not only with the technology but with the disruptions that accompany any change. It will take all of the ingenuity of managers to adapt within their organizations, and all of the ingenuity of society as a whole to adapt to the adjustments that must, and will, occur.

The pace of change is accelerating. Every new technological development spawns a host of spin-offs. What is cutting-edge technology today will be obsolete and superseded by improvements or even by complete replacement within a few years at most. Managers not only must prepare themselves and their organizations for current technology but they also must try to envision what changes will occur in the years immediately ahead. Those that have sufficient current information coupled with sufficient creativity and innovativeness will thrive; those that lack these qualities will suffer decline and may disappear, having been overtaken by their competitors. In many cases it would be foolhardy to attempt to predict *what* specific technology will be developed. Instead, managers must develop and perfect the management skills that have been described in this book—to make the best use of opportunities, to ensure the best atmosphere for encouragement of innovation and dedication of their employees, and to remain ever alert to ways to retain flexibility to adapt to changing times. The challenges are formidable; the opportunities are almost unlimited.

## Summary of Learning Objectives

▷ **Distinguish between** *technology* **and** *innovation* **and describe** *technology transfer.*
Technology is the totality of means used by people to accomplish tasks that bring comfort and sustenance and to accomplish desired tasks, whereas innovation refers to bringing new technologies to applications in which they contribute usefully. Technology transfer is often used to describe the transfer from a concept or even a prototype to some more tangible application. The term is also used to describe the situation in which the source of a concept or innovation makes it available to another person, unit, or organization.

▷ **Explain the value chain analysis procedure.**
Value chain analysis is a concept developed by Michael E. Porter to identify opportunities for technology application. It identifies five primary and four support activities and links them to the overall functions of the organization. The support categories include the organization's infrastructure functions, human resource management, technology development, and procurement of inputs. The primary functions include product creation, production, marketing, delivery, and after-sale support.

▷ **Describe the managerial skills needed for managing technology.**
The skills often cited are little different from those required in any management situation: leadership, technical, and administrative skills.

▶ **Discuss the differences among technology-driven transfer, market-driven transfer, and product-and-process-improvement transfer.**

Technological discoveries in a laboratory or through other basic and commercial research can create market opportunities. The technology in essence drives the demand for the product, service, or process. In market-driven transfer, a customer need exists. The task is to find the best technology to meet the need. Product-and-process-improvement transfer centres on improving technology. Even the car and the telephone, despite having been on the market for more than a century, continually are being improved by innovative manufacturers. In all industries, improvements in technology are occurring in terms of quality enhancement and speed from the lab to the market.

▶ **Describe some important techniques that managers can use to encourage creativity.**

Some of the more widely used techniques include encouraging experimentation among employees, permitting on-the-job interaction among them, tolerating failures, providing clear objectives and the freedom to achieve them, and offering recognition for good effort and performance.

▶ **Discuss why an organization might decide either to provide or not to provide creativity training for its employees.**

There have been no compelling research findings to indicate that an organization can improve creativity or innovation by creativity training such as fluency exercises, excursion exercises, pattern breakers, and shake-up exercises. Still, creativity is so important for the health of an organization that managers try to stimulate and encourage it in the hope that exposure to creativity training may enhance it.

## KEY TERMS

brainstorming, p. 558
creativity, p. 554
data mining, p. 542
differentiation, p. 539

excursion exercise, p. 558
fluency exercise, p. 558
innovation, p. 536
shake-up exercise, p. 558

technology, p. 536
technology forecasting, p. 540
technology transfer, p. 547
value chain analysis, p. 537

## REVIEW AND DISCUSSION QUESTIONS

### Recall

1. How can a licensing agreement or a joint venture be used to acquire technology from a competitor or potential competitor?
2. What is the difference between creativity and innovation?
3. What special problems do managers face with the widespread access to e-mail and to the Internet?
4. What are the primary support activities in the value chain analysis?

### Understanding

5. Why is it difficult to determine whether creativity training actually enhances creativity and innovation?
6. Explain the S-curve and how it can be used as a guide for technology forecasting.

**7.** Why might a company that has a secret process or composition of a product decide to share that technical information with another company?

## Application

**8.** Visit a business, office, factory, or other organization and take note of the technologies being used. List those that you observe. Then pick any one of the technologies that is being used and write a brief description of how that technology improves the effectiveness of the organization, what capabilities it provides to the organization that would be difficult or impossible to generate otherwise, and whether the technology is likely to improve working conditions of the employees. Then imagine what modifications might be made in that technology to increase its effectiveness (without regard to possible cost, practicality, or whether you think it would be possible to design and build such modifications).

**9.** Select a device or process that is in common use in Canada today and that, when it was first introduced, reflected the application of creativity and innovation. Write a brief description of how you think life would be changed if suddenly all copies of that device or descriptions of that process were to disappear in a puff of smoke and not ever be able to be reproduced or replaced.

## CASE 15-1

# Dusseault Designs Company

When fashion designer Donna Dusseault started her company seven years ago, she focused on keeping her small store in downtown Toronto open long enough to build a loyal client base. Today, Dusseault Designs Company has capitalized on some of Toronto's hottest fashion trends and currently has three prominent downtown locations. The company employs a total of 28 people, including 14 sales associates, 10 seamstresses, 2 managers, 1 systems administrator/designer, and 1 accountant.

The sales associates she has hired are fashion-design students at a local college, and are fully trained wardrobe consultants. The students work in the store and also respond to the multiple e-mail questions and orders that arrive daily via the company's new Web site.

Last year, Dusseault had a professional Web site designed for her company. She placed some of the same designs found in her three stores on her Web pages, as well a line of casual wear sold exclusively via the Internet. She worked with the Web-design team to create self-assessment quizzes that link wardrobe pieces to traditional style preference indicators.

As the clients surf Dusseault's Web page, they have the option of using the embedded test to help them make sensible wardrobe decisions. The clients even can add pieces they have in their existing wardrobe to help determine their fashion needs. While these helpful self-tests and wardrobe profiles are free, value-added services to clients, they allow Dusseault to obtain market research or data-mining information easily.

Dusseault's systems designer downloaded monthly trend reports and listed new special-request items, giving the company a direct link to the ebbs and flows of her customers. Hits on her Web site reached 20,000 after just two months. This instant online success boosted profits by a staggering 51 percent after the first year. The Web site created an instant international profile for Dusseault. Her client roster has grown from servicing mainly local Canadian clients to reaching an international client base.

When reviewing costs with her accountant, Dusseault realized that the majority of her business costs still was related to maintaining the three traditional stores, while the majority of her revenue was coming from Internet sales.

Dusseault needs to determine if the benefits associated with maintaining the traditional Dusseault Designs Company stores are valuable enough to continue maintaining them. Would she be better off closing one or all of the stores—relying on "virtual sales" only?

## Questions

1. What are the benefits of leaving the stores open?
2. What would Dusseault gain and/or lose by closing the stores?
3. What do you recommend she do? Explain your choice by listing all of the opportunity cost factors associated with your approach.
4. What information does Dusseault need to know about her virtual clients before making a decision?
5. How many employees do you think she'll need in both scenarios (leaving the stores open and deciding to close them)?
6. How else could Dusseault use technology to increase her sales and profile? Be creative.

Contributed by Marnie Wright, British Columbia Institute of Technology.

## APPLICATION EXERCISE 15-1

### Dividing the Farmer's Land

A farmer owns land that is a perfect rectangle, 800 metres long and 400 metres wide. He wishes to divide the land, giving exactly one-quarter to each of his four children. What are three ways that he can divide the land so that each parcel will be identical to the others in size and in shape? The keys will be found in the Appendix to this chapter, but should not be consulted until three solutions have been found, or the person solving the problem has given up in despair.

800 metres

400 metres

### Questions

**1.** What previous experiences have you had that made it harder or easier for you to solve this problem?

**2.** What general type of problem is this? What other problems are like this?

**3.** What general principle(s) could you use to help you solve similar future problems?

Source: Adapted from N.R.F. Maier, *Problem Solving and Creativity in Individuals and Groups* (Belmont, CA: Brooks/Cole, 1970): 96-97.

## ► *APPLICATION EXERCISE*  **15-2**

### Understanding the Value Chain

Marion Smith is holding a profit-making barbecue for her favourite charity, the Manitoba Sewing Club. Her goal is to make as much money as possible for the organization, keeping in mind that her modest volunteer pool currently sits at seven. She has two suppliers to choose from:

- Supplier A is a catering company that will barbecue the chicken and hamburgers for her and provide the condiments and beverages at a 15 percent markup over their cost of $8 per person.
- Supplier B will deliver the frozen patties, buns, condiments, and beverages to the event. Marion and her team of volunteers will need to staff the barbecue themselves. The cost will be $5 per person.

Marion needs to determine how many people she will invite to her function. Use Porter's value chain analysis to determine how each of these suppliers adds value to Marion's organization. In what situations would Marion choose Supplier A or B—recognizing that they "add value" at different parts of the chain.

Contributed by Marnie Wright, British Columbia Institute of Technology.

## ► *INTERNET APPLICATION*  **15-1**

Enter the Web site of United Parcel Service (UPS) (www.ups.com).

1. What kinds of information systems and technologies does UPS use to improve services to customers?

2. In what ways does the use of these information systems and technologies provide UPS with a competitive advantage?

Search for a Web site of an organization that makes extensive use of information systems to deliver its goods and services to customers. What systems does it use and how do they give the organization a competitive advantage?

# Appendix: Solutions for Application Exercise 15-1

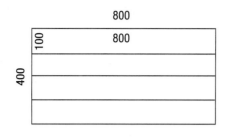

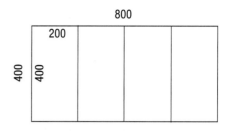

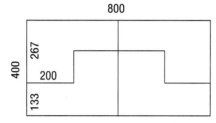

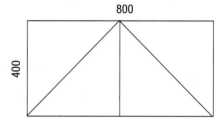

# Endnotes

## Chapter 1

1. "Seventeenth Annual Franchise 500," *Entrepreneur* (January 1996): 249.
2. "Annals of Marketing," *The Report on Business Magazine* (October 1998): 16.
3. *UN Handbook of International Trade and Development* (1997).
4. Brian Dumaine, "The New Non-Manager Managers," *Fortune* (February 22, 1993): 80-84; "A Checklist of Qualities That Make a Good Boss," *Nation's Business* (November 1984): 100.
5. Luis R. Gomez-Mejia, Joseph E. McCann, and Ronald C. Page, "The Structure of Managerial Behaviors and Rewards," *Industrial Relations*, 24 (1985): 147-54.
6. See Robert L. Katz, "Skills of an Effective Administrator," *Harvard Business Review* (September-October 1974): 91-102.
7. Del Marth, "Keeping All the Lines Open," *Nation's Business* (October 1984): 85-86.
8. "Trying to Climb the Corporate Ladder? Without Basic Computer Skills, You Risk Falling Off, Survey Shows," *PR Newswire* (January 20, 1988).
9. Henry Mintzberg, *The Nature of Managerial Work* (Englewood Cliffs, NJ: Prentice-Hall, 1980).
10. See also Henry Mintzberg, "The Manager's Role: Folklore and Fact," *Harvard Business Review* (July-August 1975): 49-61; Jay W. Lorsch, James P. Baughman, James Reece, and Henry Mintzberg, *Understanding Management* (New York: Harper & Row, 1978); Neil Snyder and William F. Glueck, "How Managers Plan—The Analysis of Managers' Activities," *Long Range Planning* (February 1980): 70-76.
11. Frederick W. Taylor, *Principles of Scientific Management* (New York: Harper, 1911).
12. Lyndall Urwick, *The Golden Book of Management* (London: Newman Neame, 1956): 36-37.
13. Charles D. Wrege and Anne Marie Stotka, "Cooke Creates a Classic: The Story Behind F.W. Taylor's Principles of Scientific Management," *Academy of Management Review*, 3(4) (1978): 736-49, in which the authors make a convincing case, complete with copies of pages of manuscript drafts, that Taylor lifted at least three chapters from his colleague Morris L. Cooke's book entitled *Industrial Management*, which Cooke never published, in part because of advice received from Taylor to defer its publication.
14. Claude S. George, Jr., *The History of Management Thought* (Englewood Cliffs, NJ: Prentice-Hall, 1968). See also Edwin A. Locke, "The Ideas of Frederick W. Taylor: An Evaluation," *Academy of Management Review*, 1 (1982): 14-24.
15. *See* James D. Mooney and Alan C. Reiley, *Onward Industry* (New York: Harper & Row, 1931); Lyndall F. Urwick, *The Elements of Administration* (New York: Harper & Row, 1943).
16. Henri Fayol, *Administration Industrielle et General* (1919). Trans. by J.A. Coubrough under the title *General and Industrial Management* (New York: General and International Management Institute, 1930); revised by Irwin Gray under the same title (New York: Institute of Electrical and Electronics Engineers, c. 1984).
17. Weber, *Wirtschaft und Gesellschaft*, III(6), as translated and edited by A.M. Henderson and Talcott Parsons under the title *The Theory of Social and Economic Organization* (New York: Oxford University Press). For a critique of this interpretation see R.M. Weiss, "Weber on Bureaucracy: Management Consultant or Political Theorist?" *Academy of Management Review*, 8 (1983): 242-48.
18. Fritz J. Roethisberger and William J. Dickson, *Management and the Worker* (Cambridge, MA: Harvard University Press, 1931).
19. Stephen R.G. Jones, "Worker Interdependence and Output: The Hawthorne Studies Reevaluated," *American Sociological Review*, 55(2) (1990): 176-90; *see also* Richard Herbert Franke and James D. Kaul, "The Hawthorne Experiments: First Statistical Interpretation," *Sociological Review*, 43 (1978): 623-43.
20. Ludwig Von Bertalanffy, "The History and Status of General Systems Theory," *Academy of Management Journal* (December 1972): 411.
21. *Finning Ltd. Annual Report* (1995).
22. Chester I. Barnard, *The Functions of the Executive* (Cambridge, MA: Harvard University Press, 1938): 65.
23. For further discussion of the systems approach, see Steve Cavaleri and Krzysztof Obloj, *Management Systems: A Global Perspective* (Belmont, CA: Wadsworth, 1993): 6-10; Fremont E. Kast and James E. Rosenzweig, "General Systems Theory: Applications in Organizations and Management," *Academy of Management Journal* (December 1972): 447-65; Daniel Katz and Robert L. Kahn, *The Social Psychology of Organizations* (New York: John Wiley & Sons, 1966).
24. Fremont E. Kast and James E. Rosenzweig, "General Systems Theory: Applications in Organizations and Management," *Academy of Management Journal* (December 1972): 463.
25. For discussions of contingency theory, see Fred Luthans, "The Contingency Theory of Management: A Path Out of the Jungle," *Business Horizons* (June 1973): 63-72; Harold Koontz, "The

Management Jungle Revisited," *Academy of Management Review* (April 1980): 175-88.

26 William G. Ouchi, *Theory Z: How American Business Can Meet the Japanese Challenge* (Reading, MA: Addison-Wesley, 1981).

27 Harold Geneen, *Managing* (New York: Avon Books, 1984): 17.

28 Thomas J. Peters and Robert H. Waterman, Jr., *In Search of Excellence* (New York: Harper & Row, 1982).

29 Thomas J. Peters, *Liberation Management* (New York: Alfred A. Knopf, 1992).

30 John Case, *From the Ground Up* (New York: Simon and Schuster, 1992): 45-46.

31 Peter F. Drucker, *Management: Tasks, Responsibilities, Practices* (New York: Harper & Row, 1973).

32 Peter F. Drucker, *The Practice of Management* (New York: Harper & Row, 1954).

33 Peter F. Drucker, *Innovation and Entrepreneurship* (London: William Heinemann, 1985).

34 Peter F. Drucker, *Post-Capitalist Society* (New York: Harper-Collins, 1993).

35 W. Edwards Deming, *Out of the Crisis*, 2nd ed. (Cambridge, MA: MIT Center for Advanced Engineering Study, 1986).

36 *Ibid.*

37 Philip B. Crosby, *Quality without Tears* (New York: McGraw-Hill, 1984): 12. See also Philip B. Crosby, *Quality Is Free* (New York: McGraw-Hill, 1979).

38 Henry Mintzberg, *The Rise and Fall of Strategic Planning* (Toronto: Maxwell-Macmillan Canada, 1995).

## Chapter 2

1 Konrad Yakabuski, "Quebec Cement Firms Socked," *Globe and Mail* (August 20, 1996): A1, A3.

2 Jennifer Wells, "Hunters for Gold, Pursuers of Fame," *Report on Business Magazine* (October 1998): 85-99.

3 Andrew Willis and Andrew Goold, "Bre-X: The One-Man Scam," *Globe and Mail* (July 22, 1997): A1, A10.

4 Paul Waldie and Allan Robinson, "Timbuktu Tampering Preceded Test," *Globe and Mail* (June 12, 1996): B1.

5 Reed Abelson, "Justice—Corporate Style," *Globe and Mail* (August 8, 1996): B6.

6 John Saunders, "TSE Queries Bre-X Ownership," *Globe and Mail* (February 21, 1997): B1, B7.

7 James Christie, "Samaranch Linked to Olympics Scandal," *Globe and Mail* (January 6, 1999): S1.

8 Canadian Pacific, *Code of Business Conduct* (1995).

9 Staff, "Food Poisoning: Killer Hamburgers," *The Economist* (February 13, 1993): 27-28; Ronald Grover, Dori Jones Yang, and Laura Holson, "Boxed in at Jack in the Box," *Business Week* (February 15, 1993): 40.

10 Edgar H. Schein, *Organizational Culture and Leadership* (San Francisco: Jossey-Bass, 1985): 168.

11 T.A. Deal and A.A. Kennedy, "Culture—A New Look Through Old Lenses," *Journal of Applied Behavior Science* (November 1983): 50.

12 K.L. Gregory, "Native-View Paradigms: Multiple Cultures and Culture Conflicts in Organizations," *Administrative Science Quarterly* (September 1983): 359-76.

13 G.S. Saffold, "Culture Traits, Strength, and Organizational Performance: Moving Beyond 'Strong' Culture," *Academy of Management Review* (October 1988): 546-58.

14 Mike Maremont, "Blind Ambition," *Business Week* (October 23, 1995): 78-92.

15 Anthony Sampson, *Company Man* (New York: Times Business, 1995) cited in Glasgall, "The Dinosaur in the Gray Flannel Suit," *Business Week* (October 30, 1995): 19.

16 Janice Acton, Penny Goldsmith, and Bonnie Shepard (eds.), *Women at Work, Ontario, 1850-1930* (Toronto: Canadian Women's Educational Press, 1974): 280.

17 Kathleen Gerson, *Hard Choices: How Women Decide about Work, Career and Motherhood* (Berkeley, CA: University of California Press, 1985): 233.

18 Paul Phillips and Erin Phillips, *Women and Work: Inequality in the Canadian Labour Market* (Toronto: James Lorimer & Company, 1993): 35.

19 Peter Drucker, *The Age of Discontinuity* (New York: Harper & Row, 1969): 12.

20 Anne McIlroy, "Hepatitis C Victims Deserve Aid, Krever Says," *Globe and Mail* (November 27, 1997): A10.

21 Scott McMurray, "Wounded Giant: Union Carbide Offers Some Sober Lessons in Crisis Management," *The Wall Street Journal* (January 28, 1991): A1.

22 Carey French, "Globetrotters at Increasing Risk of Malaria," *Globe and Mail* (February 25, 1997): C5

23 Tom Dunkel, "Affirmative Reaction," *Working Woman* (October 1995): 39-43.

24 Milton Friedman, *Capitalism and Freedom* (Chicago: University of Chicago Press, 1962).

25 Milton Friedman, "The Social Responsibility of Business Is to Increase Its Profits," *New York Times Magazine* (September 1970): 33, 122-26.

26 Michael Deck, as quoted in *Globe and Mail* (May 17, 1996): B8.

27 Suggested by S. Prakash Sethi, "A Conceptual Framework for Environmental Analysis of Social Issues and Evaluation of Business Response Patterns," *Academy of Management Review* (January 1979): 66.

28 *Ibid.*

29 Peter Arlow and Martin J. Gannon, "Social Responsiveness, Corporate Structure, and Economic Performance," *Academy of Management Review* (April 1982): 235.

30 Laurence D. Hebb, "Consider the Other Stakeholders," *Globe and Mail* (July 2, 1996): B2.

31 Alex Cutler, *Eco-Management Strategies for the Future* (London: New Academy of Business, 1996).

32 H. Gordon Fitch, "Achieving Corporate Social Responsibility," *Academy of Management Review* (January 1976): 45.

33 Janet McFarland, "How Canadian Companies Stack Up on Ethics," *Globe and Mail* (July 25, 1996): B4.

34 Gabriella Stern and JoAnn S. Lubin, "GM Gets Tough with Ethics," *Globe and Mail* (June 5, 1996): B10.

35 "Do Corporate Executives Think Ethics Matter?" *HR Magazine* (October 1995): 90.

36 John Heinzl, "Survey Finds Few Firms Act on Code of Conduct," *Globe and Mail* (February 21, 1997): B11.

37 Fred Luthans, Richard M. Hodgetts, and Kenneth R. Thompson, *Social Issues in Business* (New York: Macmillan, 1984): 97-105.

38 For a negative view, see Rick Wartzman, "Nature or Nurture? Study Blames Ethical Lapses on Corporate Goals," *The Wall Street Journal* (October 9, 1987): 21.

[39] Beverly Gebert, "Unethical? Who Me?" *Training* (October 1995): 104.

## Chapter 3

[1] Paul S. Adler, "Time-and-Motion Regained," *Harvard Business Review* (January-February 1993): 97-108.

[2] C.A. Knox Lovell, "Econometric Efficiency Analysis: A Policy-Oriented Review," *European Journal of Operational Research* (February 2, 1995): 452-61.

[3] D. Keith Denton, "Creating a System for Continuous Improvement," *Business Horizons* (January/February 1995): 16-21.

[4] C. Jackson Grayson, Jr., and Carla O'Dell, *American Business: A Two-Minute Warning* (New York: Free Press, 1988): 211-12.

[5] Paul Hersey and Kenneth Blanchard, *Management of Organizational Behavior* (Englewood Cliffs, NJ: Prentice-Hall, 1993): 19.

[6] Joel Barker, *Future Edge* (New York: Morrow, 1992): 15-17.

[7] Robert Melnbardis, "A Factory Takes Off," *Canadian Business* (November 1994): 44-45.

[8] Sarah Kennedy, "Waking Up to the Realities of Customer Satisfaction," *CMA Magazine* (February 1977): 28.

[9] Sandy Jap, "The Employee's Viewpoint of Critical Service Encounters," *Stores* (January 1995): RR4-RR6.

[10] Salem Alaton, "CEOs Shed Their Armour to Share Managing Expertise," *Globe and Mail* (September 22, 1998): C6.

[11] R.A. Cozier and C.R. Schwenk, "Agreement and Thinking Alike: Ingredients for Poor Decisions," *Academy of Management Executive* (February 1990): 69-74.

[12] P.A. Renwick and H. Tosi, "The Effects of Sex, Marital Status, and Educational Background on Selected Decisions," *Academy of Management Journal* (March 1978): 93-103; A.A. Abdel Halim, "Effects of Task and Personality Characteristics on Subordinates' Responses to Participative Decision Making," *Academy of Management Journal* (September 1983): 477-84.

[13] Leon Festinger, *A Theory of Cognitive Dissonance*, Chapter 1 (New York: Harper & Row, 1957).

[14] B.M. Staw, "The Escalation of Commitment to a Course of Action," *Academy of Management Review* (October 1981): 577-87.

[15] For example, see Staw, "The Escalation of Commitment to a Course of Action," *op. cit.* and Max H. Bazerman and Alan Appelman, "Escalation of Commitment in Individual and Group Decision Making," *Organizational Behavior and Human Decision Processes* (Spring 1984): 141-52.

[16] Richard A. Guzzo and James A. Waters, "The Expression of Affect and the Performance of Decision-Making Groups," *Journal of Applied Psychology* (February 1982): 67-74; D. Tjosvold and R.H.G. Field, "Effects of Social Context on Consensus and Majority Vote Decision Making," *Academy of Management Journal* (September 1983): 500-06; Frederick C. Miner, Jr., "Group versus Individual Decision Making: An Investigation of Performance Measures, Decision Strategies, and Process Losses/Gains," *Organizational Behavior and Human Decision Processes* (Winter 1984): 112-24.

[17] Alex F. Osborn, *Applied Imagination: Principles and Procedures of Creative Thinking* (New York: Charles Scribner's Sons, 1953); James L. Adams, *Conceptual Blockbusting: A Guide to Better Ideas* (Menlo Park, CA: Addison Wesley Publishing, 1974/1979).

[18] Carolyn Leitch, *Globe and Mail* (July 23, 1996): C1.

[19] Irene Kim, "The Virtual Engineer: Brainpower to Go," *Chemical Engineering* (October 1995): 35-43.

[20] V. Thomas Dock and James C. Wetherbe, *Computer Information Systems for Business* (St. Paul, MN: West, 1988): 36.

[21] C. Jackson Grayson, Jr., and Carla O'Dell, *American Business: A Two-Minute Warning* (New York: Free Press, 1988): 211-12.

[22] Alan P. Crawford, "No Computer is an Island," *American Gas* (November 1994): 24-27.

[23] Susan Concilla, "Groupware Competition Targets Lotus Notes Market Dominance," *Info Canada* (January 1995): IC15-17.

[24] Barbara Darrow, "Lotus Builds on Groupware," *Computer Reseller News* (January 9, 1995): 3, 8.

[25] Leslie Meall, "The Power to Make Progress," *Accountancy* (January 1992): 78-79.

[26] Frederick Stodolak and Joseph Carr, "Systems Must Be Compatible with Quality Efforts," *Healthcare Financial Management* (June 1992): 72-77C.

[27] Robert J. Mockler, "Strategic Intelligence Systems: Competitive Intelligence Systems to Support Strategic Management Decision Making," *SAM Advanced Management Journal* (Winter 1992): 4-9.

[28] *Globe and Mail* (January 2, 1999).

[29] William M. Bulkeley, "Databases are Plagued by Reign of Error," *The Wall Street Journal* (May 26, 1992): B6.

[30] G. Michael Ashmore, "Telecommunications Opens New Strategic Vistas," *Journal of Business Strategy* (March-April 1990): 58-61.

[31] Michael W. Miller, "Computers May Get Vast Ability to Blend Data, Images, Sound," *The Wall Street Journal* (June 7, 1989): A1, A4.

[32] Amy Cortese et al., "Cyberspace," *Business Week* (February 27, 1995): 78-86.

[33] Kelly Shermach, "Business Marketers Are Heavy Users of Interactive Catalogs," *Marketing News* (1995): 15.

[34] Betsy Spethmann and Eric Hollreiser, "Brand Builders," *Brandweek* (February 20, 1995): 18-19.

[35] Mark Berniker, "Sony Online Debuts Internet Site," *Broadcasting & Cable* (February 20, 1995): 51.

[36] Cliff Stoll, *The Cuckoo's Egg* (New York: Pocket Books, 1990).

[37] For instance, see David C. Rudd, "IBM Prepares 'Vaccine' for Computer Virus," *Chicago Tribune* (October 6, 1989): 1-2.

## Chapter 4

[1] See Dalton E. McFarland, *The Managerial Imperative: The Age of Macromanagement* (Cambridge, MA: Ballinger, 1986).

[2] David A. Fischer, "Strategies Toward Political Pressure: A Typology of Firm Responses," *Academy of Management Review* (January 1983): 71-78.

[3] Armand Feigenbaum, *Total Quality Control* (New York: McGraw-Hill, 1961): 134.

[4] Howard Gleckman and Susan B. Garland, "Downsizing Government," *Business Week* (January 23, 1995): 34-39.

[5] Daryl R. Connor, *Leading at the Edge of Chaos: How to Create the Nimble Organization* (Toronto: John Wiley & Sons, 1998).

[6] Carole King, "Equitable Tightens Reins on Agencies," *National Underwriter* (January 9, 1995): 7-8.

[7] Jon M. Ivancevich, James H. Donnelly, Jr., and James L. Gibson, *Management: Principles and Functions*, 5th ed. (Homewood, IL: Richard D. Irwin, 1989): 69-70.

[8] James C. Wetherbe, "Principles of Cycle Time Reduction: You Can Have Your Cake and Eat It Too," *Cycle Time Research* (1995): 1-24.

9 Mary Driscoll, "Never Stop Learning," *CFO* (February 1995): 50-56.

10 Staff, "Aligning the Process with the People," *Chief Executive* (March 1995): 8-13.

11 John H. Zimmerman, "The Principles of Managing Change," *HR Focus* (February 1995): 15-16.

12 Burt Nanus, *Visionary Leadership* (San Francisco, CA: Jossey-Bass, 1992): 8.

13 Chips Klein, "Take SWOT Approach to Strategy," *Globe and Mail* (November 6, 1998): B11.

14 John Naisbitt and Patricia Aburdene, *Megatrends 2000* (New York: William Morrow, 1990).

15 Frank Beacham, "Getting It Wrong—in Great Style," *Globe and Mail: User Friendly,* Number 2 (April 1996): 1.

16 From Dick Wilson, *China: The Big Tiger* (London: Little Brown & Company, 1996) as extracted in *South China Morning Post International Weekly* (May 11, 1996): 6; and from Lester Brown, WorldWatch Institute, as referred to in *South China Morning Post International Weekly* (October 7, 1995): 3.

17 W. Edwards Deming, *Out of the Crisis* (Cambridge, MA: Center for Advanced Engineering Study, Massachusetts Institute of Technology, 1986): 175.

18 Lindley H. Clark, "The Outlook: Diversification, Aid to Productivity," *The Wall Street Journal* (May 14, 1990): A1.

19 Philip B. Crosby, *Running Things: The Art of Making Things Happen* (New York: McGraw-Hill, 1986): 78-80.

20 William E. Halal, *The New Capitalism* (New York: John Wiley & Sons, 1986): 201.

21 Peter P. Pekar, "Setting Goals in the Non-Profit Environment," *Managerial Planning* (March-April 1982): 43-46.

22 D. Quinn Mills, "Planning with People in Mind," *Harvard Business Review* (July-August 1985): 97-195.

23 For relevant discussions of these and related management problems, see M.L. Gimpl and S.R. Daken, "Management and Magic," *California Management Review* (Fall 1984): 125-36; R.T. Pascale, "The Paradox of Corporate Culture: Reconciling Ourselves to Socialization," *California Management Review* (Winter 1985): 26-41; and Frederick D. Sturdivant, *Business and Society: A Managerial Approach*, 3rd ed (Homewood IL: Richard D. Irwin, 1985).

24 Peter F. Drucker, *The Practice of Management* (New York: Harper & Row, 1974): 64.

25 A. Parasuraman, Valerie A. Zeithaml, and Leonard L. Berry, "A Conceptual Model of Service Quality and Its Implications for Future Research," *Working Paper 84-106* (Cambridge, MA: Marketing Science Institute, 1984): 13-14, cited in Daniel T. Seymour, *On Q: Causing Quality in Higher Education* (New York, Macmillan, 1992): 130.

26 Greg Kennan, "Magna Announces Plans for Its Future," *Globe and Mail* (December 5, 1997) and Douglas Goold, "The Keys to Magna's Success" *Globe and Mail* (December 6, 1997): B22.

27 Thomas A. Stewart, "Why Budgets Are Bad for Business," *Fortune* (June 4, 1990): 179-90.

28 Mark Maremount, "Kodak's New Focus," *Business Week* (January 30, 1995): 62-68.

29 Toyohiro Kono, "Japanese Management Philosophy: Can It Be Exported?" *Long Range Planning* (Fall 1982): 90-102.

30 J.M. Juran, *Juran on Leadership for Quality: An Executive Handbook* (New York: Free Press, 1986): 186.

31 Karen Howlett and Allan Robinson, "Mining Expert Warns Against Corruption," *Globe and Mail* (March 18, 1997): B1, B15.

32 Jeff Sallot, "Ottawa Takes Middle Road on Ethics," *Globe and Mail* (September 6, 1997): B7.

33 Glenn R. Simpson, "Anti-bribery Treaty Hits U.S. Snag," *Wall Street Journal*, quoted in the *Globe and Mail* (October 19, 1998): B12.

34 Shawn Tully, "So, Mr. Bossidy," *Fortune* (August 21, 1995): 70-80.

35 J.M. Juran, *Juran on Leadership for Quality: An Executive Handbook* (New York: Free Press, 1986): 81-144.

36 W. Edwards Deming, *Out of Crisis* (Cambridge, MA: MIT Center for Advanced Engineering Study, 1986): 175.

37 David A. Garvin, *Managing Quality: The Strategic and Competitive Edge* (New York: Free Press, 1988): 183.

38 Mary Walton, *Deming Management at Work* (New York: G.P. Putnam's Sons, 1990): 21-22.

39 Karen Bemoski, "Carrying on the P&G Tradition," *Quality Progress* (May 1992): 24.

40 George Stalk, Jr., and Thomas M. Hout, *Competing Against Time: How Time-Based Competition Is Reshaping Global Markets* (New York: Free Press, 1990).

41 Joseph D. Blackburn, "The Time Factor." In Joseph D. Blackburn, (ed.), *Time-Based Competition: The Next Battleground in American Manufacturing* (Homewood, IL: Business One Irwin, 1991): 19.

42 J.M. Juran, *Juran on Quality Planning* (New York: Free Press, 1988): 1-2.

43 J.M. Juran, "The Quality Trilogy," *Quality Progress* (August 1986): 19-24.

44 J.M. Juran, "The Quality Trilogy," *Quality Progress* (August 1986): 19-24; also J.M. Juran, *Juran on Quality Planning*, Chapter 1 (New York: Free Press, 1988).

## Chapter 5

1 Hugh C. Willmott, "The Structuring of Organizational Structures: A Note," *Administrative Science Quarterly* (September 1981): 470-74.

2 Jerry Bowles, "Is American Management Really Committed to Quality?" *Management Review* (April 1992): 42-45.

3 *International Quality Study* (American Quality Foundation and Ernst & Young, 1991): 16-23.

4 Wendy Zellner, Robert D. Hof, Richard Brandt, Stephen Baker, and David Greising, "Go-Go Goliaths," *Business Week* (February 13, 1995): 64-70.

5 Tom Peters, *Thriving on Chaos* (New York: Alfred A. Knopf, 1987): 467.

6 James Treece, "Doing It Right, Till the Last Whistle," *Business Week* (April 6, 1992): 58-59.

7 Frederick W. Taylor, *Principles of Scientific Management* (New York: Harper & Row, 1911).

8 Scott Madison Paton, "Joseph M. Juran—Quality Legend: Part III," *Quality Digest* (March 1992): 49-58.

9 Lloyd Dobyns and Clare Crawford-Mason, *Quality or Else* (Boston: Houghton Mifflin, 1991): 56.

10 Dobyns and Crawford-Mason (1991), *op. cit.*: 60.

11 Marshall Sashkin and Kenneth J. Kiser, *Total Quality Management* (Seabrook, MD: Ducochon, 1991): 118.

12 Charles Garfield, *Second to None* (Homewood, IL: Business One Irwin, 1992): 164.

[13] Frank Shippes and Charles C. Manz, "Employee Self-Management without Formally Designated Teams: An Alternative Road to Empowerment," *Organizational Dynamics* (Winter 1992): 48-61.

[14] John A. Byrne, "Management," *Business Week* (September 18, 1995): 122-32.

[15] Adapted from Susan Cominiti, "What Team Leaders Need to Know," *Fortune* (February 20, 1995): 93-100.

[16] "The Quality Glossary," *Quality Progress* (February 1992): 20-29.

[17] G. Christian Hill and Ken Yamada, "Motorola Illustrates How an Aged Giant Can Remain Vibrant," *The Wall Street Journal* (December 9, 1992): A1, A14.

[18] Gilbert Fuchsberg, "Decentralized Management Can Have Its Drawbacks," *The Wall Street Journal* (December 9, 1992): B1, B8.

[19] Dana Milbank, "Restructured Alcoa Seeks to Juggle Cost and Quality," *The Wall Street Journal* (August 24, 1992): B4.

[20] Gilbert Fuchsberg (1992), *op. cit.*

[21] Thomas J. Peters and Robert H. Waterman, Jr., *In Search of Excellence* (New York: Warner Books, 1982): 15-16.

[22] Marshall Sashkin and Kenneth J. Kiser (1991), *op. cit.*: 67.

[23] Tom Peters, *Thriving on Chaos* (New York: Knopf, 1988): 292.

[24] Philip B. Crosby, *Quality Is Free* (New York: Mentor, 1979): 238.

[25] W. Edwards Deming, *Out of Crisis* (Boston: MIT Center for Advanced Study, 1986): 23-24.

[26] V. Daniel Hunt, *Quality in America* (Homewood, IL: Business One Irwin, 1992): 24-25.

[27] Douglas McGregor, *The Human Side of Organizations* (New York: McGraw-Hill, 1960): 33-34.

[28] J.J. Tuinman, "Literacy," *The Canadian Encyclopedia*, Vol. II (Edmonton: Hurtig Publishers, 1985): 1011-12.

[29] Paul Knox, "Canada Praised and Blamed," *Globe and Mail* (September 9, 1998).

[30] Charles Garfield, *Second to None* (Homewood, IL: Business One Irwin, 1992): 4-5.

[31] Thomas A. Stewart, "The Search for the Organization of Tomorrow," *Fortune* (May 18, 1992): 92-98.

[32] Richard Jaccoma, "Smart Moves in Hard Times," *Dealership Merchandising* (January 1992): 164-67.

[33] Paul R. Lawrence, Harvey F. Kolodny, and Stanley M. Davis, "The Human Side of Matrix Organizations," *Organizational Dynamics* (September 1977): 4.

[34] Philip Crosby, *Completeness: Quality for the 21st Century* (New York: Dutton, 1992): 73.

## Chapter 6

[1] Quoted in Eileen C. Shapiro, *Fad Surfing in the Board Room: Reclaiming the Courage to Manage in the Age of Instant Answers* (Reading, MA: Addison-Wesley, 1995): 6.

[2] R. Tannenbaum, I.R. Weschler, and F. Massarik, *Leadership and Organization* (New York: McGraw-Hill, 1961): 24.

[3] Janet McFarland, "Bullies Cling to Old Ways," *Globe and Mail* (December 9, 1997): B12.

[4] Frances Huffman, "Role Model: She May Drive a Pink Cadillac, but She Ain't No Powder Puff," *Entrepreneurial Woman* (June 1991): 36-39.

[5] Abraham Zaleznick, "Leaders and Managers: Are They Different?" *Harvard Business Review* (1977): 31-42; Abraham Zaleznick, "Real Work," *Harvard Business Review* (1989): 52-64; and Abraham Zaleznick, *The Managerial Mystique* (New York: Harper & Row, 1989): 1-42.

[6] Stephen R. Covey, A. Roger Merrill, and Rebecca R. Merrill, "Putting First Things First," *CMA Magazine* (March 1996): 15-19.

[7] Brent Jang, "Nova's Newall a $6.3 Million Man," *Globe and Mail* (March 20, 1997): B1, B6.

[8] Gayle MacDonald and Ijeoma Ross, "Nova's Newall Keeps His Cool in Big Breakup," *Globe and Mail* (November 13, 1997): B17.

[9] Quoted in Gordon Pitts, "A Good Leader Is Hard to Find," *Globe and Mail* (May 31, 1996): B9.

[10] Janet McFarland, "Cadbury Condemns Corporate Leadership," *Globe and Mail* (June 6, 1996): B13.

[11] Robert Dahl, "The Concept of Power," *Behavioral Science*, 2 (1957): 210-15.

[12] John R.P. French, Jr. and Bertram Raven, "The Bases of Social Power." In Dorwin Cartwright (ed.), *Studies in Social Power* (Ann Arbor, MI: University of Michigan Press, 1959): 150-67.

[13] Chris Klein, "Supportive Mentors a Boon for Business," *Globe and Mail* (November 13, 1998): B12.

[14] Jim Clemmer, "What We Get Is What We Are," *CMA Magazine* (June 1996): 8.

[15] Patricia Haddock, "Communicating Personal Power," *Supervision* (July 1995): 20.

[16] Ralph M. Stogdill, "Personal Factors Associated with Leadership," *Journal of Applied Psychology* (January 1948): 35-71.

[17] Edwin E. Ghiselli, "Managerial Talent," *American Psychologist* (October 1963): 631-41.

[18] Charles C. DuBois, "Portrait of the Ideal MBA," *The Penn Stater* (October 1992): 31.

[19] Morgan W. McCall and Michael M. Lombardo, "What Makes a Top Executive?" *Psychology Today* (February 1983): 26-31.

[20] Ralph Katz, "Skills of an Effective Administrator," *Harvard Business Review* (October-November 1974): 90-101.

[21] R. Stogdill, *Handbook of Leadership* (New York: Free Press, 1974): 35-71.

[22] Henry Mintzberg, quoted in Madelaine Drohan, "What Makes a Canadian Manager," *Globe and Mail* (February 25, 1997): B18.

[23] Madelaine Drohan, *op. cit.*

[24] Madelaine Drohan, *op. cit.*

[25] Katherine Gay, "Canadian versus American Leadership Styles," *The Financial Post* (Fall 1994): 8.

[26] Madelaine Drohan, *op. cit.*

[27] Rensis Likert, *New Patterns of Management* (New York: McGraw-Hill, 1961).

[28] Philip B. Crosby, *Running Things: The Art of Making Things Happen* (New York: McGraw-Hill, 1986): 23.

[29] N.C. Morse and Edward Reimer, "The Experimental Change of a Major Organizational Variable," *Journal of Abnormal and Social Psychology*, 52 (1956): 120-29.

[30] Edwin A. Fleishman and James G. Hunt (eds.), *Current Developments in the Study of Leadership* (Carbondale, IL: Southern Illinois Press, 1973): 1-37.

[31] Julian Barling, Tom Weber, and Kevin Kelloway, referred to in "Management Briefs: Leadership Lessons," *Globe and Mail* (March 25, 1997): B12.

[32] Fred E. Fiedler and Martin M. Chemers, *Leadership and Effective Management* (Glenview, IL: Scott, Foresman, 1974).

[33] Paul Hersey and Kenneth H. Blanchard, *Management of Organizational Behavior: Utilizing Human Resources* (Englewood Cliffs, NJ: Prentice Hall, 1993).

34  O.M. Irgens, "Situational Leadership: A Modification of Hersey and Blanchard's Model," *Leadership & Organizational Development Journal*, 16(2) (1995): 36-39.

35  William R. Norris and Robert P. Vecchio, "Situational Leadership Theory," *Leadership & Organization Development Journal* (December 1992): 19-22; Warren Blank, John R. Weitzel, and Stephen G. Green, "A Test of the Situational Leadership Theory," *Group & Organization Management* (September 1992): 579-97.

36  Victor Vroom and Arthur Jago, "Decision Making as a Social Process: Normative and Descriptive Models of Leadership Behavior," *Decision Sciences* (1974): 743-70.

37  Victor Vroom and Philip W. Yetton, *Leadership and Decision Making* (Pittsburgh, PA: University of Pittsburgh Press, 1973).

38  Robert J. House and Terrence Mitchell, "Path-Goal Theory of Leadership," *Journal of Contemporary Business* (Autumn 1974): 81-97.

39  Steven Kerr and John M. Jermier, "Substitutes for Leadership: Their Meaning and Measurement," *Organizational Behavior and Human Performance* (December 1978): 375-403.

40  Gary A. Yukl, *Leadership in Organizations* (Englewood Cliffs, NJ: Prentice-Hall, 1989): 108-112.

41  J.M. Burns, *Leadership* (New York: Harper & Row, 1978): 1-52; Bernard M. Bass, *Leadership: Performance Beyond Expectations* (New York: Free Press, 1985): 43; Bernard M. Bass, "Leadership: Good, Better, Best," *Organizational Dynamics* (1985): 26-40.

42  Bernard M. Bass, *Leadership: Performance Beyond Expectations* (New York: Free Press, 1985).

43  The material on self-leadership has been adapted from Henry P. Sims, Jr. and Peter Lorenzi, *The New Leadership Paradigm: Social Learning and Cognition in Organizations* (Newbury Park, CA: Sage, 1992).

44  Marshall Sashkin, "Participative Management Remains an Ethical Imperative," *Organizational Dynamics* (Spring 1986): 62-75.

45  W. Baldwin, "This Is the Answer," *Forbes* (July 5, 1982): 52.

46  Charles C. Manz and Henry P. Sims, Jr., *Superleadership* (New York: Berkeley, 1990): xviii.

47  G. Kozmetzky, *Transformational Management* (Cambridge, MA: Ballinger, 1985).

48  J.M. Stewart, "Less Is More," *Canadian Business Review* (Summer 1989): 48-49.

49  Howard Weiss, "Subordinate Imitation of Supervisor Behavior: The Role of Modeling in Organizational Socialization," *Organizational Behavior and Human Performance*, 19 (1977): 89-105.

50  M. Sashkin, "Participative Management Is an Ethical Imperative," *Organizational Dynamics*, 12 (1984): 5-22.

51  Martha T. Moore, "Sorting Out a Mess," *USA Today* (April 10, 1992): 5B.

52  H.B. Braiker, "The Power of Self-Talk," *Psychology Today* (December 1989): 23. *See also* D.D. Burns, *The Good Feeling Handbook* (New York: William Morrow, 1989).

53  M. Porter, "Why Nations Triumph," *Fortune* (March 12, 1990): 94-98; J. Dreyfuss, "Get Ready for the New Work Force," *Fortune* (April 23, 1990): 165, 168, 172, 176, 180-81.

54  Statistics Canada, *The Labour Force Annual Averages*: 71-220, quoted in Paul Phillips and Erin Phillips, *Women and Work* (Toronto: James Lorimer & Company, 1993): 35.

55  Katherine Gay, "Smashing the Glass Ceiling," *The Financial Post* (Fall 1994): 8.

56  B. Levine, "Women Could Lead Way into 1990s," *Winnipeg Free Press* (November 13, 1990): 33.

57  Chris Argyris, *Personality and Organization* (New York: Harper, 1957).

58  D. Eden and A.B. Shani, "Pygmalion Goes to Boot Camp: Expectancy, Leadership, and Trainee Performance," *Journal of Applied Psychology*, 67 (1982): 94-99.

59  Joann S. Lublin and Rebecca Blumenstein, "She's the CEO of HP, He's the Boss at Home," *Globe and Mail* (July 23, 1999): M1.

60  Katherine Gay, "Smashing the Glass Ceiling," *The Financial Post* (Fall 1994): 9.

61  David Paris, "GM of Canada's Driving Force," *CMA Magazine* (June 1996).

62  Oliver Bertin, "Marketing VP Carries the Load at Canadian," *Globe and Mail* (July 12, 1996): B8.

63  Barbara Beck, "Cracks in the Glass Ceiling," *Report on Business Magazine* (January 1999): 78.

64  Patricia W. Hamilton, "What a Changing Work Force Means for Business," *D&B Reports* (January-February 1992): 20-23.

65  Renee Bazile-Jones, "Diversity in the Work Place: Why We Should Care," *CMA Magazine* (June 1996).

66  Taylor H. Cox and Stacy Blake, "Managing Cultural Diversity: Implications for Organizational Competitiveness," *Academy of Management Executive* (August 1991): 45-56.

67  Tim Turner, "A Woman for All Seasons: An Interview with Betty Friedan," *Hemispheres* (August 1993): 19-23.

68  David K. Foot, with Daniel Stoffman, *Boom, Bust and Echo: How to Profit from the Coming Demographic Shift* (Toronto: Macfarlane Walter & Ross, 1996): 193.

69  Laura Ramsay, "Growing Numbers Bear Elder Care Burden," *Globe and Mail* (December 1, 1998): C1.

70  Charles Garfield, *Second to None* (Homewood, IL: Business One Irwin, 1992): 286-91.

71  Lee Gardenswartz and Anita Rowe, *Managing Diversity* (Homewood, IL: Business One Irwin, 1993): 4.

72  *Ibid.*

73  F.A. Manske, Jr., *Secrets of Effective Leadership* (Memphis, TN: Leadership Education and Development, Inc, 1987).

## Chapter 7

1  Joseph M. Juran, *Juran on Leadership for Quality* (New York: Free Press, 1989): 145.

2  Walter A. Shewart, *Statistical Method from the Viewpoint of Quality Control* (Washington, DC: Graduate School, U.S. Department of Agriculture, 1939): 1.

3  W. Edwards Deming, *Out of the Crisis* (Cambridge, MA: Center for Advanced Engineering Study, Massachusetts Institute of Technology, 1986): 276-77.

4  Deming, *op. cit.*: 290-91, 294.

5  Deming, *op. cit.*

6  Michel Perigord, *Achieving Total Quality Management* (Cambridge, MA: Productivity Press, 1990): Chapter 8.

7  Perigord, *op. cit.*: 121.

8  Patricia Sellers, "Companies That Serve You Best," *Fortune* (May 31, 1993): 74-88.

9  *See* John M. Ivancevich and William Glueck, *Foundations of Personnel*, 5th ed. (Homewood, IL: Richard D. Irwin, 1992).

[10] Peter Lorange and Declan Murphy, "Considerations in Implementing Strategic Control," *Journal of Business Strategy* (Spring 1984): 27-35.

[11] George Schreyogg and Horst Stenman, "Strategic Control: A New Perspective," *Academy of Management Review* (1987): 91-103.

[12] Luis R. Gomez-Mejia, Henry Tosi, and Timothy Hinkin, "Managerial Control, Performance, and Executive Compensation," *Academy of Management Journal* (March 1987): 51-70.

[13] John M. Ivancevich and William Glueck, *Foundations of Personnel*, 5th ed. (Homewood, IL: Richard D. Irwin, 1992): Chapter 2.

[14] Frank Collins, Paul Munter, and Don W. Finn, "The Budgeting Games People Play," *Accounting Review* (January 1987): 29-49.

[15] Lawrence L. Stenmetz and H. Ralph Todd, Jr., *First-Line Management*, 3rd ed. (Homewood, IL: Richard D. Irwin, 1986).

[16] Burton A. Kolb and Richard DeMong, *Principles of Financial Management*, 2nd ed. (Homewood, IL: Richard D. Irwin, 1988); *and* Diane Harrington and Brent D. Wilson, *Corporate Financial Analysis*, 2nd ed. (Homewood, IL: Richard D. Irwin, 1986).

[17] Avi Rushinek and Sara F. Rushinek, "Using Financial Ratios to Predict Insolvency," *Journal of Business Research* (February 1987): 74-77.

[18] Ralph H. Garrison, *Managerial Accounting: Concepts for Planning, Control and Decision Making*, 5th ed. (Homewood IL: Richard D. Irwin, 1988).

[19] Kathleen Kerwin and David Woodruff, "Is Detroit Pulling Up to Pass?" *Business Week* (January 11, 1993): 63.

[20] Kenneth R. Thompson, "A Conversation with Robert W. Galvin," *Organizational Dynamics* (Spring 1992): 56-69.

[21] Gabriel A. Pall, *Quality Process Management* (Englewood Cliffs, NJ: Prentice-Hall, 1987): 94.

[22] Mark Bryson, "Experimental Design Boosts Production Yields," *Chemical Engineering* (July 1995): 155.

[23] Kevin M. Barry, "Measuring Continuous Improvement in a Project Office," (July 1995): 19-21.

[24] Lloyd Dobyns and Clare Crawford Mason, *Quality or Else* (Boston: Houghton Mifflin, 1991): Chapter 6.

[25] A.V. Feigenbaum, *Total Quality Control* (New York: McGraw-Hill, 1991); *and* Mary Walton, *The Deming Management Method* (New York: Perigree, 1986): 122-30.

[26] Kaoru Ishikawa, *What Is Total Quality Control?* (Englewood Cliffs, NJ: Prentice-Hall, 1985): 90-94.

[27] A.V. Feigenbaum, *op. cit.*

[28] Kaoru Ishikawa, *op. cit.*

[29] Thomas Pyzdek, *What Every Manager Should Know About Quality* (New York: Marcel Dekker, 1991): 3.

[30] A.V. Feigenbaum, *op. cit.*: 828-33.

[31] Thomas Pyzdek, *op. cit.*: 3-4.

[32] Thomas J. Peters and Robert H. Waterman, *In Search of Excellence* (New York: Harper & Row, 1982).

[33] "Productivity from Control," *Nation's Business* (June 1993): 38.

[34] Karen Lowry Miller, "The Factory Guru Tinkering with Toyota," *Business Week* (May 17, 1993): 95-97.

[35] W. Edwards Deming, *Out of Crisis* (Cambridge, MA: Center for Advanced Engineering Study, Massachusetts Institute of Technology, 1986): 380-87.

[36] Joseph M. Juran, *op. cit.*: Chapter 5 *and* 147-48.

[37] Joseph M. Juran, *op. cit.*: 148-50.

[38] A.V. Feigenbaum, *op. cit.*: 204-209.

[39] George E. Wollner, "The Law of Producing Quality," *Quality Progress* (January 1992): 35-40.

[40] Gilbert Fuchsberg, "'Total Quality' Is Deemed Only Partial Success," *The Wall Street Journal* (October 1, 1992): B1, B7.

[41] ISO 9000, "Canada and ISO 9000," *Globe and Mail* (May 7, 1996): Supp. 1.

[42] Dr. Tony Fattal, "ISO 9000: A Management Perspective," *Globe and Mail* (May 7, 1996): AS 1.

[43] Standards Council of Canada, *ISO Survey of ISO 9000 and ISO 14,000 Certificates* (1999).

[44] Norm Bush, *quoted in* ISO 9000, "Canada and ISO 9000," *Globe and Mail* (May 7, 1996): Supp. 6.

[45] Standards Council of Canada, *The ISO Survey of ISO 9000 and ISO 14000 Certificates* (1998).

[46] Catherine Neville, *quoted in* ISO 9000, "Canada and ISO 9000," *Globe and Mail* (May 7, 1996): Supp 3.

[47] Chris Rauwendaal, "Statistical Process Control in Extrusion," *Plastics World* (March 1995): 59-64.

[48] John Schriefer, "The Rewards of Quality," *Iron Age New Steel* (April 1995): 3-32.

[49] Stewart Anderson, "ISO 9000 Registrations on the Rise," *Globe and Mail* (May 7, 1996): AS 2.

# Chapter 8

[1] Ian Dutton, "Most Employees Feel Left Out," *Victoria Times-Colonist* (November 7, 1996): D7.

[2] Tom Peters and Robert Waterman, Jr., *In Search of Excellence* (New York: HarperCollins, 1982): 64.

[3] "Management Briefs: Employee Power," *Globe and Mail* (March 19, 1996).

[4] Edward E. Lawler III, "Human Resource Management," *Personnel* (January 1988): 24-25.

[5] Catherine A. Oliver, "Harnessing the Overqualified," *HR Focus* (June 1992): B.

[6] John M. Ivancevich, *Human Resource Management* (Homewood, IL: Richard D. Irwin, 1992): 172.

[7] Ricky W. Griffin, *Task Design: An Integrative Approach* (Glenview, IL: Scott, Foresman, 1982): 91.

[8] Bob Nelson, "Asset Appreciation Produces Best Returns," *CMA Magazine* (March 1996).

[9] Allan W. Farrant, "Job Rotation is Important," *Supervision* (August 1987): 14-16.

[10] Charles R. Walker and Robert H. Guest, *The Man in the Assembly Line* (Cambridge, MA: Harvard University Press, 1952).

[11] Frederick Herzberg, B. Mausner, and B. Snyderman, *The Motivation to Work* (New York: John Wiley & Sons, 1959).

[12] Margaret Houston and John Talbott, "Worker Empowerment Works—Sometimes," *CMA Magazine* (July-August 1996): 16, 17.

[13] J. Richard Hackman, "Work Design." In J. Richard Hackman and J.L. Suttle (eds.), *Improving Life at Work* (Santa Monica, CA: Goodyear, 1976): 96-162.

[14] T. Richard Hackman and Greg R. Oldham, *Work Redesign* (Reading, MA: Addison-Wesley, 1980): 77-82.

[15] Katherine Gay, "Poor Management Can Spawn Absenteeism," *The Financial Post* (Fall 1994): 10.

[16] Michael A. Champion and Chris J. Barger, "Conceptual Integration and Empirical Test of Job Design and Compensation Experiments," *Personnel Psychology* (Autumn 1990): 525-54.

[17] Edward E. Lawler, *Pay and Organization Development* (Reading, MA: Addison-Wesley, 1981).

[18] David A. Ralston, William P. Anthony, and David J. Gustafson, "Employees Love Flextime, But What Does It Do to the Organization's Productivity?" *Journal of Applied Psychology* (May 1985): 272-79.

[19] C.W. Proel, Jr., "A Survey of the Empircal Literature on Flexible Work Hours: Character and Consequences of a Major Innovation," *Academy of Management Review* (October 1978): 837-53.

[20] Randall B. Dunham and John L. Pierce, "The Design and Evaluation of Alternative Work Schedules," *Personnel Administrator* (April 1983): 67-75.

[21] Sue Shellenbarger, "Employees Take Pains to Make Flextime Work," *The Wall Street Journal* (August 18, 1992): B1.

[22] Gordon Arnaut, "Balancing Work and Family is Eased by the Right Technology," *Globe and Mail* (July 2, 1996): C16.

[23] Linda Russell, "Telecommuting Has Finally Hit Its Stride," *Globe and Mail* (June 26, 1998): C6.

[24] Barbara Ehrenreich and Dierdre English, "Blowing the Whistle on the 'Mommy Track.'" In E.D. Nelson and B.W. Robinson (eds.), *Gender in the 1990s: Images, Realities and Issues* (Toronto: ITP Nelson, 1995): 214.

[25] Randall Scott Echlin, "How to Avoid Traps When Hiring or Applying," *Globe and Mail* (December 7, 1998): B15.

[26] Malcolm MacKillop, "Personality Conflict Can Lead to Firing," *Globe and Mail* (January 19, 1998): B15.

[27] Sean Fine, "Sexual-Harassment Policies Softening," *Globe and Mail* (September 15, 1997): A1.

[28] Ross Howard, "Stalking Problem Larger Than Expected," *Globe and Mail* (November 24, 1996): A1, A8.

[29] *Ibid.*

[30] Theodore E. Zorn, Jr., "A More Systematic Approach to Employee Development," *Supervisory Management* (June 1983): 10-12.

[31] James W. Walker, *Human Resource Planning* (New York: McGraw-Hill, 1980): 251.

[32] Jim M. Graber, Robert E. Breisch, and Walter E. Breisch, "Performance Appraisals and Deming: A Misunderstanding?" *Quality Progress* (June 1992): 59-62.

[33] Walter Borman, "Exploring Upper Limits of Reliability and Validity in Job Performance Ratings," *Journal of Applied Psychology*, 63 (1978): 135-44.

[34] Margot Gibb-Clark, "Workers Pinpoint Bosses' Flaws," *Globe and Mail* (October 18. 1996): B12.

[35] Ann M. Morrison and Mary Ellen Kranz, "The Shape of Performance Appraisal in the Coming Decade," *Personnel* (July-August 1981): 12-22.

[36] Gay Gooderham, "Measures Must Motivate," *CMA Magazine* (October 1997): 8.

[37] Thomas Patton, *Pay* (New York: Free Press, 1977).

[38] James N. Finch, "Computers Help Link Performance to Pay," *Personnel Journal* (October 1988): 120-26.

[39] Bruce Livesey, "Provide and Conquer," *Report on Business Magazine* (March 1997): 34-44.

[40] David E. Bowen and Edward E. Lawler III, "Total Quality-Oriented Human Resource Management," *Organizational Dynamics* (Spring 1992): 29-41.

[41] Reuters News Agency, "Incentive Pay Breeds Unhappiness," *Globe and Mail* (July 9, 1998): B13.

[42] Herbert Meyer, "The Pay for Performance Dilemma," *Organizational Dynamics* (Winter 1975): 39-50.

[43] Andrew G. Spohn, "The Relationship of Reward Systems and Employee Performance," *Compensation and Benefits Management*, 6 (Winter 1990): 128-32.

[44] Victoria A. Hoevemeyer, "Performance-Based Compensation: Miracle or Waste?" *Personnel Journal* (July 1989): 64-68.

[45] *Ibid.*

[46] Herbert Meyer, *op. cit.*

[47] James N. Finch, *op. cit.*

[48] Frederick S. Hills, *Compensation Decision Making* (Chicago: Dryden Press, 1992).

[49] Carla O'Dell, *People, Performance, and Pay: America Responds to the Competitiveness Challenge* (Scottsdale, AZ: American Compensation Association, 1986).

[50] George T. Milkovich and J.M. Newman, *Compensation* (Burr Ridge, IL: Richard D. Irwin, 1993): 98; Reuters News Agency, "Incentive Pay Breeds Unhappiness," *Globe and Mail* (July 9, 1998): B13.

[51] David E. Bowen and Edward E. Lawler III, *op. cit.*: 38.

[52] Jay R. Schuster and Patricia K. Zingheim, "Improving Productivity through Gainsharing: Can the Means be Justified in the End?" *Compensation and Benefits Management*, 5(3) (Spring 1989): 207-10.

[53] Theresa M. Welbourne and Luis R. Gomez-Mejia, "Gainsharing Revisited," *Compensation and Benefits Review*, 20(4) (July-August 1988): 19-28.

[54] Jerry McAdams, "Alternative Rewards: What's Best for Your Organization?" *Compensation and Benefits Management*, 6(2) (Winter 1990): 133-39.

[55] Steven E. Markham, K. Dow Scott, and Beverly L. Little, "National Gainsharing Study: The Importance of Industry Differences," *Compensation and Benefits Review* (January-February 1992): 34-45.

[56] Janet McFarland, "Levi Offers Employees Unique Incentive Plan," *Globe and Mail* (June 13, 1996): B1.

[57] Statistics Canada (1996), cited in Alanna Mitchell, "Wage Gap Narrows Between Women, Men," *Globe and Mail* (January 28, 1997).

[58] William W. Back, *Equality in Employment: A Systemic Approach* (Ottawa: Human Rights Research and Education Centre, University of Ottawa, 1985): 3.

[59] Russel G. Juriansz, *Equal Pay Legislation and Ontario's New Pay Equity Act* (Toronto: Blake, Cassels & Graydon, n.d.): 3-5.

[60] "Equal Pay for Male and Female Employees Who Are Performing Work of Equal Value," *Interpretation Guide for Section 11 of Canadian Human Rights Act* (Ottawa: Canadian Human Rights Commission, n.d.).

[61] David Conklin and Paul Bergman (eds.), *Pay Equity in Ontario: A Manager's Guide* (Halifax: The Institute for Research on Public Policy, 1990): 32.

[62] Laurence E. Coward, *Mercer Handbook of Canadian Pension and Welfare Plans* (Toronto: CCH Canadian Limited, 1991): 184; and Frank Livesey and Robert J. McKay, "Flexible Compensation Schemes Catching on Slowly," *Financial Post* (1986).

[63] Terrence Belford, "Flex Plans Now Offer What Employees Really Want: Cash," *Globe and Mail* (May 13, 1998).

[64] Kirk Makin, "Insensitive Firings Not To Be Tolerated," *Globe and Mail* (October 31, 1997): A4.

[65] Ellen E. Mole, *Wrongful Dismissal Practice Manual* (Toronto: Butterworths Canada, 1989).

[66] Margot Gibb-Clark, "Courts Back Employees in Most Just-Cause Firings," *Globe and Mail* (May 2, 1996): B11.

## Chapter 9

[1] Gary Hamel and C.K. Prahalad, *Competing for the Future* (Boston, MA: Harvard Business School Press, 1994).

[2] Howard Isenberg, "The Second Industrial Revolution: The Impact of the Information Explosion," *Industrial Engineering* (March 1995): 15.

[3] John P. Kotter, "Leading Change: Why Transformation Efforts Fail," *Harvard Business Review* (March/April 1995): 59-67.

[4] D. Keith Denton, "Creating a System for Continuous Improvement," *Business Horizons* (January/February 1995): 16-21.

[5] Allan H. Church, Anne Margiloff, and Celeste Coruzi, "Using Surveys for Change: An Applied Example in a Pharmaceuticals Organization," *Leadership & Organizational Development Journal*, 16(4) (1995): 3-11.

[6] Doug Snetsinger and Greg Pellett, "Making Employee Research Pay Off," *CMA Magazine* (July-August 1996): 13, 14.

[7] Allan H. Church, "Managerial Behavior and Work Group Climate as Predictors of Employee Outcomes," *Human Resource Development Quarterly* (Summer 1995): 173-205.

[8] For a discussion of the positive role that change resistance may play in organizational change effort, see Perry Pascarella, "Resistance to Change: It Can Be a Plus," *Industry Week* (July 27, 1987): 45ff.

[9] Jim Clemmer, "'Change Management' Is an Oxymoron," *CMA Magazine* (October 1996).

[10] Marilyn Bruner, "Adopting an Organizational Culture of Continual Change," *CMA Magazine* (September 1996): 6.

[11] Bruce Brocka and M. Suzanne Brocka, *Quality Management* (Homewood, IL: Business One Irwin, 1992): 232-33.

[12] Margot Gibb-Clark, "Hospital Managers Gain Tool to Compare Notes," *Globe and Mail* (September 9, 1996): B9.

[13] Paul Hersey and Kenneth H. Blanchard, *Managing Organizational Behavior* (Englewood Cliffs, NJ: Prentice Hall, 1993): 368-69.

[14] Gary Hamel and C.K. Prahalad, *Competing for the Future* (Boston, MA: Harvard Business School Press, 1994): 3.

[15] Gary Hamel and C.K. Prahalad, *op. cit.*: 4.

[16] Kate Lademan, "Measuring Skills and Behavior," *Training & Development* (November 1991): 61-66.

[17] Janet McFarland, "The Mind Behind Potash Corporation," *Globe and Mail* (September 4, 1996): B9.

[18] Konrad Yakabuski, "Power Struggle at Hydro-Quebec," *Globe and Mail* (September 7, 1996): B1, B5.

[19] Shona McKay, "The Challenge in Change," *The Financial Post Magazine* (April 1992): 43-44.

[20] Roger Harrison, "Choosing the Depth of Organizational Intervention," *Journal of Applied Behavioral Science* (1970): 181-202.

[21] Wendell L. French, and Cecil H. Bell, Jr., *Organizational Development: Behavioral Science Interventions for Occupational Improvement* (Englewood Cliffs, NJ: Prentice-Hall, 1990): 120.

[22] J.L. Franklin, "Improving the Effectiveness of Survey Feedback," *Personnel* (May-June 1978): 11-17.

[23] An excellent framework for developing a team-building program is provided in Cynthia Reed Johnson, "An Outline for Team Building," *Training* (January 1986): 48ff.

[24] Richard L. Hughes, William E. Rosebach, and William H. Glover, "Team Development in an Intact, Ongoing Work Group," *Group and Organizational Studies* (June 1983): 161-81.

[25] For other strategies for team building effectiveness, see Paul S. George, "Team Building Without Tears," *Personnel Journal* (November 1987): 122ff.

[26] Kenneth P. deMeuse and S. Jay Liebowitz, "An Empirical Analysis of Team-Building Research," *Group and Organizational Studies* (September 1981): 357-78.

[27] W.J. Heisler, "Patterns of OD in Practice." In Daniel Robey and Steven Altman, (eds.), *Organization Development* (New York: Macmillan, 1982): 23-29.

[28] John Hagerman, "Teams and Measurable Results," *CMA Magazine* (March 1995): 6.

[29] John W. Kennish, "Motivating with a Positive, Participatory Style," *Security Management* (August 1994): 22-23.

[30] Margaret Houston and John Talbott, "Empowerment: What Is It?" *CMA Magazine* (July-August 1996): 18.

[31] W. Alan Randolph, "Navigating the Journey to Empowerment," *Organizational Dynamics* (Spring 1995): 19-32.

[32] Jeffrey Pfeffer, Toru Hatano, and Timo Santalainen, "Producing Sustainable Competitive Advantage Through the Effective Management of People," *Academy of Management Executive* (February 1995): 55-72.

[33] Christopher A. Bartlett and Sumantra Ghoshal, "Changing the Role of Top Management: Beyond Systems to People," *Harvard Business Review* (May-June 1995): 132-42.

[34] Carlla S. Smith and John Tisak, "Discrepancy Measures of Role Stress Revisited: New Perspectives on Old Issues," *Organizational Behavior & Human Decision Processes* (November 1993): 285-307.

[35] Jane Gadd, "Who's Got the Jobs From Hell?" *Globe and Mail* (January 13, 1999): A1, A9.

[36] Charles J. Fombrum, *Turning Points* (New York: McGraw-Hill, 1992).

[37] JoAnn S. Lublin and Alex Markels, "How Three CEOs Achieved Fast Turnarounds," *The Wall Street Journal* (July 21, 1995): B1, B12.

[38] Edward E. Lawler, *The Ultimate Advantage* (San Francisco: Jossey-Bass, 1992).

[39] Greg Keenan, "Magna Plans Spinoff of Decoma Division," *Globe and Mail* (December 4, 1997): B1, B12.

[40] Joe Shlesinger, "Why Restructuring Often Fails," *Globe and Mail* (September 25, 1998): B23.

[41] G. Sharman, "When Quality Control Gets in the Way," *The Wall Street Journal* (February 24, 1992): A16.

[42] R. Krishnan et al., "In Search of Quality Improvement: Problems of Design and Implementation," *Academy of Management Executive*, 7(4) (1993): 7-20.

[43] R. Krishnan et al., *op. cit.*: 12-13.

[44] *Quoted in* Karen Lowry Miller, "The Toughest Job in Europe," *Business Week* (October 9, 1995): 52-53; and Daniel Benjamin, "Some Germans Fear They're Falling Behind in High-Tech Fields," *The Wall Street Journal* (April 27, 1994): A1, A7.

# Chapter 10

1 V. Daniel Hunt, *Quality in America* (Burr Ridge, IL: Business One Irwin, 1992): 186.

2 Chester Barnard, *The Functions of the Executive* (Cambridge, MA: Harvard University Press, 1938).

3 Frank M. Corrado, *Getting the Word Out* (Burr Ridge, IL: Business One Irwin, 1993): 10.

4 E.A. More and R.K. Laird, *Organisations in the Communications Age* (Sydney, Australia: Pergamon Press, 1985): 1.

5 D.L. Kanter and P.H. Mirvis, *The Cynical Americans: Living and Working in an Age of Discontent and Disillusion* (San Francisco: Jossey-Bass, 1989).

6 "CEOs Say They Neglect Employee Communications," *Public Relations Journal* (May 1990): 13.

7 Stephen R. Axley, "Managerial and Organizational Communication in Terms of the Conduit Metaphor," *Academy of Management Review* (July 1984): 428-37.

8 Sim B. Sitkin, Kathleen M. Sutcliffe, and John R. Barrios-Choplin, "A Dual-Capacity Model of Communication Choice in Organizations," *Human Communications Research* (June 1993): 563-98.

9 Richard Daft and Robert H. Lengel, "Information Richness: A New Approach to Managerial Behavior and Organization Design." In Barry N. Staw and Larry L. Cummings (eds.), *Research in Organizational Behavior* (Greenwich, CN: JAI Press, 1984): 196-97.

10 Richard Daft, Robert H. Lengel, and Linda Klebe Trevino, "Message Equivocality, Media Selection, and Manager Performance: Implications for Information Systems," *MIS Quarterly*, 1 (1987): 353-64.

11 Richard K. Allen, *Organizational Management through Communication* (New York: Harper & Row, 1977): 2.

12 Gary L. Kreps, *Organizational Communication* (New York: Longman, 1986): 53-54.

13 K. Weick, *The Social Psychology of Organizing* (Reading, MA: Addison-Wesley, 1969).

14 Cheryl Hamilton and Cordell Parket, *Communicating for Results* (Belmont, CA: Wadsworth, 1990): 127.

15 S.M. Jourard, *Disclosing Man to Himself* (Princeton, NJ: Van Nostrand, 1968).

16 Ted Holden and Suzanne Wooley, "The Delicate Art of Doing Business in Japan," *Business Week* (October 2, 1989): 120.

17 Stephen R. Covey, *The 7 Habits of Highly Effective People* (New York: Fireside, 1990): 237.

18 John R. Ward, "Now Hear This," *IABC Communication World* (July 1990): 20-22.

19 Kenneth R. Thompson, "A Conversation with Robert W. Galvin," *Organizational Dynamics* (Spring 1992): 56-69.

20 Carol Birkland, "Huh? Or the Art of Good Communication," *Fleet Equipment* (January 1992): 36-37.

21 Staff, "A Whistle Stop," *Globe and Mail* (November 27, 1997): A24.

22 John Naisbitt and Patricia Aburdene, *Re-Inventing the Corporation* (New York: Warner Books, 1985): 62.

23 Margot Gibb-Clark, "E-mail Knocks Over the Water Cooler," *Globe and Mail* (July 23, 1998): B13.

24 J. McKeand, "GM Division Builds a Classic System to Share Internal Information," *Public Relations Journal* (November 1990): 24-26, 41.

25 Thomas Stirr, "Communication Starts with Rapport," *CMA Magazine* (March 1997): 8.

26 Richard G. Charlton, "The Decade of the Employee," *Public Relations Journal* (January 1990): 26, 36.

27 John Hendren, "Boardroom Breeds Atrocious Language," *Globe and Mail* (August 22, 1996).

28 Ruth King, *Talking Gender* (Mississauga, ON: Copp Clark Pitman, 1991).

29 Francine Wattman Frank and Paula A. Treichler, *Language, Gender, and Professional Writing: Theoretical Approaches and Guidelines for Nonsexist Usage* (New York: Modern Language Association of America, 1989).

30 Government of British Columbia, *Communicating Without Bias* (Victoria, BC: Crown Publications, 1992).

31 "Public Relations Must Pave the Way for Developing Diversified Workforce," *Public Relations Journal* (January 1992): 12-13.

32 Eleanor Davidson, "Communicating with a Diverse Workforce," *Supervisory Management* (December 1991): 1-2.

33 Catherine Hardwick, *Literacy, Economy and Society: Results of the First International Adult Literacy Survey* (Ottawa: Labour and Household Survey Analysis Division, Statistics Canada, 1996).

34 E.A. More and R.K. Laird, *Organisations in the Communications Age* (Sydney, Australia: Pergamon Press, 1985): 1.

35 Gary F. Grates, "Communication in the Second Half of the Nineties: Strategy—Not Creativity—Drives Everything," *Communication World* (April 1995): 16-19.

# Chapter 11

1 Alicia Swasey and Carol Hymowitz, "The Workplace Revolution," *Wall Street Journal Reports* (February 9, 1990): R6.

2 Vincent Al Mabert, "Operations in the American Economy: Asset or Liability," *Business Horizons* (July-August 1992): 3-5.

3 Samuel Huber, *Efficiency and Uplift* (Chicago: University of Chicago Press, 1964).

4 Richard B. Chase and Nicholas J. Aquilano, *Production and Operations Management: A Life Cycle Approach* (Homewood, IL: Richard D. Irwin, 1989): 19-20.

5 Peter F. Drucker, "The Emerging Theory of Manufacturing," *Harvard Business Review* (May-June 1990): 94-102.

6 "Telecommunications Spin-Off Thrives," *Globe and Mail* (December 4, 1996): S1.

7 Gary Reiner, "Lessons from the World's Best Product Developers," *The Wall Street Journal* (August 6, 1990): A12.

8 Magna International, *Annual Reports* (1994, 1995, 1996).

9 Gerald Levitch, "Pizzas and Piazzas: 'Workplace of the Future'," *Globe and Mail* (October 12, 1996): C7.

10 Michael Fredericks, "MRP into the Next Century," *Logistics Focus* (June 1995): 36-37.

11 William J. Stevenson, *Production and Operations Management* (Homewood, IL: Richard D. Irwin, 1990): 624.

12 Peter Turnbull, Nice Oliver, and Barry Wilkinson, "Buyer-Supplier Relations in the UK Automotive Industry," *Strategic Management Journal* (February 1992): 159-68.

13 Sal Aliotta, "Do You Really Want to Distribute?" *Industrial Distribution* (March 1995): 88.

14 Ronald Henkoff, "Delivering the Goods," *Fortune* (November 28, 1994): 34-37.

15 Philip B. Crosby, *Quality Is Free* (New York: McGraw-Hill, 1992): 200-201.

16. Mark Maremont, Thane Peterson, and Lori Bongiorno, "These Repair Jobs Are Taking a Little Longer than Expected," *Business Week* (April 27, 1992): 117-21.

17. Marina Strauss, "Zellers Amends Its Price Law," *Globe and Mail* (September 12, 1996): B14.

18. Tim Studt, "CAD Systems Get Even Smarter, Speed Up Product Development," *R&D* (April 1995): 25-27.

19. Fleur Templeton, "May Tailor? Kind of a By-the-Numbers-Type—But Good," *Business Week* (May 11, 1992): 101.

20. William H. Miller, "CADs Becoming Universal," *Industry Week* (February 20, 1995): 22.

21. Robert Mills, "The Inevitability of CAE," *Computer-Aided Engineering* (July 1995): 4.

22. James Aaron Cooke, "Agility Counts! Part IV," *Traffic Management* (August 1995): 27-31.

23. Barbara Schmitz, "Under-the-Wire Designs," *Computer-Aided Engineering* (July 1995): 8.

24. Fleur Templeton, "A Dial-Twisting Robot That Keeps Testing Gear Honest," *Business Week* (July 6, 1992): 65.

25. Mark Hornung and Richard A. Moran, *Opportunities in Micro-electronic Careers* (Lincolnwood, IL: NTC Group, 1985): 27-28.

26. Vivian Manasc, quoted in "Dancing on the Bleeding Edge," *Profit* (November 1998): 20.

27. David M. Upton, "What Makes Factories Flexible?" *Harvard Business Review* (July/August 1995): 74-79.

28. Susan Moffat, "Personalized Production," *Fortune* (October 22, 1990): 132-35.

29. Philip B. Crosby, *Quality Is Free* (New York: McGraw-Hill, 1979): 200-201.

30. "Telecommunications Spin-Off Thrives," *Globe and Mail* (December 4, 1996): S1.

31. Gary Beasely and Joseph Cook, "The 'What,' 'Why,' and 'How' of Benchmarking," *Agency Sales Magazine* (June 1995): 52-56.

32. Robert C. Camp, "Learning from the Best Leads to Superior Performance," *Journal of Business Strategy* (May-June 1992): 3-6.

33. Charles Garfield, *Second to None* (Homewood, IL: Business One Irwin, 1992): 215-17.

34. Jan Matthews and Peter Katel, "The Cost of Quality," *Newsweek* (September 7, 1992): 48-49.

35. Gilbert Fuchsberg, "Total Quality Is Termed Only Partial Success," *The Wall Street Journal* (October 1, 1992): B1, B7.

36. Philip B. Crosby, *Completeness: Quality for the 21st Century* (New York: E.P. Dutton, 1992): 116.

37. *Ibid.*

38. Thomas J. Peters and Robert H. Waterman, *In Search of Excellence: Lessons from America's Best-Run Companies* (New York: Harper & Row, 1982): 249.

39. *Ibid.*

40. Albert R. Karr, "The Corporate Race Belongs to the Safest," *The Wall Street Journal* (July 5, 1990): B1, B5.

41. Tom W. Ferguson, "Job Injury Burden Could Disable Some Companies," *The Wall Street Journal* (July 10, 1990): A17.

42. Michael D. Lemonick, "The Ozone Vanishes," *Time* (February 17, 1992): 60-63.

43. Nancy C. Morey and Robert V. Morey, "Business and the Environment in the 21st Century," *Business Forum* (Winter 1992): 51-55.

44. Paul Hofheinz, "The New Soviet Threat: Pollution," *Fortune* (July 27, 1992): 110-14.

45. Caleb Solomon, "Refiner Begins Making Gasoline from Used Oil," *The Wall Street Journal* (February 11, 1992): B1-B2.

46. Dianna Solis and Sonia L. Nazario, "U.S., Mexico Take on Border Pollution," *The Wall Street Journal* (February 25, 1992): B1, B8.

47. Jeffrey Taylor, "New Rules Harness Power of Free Markets to Curb Air Pollution," *The Wall Street Journal* (April 14, 1992): A1, A4.

48. "Forward Conveyor Speed Testing at Hotpoint," *Material Handling Engineering* (August 1995): 76.

## Chapter 12

1. Michael Hepworth, "How to Stem Revenue Loss Resulting from Customer Dissatisfaction," *CMA Magazine* (October 1997): 31.

2. Paula M. Saunders, Robert F. Scherer, and Herbert E. Brown, "Delighting Customers by Managing Expectations for Service Quality: An Example from the Optical Industry," *Journal of Applied Business Research* (Spring 1995): 101-109.

3. James Brian Quinn and Christopher E. Gagnon, "Will Services Follow Manufacturing into Decline?" *Harvard Business Review* (November-December 1987): 95-193.

4. James L. Heskett, W. Earl Sasser, Jr., and Christopher W.L. Hart, *Service Breakthroughs* (New York: Free Press, 1990): 1.

5. Steven J. Skinner, *Marketing* (Boston: Houghton Mifflin, 1990): 631.

6. Rob Muller, "Training for Change," *The Canadian Business Review* (Spring 1995): 16-19.

7. Peter K. Mills and James H. Morris, "Clients as 'Partial' Employees of Service Organiztions: Role Development in Client Participation," *Academy of Management Journal* (December 1986): 726-35.

8. Sandy Jap, "The Employee's Viewpoint of Critical Service Encounters," *Stores* (January 1995): RR4-RR6.

9. Choy L. Wong and Dean Tjosvold, "Goal Interdependence and Quality Marketing Services," *Psychology & Marketing* (May 1995): 189-205.

10. Carol A. Reeves and David A. Bednar, "Quality as Symphony," *Cornell Hotel & Restaurant Administration Quarterly* (June 1995): 72-79.

11. Christopher H. Lovelock, "Classifying Services to Gain Strategic Marketing Insights," *Journal of Marketing* (Summer 1983): 9-20.

12. Jagdip Singh, Jerry R. Goolsby, and Gary K. Rhoads, "Employee Burnout and Its Implications for Customer Service Representatives," *Stores* (April 1995): RR8-RR9.

13. Hollie Shaw, "Art of Service on the Decline, Retail Analysts Fear," *Globe and Mail* (January 11, 1999): A5.

14. Wallace Immen, "The Cruise Industry's Fountain of Youth," *Globe and Mail* (September 1, 1998): A1, 4.

15. "G.A.P. Adventures," *Profit* (June 1998): 139.

16. Leonard L. Berry, David R. Bennett, and Carter W. Brown, *Service Quality: A Profit Strategy for Financial Institutions* (Homewood, IL: Dow Jones-Irwin, 1989): 26.

17. Stephen W. Brown, "Building Quality into Service Calls for More than Just 'Smile Training,'" *Marketing News* (September 26, 1988): 16.

18. Karl Albrect, "Total Quality Service," *Quality Digest* (January 1993): 18-19.

19. Gregg Fields and Joan Chrissos, "Service Without a Smile: A Growth Industry," *Herald-Leader* (Lexington, Kentucky) (October 4, 1987): A1, A14.

20 Barrie Whittaker, "Customer Delight by Design," *CMA Magazine* (July-August 1996): 5.

21 *Ibid.*

22 Monci Jo Williams, "Why Is Airline Food So Terrible?" *Fortune* (December 19, 1988): 169-72.

23 Patricia Sellers, "How to Handle Customers' Gripes," *Fortune* (October 24, 1988): 88-100.

24 Michael Hepworth, "How to Stem Revenue Loss Resulting from Customer Dissatisfaction," *CMA Magazine* (October 1997): 31.

25 Leonard L. Berry and A. Parasuraman, *Marketing Services* (New York: Free Press, 1991): 15-16.

26 John Chidchester, "Tailoring Your Survey," *Credit Union Management* (April 1995): 30-31.

27 Elizabeth Church, "Service Firms Follow the Flow to ISO," *Globe and Mail* (August 24, 1998): B11.

28 Peter F. Drucker, "The New Productivity Challenge," *Harvard Business Review* (November-December 1991): 70-79.

29 Curtis R. McClaughlin and Sydney Coffey, "Measuring 'Productivity' in Services," in Christopher H. Lovelock (ed.), *Managing Services* (Englewood Cliffs, NJ: Prentice Hall, 1992): 395-96.

30 C. Jackson Grayson, Jr., and Carla O'Dell, *American Business: A Two-Minute Warning* (New York: Free Press, 1998).

31 Peter F. Drucker, *op. cit.*: 70-79.

32 Oliver Bertin, "Chief Leads Railway With New Train of Thought," *Globe and Mail* (January 11, 1999): B1, B4.

33 Ronald Henkoff, "Piety, Profits and Productivity," *Fortune* (June 29, 1992): 84-85.

34 Christine V. Bullen, "Productivity CSFs for Knowledge Workers," *Information Strategy: The Executive's Journal* (Fall 1995): 11-20.

35 Michael J. Roche and Mary Porter, "Technology Provides Competitive Edge," *Corporate Cashflows* (July 1995): 30-34.

36 Regina Eisman, "Higher Education, Higher Output," *Incentive* (July 1995): 15.

37 Christopher H.L. Hart, James L. Heskett, and W. Earl Sasser, "The Profitable Art of Service Recovery," *Harvard Business Review* (July-August 1990): 148-56.

38 James H. Donnelly, Jr., and Steven J. Skinner, *The New Banker* (Homewood, IL: Dow Jones-Irwin, 1989): 21-26.

39 Scott W. Kelley, "Discretion and the Service Employee," *Journal of Retailing* (Spring 1993): 104-26.

40 Ronald Henkoff, "Finding, Training & Keeping the Best Service Workers," *Fortune* (October 3, 1994): 110-22.

41 James Brian Quinn, Thomas L. Doorley, and Penny C. Paquette, "Technology in Service: Rethinking Strategic Focus," *Sloan Management Review* (Winter 1990): 79-87.

42 John Haywood-Farmer, "Expanding Your Service Business," *Globe and Mail* (December 4, 1997): C7.

43 Jeffrey Pfeffer, Toru Hatano, and Timo Santalainen, "Producing Sustainable Competitive Advantage Through the Effective Management of People," *Academy of Management Executive* (February 1995): 55-72.

44 Fanglan Du, Paula Mergenbagen, and Marlene Lee, "The Future of Services," *American Demographics* (November 1995): 30-47.

45 Gustavo Vargas and Shasem H. Manoochehri, "An Assessment of Operations in U.S. Service Firms," *International Journal of Operations & Production Management*, 15(1) (1995): 24-37.

46 "Xerox Canada, Ltd. Offers Seamless Customer Service in New Brunswick," *Telemarketing* (June 1995): 54.

# Chapter 13

1 Geoffrey Rowan, "Businesses Moving into the New Age of Computing," *Globe and Mail* (May 7, 1990): B1.

2 *Modified from a definition appearing in* Robert S. Ronstadt, *Entrepreneurship: Text, Cases and Notes* (Dover, MA: Lord, 1984): 28.

3 Royal Bank, "Twelve Who Dared," *Royal Bank Business Report* (1995): 7, 12.

4 K.R. Blawatt, "Entrepreneurship in Estonia: Profiles of Entrepreneurs," *Journal of Small Business Management* (April 1995): 74-79.

5 Bruce Little, "Study Finds Large Firms Play Bigger Role in Job Creation," *Globe and Mail* (April 17, 1996): B1.

6 John J. Kao, *The Entrepreneur* (Englewood Cliffs, NJ: Prentice-Hall, 1991): 16.

7 Ralph Waldo Emerson, "On Self-Reliance." In Eugene F. Irey (ed.), *Essays* (New York: Garland, 1981).

8 Robert Kaplan, "Entrepreneurship Reconsidered: The Anti-management Bias," *Harvard Business Review* (May-June 1987): 89.

9 Robert B. Reich, "Entrepreneurship Reconsidered: The Team as Hero," *Harvard Business Review* (May-June 1987): 89.

10 Foard F. Jones, Michael H. Morris, and Wayne Rockmore, "HR Practices that Promote Entrepreneurship," *HR Magazine* (May 1995): 86-91.

11 Gifford Pinchot III, *Intrapreneuring* (New York: Harper & Row, 1985).

12 Tom Peters and N. Austin, *A Passion for Excellence: The Leadership Difference* (New York: Random House, 1986).

13 Gifford Pinchot III, *op. cit.*

14 Hollister B. Sykes, "Lessons from a New Venture Program," *Harvard Business Review* (May-June 1986): 69-74.

15 Shaker A. Zahra and Jeffrey G. Covin, "Contextual Influences on the Corporate Entrepreneurship-Performance Relationship: A Longitudinal Analysis," *Journal of Business Venturing* (January 1995): 43-58.

16 Hans Schollhammer, "Internal Corporate Entrepreneurship." In Calvin A. Kent, Donald Sexton, L. Donald and Karl H. Vesper (eds.), *Encyclopedia of Entrepreneurship* (Englewood Cliffs, NJ: Prentice-Hall, 1982): 209-23.

17 Royal Bank, *op. cit.*

18 Anne Reifenberg, "How Secret Formula for Coveted Slick 50 Fell into Bad Hands," *The Wall Street Journal* (October 25, 1995): A1, A6.

19 Peter F. Drucker, *Innovation and Entrepreneurship* (New York: Harper & Row, 1985): 143.

20 Figures adapted from Supply and Services, Canada, *Small Business in Canada: Growing to Meet Tomorrow* (Ottawa: Supply and Services, Canada, 1989 et seq.) *and Statistics Canada* (Ottawa: Statistics Canada, 1992 et seq.).

21 *Ibid.*

22 Elizabeth Church, "Women Make Move Into New Sectors," *Globe and Mail* (August 22, 1996): B14.

23 Larry Ginsberg, "Neglecting Basics the Kiss of Death," *Globe and Mail* (September 21, 1998): B13.

24 Dawn Walton, "The Cost of Self-Made Success," *Globe and Mail* (October 15, 1998): B13.

25 Patrick R. Liles, *New Business Ventures and the Entrepreneur* (Homewood, IL: Richard D. Irwin, 1974): 14-15.

26 William Harrell, "Entrepreneurial Terror," *Inc.* (February 1987): 74-76.

27 Staff, "It's a Tough Row to Hoe," *CMA Magazine* (April 1998): 9, 10.

28 Peter Metcalf, "Lessons Learned," *Inc.* (April 1995): 35-36.

29 Curtis Hartman, "Main Street, Inc.," *Inc.* (June 1986): 56.

30 Jeremy Main, "Breaking Out of the Company," *Fortune* (May 25, 1987): 83; and Henry Bacas, "Leaving the Corporate Nest," *Nation's Business* (March 1987): 14ff.

31 Susan Fraker, "Why Women Aren't Getting to the Top," *Fortune* (April 16, 1984): 40-44; and Alex Tayler III, "Why Women Managers are Bailing Out," *Fortune* (August 18, 1986): 16-23.

32 Curtis Hartman, *op. cit.*

33 Konrad Yakabuski, "Greasing the Wheels for Their Gender," *Globe and Mail* (November 27, 1997): A2.

34 Quoted in "Women in Business," *Globe and Mail* (April 29, 1997): A24.

35 Donald Sexton and Nancy Bowman, "The Entrepreneur: A Capable Executive and More," *Journal of Business Venturing*, 1(1) (1985): 129-140.

36 Janice Langan-Fox and Susanna Roth, "Achievement Motivation and Female Entrepreneurs," *Journal of Occupational and Organizational Psychology* (September 1995): 209-18.

37 Kathleen Allen, *Launching New Ventures* (Chicago, IL: Upstart Publishing Company, 1995): 83.

38 John Heinzl, "Can Sporting Life Do It Again?" *Globe and Mail* (November 15, 1995): B11.

39 Personal interviews with Lloyd Milner, co-founder of Aftech, Inc., May 1996 and May 1998.

40 *Ibid.*

41 Dun & Bradstreet, *Business Failures Record* (New York: Dun & Bradstreet Business Economics Department, 1986): 1-10.

42 John Ablett, "One in Five: Are You Going to be the One Who Succeeds?" *LawNow* (October/November 1995): 7-9.

43 Erik Larson, "The Best-Laid Plans," *Inc.* (February 1987): 60-64; and Bruce G. Posner, "Real Entrepreneurs Don't Plan," *Inc.* (November 1985): 129-35.

44 Gary Brenner, Joel Ewan, and Kenry Custer, *The Complete Handbook for the Entrepreneur* (Englewood Cliffs, NJ: Prentice-Hall, 1990).

45 Richard L. Osborne, "Planning: The Entrepreneurial Ego at Work," *Business Horizons* (January-February 1987): 20-24.

46 "Small Business Briefs—Franchise Info," *Globe and Mail* (June 24, 1996): B6.

47 Dawn Walton and Margot Gibb-Clark, "Home Fires Are Burning Late," *Globe and Mail* (September 10, 1998): B12.

48 Elizabeth Church, "Leadership Crisis Foreseen for Family Firms," *Globe and Mail* (January 18, 1999): B14.

49 Gordon Pitts, "How Mintsberg Sees Succession," *Globe and Mail* (March 6, 1997): B13.

50 Royal Bank, *op.cit.*

## Chapter 14

1 Royal Bank of Canada, "Twelve Who Dared: Canada's Small Business Heroes and the Secrets of Their Winning Ways," *Business Report* (1995): 8-9, 13.

2 Andy Gilbert, "War on Mainland Pirates Gets a Lift," *South China Morning Post International Weekly* (August 26, 1995): 2.

3 Kenichi Ohmae, *The Borderless World* (New York: HarperPerennial, 1991): 10.

4 Fernand Braudel, *The Perspective of the World: Civilization & Capitalism, 15th-18th Century, Volume III* (translated by Sian Reynolds) (New York: Harper & Row, 1979): 25-27.

5 *Ibid.*: 92-385.

6 Statistics Canada, quoted in *Globe and Mail* (April 26, 1997): D9.

7 *The Canadian Encyclopedia* (Edmonton: Hurtig Publishers Ltd., 1985): 277-278.

8 James D. Wolfensohn, president of World Bank, quoted in *Globe and Mail* (June 30, 1995): 7.

9 John S. McClenahen, "How U.S. Entrepreneurs Succeed in World Markets," *Industry Week* (May 2, 1988): 47-49.

10 Joseph V. McCabe, "Outside Managers Offer Packaged Export Expertise," *Journal of Business Strategy* (March-April, 1990): 20-23.

11 *The Economist*, quoted in "Asians Crave Brands: Region Now a Hot Market for Luxuries," *Globe and Mail* (August 16, 1996): B4.

12 "The Giants That Refused to Die," *The Economist* (June 1, 1991): 72.

13 Diani Luciani, "Partners with Established International Companies to Tap Into Their Highly Developed Relationships in Foreign Countries," *Profit* (October 1988): 89.

14 Shelley Neumeier, "Why Countertrade is Getting Hotter," *Fortune* (June 29, 1992): 25.

15 Stratford Sherman, "Are Strategic Alliances Working?" *Fortune* (September 21, 1992): 41.

16 Gerald Albaum et al., *International Marketing and Export Management* (Don Mills, ON: Addison-Wesley Publishing Company, 1994): 242.

17 *South China Business Post,* International Edition (August 26, 1995): 1.

18 "Dynapro Systems," *B.C. Business* (January 1989).

19 Bart Ziegler, "Light in the East," *Herald-Leader* (Lexington, Kentucky) (September 23, 1990): D1, D5.

20 Kazuo Nukazawa, "Japan and the USA: Wrangling toward Reciprocity," *Harvard Business Review* (May-June 1988): 42-52.

21 Nancy J. Adler, *International Dimensions of Organizational Behavior* (Boston: Kent, 1986): 10-11.

22 Philip R. Harris and Robert T. Moran, *Managing Cultural Differences* (Houston: Gulf Publishing Co., 1987): 189.

23 Richard Gibson and Matt Moffett, "McDonald's Feels Hunger Pains Abroad," excerpt from *The Wall Street Journal* appearing in the *Globe and Mail* (October 23, 1997): B18.

24 "Tires Recalled So They Don't Tread on Allah," *Herald-Leader* (Lexington, Kentucky) (July 25, 1992): A3.

25 Shona McKay, "Outward Bound," *Report on Business Magazine* (March 1996): 74-80.

26 Madelaine Drohan, "OECD's Efforts Pay Off with Bribery Deal," *Globe and Mail* (December 15, 1997): B1, B3.

27 John Partridge, "Olympics Scandal Upstages Bribery Law," *Globe and Mail* (February 1, 1999): B12.

28 Karen Howlett and Allan Robinson, "Mining Expert Warns Against Corruption," *Globe and Mail* (March 18, 1997): B1, B15.

29 Laura Pratt, "School for Scandal," *Report on Business Magazine* (October 1997): 17.

30 Dawn Anfuso, "Coca-Cola's Staffing Philosophy Supports Its Global Strategy," *Personnel Journal* (November 1994): 116-121.

31 Charlene Marmer Solomon, "Are Companies Doing Enough?" *Personnel Journal* (July 1994): 50.

[32] For example, Phillip R. Harris and Robert T. Moran, *Managing Cultural Differences* (Houston: Gulf Publishing Co., 1987); and Rosalie Tung, "Strategic Management of Human Resources in the Multinational Enterprise," *Human Resource Management* (Summer 1984): 129

[33] Gayle MacDonald, "Expatriates May Lose Footing on the Fast Track," *Globe and Mail* (March 21, 1997): B8.

[34] International Monetary Fund, *International Monetary Statistics* (Washington: 1994) and *U.N. Statistical Yearbook, 1992* (Washington).

[35] *Statistical Abstract of the United States, 1994* (Washington): 862-63.

[36] Carey French, "The Fatal Attraction of a Luxury Car," *Globe and Mail* (February 25, 1997): C3.

[37] *Ibid.*

[38] Quoted in Joseph V. Miscallef, "Political Risk Assessment," *Columbia Journal of World Business*, 16 (January 1981): 47.

[39] "Country Risk Rankings," *Euromoney* (September 1992).

[40] RSC 1989, Ch. C-34, ss. 45(5).

[41] *Globe and Mail* (April 16, 1994).

[42] For a discussion of the political scene and of the negotiations leading up to the FTA, as well as a summary of its provisions, see G. Bruce Doern and Brian W. Tomlin, *The Free Trade Story, Faith and Fear* (Toronto: Stoddart Publishing Co. Limited, 1991).

[43] Terence Corcoran, "No Mystery to Job Creation," *Globe and Mail* (April 2, 1996): B2.

[44] Jonathan Friedland and Helene Cooper, "Chile Forges Non-NAFTA Ties," *Wall Street Journal*, quoted in *Globe and Mail* (February 24, 1997): B1.

[45] Madelaine Drohan, "A Partnership of Wealth?" *Globe and Mail* (July 15, 1995).

[46] World Economic Forum, *The World Competitiveness Report, 1993.*

[47] Australia, Brunei, Chile, Hong Kong, Indonesia, Malaysia, Mexico, New Zealand, Papua New Guinea, the Philippines, Singapore, South Korea, Taiwan, and Thailand.

[48] Laura Eggertson, *Globe and Mail* (May 12, 1997): B1, B7.

[49] *Globe and Mail* (August 30, 1995): B20.

[50] Paul Krugman, "Bric-a-Bloc," *Report on Business Magazine* (January 1994): 116-117.

## Chapter 15

[1] Blake L. White, *The Technology Assessment Process* (New York: Quorum Books, 1988): 24.

[2] C.L. Herlin and M. Roznowski, "Organizational Technologies: Effects on Organizations' Characteristics and Individuals' Responses," in Larry L. Cummings and B.M. Shaw (eds.), *Research in Organizational Behavior* (Greenwich, CN: JAI Press, 1985): 47.

[3] F. Berniker, "Understanding Technical Systems." Paper presented at Symposium on Management Training Programs: Implications of New Technologies (Geneva, Switzerland, 1987): 10.

[4] Robert Fisher, *Science, Man, & Society* (Philadelphia, PA: W.B. Saunders, 1975): 5-7.

[5] Gordon Arnaut, "Video Conferencing Gains Converts as Prices Fall," *Globe and Mail* (February 27, 1996): C10.

[6] "High Technology," *Business Week* (January 11, 1993): 78-82.

[7] Michael E. Porter, *Competitive Advantage: Creating and Sustaining Superior Performance* (New York: Free Press, 1985): 33-200; and Michael E. Porter, *The Competitive Advantage of Nations* (New York: Free Press, 1990): 41-46.

[8] Blake L. White, *op. cit.*: 61.

[9] "Cafe Owner Hedges His Bets," *Globe and Mail* (February 26, 1997): C4.

[10] Michael E. Porter (1985), *op. cit.*: 33.

[11] Geoffrey Rowan, "You Can Tech It With You: The Personal Navigator," *Report on Business Magazine* (May 1997): 101.

[12] Nathan Rosenberg, "Why Technology Forecasts Often Fail," *Futurist* (July/August 1995): 16-21.

[13] Richard N. Foster, *Innovation: The Attacker's Advantage* (New York: Summit Books, 1986): 31.

[14] Daniel Prosser and Don O'Neal, "Two Views on Telecommunications," *Hotel & Motel Management* (October 16, 1995): 36-38.

[15] "The Most Dangerous Game," *Nation's Business* (September 1995): 20.

[16] Robert N. Lussier, "Startup Business Advice from Business Owners to Would-Be Entrepreneurs," *Sam Advanced Management Journal* (Winter 1995): 10-13; and Robert N. Lussier, "A Nonfinancial Business Success Versus Failure Prediction Model for Young Firms," *Journal of Small Business Management* (January 1995): 8-20.

[17] Richard N. Foster, *op. cit.*: 214-17.

[18] Geoffrey Rowan, "Few Benefits Emerge From Dubious IT Spending," *Globe and Mail* (April 15, 1998): B25.

[19] Les Gasser, quoted in "Beyond the Internet, Generation 2," *Discover* (May 1997): 42.

[20] Hans J. Thamkain, "Developing the Skills You Need," *Research, Technology, Management* (March-April 1992): 42-47.

[21] Chris Pappas, "Strategic Management of Technology," *Journal of Product Innovation Management* (Spring 1984): 30-35.

[22] *Ibid.*: 34.

[23] John Teresko, "IT Leadership: CEO's Toughest Role," *Industry Week* (September 18, 1995): 53.

[24] Amit Chatterjee and Tridibesh Mukherjee, "Staying Ahead of Global Competition: The Tata Steel Strategy," *Journal of General Management* (Autumn 1995): 71-88.

[25] Linda Stasko, "Computers Alone Are Not Always a Solution," *Machine Design* (September 18, 1995): 73-80.

[26] Richard S. Rosenbloom and William J. Abernathy, "The Climate for Innovation in Industry: The Role of Management Attitudes and Practices in Consumer Electronics," *Research Policy* (Spring 1980): 209-25.

[27] Modesto A. Maidique and Robert B. Hayes, "The Art of High Technology Management," *Sloan Management Review* (Winter 1984): 19.

[28] Tom Stevens, "Tool Kit for Innovators," *Industry Week* (June 5, 1995): 28-34.

[29] Jacqueline Swartz, "The Right Chemistry," *Report on Business Magazine* (May 1997): 68-74.

[30] Tom Trainer, "Listening to Your Customers," *Informationweek* (September 18, 1995): 236.

[31] Louis N. Mogavero and Robert S. Shane, *Technology, Transfer and Innovation* (New York: Marcel Dekker, 1982): 1.

[32] Barbara Ettorre, "A Talk with Xerox's Top Scientist," *Management Review* (February 1995): 9-12.

[33] Paul Pihichyn, "Some Can't Wait to Get on the 'Gooey' Highway," *Victoria Times-Colonist* (October 22, 1994).

[34] Robert Lucky, paper presented at the National Academy of Engineering Symposiums on Engineering as a Societal Enterprise (Washington: October 3, 1990).

[35] The discussion of market-driven transfer and process-and-product-improvement transfer is based on and draws from

William G. Howard, Jr. and Bruce R. Guile, *Profiting from Innovation* (New York: Free Press, 1991): 19-30.

36 Lawrence Surtees, "Telemedicine Comes of Age," *Globe and Mail* (April 16, 1996): C1, C6.

37 "University of Manitoba Views Medical Solutions," *Globe and Mail* (December 8, 1996): C2.

38 Fred Hewitt, "Business Process Innovation in the Mid-1990s," *Integrated Manufacturing Systems*, 6(2) (1995): 18-26.

39 Beppi Crosariol, "The Emperor's New Web," *Report on Business Magazine* (August 1996): 19-20.

40 Kevin Marron, "Recipe for I-Business Success," *Globe and Mail* (December 9, 1997): B1.

41 Beppi Crosariol, *op. cit.*: 20.

42 Marina Strauss, "Chapters Expects Losses at On-Line Division Awaiting IPO," *Globe and Mail* (August 6, 1999): B1, B5.

43 Geoffrey Rowan, "How to Sell on the Internet," *Globe and Mail* (September 4, 1996): B9.

44 Ajit Kambil, "Electronic Commerce: Implications of the Internet for Business Practice and Strategy," *Business Economics* (October 1995): 27-33.

45 Theo Ling, quoted in "Legal Whirlwind Over Web Sales," *Globe and Mail* (November 10, 1998): C12.

46 Bernard F. Mathaisel and Jeff Kvall, "Information Superhighway: Road to the Future," *Chain Store Executive* (September 1995): 42-44.

47 Cheryl Pellerin, "Growth, Change and Bright Horizons," *The Industrial Robot*, 22(1) (1995): 34-35.

48 Charlotte Snow, "Technology Keeps Food Costs on Diet," *Modern Healthcare* (October 9, 1995): 92-94.

49 R.E. Gomory, "From the Ladder of Science to the Product Development Cycle," *Harvard Business Review* (November-December 1989): 102.

50 Catherine M. Banbury and Will Mitchell, "The Effect of Introducing Important Incremental Innovations on Market Share and Business Survival," *Strategic Management Journal* (Summer 1995): 161-82.

51 George Stalk, Jr., "Knowing Rivals' Costs Clears Profit Picture," *Globe and Mail* (April 10, 1998): B19.

52 Ben L. Kedia and Rabi S. Bhagat, "Culture Constraints on Transfer of Technology Across Nations: Implications for Research in International and Comparative Management," *Academy of Management Review* (October 1988): 559-71.

53 For an excellent discussion of international technology transfer, see Robert T. Keller and Ravi R. Chinta, "International Technology Transfer: Strategies for Success," *Academy of Management Executive* (May 1990): 33-43.

54 Staff, "International Jet Bet," *Fortune* (November 23, 1983): 7.

55 Jay Peterzel, "When Friends Become Moles," *Time* (May 1990): 50.

56 Bob Sablatura and Jim Dalgleish, "Businessmen Arrested for Allegedly Trying to Buy Dow Trade Secrets," *Midland Daily News* (August 1, 1988): 1.

57 William M. Carley, "How the FBI Snared Two Scientists Selling Drug Company Secrets," *The Wall Street Journal* (September 5, 1991): 1.

58 "Keeping Secrets: What Privacy Is Worth," *Globe and Mail* (August 16, 1996): C4.

59 Margot Gibb-Clark, "Staff Brain Power Becomes Security Focus," *Globe and Mail* (July 2, 1996).

60 Alex F. Osborn, *Applied Imagination: Principles and Procedures of Creative Thinking* (New York: Charles Scribner's Sons, 1953): 57.

61 Teresa Amabile, *The Social Psychology of Creativity* (New York: Springer Verlag, 1983).

62 E. Raudsepp, "Profile of the Creative Individual," *Creative Computing* (August 1983): 62.

63 Ted Pollock, "Minding Your Own Business," *Supervision* (January 1995): 21-23.

64 W. Guzzardi, "The National Business Hall of Fame," *Fortune* (1990): 19.

65 Thomas Kiely, "The Idea Makers," *Technology Review* (January 1993): 32-40.

66 Ann Kerr, "2 Cheers for the Latest Trend," *Globe and Mail* (June 2, 1998): C1, C9.

67 Carolyn Leitch, "Internet Use Soars to 29% Among Adult Canadians," *Globe and Mail* (July 23, 1996): C1.

68 Janet McFarland, "Firms Set Course for Cyberspace," *Globe and Mail* (July 10, 1996): B9.

69 John Bucher, "Breathless in Oberlin: The Aftermath of User Friendliness," *The Observer* (Oberlin College Newsletter) (February 28, 1997): 4.

70 Bruce Little, "Productivity Paradox Puzzles Experts," *Globe and Mail* (April 14, 1997): B7.

71 *Ibid.*: B7.

72 Joan Indiana Rigdon, "Employers Crack Down on Wired Workers," *Globe and Mail* (November 15, 1996): B4.

73 Geoffrey Rowan, "Surfers Beware: Bosses Can Now Watch You On-line," *Globe and Mail* (July 10, 1996): B1.

74 Mary Gooderham, "Electronic Messages Burying Workers," *Globe and Mail* (May 14, 1997): A9.

75 Joan Indiana Rigdon, *op. cit.*: B4.

76 Beppi Crosariol, "Insidious E-junk," *Report on Business Magazine* (May 1997): 25-27.

77 Geoffrey Rowan, "Computer Viruses Cost Firms: Study," *Globe and Mail* (December 17, 1996): B15.

78 *Ibid.*: B15.

# Glossary

## A

**accounts receivable turnover**
The total of annual sales for credit, divided by the average accounts receivable balance (the inverse of which, when multiplied by 360 or 365, expresses the average number of days that elapse between a sale and payment by the credit customer).

**acid test ratio**
Liquid current assets (such as cash and near-cash items, but not including less liquid items such as inventories and prepaid expenses) divided by current liabilities.

**activity-based accounting**
A control system based on the allocation of all costs, including those not directly related to production or the provision of service, to each unit of product or service.

**analytical skill**
The ability to solve problems by applying basic principles in a logical manner.

**assembly line**
A conveyor belt or track that carries goods and materials that are being assembled or manufactured and moves the items from work station to work station.

**attitudes**
A manner of thinking, feeling, or holding an opinion.

## B

**authority**
Decision-making power that stems from a formal position in the hierarchy of an organization, as contrasted with persuasive power that stems from the personal attributes of the person holding the position.

**balance sheet**
A financial statement that reports the organization's assets, liabilities, and equity (including retained earnings) at a particular time, usually at the end of a fiscal period.

**behavioural science approach**
The approach to management that attempts to incorporate findings of social scientists, recognizing the complexity of individuals and what interests and motivates them.

**behavioural self-management**
The use of activities such as self-set goals, self-observation, self-rewards, self-cueing, and self-designed jobs to help people gain greater control over their lives.

**beliefs**
Conscious or subconscious convictions or expectations that something is true.

**benchmarking**
Studying operations in other organizations or other divisions of the company to learn what techniques are successful and to establish high standards for operations.

**bounded rationality**
The concept that a manager's freedom to make totally rational decisions is restricted by internal and external environmental factors and by the manager's own characteristics and decision-making abilities.

**brainstorming**
A small group process designed to free participants from stereotypical thinking by having them uncritically express ideas, no matter how seemingly bizarre, and in which evaluation and judgement are deferred until the end of the process.

**budget**
A document that both predicts future resources and allocates resources for various purposes within the organization.

**bureaucracy**
Management of an organization by specialization of labour, a hierarchy of authority, specific selection and promotion criteria, and adherence to a rigid set of rules; also the people who manage an organization that follows this pattern.

**business plan**
A document that describes the business idea and how it is expected to be achieved, including primary aspects of

the product or service, marketing and promotion, operations, management and staffing, and financing.

### career development plan
An individualized outline of training, experience, and possibly education designed to facilitate an employee's growth and enhance opportunities for advancement.

### centralization
Assigning most authority to senior executives and other central figures, so that they make most major decisions; also, consolidating decision-making authority in a central core of the organization.

### centralized planning
A system in which responsibility for planning lies with the organization's highest level, or top management.

### chain of command
The formal channel that defines the lines of authority and accountability in a hierarchical organizational structure.

### champion
A person who is highly committed and enthusiastic about an idea or innovation, who continues to present and defend it, and who authorizes or helps to secure needed resources to develop it and to move it from the laboratory to the market.

### change agent
An individual or group of individuals whose intention is to initiate and manage change within an organization.

### classical organizational theory
The management theory that is primarily focused on the organization, its functions, and how it should be organized for greatest efficiency.

### classical theories of management
The general category describing early studies of management.

### cognitive dissonance
The mental state caused by the realization that the current situation is different from what has been desired.

### cognitive self-management
A mental process in which the employee creates images and aspirations that are consistent with achieving the organization's goals and objectives.

### common cause variation
A random variation from planned outcomes that results from occasional and often unpredictable causes.

### common market
In addition to the provisions of a customs union, the members of a common market provide for free movement among themselves of the factors of production, that is, labour, capital, and technology.

### communication
The exchange of information between a sender (the source) and a receiver (the audience or reader).

### communication audit
A systematic program for collecting and evaluating information about the effectiveness of an organization's communication efforts.

### communication medium
The channel through which a message is transmitted. The term includes face-to-face discussions; oral presentations to groups; telephoned messages; written memos, letters, notices, and instructions; printed matter; radio and television broadcasts; and electronic media such as e-mail, teleconferencing, and Web sites.

### communication skill
The ability to listen actively and to transmit to others ideas, concepts, and directions.

### compensation
The total of all rewards having a monetary value that are received by an employee in exchange for working for the employer.

### competitiveness
The capacity of an organization, in a free and fair market, to produce goods and services that meet the needs and wishes of customers, without causing environmental degradation, while simultaneously maintaining or expanding the real incomes of its employees and owners. It is the ultimate measure of potential for effective operations.

### computer skill
Having sufficient understanding of how computers can facilitate decision making, in order to be able to make effective selection and use of hardware and software.

### computer-aided design (CAD)
The use of computers to draw plans for a product or service applying preprogrammed parameters that describe the desired finished product.

### computer-aided engineering (CAE)
The use of computers to plan engineering processes and test designs, permitting managers to forecast the changes that would occur if various parameters were varied.

### computer-aided manufacturing (CAM)
The use of computer systems to monitor and control manufacturing processes.

### conceptual skill
The ability to think in abstract terms, to analyze and diagnose problems, and to make use of lateral thinking when appropriate.

### concurrent control
Monitoring ongoing operations to ensure that standards are met and objectives are pursued.

### confiscation
Expropriation without payment of compensation.

### constraint
Any circumstance that limits freedom of action; in this context, a situation that hinders the leader from acting effectively to accomplish desired goals and objectives.

### contingency leadership model
The analysis of leadership that assumes that different situations require different leadership actions and attitudes.

### contingency management approach
The theory of management that recognizes that the appropriate managerial response to a particular situation is contingent on the specific characteristics of the situation.

**contingency models of leadership**
Models that suggest that the most effective leaders are those whose leadership style best fits the situation within the organization.

**control**
The processes involved in maintaining conformance of the system with standards, objectives, and goals.

**control chart**
A graphical display of statistics, often used to highlight variation.

**controlling**
The function of management that involves monitoring performance, comparing results with planned objectives, and providing feedback and, if necessary, correction.

**countertrading**
A bartering arrangement that provides for the exchange of goods for other goods, or the exchange of goods for other obligations that do not require direct payment.

**creativity**
The ability to create new and useful ideas.

**critical service encounter**
An element of the delivery of a service that likely will lead the recipient of the service to form an opinion as to its quality.

**critical success factors**
The elements involved in the delivery of a service that are essential to the success of the effort.

**cultural diversity**
The differences in language, perceptions of time and authority, mannerisms, and attitudes that exist both within and among different societies.

**culture**
An organization's way of life, including the meanings and practices shared by members of the organization, as shown in common ways of thinking, traditions, customs, manners, and ways of dealing with each other and with "outsiders," all of which are transmitted to new members of the organization by example, and sometimes by directives.

**current ratio**
Current assets divided by current liabilities.

**customer departmentalization**
Departmentalization by type of customer, such as industrial, retail outlets, consumer, government, hospitals, and, in some cases, a single major customer.

**customs union**
Multinational agreement that goes beyond a free trade agreement and provides that the member nations will establish common trade policies with respect to non-member countries.

**cycle time reduction (CTR)**
Actions to reduce the time required to complete a process and to be ready to begin the cycle anew.

**data mining**
Drawing useful inferences from information that is available.

**debt/asset ratio**
The total of long-term and short-term debt divided by total assets.

**debt/equity ratio**
The total of long-term and short-term debt divided by the total of owner's equity plus retained earnings.

**decentralization**
Distributing authority throughout the organization, reducing the degree of direct control exerted by senior executives and other central figures; also, developing semi-autonomous divisions in which decisions are made within only general guidelines.

**decentralized planning**
A system in which responsibility for planning lies with employees at several levels of the organization and participation in the planning process is widespread.

**decision**
A choice, whether conscious or not, among available alternatives.

**decision formulation**
The process of (1) establishing specific goals and objectives; (2) identifying the need for a decision; (3) establishing priorities; (4) determining the causes of the problem; (5) collecting information and developing possible alternative courses of action; (6) evaluating the alternatives; and (7) selecting one of the alternatives.

**decision implementation**
The process of putting the decision made into action, and of following up the results and possibly communicating feedback and deciding on modifications in the ways in which the decision is being applied.

**decision-making process**
A series of related steps that lead to a decision, its implementation, and follow-up.

**decision-making skill**
The ability to choose solutions from alternatives, and to have the courage to take definitive action when required.

**decoding**
The process by which the receiver interprets the symbols used by the source of the message by converting them into concepts and ideas.

**Delphi technique**
A process for arriving at an evaluation of decisions, in which selected individuals are asked to respond individually to key questions about a problem, then are provided with a summary of the responses all members have given and invited to respond again.

**demography**
The study of the people of a society, including factors such as education and literacy, age, ethnic and language preferences, and other distinguishing features.

**departmentalization**
Grouping jobs according to some similarities, in order to simplify and clarify the chain of command and authority and to facilitate cooperation among

those with similar responsibilities or tasks.

**depth of intervention**
The extent to which the intended intervention involves changing employee attitudes and behaviours.

**descriptive essay**
A brief statement describing a manager's evaluation of an employee's job performance.

**descriptive statistics**
Statistics that directly state measured facts.

**differentiation**
The ability to provide superior value to a buyer or user in ways that are different from competitors. These advantages may be in terms of the availability of the service or product, its special features, its quality, or the after-sale service.

**direct ownership**
A form of entry into business by purchasing all or a portion of an existing business or by establishing and operating a new business.

**direction**
Communication from managers to subordinates, whether managerial or non-managerial, to instruct how, when, or to what standards work is to be performed.

**discretionary effort**
The range in which an employee can decide to function with the minimum amount of effort and effectiveness required to avoid direct or indirect punishment, or with the maximum feasible effort and effectiveness.

**discrimination**
Making decisions or taking actions based on an individual's personal characteristics that do not directly impinge on fitness for a job.

**dominant culture**
An organization's core values that are shared by a majority of its members.

**downward communication**
Messages that flow from those farther up to those more subordinate in the organizational hierarchy.

**driving forces**
Forces, either internal or external, that would facilitate change.

**E**

**economic integration**
The situation that exists when two or more countries agree to reduce tariffs and non-tariff barriers on goods or products passing from one to another and, in some cases, including other forms of economic cooperation.

**economic union**
An arrangement that combines the features of a common market and in addition covers harmonization among the members of economic policies relating to government spending, taxation, and monetary policy.

**economy of time**
Saving time through reducing lost time, as in having faster inventory turns or quicker turnover of customer seats in a restaurant.

**effectiveness**
Doing the right thing, at the right time, to achieve the right results.

**efficiency**
The ability to achieve business objectives with the minimum of effort, expense, or waste.

**embargo**
A legal prohibition on bringing specified goods or products into a country.

**empathic listening**
Listening from the standpoint of the sender of a message to receive the full message that the sender intends without distorting it because of personal interests, biases, or inattention.

**employee training**
An organized program in which employees are provided with information, concepts, and skills that the organization believes will help them to become more effective in their jobs, or in jobs to which they may later be assigned.

**empowerment**
Delegating decision-making authority to individuals, usually to people in what traditionally were relatively subordinate positions.

**encode**
To convert a message into groups of words, symbols, gestures, or sounds that represent ideas or concepts.

**entrepreneur**
A person who assumes the major risks of starting a new business by committing equity, time, and often career to the venture.

**environment**
The factors that affect an organization, and the situations within which the organization functions.

**environmental analysis**
Applying rationality to understand the sources and possible effects of environmental factors and to determine the organization's opportunities and threats.

**equal pay**
Wage or salary schedules based on the concept of paying the same amounts for identical jobs, regardless of the gender of the employees doing those jobs.

**escalation of commitment**
An increased desire to support a decision that has been made, despite having received evidence that it may not be the optimum decision.

**ethics**
Standards of conduct that are reflected in behaviour that is fair and just, including but also extending over and above what is required by laws and regulations.

**evaluative criteria**
The factors that the recipient of a service may use, either consciously or unconsciously, to judge the quality of the service.

**excursion exercise**
A technique designed to take participants' minds away from the problem at hand in order for them to approach possible solutions from different and unexpected directions.

**executive summary**
An abstract or summary of all of the fundamental facts included in the business plan.

**expert power**
Power arising from expertise in a specific area, or from knowledge of specific circumstances or situations.

**exporting**
Transporting goods produced in one country to another country for sale.

**expropriation**
The taking by a government of property that belongs to private individuals or companies in exchange for some form of compensation.

**external environment**
All factors, such as laws, competition, technology, social-cultural norms and trends, and ecology, that are outside the organization and that may affect it.

**feedback**
(1) Information concerning results of activity that is conveyed to the policymakers or authority figures, enabling them to confirm, amend, or abandon the policy in question; (2) The receiver's response to the sender's message, communicated back to the sender.

**feedback control**
In terms of control, communication back to the originator of a process that is intended to indicate whether the process is functioning according to the established standards or whether some adjustments should be made.

**Fiedler's LPC theory**
An approach to leadership in which the leader's behaviour is first categorized on a scale from task orientation to people orientation, and then efforts are made to find a work situation to which that particular style is best suited.

**flex benefits plans**
Benefits plans in which employees are assigned a certain amount and can allocate that amount to the benefits that best suit their own personal circumstances.

**flexible manufacturing system (FMS)**
A system in which computerized controls, and often robots, can be programmed to permit rapid changes in production to accommodate frequent changes in specifications of the products being manufactured.

**flextime**
A plan in which employees can set their own work hours, within limits set by management.

**fluency exercise**
An exercise that is designed to open participants' minds to new ideas.

**force field analysis**
Analysis of the forces that might have a positive or negative effect on change.

**forecast**
A prediction of future events, based on experience, past and current, and expectations for the future.

**franchise**
A contractual arrangement in which the entrepreneur, as franchisee, is permitted to use the name of the franchisor in business, the operations of which are controlled to some degree by the franchisor, in exchange for payment of royalties calculated as a percentage of the gross revenues of the business.

**franchising**
A contractual arrangement in which one company, the franchisor, grants to the franchisee the right to use the franchisor's name, and its business and operating techniques, within a specified area in exchange for a fee based on the volume of sales generated.

**free trade area**
A combination of countries that have agreed to reduce or eliminate tariffs and non-tariff barriers that apply to goods and products passing from one country to another.

**functional departmentalization**
Departmentalization by function, such as finance, human relations, production, and marketing.

**functional illiteracy**
Inability to read and understand relatively simple written communications such as memos, instructions, and descriptions and to understand and complete typical business forms.

**gainsharing incentive plan**
A compensation system in which the remuneration paid to employees is calculated on the basis of a pre-announced formula the results of which are dependent at least in part on the financial success of the employer, usually as a result of increased competitiveness arising from improved productivity or cost reduction.

**gender-exclusive language**
Masculine words or terms that are used to encompass both men and women or that inappropriately disregard the inclusion of one of the genders. An example is the use the male singular pronoun (*he* or *him*) to signify all people regardless of gender.

**geographical departmentalization**
Departmentalization by municipality, province, region, country, or international region.

**global corporation**
A company that operates as if the world were a single entity and that has corporate headquarters, manufacturing facilities, and marketing operations throughout much of the world. While similar to an MNC, it is not as directly anchored in a single country, and its operations in several countries are as important as in the country in which it originated.

**goal**
Specific achievements that the organization intends to accomplish, based on its mission statement.

**grapevine**
An informal and unstructured communication channel that cuts across formal channels of communication in almost all organizations and that usually is characterized by rumour, gossip, and even outright fabrication, but that sometimes conveys factual information that has not been officially released.

**graphic rating scale**
A listing of performance characteristics and behaviours that is used to evaluate numerically the performance of an employee and arrive at a total that is intended to rate that performance in terms of value to the organization.

**greenfield**
A colloquial term used to describe an operation that starts from little but an idea—as contrasted with the purchase of an existing business or a franchise.

**Hawthorne effect**
The tendency of workers to increase their productivity when management pays attention to them, and also to respond as they believe researchers intend them to.

**heterogeneity**
The quality of services reflecting the fact that because they are delivered by different individuals at different times to different recipients, they will not be identical.

**hierarchical or position power**
Power that is the result of the leader's position in the organizational hierarchy.

**horizontal communication**
Messages that flow, either formally or informally, between or among peers, that is, those who are not in positions of subordinate/superior to each other.

**human relations approach**
The management approach that focuses on the interaction of individuals within groups, and pays heed to the individual's needs, goals, and expectations.

**human resource management (HRM)**
In an organization, the management of people and systems that pertain directly to employees.

**human resource planning**
Forecasting the numbers and qualifications of employees and support services that will be required by the organization, and determining how those sources will be made available.

**implementation**
Putting a plan into action by assigning people and other resources to it, and by acting to achieve its design.

**income statement**
A financial statement that reports the organization's revenues and expenditures during a stated fiscal period.

**industry foresight**
Predicting the future of an industry in order to shape the present so that the organization will function effectively and competitively in the future.

**inferential statistics**
Statistics that, when subjected to analysis, lead to conclusions or inferences but do not directly reveal them.

**infrastructure**
The facilities that support operations, including utilities, transportation, and communication facilities, and controls of the working environment.

**innovation**
The generation of a new idea, and its implementation into a new product, process, or service.

**inputs**
The influences on an organization from various aspects of its environment, including reactions of suppliers, customers, the general public, shareholders, and employees; effects of competition; governmental actions; and economic factors.

**inseparability**
An identifying quality of a service, that the production and consumption of the service occur simultaneously, not at different times.

**intangibility**
Having no inherent physical substance.

**internal change forces**
Forces for change that arise within the organization, such as problems in communication, morale, and decision making, and including financial stresses and changes in key personnel.

**internal environment**
The factors within an enterprise, such as employees, structure, policies and practices, and system of rewards, that influence how work is done and how goals are accomplished.

**international business**
The conduct across national boundaries of business of all kinds, including financial transactions, expenditures by tourists, and transactions such as the purchase of insurance.

**international management**
The process of management when conducted across national lines.

**international trade**
The exchange across national boundaries of goods for money or for other goods.

**interpersonal communication**
Communication between two people or among a relatively small group of people.

**intervention method**
The technique or means used to effect change within an organization.

**intrapreneur**
An employee of an organization who exhibits the characteristics and actions of an entrepreneur.

**intuitive decision**
A decision based primarily on an almost unconscious reliance on the decision maker's experience, without a conscious rational analysis having been made.

**inventory turnover**
The total cost of goods taken out of inventory for sale or to be incorporated as a component into a product for sale, divided by the average inventory levels.

**ISO 9000**
A worldwide system of registration of an organization's operating sites that have been shown by independent audit to meet specified levels of quality and that continue to make effective efforts towards further quality improvement.

**jargon**
Words or terms that sound superficially as if they had precise meanings but, in fact, do not. Often used by people within particular groups, kinds of work, or professions, and relatively unintelligible to people not in those groups.

**job analysis**
Systematically gathering and analyzing the duties and skills required for a job.

**job description**
A written statement of the job's activities, the equipment required for it, and the working conditions in which it exists.

**job design**
The tasks required to complete the job, including how it relates to other jobs.

**job enlargement**
Increasing the number and variety of tasks assigned to a job.

**job enrichment**
Giving employees more control over their work to make it more interesting and address their needs for growth, recognition, and a sense of achievement.

**job posting**
Making available to all employees written notice of job vacancies within the organization to permit those interested to apply for the positions.

**job rotation**
Systematically moving employees from job to job.

**job specialization**
Assigning to one job a small number of different tasks, which will be repeated.

**job specification**
A written statement of the skills, knowledge, abilities, and other characteristics needed to perform a job effectively.

**joint venture**
A form of business organization similar to a partnership, in which the co-venturers each agree to contribute funds, expertise, or other benefits or assets and to divide the products produced.

**just-in-time (JIT) inventory control**
A system that coordinates procurement and delivery of materials so that items are delivered by suppliers at the precise time that they are needed by production.

**leader-manager**
An individual who is able both to exert leadership and to manage an operation.

**leadership**
The ability to influence people to act in ways the leader prefers—usually to achieve the organization's goals and objectives.

**leading**
The function of management concerned with demonstrating by example and by teaching, directing, and motivating employees to perform effectively to achieve the objectives of the organization.

**level of detail**
The degree of specificity.

**licensing**
A contractual arrangement in which one company, the licensor, grants to the licensee the rights to use specified technology or manufacturing processes or components in exchange for a fee, called a royalty, based on the volume of sales or usage.

**line position**
A position to which decision-making authority has been delegated, within the chain of command from senior managers to front-line production or service employees.

**liquidity**
The extent to which an organization's assets could quickly and without material loss be converted into cash.

**local area network (LAN)**
A system in which separate computers are linked for communication.

**management information system (MIS)**
A composite system that entails collecting, recording, and storing information for later retrieval to assist in management decision making.

**managerial role**
The behaviour pattern of a manager, incorporating interpersonal, informational, and decisional roles.

**managers**
Top-level managers are responsible for developing long-range plans for the business; middle managers are responsible to top-level managers for directing and managing one or more business units or functions; first-line managers are responsible to middle managers for direct supervision of the performance of non-management employees.

**manufacturing**
The physical process of making something tangible by hand, by machine, or by a combination of the two.

**mass production**
A system permitting the manufacture of large quantities of identical goods, using repetitive actions by people or machines.

**materials requirements planning (MRP)**
A computer-driven system for analyzing and projecting materials needs and then scheduling their arrival at the work station at the right time.

**matrix form of organization**
A cross-functional organizational structure in which individuals performing one function, such as accounting, are accountable to the senior executive in finance and also to the senior executive in a geographical, product, or customer department.

**media richness**
The extent to which media convey all of the message, including not only the express words but also the associated characteristics such as tone of voice, volume and speed, body language, and other attitudinal factors.

**medium of transmission**
A means of carrying an encoded message from the source or sender to the receiver.

**message**
The content of the communication.

**mission statement**
A statement of the organization's purpose and intentions, its long-term vision, that distinguishes it from other organizations.

**mixed departmentalization**
A hybrid form in which more than one type of departmentalization is employed within the same organization.

**multinational corporation (MNC)**
A company that conducts business in two or more countries. MNCs usually are based in one country, with some operations, production facilities, and perhaps marketing functions in one or more other countries.

**niche**
The special characteristics of the planned business that set it apart from all of the similar businesses that presently exist and that, for a reasonable period, will set it apart from the new competitors that will enter the market.

**niche strategy**
The strategy of finding a unique characteristic such as design, form and speed of service, or attractiveness to a particular segment of the market.

**noise**
Interference that reduces the possibility that the receiver will receive the same message as the sender sends or that makes it more difficult to interpret and understand.

**nominal group technique (NGT)**
A group decision-making process in which selected individuals each submit possible solutions to a problem, then discuss them and attempt to reach consensus.

**non-tariff barriers (NTBs)**
Legal methods other than tariffs that are used to discourage, delay, or prevent goods from entering a country.

**nonverbal communication**
Conveying a message by means other than words, and including factors such as tone of voice, facial expression, and body language.

**objective**
Detailed steps that the organization intends to take in achieving its goals, stated in specific terms and accompanied by the dates on which each step is to be commenced and completed.

**operational planning**
Short-term, focused, specific planning that provides direction for implementing the organization's broad concepts in the strategic plan into clear objectives for operations.

**operations**
All of the functions involved in producing and delivering goods or services, including all support functions.

**opportunity building**
Seeking and developing possibilities for success, either as individuals or as an organization.

**oral communication**
Communication using the spoken word to convey a message.

**organizational structure**
The framework of interrelationships among individuals and departments that describes relationships of reporting and accountability.

**organizing**
The function of management that arranges appropriate staffing and assigns responsibilities and tasks to individuals and groups, in order to best achieve the objectives established by planning.

**original equipment manufacture (OEM)**
A contractual arrangement in which one company produces goods and a second company markets those goods under its own name.

**outputs**
The products or services produced by an organization.

**path-goal theory**
A leadership theory, based on the expectancy theory of motivation, that suggests that the leader's role is to discover what rewards the workers value and to ensure that they realize that earning those rewards will depend on actions that meet the organization's goals and objectives.

**pay equity**
The concept of setting wage and salary rates that are identical for jobs of equal value or equal worth to the employer, regardless of the gender of the employees doing those jobs.

**peak performance**
The highest level of performance an employee or an organization can achieve.

**people skill**
The ability to work effectively with and motivate others.

**people-oriented behavioural style**
The type of management in which the leader's primary focus is on relationships with and among people, with most emphasis placed on employee needs and morale.

**performance culture**
In an organization, the internal environment in which there is widespread commitment to the effective and satisfactory delivery of service.

**performance evaluation**
A formal, systematic appraisal of the qualitative and quantitative aspects of an employee's performance.

**performance standards**
Levels of behaviour or output that are defined by plans.

**perishability**
An identifying quality of many types of service, that they are time-sensitive and cannot be stored or deferred if not delivered at the relevant time.

**personal power**
The combination of referent power and expert power.

**personnel benefits**
Forms of employee compensation that are measurable in dollars but that are not part of wages or salaries.

**persuasion**
The process of convincing others to accept one's ideas, beliefs, or plans for the future.

**PERT chart**
A graphical display of all of the steps required to complete a project, showing the interrelationships among the steps, the order in which they must occur, and the times require to complete each.

**piggyback distribution**
An arrangement in which a company that produces goods in one country contracts with a distribution organization in another country for marketing in the second country.

**planning**
The function of management that determines the objectives of the business, and how best to achieve those objectives.

**policy**
A governing principle, either written or simply understood by the individuals in an organization, that is intended to guide individual or group action in specific circumstances.

**political union**
A combination of what were formerly independent countries into a single country.

**positive self-talk**
Creative mental imagery that enhances the individual's sense of ability, capacity, and self-worth.

**power**
The capacity to influence people and accomplish desired objectives.

**preliminary control**
Control that focuses on preventing deviation in the quantity and quality of resources used in the operations of the organization.

**prestige strategy**
The strategy of setting high prices relative to the competition on the basis of high quality or an unusually attractive image in the market.

**price penetration strategy**
The strategy of setting low prices to create a mass market rapidly.

**proactive decision**
A decision made in anticipation of an existing situation or an expected change in conditions.

**product departmentalization**
Departmentalization by type of product, such as men's suits, women's shoes, housewares, and hardware.

**production**
The total process by which an organization creates its finished goods, often applied to the divisions of a company that transform raw materials and components into finished products. Also, the output of a service organization.

**productivity**
The measure of units of output, such as the number of items produced, against units of input, such as the hours of labour worked or dollars expended.

**process improvement team**
A group brought together from different functions and levels of an organization, to consider ways in which the organization's activities could be improved.

**programmed decision**
A decision for repetitive or routine problems, for which the responses have been decided already and made known to the persons who will make the decisions.

**progressive discipline**
A connected series of escalating disciplinary measures applied to an employee who is failing to meet the organization's standards and policies.

**quality circle**
A group of perhaps six to ten employees who do similar work within an organization and meet regularly to discuss the effectiveness of their work and possible solutions to problems that arise.

**quota**
In international trade, a specified limit as to the amount or value of goods or products that can be brought into a country during a stated period.

**R**

**ranking**
Comparing the performances of employees by listing them in rank order of their contribution to the organization's effectiveness.

**rate of return**
A control ratio calculated by dividing net income (that is, profit) by the value of sales, owner's equity, or total assets invested in the enterprise.

**reactive decision**
A decision made in response to a change or situation.

**recruitment**
Searching for and selecting suitably qualified and motivated candidates for positions within the organization.

**recruitment plan**
A systematic description of the need for recruitment and how, when, and by whom it will be accomplished.

**referent power**
Power that depends on the personal characteristics of the leader, as seen by those whom the leader seeks to influence.

**regulation**
A ruling, often relating to administrative procedures, that specifies how individuals within an organization shall act when certain foreseen circumstances arise.

**repetitive strain injury**
A physical injury suffered by individuals who repeatedly perform activities that require the same movements, postures, and muscle strains.

**resources**
Financial, physical, human, time, and other assets of an organization that can

be used to fulfil its mission, goals, and objectives.

**restraining forces**
Forces that would inhibit, delay, or prevent change.

**reward power**
Power that stems from the ability to influence people through granting or withholding benefits that are of interest to them.

**robot**
A reprogrammable, computer-controlled machine that can function without direct moment-by-moment control by an operator to manipulate objects and materials and perform specified functions in accordance with detailed instructions.

**role**
A behaviour pattern expected of, or exhibited by, an individual in a given situation.

**role modelling**
Leadership by example, that is, demonstrating in daily work patterns the attitudes and behaviours wished for in the rest of the staff.

**rolling budget**
A budget that is set for a period such as a year, and then is adjusted after each period of operations, such as a month, to reflect actual results and to function for the succeeding 12 months, until amended the following month.

**S**

**scientific management**
The theory that there is one best way to do any particular job, that it can be ascertained and taught to employees, and that workers are motivated primarily by money.

**scope**
In planning, the range of activities covered by a plan.

**screening**
Analyzing résumés and associated information to sort applicants and select those who appear most suitable for employment in the organization.

**selective perception**
The subconscious process through which receivers screen out all or some parts of a message that are inconsistent with their assumptions, beliefs, or background, or that they particularly do not want to hear.

**self-cueing**
Planning and making arrangements required to complete a task or project before embarking on it.

**self-designed job**
A job for which parameters and specifications have been established in whole or in part by the employee who will fill the job.

**self-leadership**
A strategy in which employees at all levels motivate themselves to accomplish not only the tasks that are interesting to them, but others as well that are required to meet the organization's goals and objectives.

**self-management**
A strategy that encourages all employees to arrange and control their personal activities and resources, with little input from external sources.

**self-observation**
Monitoring one's own behaviour, actions, and outcomes.

**self-rewards**
Desired benefits, usually of a minor nature, that employees award to themselves for having reached pre-set goals or stages in their work.

**self-set goals**
Goals that are developed by the employee rather than by the manager.

**service**
An intangible result of human or mechanical effort that is designed to meet the wants or needs of customers, clients, or other potential recipients.

**service productivity**
The relationship between the services delivered and the resources used to produce them.

**service quality**
The extent to which a service meets the recipient's reasonable expectations.

**sexual harassment**
Any act, word, gesture, or situation that diminishes an individual's sexual dignity or integrity.

**shake-up exercise**
A technique designed to break down barriers among participants and to develop a sense of cooperation and community among them.

**short list**
The small number of preferred applicants who remain of interest to the organization after various stages of screening.

**single-use plan**
A plan for a defined project or purpose that will exist for a short period and become redundant when the project is completed or the purpose is fulfilled.

**skill**
Ability or proficiency in performing a particular task or kind of task.

**skimming strategy**
The strategy of setting a high price when a product is new and before competitors enter the market, with the realization that the high price will attract competitors, and that when they enter the market the price will have to be lowered.

**skunkworks**
An informal group of innovative employees who are permitted to digress temporarily from their regular tasks and "waste time" by dreaming of innovative ideas and trying them out in pilot experiments using equipment and supplies that may have been "borrowed" from conventional operations.

**social responsibility**
The practices of a company for which it is accountable, in relation to other parties such as customers, competitors, governments, employees, suppliers, creditors, and the general public.

**solvency**
The organization's ability to meet its financial obligations when they are due.

**source credibility**
The degree of confidence and trust the receiver has in the sender or the source of the message.

**span of control**
The number of people who are accountable to a single manager.

**special cause variation**
A variation from planned outcomes that results from identifiable causes that are external to the system.

**stable system**
A system in which special cause variation has been almost entirely eliminated (for the time being) and the effects of common cause variation have been minimized, so that results are reasonably predictable.

**staff position**
A position that does not entail authority over people in line positions but that provides support and advice to those in line positions.

**standard cost system**
A control system based on setting the desired cost of each step or activity in the operation, in terms of the unit of output product or service.

**standing plan**
A plan intended to have ongoing meaning and to be applied in an organization for a significant period.

**statistical process control**
A control system that uses statistical analyses to detect and correct variations from plan.

**strategic alliance**
An agreement between two businesses in which they share technology, market connections, or some other advantage that one has and the other lacks.

**strategic planning**
Comprehensive, long-range planning, focusing on broad, enduring issues to increase the organization's effectiveness.

**stretch target**
A goal or objective that is achievable, but only by the application of considerable effort and energy, and that exceeds the

change that would come from a series of small incremental changes.

**survey feedback**
A shallow intervention method that reports the results of a survey, usually including analysis of the implications of the information.

**system**
A collection of individual parts that are coordinated to accomplish a common purpose.

**systematic decision making**
An organized, exacting, information-driven process, applying logic in choosing among alternatives.

**systems approaches**
Approaches to management based on the assumption that an organization is a collection of parts, and that is primarily concerned with the interactions of those parts.

**tactical planning**
Planning that is more specific and for a shorter period than strategic planning but less specific and for a longer period than operational planning.

**tariffs**
Customs duties established by law that require payment of fees to the government to bring products into a country, with the payment being based on the value of the products, their number or physical amount, or a combination of the two.

**task-oriented behavioural style**
The type of management in which the leader is concerned primarily with accomplishing goals and objectives and concentrates on the task itself and only incidentally on the people doing it.

**team building**
A moderate-depth intervention that is designed to create a sense of belonging to a "team" and, consequently, a willingness to work cooperatively to achieve the established goals.

**technical skill**
The ability to apply specific knowledge,

technique, or expertise to perform a task.

**technological innovation**
The translation of technical knowledge into physical reality that can be used to achieve a purpose.

**technology**
The totality of the means people employ to accomplish desired tasks.

**technology forecasting**
Predicting the direction and impact of a new technology.

**technology transfer**
A transfer of knowledge from a concept or even a prototype to some more tangible application. Also used to describe the situation in which the source of a concept or innovation makes it available to another person, unit, or organization.

**telecommuting**
Doing work at home or in other locations but staying in communication with the workplace and other employees through networks, computers, and modems.

**time and motion studies**
Timing each aspect of a job to determine the actual physical movements that will allow it to be done most efficiently.

**time frame**
The period of time covered.

**total quality control**
A system that focuses on customer satisfaction by applying methods to improve and maintain quality of product or service.

**total quality management**
A system of control that focuses on improvements in the system rather than in the way that employees perform to accomplish improvement and maintenance of quality of a product or service.

**trading company**
A company that purchases goods or products from a company that has produced them and then sells them for its own account, often in another country.

**trait**
An individual's personal attributes,

including both physical and psychological aspects.

**trait theory of leadership**
The analysis of leadership that attempts to identify specific traits that indicate that a person will or will not be a successful leader.

**transactional leadership**
A leadership style that focuses on activities, that is, the traditional management roles of planning, organizing, leading, and controlling.

**transformation**
The process of change that occurs as an organization processes inputs and changes a product or service from the form in which it was received to the form in which it is delivered to a customer, or to the next stage of production.

**transformational leadership**
A leadership style designed to change (or transform) the culture of the organization by communicating to employees and others a new vision, and enlisting their support in moving towards it.

**universalist management approach**
The theory of management that presupposes that for every problem there is a "best" answer, and that the manager's task is to find that answer and apply it universally.

**upward communication**
Messages that flow from those more subordinate to those farther up in the organizational hierarchy.

**value chain analysis**
A system designed to analyze the sources of competitive advantage.

**values**
Convictions about what is good or desirable; beliefs that a specific mode of conduct is personally or socially preferable to other modes of conduct.

**variable budget**
A budget that reflects the fact that actual results are likely to deviate from those

predicted and that allows for adjustment accordingly.

**verbal communication**
Any communication that conveys a message by means of words. Often mistakenly used to mean *oral communication.*

**Vroom-Jago model**
A leadership theory that postulates that an effective leader is one who develops a variety of leadership styles, and in each situation applies the style that best fits the circumstances.

**written communication**
Communication using written words, symbols, or designs to convey a message.

**zero defects**
The concept of producing goods or providing services, all of which conform 100 percent with specifications and plans.

# Name/Company Index

# Subject Index

creating action plan, 150–51
implementing plan, 152–55
mission statement, 143–50
steps in, 141–56
Point of sale systems, 539
Policy, 153
    effective, characteristics of, 153–54
    setting vs. implementing, 252
    standard operating procedures (SOPs), 153
Political climate, and planning, 143
Political union, 522
Political-legal environment. *See* Environment, political-legal
Population, and market opportunities, 134
Position power, 212
Positive self-talk, 231
Post-it notes, 463, 492
Power
    in change program, 344
    coercive, 210
    defined, 210
    expert, 212
    hierarchical, 212
    and leadership, 210–12
    personal, 212
    punishment, 211
    referent, 212
    reward, 210, 212
    sources of, 210, 212
Preliminary control, 251–53
    financial resources, 253
    human resources, 252
    material, 252–53
Prestige strategy, 138
Price fixing, 511
Price of nonconformance (PONC), 9
Price penetration strategy, 137
Pricing, and perishability, 431
Proactive decision, 91
Problems, solving. *See* Decision making; Decision-making process
Process improvement teams, 106
Product departmentalization, 188
Production, defined, 248
Productivity
    defined, 55
    and inflation, 55
    objectives, 149
    rates, 56
Profitability objectives, 147
Programmed decisions, 89
Progressive discipline, 314
Prosumer, 272
Prozac, 546
Punishment power, 211

**Q**

Quality. *See* Service quality
Quality circles, 180–81
Quality control, 258–68. *See also* Total quality control
    ISO 9000 standard, 268–69
    statistical process control, 259–63
    total quality control, 263–65
    total quality management, 265–68
Quality objectives, 149
Quebec Pension Plan, 313
Quotas, 517, 521

**R**

Rate of return, 255
Reactive decisions, 91
Record of Employment (ROE), 314
Recruitment (job), 295–30. *See also* Selection of candidates
    checking references, 299
    job posting, 296
    pre-interview contact, 299
    selection, 297–301
    sources of candidates, 296–97
Recruitment plan, 295
Red bead experiment, 245–46
References, checking, 299
Referent power, 212
Regulation, 154
    of business, by government, 59–60
*Re-inventing the Corporation*, 373
Research and development grants, 60
Resources, allocating, 151–52
Restaurants, 539
Restraining forces against change, 340
Restructuring, 175
Retail industry, competitive advantage, 541–42
Reward power, 210, 212
*Riding the Tiger*, 546
Rightsizing, 267
*Road Ahead, The*, 535
Role, 15
Role-modelling, 229
Rolling budget, 152
Royalty, 506

**S**

Sabotage, internal, 562
Safety of employees, 54
Satellites, 540
Scientific management, 18–19, 21
Scope, of planning, 137

Screening, job applicants, 297
    group interview, 300–301
    interview, 300
    pre-interview contact, 299
    references, checking, 299
    résumés, detailed analysis of, 297–00
    short list, 297
S-curve, 540–42
    vs. craftsmanship, 177–78
Selection of candidates
    detailed analysis of résumés, 297–99
    preliminary screening, 297
    short list, 297
Selective perception, 376
Self-administered rewards, 229–30
Self-cueing, 230
Self-designed jobs, 230
Self-directed Automated Machine (SAM), 552
Self-leadership, 226–31
    behavioural, 229
    cognitive self-management, 230–31
    concepts, implementing, 226
    culture, developing, 231–32, 234
    defined, 227
    empowerment, 228
    role-modelling, 229
    self-cueing, 230
    self-designed jobs, 230
    self-observation, 229
    self-rewards, 229–30
    self-set goals, 229
    telecommuting, 227
Self-leadership culture, 231–32, 234
    reinforcement, 231
    sharing information, 231
    training, 231
Self-management, 228–29
Self-observation, 229
Self-responsibility, encouraging, 11
Self-rewards, 229–30
Self-set goals, 229
Servers, 117
Service companies, Canada's largest (table), 428
Service quality, 149–50
Service(s)
    characteristics of, 429–32
    classifying, 432–35
    defined, 427
    degree of customer contact, 433, 434
    degree of urgency in time, 434
    employee burnout, 433
    goal of service provider, 434–35
    heterogeneity, 431–32
    inseparability of production and consumption, 430–31

# Photo Credits

## Chapter 1

Page 5: Don Spiro/Tony Stones Images
Page 7: Photo Disc
Page 21: CORBIS/Bettman
Page 23: Property of AT&T Archives. Reprinted with permission of AT&T.
Page 25: CP Picture Archive (Ryan Remiorz)
Page 28: "Coca-Cola" trademarks appear courtesy of Coca-Cola Ltd. and The Coca-Cola Company

## Chapter 2

Page 47: Don Smetzer/Tony Stone Images
Page 50: Photo Disc
Page 53: Photo CD Steve Skjold
Page 54: Photo Disc
Page 56: CP Picture Archive (Frank Gunn)
Page 57: Photo Disc
Page 61: CP Picture Archive
Page 65: Photo by Iain Mellows. Courtesy of Girl Guides of Canada—Guides du Canada.

## Chapter 3

Page 85: Photo by Sam Ogden
Page 95: CP Picture Archive (Charlie Neibergall)
Page 100: Photo Disc
Page 111: Brian Losito, Air Canada
Page 117: Photo Disc

## Chapter 4

Page 127: CP Picture Archive (Mike Ridewood)
Page 143: CP Picture Archive (Frank Gunn)
Page 149: Photo Disc
Page 154: Canadian Wheat Board photograph by Robert Tinker
Page 157: Photo Disc

## Chapter 5

Page 174: Photo Disc
Page 178: John Millar/Tony Stone Images
Page 181: Charles Gupton/Tony Stone Images

## Chapter 6

Page 219: Microsoft Corporation
Page 222: Courtesy of Toronto Maple Leaf Hockey Club
Page 227: The Lincoln Electric Co.
Page 230: Tervor Main/Tony Stone Images
Page 232: Frank Herholdt/Tony Stone Images

## Chapter 7

Page 249: Reprinted with kind permission of De Beers
Page 250: The Home Depot Canada
Page 253: Photo Disc
Page 262: Courtesy of Motorola Museum © 1999
Page 265: Courtesy of Johnson Controls
Page 269: Courtesy of Pioneer Hi-Bred Limited

## Chapter 8

Page 279: Bruce Ayres/Tony Stone Images
Page 286: Photo Disc
Page 291: Photo Disc
Page 294: Photo Disc
Page 297: Courtesy of KPMG LLP
Page 301: Loren Santow/Tony Stone Images
Page 303: Bob Handelman/Tony Stone Images

## Chapter 9

Page 329: "Coca-Cola" trademarks appear courtesy of Coca-Cola Ltd. and The Coca-Cola Company.
Page 331: Photo Disc
Page 337: CP Picture Archive (Frank Gunn)
Page 338: Copyright © 1995-1999 Federal Express Corporation. All Rights Reserved.
Page 341: Used with permission of CSX Transportation, Inc.
Page 347: Canadian Outward Bound Wilderness School
Page 349: Bruce Ayres/Tony Stone Images

## Chapter 10

Page 361: Photo Disc
Page 364: Photo Disc

Page 366: Bruce Ayres/Tony Stone Images
Page 369: Digital Stock
Page 374: Bruce Ayres/Tony Stone Images
Page 378: Mark Segal/Tony Stone Images
Page 379: Photo Disc

## Chapter 11

Page 391: Ed Simpson/Tony Stone Images
Page 398: Photo by Jack Cornelis
Page 407: Courtesy of Cominco Ltd.
Page 409: Tony Stone Images
Page 415: City of Toronto, Works and Emergency Services Department

## Chapter 12

Page 429: Digital Stock
Page 434: Photo Disc
Page 435: Photo Disc
Page 439: Brian Losito, Air Canada
Page 442: Steven Peters/Tony Stone Images
Page 443: Photo Disc

## Chapter 13

Page 460: CORBIS/Jeremy Horner
Page 467: Photo Disc
Page 469: Photo Disc
Page 471: Photo Disc

## Chapter 14

Page 501: CORBIS/Steve Raymer
Page 505: Hugh Sitton/Tony Stone Images
Page 511: Ken Fisher/Tony Stone Images
Page 514: CP Picture Archive (Ed Bailey)
Page 522: CP Picture Archive (Frank Gunn)

## Chapter 15

Page 533: Sun Microsystems
Page 535: Rich La Salle/Tony Stone Images
Page 539: David Frazier/Tony Stone Images
Page 540: Courtesy of NASA
Page 541: B.C. Ferries
Page 545: Tony Stone Images
Page 551: Hyundai Motor America, Click Interactive Inc., and Bell and Howell Catalog Systems
Page 561: Photo Disc